Argentine Theme Issue

The Journal of Decorative and Propaganda Arts is published annually by The Wolfson Foundation of Decorative and Propaganda Arts, Inc. and distributed by Rizzoli International Publications. U.S. subsciption rate (1 issue): individuals $19, institutions $25. Foreign subscription rate (payable in U.S. dollars): individuals $22, institutions $28. Back issues available at $19 U.S., $22 foreign (payable in U.S. dollars).

Send address changes to *The Journal of Decorative and Propaganda Arts,* 2399 N.E. Second Avenue, Miami, Florida 33137 U.S.A. Fax 305/573-0409.

For advertising rates and schedules, write to *The Journal of Decorative and Propaganda Arts* or call 305/573-9170.

 ISSN 0888-7314, ISBN 0-9631601-0-9. Indexed in DAAI and RILA.

Printed by Toppan Printing Company (America), Inc.

Cover: Francisco Salamone, angel, sculpture in reinforced concrete, ca. 1937. Photograph by Alberto Bellucci. (See page 112.)

Argentine Theme Issue

1992

18

The Journal of Decorative and Propaganda Arts 1875–1945

Acknowledgments

Creating this issue has been a fascinating and challenging endeavor, made possible by the expert advice and assistance of many colleagues and dignitaries who deserve special recognition. Notable among them are:

Carlos Ortiz de Rozas, Ambassador, and José Vignolo, Cultural Affairs Counselor, Argentine Embassy, Washington, D.C.

Francisco Thompson-Flores, Ambassador, Mrs. Francisco Thompson-Flores, and María Angélica Menéndez Pinto, Brazilian Embassy, Buenos Aires.

Domingo Cullen, Minister, Argentine Embassy, The United Kingdom.

Juan Carlos Vignaud, Argentine Consul General, Argentine Consulate, Atlanta, Georgia.

Ernesto Uribe, Public Affairs Officer, Raymond D. Anderson, Jr., Cultural Affairs Officer, and Federico González del Pino, Cultural Affairs Specialist, USIS, American Embassy, Buenos Aires.

Sigrid Maitrejean, Director, and Maria Estella Corrêa, Cultural Assistant, USIS, American Consulate, São Paulo.

Frances F. Switt, Director, USIA, Miami Reception Center, Miami, Florida.

Charles Dusseau, Commissioner, Metropolitan Dade County, Miami, Florida.

Elsa Kelly, Former Director of Cultural Relations, Ministry of Foreign Affairs, Buenos Aires.

Nelly Arrieta de Blaquier, President, and the Friends of the National Museum of Fine Arts, Buenos Aires.

Juan Carlos Ahumada Sérè, President, Inés Zavalia Bunge de Herrera Vegas, and the Friends of the National Museum of Decorative Art, Buenos Aires.

Lucrecia de Oliveira Cézar de García Arias, President, and the Argentine Federation of the Friends of Museums, Buenos Aires.

Jorge S. Helft, Director, Antorchas Foundation, Buenos Aires.

We join Alberto Bellucci in thanking the Antorchas Foundation for their grant furthering his research on the urban art of Francisco Salamone.

Also, to those who in a private capacity acted as advisors, supportive friends, or both, we remember Roberto Behar, Fatima Bercht, James A. Findlay, Alejandro Furlong, Miranda Kenny de Green, Rodolfo Machado, David A. Morton, Cynthia de Oliveira Cézar, Rafael de Oliveira Cézar, Samuel Paz, Dianne H. Pilgrim, Nicholas Pisaris, Socorro Salvador Prieto, Waldo Rasmussen, Luis Santeiro, Nicolas Sapieha, Domingo I. Tellechea, Susana Torre, Joseph Tulchin, and Julia Valentine. For inadvertent omissions, we beg forgiveness.

A Spanish supplement to this issue was edited by José Monleón, Associate Professor of Spanish at the University of California at Los Angeles. His sublime calm during the perilous process of conforming English and Spanish texts was a joy to behold. Through his consummate skill, we can reach a wider audience, for which we are grateful.

It is not an exaggeration to say that without Edward Shaw our idealistic plans for this issue could never have been realized. As our liaison in Buenos Aires, he gave unstintingly of his time. His practical help and wise counsel shaped the work in innumerable ways, and we salute him fondly.

Introduction

By Pamela Johnson

This issue of *The Journal of Decorative and Propaganda Arts* focuses on Argentina in an age of self-generation hardly matched in the history of nations. From 1875 to 1945, a radically new Buenos Aires was built and its great port established. Industry and transportation were structured, meat packing and agriculture burgeoned, fabulous fortunes amassed. And, in the first half of the twentieth century, Argentina led the world in population increase with an astounding 251 percent.[1]

To declare it a golden age, however, is romantic indulgence, and there are a swarm of gadflies to tell us so. Eduardo Mallea in his fervid *History of an Argentine Passion*[2] posited a visible and an invisible Argentina: the spiritual subsurface "generously exalted,...severe and stately [in its] living, enjoying, and suffering" but estranged from the crass surface—materialistic, exploitive, vain. In *The Argentine Republic,*[3] Ysabel F. Rennie also proclaimed "there are two Argentinas," though her intuition was more pragmatic. "The dichotomy in the country is that of creole and European, protectionist and free trader, the provinces and Buenos Aires.... Until the two Argentinas are brought together, that nation will have no peace." The image of a split appeared again in the truism that Argentine culture was not Argentine at all but merely an imitation of European culture. The contention ran that this European persona must dissolve before Argentina could be "national," "authentic."

Theories make life intelligible, but often at the cost of truth. Despite the alleged split in body, mind, and spirit, Argentine painters, architects, sculptors, designers, and decorative artists went about their business, transforming the reality they knew into art. When they emulated European models, national character was not lost. How could it be? What they chose to emulate reflected national character exquisitely. Their desire to move from what they called barbarism to what they called civilization had been fired by an ardent patriot, Domingo F. Sarmiento, and was a principle like so many (equality under the law, religious freedom, Manifest Destiny) that have shaped a country's identity. Further, in what they produced there was the inevitable stamp of Argentine materials, topics, customs, and, above all, idiosyncratic reading of foreign concepts.

1. United Nations Educational, Scientific and Cultural Organization survey, 1951.
2. Eduardo Mallea, *History of an Argentine Passion,* ed. and trans. Myron I. Lichtblau (Pittsburgh, Pa.: Latin American Literary Review Press, 1983), 181.
3. Ysabel F. Rennie, *The Argentine Republic* (New York: The Macmillan Company, 1945).

In the essays that follow, architecture of the period is delineated not by conventional buildings but by experiments in three dramatic modes. Martha Levisman de Clusellas documents the evolution of construction styles in San Carlos de Bariloche, culminating in the creation of the Llao-Llao Hotel where architect Alejandro Bustillo put Greek classical principles under the sway of the Argentine landscape. Equally important is Levisman's discussion of the hotel's interiors, especially its furniture incorporating local woods and native leathers. Here Bustillo collaborated with the remarkable Comte group which, after 1939, included Jean-Michel Frank.

Architecture of the thirties—with emphasis on the contributions of Alejandro Virasoro, Alberto Prebisch, Antonio Vilar, and Wladimiro Acosta—is the theme of Ernesto Katzenstein. He traces the development of the modern movement through a decade that saw landmark skyscrapers rise above Buenos Aires. The influence and observations of Le Corbusier (who visited the city in 1929 and was captivated by its "hopeless streets" and "immense skies") are woven through this brilliant study.

A third revelation is Alberto Bellucci's original investigation of what he dubs monumental deco—the government-sponsored buildings of Francisco Salamone. In Buenos Aires Province, Salamone devised town halls, cemetery portals, and municipal slaughterhouses that combine, in Bellucci's words, "authoritarianism, art deco, functionalism, and propaganda value on a colossal scale." Bellucci links these neglected often forsaken structures to realms as diverse as sixteenth-century Italy and twentieth-century Germany.

Decorative painting is encompassed by another trio. Guillermo Whitelow presents a distinguished critique of Spanish muralist José Mariá Sert and his presence in Buenos Aires, highlighting the Sert ceilings at the Brazilian ambassador's residence, once the Pereda Palace. There Argentine *estanciero* Celedonio Pereda exercised avant-garde taste by commissioning decorations that broke with the academicism of the day. Whitelow also comments on murals by Sert's predecessors in Buenos Aires.

Emilio Basaldúa charts the odyssey of his father, Héctor Basaldúa, who studied painting in Paris before returning to his homeland to spend thirty years as resident stage designer at the Colón Theater. European training was prototypical, but Basaldúa's stage design sprang from deeper sources. Late in life, he recognized the overpowering effect of "the simple and naive atmosphere of [earlier] times, the moon over the village's main square, the streets during carnival, the obsessing characters, the social gatherings where conversations were forever repeated, the ennui, and all the mythology." In his graceful, pure designs, we have reason to celebrate the Europe/Argentine gestalt.

An indigenous form of decorative painting is explored by María Estenssoro—the *filete porteño,* once adorning the carts, trucks, and buses of Buenos Aires. Drawing on extensive research by painter Nicolás Rubió and his wife, sculptor Esther Barugel, Estenssoro gives testimony to folk art of the highest caliber. She distinguishes the *filete* from Sicilian *carretto* painting and other similar expressions, and mentions the ways *filete* motifs persist in contemporary art and design.

Painting and propaganda meet in Marcelo Pacheco's substantial survey of social realism. He introduces his subject with an outline of political and economic history which serves as a valuable referent for the journal as a whole. He then analyzes how artists responded to the darker realities of Argentine expansion—the oppressed workers, the beggars, the teeming slums. Certain painters like Antonio Berni worked consciously, (he asserted, "I think that the political reading of my work is fundamental.... [A] merely esthetic reading would be a betrayal"), while others espoused social realism not always consciously or with an explicit goal. But a keener sense was emerging of the need to balance the demands of justice with the demands of vision.

Growth in the Argentine textile industry is mapped by Elena Moreira, with an overview of Argentine fashion and its symbolic significance in a changing milieu. For the upper class *porteña,* high fashion meant Paris. The *porteño* looked to London for his elegant attire. Yet these conformists survive in the collective imagination as unique beings. Moreira reminds us that the women were lauded by poets like Apollinaire, Cendrars, and Darío. The men were deified by Broadway and Hollywood. English suits and French gowns could not disguise what was unmistakably—mysteriously—Argentine.

Our final section, again a triad, begins with an interview—museum director José María Peña revealed as gentleman/warrior by Edward Shaw. The Argentine ethos is Peña's concern, and he has dedicated his life to defining and promulgating it through the Museum of the City of Buenos Aires. After the interview, which plumbs his philosophy, come two essays in which Peña traverses public sculpture and *art-nouveau* stained glass and ironwork. Evaluating both European and Argentine artists, he gives an appreciation of the work done between 1875 and 1945, disclosing with precision—and not without humor—the national mentality.

Read, and let Argentina speak for herself. Her voice is inimitable.

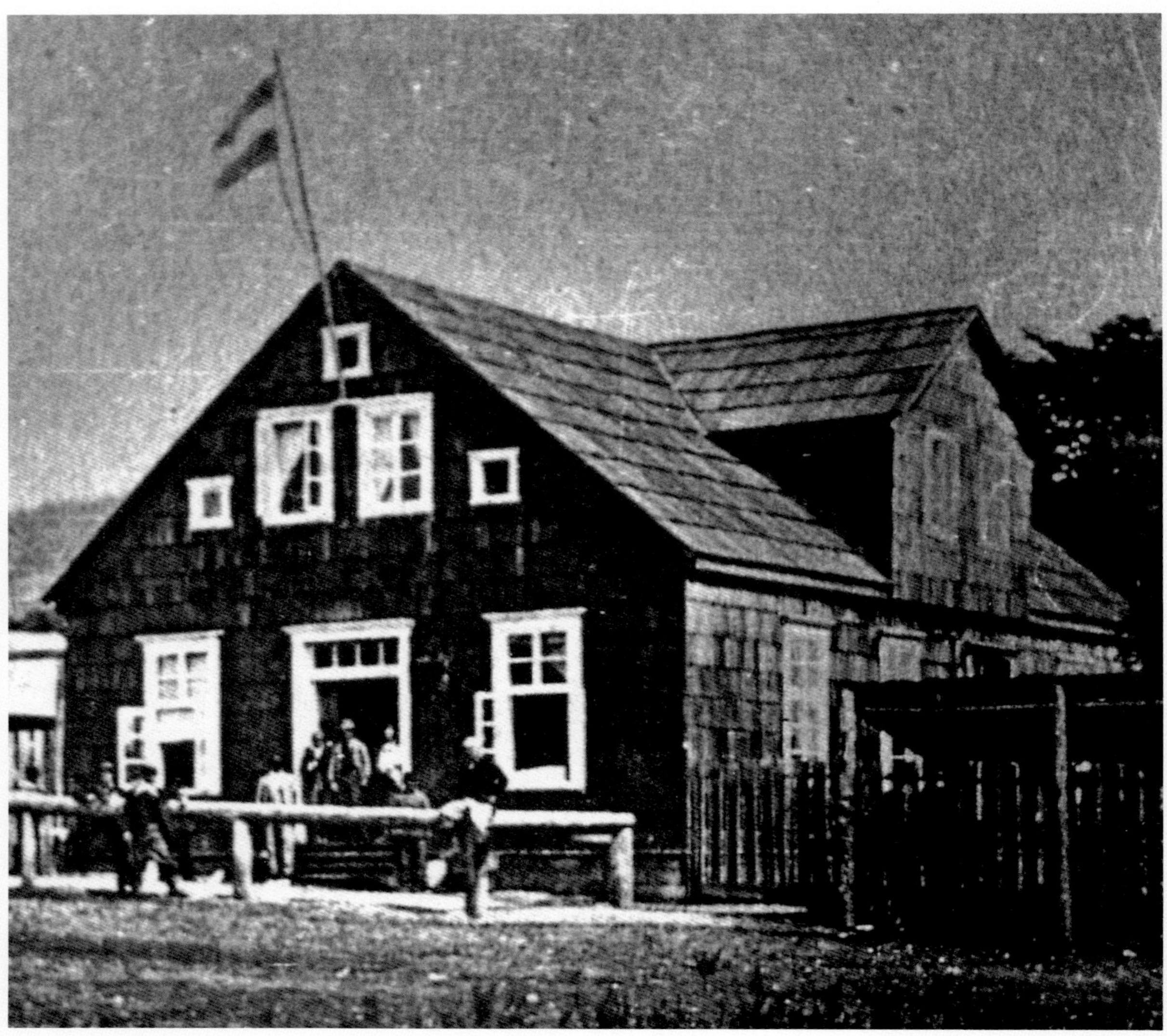

Fig. 1. Early shingle-style construction, Bariloche.

(See page 12.)

The Bariloche Style

By Martha Levisman de Clusellas

Translated by Theodore McNabney

Martha Levisman de Clusellas is a graduate of the National University of Buenos Aires School of Architecture and a practicing architect specializing in offices and banks. Recently, she has focused on major restoration projects. She has curated and directed architecture exhibitions at the National Museum of Fine Arts and the San Telmo Foundation and is custodian of the Alejandro Bustillo archives.

San Carlos de Bariloche, located in the southern Patagonia lake region in the province of Río Negro, was originally inhabited by the Pehuenches, Tehuelches, Puelches, and Pogyas (or Patagones from the North) when the area was known as Araucania.

By the end of the sixteenth century, before the first missionaries arrived, Lake Nahuel Huapí (Lake of the tigers) was being used as a means of communication with indigenous populations from the Pacific.

> The route to Bariloche deserves to be called legendary because of the mystery surrounding it. After use by the Spanish Conquistadors, its location was forgotten, to be rediscovered by Father Guillelmo at the beginning of the eighteenth century. As time passed and new attempts to reopen the route failed, a halo of mystery grew around it. It was strategically important for missionaries, traders, explorers, and the military because it connected the Pacific Ocean with Nahuel Huapí in three days.[1]

The City of the Caesars, capital of the Araucanian kingdom, was a myth that stimulated Spanish expeditions from Chile beginning in 1620. This enchanted city, which no one had ever seen, was located somewhere in Patagonia on the banks of a great lake in the midst of the mountains. It stimulated greed and the thirst for adventure.

> [I]t is inhabited by beautiful blond people with thick beards and blue eyes who peer from beneath the brims of three-cornered hats, seated in their houses on gold benches, speaking a language not understood by either the Spaniards or the Indians....
>
> To cross the city required many hours along stone-paved streets laid on the banks of a large blue lake. The stone buildings were sumptuous, with their Spanish-style roofs. Nothing equaled the magnificence of its temples covered in solid silver. Silver was also used for pots, knives, and even garden fences.[2]

In 1881, when the desert was finally cleared of Indians during the presidency of General Julio A. Roca, Patagonia was militarily incorporated into the nation. The first construction was in the Chilean style because the Pacific coast was

Photographs courtesy of the author.

1. Juan M. Biedma, *Crónica histórica del lago Nahuel Huapí* (The historical chronicle of Lake Nahuel Huapí) (Buenos Aires: Editorial Emecé, 1987).
2. Data about the City of the Caesars was drawn from Biedma, *Crónica histórica,* and Emilio B. Morales, *Nahuel Huapí*, ed. L. J. Russo (Buenos Aires: Taller Gráficos Argentinos, 1929). Another source is stories by Pedro de Angelis in Richard Vallmitjana's *Bariloche, mi pueblo* (Bariloche, my village) (Buenos Aires: Fundación Antorchas, 1989).

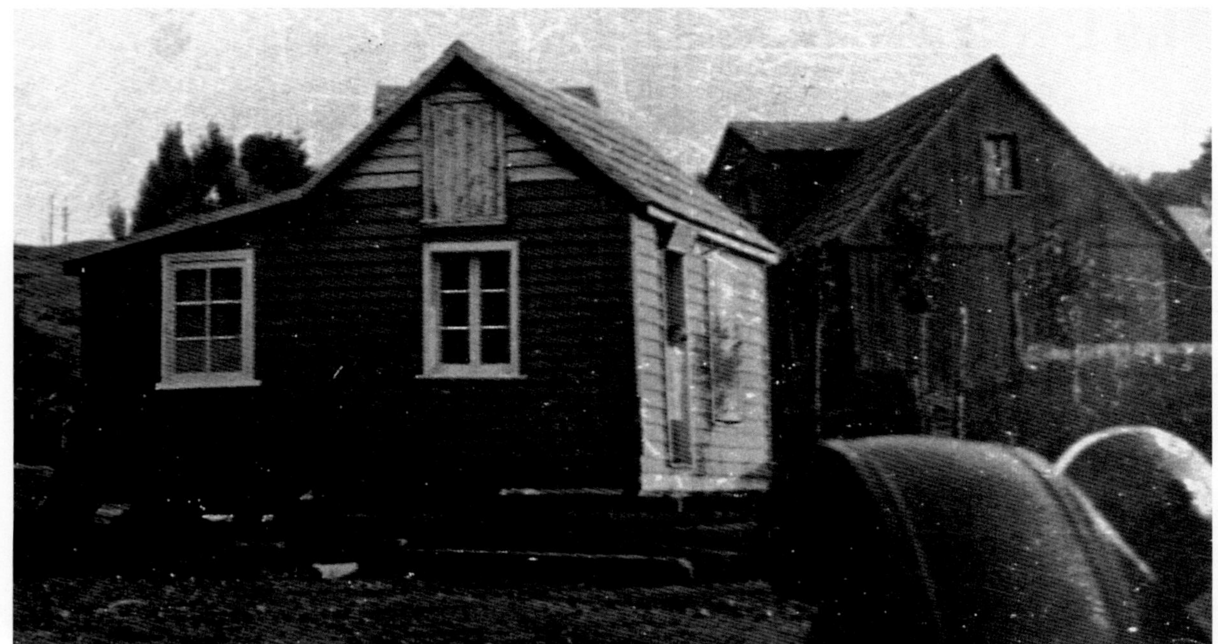

Fig. 2. Settlers' cabins, Bariloche. Photograph from Ricardo Vallmitjana's book *Bariloche, mi pueblo.*

only three days by horse from Lake Nahuel Huapí. Hotels, businesses, and *estancias* were built with local wood—*lenga*, larch, and cypress. An excellent example of this style of construction is in the south of Chile and, above all, in Chiloé (fig. 1).

With the first settlers, almost all foreigners, came an increase in every kind of enterprise. Lumbering was developed, the sawmill was mechanized, and from that came the utilization of overlapping planks in construction, either vertical or horizontal, with or without bark (fig. 2).

When, in 1902, the Agricultural Colony of Bariloche was set up, there already existed a country store founded in 1894 by Carlos Wiederhold. The building of new homes and *estancias* increased, using local systems of construction.

By 1920, several hotels had been installed in various spots of tourist interest in Bariloche (fig. 4). The first borders of the National Park of the South were established on land donated by Perito Moreno, a government consultant on boundary questions. The first studies had begun on the development of water power and the distribution of potable water. The railroad came to within eighty kilometers of Bariloche.

Foreigners, who comprised 90 percent of the population until the 1940s, were mainly Swiss, German, English, and North American. They had settled villages in the best locations, including the site where the Bariloche Civic Center would later be built, thus deciding the layout of the streets (fig. 3).

According to Exequiel Bustillo in the first chapter of his book *El despertar de Bariloche*,[3] a group of Argentines met in Paris in 1930. They were awaiting the announcement of the fall of President Hipólito Yrigoyen (the first president elected by popular vote at a moment of political change following a cycle of Conservative governments) so they could return to Argentina. Fascinated by

3. Exequiel Bustillo, *El despertar de Bariloche* (The awakening of Bariloche), 1st ed. (Buenos Aires: Editorial Sudamericana, 1968).

the description of Lake Nahuel Huapí given by an Argentine living on the island of Huemul, they signed a formal agreement to visit the area.

This group, representative of the Generation of the '80s and inspired by the "colonization illusion or fantasy,"[4] led the country according to their class interests, changing it into a rich and flourishing organism. An inspection tour of Bariloche and its surroundings was undertaken by a group of friends (Bustillo called it a party) made up of Carlos and Luis Ortiz Basualdo who, along with Aaron Anchorena, owned Huemul Island; and the Bustillo, Lynch, Pacheco, Santamarina, and Uribelarrea couples. The history of Llao-Llao began with this trip and, with it, the touristic and civic development of Bariloche.

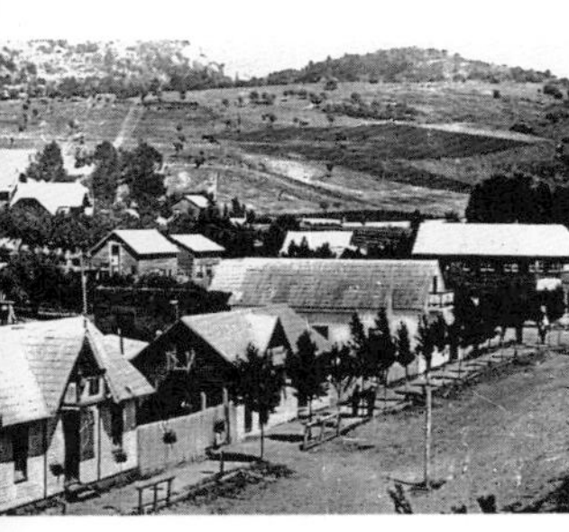

Fig. 3. Original site of the civic center, Bariloche.

The railroad went through a landscape that Bustillo called "deceptive," but the description that follows from his book clearly shows his passion for Nahuel Huapí and the "cult" that was established there.

> We went along...for awhile until, on the left flank, the great bowl of the lake appeared, dry on its eastern side; but because of its color and huge size, we had an idea of its superb beauty.... This is the highest point, the meridian of loveliness from which the forest, with its mixture of trees, fills the soul. We do not know what to say, how to express our admiration of the scene as we contemplate the great blue expanse of the lake and, behind, rising majestically, the snow-covered peak of Tronador.[5]

Exequiel Bustillo would not leave the region. He bought a piece of land in Correntoso on the banks of the lake and called it Cumelén, which in the Araucanian tongue is equivalent to the French *sans-souci*. Single-handedly, he transformed it into a private paradise.[6] Then he worked to complete many projects that were part of the "colonization illusion": the first radio-telegraph in Correntoso, the arrival of the railroad at Bariloche in 1934, the creation of

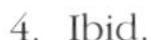

4. Ibid.
5. Ibid.
6. Today Cumelén is a country club.

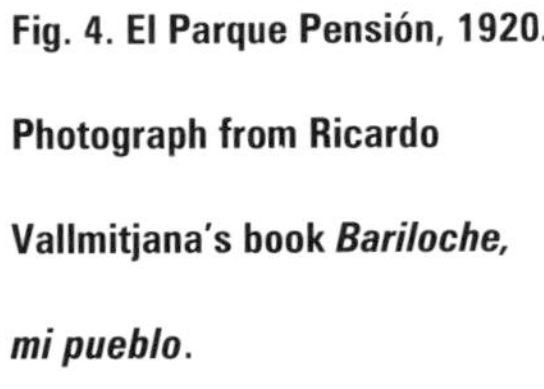

Fig. 4. El Parque Pensión, 1920. Photograph from Ricardo Vallmitjana's book *Bariloche, mi pueblo*.

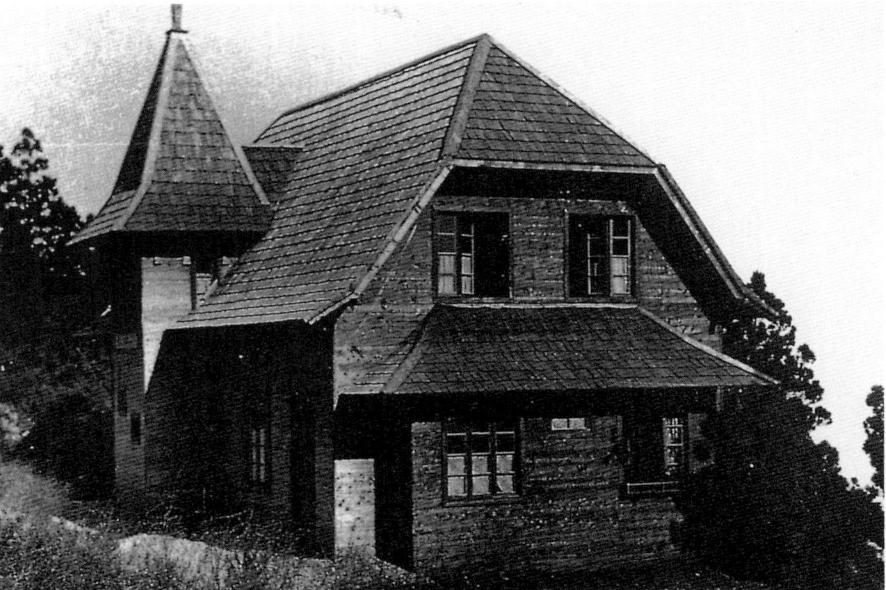

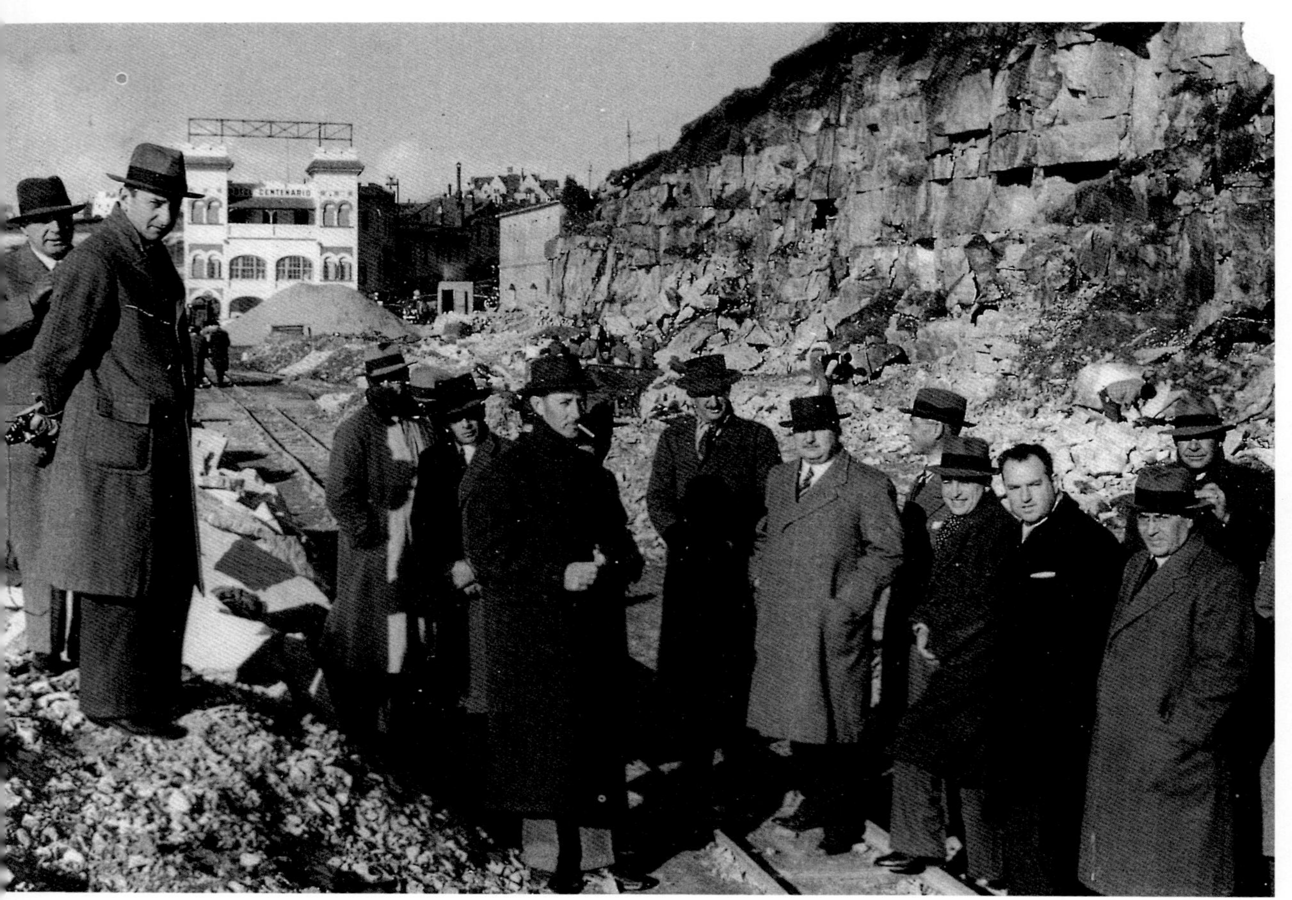

Fig. 5. Alejandro Bustillo, *upper left foreground*, directing construction in Mar del Plata Casino.

the national parks law in the same year with Bustillo as Parks president, succeeding Angel Gallardo. The Parks Commission also included Antonio Lynch, Víctor Pinto, E. Huergo representing the railroad, Germán Frers representing the Highway Department, Enrique Butty for the army, Carlos Ortiz Basualdo, [?] Serigós, and Antonio Baldrich. They planned a program of activity for the park, including houses for park rangers, administration, docks, port buildings, and roads, with the intention of promoting progress in the zone, thus creating a regional architectural style.

This style was spread by the National Parks in their desire to make Bariloche a special city, not like other towns and cities of the country that were laid out on the typical Spanish grid, but rather like one of the quaint mountain towns that were the pride of Switzerland and the Tyrol.

Later, the urbanization of Bariloche and zoning regulations were developed with the advice of Alejandro Bustillo, architect and brother of Exequiel, and with the direction of Miguel Angel Cesari, an architect from the École des Beaux-Arts who designed the civic center. The choice of a style was set.

One month after the railroad reached Bariloche, some of the Commission, among them Alberto del Solar Dorrego, a golf expert, and Alejandro and Exequiel Bustillo, traveled there to ascertain the location and architecture most appropriate for a hotel. The story of their trip is repeated here.

> We reached Bariloche and, before continuing to Huemul, we attacked the task of locating the hotel. We examined practically the entire town for this purpose but did not find a place.
>
> Then we continued on to Llao-Llao where Alejandro, like one who had discovered a diamond, did not waver a moment and, discarding any other location, recommended a small plateau covered with a burned forest as the site for the hotel.
>
> The spot could not have been better because, even though the wind from the mountains on this side of the lake was an inconvenience, it was more than compensated for by the breathtaking view.[7]

Alejandro Bustillo was born in Buenos Aires in 1889 and lived almost ninety-four years, during which he projected and directed approximately 250 works in different parts of the country (fig. 5) as well as in France. He was a painter, sculptor, builder, and architect, a member of the Fine Arts, Sciences, and Hellenic Academies. His first prize was in the Buenos Aires Salón Nacional of 1912 for one of his self-portraits. He constructed his first buildings in Plátanos in Buenos Aires Province, the rural area where he lived and learned about local materials and their traditional uses, applying his ideas of proportion to chicken houses and barns.

His first important works were planned in Paris where he and his family were sent by Don Carlos Tornquist. He constructed two buildings in Buenos Aires for this client in 1923 and 1928: the family's house, currently the Belgian Embassy, and the Tornquist Bank (fig. 6), currently Credit Lyonnais. Both buildings are in the French neoclassic style.

His great admiration for Greek Culture dated from his childhood and is shown in his ideals of Perfection, Beauty, and the Search for Truth without conflict: abstract, universal, and absolute.[8] These define him as a classicist, respecting all that the École des Beaux-Arts stamped on architecture well into the twentieth century.

In 1800, in Argentina, the architectural return to the Greek and Roman style, following the Spanish colonial period, was a sign of liberty and republicanism and a standard for the movements of liberation. Alejandro Bustillo said, "I began with classic, but then followed the neoclassic because it is closest to Greek architecture."[9]

In 1935, Bustillo took part in a competition sponsored by the Parks Commission for the construction of a hotel in Bariloche. It was projected that the work could be completed with two and a half million pesos to be raised by a bond issue. The amortization of the debt and the interest was the responsibility of the National Parks.

The projects were presented on 14 February 1935 and judged by a jury composed of J.A. Hortal, national director of public works; E. Huergo; and Antonio Lynch, the latter two already mentioned as members of the Parks Commission. The president of the country, Augustín P. Justo, also attended the exposition of the projects held in the Palais de Glace where the entries

7. Bustillo, *El despertar*.

8. In Alejandro Bustillo's original texts, these terms are capitalized.

9. Alejandro Bustillo, conversation with author.

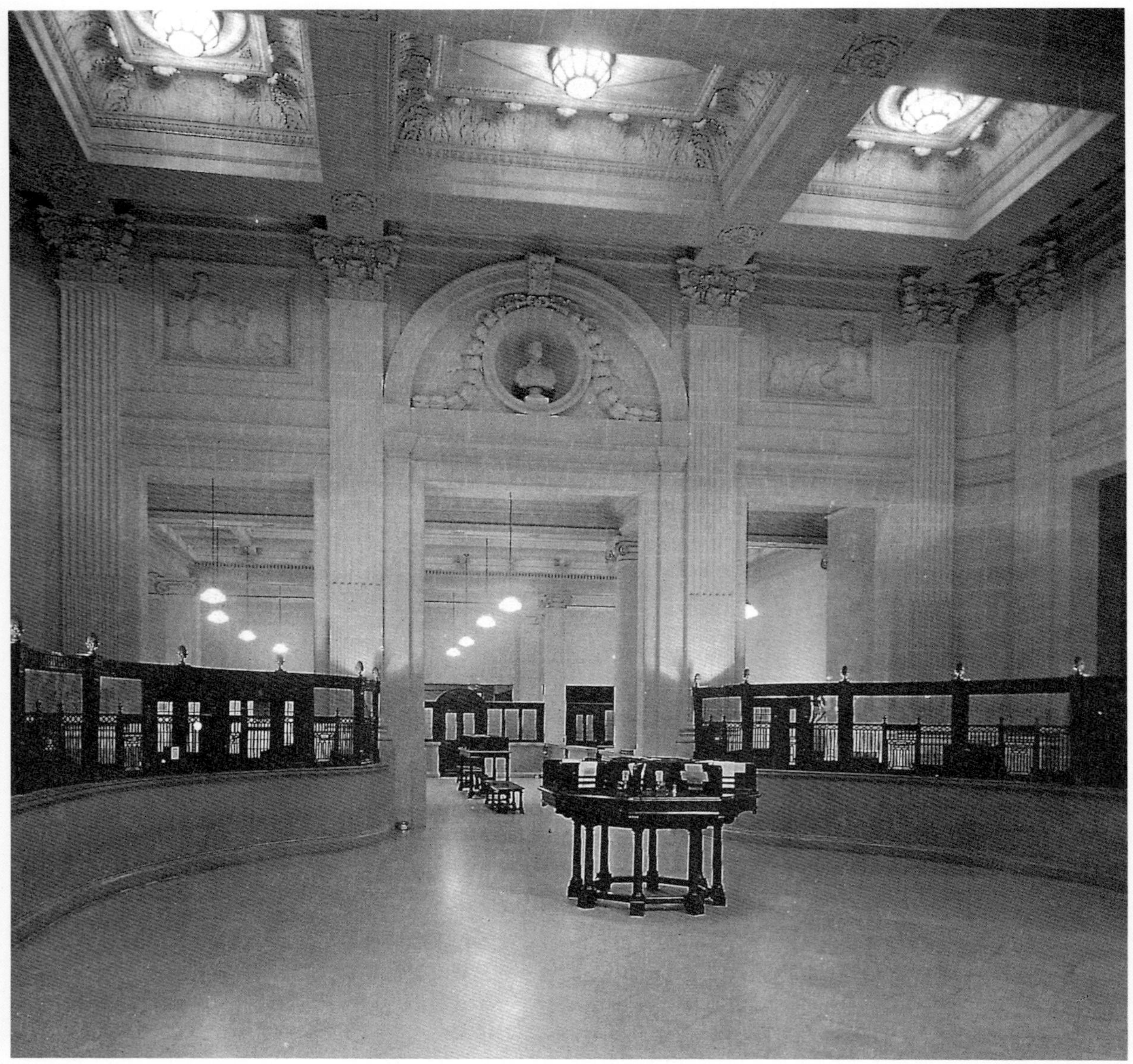

Fig. 6. Alejandro Bustillo,

lobby of the Tornquist Bank,

Buenos Aires, 1928.

were judged. Alejandro Bustillo, author of the winning project, said of his design, "The problem is to make something impeccable.... I think it would be very difficult for someone to do this better than I.... [I]t is such a complex matter that no one could solve it by chance."

In the years during which he told me of some of his achievements, this description of what motivated his winning project was included: "On the visit to Bariloche with my initial partners, study companions (a group that did not last long), Dates and Jacobs and two of my sons, Alejandro and César, our path took us to Puerto Pañuelo. There we stayed at the Hotel Entrelagos, from which we surveyed the area previously photographed by Thorlichen" (fig. 7).

From this site, as he would do with the hotel and casino in Mar del Plata, with his eyes half-closed in the semidarkness of his room, he drew the silhouette of Llao-Llao, following the profile of the mountain. These drawings and sketches, further developed on the train to Bariloche, are exactly the same as the final project presented in the competition (fig. 8).

According to local historians, the architects of the Generation of the '80s used the French style unreservedly as an expression of conservatism. At the same time, in the interior of the country, the local traditions—the native, the picturesque, the popular—prevailed. Nevertheless, the changes begun in that decade, combined with an emerging cosmopolitanism, were expressed in the historicist eclecticism dominating all of western Europe.

The School of Architecture at the University of Buenos Aires was established in 1901, under Exact Sciences, following the model of Beaux-Arts in Paris. Bustillo graduated as architect in 1914. In his writings, published as reflections after the almost simultaneous accomplishment of his three major works—Mar del Plata, Llao-Llao, and the National Bank—Bustillo said the following about the question of styles: "It is necessary to *think* what architecture is in order to *decide* what architecture is and to be able to choose with certainty and precision the architecture best suited to the place and time."[10]

10. Alejandro Bustillo, *La belleza primero: hipótesis metafísica* (Beauty first: a metaphysical hypothesis) (Buenos Aires: Guillermo Kraft, Ltd., 1957).

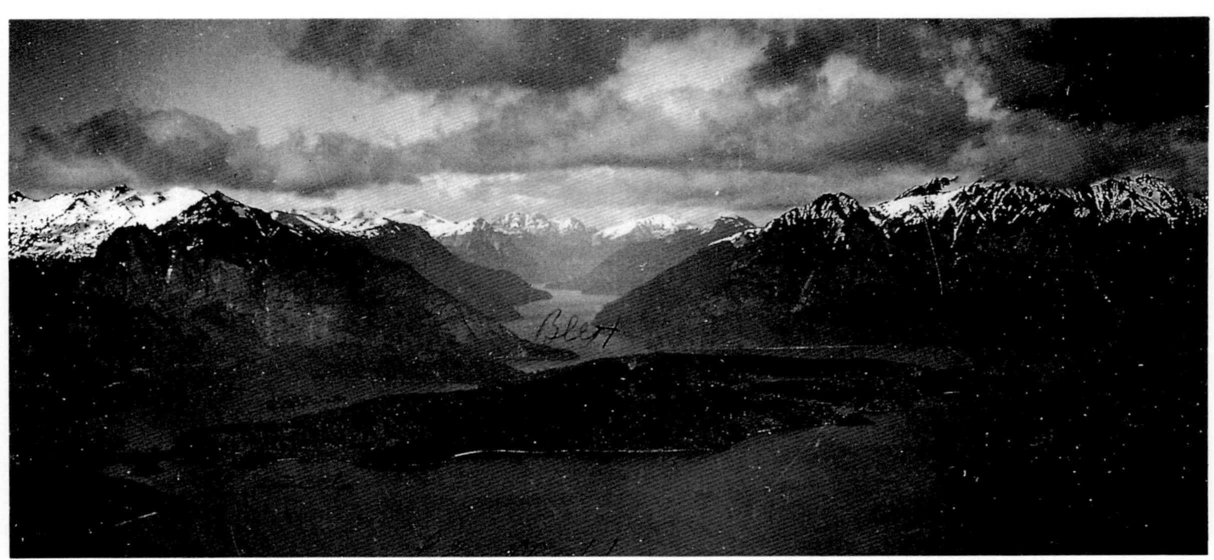

Fig. 7. Site of the Llao-Llao Hotel. Photograph by Thorlichen.

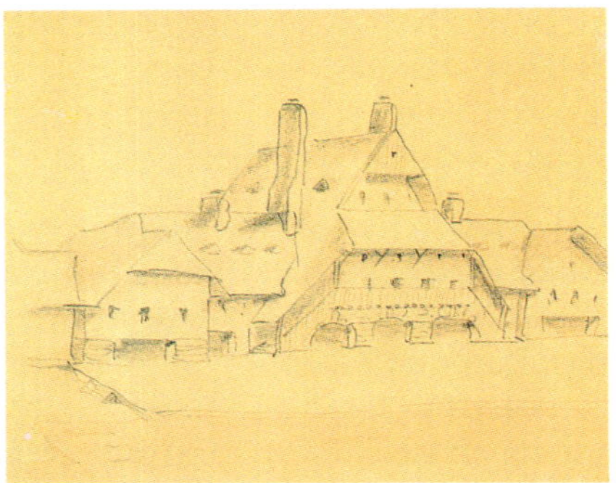

Fig. 8. Alejandro Bustillo, early sketch of the Llao-Llao Hotel.

The development of these three grand works caused him to think of the possibility of an Argentine monumental architecture. "Monumental architecture is architecture as essence and as art, putting aside the technical aspects of construction and function.... [T]o understand the question of style in architecture, which is an art that comes from the social and cultural, one must remove oneself from controversies and antagonisms.... Architecture is something like a skeleton that supports everything man needs to live, dream, create, and to be man."[11]

The Llao-Llao Hotel, constructed in 1939 and rebuilt after a fire the following year, is a monument to nature, a container for the dazzling elegance of the wealthy society of the time. It is possible to think that it was conceived for that unknown race of beautiful blond people with thick beards and blue eyes who peered from under the brims of three-cornered hats and spoke a language the Spaniards and the Indians could not understand. With his eyes half-closed, Bustillo drew a unique building, asymmetrical like the Greek complexes, reinventing the City of the Caesars, giving it a real life (figs. 9 and 10).

The foundation and the walks were of stone. The luxurious building was made of carved stone, the walls were overlapping wooden panels with bark still attached, as in the first local constructions offered by the lumbering industry at the turn of the century. The roofs were inspired, as he remembers, by a book of engravings that his mother gave him. With their multiple slopes, they almost exactly copy the El Parque Pensión in the Argricultural Colony of Bariloche built in 1920.

▸

Figs. 9 and 10. The original Llao-Llao Hotel, 1939.

After the fire, when all that remained was the stone base, the hotel was reconstructed (fig. 11). The wood disappeared; the log walls and shingle roofs were replaced by reinforced concrete and tiles. But the shape was the same because it pertained to the landscape that it imitated. From that moment, Llao-Llao became the symbol of Bariloche. Its useful life was forty short years, and this marvel, placed so solidly on the edge of the lake, would represent a synthesis of traditional construction and modern function.

The use Bustillo made of the landscape, integrating the new image of the building with nature, is easily understood when he speaks about the Parthenon, for him an example of perfect architecture. "[I]t is not a monument made with straight and level lines but rather with ingenious deformations and the most subtle modulations of lines; the rhythm of the hill follows the rhythm of the work" (fig. 12).[12]

11. Ibid.

12. Ibid.

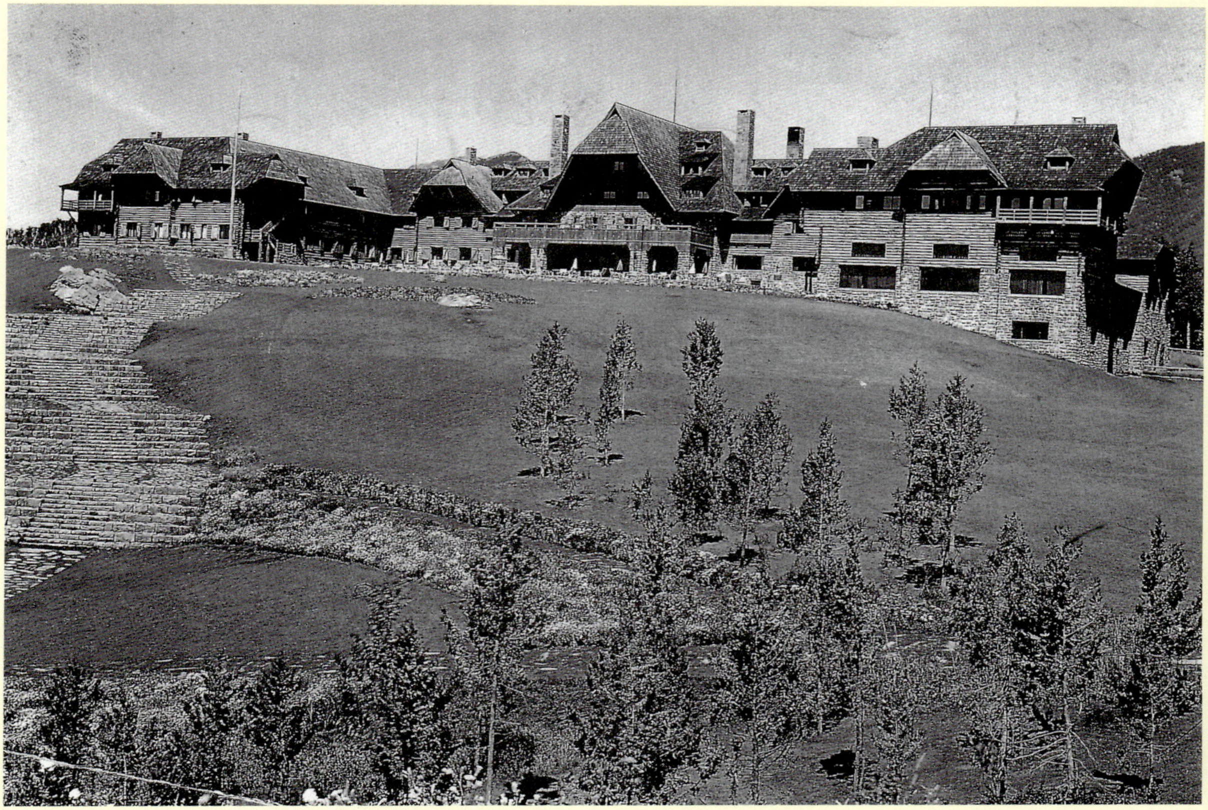

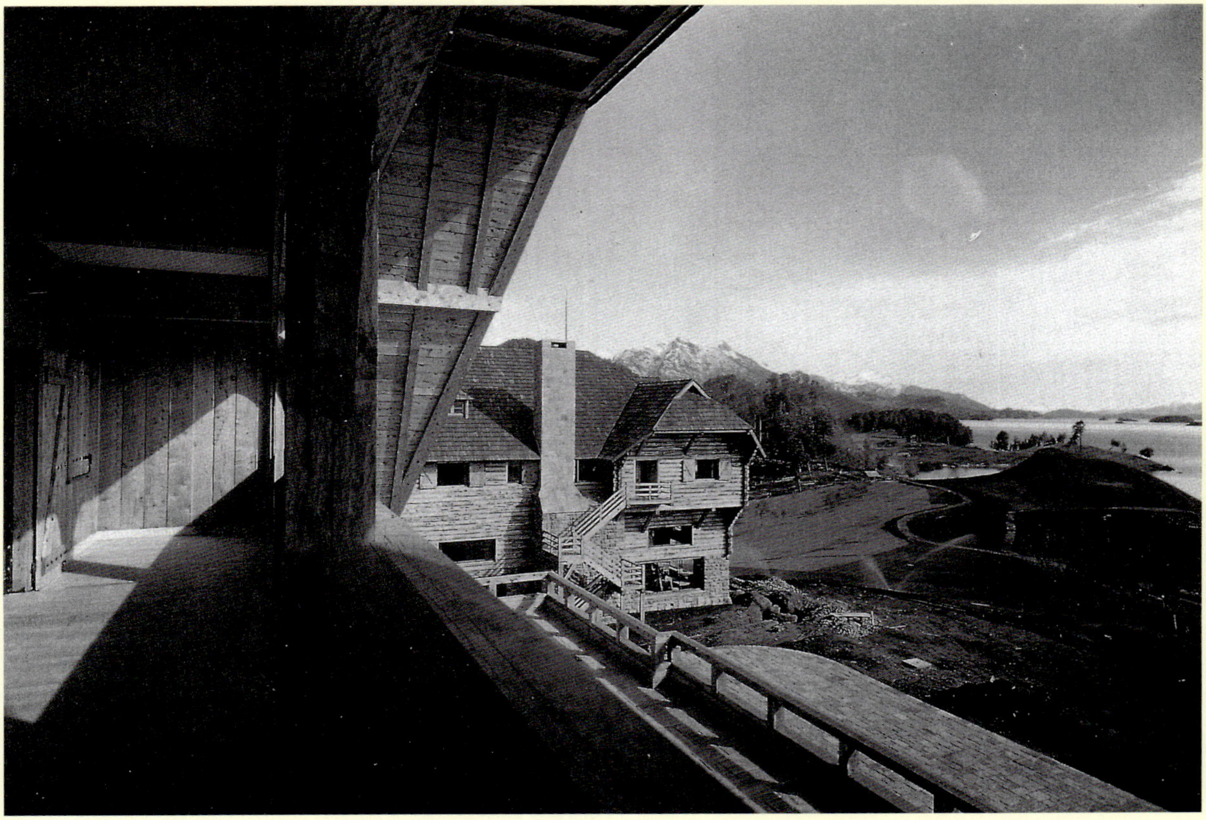

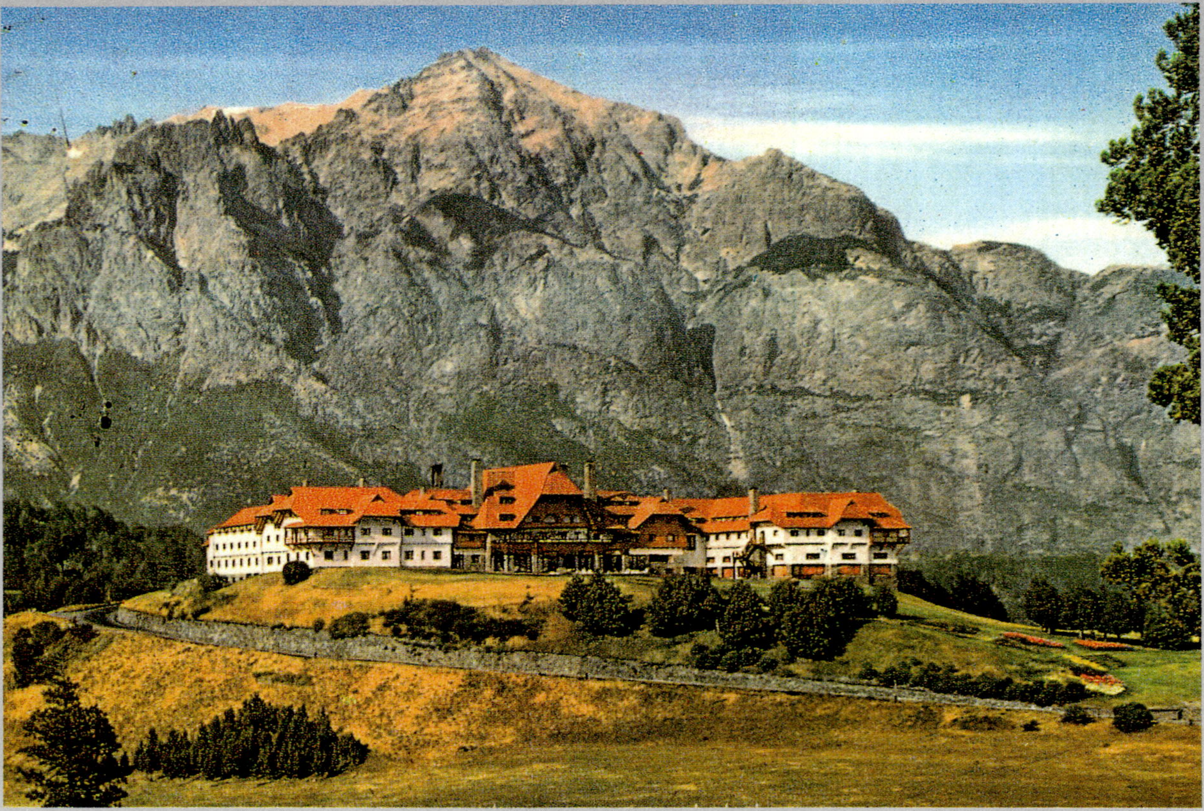

Figs. 11 and 12. The rebuilt Llao-Llao Hotel, 1945.

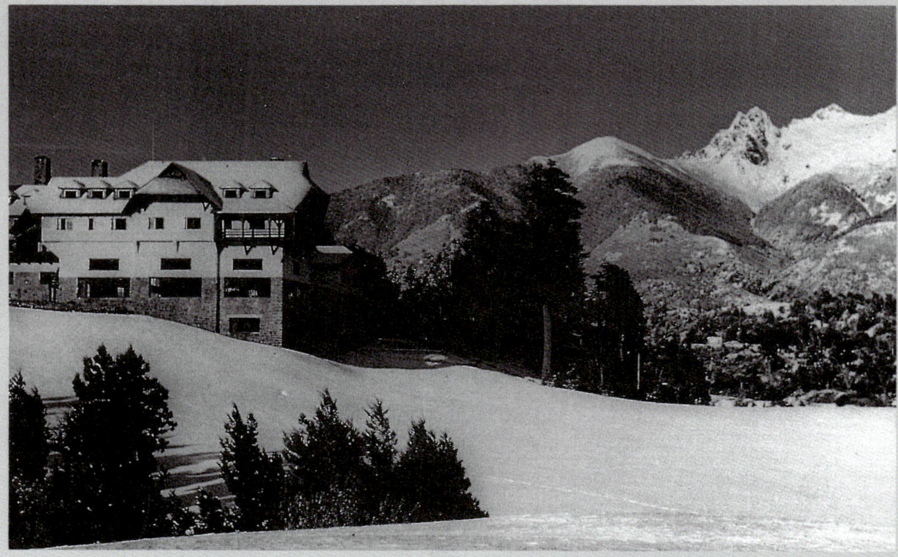

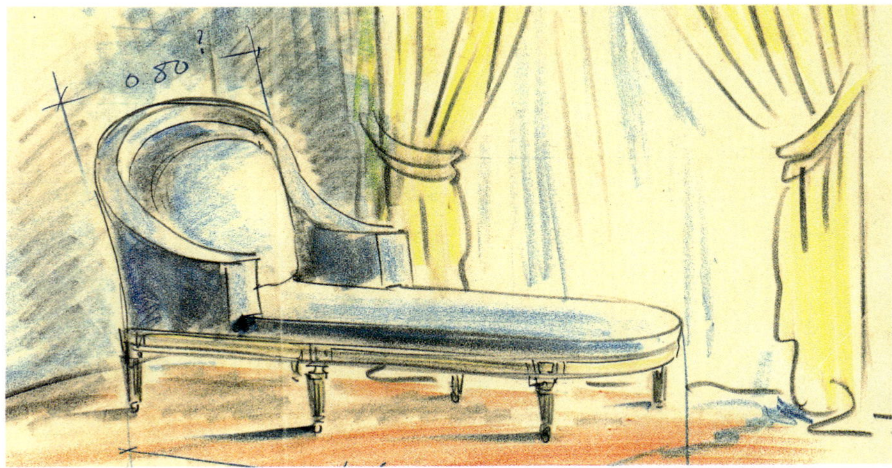

Fig. 13. Alejandro Bustillo, chaise-lounge, 1940.

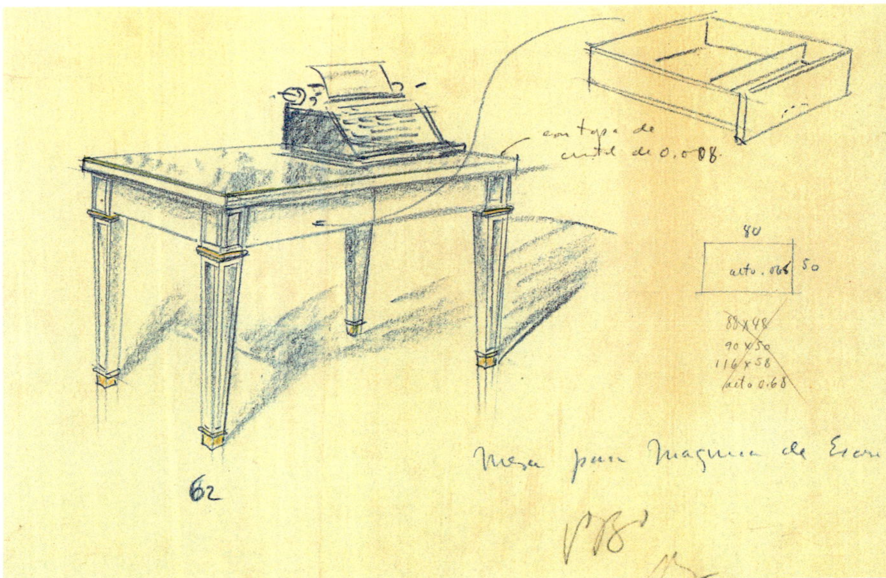

Fig. 14. Alejandro Bustillo, desk for the National Bank, ca. 1941.

The project for the interior of the Llao-Llao Hotel is also Alejandro Bustillo's. It is connected with the history of Argentine furniture and the Comte group, formed in the thirties by the architects Mariano Mansilla Moreno, José Enrique Tivoli, Ricardo Pirovano, and the lawyer Ignacio Pirovano.[13]

Bustillo designed the furniture for all his French neoclassic buildings, for the *petit hotels* (fig. 13), and the National Bank (figs. 14 and 18). The Comte group collaborated on many of these works. Comte specialized at that time in grand government buildings which bear their stamp. They worked in the Presidential Residence, the National and Provincial Banks, the Foreign Office, the Ministries, and even on a scale model of the D.L.22 airplane for the Aeronautic Institute of Córdoba.

In the same way that the architecture of Llao-Llao looked to traditional, colonial, and missionary models, for the designs of the furniture Bustillo and

13. Celina Arauz de Pirovano inherited Comte's archives and has generously provided the information transcribed here.

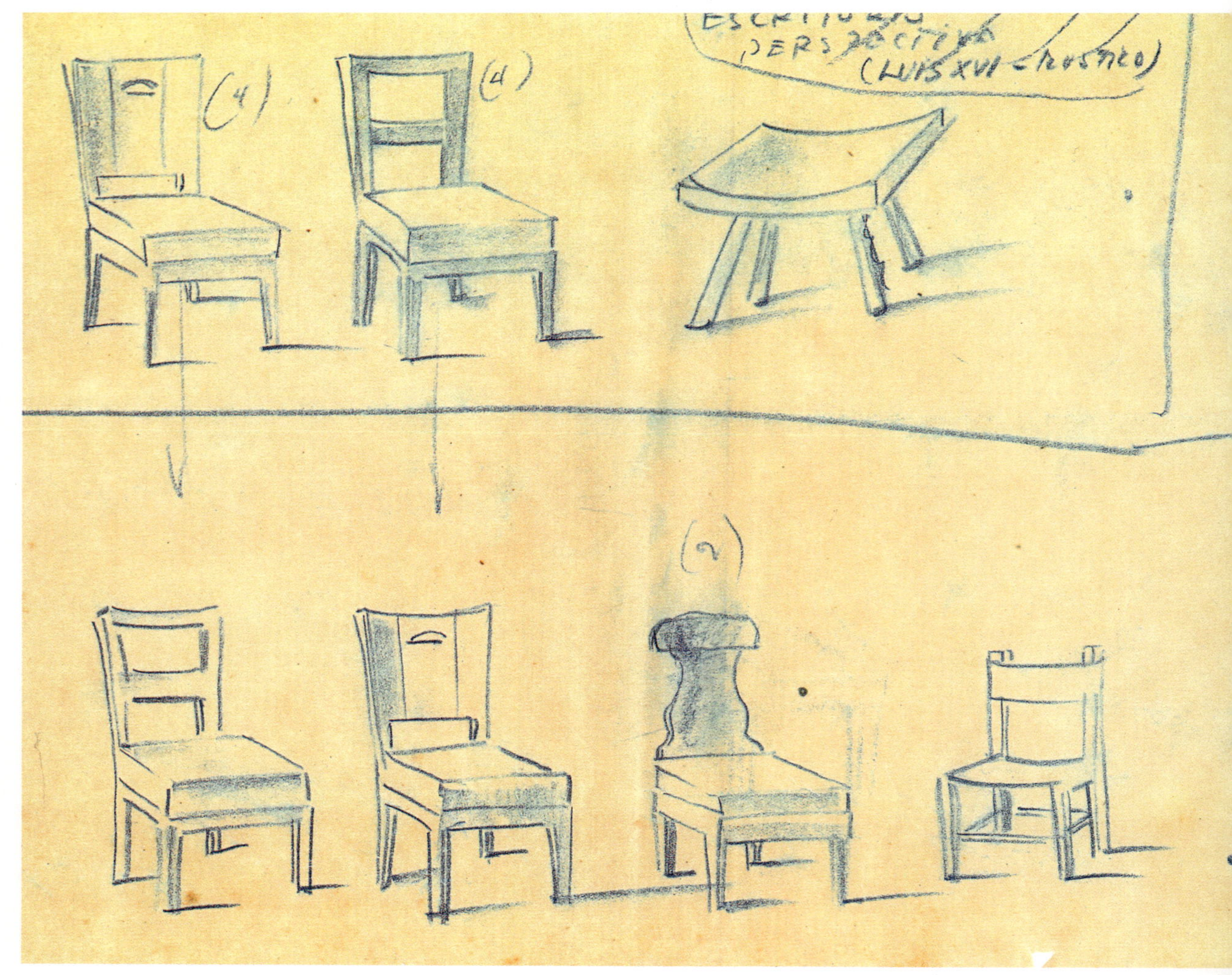

Fig. 15. Alejandro Bustillo, sketches for Llao-Llao Hotel furniture. **(See page 25.)**

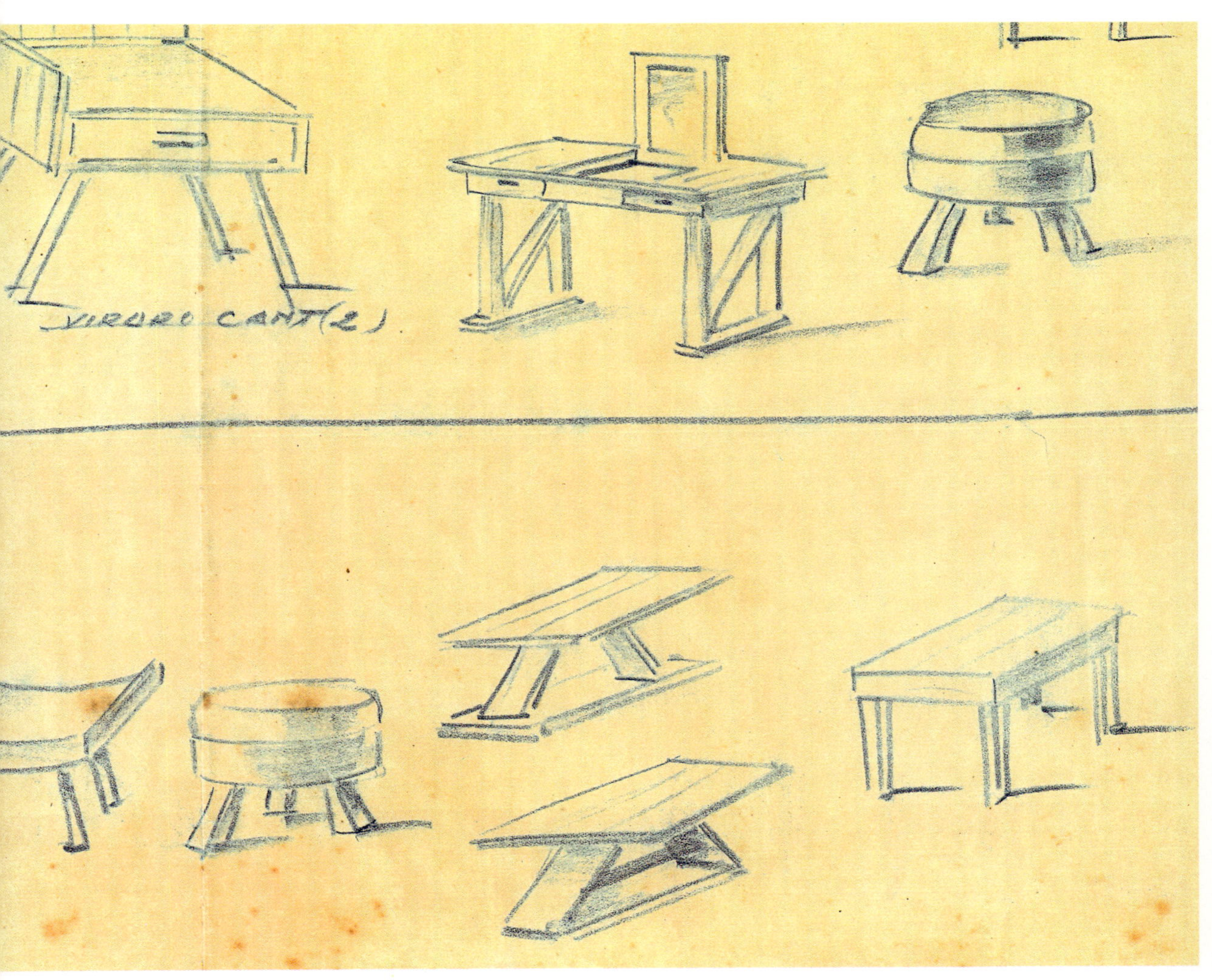
VIRORO CANT(2)

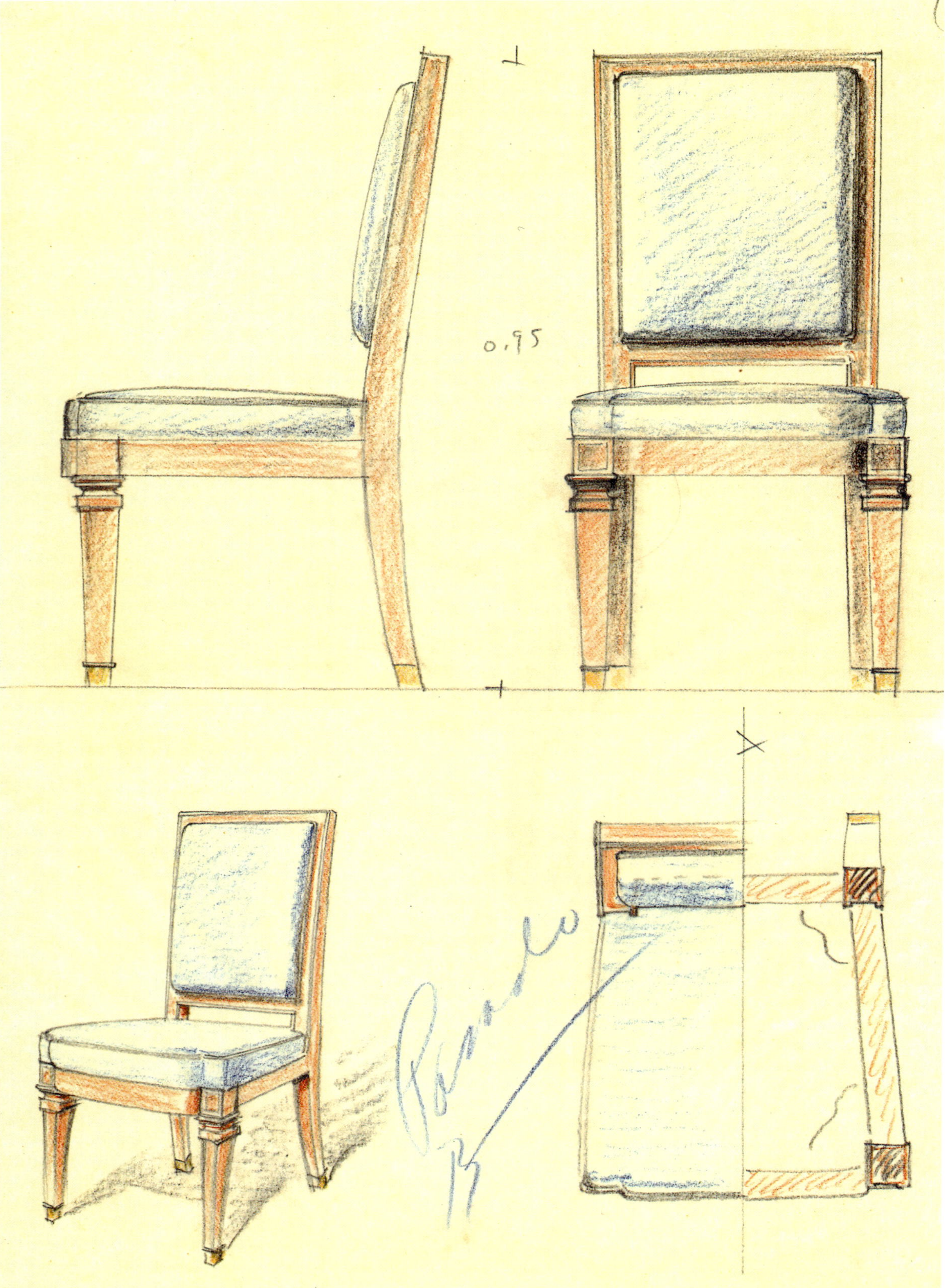
0,95

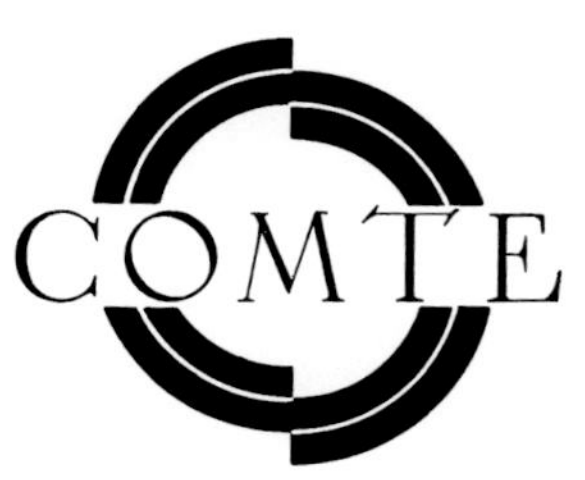

Fig. 16. Comte logo.

Comte used the materials available in the country (fig. 15). The Comte group (figs. 16 and 17) won a competition for the furnishing and decorating of the hotel and put rustic prototypes to the test. New designs were created for *algarrobo* and *palo santo* (two native trees), and well-known Louis XVI designs were modernized and stripped—or "cleaned," according to Comte—of all excess decoration to create the Llao-Llao style.

In an unpublished article about Comte, Ignacio Pirovano wrote, "The character of Llao-Llao, inspired by Bustillo, was that of a great country house of exceptional proportions.... [C]ompletely new bedroom sets, all different, were designed where primary colors alternated with their variations. Sky blue, canary yellow, pink, and Nile green combined with the dark and light woods of the furniture.

"For upholstery they chose handmade fabrics, woven by Alfredo Peña Unzué, dyed in monochromatic blue, yellow, green, and red. These colors were chosen so as not to compete with the flowered landscape outside or the admirably worked raw leathers of deer, axis, capybara, horse, and Aberdeen Angus and Jersey cattle. This beautifully toned leather was used to cover the great sofas and comfortable easy chairs, with their simple and severe lines."

The Llao-Llao collection was made up of a group of models that attempted a national furniture design. The dining room chair came from the simplification of a French chair (fig. 19), with the hand hole in its back, a theme repeated in the dressing-room chair (fig. 20). This detail is traditional in the rural furniture of Argentina. It lightens the weight and makes the piece easily transportable.

The dining room had been carefully designed without columns. Large and decorative pieces of wood were placed like curved ribs as divisions between the sectors (figs. 21 and 22). The bases of the dining tables were, in some cases, in the shape of a fixed cross, inspired by army furniture that can be taken apart. Other tables were made from entire cylindrical logs with the bark still attached (fig. 24).

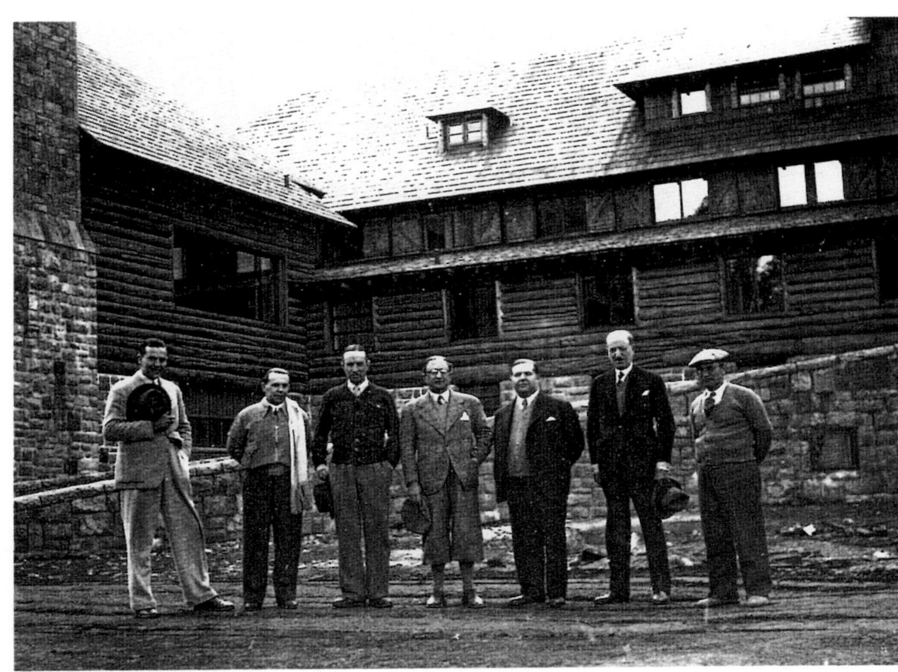

Fig. 17. Ricardo Pirovano, *far left*, Exequiel Bustillo, *third from left*, Llao-Llao, 1939.

◀

Fig. 18. Alejandro Bustillo, chair for the National Bank, ca. 1941.

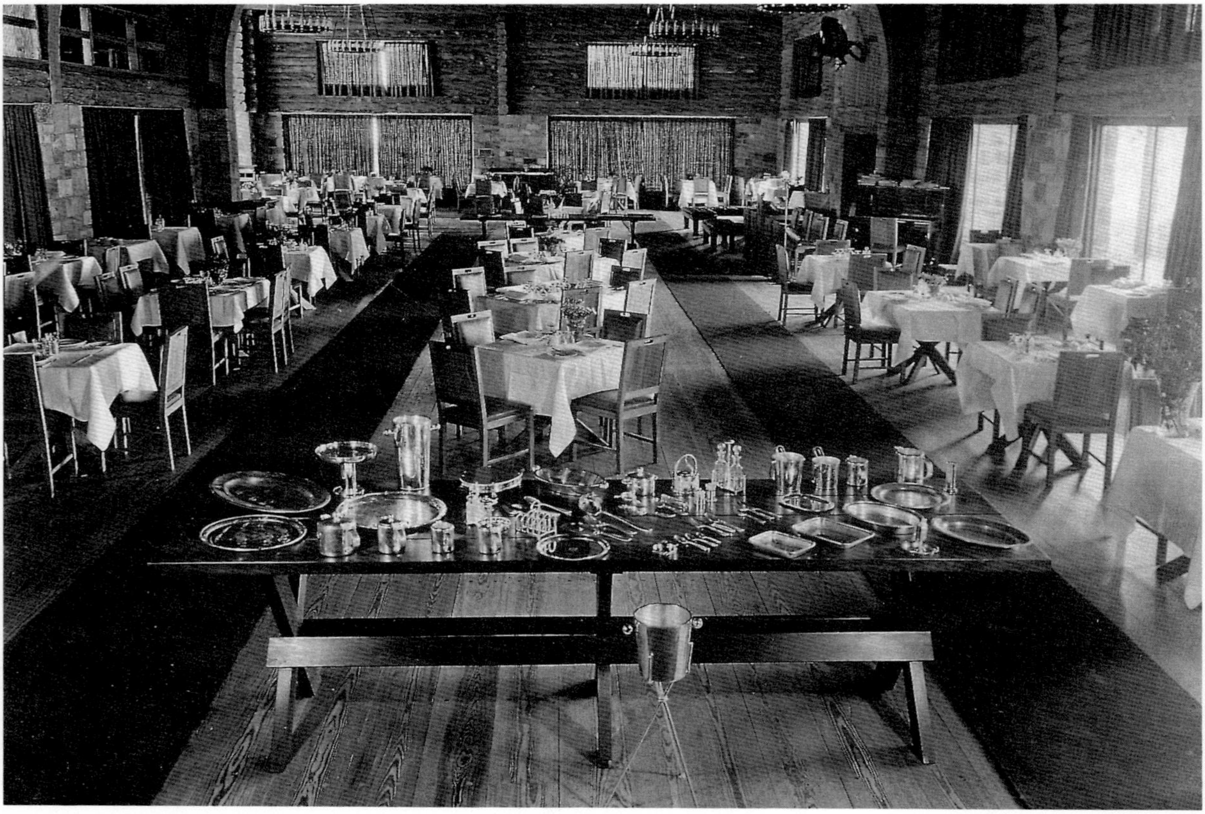

Fig. 19. Formal dining room, Llao-Llao Hotel, 1939.

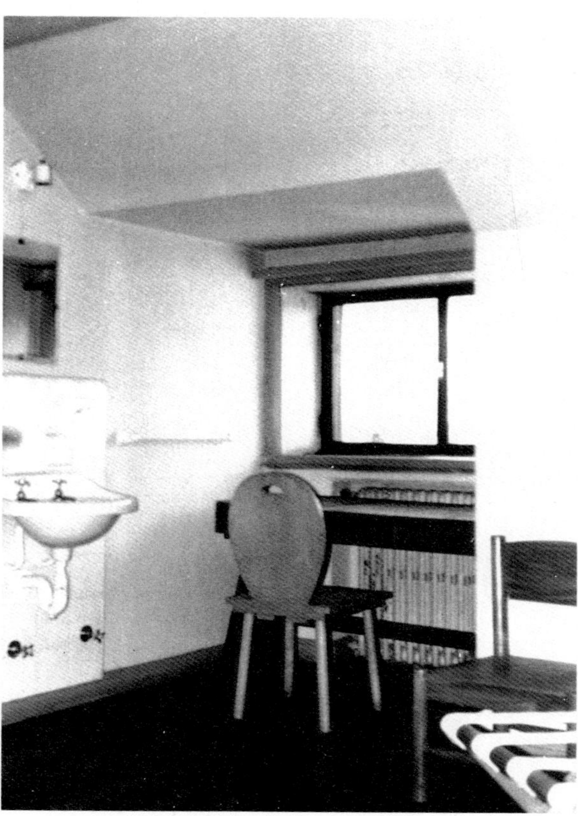

Fig. 20. Dressing-room chair, Llao-Llao Hotel, 1939.

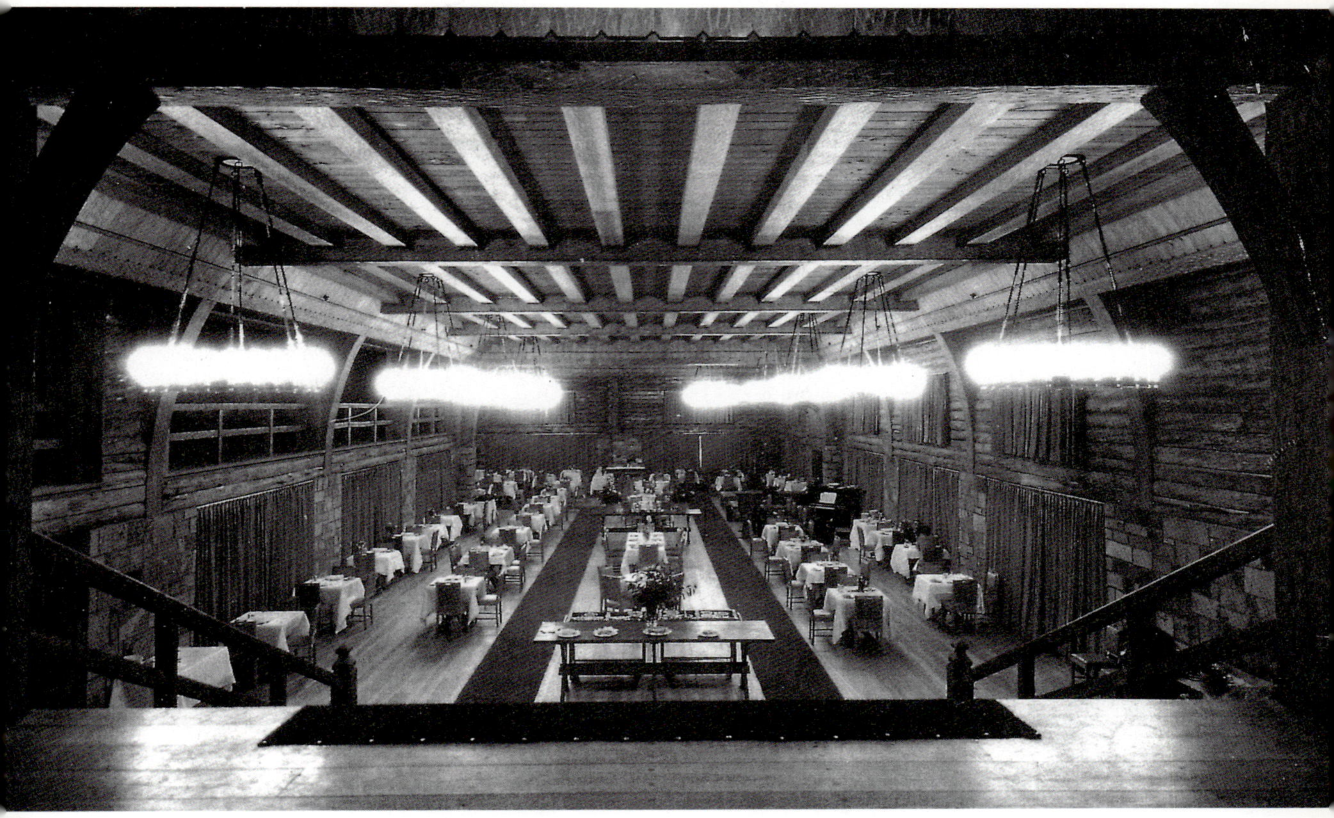

Fig. 21. Formal dining room, Llao-Llao Hotel, 1939.

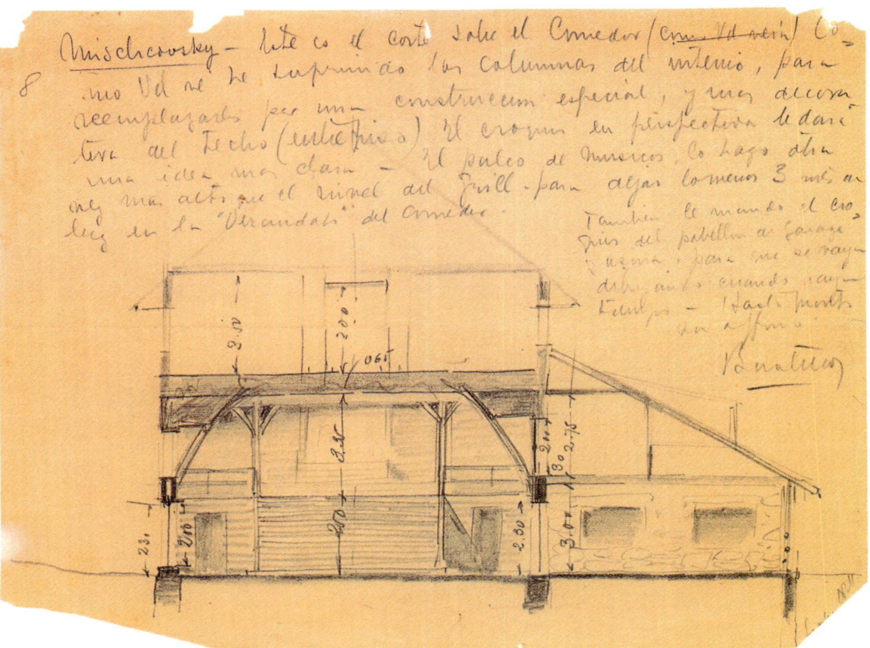

Fig. 22. Alejandro Bustillo, sketch of the formal dining room, Llao-Llao Hotel, 1939.

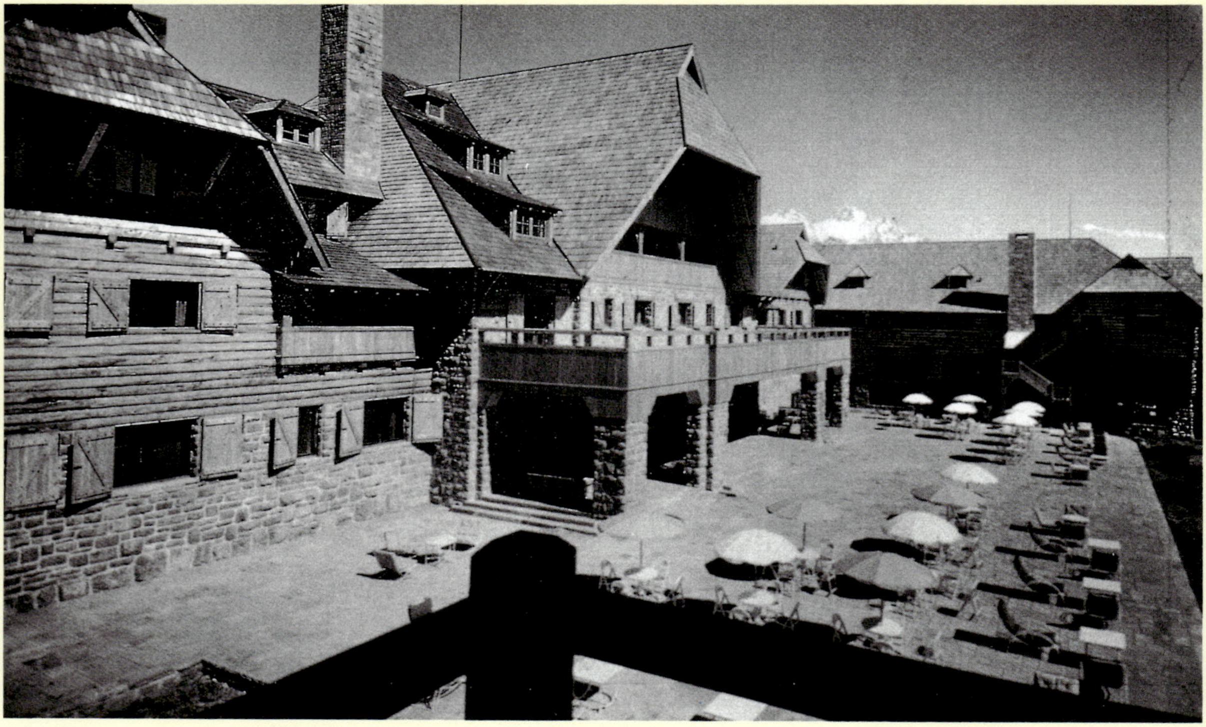

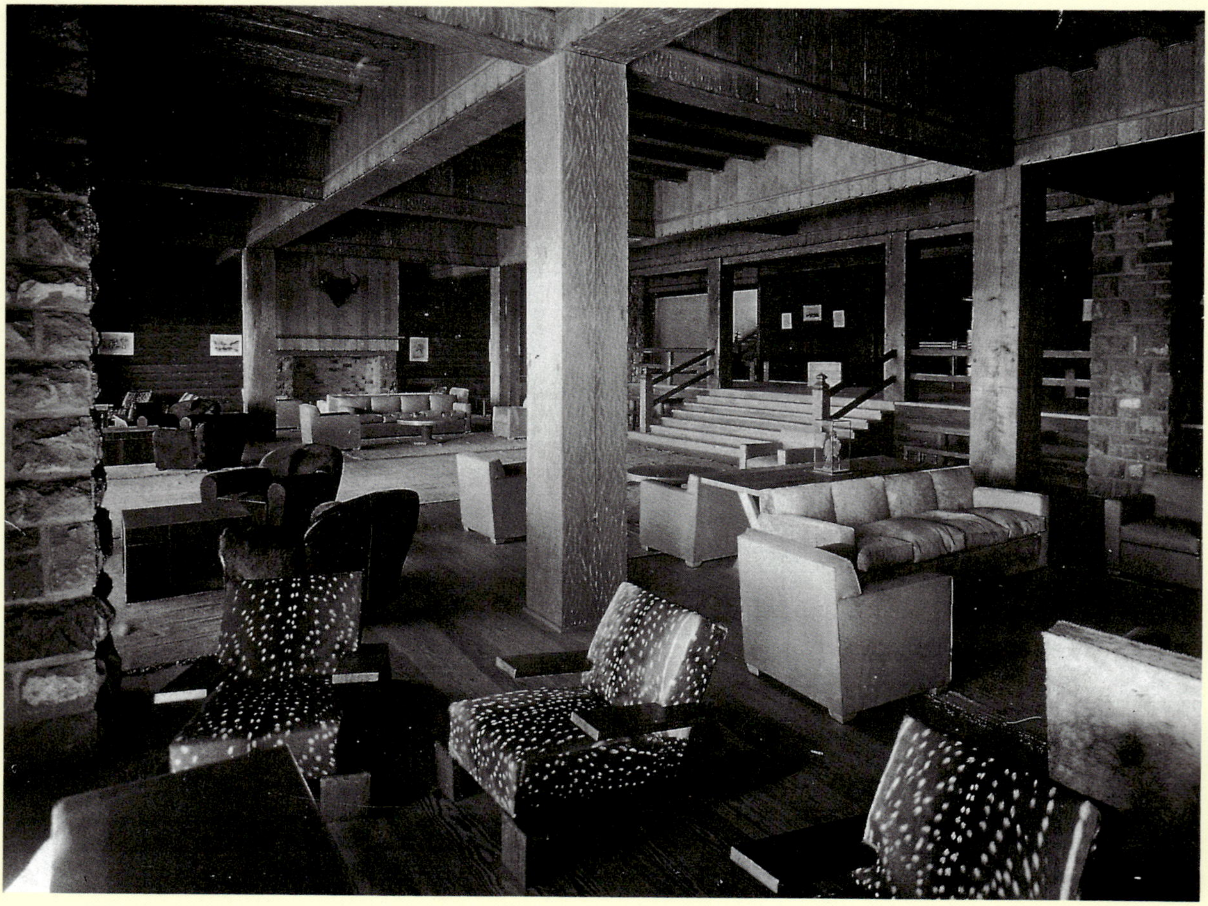

◂

Fig. 23. Terrace, Llao-Llao Hotel, 1939. (See page 30.)

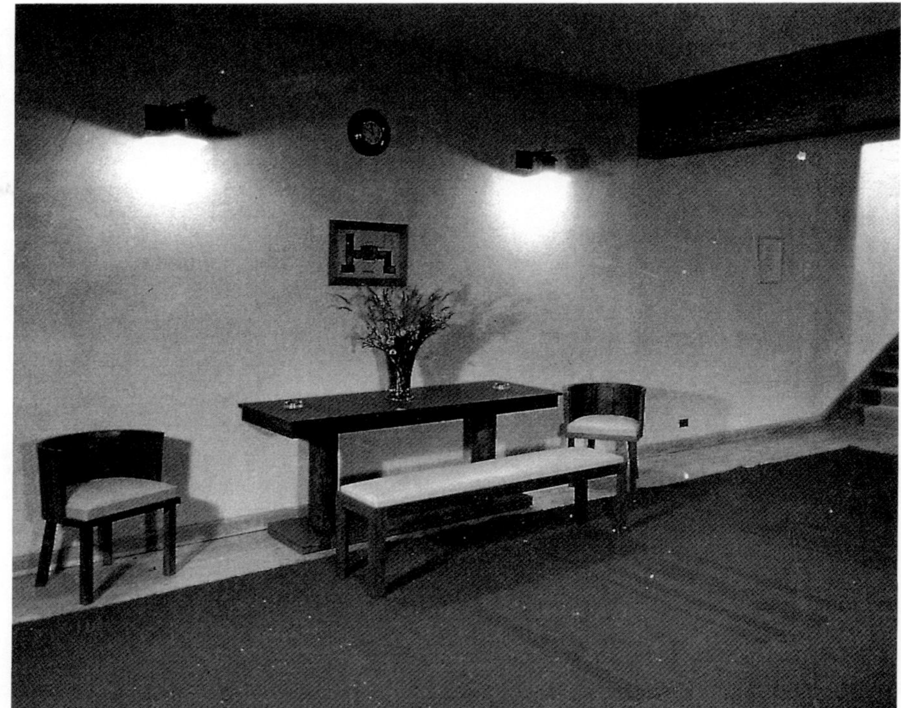

Fig. 24. Table with tree-trunk legs, Llao-Llao Hotel, 1939.

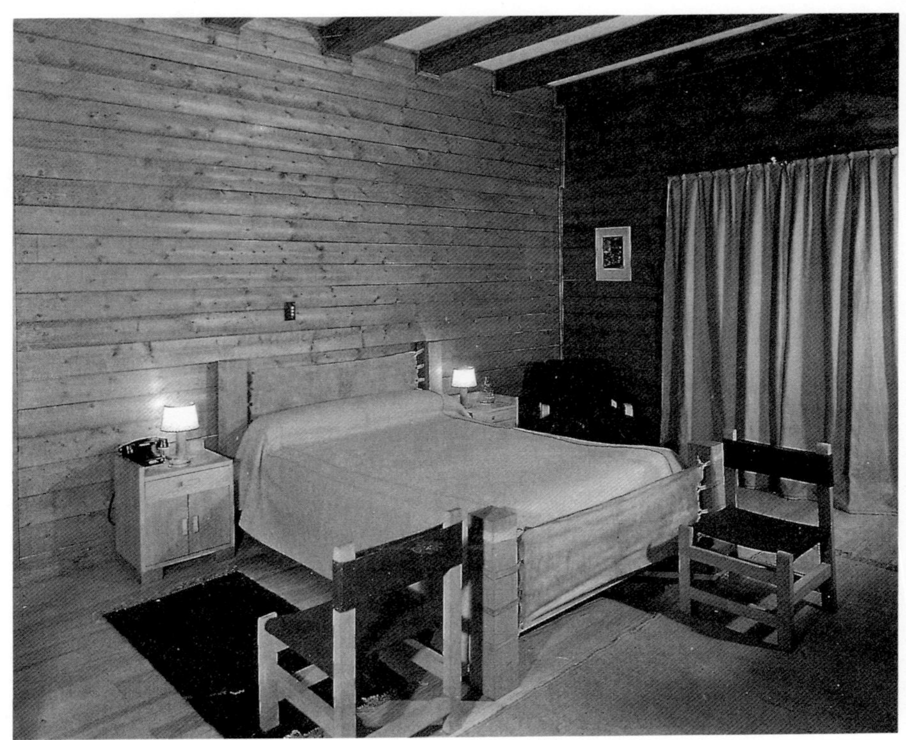

◂

Fig. 25. Jean-Michel Frank, "elephant" chair, Llao-Llao Hotel, 1939. (See page 30.)

Fig. 26. Bedroom, Llao-Llao Hotel, 1939. (See page 30.)

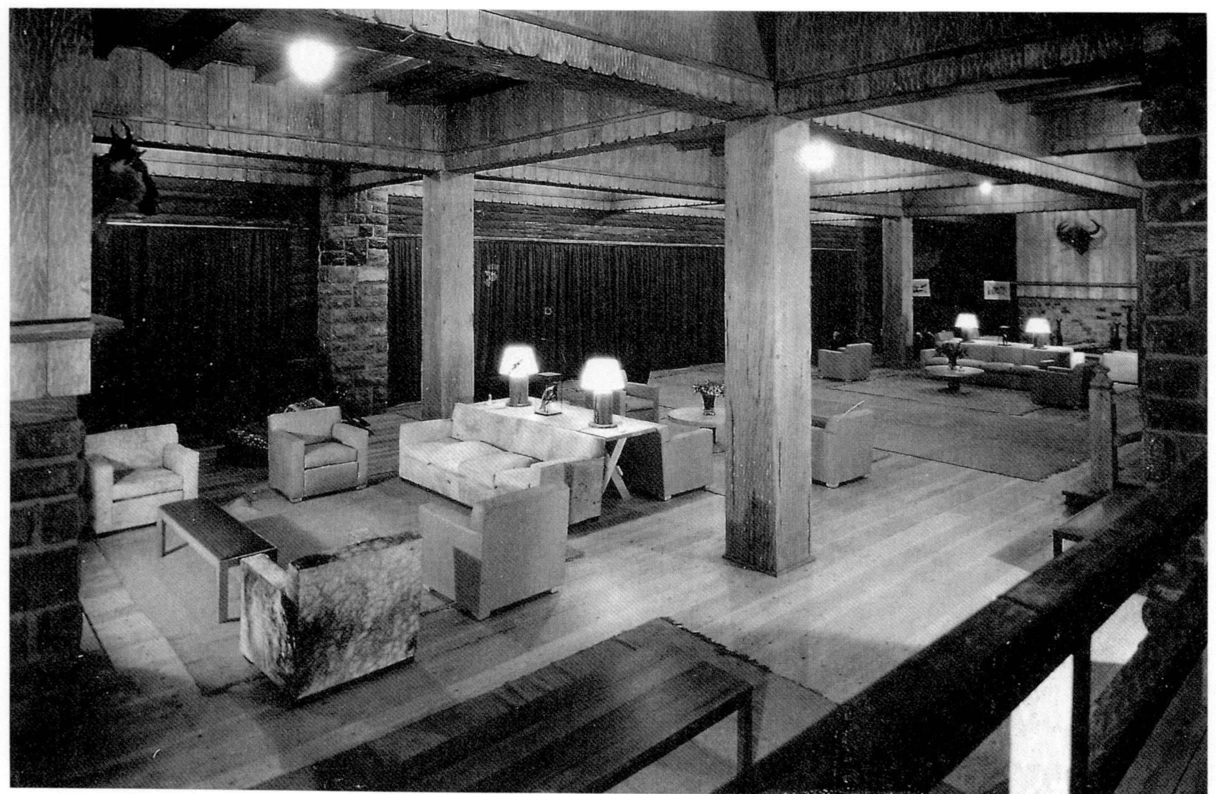

Fig. 27. Jean-Michel Frank, furniture upholstered with rare animal hides, Llao-Llao Hotel, 1939.

The bedroom chair, redesigned from the familiar Jesuit or Spanish colonial chair, with or without stretched leather, had an additional crosspiece as a footrest for the guitar player (fig. 26). Recently created modern designs of Le Corbusier and Mies van der Rohe were used on the terraces (fig. 23).

Variations in the chair designs and the entire collection of the Llao-Llao style can be seen in Bustillo's drawings. This would later spread throughout the whole Nahuel Huapí region, becoming a regional type. The Comte group continued with its repertory of rustic forms—the missionary style and the Argentine rural style—until the end of the Second World War when it changed production methods and began to manufacture built-in furniture.

In 1939, Jean-Michel Frank, the great "recreator of French designs,"[14] joined Comte (figs. 27 and 28). With him, the prestige of the French vanguard and the influence of the 1925 Exposition Internationale des Arts Décoratifs et Industriels Modernes were incorporated. One testimony to his work and his contribution to Llao-Llao is an "elephant" model chair (fig. 25), characterized by the plainness of its lines and its originality.

The influence of Frank in Llao-Llao is definite, through his writing and his lectures, and even more when he came to Argentina as Comte's collaborator.

14. Leopoldo Diego Sánchez, *Jean-Michel Frank* (Paris: Éditions Du Regard, 1980).

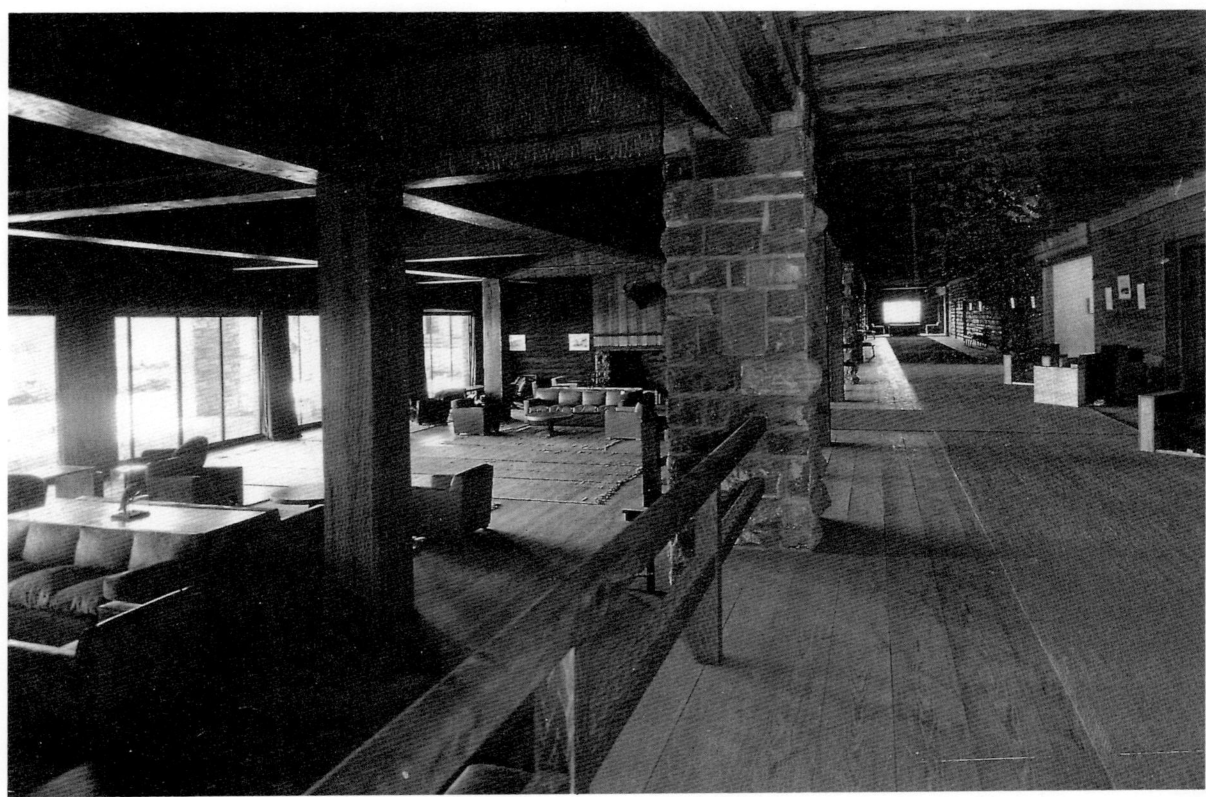

Fig. 28. Jean-Michel Frank, furniture upholstered with rare animal hides, Llao-Llao Hotel, 1939.

Josette Devin wrote about Frank:

> [I]f he preferred expensive materials, he also knew how to cover walls or furniture with burlap and put raffia mats on the floor without losing his secure sense of harmony and togetherness. His taste tended toward handcrafted iron, leather, and wood. He had to "feel the hand," as they say. He preferred fabrics and rugs that were made by hand. He used natural cowhide to cover small commodes.... He had no prejudices...and liked to create unexpected situations.... He used many elements made by local craftsmen in his installations. He liked the thick saddle harnesses, decorated with studs and bronze adornments, and used them in screens, mirror frames, and clothes racks.[15]

Paris 1930–Bariloche 1940 represents a fusion experience, one which has been constantly repeated in the history of our country.[16] □

15. Josette Devin, "Un decorador olvidado," *L'Oeil*, no. 101 (May 1963). This material was lent for use in this article by Celina Arauz de Pirovano and translated by Ignacio Pirovano.

16. The Llao-Llao Hotel, which closed 1 April 1980, has been sold to Quality Inn Sur S.A. It will be restored, modernized, and reopened in 1993.

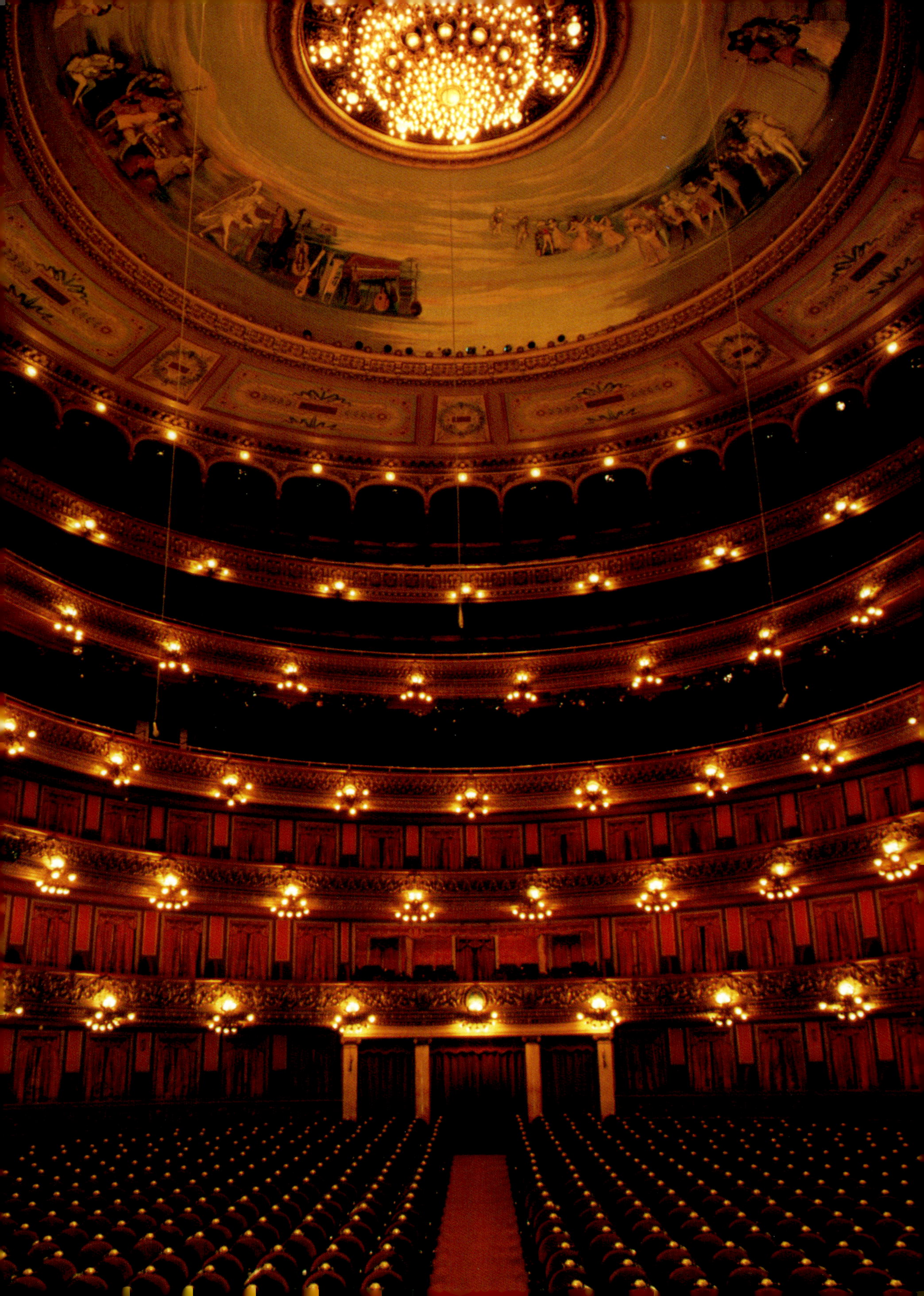

Héctor Basaldúa and the Colón Theater: Thirty Years of Stage Design

By Emilio Basaldúa

Emilio Basaldúa is a film and stage designer. His most recent work was *El milagro secreto* for the Colón Theater, and Falla's *La vida breve* will follow next season. A graduate of the National University of Buenos Aires School of Architecture, he took post-graduate courses at the Hornsey College of Art, the Sorbonne, and New York University as a Fulbright scholar. He is Héctor Basaldúa's son.

In 1910, Buenos Aires celebrated the one-hundredth anniversary of the Revolución de Mayo. The city had changed dramatically in fifteen years, from a provincial town with a colonial aspect to a new and proud capital of what had become, due to its exports of meat and grain, a wealthy country.

To mark the important anniversary, many public and private buildings were hastily erected. Buenos Aires was transformed into a "European" city, the "Paris of America." Architectural sources of inspiration were European revivals—classical, medieval, or Renaissance—and the great Parisian houses of the late eighteenth century.

The Avenida de Mayo was opened as a wide boulevard to connect Government House with the new Congress Building (after the American Capitol); a modern underground system was built, and also railway terminals (after Victoria Station), the docks, the zoo (after different Indian revivals), the Parque de Palermo (after the Bois de Boulogne), splendid palaces for the affluent new bourgeoisie (after eclectic versions of the Parisian *hotel particulier*), and the Colón Theater (after the Paris Opera) which was finished in 1908 (fig. 1).

Construction of the theater had been ordered by the government as far back as 1888, but due to financial difficulties the work started much later (in 1904), on the site formerly occupied by a railway station. Designed by architect Julio Dormal, among others, the house accommodates three thousand people in a horseshoe plan with excellent acoustics. The stage is twenty meters wide, fifteen meters high, and twenty meters deep. Although not everything was finished (*vitraux* were not there, curtains were missing, some furniture had not arrived), the theater opening took place on 25 May 1908 (Independence Day), and the opera chosen for the grand occasion was *Aida*. The sets the audience saw for the first time on that stage were designed by Angelo Parravicini, considered then to be one of the best scenographers of the Scala in Milan.

From 1908 to 1925, the theater was in the hands of private impresarios who brought entire companies from Europe, mainly from Italy, including the sets. All were done in a *trompe l'œil* manner: "realistic" decor designed according to the taste of the times.

Fig. 1. Colón Theater, Buenos Aires. Photograph by Aldo Sessa.

> In 1912, at Callao Street, a few blocks away from home, Bolognini, an Italian painter, had opened a night school to give drawing lessons. Seated next to me, a very alert and bright young man dazzled me with his conversation. Some time later another [young man], recently arrived from Italy, joined us, showing great sensibility and reserve. Uninterested by the low

standards of the school, I lost sight of them. The next year, I was overjoyed when I met them again as we started courses together at the old Fine Arts Academy. Only then did I learn that they were Héctor Basaldúa and Aquiles Badi, my first friends, with whom destiny contrived a long and transcendent friendship.[1]

So says Horacio Butler (1897–1983), an Argentine fellow painter. Basaldúa (1894–1976), Butler, and Badi (1894–1979) would become known as "The Three B's," forming a part, with other Argentine artists, of the Paris Group.

Fig. 2. Héctor Basaldúa, Buenos Aires, 1970. Photograph courtesy of the author.

Héctor Basaldúa (fig. 2) was born in Pergamino, a small town one hundred miles northwest of Buenos Aires. There he spent his childhood, and this context influenced his later painting. When he was in his teens, his family moved to Buenos Aires to a neighborhood called Flores, a kind of lower-middle-class suburbia, with Italian one-storied houses, and neighbors gazing through grated windows. This atmosphere is also crucial in his later work. It is important to mention now that although Basaldúa's relationship with the Colón Theater, as resident stage and costume designer, was going to be a long and intense one (1931–1952 and 1956–1964) during which he designed more than a hundred operas and ballets, he always saw himself mainly as a painter.

Buenos Aires in 1915 was "a flat and conventional city with enormous skies and very long streets not leading anywhere. The atmosphere was melancholic. Men spent all their time standing on street corners waiting for something that never arrived. Only later in Sicily have I seen similar scenes."[2] Although rather exaggerated, Butler's remarks dramatize the cultural vacuum in which young artists had to move.

The Fine Arts Academy gave only drawing lessons.

> The teaching was in the hands of Italians who had studied in Rome or Milan. For them, Art, with a capital *A*, started and ended in the Renaissance; the rest didn't exist. Their ideas were completely wrong. They expected academic and analytical drawings from us. In an anatomy course, the professor criticized a Christ by Velázquez because the insertion of the biceps was misplaced. But the hardest part was the complete lack of artistic information, and we were very conscious of it. There were no art magazines with color reproductions; only by intuition we guessed that something unknown was happening in Europe, through the remarks of travelers coming back.[3]

Basaldúa echoed this opinion in a radio interview in 1958: "We didn't know very much about foreign painters. Just a little about French impressionism through the few canvases hanging at the Fine Arts Museum. The taste then was for a more conventional type of painting. Of course, European art magazines and the reports of people coming back informed us about another kind of art, showing us reproductions of van Gogh, Renoir, Cézanne, of the cubists, of the Italian futurists. All this disturbed us, but many times when we asked our teachers about the value of these works that reached us in such an incomplete way we were answered: "They are...'isms'."[4]

1. Horacio Butler, *La pintura y mi tiempo* (Buenos Aires: Editorial Sudamericana, 1966), 23–24.

2. Horacio Butler, *Conversaciones con María Esther Vázquez* (Buenos Aires: Ediciones de Arte Gaglianone, 1982), 45.

3. Ibid., 46–48.

4. Interview script, Radio Splendid, Buenos Aires, 29 October 1958.

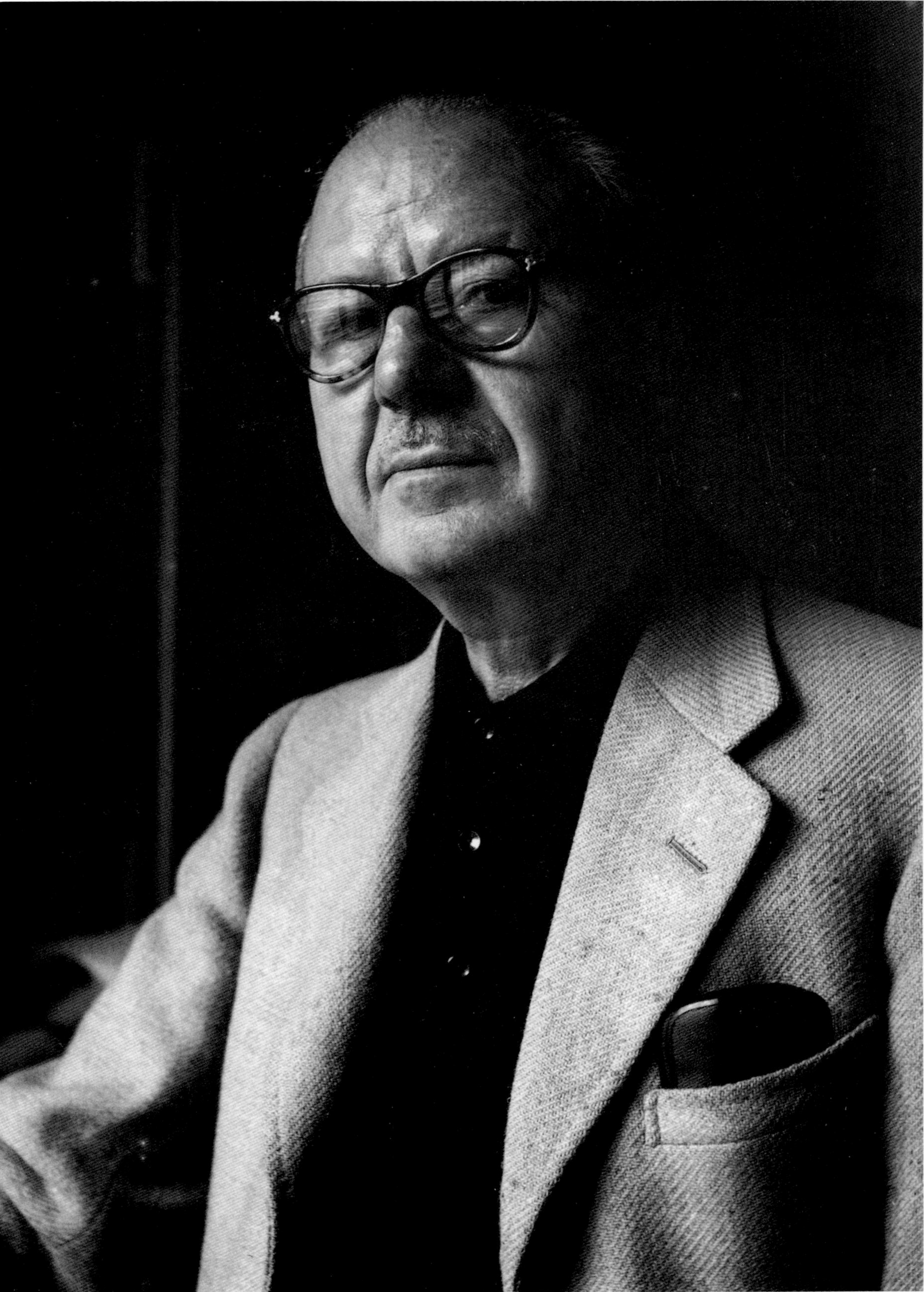

In 1917, Diaghilev's Ballets Russes visited Buenos Aires for the second time. "This was an event that greatly influenced our generation. Suddenly, we were in contact with the great figures of the time in music, painting, and choreography, and a totally new concept of theater. The sets by Braque, Picasso, Matisse; the music of Stravinsky, Debussy, Rimsky-Korsakov were revelations that made us feel the ignorance in which we were living. Furthermore, Badi, our great friend, was in Italy and in his very enthusiastic letters urged us to leave. The trip to Europe became an obsession."[5]

Another important event for Basaldúa and his group was the exhibition, held in 1920 in Buenos Aires, by the Uruguayan painter Pedro Figari. "When we saw Figari's work for the first time, we felt overpowered. It was not only the color but a great freedom in composition. We sensed that he was right. His horses, that seemed badly drawn, were much more expressive than the most accurate and academic sketch. Nowadays, this seems obvious, but then and in that milieu, it meant a revolution."[6]

Butler left for Europe in 1922, and Basaldúa went in 1923 on a very modest scholarship (from the government of Buenos Aires Province). Butler tells about Basaldúa's arrival at the Gare d'Orsay: "[S]uddenly we see him, dressed as a dandy, with bowler hat, hard collar, patent leather shoes, leggings, and a walking stick. I was very shocked because, in one year without seeing him, he had become a dreadful bourgeois. When later, at my studio, I showed him a still life (after Cézanne) I was working on, he answered me very abruptly: 'I didn't come to Paris to do *petit*-Cézanne.' Shortly after, he starts going to André Lhote's atelier, he dresses like a workman, he reduces his palette to earthy colors, and he adopts the principle of Cézannian construction."[7]

From 1923 to 1930, Basaldúa lived in Paris and attended the courses of André Lhote, Charles Guérin, and Othon Friesz. As money was very scarce, he also drew some covers for *Fairchild* and *Vogue*. In 1924, Basaldúa explained his feelings in a letter to friends:

> I arrived in Paris ready to start painting. I went to the Louvre, and there...I was completely shocked. I discovered that the masters were great because they were formidable painters; if their work is alive today, it is because of their plastic qualities that have nothing to do with feeling or technique. I went on to see the paintings of those I considered my gods in Buenos Aires, like Zuloaga, Anglada, even Whistler, and for the same reasons I mentioned above, they completely vanished; and in the third place, I found out that the 'moderns,' unknown and exposed to ridicule in Buenos Aires, were the only artists that fought for freedom, honesty, and sincerity in their work. I realized I knew nothing, and that what was best for me was to start again very humbly, like a schoolboy.[8]

Basaldúa rented a studio in the rue Daguerre "where he lived like a monk, completely dedicated to his work. He met a young Belgian student of philosophy at the Sorbonne, Marguerite Marechal, who persuaded him to read the novels of Marcel Proust. The Proustian world was almost handmade for Basaldúa, and he dreamt with Mme. de Guermantes."[9] Much later, the childhood memories of

5. Horacio Butler, taped conversations with author, 25 and 28 October 1978.
6. Butler, *Conversaciones*, 53.
7. Butler, taped conversations.
8. Héctor Basaldúa, letter to unnamed friends ("Queridos amigos"), Paris, 27 June 1924.
9. Butler, taped conversations.

the Argentine pampas, with its small village scenes and personalities, and the houses and people of Buenos Aires's suburbia combined with the teachings of Friesz, Lhote, and Guérin and the nostalgic atmosphere of the Proustian *temps perdu* to develop into a highly personal pictorial language, greatly influencing his future stage designs.

Basaldúa, in the 1924 letter, explained his feelings about his French teachers: "I started going to Charles Guérin's atelier.... I considered [him] a link between what I had learned in Buenos Aires and what I wanted to do next; and this was so because Guérin, who is regarded as a very sensitive painter and a good colorist, also is, from my point of view, somewhat dull. [But] this gentleman gave me precious advice. He made me drop all exaggerated harmonies and overblown technique, and I made a lot of progress. In the end I realized it wasn't enough to express myself, and so I went to André Lhote's atelier (former cubist, theoretician, a very bad painter, and an excellent but very dangerous teacher)."[10]

Lhote went two or three times a week to his atelier on the rue Odessa, supervising students from all over the world who crowded the dirty and decrepit studio to be initiated into the "modern" laws of painting. To Basaldúa's astonishment, Lhote's theories were exemplified by the classics: Tintoretto, Ingres, Greco. He made his students reduce all shapes to basic geometric elements and start from there. Furthermore, the idea of using only earthy colors was a reaction against impressionism. The obsession of the day was "construction." Basaldúa and his friends had discovered Cézanne some time before, and Lhote had been one of his disciples.

Othon Friesz, the third painter to be Basaldúa's teacher, was the opposite of Lhote. "Maybe a less brilliant professor, he took great pains in front of his pupil's works to find the exact words that would express his precise diagnosis; but that discreet shyness conveyed the presence of a true artist. If I had to summarize his teachings, I would say he made us realize the sense of unity in painting."[11]

From 1924 onward, Basaldúa, Butler, and Badi (already referred to as the Paris Group) started sending their work from Paris to the Buenos Aires Salón Nacional, which was the main showcase for Argentine painters. Their canvases, hung in the worst rooms, were ill received and sharply criticized because, according to Butler, "the city was infected with postimpressionist smallpox."[12]

During the twenties, new trends of stage design were seen at the Colón Theater. The modern ideas of Gordon Craig and Adolph Appia and the spectacular sets of Diaghilev's Ballets Russes had dealt a death blow to the Italian tradition of opera design. Instead of conventional painted backdrops, volumes, different levels, and interconnecting staircases filled the stage. Still, there was an aftertaste of the former school in a rather old and messy pictorial technique unmatched to the stage's new simplicity.

In 1925, the management of the Colón continued buying all their sets in Europe, paying high prices for them and not always acquiring the best.

10. Basaldúa, letter to unnamed friends.

11. Butler, *La pintura*, 59.

12. Ibid., 28.

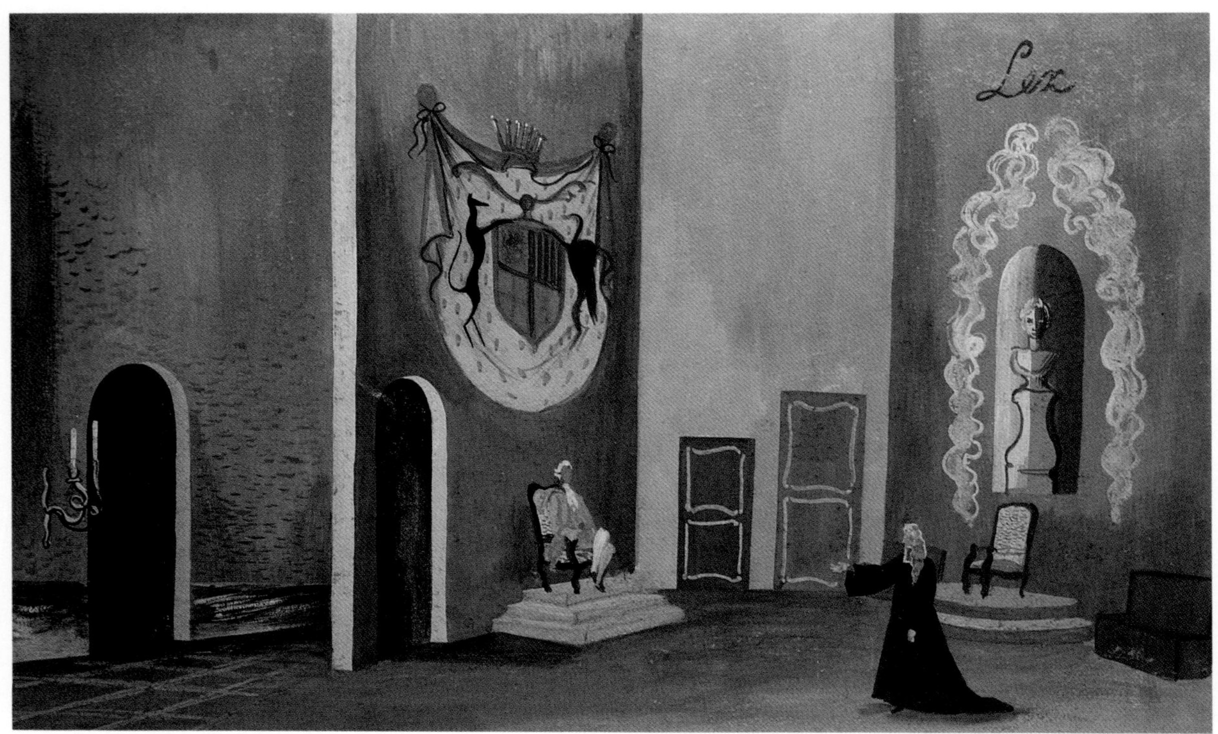

Fig. 3. Héctor Basaldúa, *Le nozze di Figaro*, gouache on board, approx. .50 x .70 m, 1931. Collection of Emilio Basaldúa. Photograph by Pedro Roth. **(See page 40.)**

But during that year, the role of resident stage designer was created, and Rodolfo Franco, an Argentine artist recently returned from Europe, took the job. He came with fresh ideas; from then on, different forms and colors were incorporated. He renovated the lighting system of the theater, and planned a reformation of the stage, although that never occurred. Franco stayed as designer until 1930.

"Little by little, the B.A. critics were taking our work more seriously, so every October we went to the Parisian branches of the Argentine newspapers to read the vituperations that our remittances produced. Until one day [in 1926], we received a new avant-garde magazine called *Martín Fierro*, with art criticism written by Alberto Prebisch who pointed out the sincerity of our artistic efforts. From then on, we could count on [his] almost unconditional support."[13] Alberto Prebisch (1899–1971) was an Argentine architect who had met "The Three B's" in Paris, while going regularly to Le Corbusier's studio on the rue des Sèvres. Returning to Argentina, he became a staunch supporter of rationalist architecture, leaving many good examples of his work in Buenos Aires. He was also going to be a firm supporter of Basaldúa in the next few years as a member of the board of directors of the Colón Theater.

In 1928, the Paris Group (joined by the painters Antonio Berni and Lino Enea Spilimbergo) had its first solo exhibition in Buenos Aires on the premises of a new private institution called Amigos del Arte. Although the critics were mainly against the artists, accusing them of lack of personality, having basically the same approach, and being revolutionaries who destroyed without offering alternatives, the seed had been planted.

13. Ibid., 73–74.

In autumn 1929, the New York Stock Market crashed. Americans and other potential art buyers hurried back to their home countries. Artists who filled Montparnasse's cafes also started to leave. Galleries closed down, and poverty was so extreme that soup kitchens were set up to help hungry artists. "The hour struck for the Argentine group to disband, and Basaldúa, not being able to take it any longer, decided to go back. We were all devastated, as we felt that a very important part of our life was over.... And so it was, because when we returned to Buenos Aires everyone began to struggle for himself, and the strong link that existed in the ateliers, the academies, and the life in Paris was forever broken."[14]

Basaldúa wrote a letter to Badi, who was in Italy: "Strange as it may seem, Buenos Aires doesn't give me the impression of a hopeless place as I was expecting. The whole city is full of life, with many people walking in the streets, and new cinemas showing very interesting films; but with the few exceptions of the friends one appreciates, the rest of the people are impossible."[15] Buenos Aires had changed indeed. Amigos del Arte was not only a place where new painters and sculptors had their work exhibited, but also on its premises visiting European intellectuals such as Ortega y Gasset, Paul Morand, Federico García Lorca, and Le Corbusier, among others, gave lectures and expressed their ideas.

Another vital personality of the time was Victoria Ocampo (1890–1978). Born to a wealthy and traditional Argentine family, she had learned to read and write in French before Spanish, a fact her future critics would take as a sign of not being sufficiently "Argentinean." Regardless of what was expected of a woman in such a narrow-minded society, she wanted to be a writer and courageously stood her ground. Because of her, foreign musicians and writers like Pierre Drieu La Rochelle, Hermann Keyserling, Waldo Frank, Rabindranath Tagore, and Igor Stravinsky came to Buenos Aires, enhancing the local scene. In addition, she founded and financially supported the literary magazine *Sur* that for decades would publish the most important American and European writers.

Also, during the thirties many European artists had to leave their homelands because of the Spanish Civil War, such as Margarita Xirgu, Rafael Alberti, Manuel de Falla, and Ramón Gómez de la Serna; and because of nazism, such as Joseph Gielen, Erich Kleiber, Falconetti, Roger Caillois, Albert Wolff, and Margarita Wallman. All these circumstances combined to make Buenos Aires an outstanding center.

Furthermore, the Colón Theater had changed its policies. From 1930 on, it was no longer in the hands of private impresarios who often based decisions on commercial rather than artistic considerations. The new board of directors was an autonomous entity, with its own budget paid by the Buenos Aires municipality. Its aim was to achieve high artistic levels almost regardless of financial cost. Raymond Cogniat, a French critic, wrote in *Beaux Arts* in 1938:

> It is well known that the theater plays a prominent role in Argentina's cultural life. Buenos Aires has welcomed the best companies in the world, the most celebrated actors, the most highly reputed plays. Every year touring companies from France, Italy, Germany, defend each nation's prestige.... Argentina has become an arena for a vast competition among opposing trends and theatrical esthetics. The Colón Theater occupies the front line in

14. Butler, taped conversations.

15. Héctor Basaldúa to Aquiles Badi, 21 February 1931.

this combat. On its stage, the most daring creations are shown. It is the oldest theater in South America, the most active, and the one that has made the greatest effort to renovate stage design and to achieve productions worthy to be judged with the best seen in European theaters.[16]

Basaldúa gave his own account of his first years at the opera house, in a 1949 interview for an art magazine: "My debut at the Colón Theater took place in 1921 [when I designed] the sets for *Ariadna y Dionysos*, an opera by the Argentine composer Felipe Boero, followed in the next year by *Raquela*, by the same author. Both operas, a vision of mythological Greece and of our pampas, were performed to total indifference. I am mainly referring to the visual results of both works because, if the decor was conceived by the ingenuity of a beginner, its construction and painting (very mediocre, from my point of view) was in the hands of the theater's impresario." After recounting the years in Europe, Basaldúa continued: "I went back to the theater in 1931, together with other painters to participate in that season.... I designed *Le nozze di Figaro* (fig. 3). With stage director Natasha Satz, I decided on the use of the revolving stage, showing a succession of small sets with simple shapes and subdued colors. This produced, in my opinion, a change in our theater decor which, up to then, used an excess of ornamentation."[17]

Although the critics were mixed, many against but others very enthusiastic, one thing was certain: for the first time, and thanks to a rather naive theatrical point of view, a painter with a personal vision broke the rules by not presenting the naturalistic sets that audiences expected.

Raymond Cogniat summed it up correctly:

> It seems that Basaldúa doesn't give much importance in his sets to historic accuracy; rather, he tries to capture an atmosphere, he evokes a certain period without doing an imitation. In this sense, he is a true creator, more faithful to the spirit of each opera than to its [literal] value. One can only rejoice at this conception that renews the stage, adapting it to present times without betraying the author. His sets for *Le nozze di Figaro* are a good example of this. He takes a different approach from what we would have done in France, and shows us what a foreigner can draw from our eighteenth century, its grace and refinement.[18]

In 1932, Basaldúa designed *Il segreto di Susanna*, *Il matrimonio segreto*, and two ballets—*La Boîte à joujoux* with music by Claude Debussy and *Bolero* (fig. 4), "the former set as a small scene with successive painted backdrops in a fresh and spontaneous style, and the latter in different levels and very contrasting colors."[19]

"Some thirty-five years ago, we were discussing with friends how to stage a little play I had written and with what sets. One of them said, 'I will ask a gifted young man who paints. He will do something, if he wants to.' The young man I was introduced to was you, Basaldúa. Years went by, and one day Buenos Aires's Lord Mayor asked me who, to my knowledge, could be responsible for set designing at the Colón. I answered (here history repeats itself), 'I will ask

16. Raymond Cogniat, "L'art à l'étranger. Le théâtre en République Argentine. L'œuvre d'Héctor Basaldúa," *Beaux Arts* (18 February 1938).

17. Héctor Basaldúa, "Mis escenografías en el Teatro Colón de Buenos Aires," *Boletín del Museo Nacional de Arte Decorativo* IV, no. 10–11, June 1949.

18. Cogniat, "L'art à l'étranger."

19. Basaldúa, "Mis escenografías."

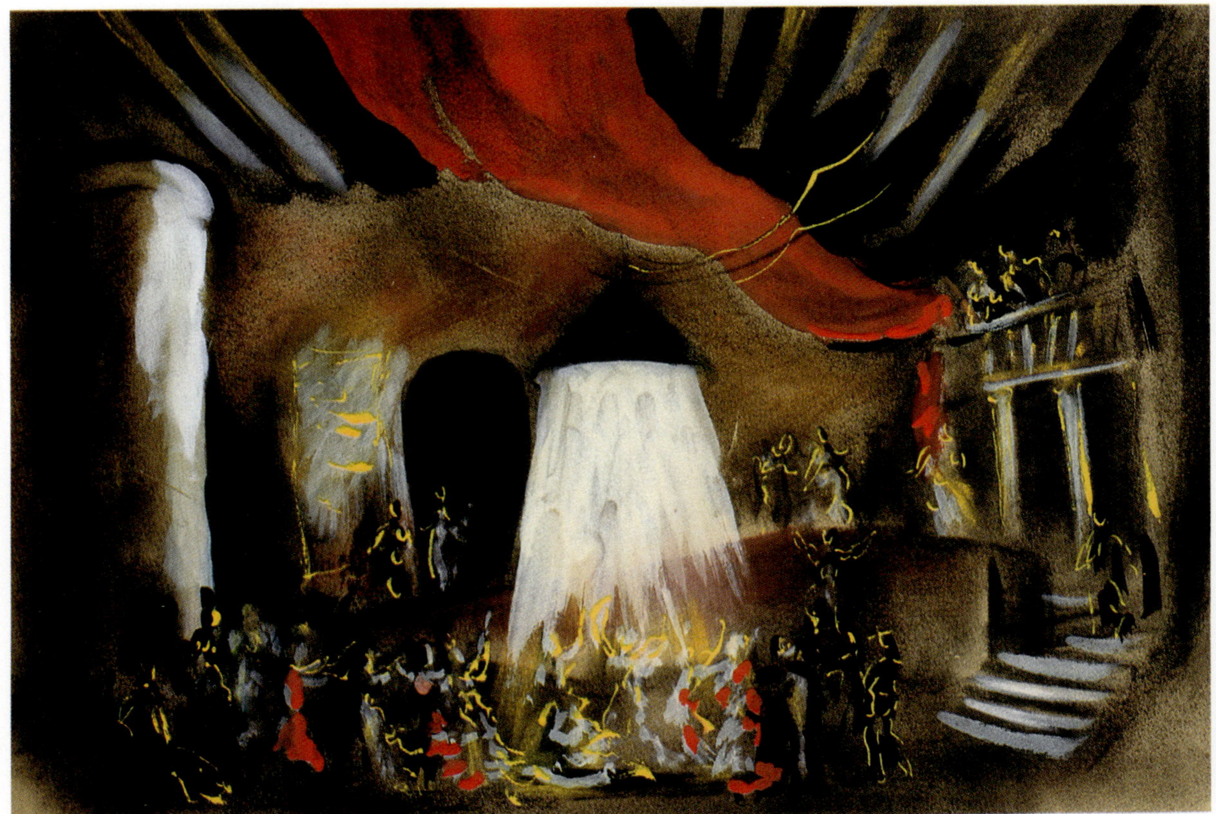

Fig. 4. Héctor Basaldúa, *Bolero*, gouache on board, approx. .50 x .70 m, 1932. Collection of Emilio Basaldúa. Photograph by Pedro Roth.

a talented man I know. He will do something, if he wants to.' The talented man was named head designer."[20] So said Victoria Ocampo in a catalogue for a Basaldúa painting exhibit.

In 1933, a new board was named at the Colón. Ocampo and the already mentioned Alberto Prebisch were appointed, among others. The chairman of the board was the young composer and conductor Juan José Castro (1895–1968), who also widely promulgated Manuel de Falla's music in Argentina. This board was particularly concerned with high standards. They were determined to make the Colón one of the best opera houses in the world, and they didn't hesitate to take artistic risks if they thought the results worthwhile.

In Basaldúa's case, the appointment was particularly risky because he had no technical background to fall back on. In the beginning, this fact was used against him, as can be read in newspapers of that time. Nevertheless he remained until 1952. "For some years, the Colón Theater has deepened its aim of renewal and its will to accomplish personal creations by entrusting all its stage decor to a young artist, Héctor Basaldúa, who since 1933 has designed many first-rate productions. He has asserted his personality, and his decor bears a strong trademark. In spite of this, his output is varied as he lets himself be carried away by the atmosphere of each new work. He is, above all, a strong colorist, with a taste for light tonalities or for dramatic contrasts with multiple colors."[21]

20. Victoria Ocampo, introduction to a catalogue of Héctor Basaldúa's paintings at Galería Bonino, San Isidro, October 1957.

21. Cogniat, "L'art à l'étranger."

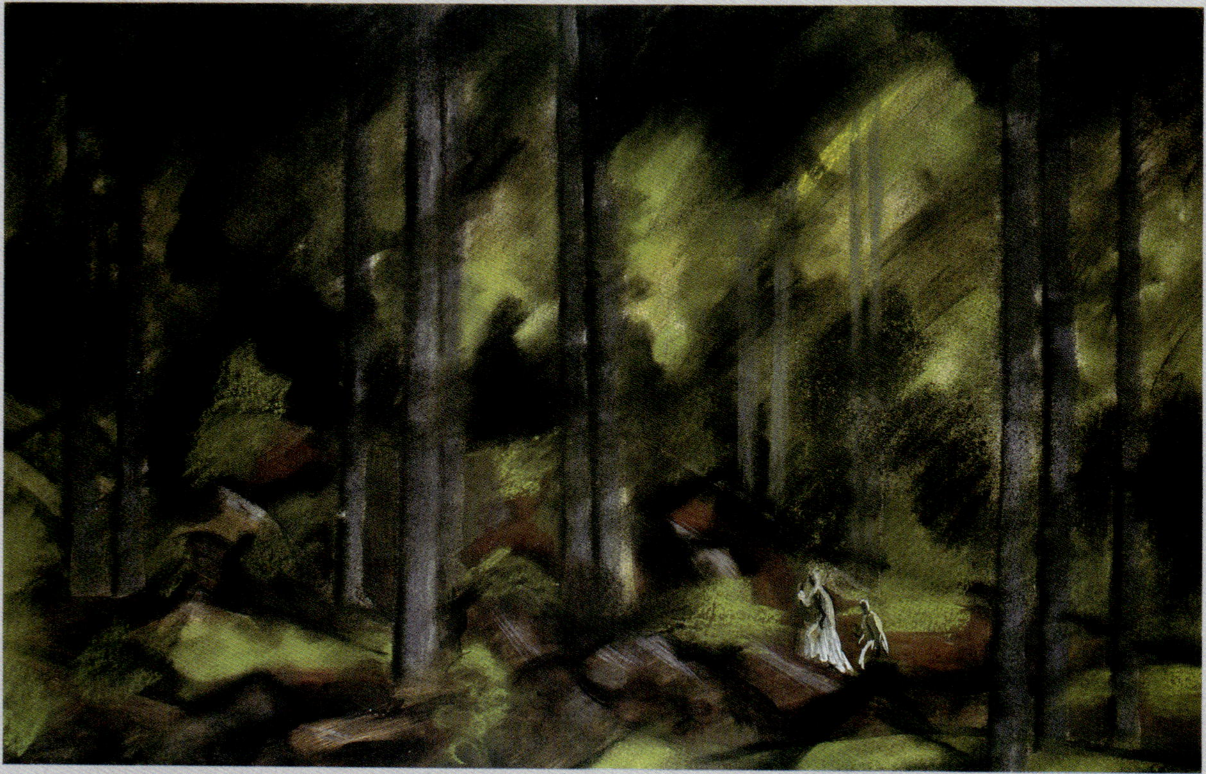

Fig. 5. Héctor Basaldúa, *Parsifal*, gouache on board, approx. .50 x .70 m, 1933. Collection of Emilio Basaldúa. Photograph by Pedro Roth.

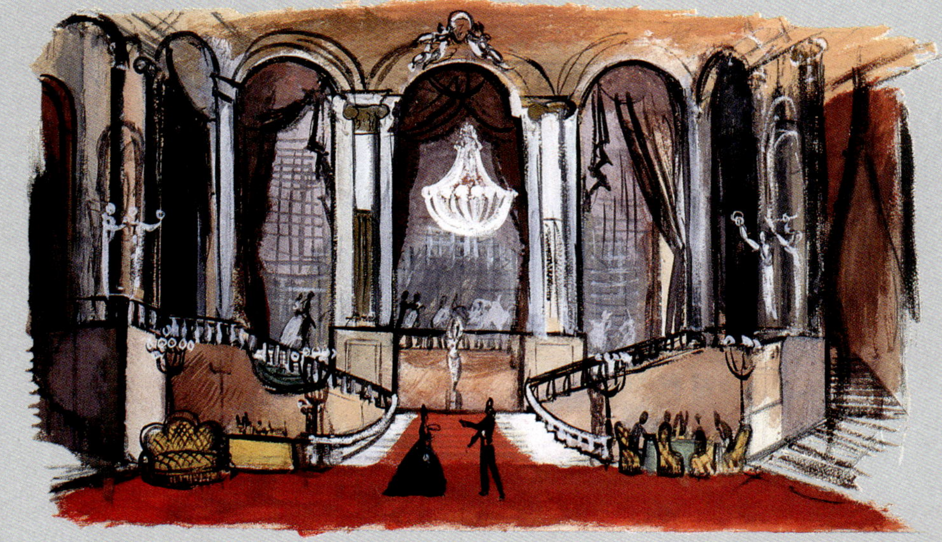

Fig. 6. Héctor Basaldúa, *La Traviata*, gouache on board, approx. .50 x .70 m, 1933. Collection of Emilio Basaldúa. Photograph by Pedro Roth.

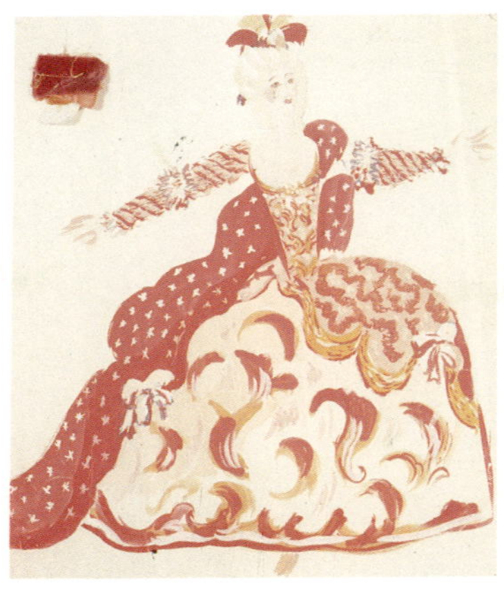
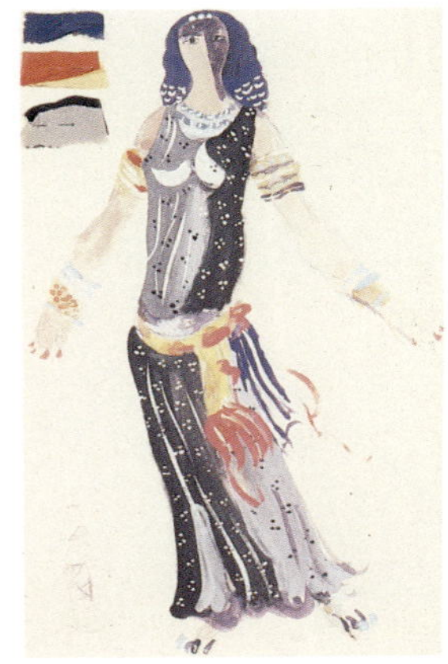
Fig. 7. Héctor Basaldúa, *Castor et Pollux*, watercolor on paper, 1936. Collection of Emilio Basaldúa. Photograph by Pedro Roth.

La Traviata (fig. 6) was produced in 1933, the leading role sung by Claudia Muzio. According to the critics, it was visually very successful. Nonetheless, Basaldúa remarked that "the corporeal sets were done with a simplified realism, perhaps a trifle heavy."[22]

A totally different approach was used for *Parsifal* (fig. 5), a production conducted by Fritz Busch. Although there were some mechanical problems with the revolving stage, the result was very positive. "For *Parsifal*, I used corporeal elements on top of the revolving disc that worked as tree trunks and back projections onto the cyclorama. From that first version [1933], few things are left because the machinery was very complicated. We used light projections for the first time at the Colón. Although the results were far from perfect, we saw the enormous potential of the system. I used projections again that same year for different sequences of *Le Baiser de la fée* (fig. 8), choreographed by the celebrated Bronislava Nijinska.

"After doing [the Stravinsky], I designed several ballets in 1934: *Homenaje a Schubert*, a set with small folding screens in the foreground and a big painted backdrop, and Serge Lifar's three ballets: *Prometée* (fig. 9), *Le Prelude à l'après-midi d'un Faune,* and *Le Spectre de la Rose*."[23]

"We talked a lot with Lifar about Diaghilev and his tragic death. As you may know, I was in Venice in 1929 with Badi, and one afternoon we saw Diaghilev strolling with Lifar in the Piazza San Marco. A few days later, we were shocked when we read in the papers that he had died. The funeral was going to take place in the small orthodox church of San Giorgio dei Grecci. We went there with Badi. Diaghilev's coffin arrived on a huge black gondola. His sudden death was the reason that very few people were at his grave: Mme. Chanel, Serge Lifar, Etienne de Beaumont, and some others I don't remember; maybe a total of eight people, two curious and moved Argentines among them."[24]

It is important to note that Basaldúa's painterly approach was not restricted to set design. In the still-existing costumes for *Castor et Pollux* (1936) (fig. 7) and *Samson et Dalila* (1936), a sort of collage of different materials was used in the former, and very light, dyed and painted gauzes in the latter.

22. Basaldúa, "Mis escenografías."

23. Ibid.

24. Interview script.

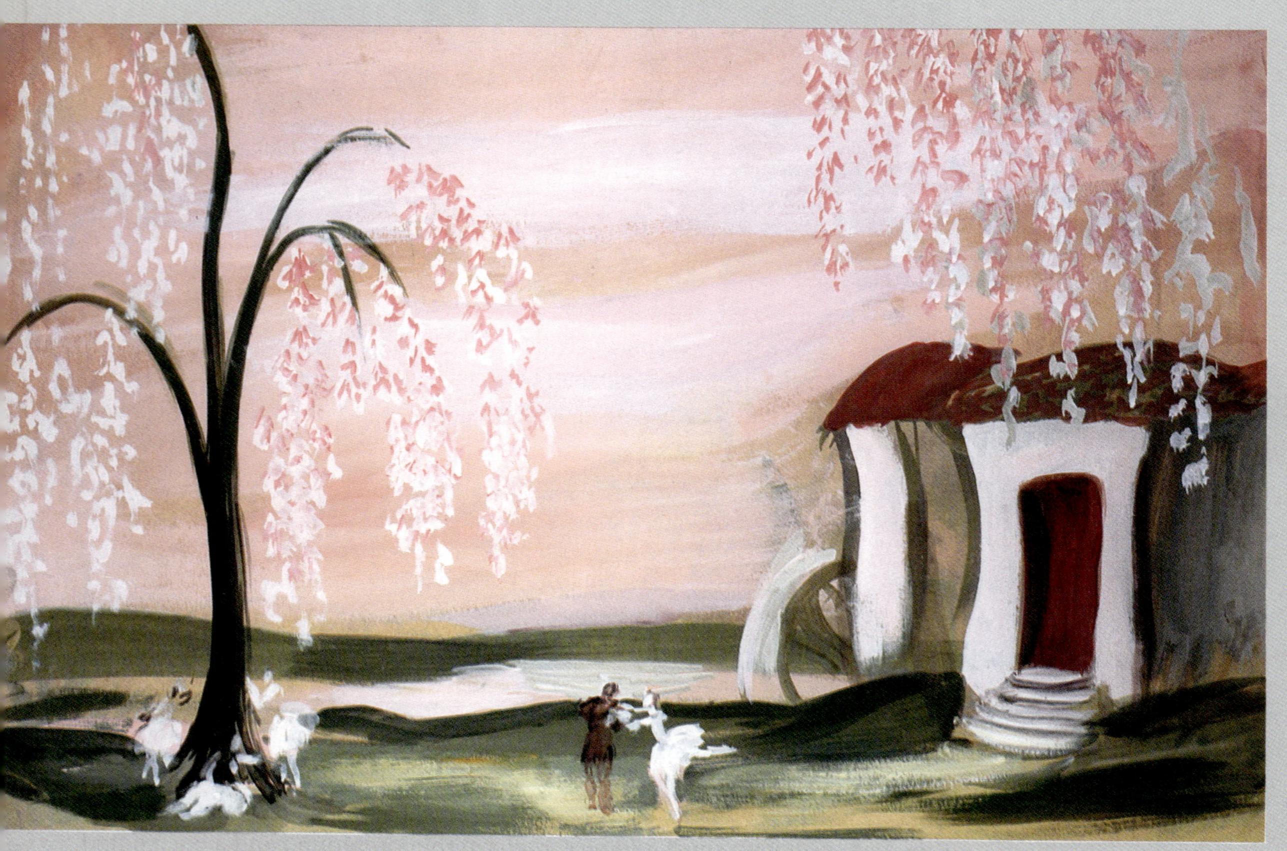

Fig. 8. Héctor Basaldúa, *Le Baiser de la fée*, gouache on board, approx. .50 x .70 m, 1933. Collection of Emilio Basaldúa. Photograph by Pedro Roth.

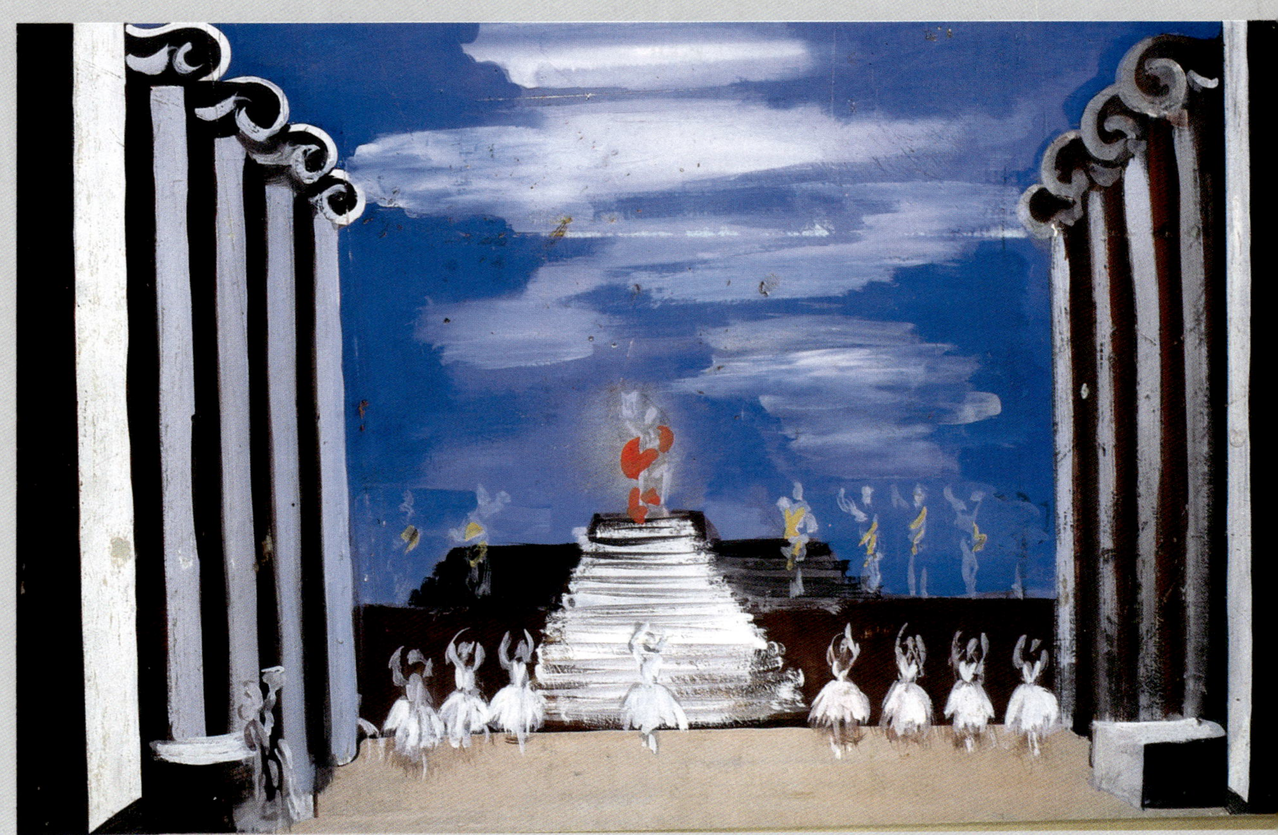

Fig. 9. Héctor Basaldúa,

Prometée, gouache on board,

approx. .50 x .70 m, 1934.

Collection of Emilio Basaldúa.

Photograph by Pedro Roth.

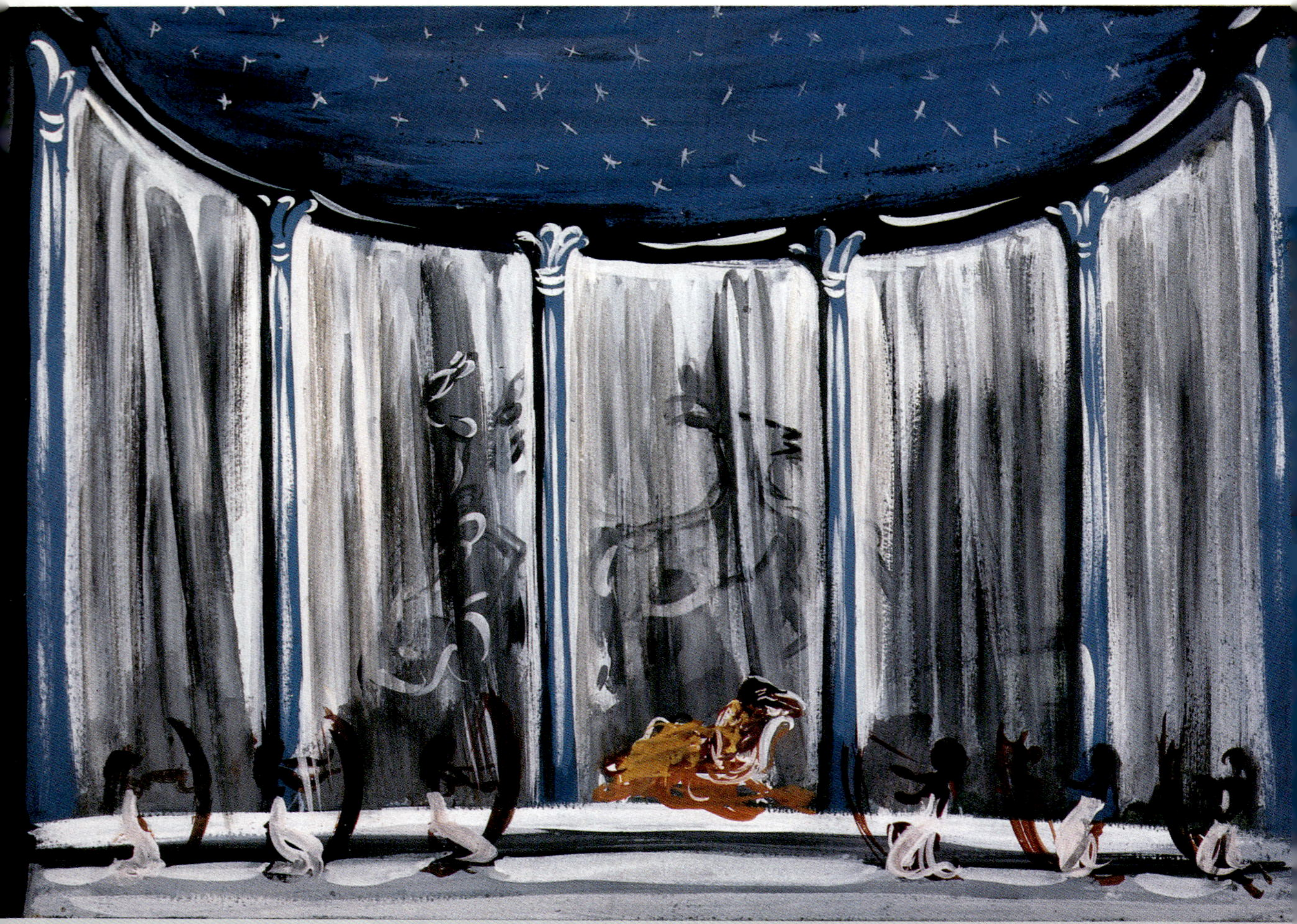

▲

Fig. 10. Héctor Basaldúa, *Aida*, gouache on board, approx. .50 x .70 m, 1937. Collection of Emilio Basaldúa. Photograph by Pedro Roth.

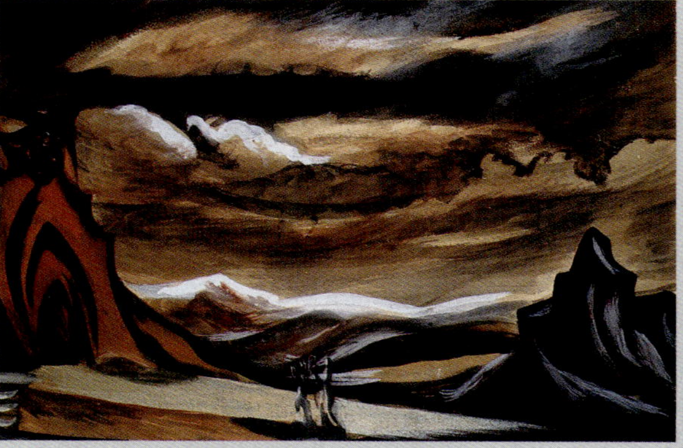

Fig. 11. Héctor Basaldúa, *Alleluia*, gouache on board, approx. .50 x .70 m, 1936. Collection of Emilio Basaldúa. Photograph by Pedro Roth.

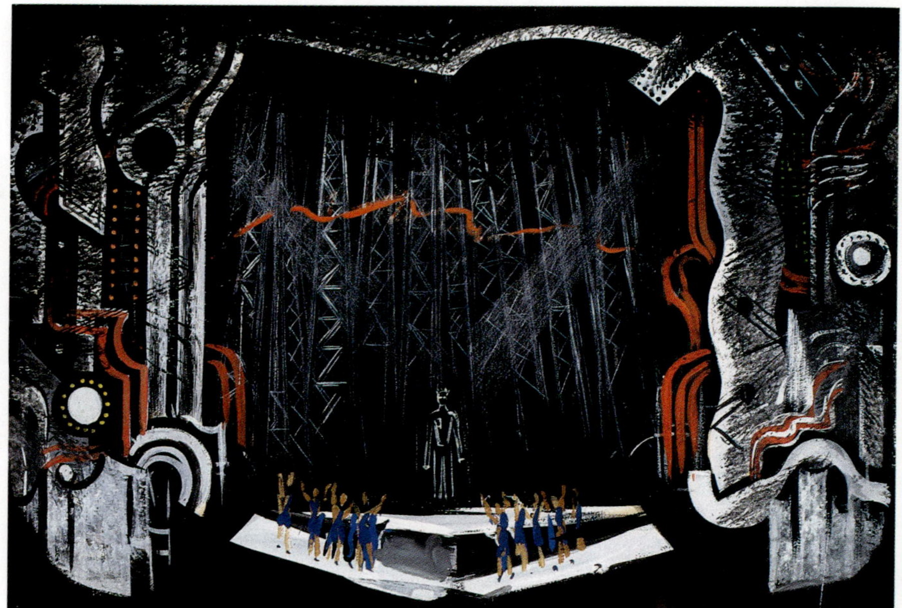

Fig. 12. Héctor Basaldúa, *Mêkhâno*, gouache on board, approx. .50 x .70 m, 1937. Collection of Emilio Basaldúa. Photograph by Pedro Roth.

"Basaldúa's solutions for more dramatic [operas] are also interesting. His sets for *Alleluia* (fig. 11) and *Aida* (fig. 10), with their violent contrasts and their vigorous architectures, show his resources in this area, as well as an intelligent use of platforms, by organizing stage areas that permit singers to move at different levels with great freedom."[25]

The case of the 1937 ballet *Mêkhâno* (fig. 12) was different. An expressionist ballet of sorts, with music by Juan José Castro, it looked as if Basaldúa felt uncomfortable designing it. In a letter sent to him by the ballet's author, she complained: "I don't deny its elegance, but I don't think black and red evoke the gaiety I tried to express."[26]

In that same year, he won first prize for stage design at the Paris International Exhibition, and a book was published with color reproductions of his designs for the Colón. In a foreword to that edition, Basaldúa wrote:

> Being a painter, I later became a stage designer, and, although the end and means are different, I have tried to apply to the stage the principles learned in painting regarding the problems of color and composition.
>
> The theater set is not an end in itself; as beautiful and striking as it may be, it will fail if its aim is not accomplished, that is: to follow the dramatic idea as closely as possible, creating the required atmosphere. All theories...from the heroic days of the end of the last century to our 1937 agree to abolish the false tradition of banal realism and *trompe-l'œil*. Following this great truth, I have always tried to create sets with simplicity, suggesting atmospheres and choosing the plastic elements very carefully so as to merge the illusion with the dramatic idea by means of analogies of form and color. To achieve this, I have not excluded any alternative: decorative fantasy or expressive synthesis, depending on the case. Sometimes I have used

25. Cogniat, "L'art à l'étranger."

26. Josefina Cruz to Héctor Basaldúa, 7 May 1937. Cruz conceived the ballet; Paul Petroff did the choreography.

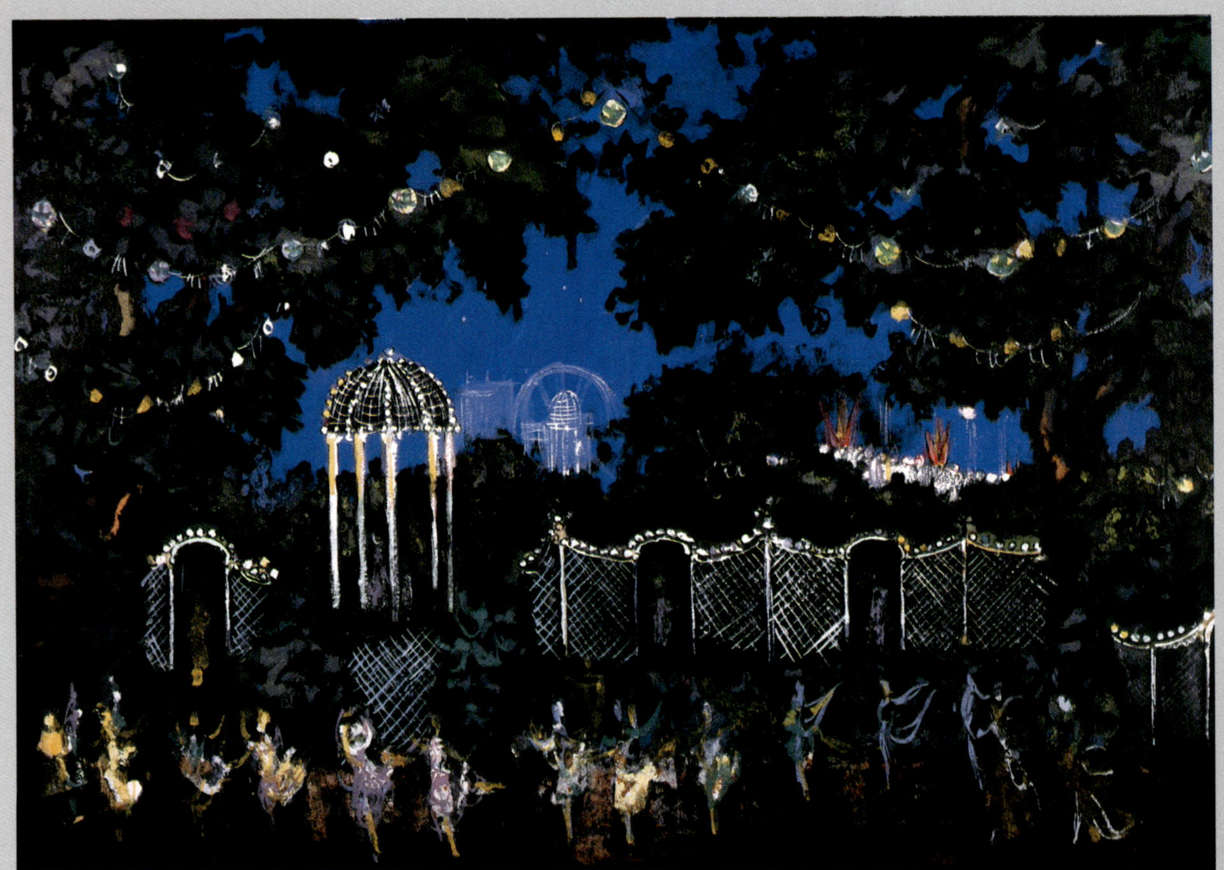

Fig. 13. Héctor Basaldúa, *Offenbachiana*, gouache on board, approx. .50 x .70 m, 1940. Collection of Emilio Basaldúa. Photograph by Pedro Roth. **(See page 51.)**

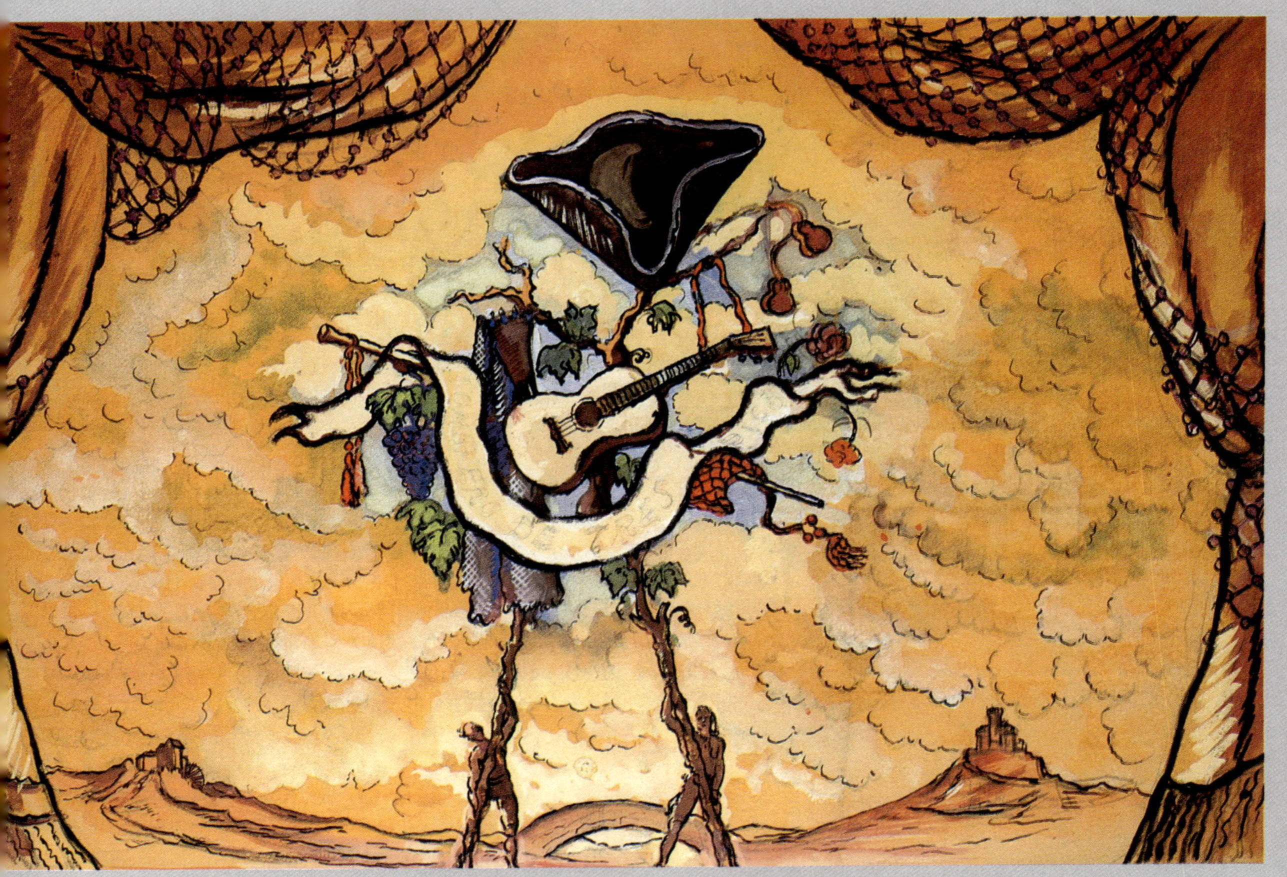

Fig. 14. Héctor Basaldúa,
El sombrero de tres picos**,**
gouache on board, approx.
.50 x .70 m, 1941. Collection of
Emilio Basaldúa. Photograph by
Pedro Roth. **(See page 51.)**

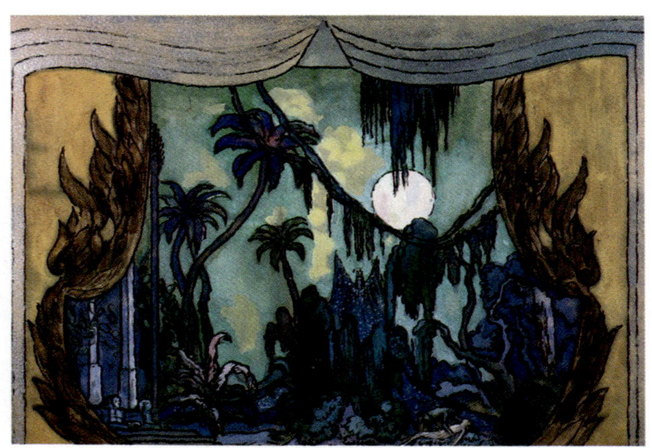

Fig. 15. Héctor Basaldúa, *Die Zauberflöte*, gouache on board, approx. .50 x .70 m, 1941. Collection of Emilio Basaldúa. Photograph by Pedro Roth.

> volumetrical sets, to enhance the actor's presence; at other times I use painting that, powerfully or subtly, can suggest atmospheres by pure plastic means and not by the subordinate formulas of realistic imitation.[27]

In 1938, the Colón Theater sent him on a long tour of Europe to take a closer look at the principal opera houses of Germany, Italy, and France. He wrote a letter from Bayreuth to a friend in July 1939:

> I arrived here on schedule, with a free pass that the very charming Winifred Wagner gave me. I saw *Die Walküre* and *Siegfried* and tomorrow I am going to see *Götterdämmerung*. Bayreuth's productions are perfect.... What an orchestra! You can almost feel plastically the different musical *Leitmotivs*, their struggles and developments. What singers and what actors! The decor is very realistic, but perfect. What is extraordinary is the stage lighting, especially in the forest scene with the trembling of the leaves and the constant change of the *sous-bois*. Also very interesting is the *Walküre* awakening and Sigfried's scene. I am very short of cash because I didn't plan to stay in Germany for so long, but though life here is very expensive, I think I will stay to see the rehearsals of *Parsifal* and *Tristan*, even though I might have to walk back to Paris.[28]

Actually, Basaldúa was considering staying in Paris—a city he always loved—when war was declared. Finally, due to considerable pressure from friends and family, he decided to return to Argentina at the end of 1939.

The war years marked the zenith of Buenos Aires as a cultural center. Although the world was living under tragic circumstances, Buenos Aires continued to be the shelter for a now greatly enlarged number of exiled artists. "Alfredo Bigatti and Alberto Lagos (sculptors); Raquel Forner, Manuel Angeles Ortiz, Emilio Centurión, Héctor Basaldúa, and Susan Aguirre (painters); Alberto Prebisch, Alejo Martinez, and Eduardo Sacriste (architects); Emiliano Aguirre, Juan José Castro, and Jacqueline Ibels (musicians); Gloria Alcorta and Susana Bombal (writers); and the French singer Jane Bathori were very much together, forming a group of friends trying to cope with the confusion and anguish of those terrible years."[29]

27. Héctor Basaldúa, *Escenografías de Héctor Basaldúa* (Buenos Aires: Teatro Colón, Municipalidad de la Ciudad de Buenos Aires, 1938), 10–12.

28. Héctor Basaldúa to unnamed friend ("Mi querida amiga"), 10 July 1939.

29. Butler, *La pintura*, 179.

In 1940, and for many years thereafter, Margarita Wallman would be the principle choreographer for the Colón ballet. She wrote in 1979: "The ballets were very different in character. They went from the classic repertoire to modern expressionism, from Spanish folklore to ethnic ballets, from the Belle Époque to Poulenc's and Stravinsky's neoclassicism. They were complicated, with many scenes, and often they were staged on the revolving disc with the whole corps de ballet, which at that time had more than a hundred dancers. Many of the most successful ones, like the 1940 *Offenbachiana* (fig. 13) and *El sombrero de tres picos* (fig. 14), were born from an harmonious collaboration between Basaldúa and myself."[30]

Other examples of Basaldúa's sets in the forties are *Die Zauberflöte* (fig. 15) and more specially *Armide* (fig. 16), where the blues used in a very refined way would be seen afterwards in his painting. In 1952, after more than twenty years of uninterrupted work by Basaldúa at the Colón, the role of resident stage designer was declared vacant by the Peronist administration. In those twenty years, Basaldúa almost had to take his painting as a hobby due to lack of time. As Butler says: "Basaldúa was a very poor administrator of his own talent, and this made him waste twenty years of his artistic life as a designer at the Colón in an exhausting effort that, like everything connected with the theater, leaves no trace."[31]

For the rest of his life, he concentrated on his painting, developing his particular plastic language with blacks and greys in the fifties and an explosion of color in the sixties and early seventies.

Once again, he was named resident designer of the Colón from 1956 to 1964. Examples of that period are *Bodas de sangre* (fig. 17), music by Juan José Castro, based on García Lorca's play, with a total absence of color due to the dramatic requirements of the opera; *Carmen* (fig. 18), with a very interesting use of the revolving stage and light projections painted by himself; and the 1958 version of Menotti's *The Consul* (fig. 19), in an expressionist style. Then, in 1963, there was the premiere of Falla's *Atlántida* (fig. 20), where Basaldúa based the whole design on huge projections drawn by himself on glass plates in a style very close to his painting.

One of his last designs for the Colón was, again, *Il segreto di Susanna*. It was done in a sort of *art-nouveau* style, but in a very personal way, with considerable humor. Although simpler and more refined, it resembled in spirit the atmosphere of the other version of 1932.

30. Margarita Wallman to author, "Recuerdo de Héctor Basaldúa," 3 August 1979.

31. Horacio Butler, homage to Basaldúa at the opening of a memorial exhibition, Santa Fe, September 1976.

Fig. 16. Below. Héctor Basaldúa, *Armide*, gouache on board, approx. .50 x .70 m, 1943. Collection of Emilio Basaldúa. Photograph by Pedro Roth.

Fig. 17. Below right. Héctor Basaldúa, *Bodas de sangre*, gouache on board, approx. .50 x .70 m, 1956. Collection of Emilio Basaldúa. Photograph by Pedro Roth.

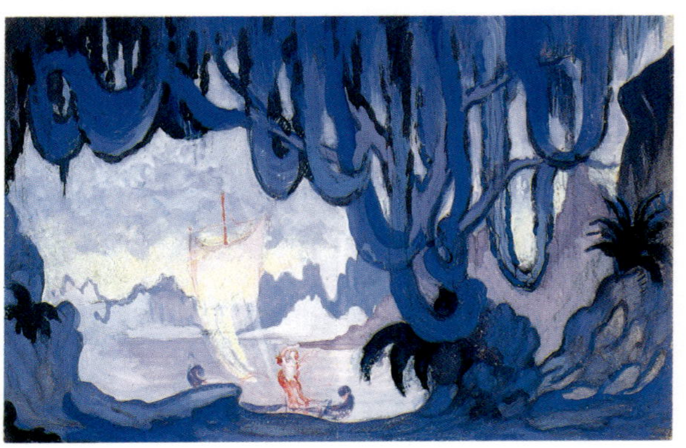

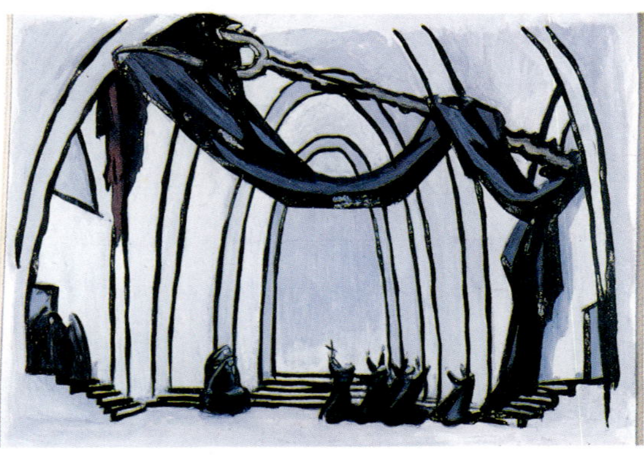

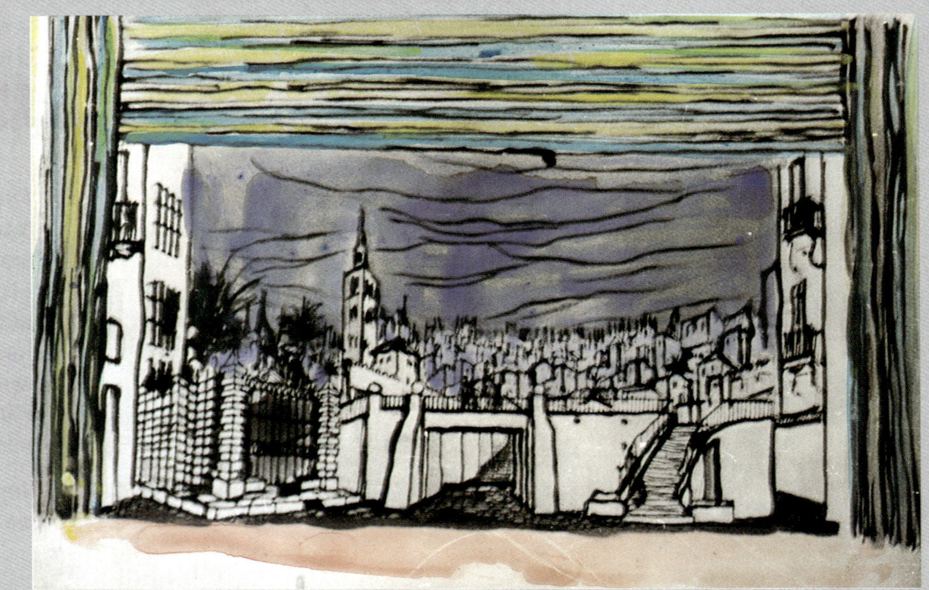

Fig. 18. Héctor Basaldúa, *Carmen*, watercolor and ink on paper, 1958. Collection of Emilio Basaldúa. Photograph by Pedro Roth.

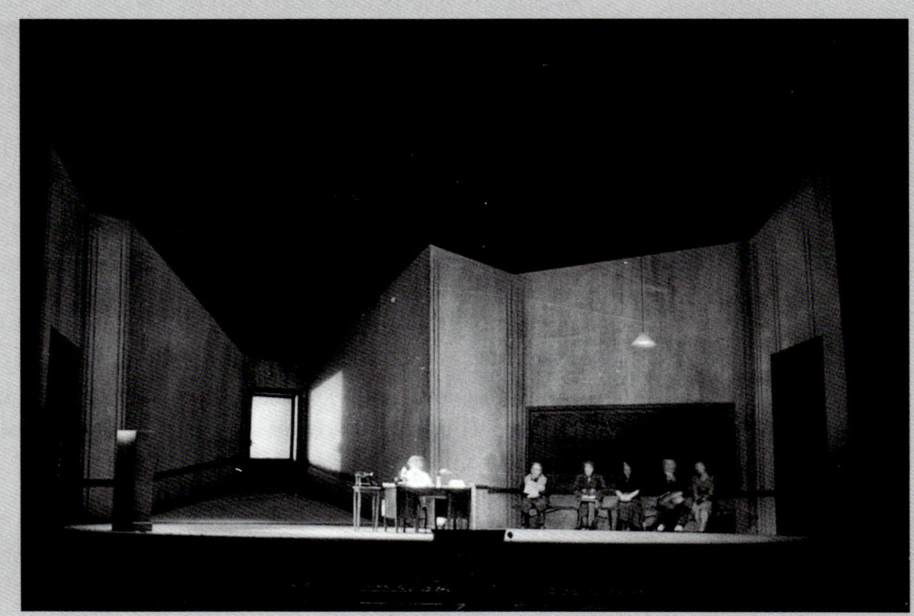

Fig. 19. Héctor Basaldúa, *The Consul*, rehearsal, 1958. Photograph courtesy of the Colón Theater.

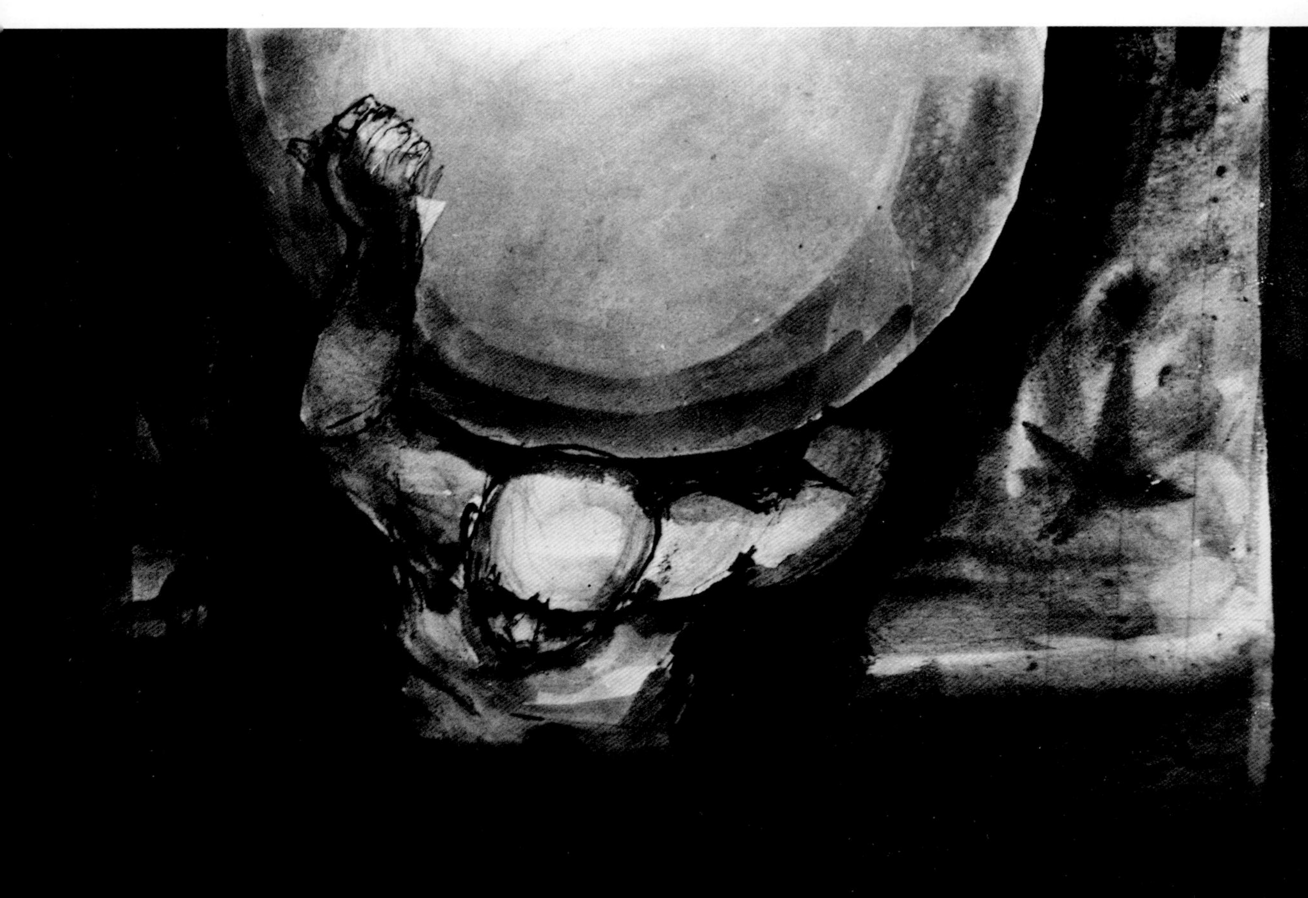

Fig. 20. Héctor Basaldúa, *Atlántida*, watercolor and ink on paper, 1963. Collection of Emilio Basaldúa. Photograph courtesy of the Colón Theater.

> I started to paint many years ago in Argentina, when artistic trends that later conquered us hadn't yet arrived. Later, we couldn't or we didn't want to avoid the inevitable contagion.... In Paris, in a whirlwind of contradictory theories, a nostalgic feeling for my country grew silently inside of me. I tried to evoke it in my paintings, perhaps in a coarse and clumsy way, but expressing essentially the truth that inside me was striving to come out.... Back in Argentina, life circumstances took me to the theater, with an enormous responsibility, facing permanent prearranged deadlines, reduced budgets, and conflicting ideas.... I didn't stop painting, although time was practically nonexistent.... So, little by little, I started to express in my own way the simple and naive atmosphere of [earlier] times, the moon over the village's main square, the streets during carnival, the obsessing characters, the social gatherings where conversations were forever repeated, the ennui, and all the mythology.... I still don't know if it was seen or dreamed.[32]

Héctor Basaldúa died in Buenos Aires on 21 February 1976. □

32. Héctor Basaldúa, collección audiovisual *Color y Línea*, Serie Pintores Argentinos Contemporáneos, Buenos Aires, Editorial Alexkraft, 1967.

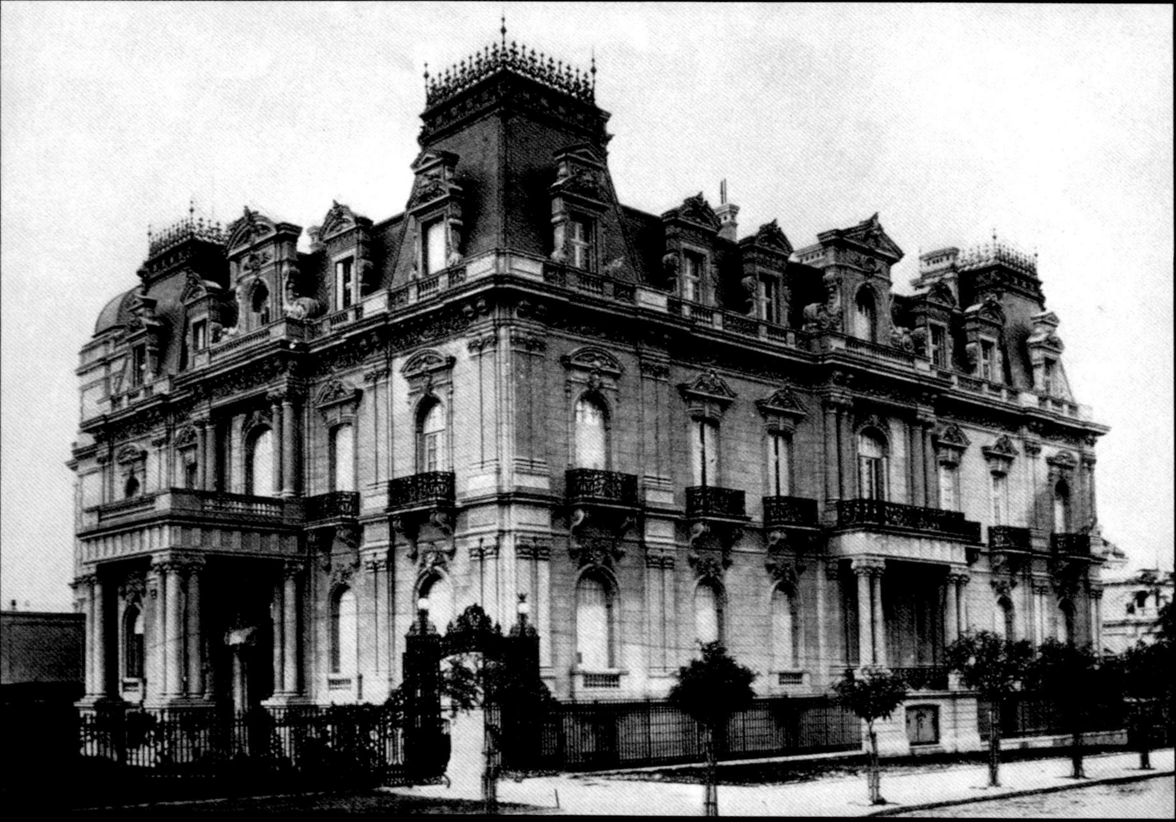

Fig 1. Julio Dormal, residence, Buenos Aires, 1880.

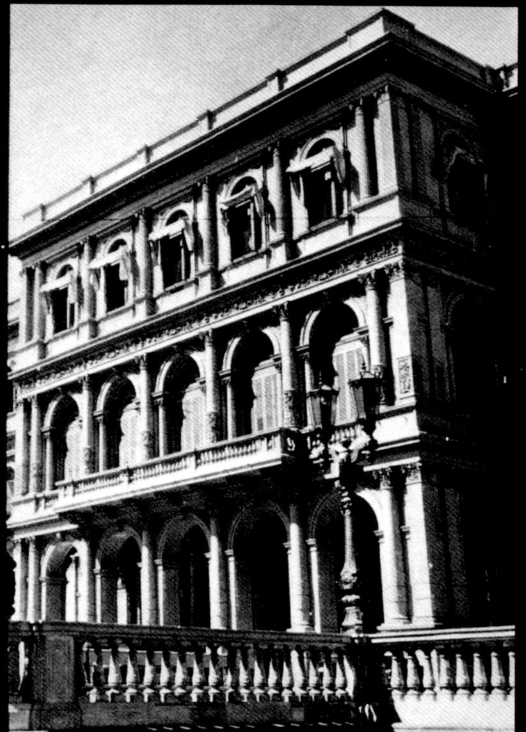

Fig. 2. Francisco Tamburini, Government House, Buenos Aires, built 1883–1889.

Argentine Architecture of the Thirties

By Ernesto Katzenstein

Translated by Edward Shaw

Ernesto Katzenstein is a practicing architect in Buenos Aires. A lecturer at the National University of Buenos Aires School of Architecture, he also has lectured throughout South America and the United States and has written on modern architecture and related subjects.

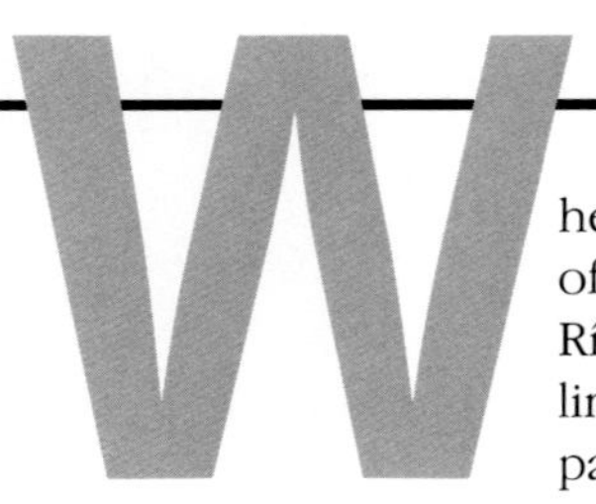

hen Le Corbusier arrived in Buenos Aires in the spring of 1929, after crossing the immense estuary of the Río de la Plata, he found a flat city with no precise limits leaning against the endless vastness of the pampas, whose coast was just a line on a map.

At that time, this city of two million inhabitants, capital and financial center of a sparsely populated country, was the point of exit, through its port, of a huge agricultural production that placed Argentina among the leading nations of the world in any economic ranking.

The city was then, and still is, built on an inflexible grid network designed four centuries before by Spanish conquerors. Lacking an important native culture, of secondary status in the Spanish colonial empire, the population of Buenos Aires did not inherit any historic monuments comparable to those of other colonial cities, not to mention the marvels of Mexico or Peru.

The Buenos Aires that Le Corbusier first saw was a city that had been given its formal structure between the end of the nineteenth and the beginning of the twentieth centuries. It was then that the port and many of the city's grand buildings were built and the country received its largest immigratory influx, which peaked by 1914 with almost half of the city's population made up of foreigners.

Thus the city had a hybrid appearance. With certain features imposed by colonial city planning, public buildings and large residences of the most varied European styles were mixed together with old houses of strictly local cast and tenements where poor immigrants seemed, literally, to be stacked on top of each other.

The important buildings were built by the government and the country's leading citizens who emerged as such, after a complex transculturalization, to turn the country into a modern and European nation, at least in appearance. Housing was considered an outlet for private speculative funds, an investment of the surplus collected from exporting the interior's agricultural products.

Official architecture, and that of the social class connected with the country's rulers, had gone from a somewhat naive academicism to an opulent eclecticism in the fifty years prior to Le Corbusier's arrival (fig. 1). Eclecticism was, on the whole, the architecture of the state (fig. 2). In its different guises, in its own evolution and continual updating of itself, were reflected the social and economic pressures characterizing the structural crises of the country's socio-economic system in those years. The crises sparked new programs

Photographs courtesy of the author.

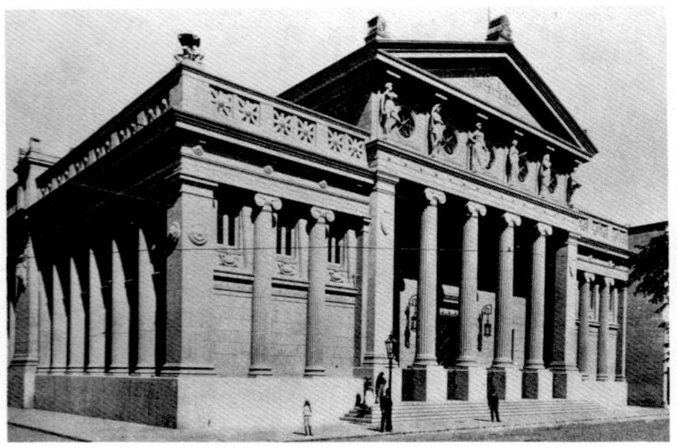

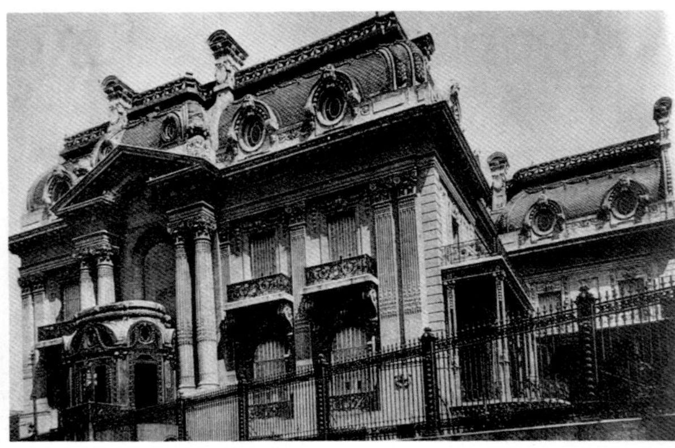

▲

Fig. 3. Carlos Morra, secondary school, Buenos Aires, 1900.

Fig. 4. Alejandro Christophersen, residence, Buenos Aires, 1909.

triggering alternative styles that were quickly assimilated, giving a spirit of continuity and vitality to the process.

By the end of the twenties in Buenos Aires, many buildings imitated fashionable French styles, from Gothic to neoclassic, designed either by local architects schooled in Europe or by foreign architects, some of whom had never even seen Argentina (figs. 3 and 4). Alongside these buildings, there were occasional examples adapted from anti-academic efforts to produce buildings in historic English modes, or others that expressed the almost always unfortunate search for a neo-Hispanic style. This last was supposed to be a more adequate manifestation of cultural tradition, but it was finally determined that such searches only changed one anachronism for another.

These formal excesses were complemented by a few often excellent examples of *art nouveau* (figs. 5, 6, 7, and 8) and by many, though tentative, examples of art deco (fig. 11). A principal advocate of the latter was Alejandro Virasoro (1892–1972), who was perhaps the first knowingly to suggest an architecture without historic antecedents, that is, to show his concern for modernism, a concern that would become the main motivation of architects in the coming decade.

Virasoro's architecture, influenced, as he himself admitted, by the Russian ballet in general and decoration by Lev Bakst in particular, reached its peak from 1925 to 1930. Characteristic of his works were his unusual telescopic treatment of spaces, and an obsessive use of decoration limited to the repetition of the most elemental geometrical shapes in the manner of Josef Hoffmann (figs. 9 and 10).

The first references to a more rationalist climate began to appear in the mid-twenties with Alberto Prebisch (1899–1971), in his articles published by a magazine called *Martín Fierro*. The texts were evidently influenced by material that appeared in the Paris periodical *L'Esprit nouveau*, and also by the activities of new groups such as Amigos del Arte who, together with other intellectuals, musicians, and writers, invited Le Corbusier to lecture in Buenos Aires.

The set of ten lectures Le Corbusier gave (that he would compile, together with other writings, in *Précisions* [Paris: Les Éditions G. Crés, 1930]) dealt with the central subjects of his personal concerns from furniture to town planning. His diagnoses respecting the city and its architecture were definitive and pessimistic. But his words were filled with a visionary and optimistic lyricism which, in the long run, proved to be more the latter than the former, since he imagined Buenos Aires developing in the future according to his rigorous poetical-mechanistic vision.

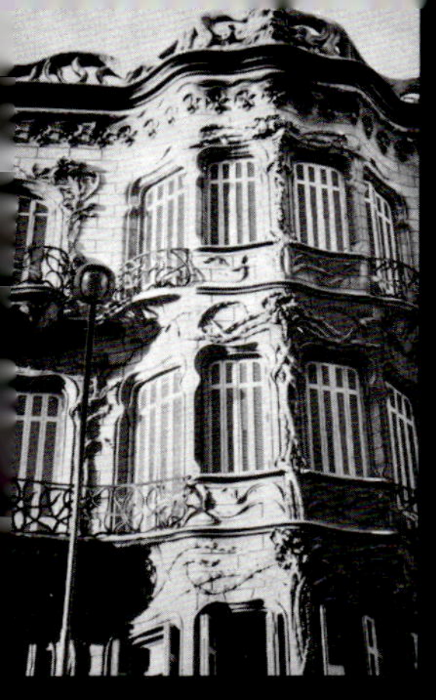

Fig. 5. Anonymous, *art-nouveau* building, Buenos Aires, ca. 1910.

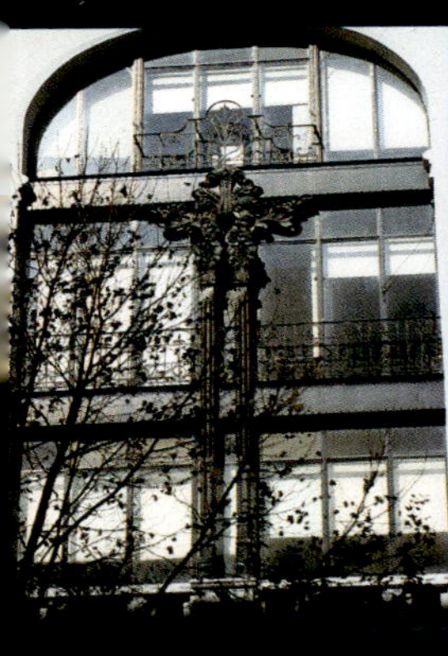

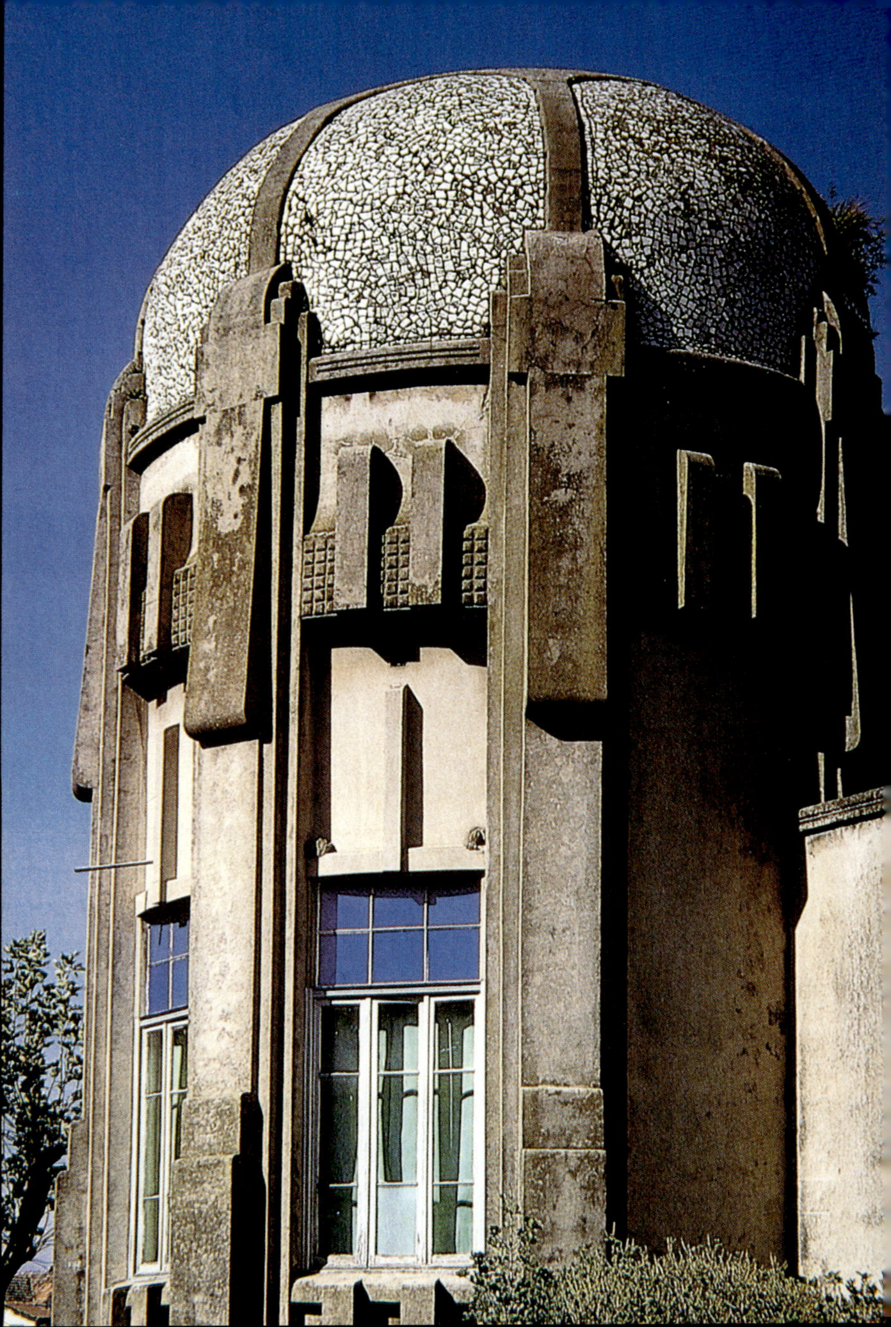

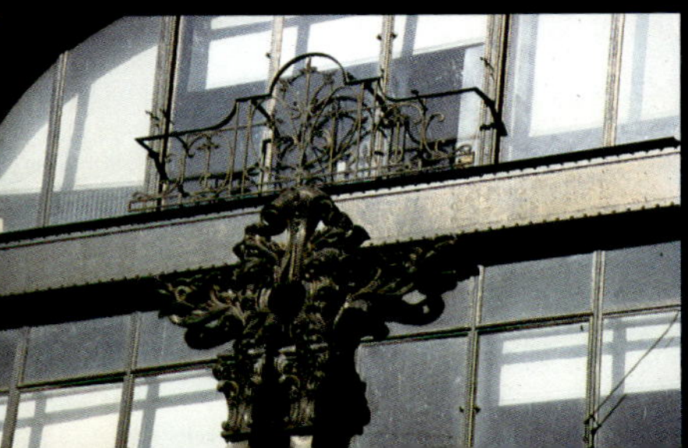

Figs. 6 and 7. Anonymous, *art-nouveau* office building, details, Buenos Aires, 1910.

Fig. 8. Julián García, home for the elderly, Temperley, 1913.

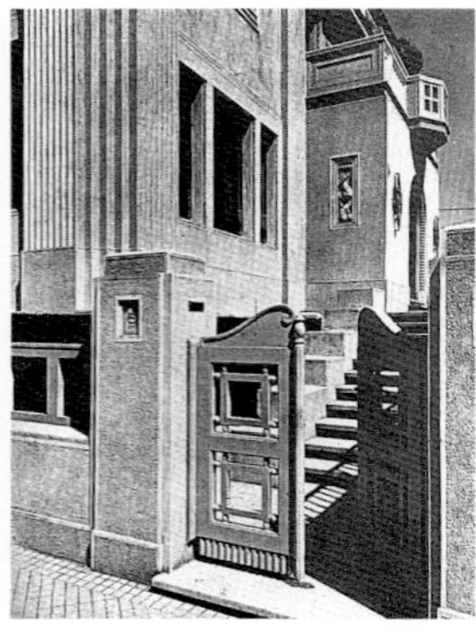

Fig. 9. Alejandro Virasoro, his residence, Buenos Aires, 1929.

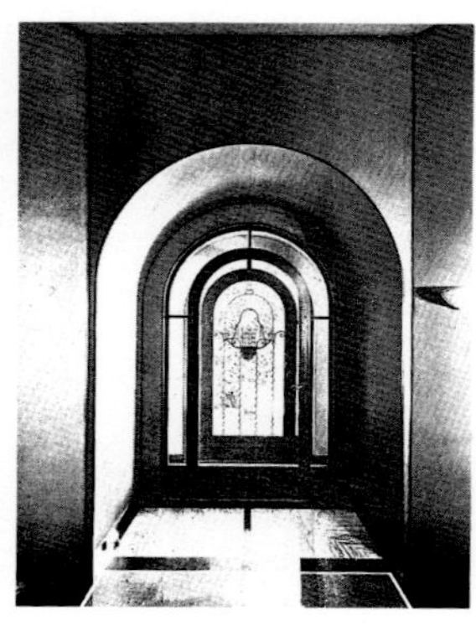

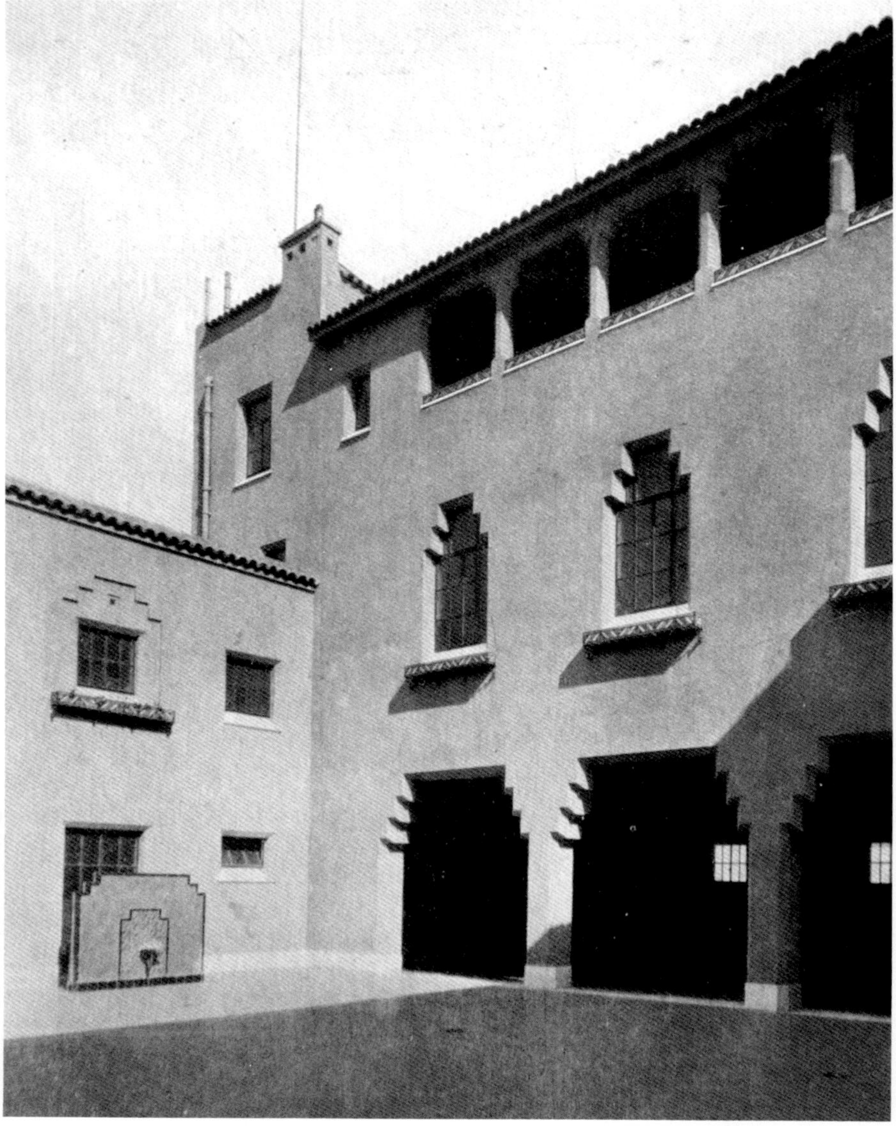

Fig. 10. Alejandro Virasoro, his residence, interior, Buenos Aires, 1929.

He came to know the geography of the country and its cityscape: Buenos Aires fascinated him. It was, as he said in *Précisions*, "the most inhuman city" he had ever seen. He walked along "its hopeless streets" and admired the Río de la Plata and its immense skies as perhaps no other foreign visitor has admired them.

He met writer Victoria Ocampo, "a tall woman of classical beauty: a rich, powerful woman, but very unhappy in her private life," as Waldo Frank described her (*Memorias* [Buenos Aires: Editorial Sur, 1975]) when she was working so hard to transform Buenos Aires into a center for culture.

She entertained in her new, modern house, reluctantly built by Alejandro Bustillo (1889–1982), an eclectic architect. We might wonder why Ocampo, who represented at that time a certain avant-garde, wanted Bustillo to build her house, a "manifesto-house" of her ideas, since Bustillo was an architect who detested those ideas and preached a return to the most rigorous classicism.

Why not accept Le Corbusier's offer (his sketches are dated September 1928) or ask her friend Prebisch to do it, since he was someone who was at ease with her position? The answer is, she needed an experienced professional more than a difficult artist or a polemic youth to carry out her ideas which, in effect, were already developed in two houses built previously.

Keeping in mind this complex, even violent relationship between architect and client, we approach this project where all design decisions were thought out in terms of balance between tradition and modernity, solved by the ahistoric aspect of the forms, including references both to the past and to the modern movement.

This effort to create a silent testimony of timeless architecture was materialized in the home's exterior through a relationship of volumes, solids and voids that gives a sensation of *gravitas* to the house, depriving it of any experimental characteristics. This situated the project near contemporary examples of Adolf Loos and especially close to another recently "rediscovered" house: one built by Ludwig Wittgenstein for his sister in Vienna.

Any sense of dynamism was dampened by the partial symmetries achieved by regulating lines reiterated in different geometric forms (cubes, prisms, the cylinder of the only visible column) that were found again in the interior spaces (figs. 12, 13, and 14). The interiors were, however, organized more conventionally: the different rooms were connected axially, their main elements (such as fireplaces or windows and doorways) being distributed in a regular, repetitive, and symmetrical way (fig. 15).

Nevertheless, the absolute consistency in treatment and, in every case, the total absence of decoration, the austerity of its light-colored walls, the striking presence of a constant lighting and, finally, the stark anonymity of its furniture made Le Corbusier admit, in *Précisions*, that "he had seen Picassos and Légers framed by a seldom-to-be-found purity."

◂

Fig. 11. Alberto Gelly Cantilo, secondary school, Buenos Aires, 1929.

This house has been dealt with in depth because all this complexity in the service of simplicity, all these anomalies and contradictions, were also to a certain extent those facing the local avant-garde emerging in those years. They were torn between a search for authenticity ingrained in a national tradition and the unavoidable acceptance of modern European culture, a subject still at the heart of our current state of affairs.

The stirring of an Argentine avant-garde took place in the twenties and was evident in the polemic activity of magazines and small groups of enthusiasts. In the following years, the leading influences were closer to German rationalism or to the work of Rob Mallet-Stevens than to Le Corbusier's purism. These influences, however, would be assimilated and adapted in a simple, at times austere, language that rejected either technological or scenic experiments or spectacular effects.

The development of the modern movement in Argentina was linked to the work of its main advocates like Alberto Prebisch, Antonio Vilar (1887–1966), and Wladimiro Acosta (1900–1967), as well as to the large number of accomplished architects who would mix modern design with traditional styles.

We already know of Prebisch's polemics, his critical articles, and his elated support of modernism after his return from Europe in 1924. On the other hand, his buildings show us his real personality, that of a self-effacing and often timid man.

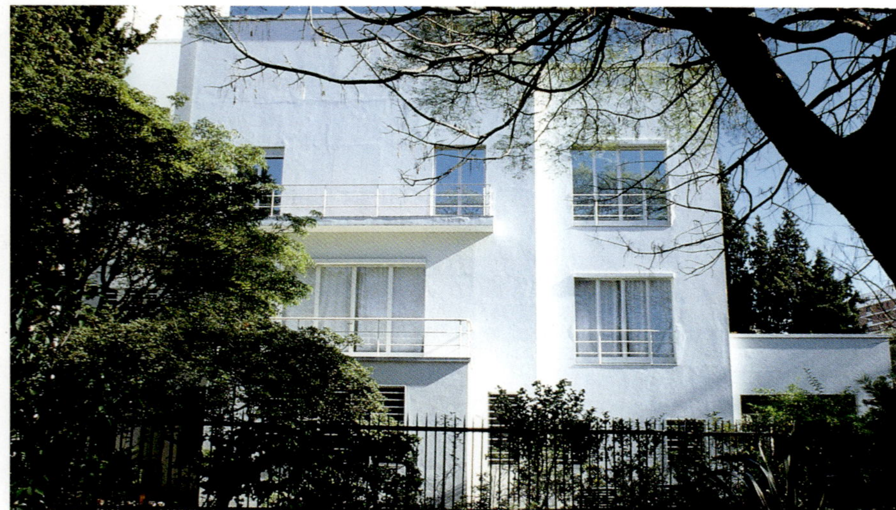

Figs. 12, 13, and 14. Alejandro Bustillo, house of Victoria Ocampo, Buenos Aires, 1929.

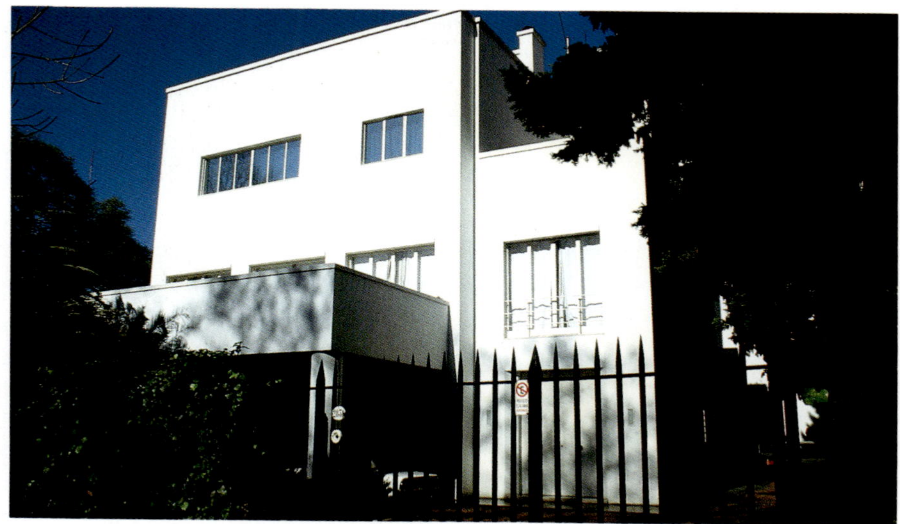

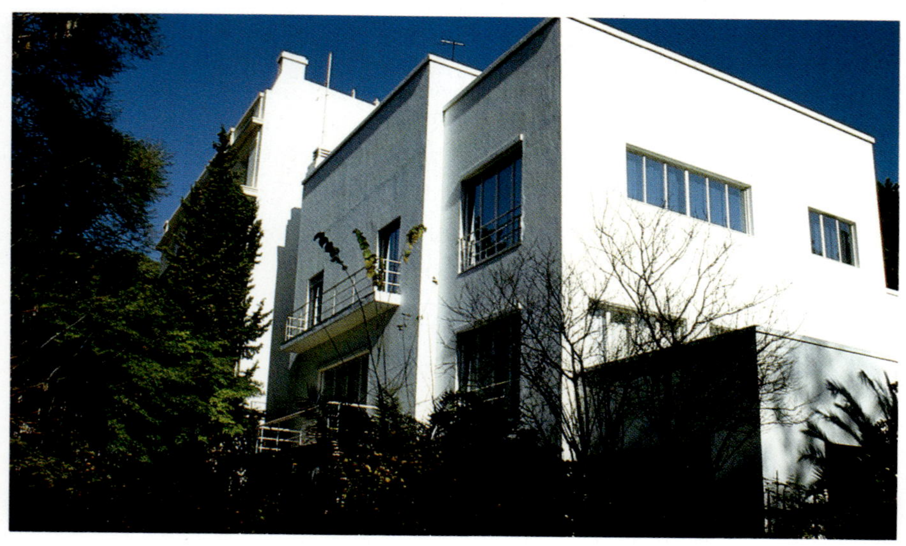

▸

Fig. 15. Alejandro Bustillo, house of Victoria Ocampo, staircase, Buenos Aires, 1929.

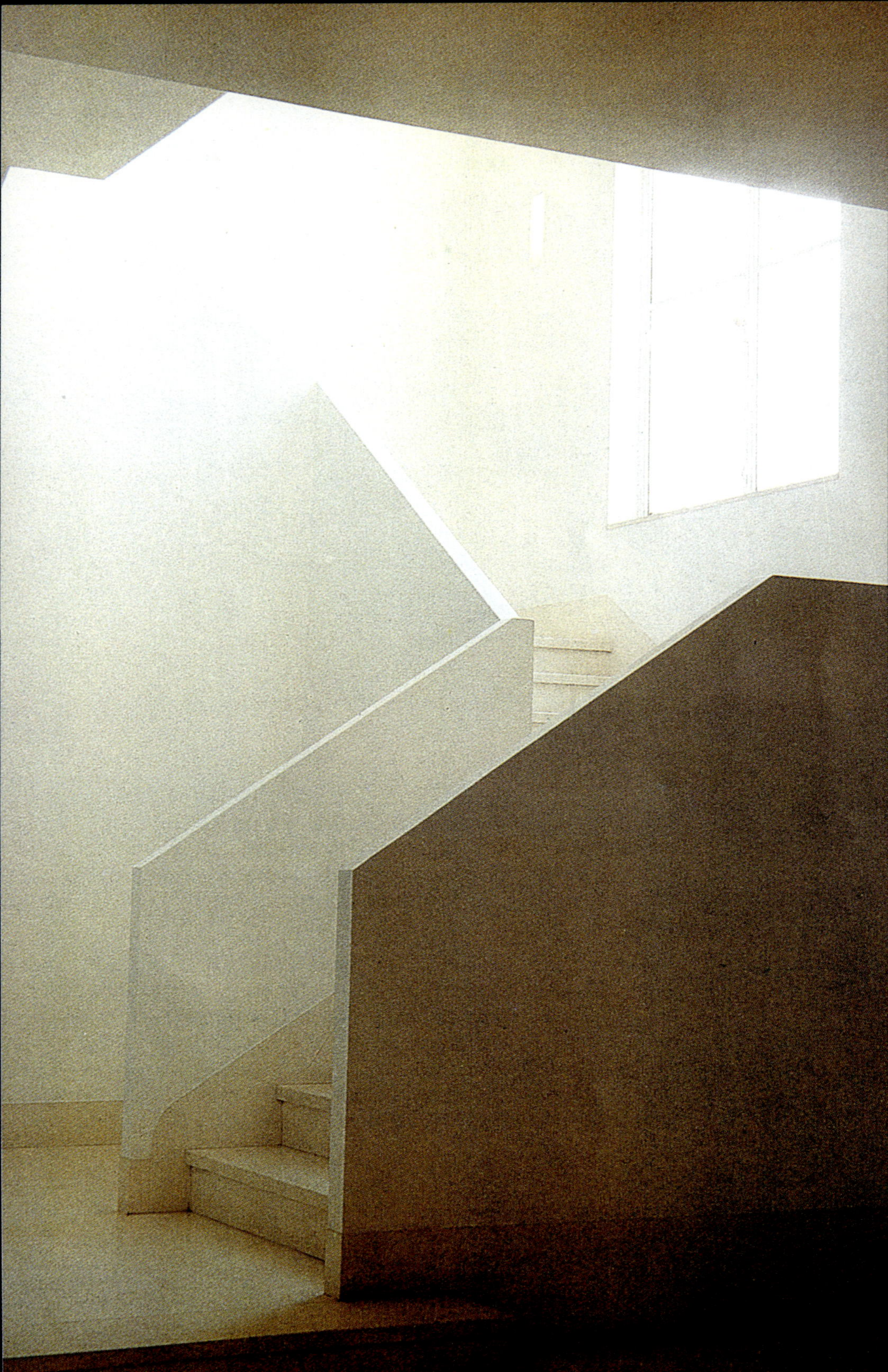

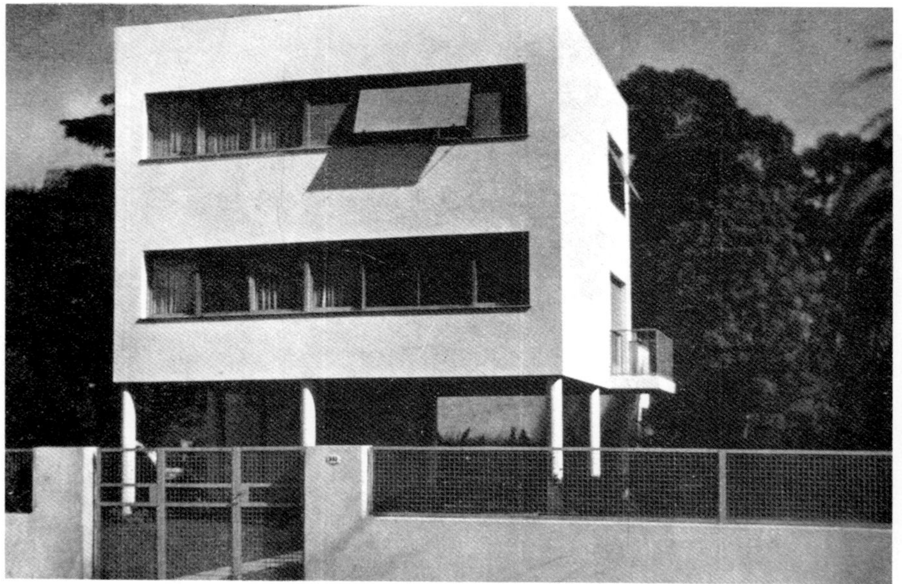

Fig. 16. Alberto Prebisch, suburban house, Buenos Aires, 1937.

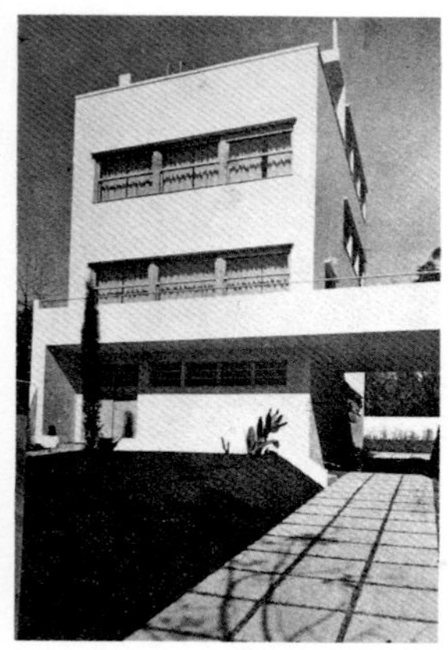

Fig. 17. Alberto Prebisch, town house, Buenos Aires, 1930.

In his early houses, the expressive vigor of their referentials was done away with by a systematic elimination of everything that meant density or tension. This fact is particularly clear in two houses. The first, dated 1930, is obviously derived from Le Corbusier's Maison Citrohan, in its first version, corresponding to the plaster model shown at the Salon d'Automne in 1922, which Prebisch had surely seen during his stay in Paris (fig. 17).

A similar volumetry, the roof garden, horizontal windows, a suggestion of piles, all belonged to Le Corbusier's prototype. Nevertheless, the inexpressive treatment of the formal elements of its interiors made Prebisch's house into a lackluster translation of the original.

The same could be said of a later house (fig. 16), one from 1937, in which all the canonical elements of the purist's language were present but seemingly frozen in an inflexible plan, where tensions and transgressions that enrich this language were eliminated in favor of a rigid distribution of functional spaces, enclosed in a simple, if not simplistic, volume.

That same year, 1937, Prebisch designed what would be one of the most important buildings of the decade, and by far his best work: the Gran Rex Cinema (fig. 19). Once we pass through the large Travertine marble facade which is, in fact, a structural frame that permitted the entrance to be built without columns, we reach the hall, three stories tall, lit by a huge glass wall (fig. 18). The hall can be seen from the outside, and the street can be seen from the balconies that are interconnected by broad staircases leading to the theater's various levels.

The interior is reminiscent of Radio City Music Hall in New York, with its parallel curves which converge on the stage, reinforced by lines of artificial lightning. Even though he was dealing with a subject that often stimulates fantasies or modernistic rhetoric, Prebisch showed himself again to be a master of sobriety.

In 1936, he had designed the best known monument in Buenos Aires: the obelisk. It was built to commemorate the four-hundredth anniversary of the founding of the city (figs. 20 and 21). Typically, he selected an historical form to celebrate this event, bringing it up-to-date by the adjustment of its size and the

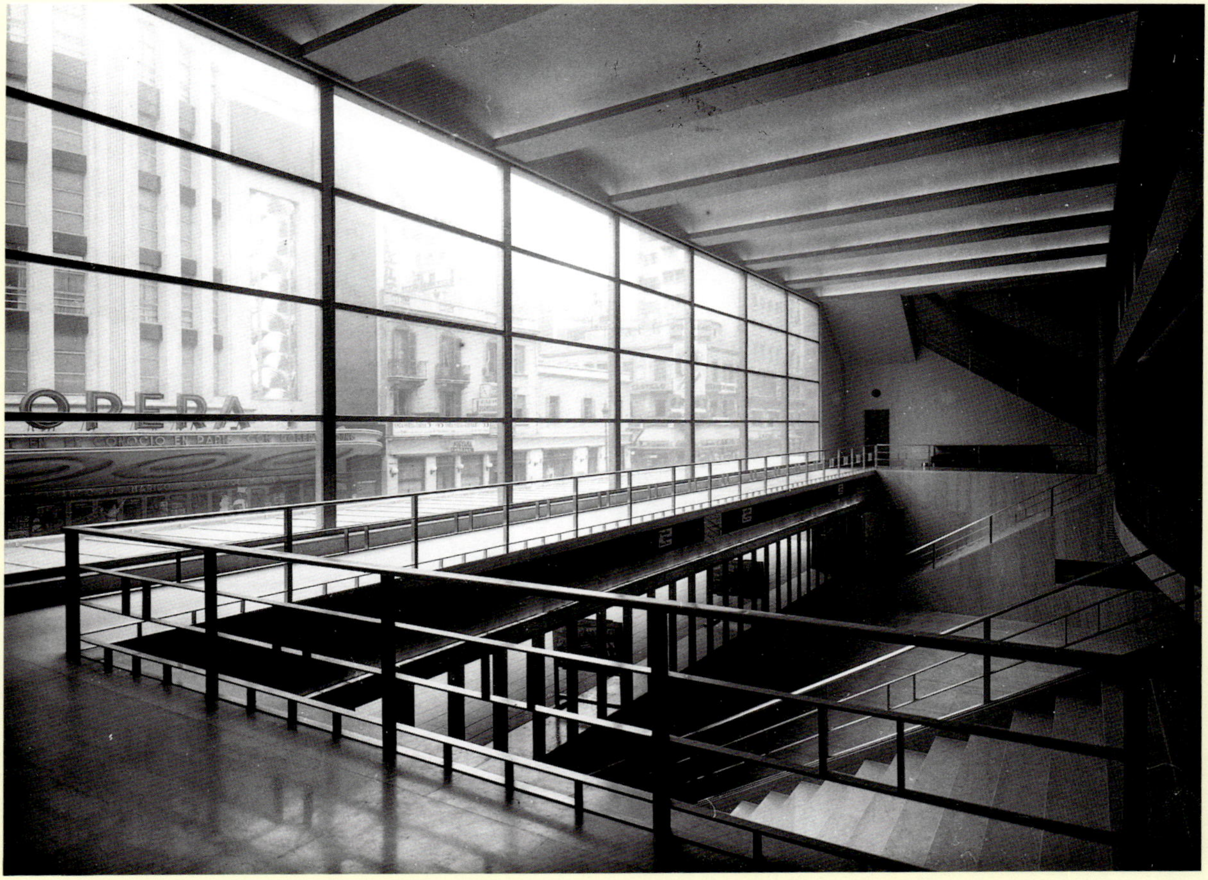

▲

Fig. 18. Alberto Prebisch, Gran Rex Cinema, lobby, Buenos Aires, 1937. Photograph by N. Gomez.

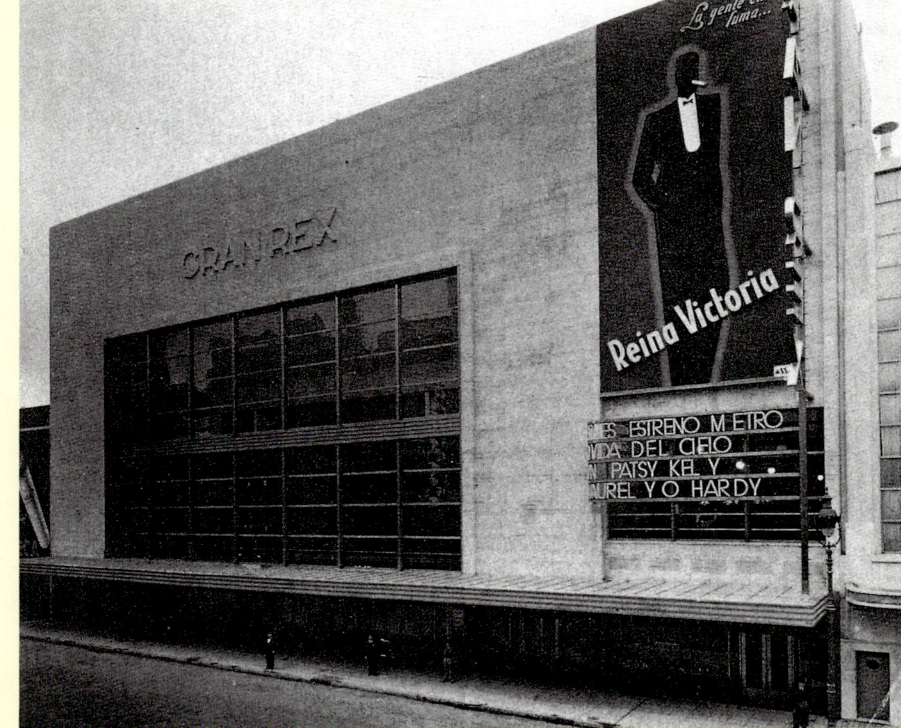

Fig. 19. Alberto Prebisch, Gran Rex Cinema, Buenos Aires, 1937.

absolute simplicity of his treatment of it, as if it were a geometric solid visualized in an almost metaphysical context. In his later work he did away with progressive influences, often finding shelter in a refined nostalgia, or, as mentioned before, in a pared-down classicism in which his complex personality finally found its true expression.

If it were necessary to choose just one name exemplifying the linguistic innovation that rationalism meant to our country, it would be that of Antonio Vilar. His work, some of which was done together with his brother Carlos, satisfied the search for homogeneity of taste by adopting a neutral language, that of the reiteration of unembellished forms and a deep adhesion to function and, more precisely, to objective conditions.

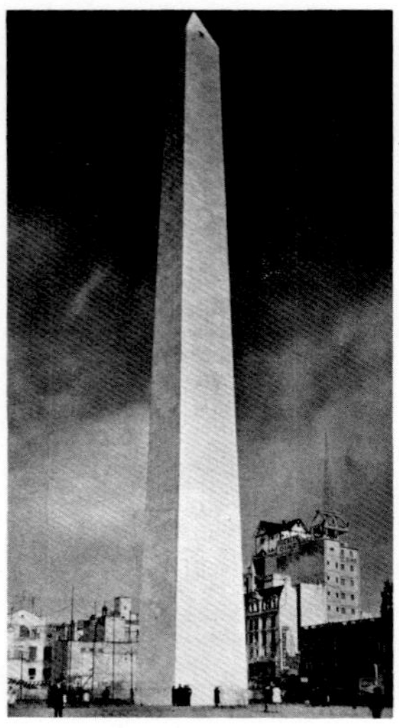

Fig. 20. Alberto Prebisch, obelisk, Buenos Aires, 1936.

▶

Fig.21. Alberto Prebisch, obelisk, Buenos Aires, 1936.

It was through this studied neutrality that he became our prototype of the modern architect. His figurative language did not renounce, as in the case of Prebisch, the expressivity of modern forms. On the contrary, he purified them in a systematic search for an economy of formal means: it is in the silent spaces of his architecture that we should seek his poetry.

His early work was representative of the eclecticism of the twenties. His last traditional building, a bank built in 1926, followed the typical pattern of the American skyscraper but already suggested, in its rigorous functional solution and in the anonymous treatment of the building's core, the characteristics that would be found in his later work. Take, for example, his apartment house of 1929 (fig. 22), a club done in 1930, and his truly modern buildings of the thirties.

He built a large number of houses on the outskirts of Buenos Aires. Among them his own, designed in 1935, stands out (fig. 24). Having an extended view of the river, the house is built partially on piles. The main floor opens to a curved terrace defined by a beam that follows its profile and suggests a double facade which defines the space.

The consistency between the ideas generating the project and the final design was such that all the elements, even in the cases where they were not so evidently functional (as in that of the abovementioned beam), were of a singular objectivity. Many of his numerous houses may not have had the poetical qualities that this house had, but all of them had their own coherence due to the systematic rejection of all that was gratuitous, plus a rigorous and imaginative adherence to the most advanced forms of a new way of living.

Thus, his focus was concentrated less on an investigation of space than on an efficient and rational organization of the plan, in a search for answers allied to the most radical solutions of his time, such as those suggested in the studies of Klein and Neufert in the late 1920s.

Other than residences, which were mostly suburban, Vilar designed a large number of apartment houses, trying to codify this typical element of our cities (fig. 23). His office buildings and a hospital (fig. 26), surely the best built in that decade, were of similar high quality.

Toward the end of the thirties, he projected and built over 150 service stations for the Automobile Club of Argentina (fig. 25). This work, well-constructed and of fine formal quality, spread modern design throughout the country, masterfully resolving the balance between unity of design and the necessity of adapting to local conditions.

Some of his works later in the decade, like those of his colleagues at the time, were marked by the influence of reactionary trends in European architecture.

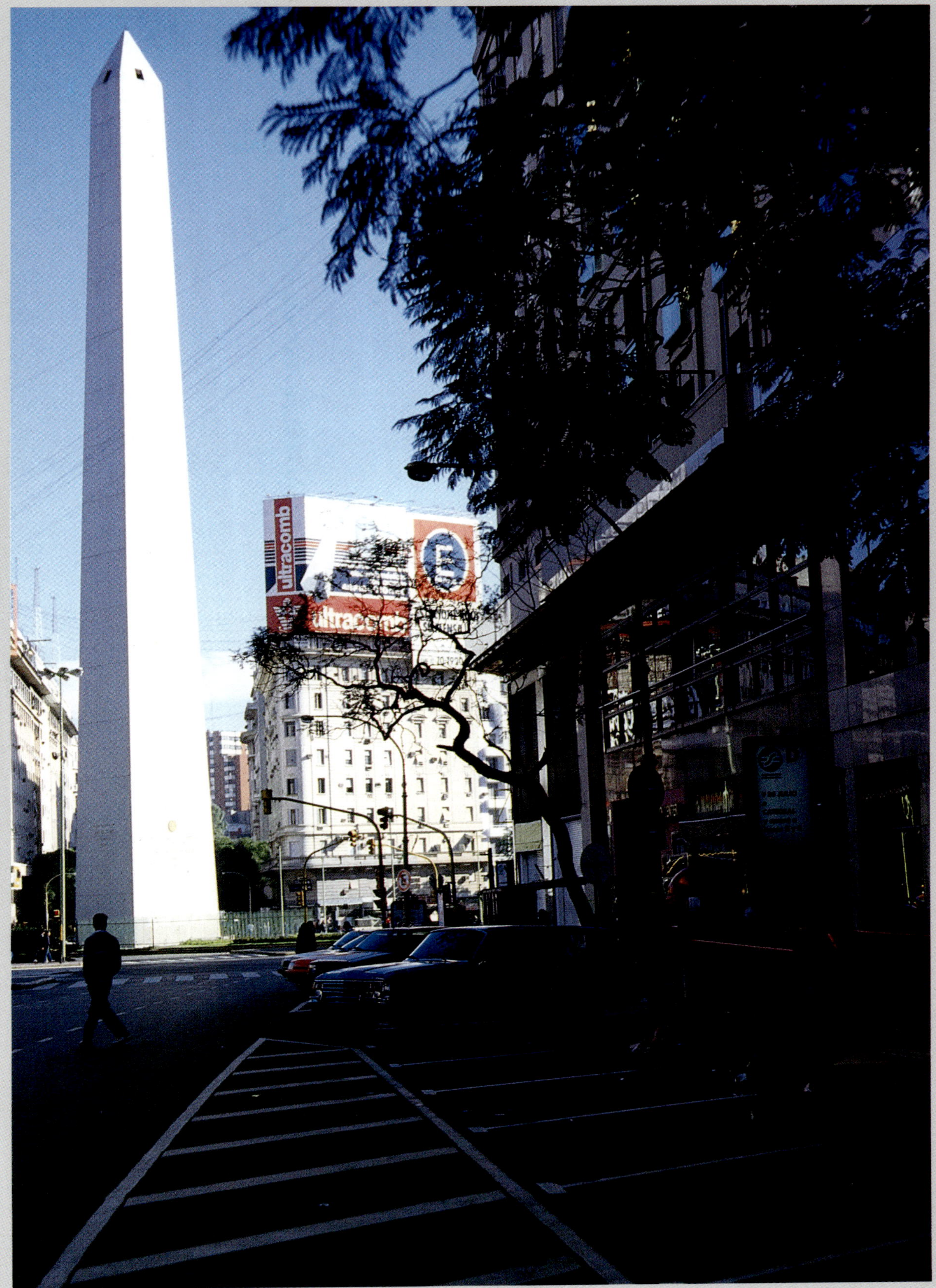
ultracomb
ultracomb

Fig. 22. Antonio Vilar, his apartment, living room, Buenos Aires, 1929. Photograph by N. Gomez.

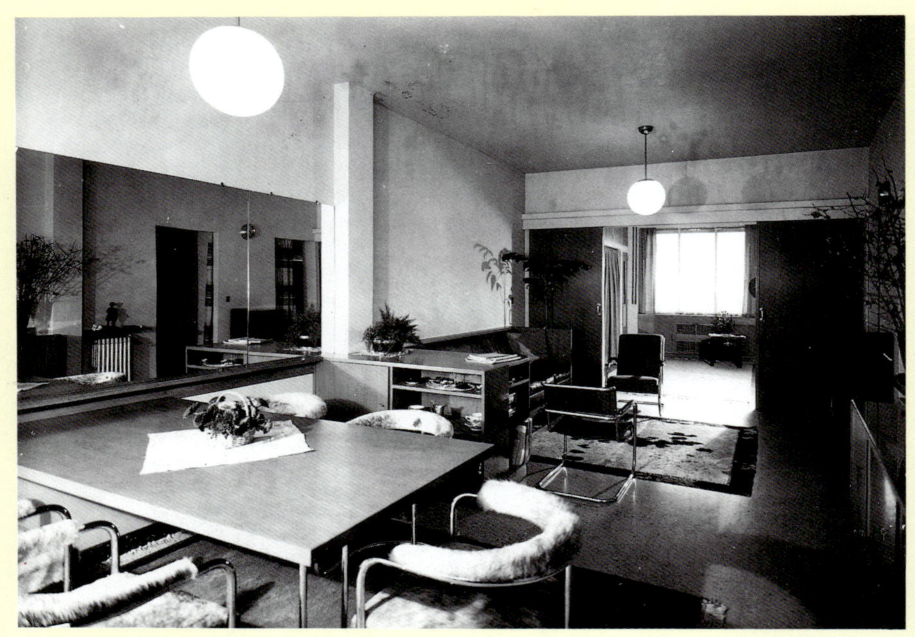

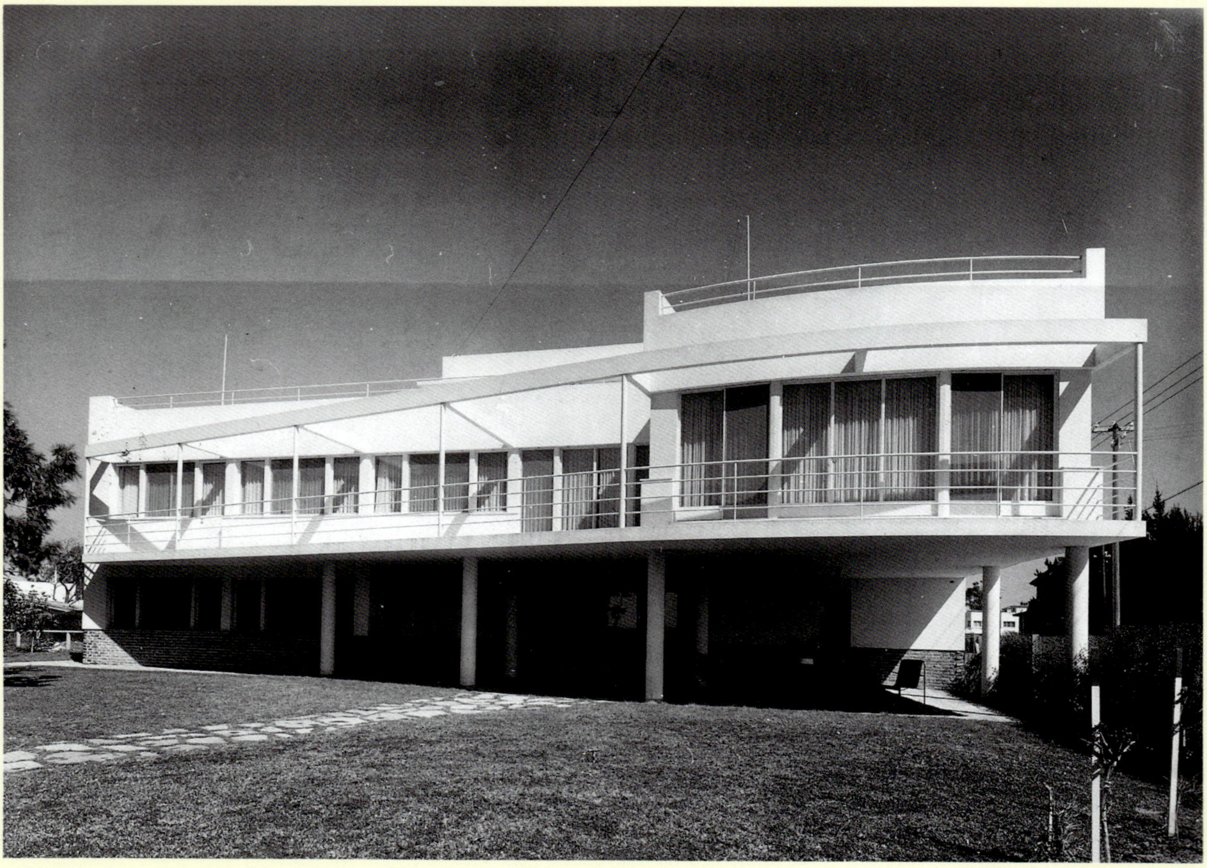

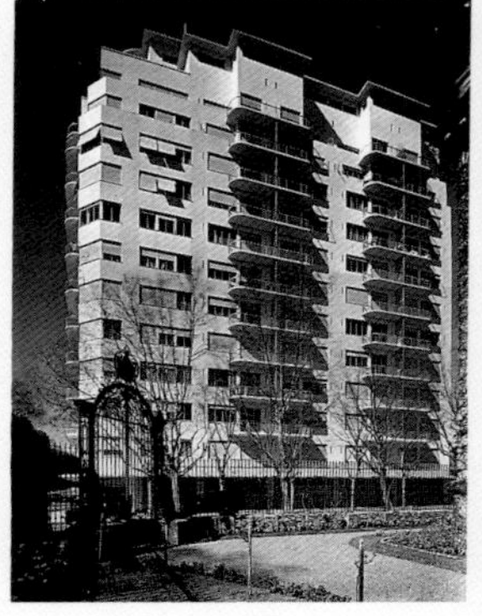

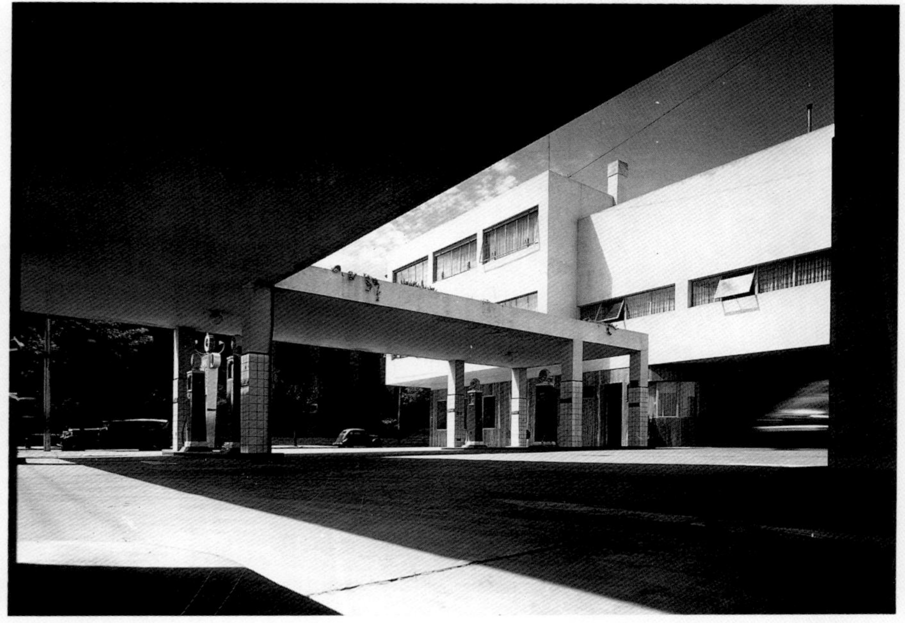

Fig. 23. Antonio Vilar, apartment house, Buenos Aires, 1936. Photograph by N. Gomez.

▲

Fig. 25. Antonio Vilar, Automobile Club gas station, Mar del Plata, 1937. Photograph by N. Gomez.

▼

Fig. 26. Antonio Vilar, Churruca Hospital, Buenos Aires, 1935. Photograph by N. Gomez.

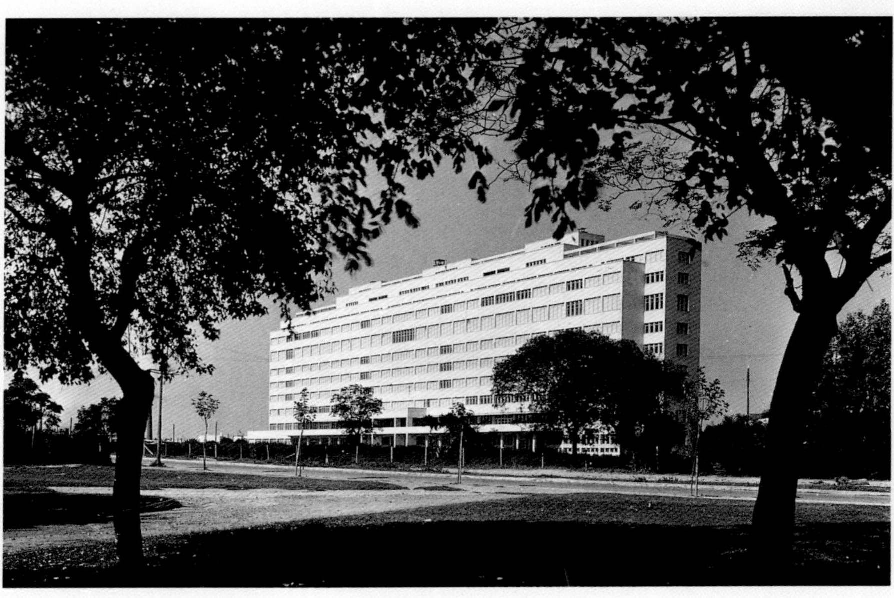

◄

Fig. 24. Antonio Vilar, his residence, San Isidro, 1935. Photograph by N. Gomez.

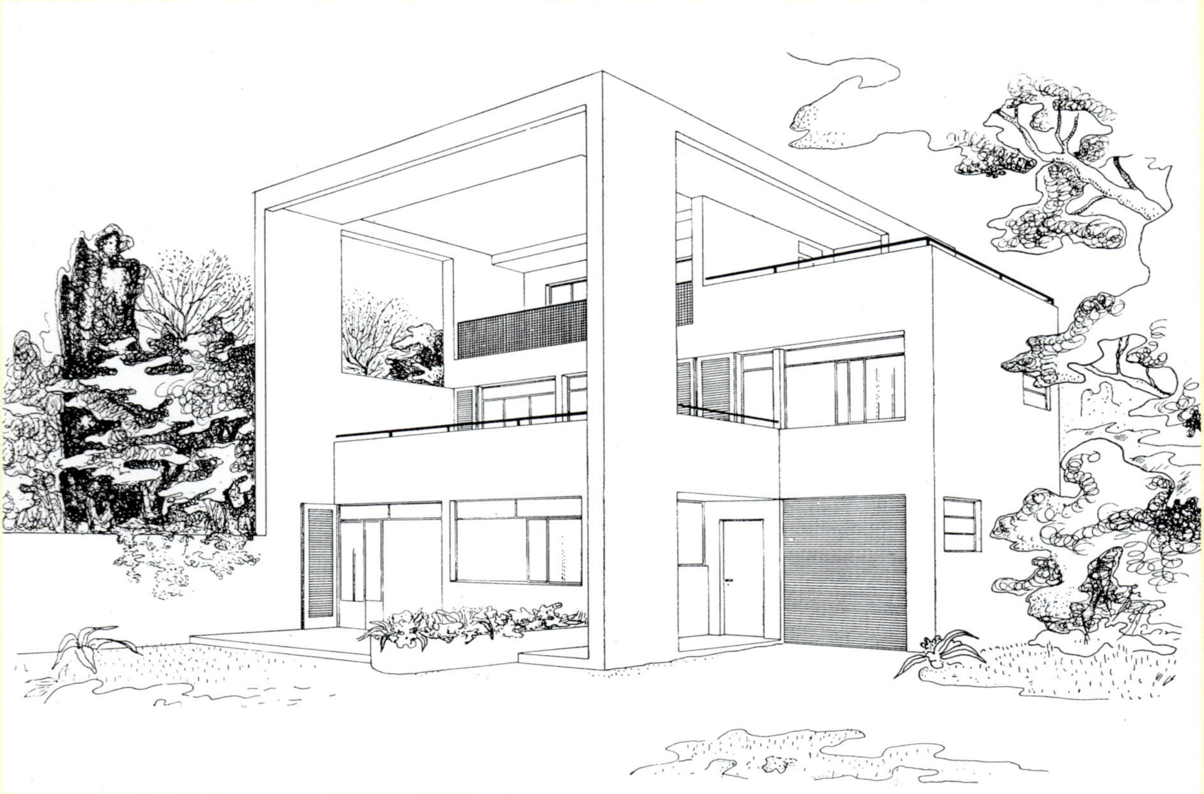

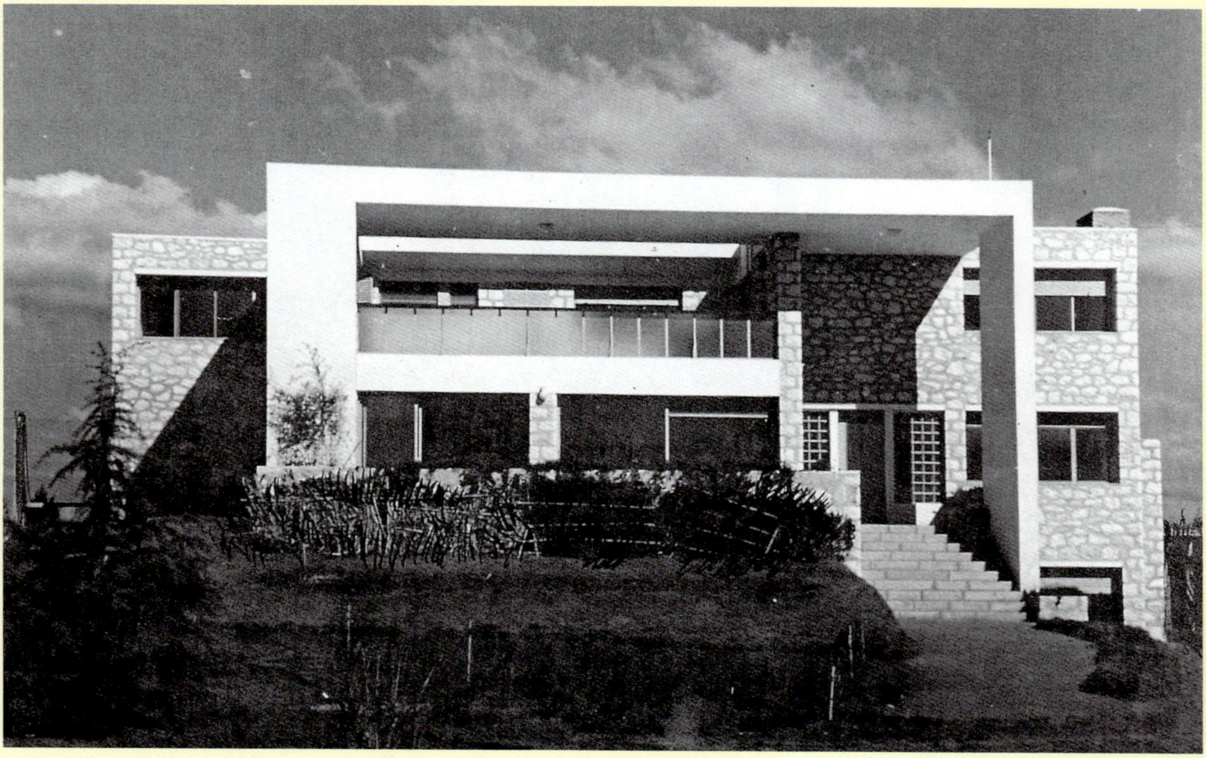

◂

Fig. 27. Wladimiro Acosta, suburban house, 1934–1935.

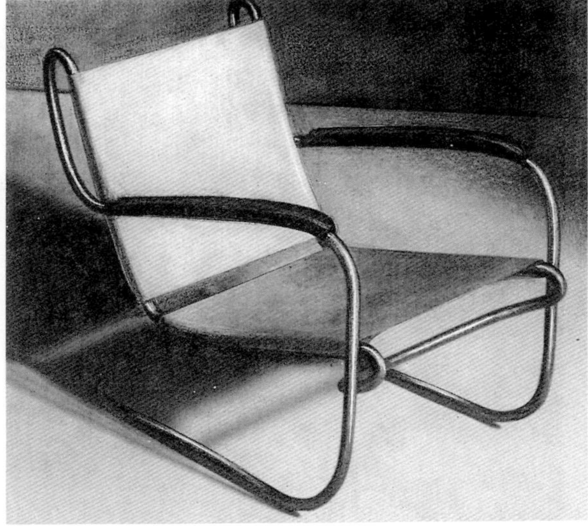

Fig. 28. Wladimiro Acosta, armchair, 1928.

Certain later examples show him compromising with local architecture, a problem perhaps caused by local conditions or, as in the case of the headquarters of the Automobile Club where he adopted a chaste monumentalism, already present in earlier buildings.

Wladimiro Acosta is a completely different man. Acosta has his own place in Argentine architecture, out of the mainstream. He was born in Russia and studied architecture and engineering in Italy and Germany in the twenties. In his German period, Acosta was influenced by the most radical ideas of German rationalist groups and by figures like Hannes Meyer, Ernst May, and Martin Wagner, who left their ideological mark on him for the rest of his life.

◂

Fig. 29. Wladimiro Acosta, vacation house, La Falda, Córdoba, 1937.

In those difficult formative years, he worked as an apprentice for important design firms in Berlin, at the same time showing an interest in fencing, expressionist dance, films, furniture (fig. 28), and especially stage design. With this unconventional background, he went to Brazil and then, in 1929, to Buenos Aires, where he published several of his projects and a book on housing and the city (*Vivienda y ciudad*, [Buenos Aires: Anaconda, 1937]).

His main concern was man's destiny in the city, being convinced that architecture was a social phenomenon whose forms developed with technical progress. To this materialistic approach must be added an original conception of space and light that led him to elaborate his own system of sun control. The problem was ingeniously resolved by the creation of an independent structure made of protective slabs which, umbrellalike, shielded the house itself (fig. 27).

In Acosta's architecture, a rich spatial interaction was created, replacing the usual volume by a complex dialectic relationship of external, internal, and intermediate spaces. The natural environment, the lighting, the shadows projected by the plans defining these spaces were the main elements which, in this way, went beyond the neoplasticist search, achieving a purpose not just by a formal mandate but rather through a rigorous adaptation to the objective conditions required by a contemporary dwelling (fig. 29).

This radical position removed him not only from the narrow professionalism of his local colleagues but also from a socio-economic environment not ready

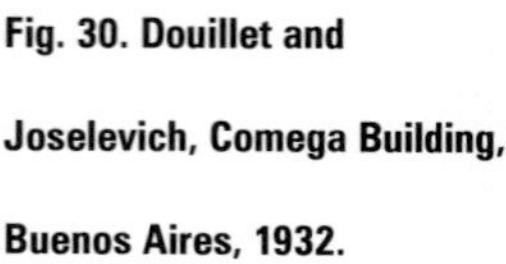

Fig. 30. Douillet and Joselevich, Comega Building, Buenos Aires, 1932.

Fig. 31. Douillet and Joselevich, Comega Building, entrance, Buenos Aires, 1930. Photograph by N. Gomez.

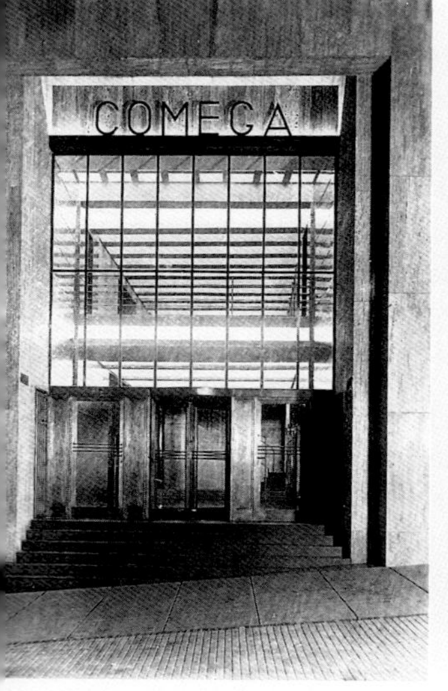

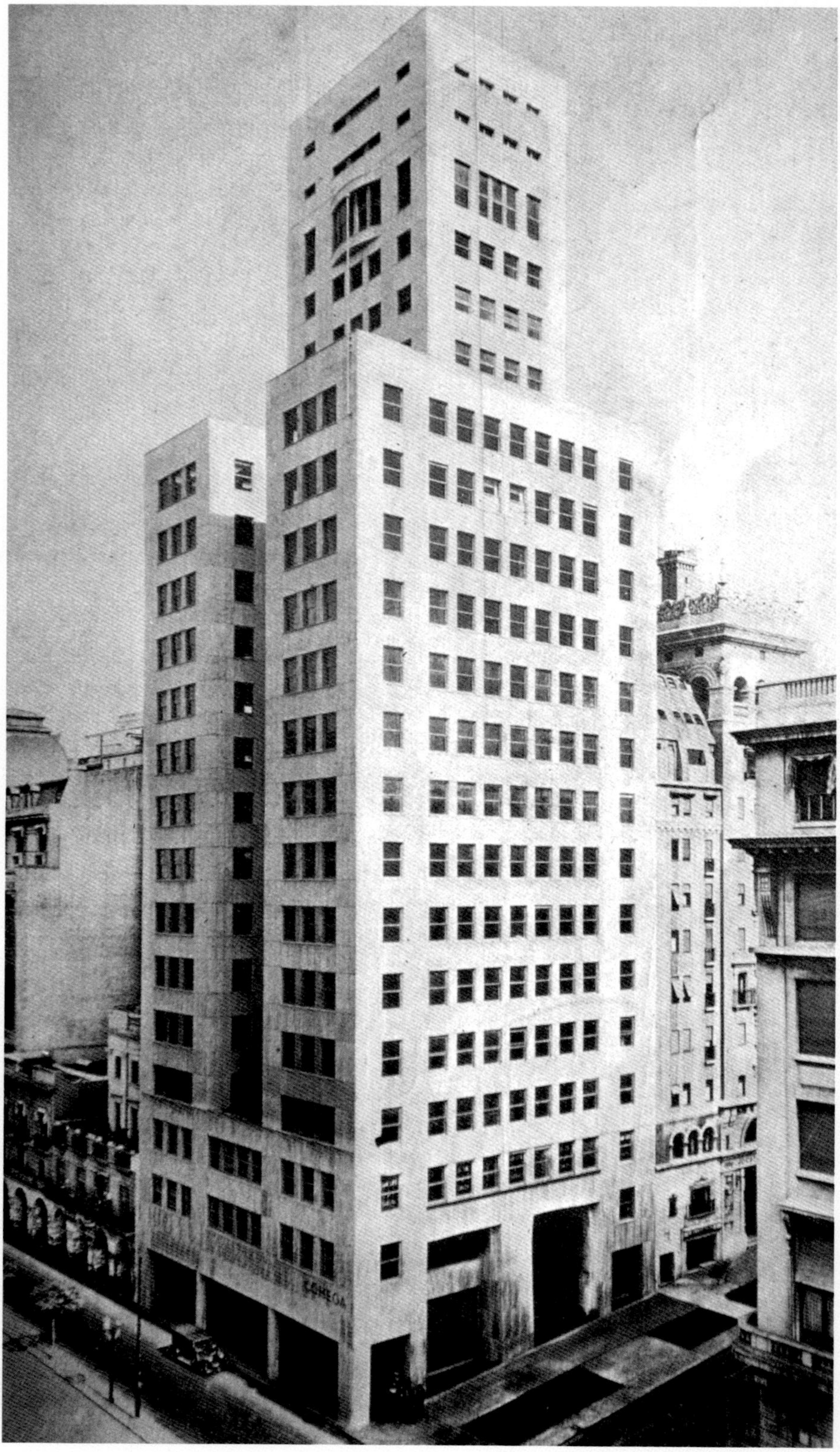

to receive him. That was why many of the projects were not carried out; finally he built just a few houses, a hospital, and an apartment building.

True to his principles, Acosta was the only one at that time to suggest an urban utopia called the integral city block. It was based, in its final version, on the juxtaposition of apartments and working areas, with uniform orientation and differentiated systems of circulation, placed lineally in the midst of large communal parks. This was a conception akin to certain Soviet proposals or to Ludwig Hilberseimer's city.

The adoption and, in many cases, the re-elaboration of the principles of European rationalism, other than in the projects of the architects already mentioned, resulted in the appearance of numerous works, often more than adequately well-designed by professionals who were not necessarily ideologically committed to the modern movement. These works achieved a serene urbanness, being linked to the most contemporary methods of production and expressing an awareness of the most advanced artistic imagery.

There are very few monuments stemming from this architecture, that is to say, works that, due to their outstanding individuality, became landmarks on the urban scene. Of all that was produced by architectural rationalism in Argentina, skyscrapers were perhaps the only monumental achievements. What made those buildings outstanding was the fact that they successfully combined the requirements of monumentality (singularity, strong formal definition, relative independence from their context) with a voluntary submission to urban morphology, through an ingenious adaptation of their volumetry and surfaces to the already-existing profile of the city.

The three most important skyscrapers built in Buenos Aires in the thirties were the Comega by Douillet and Joselevich, done in 1930; the Safico designed by Walter Moll in 1934; and the Kavanagh built by Sánchez, Lagos, and de la Torre in 1936. We will briefly analyze the relationship of each of these buildings with its environment and setting as well as investigate their main formal characteristics.

The Comega is a tall office building, placed on a downtown corner looking out on two avenues, Corrientes and Alem (fig. 30). Its two facades are differently composed so that the facade containing the main entrance predominates over the other (fig. 31). However, this apparent overvaluation of one particular facade facing a major artery is softened by the similar treatment given to both fronts, symmetrically composed with a strong emphasis on the plenitude of the arris. The upper part of the tower, with its identical facades, definitely affirms its function as a focal point on the urban landscape.

The Safico Building, set two blocks further along Corrientes Avenue, was originally projected as an apartment house (fig. 32). Built between the walls of neighboring buildings, clearly fitting into its context, it demonstrates with its volumetric composition that it has no intention of interrupting the harmony of the street's building line. The Safico's height and compactness assure the ongoing integrity of the city block on which it stands, without either a break in the symmetry or an outcropping that could affect the continuity of the block. Atop this tall foundation and set in from the building line, a stepped tower rises which respects the established building codes and regulations of the time, resulting in a design that makes a strong impact on its urban surroundings. This interplay of volumes, more complex and controlled than in the Comega Building, is maintained by an extremely synthetic figurative language. The architect uses two types of openings, one where they are grouped and another

Fig. 32. Walter Moll, Safico Building, Buenos Aires, 1934.

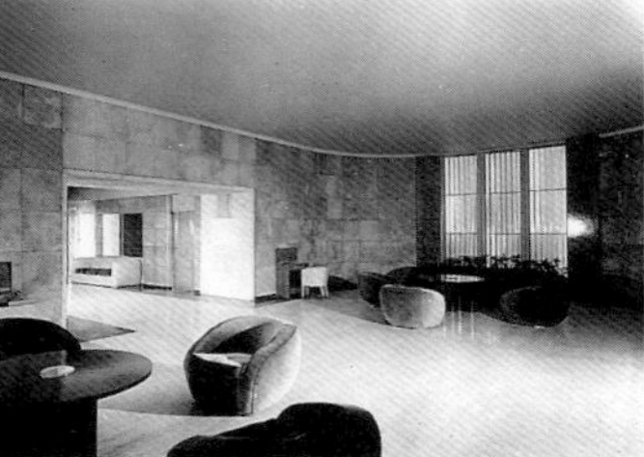

Fig. 33. Sánchez, Lagos, and de la Torre, Kavanagh Building, lobby, Buenos Aires, 1934. Photograph by N. Gomez. (See page 74.)

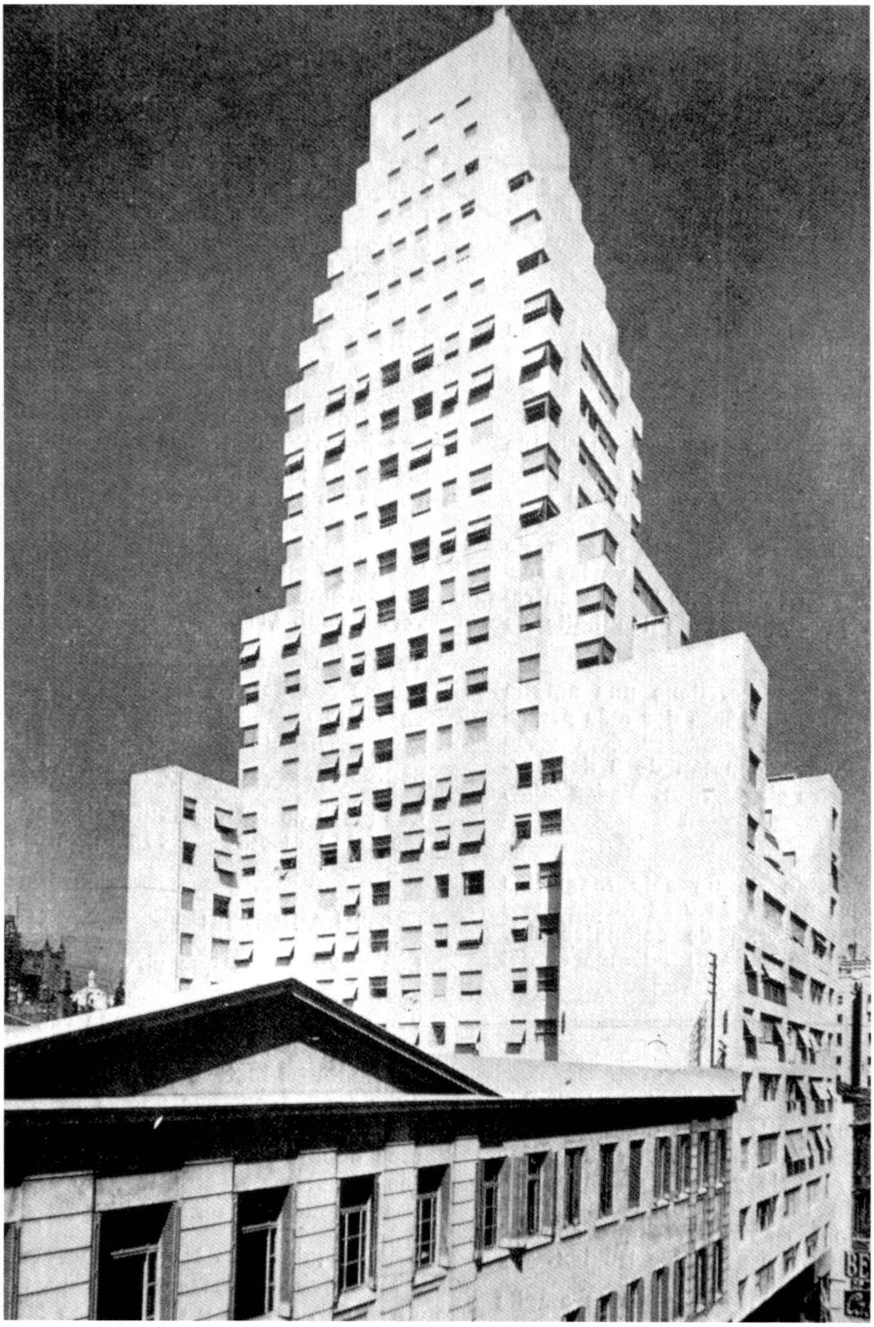

▸

Fig. 34. Sánchez, Lagos, and de la Torre, Kavanagh Building, Buenos Aires, 1936. Photograph by N. Gomez.

where they are isolated, both symmetrically organized. Each stresses, through the use of variants, the building's massiveness, underlining the enclosed character of the squat volume of the lower part of the structure trapped between its neighbors' walls, simultaneously expressing, through the windows placed in the building's corners, the isolated splendor of the tower.

Although the Kavanagh Building is more spectacular than the others mentioned, it also meets the requirements demanded by its setting (fig. 34). As a freestanding building in an exceptional location, it is treated as if it were a rare object. The internal logic used in its design adjusts to the extraordinary complexity of the

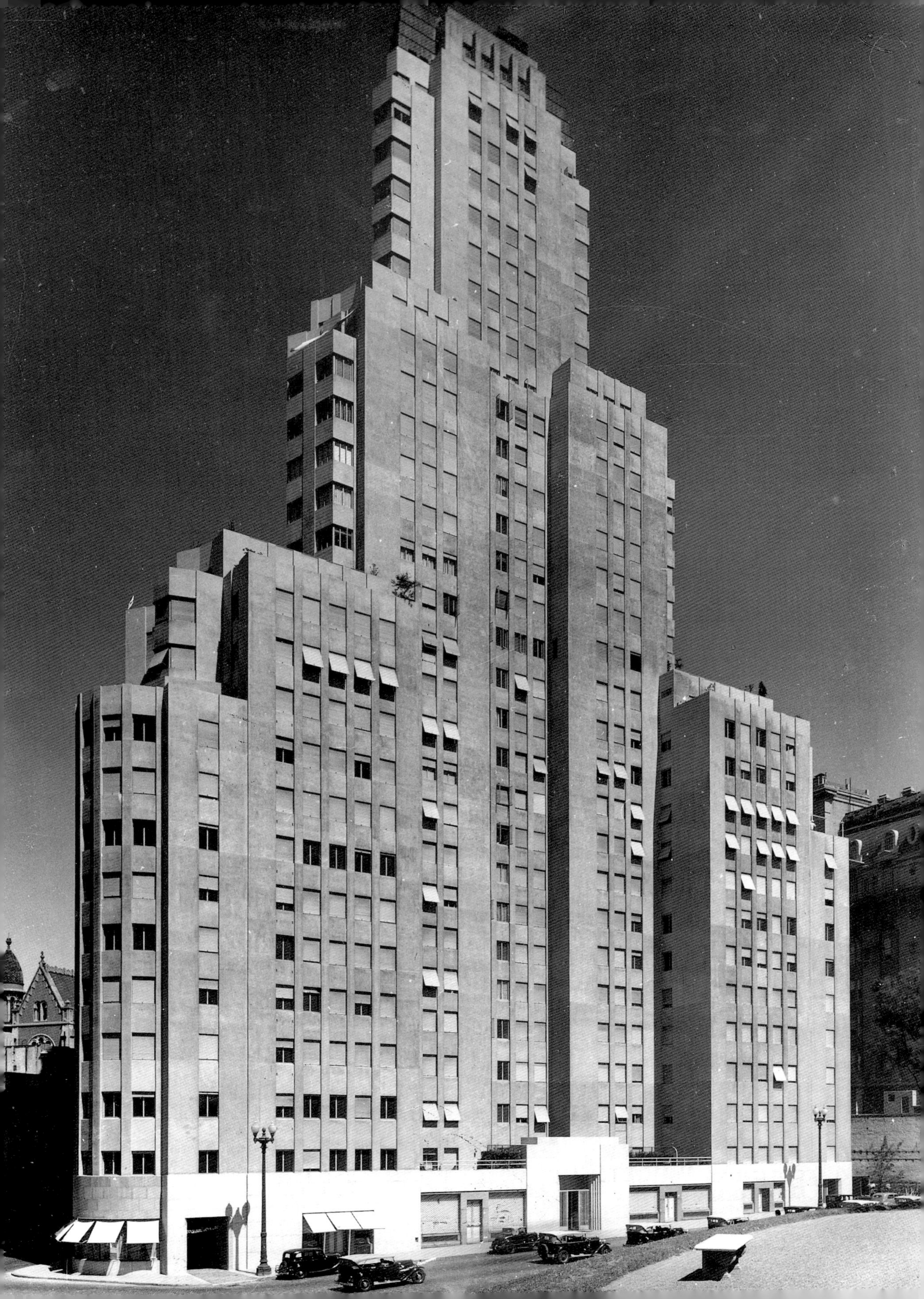

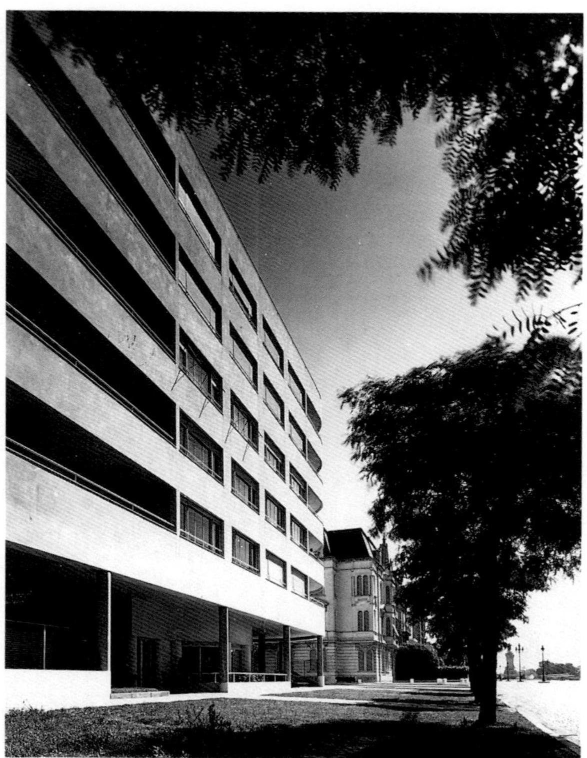

Fig. 35. Sánchez, Lagos, and de la Torre, apartment house, Buenos Aires, 1936. Photograph by N. Gomez.

irregular plot on which it stands. The result is achieved through a series of axes and partial compositions articulated in a play of volumes contained within a pyramidal whole that includes the brilliance of its repeated edges, the plasticity of a curved inflexion, and the deep convexity of the service patio. The culmination of all this is a faceted tower of expressionist overtones.

This rich compositional landmark should have inspired the most audacious formalist fantasies, but it was once again planned with a restrictive selection of extremely simple elements. Voids and solids follow the play of the different volumes, materializing the continuity or reinforcing the relative autonomy of the structure in an austere statement in which there were still traces of the stylistic resources employed in this architect's previous works (fig. 33).

The team of architects who designed the Kavanagh Building demonstrated, perhaps more than any others, the lack of any ideological commitment, together with a surprising ability to handle modern design. Their previous work, at the end of the twenties, represents the most absolute eclecticism. A brief contact with art deco led them to modern architecture, which they soon abandoned for monumental academicism.

During a short period in the thirties, they produced many works—some of them very interesting—such as the Kavanagh and another elegant apartment building, where the inflexion of the bands of windows and balconies defines the continuity of the corner (fig. 35). Deep terraces and the open ground floor set on piles make the building look somewhat like a continuation of the nearby park.

In spite of its apparent vitality, this architecture exhausted itself by the end of the decade: it became isolated from sources of power and popular sensibility.

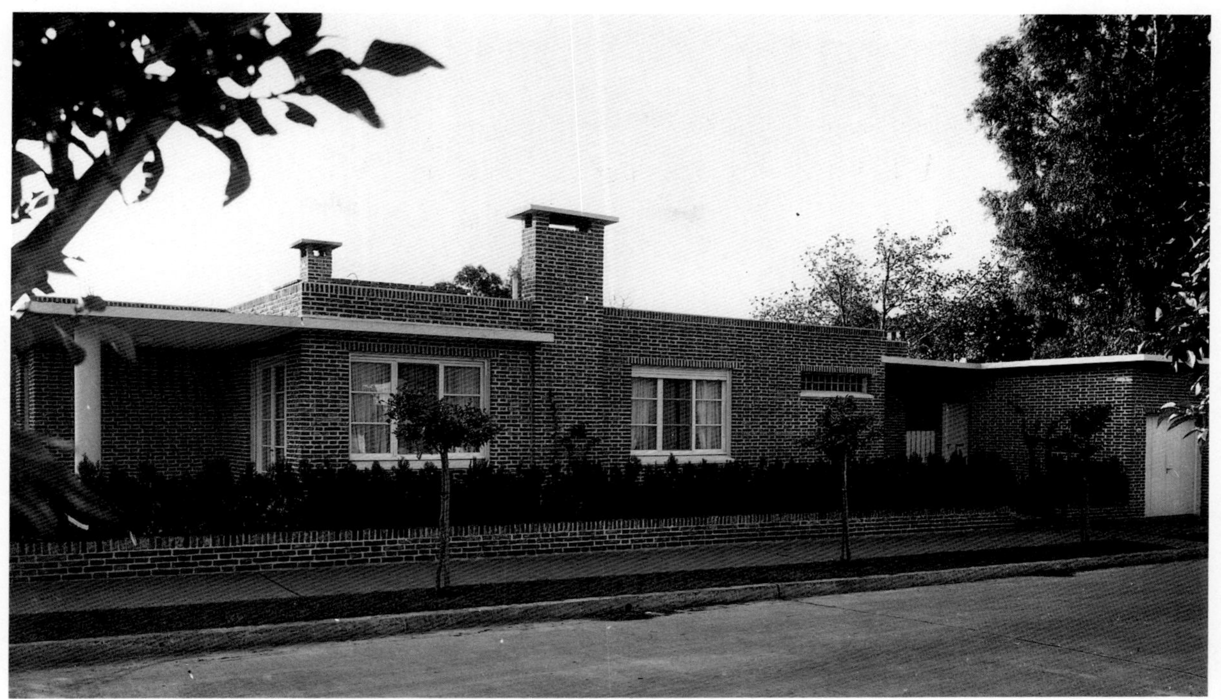

Fig. 36. Carlos Vilar, suburban house, Buenos Aires, 1940. Photograph by N. Gomez.

As it was also weakened by the lack of any ideological content that could counterbalance a driving professionalism on the part of its protagonists, it would drift into empty state monumentalism and populist anonymity.

Other important factors that worked against modern architecture in Argentina were, on the one hand, the criticism of those who were seeking a truly national architecture and, on the other hand, the fact that its traditional clients, the bourgeoisie, had abandoned their progressive tendencies in favor of more nostalgic attitudes, apparently better suited to the critical times they faced.

Natural materials, especially brick, replaced abstract white masonry, and traditional forms would shyly reappear. Some architects, like Carlos Vilar, tried a final reinterpretation of the rationalistic language cast in a new vein (fig. 36). So did Prebisch in his apartment houses of 1940, which were done with references neither to the past nor to a strictly modern style.

In the midst of a confusing panorama in which the most varied revivals coexisted with final attempts at modernity and with the arrival of several direct disciples of Le Corbusier, a new avant-garde appeared, strongly influenced by the master's latest work. Together with its concern for an authentic modernity, this group showed a renewed interest in the identity of architecture and in the less rational aspects of creation; but their focus was on the broader subjects of mass housing and town planning, topics that differentiated them from the previous generation.

Their criticism was not restricted to reactionary lines of thought but was directed in general against the modernism of the thirties, which they considered had betrayed the principles of the modern movement and become nothing more than a new academicism. □

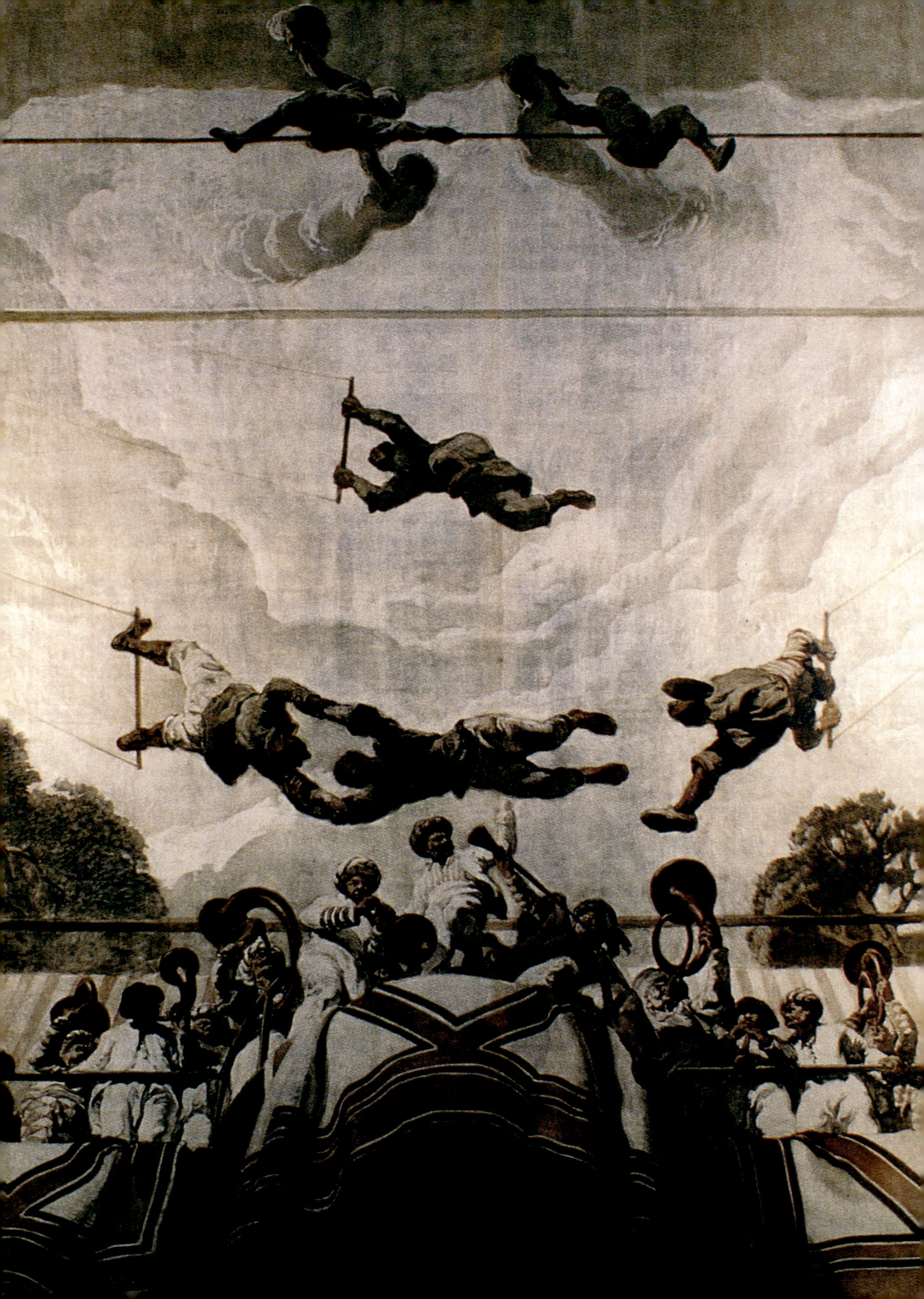

José María Sert in Buenos Aires

By Guillermo Whitelow

Translated by Edward Shaw

Guillermo Whitelow is a professor of esthetics at the National University of Buenos Aires. A former director of the Modern Art Museum in Buenos Aires, he is a member of the Foundation for the Investigation of Argentine Art, and the Argentine and International Associations of Art Critics. He is noted for books on Héctor Basaldúa and Raquel Forner, among others.

Photographs by Gustavo Sosa Pinilla

Fig. 1. José María Sert, *Los equilibristas*, detail, oil on canvas, 14 x 6 ½ m, 1932. Main hallway, Pereda Palace, Buenos Aires. (See page 84.)

Brazilian Independence Day is celebrated at the stately residence of the ambassador in Buenos Aires (fig. 2), and year after year those who attend the ceremonies are astonished when, in a moment of distraction, their gaze turns toward the ceilings of the spacious reception rooms. Many guests already know the colorful pictorial panorama that unfolds overhead, but the experience never loses its interest. It is a privilege to view these five spectacularly painted ceilings which cast an almost magic spell, bewitching the beholder.

Argentine cattleman Celedonio Pereda must have felt a degree of this ecstasy on first seeing the paintings that José María Sert had created for the Cathedral of Vich when the Spaniard exhibited them at the Jeu de Paume in Paris in June 1926. The show was composed of a polyptych to be installed in the presbytery of the cathedral, seven works that awakened reverential admiration. The exhibition had been preceded by a one-man show at the Wildenstein Gallery in New York in 1924, to be followed by subsequent shows there in 1931 and 1932. Sert was reaching the peak of his fame, the crowning triumph being his participation in decorating Manhattan's Rockefeller Center in 1933. His project replaced that of Mexican artist Diego Rivera, who was disqualified for having included a portrait of Lenin. "It is a great triumph. Not just for me, but for Europe. I have surpassed Rivera," Sert exclaimed on receiving the congratulatory telegram.[1]

In addition to the works designed for the Cathedral of Vich—a series he started in 1907 which would absorb a great proportion of his effort until just before his death—he also included forty panels for his screen *Mercado en una ciudad del Mediterráneo* (Market in a Mediterranean city) in the Jeu de Paume exhibit. This series, commissioned for the country home of Benjamin Moore, was an evocative array of picturesque scenes and vast perspectives with Goyaesque touches, set out in sienna on a silver background. It is not hard to believe that Pereda was astonished. These panels contrasted with the severity of the religious theme for which this artist from Catalonia manifested a different expressivity. Painter Miguel Utrillo, foster father of the famous Maurice, describes the impression that the works produced on viewers and comments that "the screen of the Mediterranean, which by itself would be a masterpiece, is just an elegant, flawless, exuberant, joyous bit of beauty when compared to the apocalyptical and baroque majesty of the Cathedral of Vich polyptych."[2] With these

1. Alberto del Castillo and A. C. Cirici Pellicer, *José María Sert: Su vida y su obra* (Barcelona-Buenos Aires: Editorial Argos S.A., 1947), 222.
2. Ibid., 128.

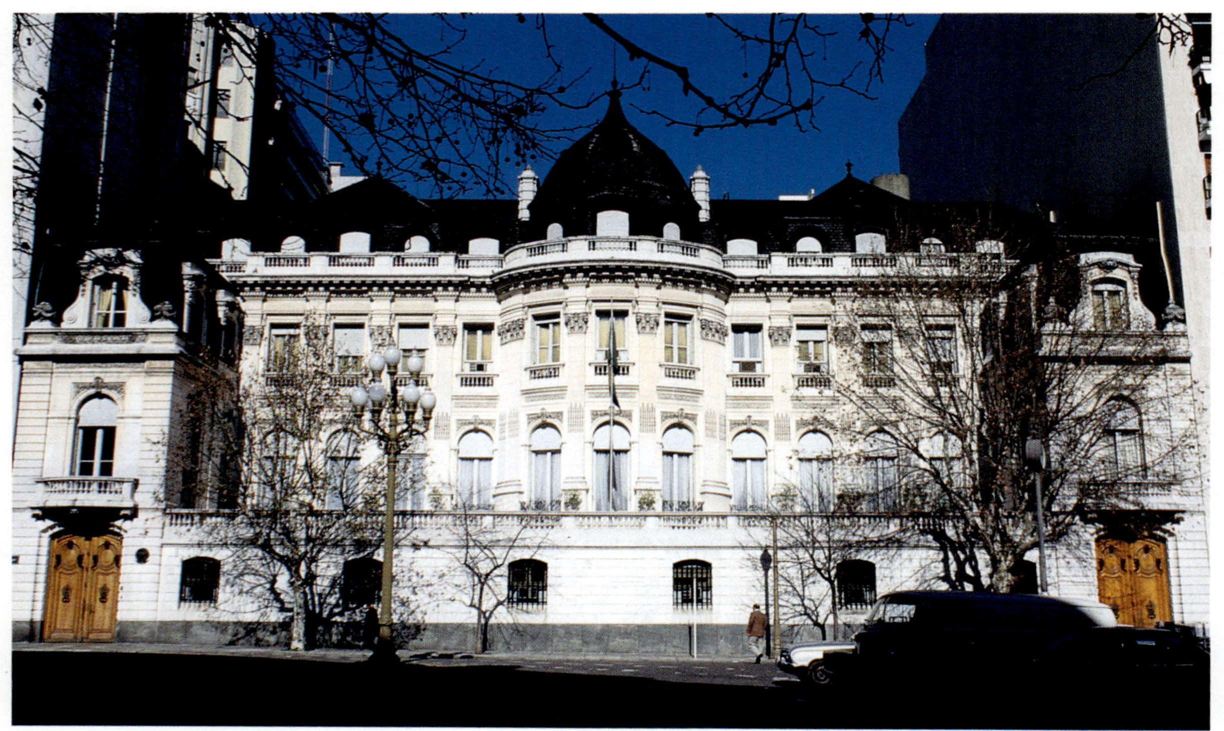

Fig. 2. Facade of the Pereda Palace, residence of the Brazilian ambassador, Buenos Aires.

words, a contradiction was revealed: the twin outpourings of Sert's inspiration covering both the religious and the profane, areas in which he was equally outstanding, each earning him immediate recognition. There were detractors, too, but they could not eclipse the halo of this brilliant muralist.

By 1919, Celedonio Pereda had decided to start building his family residence. Two years previously, he had contacted Louis Martin, the French architect, and suggested a facade similar to that of the Jacquemart-André Museum in Paris, and a grand staircase in the shape of a horseshoe like the one leading to the garden at the palace at Fontainebleau.[3] At that time, the architectural ideal for public buildings and the mansions of wealthy Argentine families was moving away from Italian style toward what could be called French style, even if the final results were not examples of absolute purity. Eclecticism was especially esteemed, perhaps reflecting a subconscious desire to hoard the rich variety of forms interpreted throughout a glorious past. As architect Federico Ortiz points out, "During the fifty years from 1880 to 1930, almost everything built in Argentina under the denomination of architecture can be classified as historicistic eclecticism."[4] Italianized architecture maintained its influence until the beginning of the twentieth century when the new style gradually imposed itself, derived from the École des Beaux-Arts in Paris, whose ideal centered on an intimate fusion of the arts of painting and sculpture. From the noble and severe lines of architects like Juan A. Buschiazzo, Francisco Tamburini, Víctor Meano, and Carlos Morra, a shift began toward buildings of sumptuous elegance, the image of solid social and economic power. Within the tenets of this style, the Pereda Palace—now the site of the Brazilian ambassador's residence—was to arise.

3. "Para visitar un palacio," *Brasil Cultura* (n.d.): 4. This issue is dedicated to the Pereda Palace.

4. Federico Ortiz, "Arquitectura 1880–1930," in *Historia general del arte de la Argentina* (Buenos Aires: Academia Nacional de Bellas Artes, 1988), 220.

Argentina's denomination at that time as the granary of the world epitomized the country's international status. Starting in 1860, many dedicated pioneering farmers and ranchers contributed to achieving this fame. Eighteen sixty was the year that Celedonio Pereda was born. He became a doctor and introduced the first vaccine against anthrax, improved the quality of the country's livestock, and organized model farms in Buenos Aires Province while developing the barren land of less hospitable areas. By 1928, he had accumulated some 300,000 acres.[5] The owner of this princely purview deserved a residence the equivalent of his rank: the house and gardens covered 40,000 square feet.

After a falling out with Louis Martin, his French architect, Pereda gave supervision of construction to Julio Dormal, a Belgian architect who was one of the first representatives of the esthetic spirit of the École des Beaux-Arts in Argentina.[6] Dormal died in 1924 and did not see the building finished. It was not until 1936 that construction was completed, but it is probable that the facade of the building and the garden staircase were built under his direction. The Government House in the city of La Plata, the final details of the Colón Theater, and the remodeling of the old Opera Theater were several of the important works in which Dormal was involved, satisfying the Europeanized taste of his wealthy clients.

With Pereda's propensity for the magnificent and the sumptuous, it is understandable that he wanted to add a flourish to the splendor of his future home: the decoration of walls and ceilings, an ancient custom which afforded a certain distinction to mansions, public buildings, temples, theaters, and stores. Few names remain of painters in Argentina who were dedicated to this task, but almost all were from Italy, possessors of a solid métier, if often dependent on stereotypes drawn from the brilliance of famous artists of the past. A general vision of the subject can be found in a study by the architect José María Peña.[7] Even today a visitor can see large panels by C. Barberis, done in 1900 to celebrate *El triunfo de la farmacia* (The triumph of pharmacy), in the Estrella Drugstore on the corner of Defensa and Alsina streets; and those of the Grand Splendid Movie Theater on Santa Fe Avenue, titled *Apoteosis de las artes* (Apotheosis of the arts), which was painted by N. Orlandi in 1919. The ceiling of the auditorium of the newspaper *La Prensa* was painted by Julio Tedini.[8] Female figures—allegories of dance, music, and theater—alternate with Cupids, all floating between gauze, garlands, and doves. A similar scene can be found in what is now the headquarters of the Center for Argentine Engineers, built in 1910 by a prolific architect, Alejandro Christophersen, who was responsible for, among many other projects, the important residence of the Anchorena family built in 1908 (today the site of the Argentine Foreign Ministry).

The pictorial genre to which we are referring had at least two other distinguished representatives, also of Italian origin. One of them, Carlos María Bonanni, arrived in Argentina around 1885 under contract to architect Carlos Morra to execute decorative work in the city of Córdoba.[9] He also took part in the construction and decoration of the Argentine Theater in La Plata, which

5. Osvaldo Salgado, "La expresión de una idea," *Brasil Cultura* (n.d.): 17.
6. Federico Ortiz, "Arquitectura 1880–1930," 260.
7. José María Peña, *Los murales*, vol. 1, no. 7 of *Argentina en el arte* (Buenos Aires: Editora Viscontea, 1966), 103–107.
8. Information given by Gustavo Brandariz, architect.
9. *Bonanni, un aporte plástico de la inmigración*, catalogue for the exhibition held at the Isaac Fernández Blanco Museum, Buenos Aires, July–August 1990.

was destroyed by fire decades ago. He was on the point of decorating the plafond of the Colón Theater when he died tragically in 1904. (The commission was delegated to Marcel Jambon, a French artist, whose paintings on the Colón's circular ceiling deteriorated little by little until they vanished. It was not until 1966 that Raúl Soldi, a contemporary Argentine, undertook the commission to paint the theater's dome, which he did masterfully.) Another artist, who worked mostly in the city of La Plata, was Rodolfo Bezzichieri. He was connected with an important construction firm. His works were varied: entryways in stucco, ceilings, walls, moldings, paneling, and tapestries. His paintings for the Provincial Bank of Credit are well remembered, as are those of the Paris Cafeteria and Mater Dei. Bezzichieri died in 1928.[10]

In those cases to which testimony remains, artists generally cultivated conventional and pleasant themes which we look upon today with a certain empathy. It would take time for a change in styles to impose itself and banish all traces of grottolike artifices and chubby nymphs from walls and ceilings in order to initiate a wave of aseptic whiteness, castrator of any possible decorative outbursts. Therefore, at this point, we must highlight the audacity Pereda demonstrated when he commissioned Sert, making a definitive break with the academicism which then reigned in the area of decoration in Buenos Aires; though it is right to mention that there were already several exceptions. Jorge Soto Acebal, a painter, had imposed a different feeling in the mural he did at the city's Plaza Hotel in 1930, composing a rural scene on a golden background with the figures drawn in sepia.[11] It is probable that Soto Acebal knew the work of Sert, given the bombastic Catalan artist's fame. Perhaps he had seen the paintings in the mansion of the Errázuriz family, a building started in 1911 according to the plans of architect René Sergent and enriched by the unusual decorations Sert invented for the boudoir. In 1922, Sert's work crossed the Atlantic for the first time. These were the panels he designed for the Errázuriz Palace, now the site of the National Museum of Decorative Art. They included five screens titled *La comedia humana* (The human comedy), a series which shows us a bizarre, carnival-like world. Alberto del Castillo, in his exhaustive book on Sert, wrote, "If Goethe married the two worlds, each so profoundly significant, of Faust and Helena, Sert united another duo, Goya and the Moulin Rouge, no less unalike, in his Argentine salon at the Errázuriz house."[12] An additional attempt at stylistic renovation which we should mention is the joint effort of a group of Argentine artists in 1933, led by the Mexican muralist David Alfaro Siqueiros, who intervened actively, (also producing a manifesto), in a mural conceived for the basement of the home of Natalio Botana in the suburb of Don Torcuato. The other artists involved were Antonio Berni, Juan Carlos Castagnino, and Lino Enea Spilimbergo, all of whom, with the passage of time, were to earn the fame they deserved in the world of Argentine visual arts.

The screens of *La comedia humana*, the ceilings of the Brazilian ambassador's residence, and a sketch belonging to Susana Pereda de Bary Tornquist of the tapestry *Riña de Gallos* (Cockfight) are pieces that can be seen in Buenos Aires. If we try to enlarge the list to include all of Sert's work that reached the city, we must add a screen titled *Escenas de pesca* (Fishing scenes) (1938),

10. Angel Osvaldo Nessi, ed., "Academias de Enseñanza Artística," *Diccionario temático de las artes en La Plata* (La Plata: Universidad Nacional de La Plata, 1982).

11. Peña, *Los murales*, 109.

12. Del Castillo, *José María Sert*, 104.

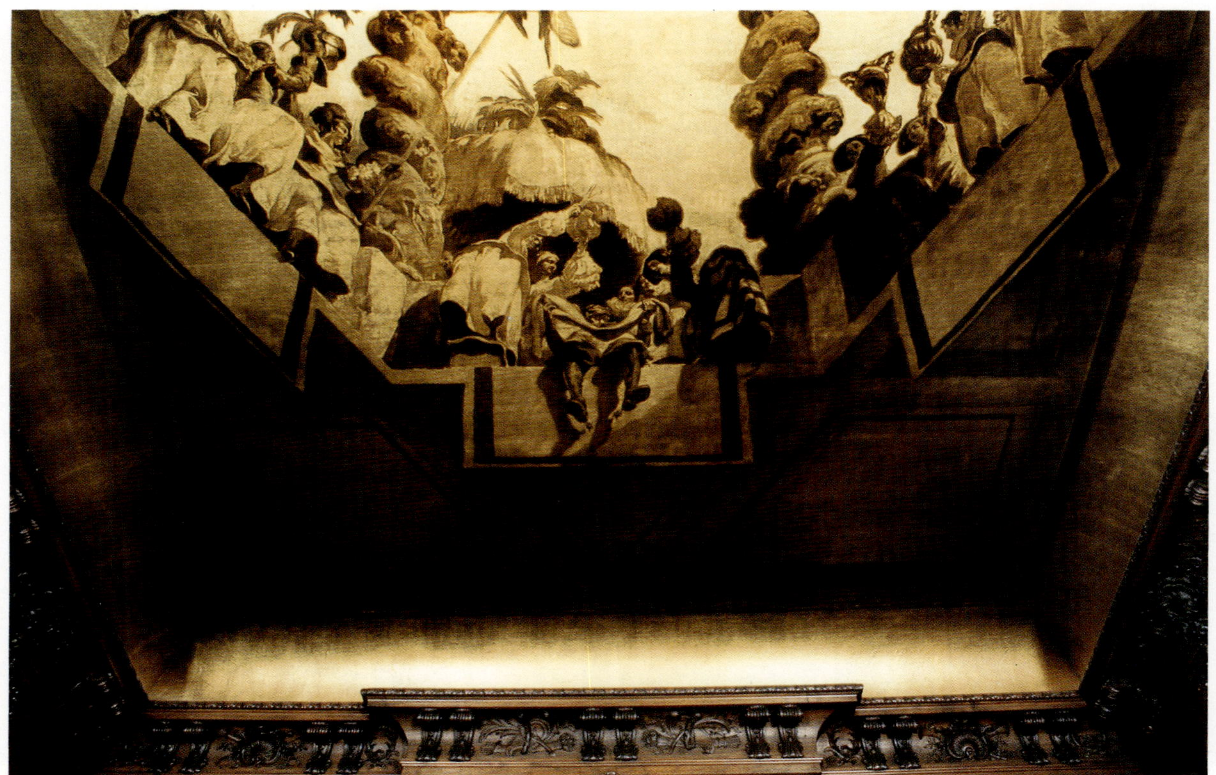

Fig. 3. José María Sert, *El aseo de don Quijote*, oil on canvas, 11 x 7 m, 1932. Main dining room, Pereda Palace, Buenos Aires. **(See page 84.)**

once in the Kavanagh Collection,[13] and the five paintings on Catalan themes (1927) that belong to Francisco Cambó and for a while resided here. Sketches for these paintings were shown in Madrid in the 1987 retrospective exhibition of Sert's work at the Velázquez Palace in the Parque del Retiro.

From conversations with Pereda's daughter, the forementioned Susana Pereda de Bary Tornquist, who accompanied her father on his trip to Europe in 1926,[14] we know that Pereda met Sert and visited his studio several times. Sert gave him brief letters of introduction which allowed him to see the ballroom of Sir Phillip Sassoon's residence in London and the home of Maurice de Wendel in Paris. This information is extremely important to our study because it gives testimony that Pereda had the opportunity to admire the ceiling of the Sassoon ballroom on the spot. This ceiling is decorated with a whirling sky which flows into a light blue "hole," similar to the sky Sert would later paint for Pereda's music room in Buenos Aires. As for the ceiling at the Wendel mansion, its description by Alberto del Castillo is worth reading. "The clouds appear to form a gigantic dome.... From the peak of this unreal space hang fourteen cords marvelously suspended from the sky-blue vault, united among themselves by garlands of crimson linen."[15] It is easy to establish a relationship between this painting and the one in the informal dining room of the Brazilian ambassador's residence, known as *La tela de araña* (The cobweb). Perhaps Pereda had expressed his desire to have the similar themes represented. What

13. Domingo I. Tellechea, *Restauración de las pinturas de Sert* (São Paulo: 1990), 31, note 3.
14. Susana Pereda de Bary Tornquist, "A la búsqueda de un artista," *Brasil Cultura* (n.d.): 23.
15. Del Castillo, *José María Sert*, 121.

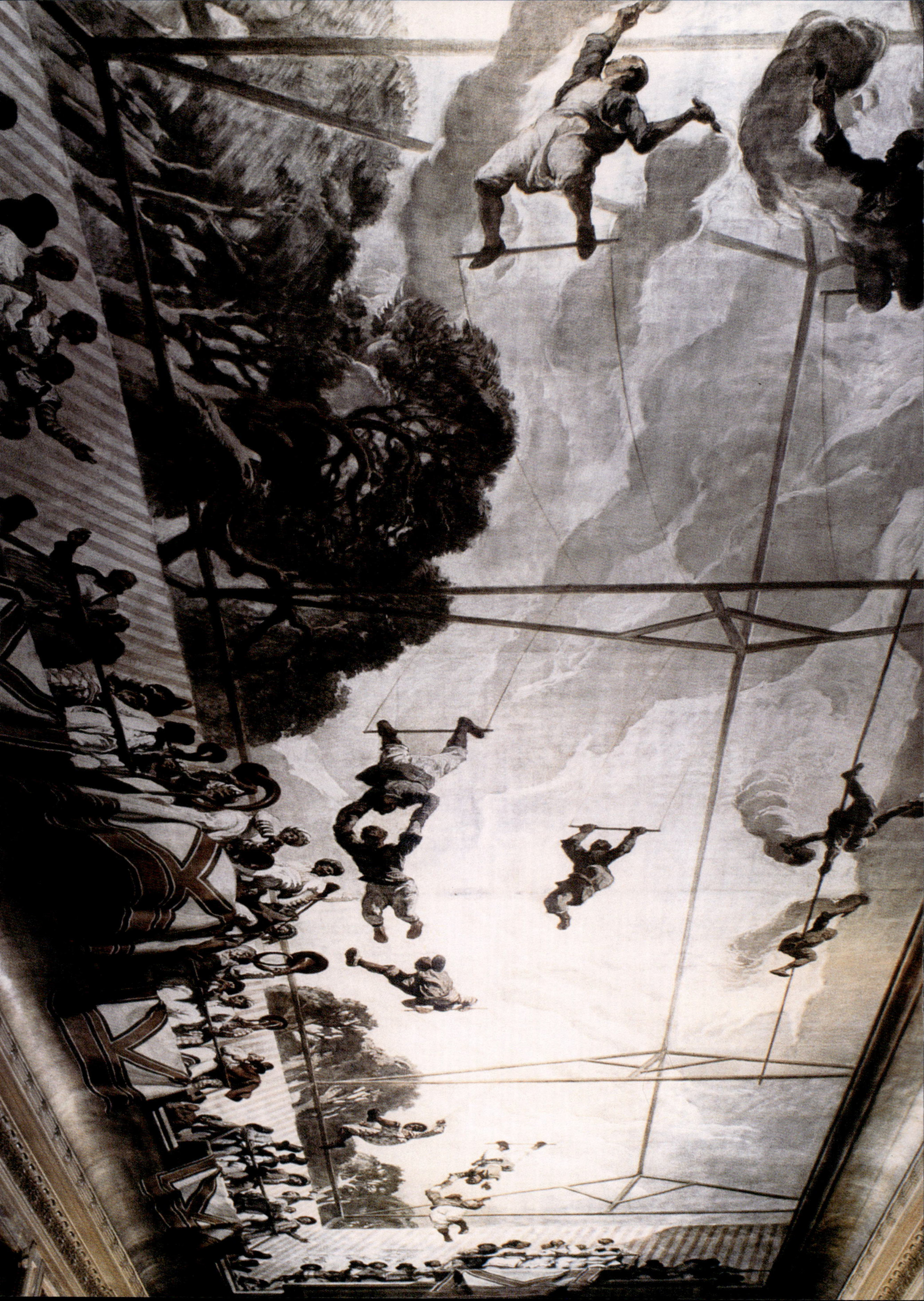

is certain is that in 1932 five canvases arrived in Buenos Aires, and at least two of them are reminiscent.

What affinity could possibly have brought this *estanciero*, submerged in the problems of his farms, together with a multifaceted personality as vital, baroque, passionate and, at the same time, as involuted as Sert? In fact, Pereda did not dedicate all his energies to making his farms productive. At home, he accumulated valuable books, works of art, tapestries, delicate carvings in ivory, semiprecious stones, and exquisite pieces of fine porcelain. The two men must have had many conversations about the world of art and its leading artists since the painter was in contact with the most brilliant celebrities of the first half of the twentieth century (Sert died at seventy-one in 1945). He settled in Paris in 1900, enjoying the friendship and admiration of Paul Claudel, to cite just one writer, and of Diaghilev, that unique name in the artistic renovation of the period for whom Sert, fascinated by the theatrical world, created costumes and set designs. He very quickly displayed a baroque genius as a muralist, revitalizing a genre which had seemed menaced with extinction. He felt himself to be one with the great fresco artists of the past, an admirer of Michelangelo and Tiepolo, and equally enthralled with the romantic fantasy of Gustave Doré. Julián Gállego listed Sert's preferences: "[He] was...a son of Venice and Naples, of Rome, Salamanca, Toledo...and of the most fabulous Orient."[16] Any list of his tastes leads, perhaps, to Goya (especially when that artist turned to popular themes, dances, and games), and the festive steps of the *verbenas* reverberate in his pictures. If we superimpose an exotic touch originating in the Orient which would satisfy his quest for the unknown, the genies of the *Thousand and One Nights*, and that strictly Spanish delight in grotesque characters and ostentatious aristocrats, we would have characterized only a part of the repertory of his complex production. We have commented that we could see in Sert the contrast between the divine and the profane, one side compensating the other. The murals he did for Vich were destroyed in 1936 during the conflict unleashed in Spain. This tragedy, instead of demoralizing him, incited him to create more work for the cathedral, with the advantage of finding himself now at the height of his maturity as an artist. Mockery and revelry on the one hand; mystical self-searching on the other.

Fig. 4. José María Sert, *Los equilibristas*, oil on canvas, 14 x 6 ½ m, 1932. Main hallway, Pereda Palace, Buenos Aires. **(See page 84.)**

Referring to Sert's ideas about muralism, writers often cite a statement of his that never loses its pertinence. "The difference between mural painting and that done on an easel is like the difference between verse and prose," Sert maintained. "The artist commissioned to decorate a monument finds himself subjected to the same tyrannical rules as those governing the poet who writes a sonnet; more so, for it is Architecture that imposes its discipline on him."[17] For Sert, muralism implied a special excellence. "I believe that in this aspect of painting there is a true language. When the human being first awoke and wanted to express his joy of living, he did not write nor did he build or sculpt: he painted on the walls of his cave."[18] At the opposite extreme from Piet Mondrian (whose neoplasticism is dated 1920), Sert declared that "man has liberated himself from the fatality of the straight line.... A future opens before us that will

16. Julián Gállego, "Servidumbre y grandeza de la pintura de Sert," in the catalogue of the retrospective exhibition of José María Sert, Palacio de Velázquez, Parque del Retiro, Madrid, 27 October –3 January 1987.

17. José María Sert, *Reconstrucciones*, Madrid (1942), reproduced in the catalogue of the 1987 retrospective exhibition in Madrid.

18. Ibid.

permit the walls of a building to be bent."[19] These opinions throw light on his esthetic creed which favored the taste for visual illusion, allied with an often uncontrolled baroqueness, allowing him to mix real and imaginary beings in a phantasmagoric carnival. Fortunately, the paintings affixed to the ceilings of the Pereda Palace offer a well-balanced set of scenes rather than a more clashing collection of elements, and his vision there is not in the least disturbing.

Fig. 5. José María Sert, *Diana cazadora*, detail, oil on canvas, 9 x 8 m, 1932. The Gold Room, Pereda Palace, Buenos Aires.

Fig. 6. José María Sert, *Diana cazadora*, oil on canvas, 9 x 8 m, 1932. The Gold Room, Pereda Palace, Buenos Aires.

We shall enumerate these works in the order in which they appear in the book by Professor Domingo Tellechea,[20] who, with a team of specialized technicians, began a scientific restoration of the panels in 1988 which was completed in six months. The works are: *El aseo de don Quijote* (The toilet of Don Quixote) in the main dining room (Fig. 3); *Los equilibristas* (The tightrope walkers) in the main hallway (figs. 1 and 4); *Diana cazadora* (Diana the huntress) in the Gold Room (figs. 5 and 6); *La tela de araña* (The cobweb) in the informal dining room (fig. 7); and *El agujero celeste* (The light blue hole), which in del Castillo's book is called *Nubarrones* (Storm clouds), in the music room (fig. 8). In the painstaking study by Tellechea on the evolution of the work the Brazilian Embassy commissioned him to do (following a report by the expert Brazilian restorer Claudio Valerio Teixeira), he explained that in 1932 the canvases were affixed to the ceilings using a method called *marouflage*, which in this case means precisely "affixing canvas to walls," according to the instructions of Sert himself. Because of their size, the panels for the ceiling of the main hallway had to be assembled in the garden.[21]

Del Castillo explains the manner in which Sert executed his works, worth quoting in order to understand the tricks of the trade the artist utilized, since he absolutely prohibited access to his studio except to a few close friends. "The master thought out the composition and transferred the idea into a drawing on a small piece of paper, which was then converted into a larger charcoal sketch by means of grid squares. The next stage was a color sketch, accompanied by a scale model of the decorations when called for, prepared by his assistants. With the sketch before them, these same assistants, always working with the grid system to enlarge the design, transferred the sketch to the canvas or panel which had been previously prepared or gilded. The work was completed under the guidance of the artist who gave the final touches and, above all, the effect, the chiaroscuro. This lack of direct execution by Sert in no way makes the paintings less personal, since the work done by his assistants was purely technical and mechanical, obeying at all times the explicit instructions of the painter himself."[22] This method of working inspired Forain to say that Sert was more an orchestra conductor than a painter. A capable and implacable photographer, Sert built many of his compositions from photographs, while also using mannequins and nude models. According to del Castillo, he did not use a paint brush, but Tellechea specifies that even though he did employ the most varied techniques (dragging cloths across the surface, using all kinds of brushlike instruments, templates, finger painting, sfumato, and other devices), brushstrokes can also be detected.[23] Del Castillo's omission now clarified, let us continue with another interesting point from his testimony: "[Sert] wrapped his thumbs with rags...and [with these pads] gave the final and decisive touches.

19. Ibid.
20. Tellechea, *Restauración*, 34.
21. Pereda de Bary Tornquist, "A la búsqueda," 24.
22. Del Castillo, *José María Sert*, 31.
23. Tellechea, *Restauración*, 47.

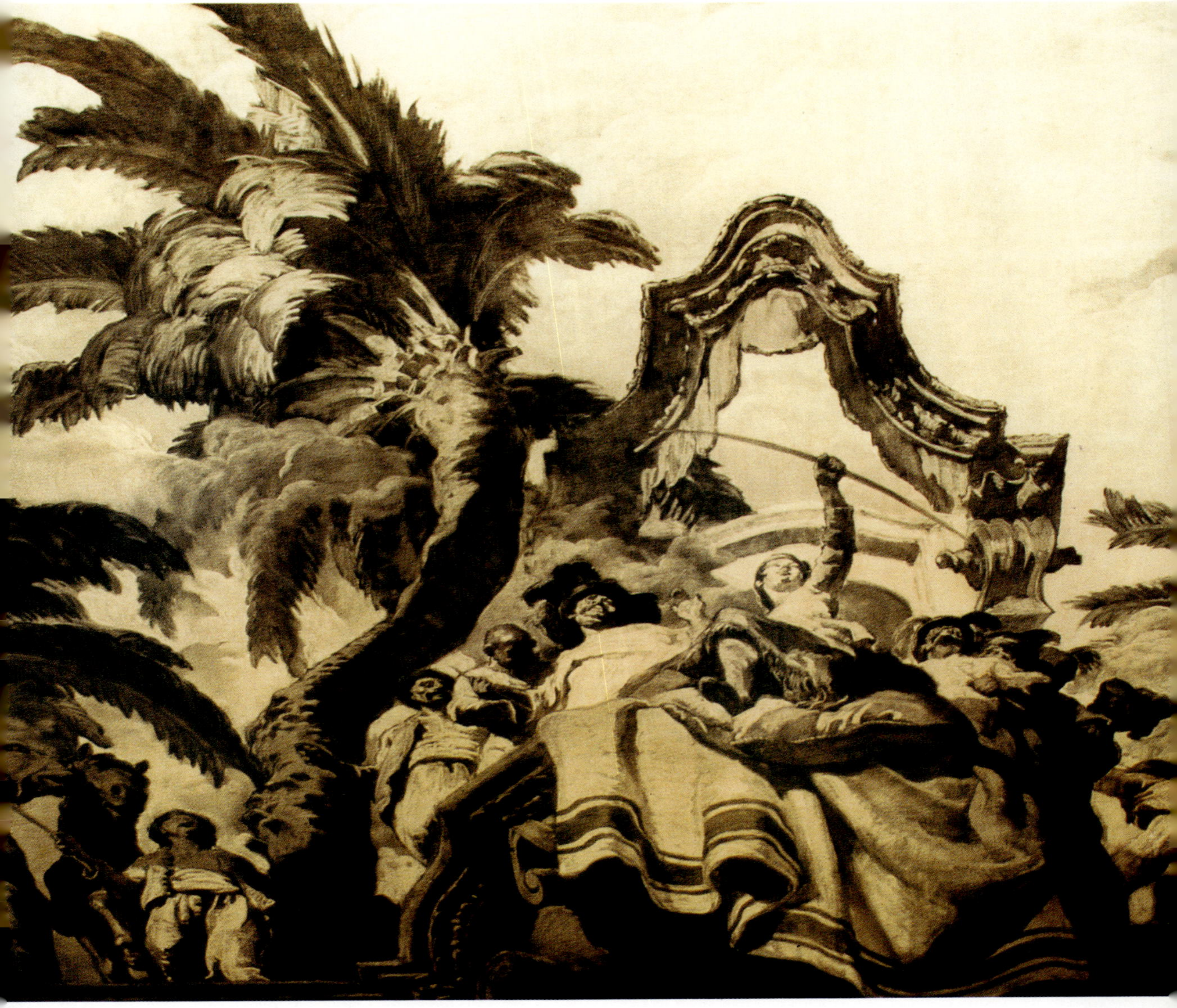

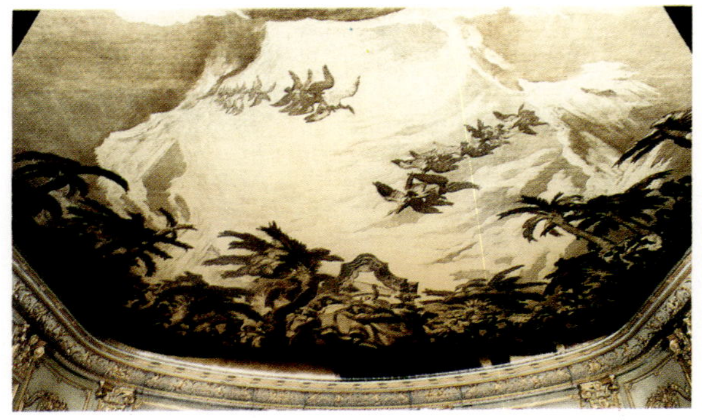

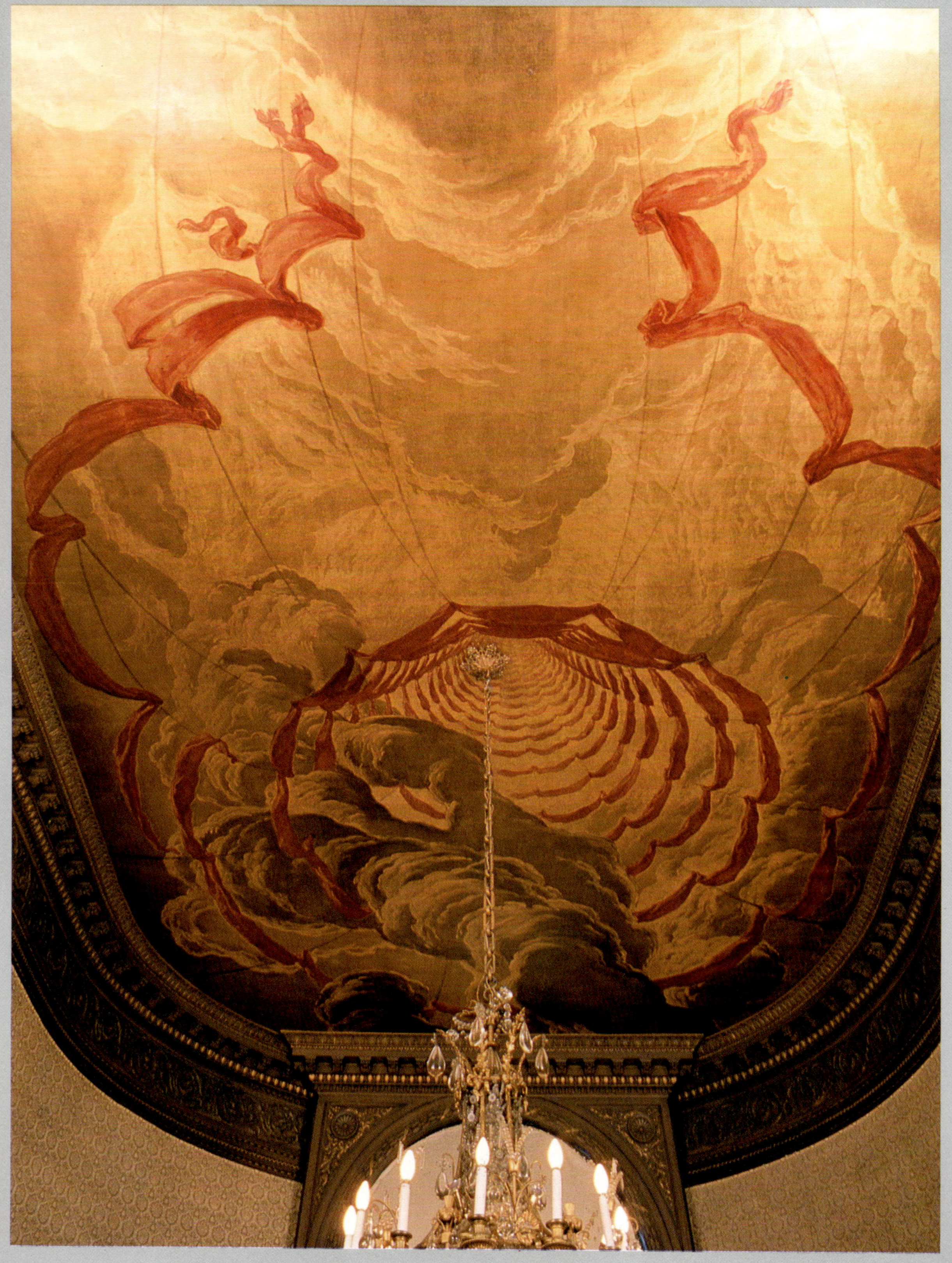

The gilding and silvering was done by applying panels of metal to the canvas which was either left untouched or veiled by thin layers of sepia."[24] The agility with which Sert handled his thumbs seems to anticipate action painting.

The paintings of the Pereda Palace do not fall into the category of overblown decorativeness and, for this reason, still produce pleasure today. How can one not feel a delightful vertigo on viewing the tightrope walkers in the main hallway? Sert had already used this theme in Kent House in London (1913), in the Palace of the Marqués of Salamanca (1920), and in the ballroom of the Wendels (1924), where tumblers pirouette with flaming torches to the blare of horns and trumpets. Equally, we find tightrope walkers, audaciously handled in reduced perspective, in the gaming room of Harrison Williams's residence in Long Island (1927). In the dining room of the Waldorf Astoria, known as the Sert Salon (1930–1931), trapeze artists, acrobats, and aerialists anticipate those of the Pereda Palace. Acrobats and aeronauts with balloons liven up the March Palace in Palma de Mallorca (1944). Popular motifs, which in the Brazilian residence accompany the feats of the acrobats, have many antecedents. Street scenes, which Sert could not renounce in spite of his fabulously Orientalizing imagination, explode in the Moore screen (1926) amidst panoramic views and, very much in the manner of Goya, in the pictures done for Francisco Cambó in 1927, and those at the Waldorf Astoria. As for *El agujero celeste* which presides over a ceiling in Baron Rothschild's castle (1920), there is a child (can it be Ganymede?) flying on an exotic bird, a scene repeated on the ceiling of Sassoon's home, discussed earlier. A swirling sky covers the ceiling of Baron de Becker's dining room in Brussels (1930), and a hallucinatory Circensian scene brightens the home of the de la Vega family in Barcelona (1927).

Fig. 7. José María Sert, *La tela de araña*, oil on canvas, 10 x 6½ m, 1932. Informal dining room, Pereda Palace, Buenos Aires.

We believe it is important to establish these comparisons (there could be many more), because the paintings at the Pereda Palace are like an anthology, a decanted selection of the author's favorite motifs. The incisive Spanish critic Julián Gállego classifies Sert's major decorative genres in four categories: "Hispanic, fantastic Oriental, religious, and classic-modern. The first two, where fantasy shines through with more confidence, respond to private commissions for mansions, palatial homes, or the elegant apartments of the international set (especially French, American, Argentine, and Spanish)."[25] The Pereda paintings are of Sert's Hispanic style, according to Gállego, who goes on to say, "A Cervantes-like theme, such as the *Tocado de don Quijote en casa de los duques* (Coiffure of Don Quixote in the home of the dukes), is treated in the Pereda Palace in Buenos Aires with the air of a Venetian festival. We can point out, in passing, the traditionalistic originality (if such a contradiction can be used) of the ceilings of this palace: the Tiepoloesqueness of the acrobats...(with a Spanish crowd); the ceiling of Diana, furrowed with flying birds; another that simulates a network or cobweb of ribbons; and one which limits itself to presenting us with what could be a hole or vortex of storm clouds, a brilliant solution which was also applied above the ballroom of Sir Phillip Sassoon in 1921, eleven years before the Argentine version. Permit me to comment that Sert has no problem in repeating themes or figures, neither does he mind borrowing personages or settings [from his favorite painters]."[26]

24. Del Castillo, *José María Sert*, 31.

25. Gállego, "Servidumbre y grandeza," 36.

26. Ibid., 39.

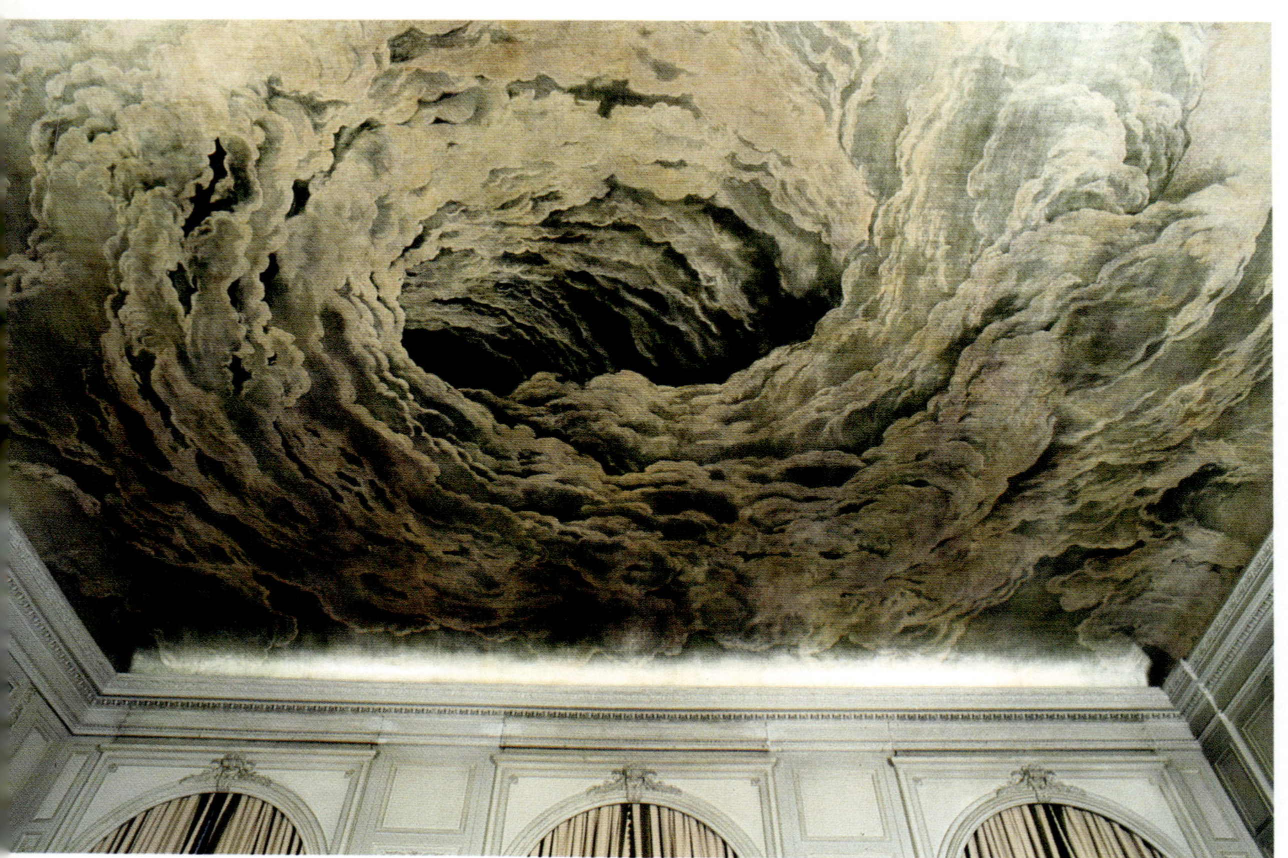

Fig. 8. José María Sert, *El agujero celeste*, oil on canvas, 10 x 6 ½ m, 1932. Music room, Pereda Palace, Buenos Aires.

Placing the canvases onto their respective ceilings did not create any major difficulties. Sert was always alert to adapting his paintings in the best possible way to their architectural surroundings. "It is essential," he said, "that the painting juxtaposes itself to the wall as the epidermis to the body."[27] When faced with the prospect that the architecture in question could be defective, he observed, "for a painter who really is just that, there is a certain pleasure even in dealing with defects, because they provoke a sensitive inventiveness capable of converting those defects into virtues.... Even when we find ourselves before ceilings and naves whose height and width are disproportionate, the painter should find an elegant solution: where there is no architectural order, he will have to give the disorder its style."[28] It is just this stylized disorder which triumphs in many of Sert's compositions, intermingled with deep-rooted dreamscapes that border on nightmare. But this is not the case with the Pereda Palace. Harmony reigns throughout the whole and facilitates a healthy communion. It is this feeling of harmony that makes the atmosphere an attractive one. Recognizing the virtues of his home, Pereda offered the use of it to the President of Brazil, Getulio Vargas, when he visited Argentina in 1938. In 1944, Brazilian Ambassador João Baptista Lusardo purchased the property from the Pereda family, most probably with the approval of his president.

If we review the decorations in their proper order, we see that in *El aseo de don Quijote* this theme of Cervantes is treated with charm, free from the

27. Julio Heller, "La pintura mural de José María Sert en el nuevo Palacio de la Sociedad de las Naciones," *La Nación,* November 1936.

28. Ibid.

complexities found in *Las bodas de Camacho* (The marriage of Camacho) at the Waldorf Astoria or the anecdotal treatment of the tapestry cartoons. This celebrated personality is leaning backward, his head barely showing, but his spurred boots and legs reeling, as are the servants who have just finished grooming him. One of these solicitous women raises the plumed crest of the knight. The drawing, done in sepia, stands out from a gold and gray background. *Los equilibristas* makes an exciting display, with men and women of different social backgrounds watching a circus performance, leaning out of balconies covered with undulating panels of fabric (a solution Sert often used, along with theater curtains). The air is crisscrossed by acrobats moving to the rhythm of horns, trumpets, and tubas; several carry flaming torches. We are united to the flight of the aerialists, suspended in a space that loses itself in an infinite silver-toned expanse. There is no diversity in the colors, which is characteristic of Sert, who thought that color was excessive in nature. There were even colors that were disagreeable to his eye! Moreover, he prided himself on his abusive sepia and was amused by the fact that a vendor of colors offered his clients a tone he called "Sert sepia." A regal *Diana cazadora* emerges out of a golden background highlighted in sepia. Sert occasionally removed mythology from its traditional context, allowing his imagination free play. The goddess, stretched out upon panels of sumptuous fabrics, shoots a virtual arrow at a group of herons. Along side, a twisted palm tree stands, seeming to mock a set of majestic Solomonic columns. A retinue of extravagant warriors and inflamed steeds completes the fantastic picture. Sert's representation of the goddess does not correspond to the iconography of the day, since he does not surround her with the required entourage: nymphs, satyrs, dogs, or deer. Sert has created a different setting for Diana, as if he were dealing with an eighteenth-century courtesan wrapped in resplendent gilt, imparting luster to this conventional cinegetic posture. The painting covering the ceiling of the informal dining room is known as *La tela de araña*, a strange composition based on a whirlpool of clouds lifting a warp of red ribbons in concentric circles toward an enigmatic, watchful eye located at the center of the ceiling (that now cannot be seen, because a lighting fixture hangs there, but can be appreciated in photographs taken earlier). *El agujero celeste*, in the music room, is no less suggestive. It could not be better suited to its site. The vortex seems to draw in sinuous sounds that emanate from invisible instruments high above. The sounds move toward the unknown. Commentary that appears in the catalogue of the Sert retrospective exhibit in Madrid in 1987 suggests that he is dealing with "that space implicit in Oriental symbolism: the light blue hole where souls circulate when searching for liberation from their karmic cycle, according to primitive Hindu symbolism."

Faced with such a profusion of diverse images created by Sert at different moments in his life, our imagination is stirred to establish all kinds of associations. Nevertheless, it is not only this we must consider. To paraphrase Susan Sontag, we could be veiling with interpretations precisely what we should enjoy directly, spontaneously, delivering ourselves to the eroticism in art, instead of losing the sensation by sterile hermeneutical interpretations. Simple delight is, in the final analysis, what justifies the existence of all great art. It goes beyond any transcribed codes intellectualizing what we know, from time immemorial, springs from undiscernible depths in the human being to surprise and disconcert his reason. □

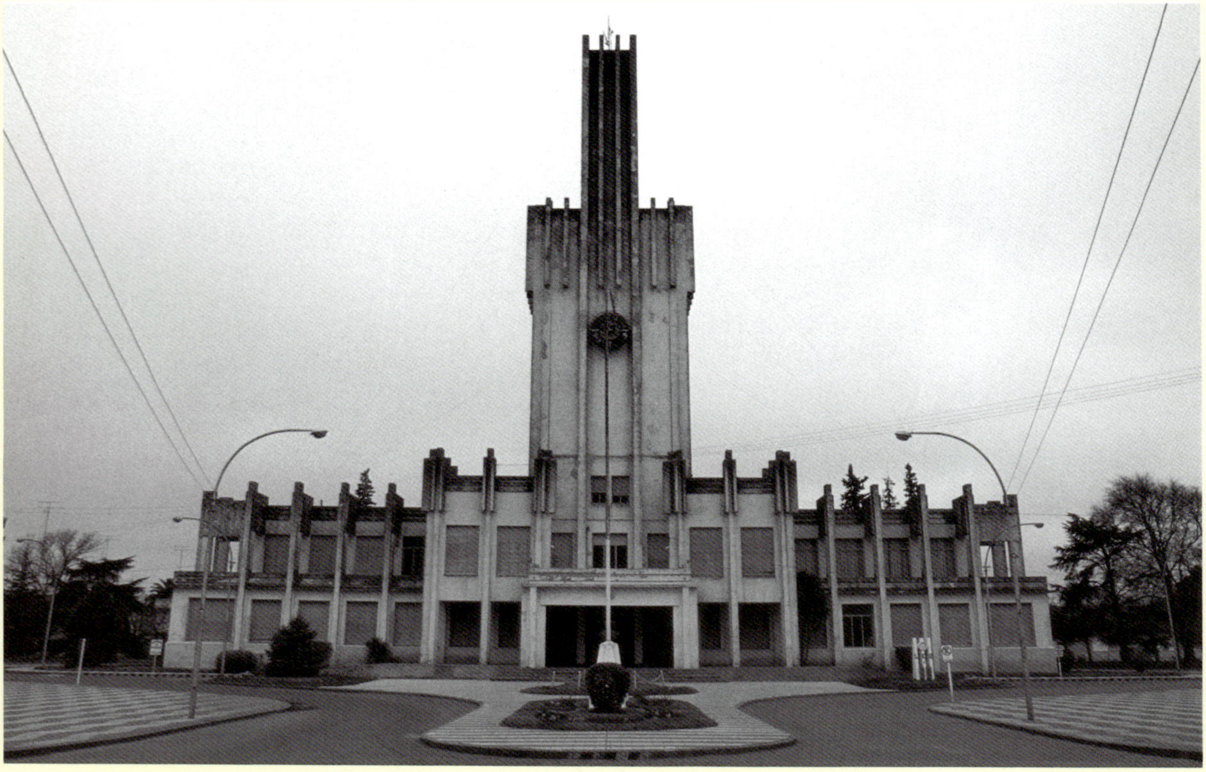

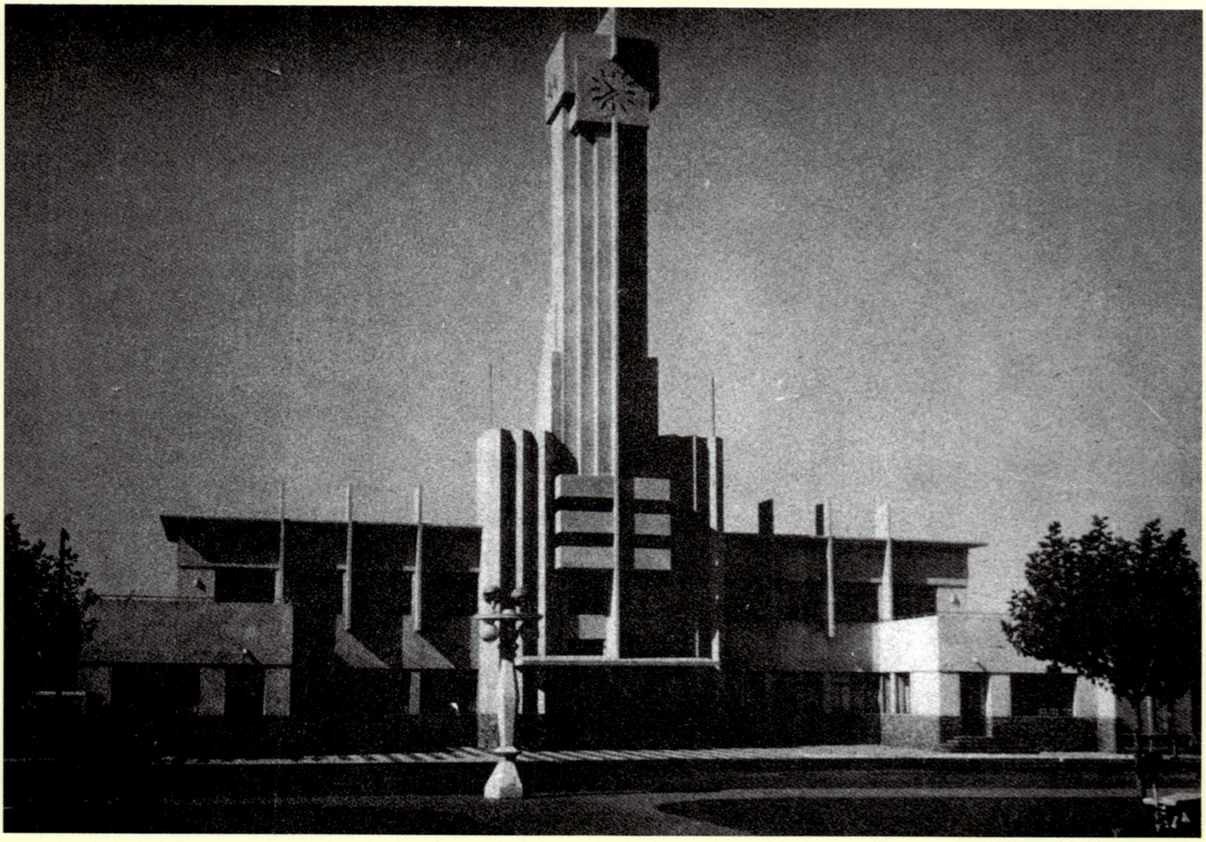

Monumental Deco in the Pampas: The Urban Art of Francisco Salamone

By Alberto Bellucci

Translated by Theodore McNabney

Alberto Bellucci is director of the National Museum of Decorative Art in Buenos Aires. He teaches art appreciation at the University of San Andrés and architectural history and design at the National University of Buenos Aires School of Architecture. He is the author of several books including *Breve historia de la arquitectura occidental.*

Photographs by the author except where noted.

Toward the end of the thirties, an intense program of public works was initiated throughout the province of Buenos Aires, the most important in the Argentine Republic. This building campaign was organized by Dr. Manuel A. Fresco, a controversial conservative politician who governed the province from 1936 to 1940. Toward the end of his term in office, a large number of new public buildings were built. Many existing buildings were enlarged and repaired, and roads, canals, and networks of communication were carried out in the 110 existing municipalities. Fresco's works, designed by the Office of Architecture of the Province of Buenos Aires, answered the common denominators officially called for by the modern movement: authoritarian character and minimal esthetic significance. Nevertheless, and despite the fact that they belong to this same representational and monumental spirit, there is a series of works Fresco commissioned directly from his friend, Francisco Salamone, that deserve to be studied for their surprising combination of authoritarianism, art deco, functionalism, and propaganda value on a colossal scale. All this on the horizon of the flat pampas (figs. 1 and 2).

A complete review of Salamone's work has never before been attempted, except for an official publication ordered by Fresco's government at the end of his term, which is not exactly a model of esthetic interpretation.[1] Ramón Gutiérrez, in his impressive history of architecture and urbanization in Latin America, says "conservative governor Manuel Fresco populated the province of Buenos Aires with town halls that, in the rationalist language, recalled the medieval *palazzi comunali* with its tower as much as the designs of Mussolini's fascism."[2] Gutiérrez asserts that the ideological should be part of the final phase of the period when the role of the state is strongly accentuated, but, due to the encyclopedic style of his book, he does not develop the topic further. Twelve years ago, architects M. Arias Incollá, A. Carrafrancq, C. Pernaut, and J. Bozzano made a valuable study concentrating on the architectural and decorative work done by Salamone in Coronel Pringles (fig. 3).[3] Unfortunately, this study was never published. Thanks to the generosity of its authors, we have been able to consult the text which has been of great help in writing this

Fig. 1. Coronel Pringles town hall, overview.

◂

Fig. 2. Laprida town hall, 1939. Photograph from *Cuatro años de gobierno, 1936–1940*, Imprenta Oficial, Buenos Aires Province.

1. *Cuatro años de gobierno, 1936–1940* (Four years of government, 1936–1940), Imprenta Oficial, Buenos Aires Province, n.d.
2. Ramón Gutiérrez. *Arquitectura y urbanismo en Iberoamérica* (Architecture and urbanism in Latin America) (Madrid: Editor Cátedra, 1983), 575.
3. M. Arias Incollá, A. Carrafrancq, C. Pernaut, J. Bozzano, *La década del 30 y la obra de Francisco Salamone* (The decade of the 30s and the work of Francisco Salamone), unpublished, ca. 1980.

essay. Previously, we personally investigated the western area of the province and published a sketch of what we observed in the municipality of Pellegrini.[4] These are the few pre-existing studies on the subject.

This is, therefore, the first published study specifically dedicated to the group of works commissioned by Fresco to be built by Salamone as representations of a curious system of urban art—the integration of architecture, decoration, and propaganda.[5]

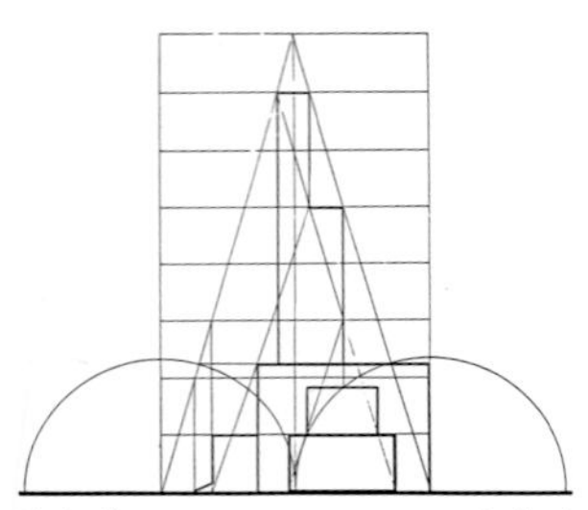

Fig. 3. Coronel Pringles town hall. Eurythmic study of an elevation, from the studio of architects M. Arias Incollá, A. Carrafrancq, C. Pernaut, and J. Bozzano.

The permanent cultural feedback inherent in our restless occidental thinking requires reconsideration of the Argentine past as a primary element of our present. In particular, the unexpected re-encounter of current postmodernism with the art deco of the thirties brings to the foreground, once again, aspects of these startling designs which, among other things, anticipated by half a century the advertising images of Las Vegas.

The small settlements Fresco tried to consolidate with this imposing urban art were 500 to 750 kilometers from the city of Buenos Aires and were, in the thirties, either what remained of a chain of forts that had been built at the end of the nineteenth century for protection against the Indians, or rail centers established every 50 kilometers in the pampa that had scarcely been conquered by the white man. This military-railroad colonization explains the actual distribution of towns all along the roads, and also the reason why the majority are named, even today, for colonels and generals who led the campaign against the Indians (ending in 1879), or for engineers who led the advance march of the railroad.

These tiny frontier towns, born between 1880 and 1910, are made up of a few square blocks. They mark the bare land with a simple checkerboard pattern which was the rule in Spanish urban development, copied from the Roman empire. This became the trademark of all Latin American cities, large and small. The central square, the church, school, health center, town hall, general store, post office, and, when the town was important enough, branch of the National or Provincial Bank were enough to condense the cattle and incipient agricultural activity into an urban concentration. Farming was extending farther, reaching the borders of the open pampa to the south and west, almost to Patagonia. It was important in the thirties to ensure that farm production would reach the capital by railroad in time and in condition to be consumed or exported to Europe and North America. The optimism of those productive years, in which Argentina was still "the breadbasket of the world," is reflected clearly in this text: "Mainly a cattle-raising country, the first step in which the potential of its basic economy lay, it now initiates another phase of perfecting agriculture. When the energies of a country concentrate and are directed toward national unity, industry must be increased. Then culture will come closer to being defined by different aspects of nationality. Architecture, perhaps more than any other activity, will reflect the influence of autonomous industry...and will acquire those nationwide attributes that only maturity can instill."[6]

With this optimistic vision, combined with a philosophy of conservative nationalism that believed in the paternalistic mission of the state and its capacity

4. A.G. Bellucci, "La municipalidad de Pellegrini" (The Pellegrini town hall), *Convicción*, 30 July 1982.

5. We must especially acknowledge the support received from the Antorchas Foundation in Buenos Aires, and the skill of Enrique Benítez Cruz, excellent pilot of his Piper Cherokee, enabling us to reach the most distant and interesting spots in order to augment this essay.

6. A. Belgrano Blanco, "La arquitectura en la República Argentina, tendencias de las construcciones" (Architecture in the Argentine Republic, building trends), *Ingeniería Internacional*, vol. XXV, no. 1, (January 1937): 15.

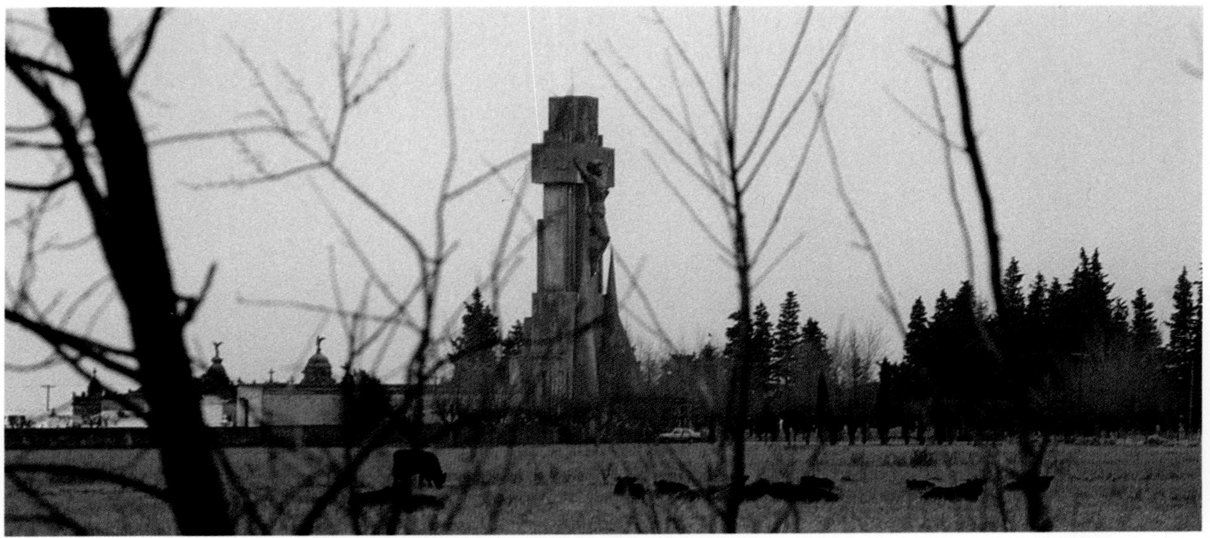

Fig. 4. Laprida monumental cemetery portal.

to generate and spread the symbols and codes of a new social order, Governor Fresco wanted each still incomplete town turned into a tiny model city. This meant electricity and running water, paved streets and sidewalks, and repairs to the church, school, police station, and hospital. Everything was to be white, cubical, flat, functional, irrelevant. But he reserved the right to build *de novo* three paradigmatic works for a new style of urban development in the cattle-raising pampa: the town hall, the slaughterhouse, and the monumental cemetery portal (fig. 4). When it was possible, he charged these to his friend Salamone, certain that he would find the most efficient and rapid interpreter, able to give physical form to his special political dream.[7] We are going to concentrate our critical attention on this trinity of urban facilities often forgotten or misunderstood, even abandoned.

Little is known of Francisco Salamone. He was born in Buenos Aires on 5 June 1898, and died there on 8 August 1959. The talent for construction was a family tradition. His father, Salvatore, was an architect from Catania, and the four sons worked in construction. Francisco graduated as a construction supervisor from the Otto Krause Industrial School in Buenos Aires and continued his studies in the city of Córdoba, graduating in 1920 as a civil engineer and—his signature stamp states—as "architect, technical director, and designer" (fig. 5).

7. The direct contracting of these works, without the intervention of the official Department of Architecture, and the special way they were paid for, caused a famous lawsuit at the end of Fresco's term and Salamone's temporary exile to Uruguay.

Fig. 5. Seal and signature of Francisco Salamone. From the work plans of the Pellegrini town hall.

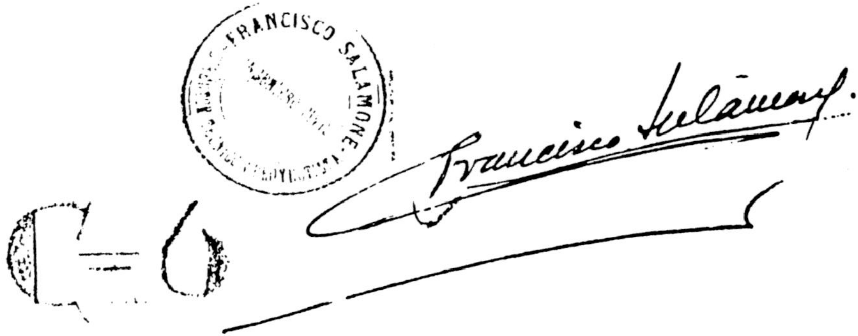

Four years later, he joined the Central Society of Architects but remained apart from the intellectual and social activities of his colleagues. He wrote nothing, but his "archi-caricatures" are remembered. They are agile drawings of strong geometrical lines that forecast the style of his designs and sculptures.

His first known work is the fountains in the main plaza of Villa María in Córdoba, forerunner of those that would be installed in the plazas of Navarro, Laprida, Azul, and Coronel Pringles (fig. 6). His relationship with Governor Fresco converted him immediately into the most active designer in the province, competing in this area—in quantity, not quality—with the architect Alejandro Bustillo, brother to the then minister of public works of Buenos Aires. Two popular sayings of the period show this unspoken rivalry; on one side "in Buenos Aires, no brick is moved unless Bustillo says so," and on the other "what Fresco orders, Salamone builds." Bustillo was given more diverse and important assignments: the casino and boardwalk of Mar del Plata, the town hall of the same city, the Llao-Llao Hotel in Bariloche, and others. Salamone took charge of designing the models for rural town halls (fig. 7), slaughterhouses, and cemeteries, inspired by his friend, Fresco.

In just four years (1936–1940), he designed and directed the construction of town halls in Carhué, Coronel Pringles, Laprida, Puán, Carlos Pellegrini (figs. 8 and 9), Rauch, Balcarce, and Tornquist (fig. 10). The town hall in Lobería was never built (fig. 11). In this same period, he did the municipal offices in Cacharí, Vedia, Saldungaray, and Chillar; the slaughterhouses of Balcarce, Carhué (fig. 12), Coronel Pringles, Azul, Laprida, Vedia, and Carlos Pellegrini; the colossal gateways to the cemeteries of Saldungaray, Laprida (fig. 13), Azul, and Balcarce; as well as crosses and lesser works in Coronel Pringles, Carlos Pellegrini, and Lobería (fig. 14), such as pergolas, ornamental flag poles, and decorative sidewalks. Several possible factors caused these works either to be forgotten or rejected: the quickness with which they were erected, the carelessness of design, the change in scale and iconography they imposed on the

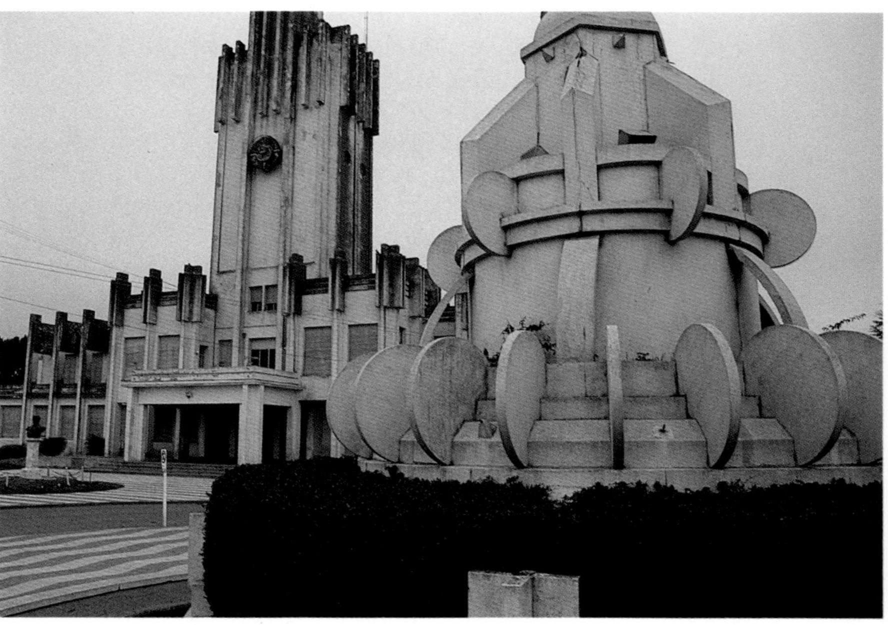

Fig. 6. Coronel Pringles town hall and fountain.

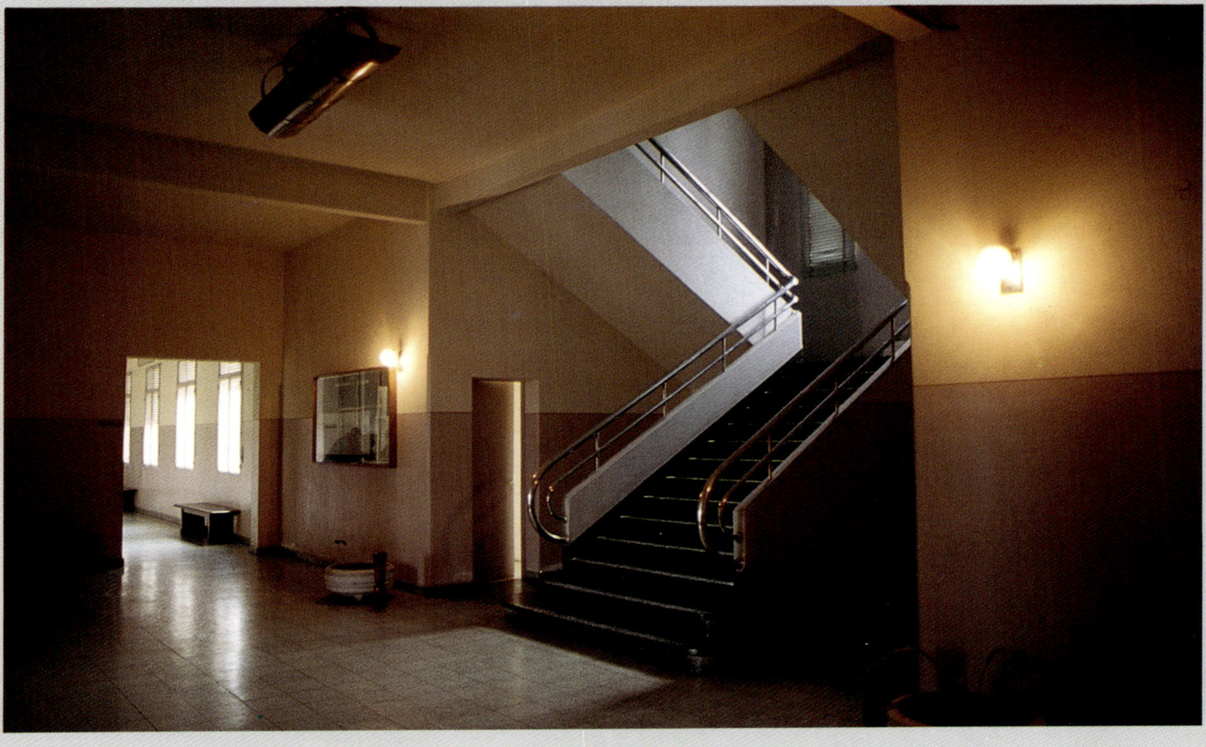

Fig. 8. Carlos Pellegrini town hall, entrance and stairway.

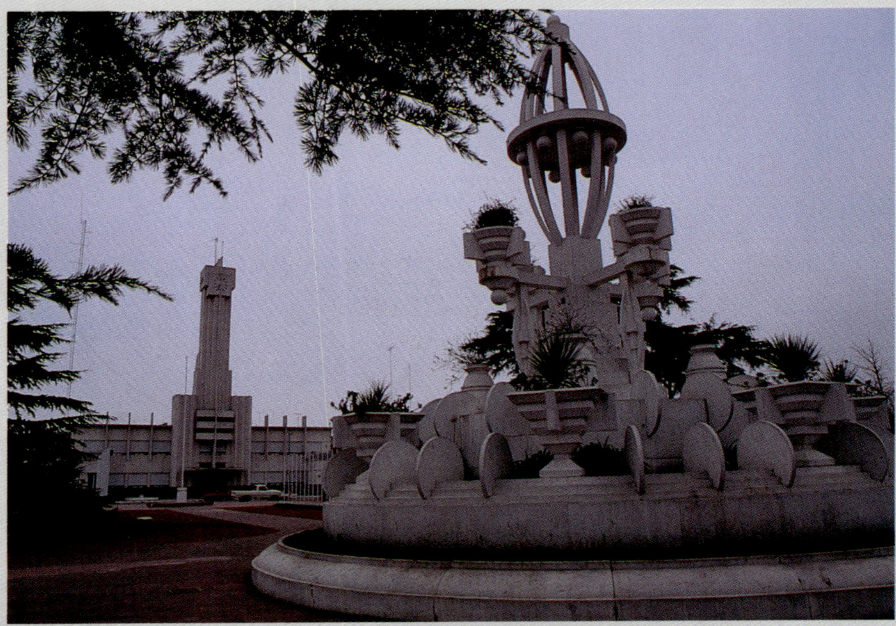

Fig. 7. Laprida town hall and fountain.

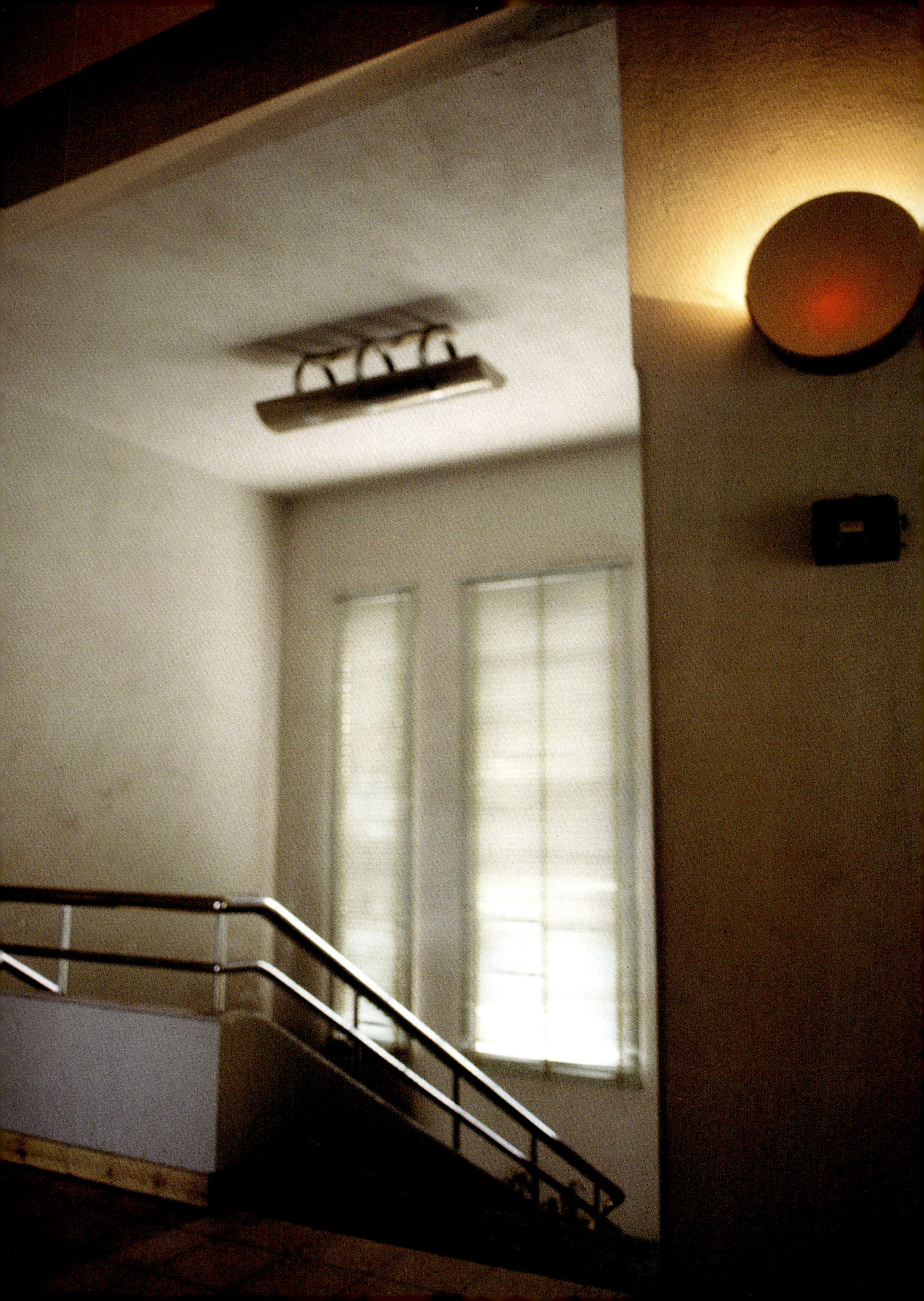

◄

Fig. 9. Carlos Pellegrini town hall, stairway.

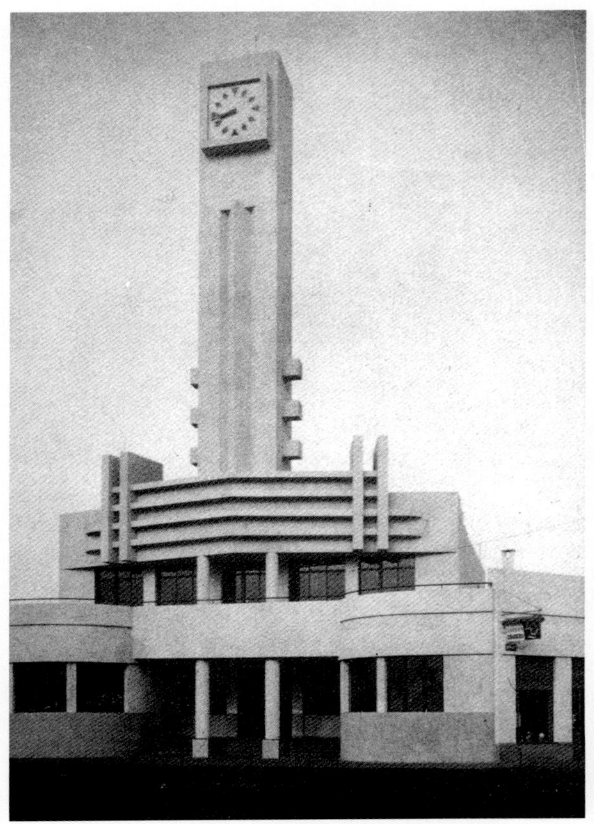

Fig. 10. Tornquist town hall, 1939. Photograph from *Cuatro años de gobierno, 1936–1940*, Imprenta Oficial, Buenos Aires Province.

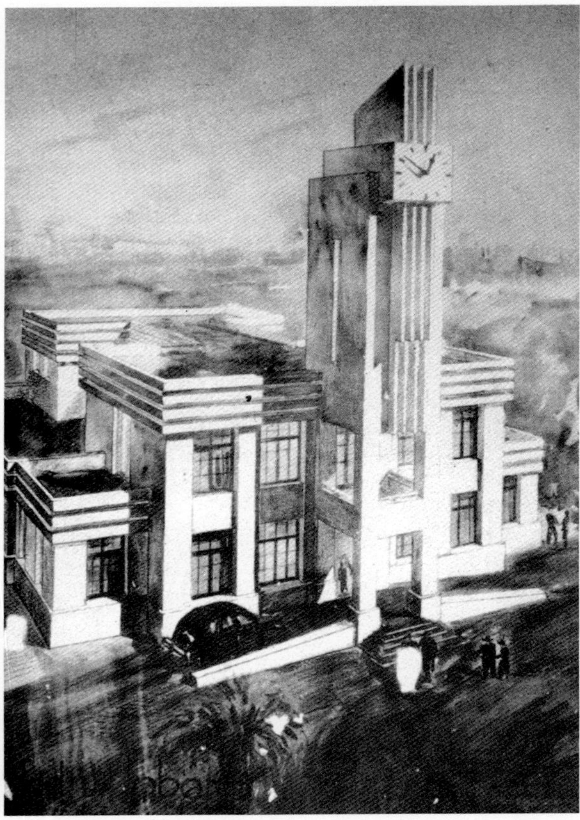

Fig. 11. Lobería town hall (unbuilt project). Photograph from *Cuatro años de gobierno, 1936–1940*, Imprenta Oficial, Buenos Aires Province.

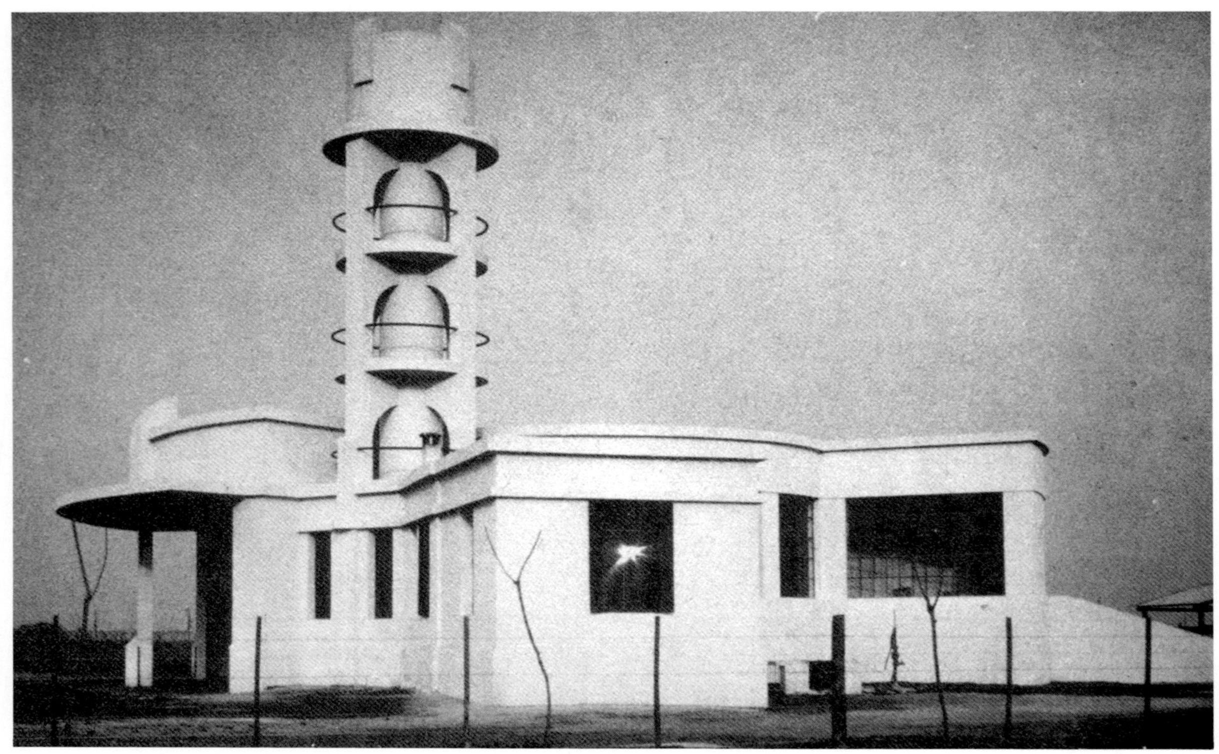

Fig. 12. Carhué slaughterhouse.

Historic photograph.

simple existing urban profile, and the lack of acceptance of these new intensive architectural expressions by the farming communities. It is also certain that the authoritative connotations inspiring them, the political changes in the country from 1945 onward and still existing today (each of them tossing their own ideological baggage onto the heap), and the progressive concentration of critical and cultural activity in the large cities abandoned these silent monuments to provincial decay, far from the everyday concerns of art leaders and critics.

Salamone's town hall designs were as far from traditional colonial buildings, with their wide gallery of semicircular arches, as they were from later Italian or French types built between 1870 and 1930. Now the town hall, focus and symbol of the state as moderator and springing from this newly productive society, should retake its position as an urban landmark, associated with an image of efficient and impersonal administration, and with a strong symbolic manifestation of its paternalistic role.

The formal contributions of the modern movement customarily incorporated in design and the recent technologies of reinforced concrete, chromed metals (fig. 18), opalines (fig. 19), and iron structures provided the basis for "functional" design. An uncomplicated plan of halls and offices with sharp, brightly lit angles, flat and uniformly white walls (a "democratic" as well as inexpensive color), granite composition or terrazzo floors (fig. 20), standardized carpentry, wide windows with panes of reinforced and translucent glass, completely tiled rest rooms with "hygienic" plumbing fixtures and hardware, no unnecessary moldings, railings of shiny tubing, and chromed indirect lighting (figs. 15, 16, and 17); here was the distant influence of Bauhaus, but even more that of the Dutch masters connected with De Stijl—van Doesburg, Rietveld, Oud—and the solitary Willem Marinus Dudok, whose plans for the Hilversum Council

Fig. 13. Laprida monumental cemetery portal. Historic photograph.

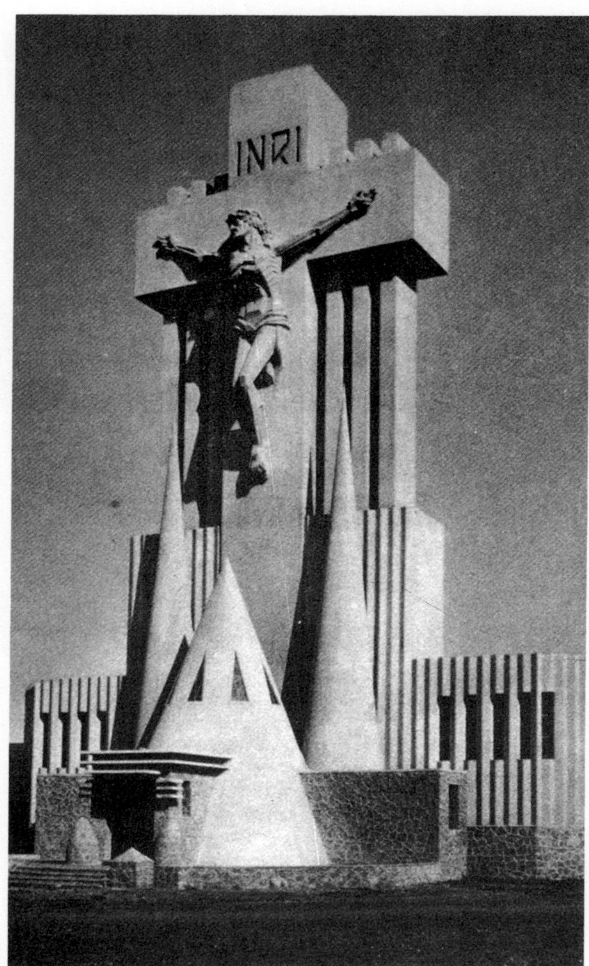

Fig. 14. Lobería monumental cemetery portal. Plan perspective.

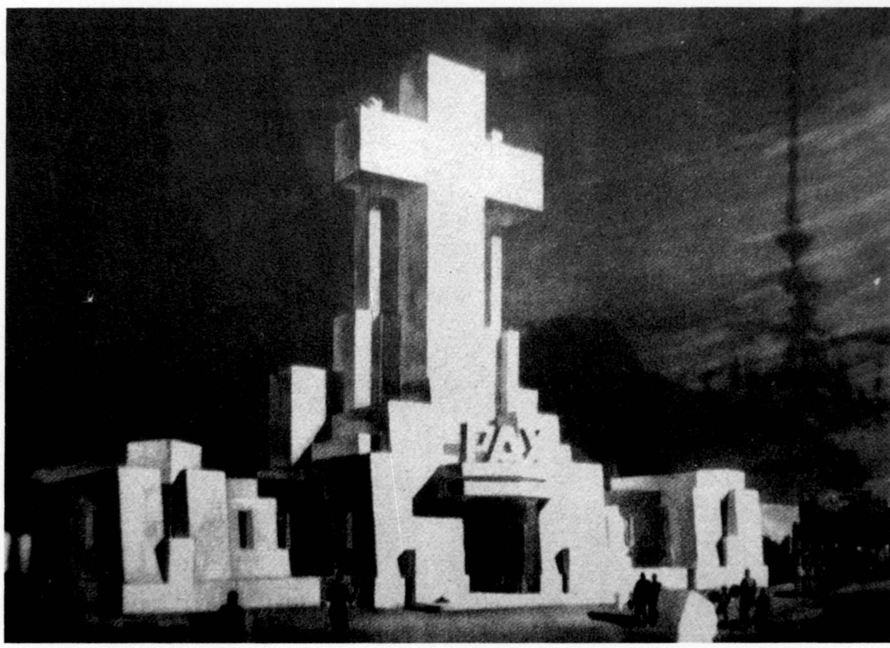

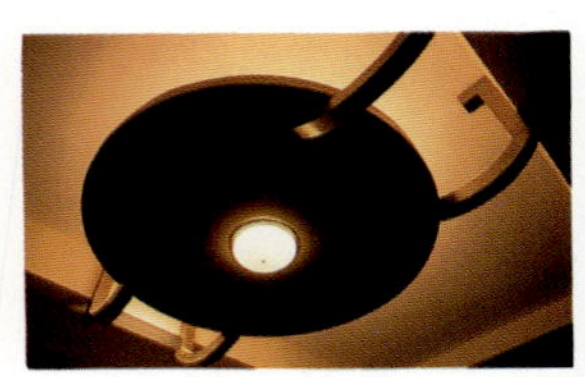

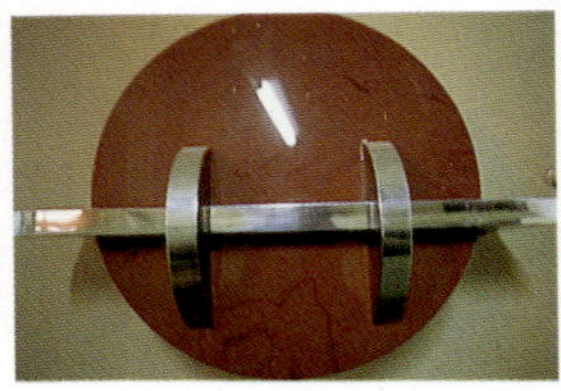

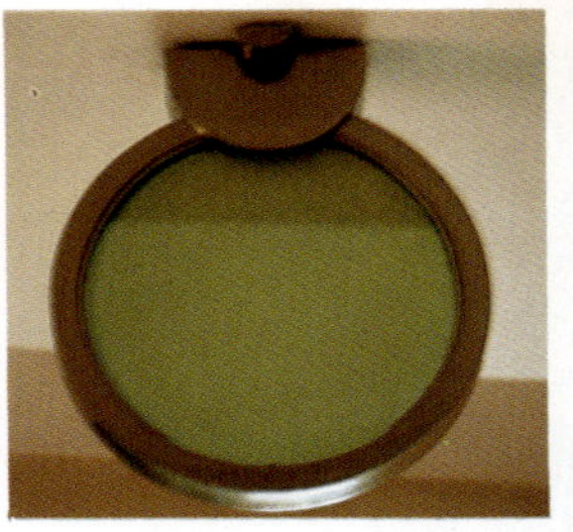

▲

Figs. 15, 16, and 17. Coronel Pringles town hall. Original lighting fixtures with colored melamine veneers. Supports and rings of chromium-plated metal.

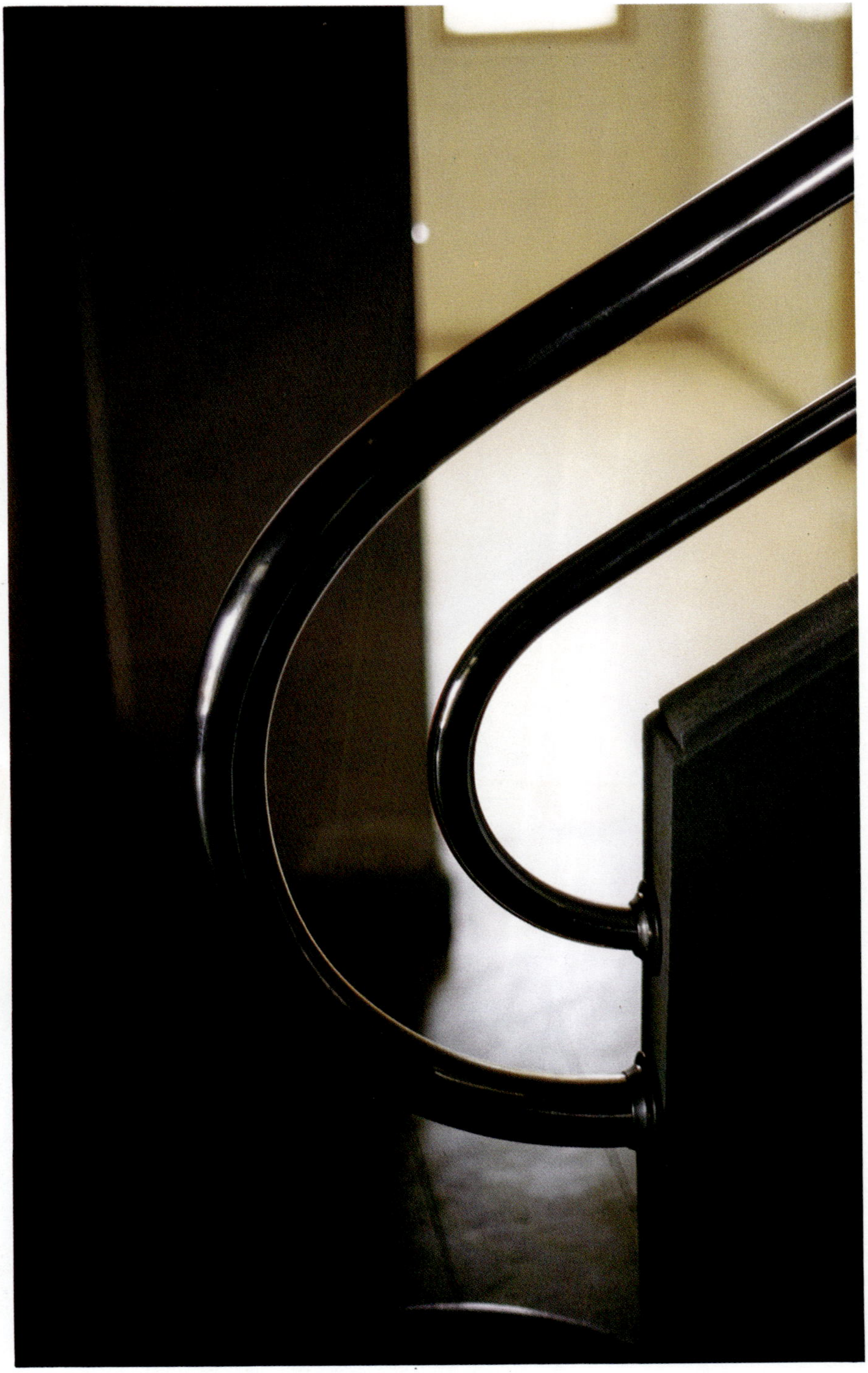

Fig. 18. Carlos Pellegrini town hall, banister of chromium-plated metallic tubing. Terrazzo floor.

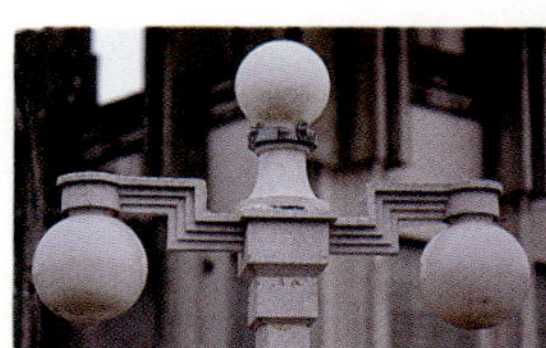

Fig. 19. Coronel Pringles, plaza street lights of premolded concrete with opaline shades.

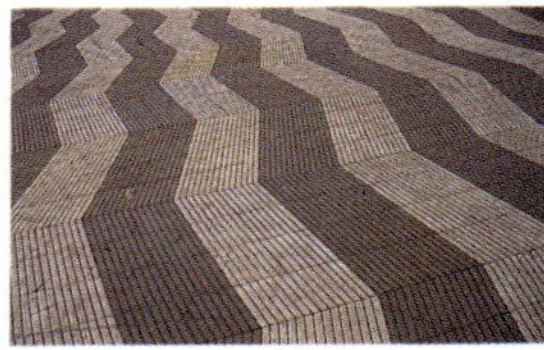

Fig. 20. Coronel Pringles town hall, zigzag tiling.

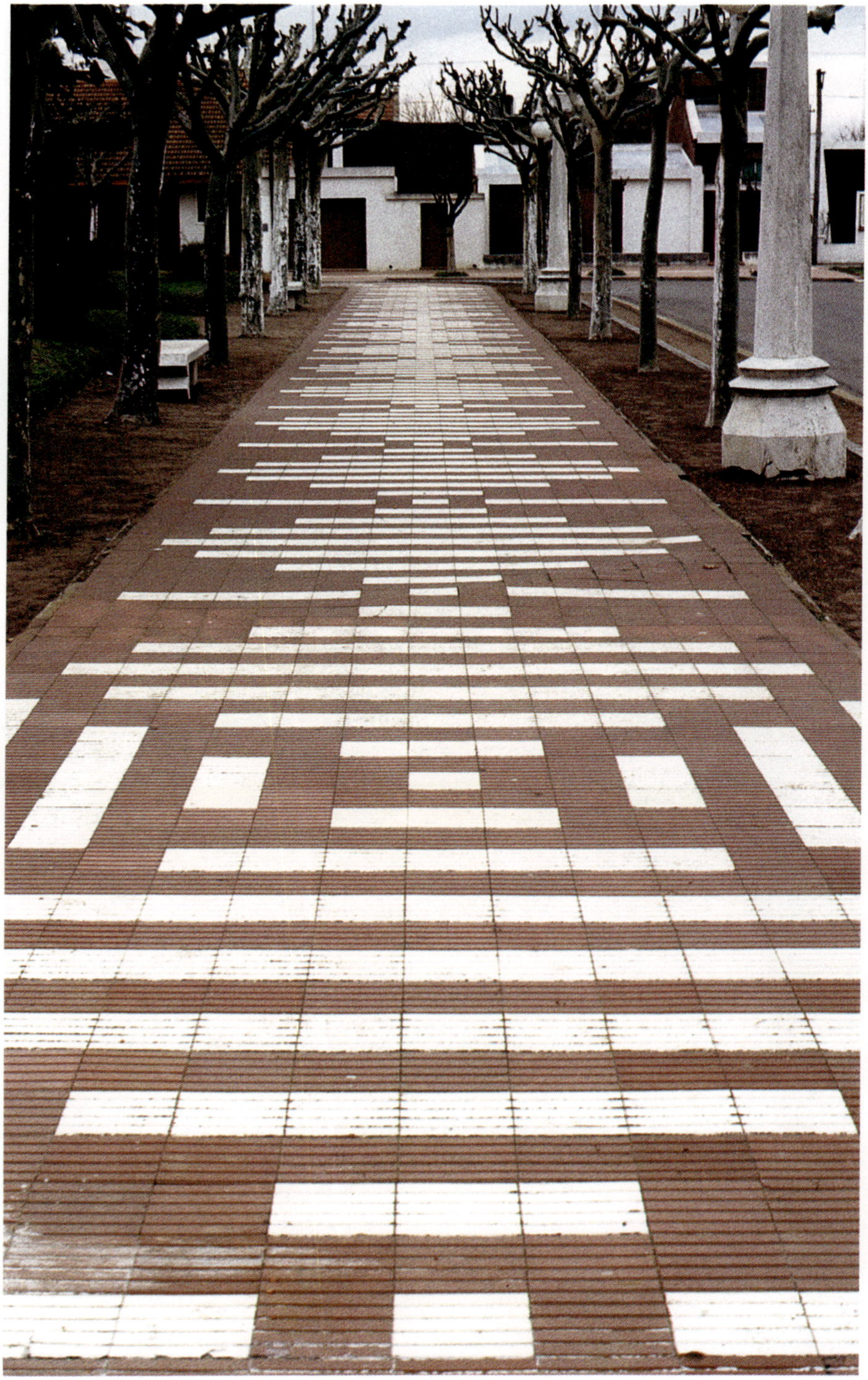

Fig. 21. Carlos Pellegrini town hall. Decorations on plaza walkway. **(See page 102.)**

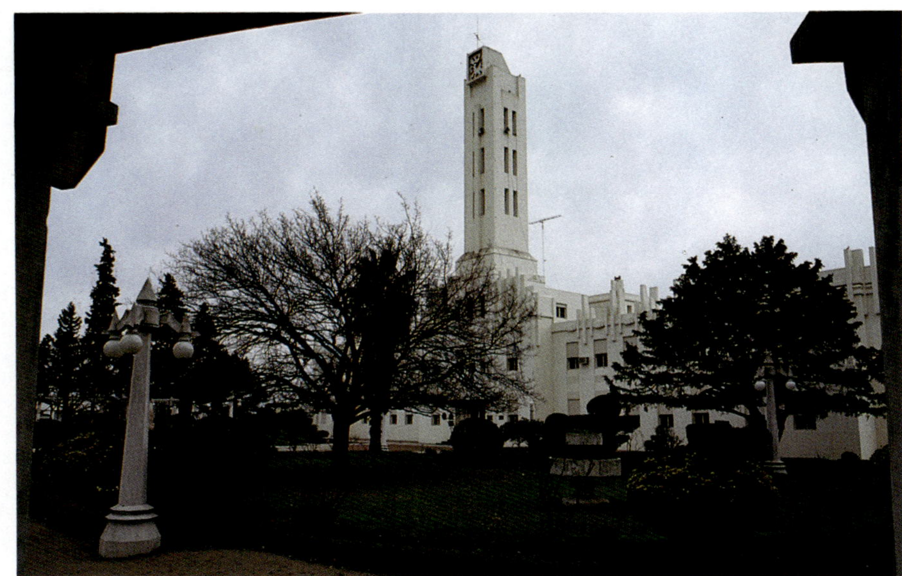

Fig. 22. Carlos Pellegrini town hall, from the center of the plaza.

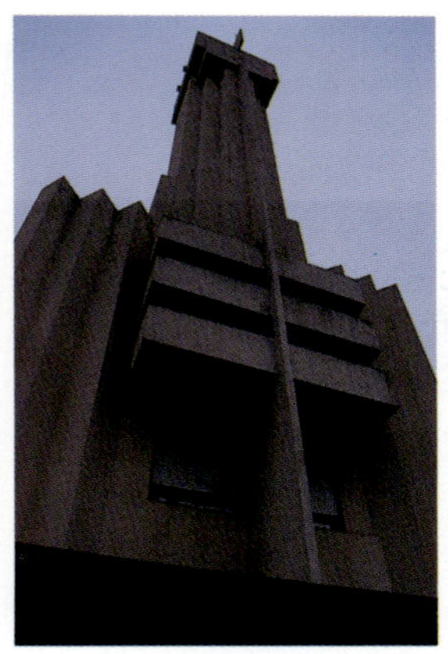

Fig. 23. Laprida town hall, central tower.

Hall were first published here in 1933, and which Salamone undoubtedly knew when he prepared his projects.

But the "elementary" asymmetry of the modern movement was not the most appropriate to project the solid image of an unchanging institution, which Fresco decided to place directly in the center of the main plaza (fig. 21) or at the intersection of the main streets. For this Salamone preferred to resort to his ancestry and rescue the image of the Umbrian-Tuscan palace of the Middle Ages with its crenelated roof line and slender central tower that tried to outdo the church spire. This is how a new kind of civil "palace" grew in the Argentine pampa, with a needlelike tower crowned by a square or circular clock, always taller than the local church, clearly signaling the center of urban life.

In the thirties, reinforced concrete made the conquest of height possible. And height, since the Biblical episode of Babel, has been a symbol of power. The magazines of that period promulgated the model designed by Robert Mallet-Stevens for the Pavilion of Tourism at the 1925 Paris Exposition, and the world delighted in competitions and projects of towers of all kinds.[8] It is no coincidence that in 1936, to commemorate the four-hundredth anniversary of the first founding of Buenos Aires, the architect Alberto Prebisch erected a sixty-meter tall obelisk in the middle of the widest avenue of the city, sitting above three intersecting subway lines. Half a century later, this obelisk has become the identifying symbol of the capital of the country.

Salamone tried to personalize each town with his treatment of the crowning tower of its town hall. This consisted of combining vertical flat surfaces and grooves rhythmically displayed in compact or open modules with unexpected horizontal grooves or bands. The decoration is generally only applied superficially and has little to do with the resistant structure of the main building itself. But we must not forget that, unlike the masters of *art nouveau*, the designers of art deco would favor an esthetic effect over construction logic. The asepsis

8. For example, in *Revista de Arquitectura* (Magazine of architecture), no 81 (February 1938), tower projects from first and fifth year students ("Volumes for ornamental towers" and "Monument recalling universal peace," respectively) were published, as well as several proposals for towers by local groups of architects, sculptors, and decorators.

called for by Adolf Loos had come to its end, and the "body" of architecture once again became a more or less neutral base for free decorative expansion.[9]

The dry symmetry of the tower in Carlos Pellegrini (fig. 22) is quite different from the almost Assyrian pyramidlike base of Puán, or the strong vertical grooves of Laprida—undoubtedly a risky design, almost futuristic (fig. 23). These pale when compared to the carefully framed work of Tornquist or the geometrical art deco of the buildings in Saldungaray and Tres Lomas and the quite heavy, predominantly horizontal lines of the designs for Lobería. Among all these perhaps the most characteristic is that of Coronel Pringles (fig. 27). It is the best representative of the series not only for the intrinsic interest of the "palace" but also for its urban location and integration into the surroundings: park, pergolas, fountains, and sidewalks.

The work of the architects Arias Incollá, Carrafrancq, Pernaut, and Bozzano, already mentioned, correctly analyzes and interprets the structural components of the whole and its relationship with the city of Coronel Pringles. It also cites the basic gracefulness of the building and concludes by saying that Salamone "translated to his work a sharp interest in finding the laws which allow regular organization of space...applying laws of selection for geometric figures and their combinations." In this sense, the composition of lines and curves, planes and spheres, so typical of art deco, reach their highest resolutions in the playful alternations of the fountains in Pringles and Laprida. In the latter case, something like the spirit of Disneyland is anticipated (figs. 25 and 26).

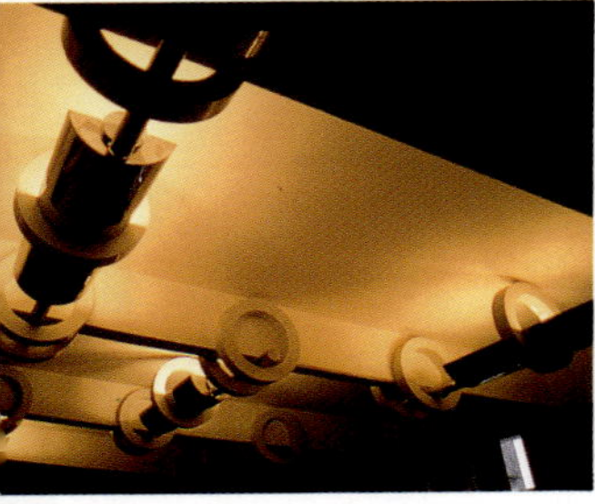

Fig. 24. Coronel Pringles town hall. Cylindrical lighting fixtures in the Council Hall ceiling, with casing of enameled veneer and rings of enameled or chromium-plated metal.

The design of the interiors was also Salamone's responsibility. His plans show not only the rapidity of the drawing but also the variety of imagination, above all in the forms and materials for lighting fixtures (fig. 24). The most common combinations are based on the rotation of cylindrical elements or those framed with rungs and chromed or painted tubes that enclose circular shades of green opaline or rose marble. Geometrical abstraction even stretched to the town clocks, which have bars and circles in place of numbers.

Cedar and walnut furniture designed by Salamone is, in general, not innovative, and when it is, it is quite uncomfortable. Only a few examples were made, among them the official chair of the Mayor of Laprida with its extremely tall back laterally grooved and topped by a triangular crown—a scaled-down reproduction of the building in which it stood. Today it is displayed in the town museum.

With architecture and decoration integrated to create a prototype of a pampa town hall, Salamone carried out contemporary ideas put forward by Alfredo Guido, an active nationalist painter, who wrote:

> One of the extremes of Argentine temperament today is represented in the work of the popular "lasting" architect. It is a classic subtype within functional construction. The designs are simple and clear. There are neither surprises nor promises in his buildings. He loves to build with hard materials like stone and granite, or make concrete seem like a noble material. He moves toward monumentality by using smooth angles, even when he should not do so.... He never puts plaster decorations on stone.... At times, his extreme severity reaches a puritanism without beauty. He is the

9. V. Arwas, *Art Deco* (London: Academy Editions, 1980).

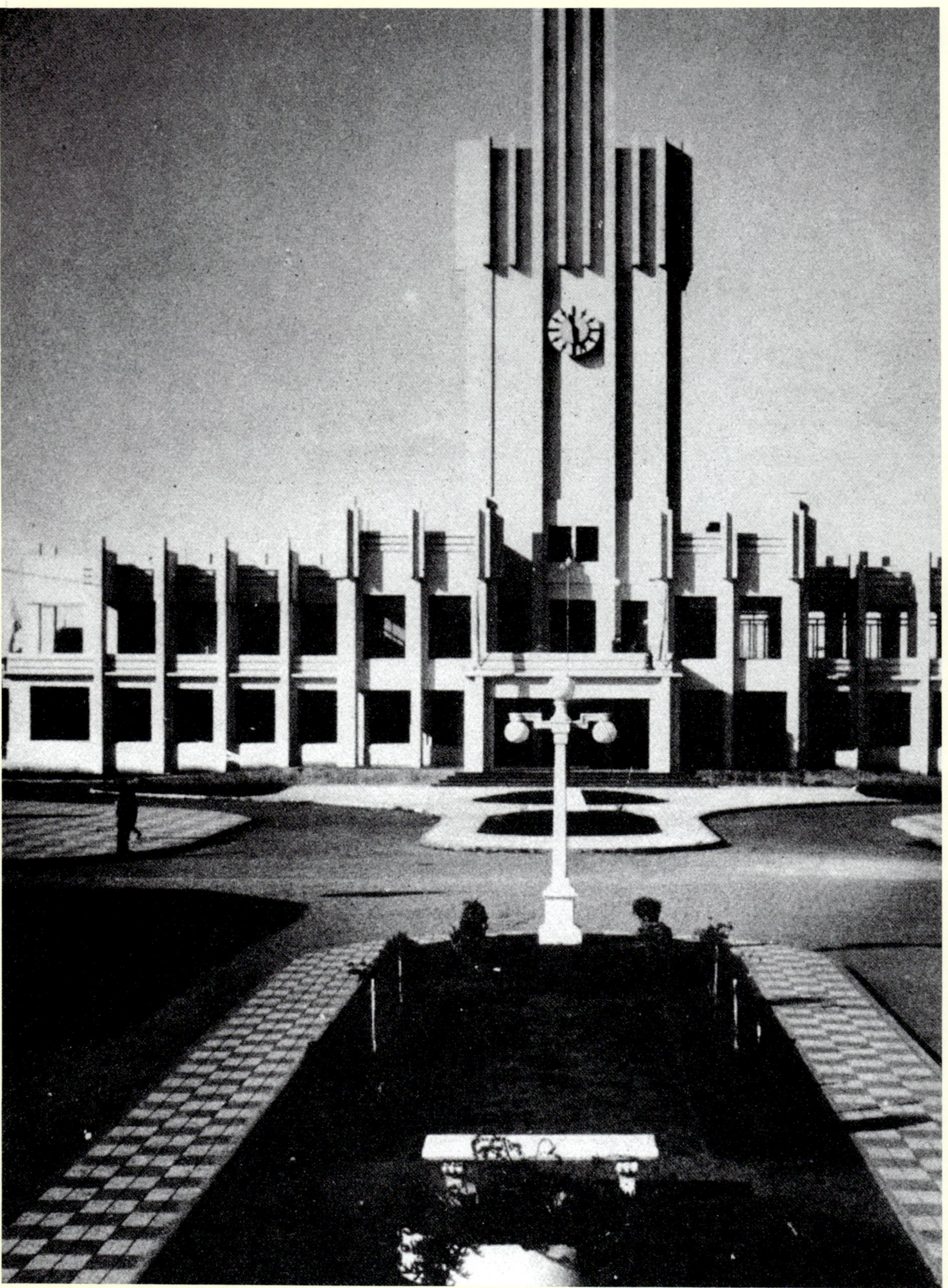

right architect to build churches and public buildings. But think of the decorator who has to work with him and ask yourself if his art is sufficiently constructive, geometrical, and austere.[10]

Toward 1935, there was further expansion in the province when municipal slaughterhouses replaced the precarious shacks of sheet metal and wood where animals were killed for local consumption. The increasing development of sanitary standards and the mechanization of the industry made it obligatory to include tiled laboratories, hooks and toothed rails, automatic gates, water troughs, washing tables, electric pumps and motors, covered corrals, and loading ramps (fig. 28). In this way, the art-deco model slaughterhouse was born in the midst of a primitive rural community. It also became a symbol of pride in the first local industry.

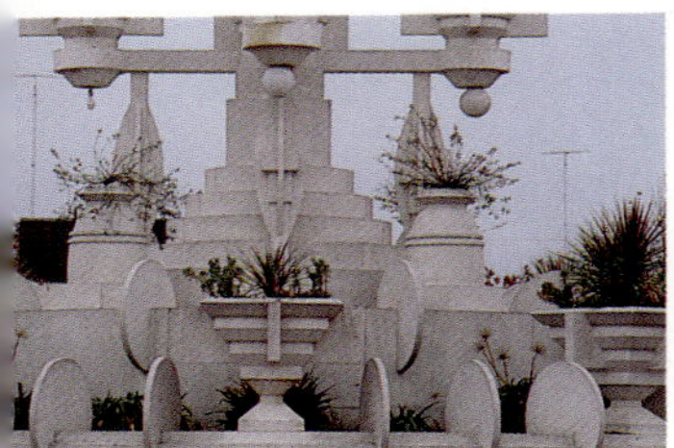

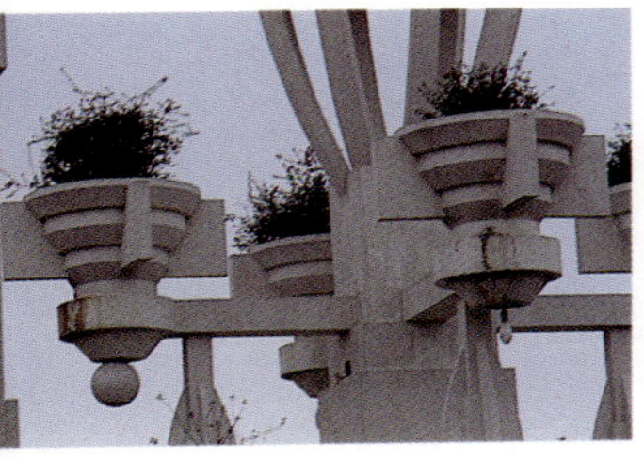

Figs. 25 and 26. Laprida town hall. Decorative details of the central fountain.

A functionalism which emphasized the mechanical placed it in the catalogue of the most innovative typologies; now it was necessary to give it a formal identity. Since there were no functional elements that characterized it sufficiently from the outside, except the corrals which could be confused with any cattle market, it was necessary to emphasize an element that would make it immediately recognizable. In this case, the most effective method was to place the word *matadero* (slaughterhouse) high up and very visible. In the case of Coronel Pringles it was *matadero modelo* (model slaughterhouse) (fig. 30). This large sign formed part of the main entrance, or marquee. Since the slaughterhouse had no symbolic importance in itself, like the town hall or the cemetery, it was impossible to invent any symbol other than its own name, simply written in large, premolded letters, usually capitals. Once more, the best solution, and the only genuinely art-deco solution of the ones we have seen, was that of Coronel Pringles, placed halfway up the tower (fig. 31).

It should be noted that in the geometrical-decorative concept of these small slaughterhouse towers (fig. 29), Salamone displayed a noteworthy artistic creativity, using different alternatives of this blend of sculpture and architecture in each town, always ruled by the principles of analytical geometry. Once more we quote Guido: "The common language between architects and decorators is geometry. It permits the decorator to order his artistic message in surface and volume. As physical exercise strengthens the muscles, the exercise of creating geometric forms strengthens and enriches the imagination."[11]

Replaced in many cases by cold-storage plants or more modern butchering methods, few of these slaughterhouses remain in use. The majority of them survive in solitude, on the outskirts of towns with their installations intact but abandoned to the slow process of deterioration.

Undoubtedly, Salamone's greatest contribution to urban decor can be found in the works he created for existing cemeteries, especially the three monumental entrances at Laprida, Azul (fig. 32), and Saldungaray. Removed by our European background from the colossal muralism of the Mexicans and Brazilians, we Argentines have an unexpected chance to appreciate this form of decorative expression in those three giant examples.

◄

Fig. 27. Coronel Pringles town hall, 1939. Photograph from *Cuatros años de gobierno, 1936–1940*, Imprenta Oficial, Buenos Aires Province.

In the thirties, Latin America was taken with an irresistible desire for regional self-expression with strong ideological characteristics from the left and the

10. Alfredo Guido, "La Decoración en la Arquitectura" (Decoration in architecture), *Revue de Arquitectura*, no. 258 (October 1941): 444.

11. Ibid.

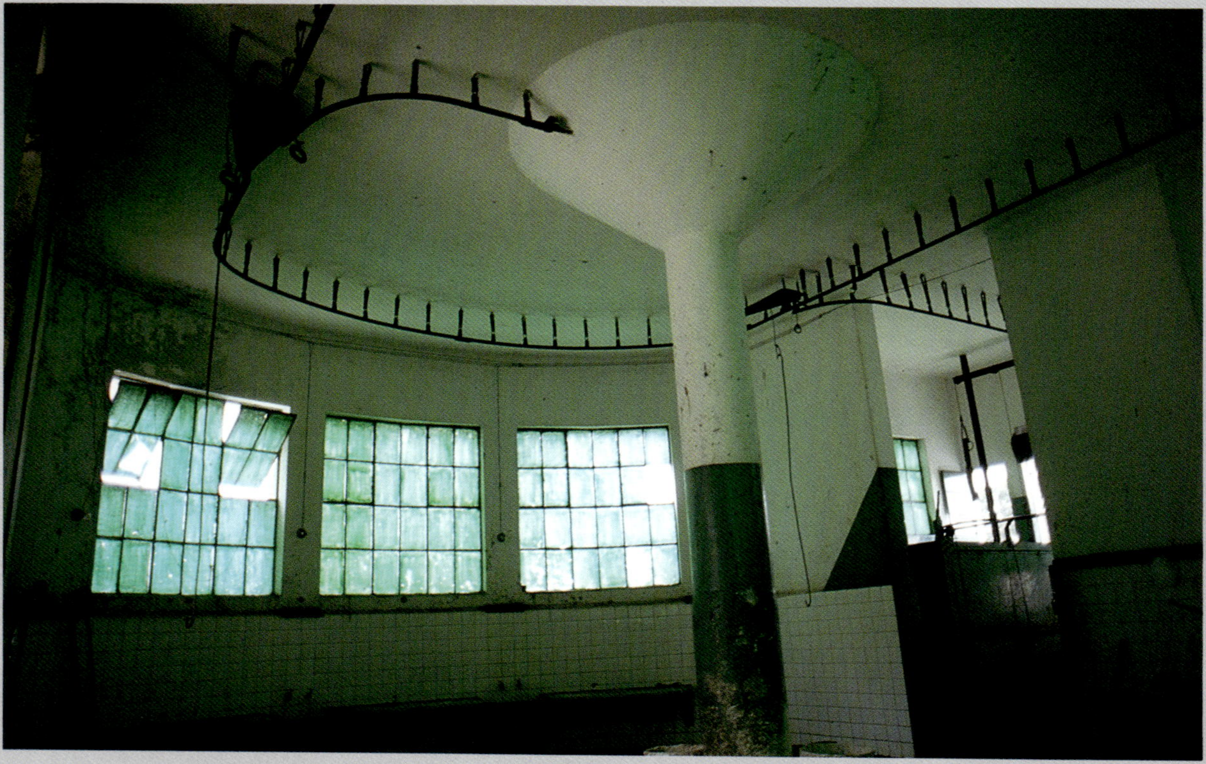

Fig. 28. Carlos Pellegrini slaughterhouse, interior.

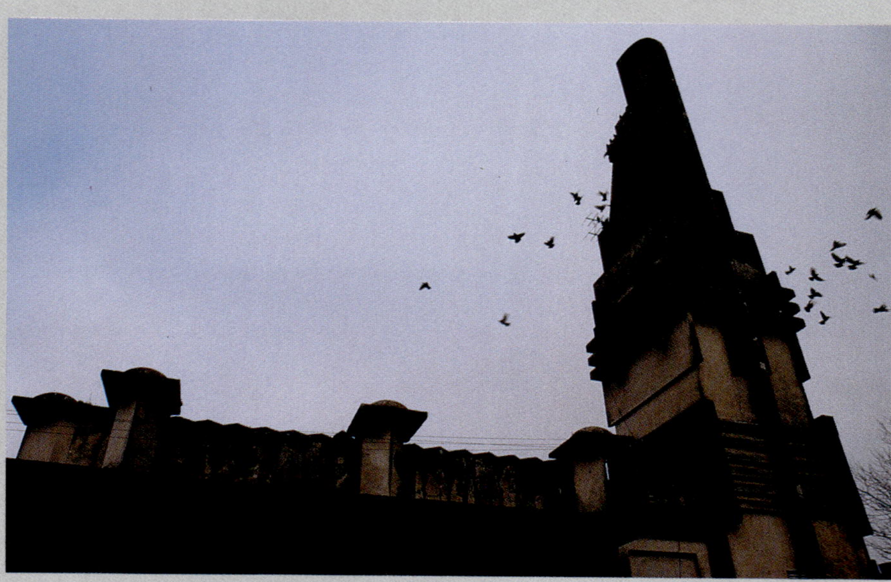

Fig. 29. Coronel Pringles slaugherhouse tower.

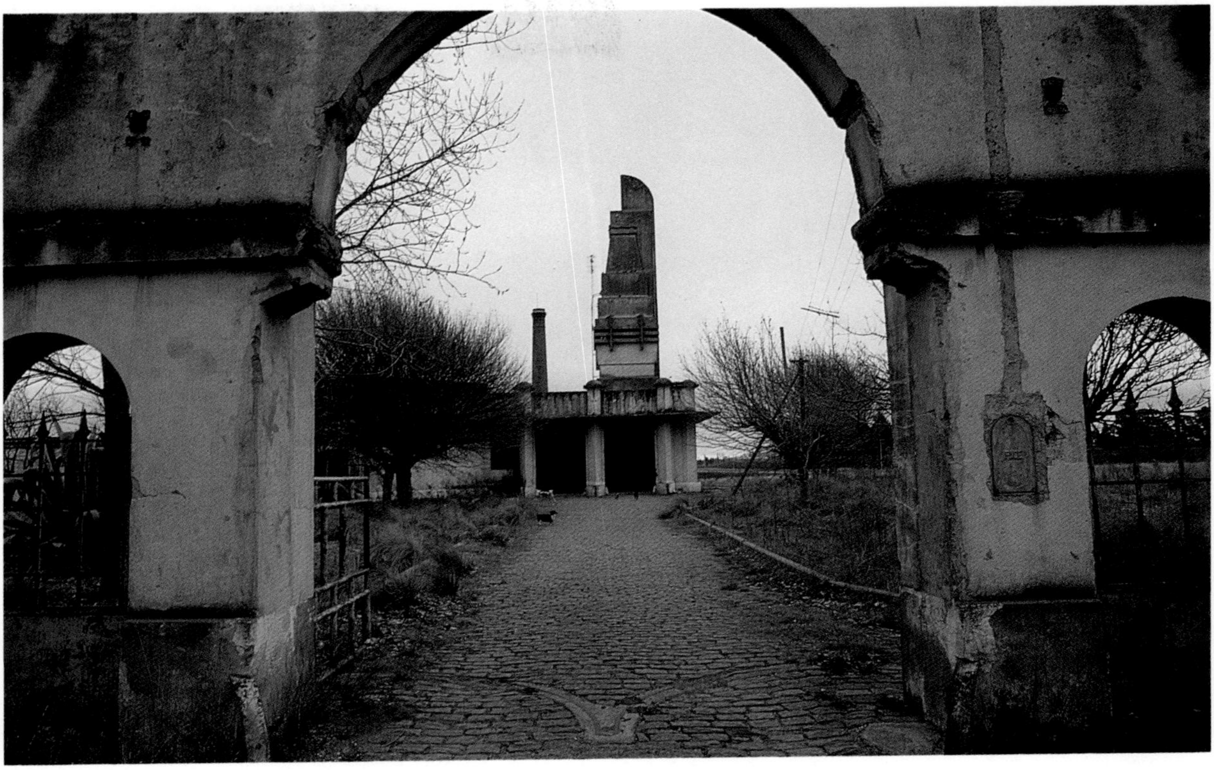

Fig. 30. Coronel Pringles slaughterhouse, now abandoned.

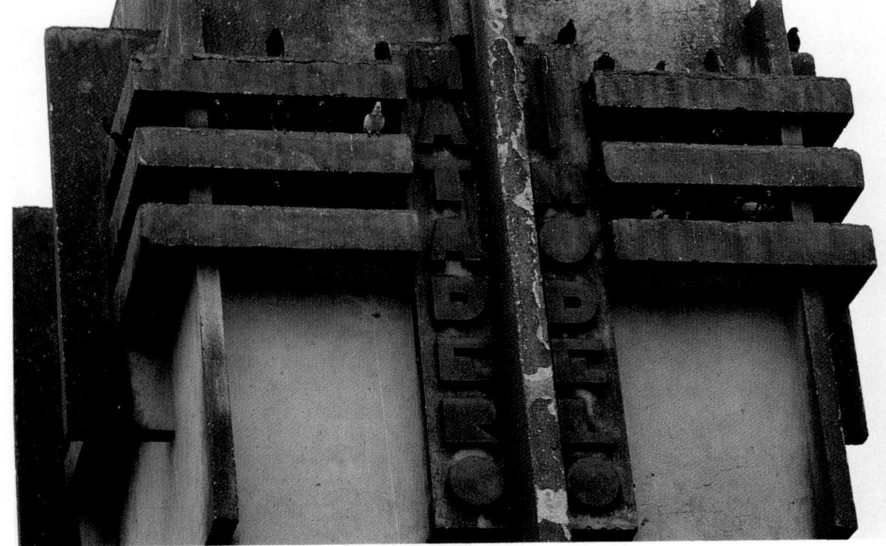

Fig. 31. Coronel Pringles slaughterhouse tower, detail. Note the inscription "matadero modelo" in art-deco typography.

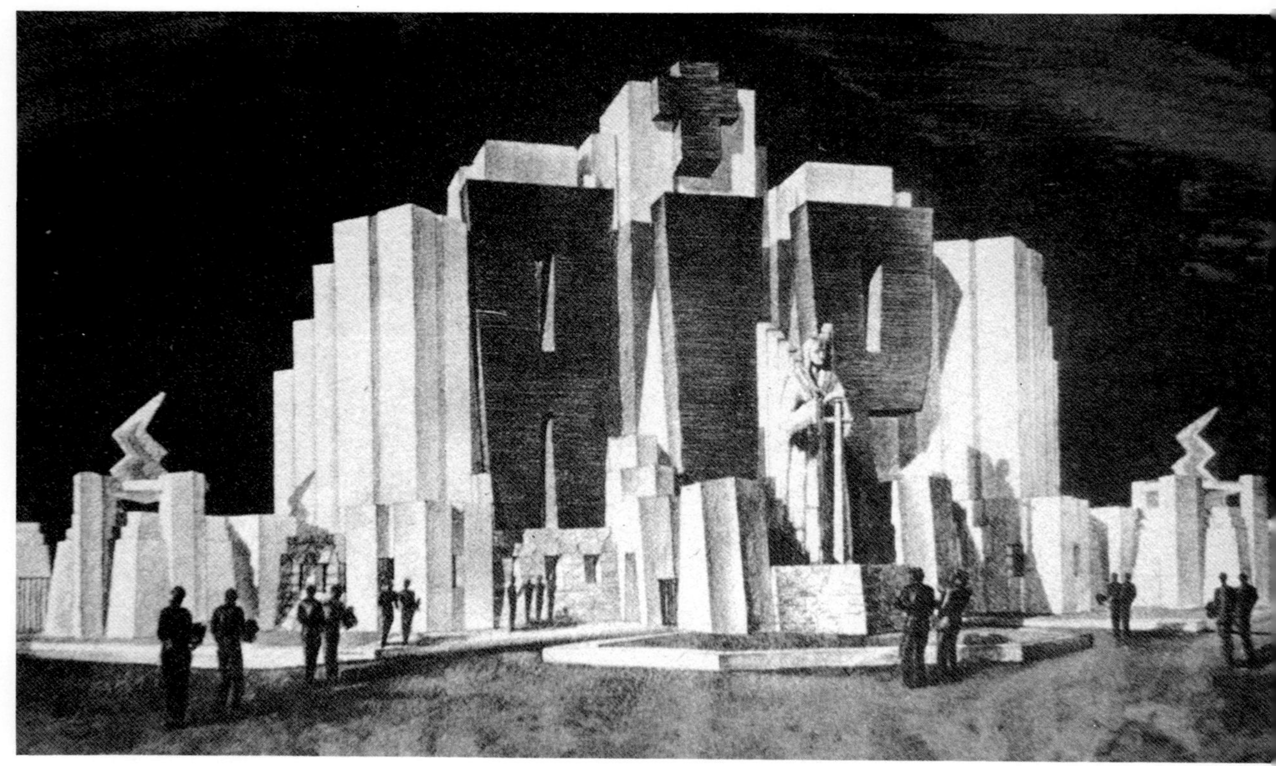

Fig. 32. Azul cemetery, monumental portal. Plan perspective, ca. 1937.

right. An urgency to establish new national codes and communicate them in the most direct form swept the continent. In this sense, monumental art took the forefront in an immediate and continuing communication with the masses. The words of Alfredo Guido are once more apt:

> It is said that decoration, in the past, was an open book for the masses, who could read into the physico-artistic representations the history of each people, [as well as] religious fundamentals...since the great majority could not read or write.... Today, although it seems paradoxical, the circle has closed, and we have reached the same conclusion. The general public needs to be presented with the equivalent of catalogues of images—as the film industry has already begun to offer us—so that [they] can discover all that those who went before also needed to know. Then man had time but did not know how to read; now man knows how to read but does not have time.... There are many ways to solve this: graphic advertising, decoration, theater.... By using the artistic decorator, the state allowed him to develop his imagination on a larger scale and exercise his experience as artisan, channeling it toward a more social and, therefore, more human art, not leaving the beaten path for the strictly individualistic path so common today.... The ever-present pictures of national history, founding fathers, national geography, customs of life and work in the different regions, religion...can greatly encourage the creation of a spirit of national unity.[12]

Here Guido states, with almost violent clarity, the connection between ideology and communication through urban art. Here, also, is the best theoretical introduction to an appreciation of the three gigantic works of stone, cement,

12. Ibid.

and plaster with which Salamone depicted the nationalistic idea of those years regarding death and immortality.

It is very difficult for Anglo-Saxon culture to understand the sense of heartbreaking tragedy with which Latins "live" death. Just as Orpheus had to cross the infernal marsh and confront Cerberus before he could find peace in the Elysian Fields, it is also necessary, beyond the certainty of a serene eternity, to confront the tragic voyage of no return. There is nothing further from the German *friedhof* and the quiet Nordic parks than Latin American cemeteries, crowded with heroic or suffering figurative and allegorical monuments. In the Latin tradition, the "city of the dead" is analogous to that of the living, only with a much more gloomy solemnness.

To have relatives buried in a specific place is a concrete sign of pertaining to that place. Therefore, in an era of frontier settlements and the affirmation of a nationalistic system, it was important to emphasize the significance of the common burial ground.

The enormous funeral settings invented by Salamone acted as literal entryways to immortality, separating daily reality from the hereafter with a little of the Arch of Triumph and a lot of the gate of Hell. If these achievements leave much to be desired—since Salamone was not a sculptor, nor did the works aspire to an independent life as sculptures—it must be realized that within the panorama of Argentine sculpture of those years they stand out as examples of a rarely attempted poetic vision. In general, Argentine sculptors like Yrurtia, Lagos, and Zonza Briano remained faithful to the classic French model, or explored a purely orthodox synthetic symbolism, as in the case of self-taught José Fioravanti, who created the monuments to Nicolás Avellanda and Roque Sáenz Peña. In any case, Salamone's model could be found in the allegorical reliefs of the German Arno Breker, directly inherited from the heroic romanticism of Rude and the synthetic carvings of Maillol, even though they were, unfortunately, used by Hitler in the service of National Socialism. Barely two years younger than Salamone, Breker had just completed the gigantic figures of the Olympic Stadium and the German Foreign Ministry in Berlin, works that were widely known in Buenos Aires.

The odd cone-shaped entrance in Laprida (fig. 33) is almost lost at the foot of this enormous monument, formed by a base more than twenty meters high on which a huge white cross is placed (fig. 35) with its crucified Christ almost eight meters tall (fig. 34). Standing guard at the sides are two conical shapes which we call "ice-cream cones," very slender, used for nothing more than to balance the base (figs. 36 and 37). In the middle of the flat pampa, from several kilometers away, the vision of what seems to be a monumental billboard is picturesque and at the same time frightening.

In Azul, the last to be finished, the design is definitely Wagnerian in its interplay of cement imitations of white and grey stones forming a wall of broken rocks which stand out from the three first initials of the Christian requiem, R.I.P. (*Requiescat in pace*) (figs. 38 and 42). It is a scene of threatening mountains, reconstructed and reordered by the sculptor. In the postcubist years, in the decade of art deco, this choice of form created a style. "Nature creates her sculptured caprices with stone and with the mountains raises her natural monuments, in a fascinatingly informal manner that never palls. Man, as sculptor, began with the menhirs, humbly copying what nature presented by chance, and, when he began the work of building monuments, he did it as

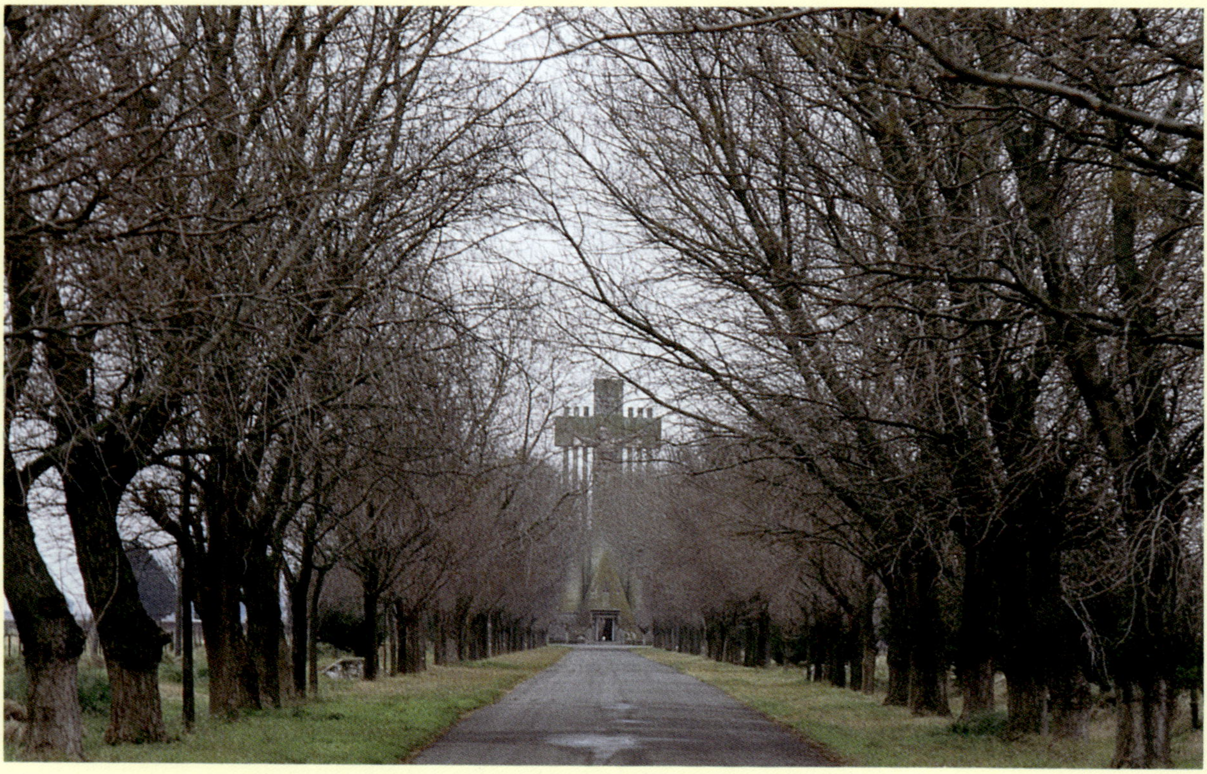

Fig. 33. Laprida cemetery, access avenue.

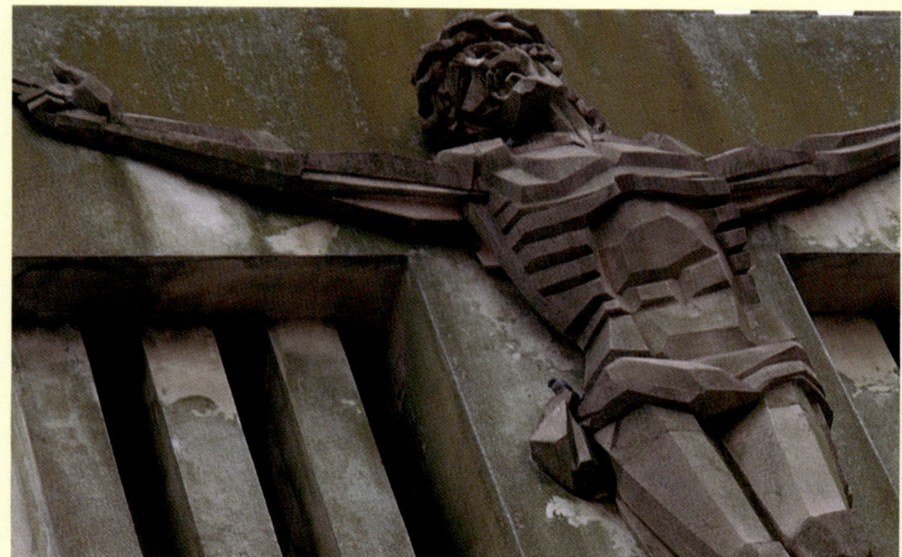

Fig. 34. Laprida cemetery, detail of Christ crucified, high relief in concrete.

Fig. 35. Laprida cemetery, nearing the portal.

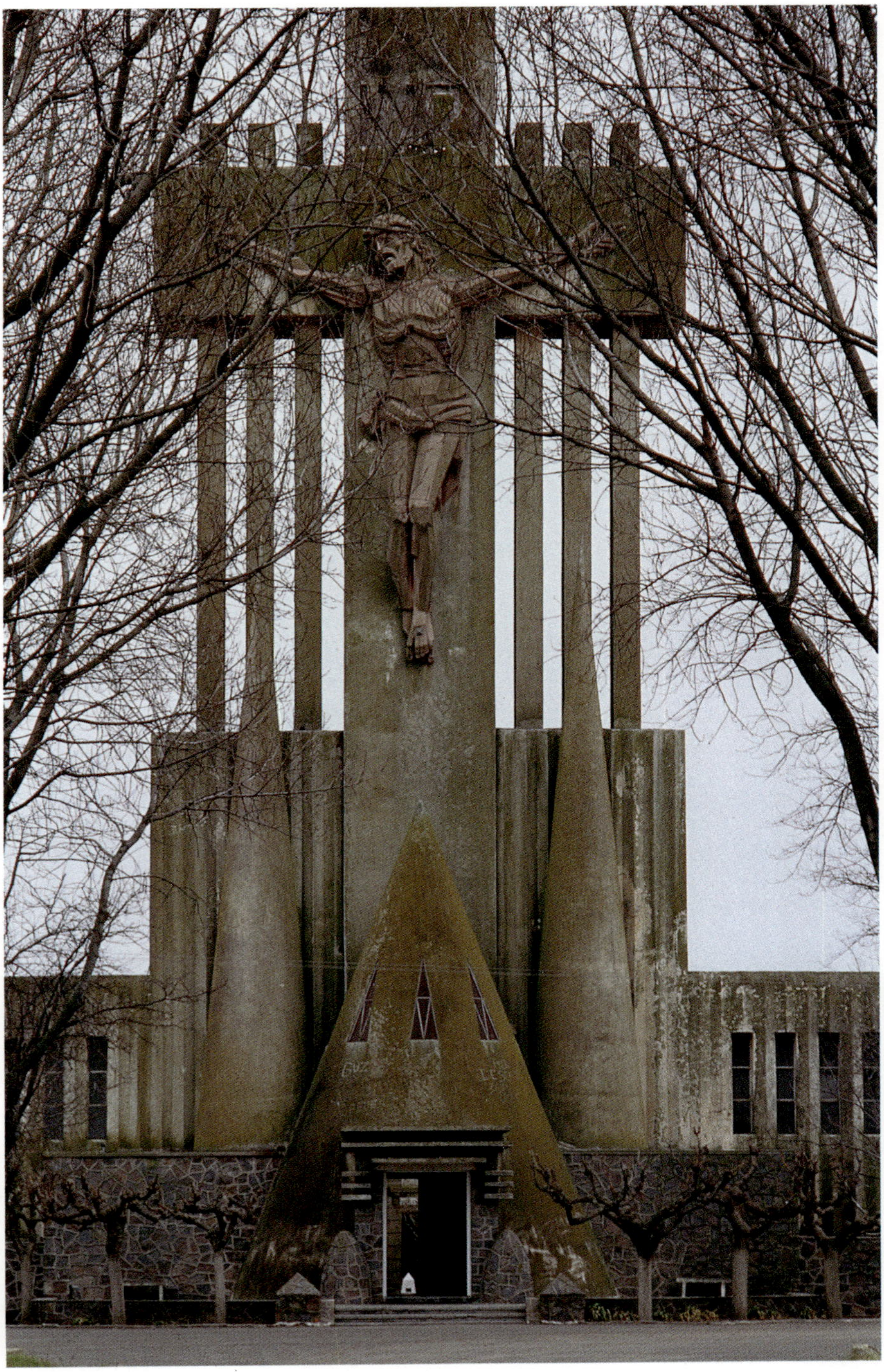

Fig. 36. Laprida cemetery, interior of the shrine, from one of the side cones.

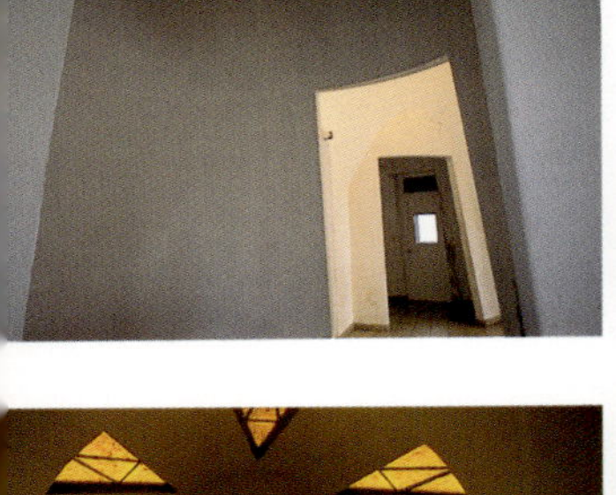

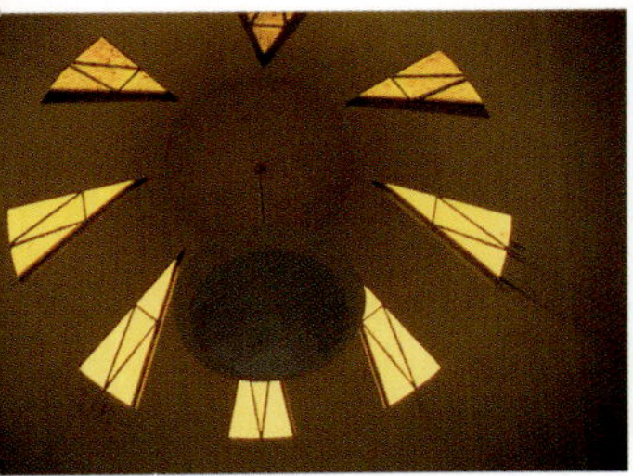

Fig. 37. Laprida cemetery, ceiling of conical central shrine.

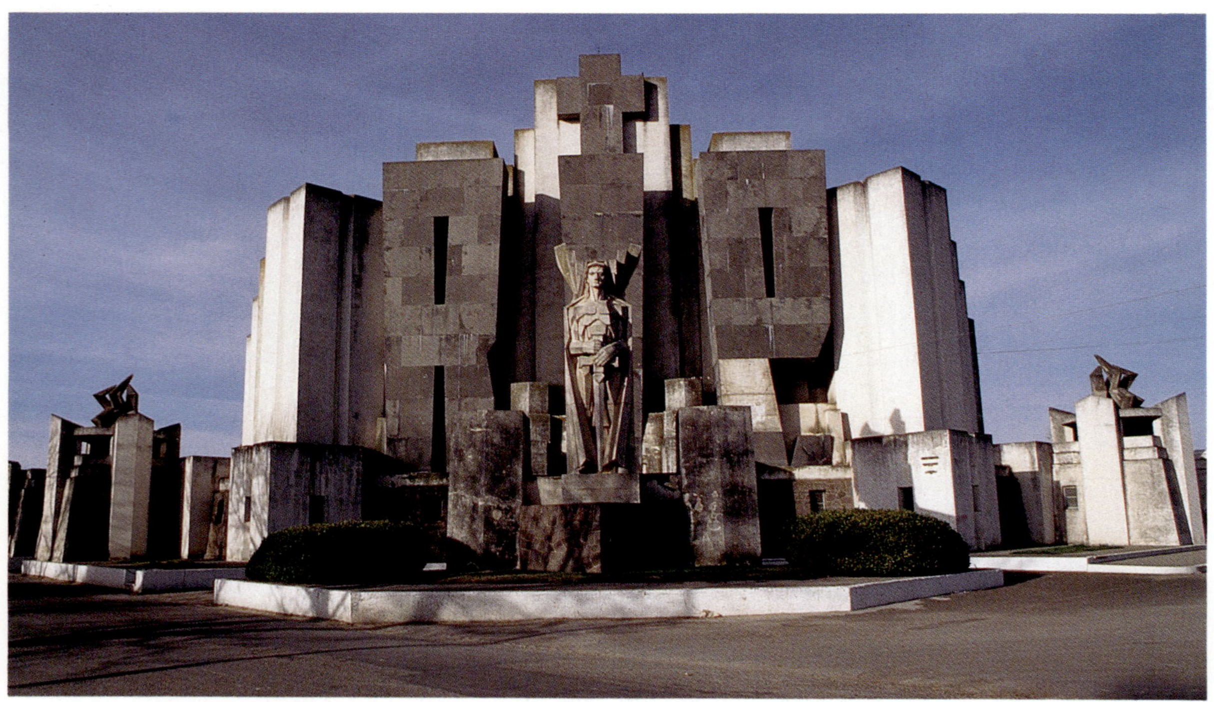

Fig. 38. Azul cemetery, the constructed portal. Note the colossal initials R.I.P. (*Requiescat in pace*).

architect, imitating, of course in human size, the grandeur of the mountains. The monument was the monolithic presence of the mountain for centuries; the mountain tamed by a geometric order and carved by the symbolic fantasy of each race. This first view of the monument-mountain has maintained its prestige to our days."[13]

The entrance is guarded by a kind of gigantic angel of death, with a wrinkled brow, wings folded, and hands on a sword (figs. 39, 40, and 41). It is made of reinforced concrete. In this sculpture, as in many Christ figures Salamone created in the province of Buenos Aires, the shape is in the form of a strong broken line, reflecting his "archi-caricatures." The mass is faceted, almost cubistic if it were not for the cuts and depressions. Under the intense light of the region, it takes on an expressionistic aspect.

But the greatest expressionistic inspiration, in our judgement, is the circular entrance to the cemetery of Saldungaray, a tiny village in the south at the foot of the mountains (figs. 43 and 45). The thick concrete disc, eighteen meters in diameter, covered on the inside with blue tiles that today are in bad condition, looks like a giant wheel fallen from the sky (fig. 44). A pathetic head of the dead Christ is incrusted in its center (figs. 46, 47, and 48). It has a faceting similar to that of Azul and more interesting than Laprida. The black entrance at the foot of the disc echoes the gate of Hell in the Park of Monsters at Bomarzo (fig. 49). Obviously, Salamone could not have known the park since the Sacred Forest of the Orsini was still hidden in weeds then; and, furthermore, he never traveled to Italy. An old municipal employee of Carlos Pellegrini remembered a comment Salamone made about the impression caused by a "round theater" on Martín García Island in the middle of the Río de la Plata. If the source is reliable, it must refer to the salon-theater, now abandoned, which

▸ **Fig. 39. Azul cemetery, angel, sculpture in reinforced concrete.**

13. E. B. Rodríguez, *Visiones de la escultura argentina* (Visions of Argentine sculpture) (Buenos Aires: Academia Nacional de Bellas Artes, 1983).

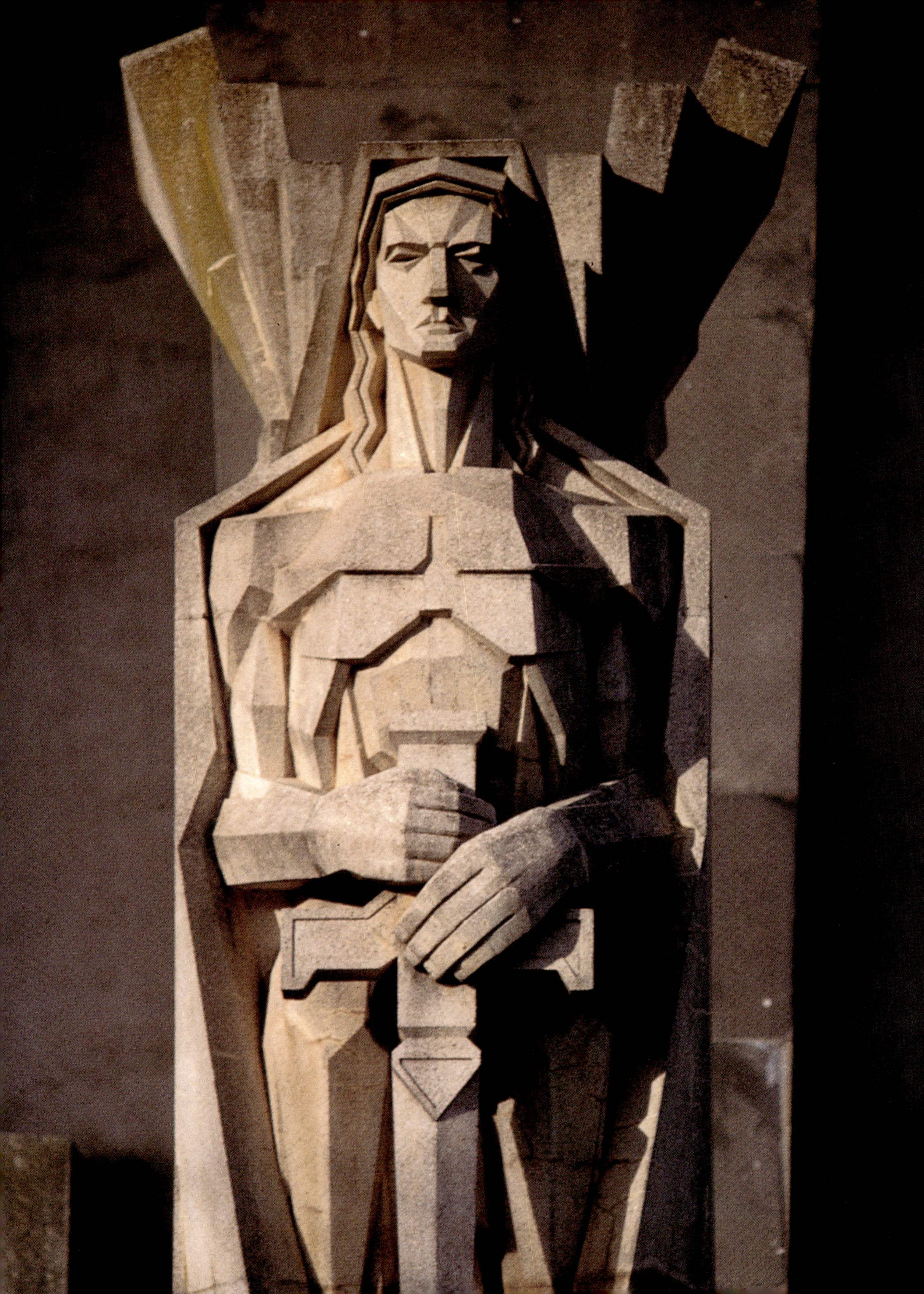

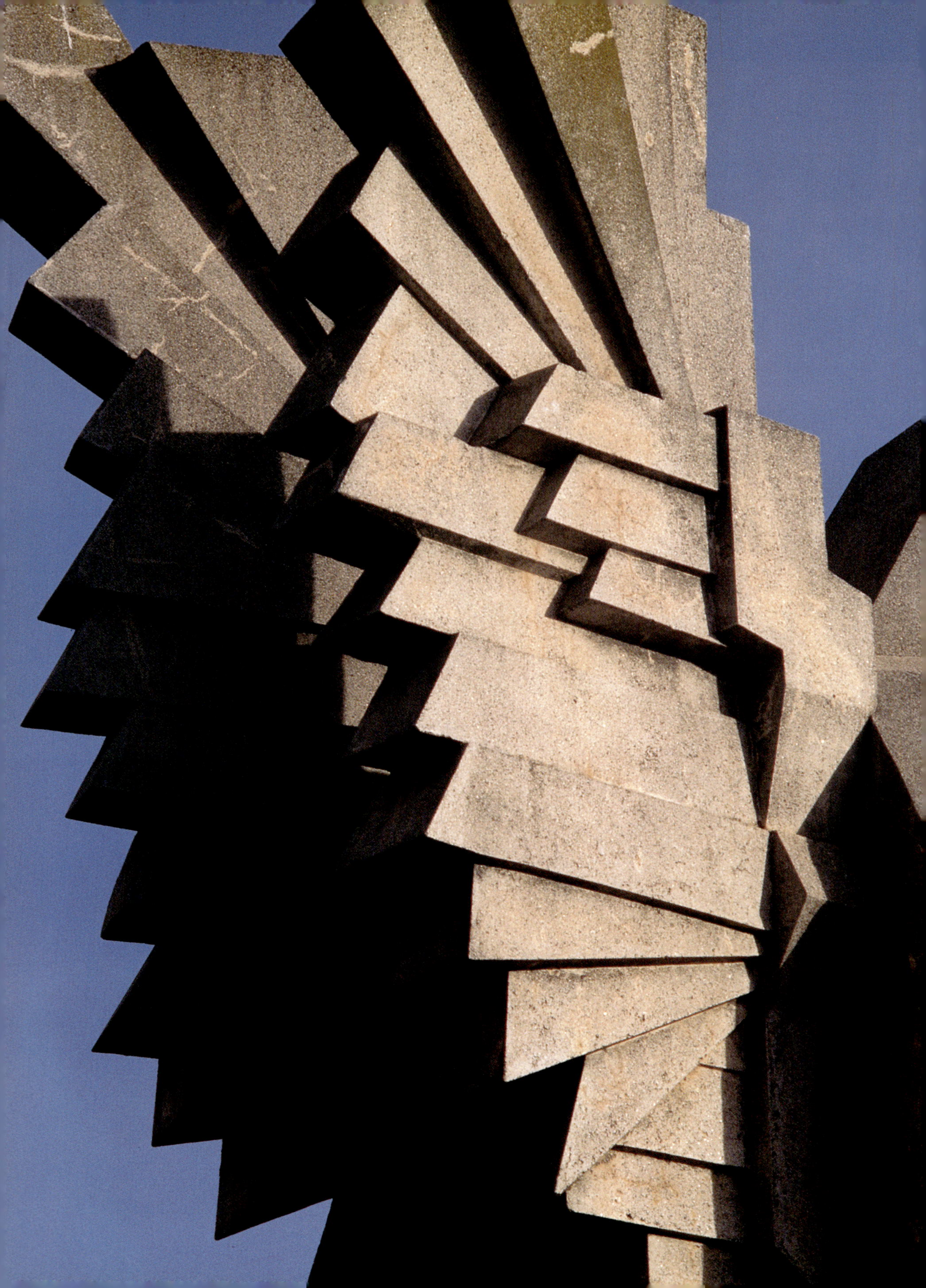

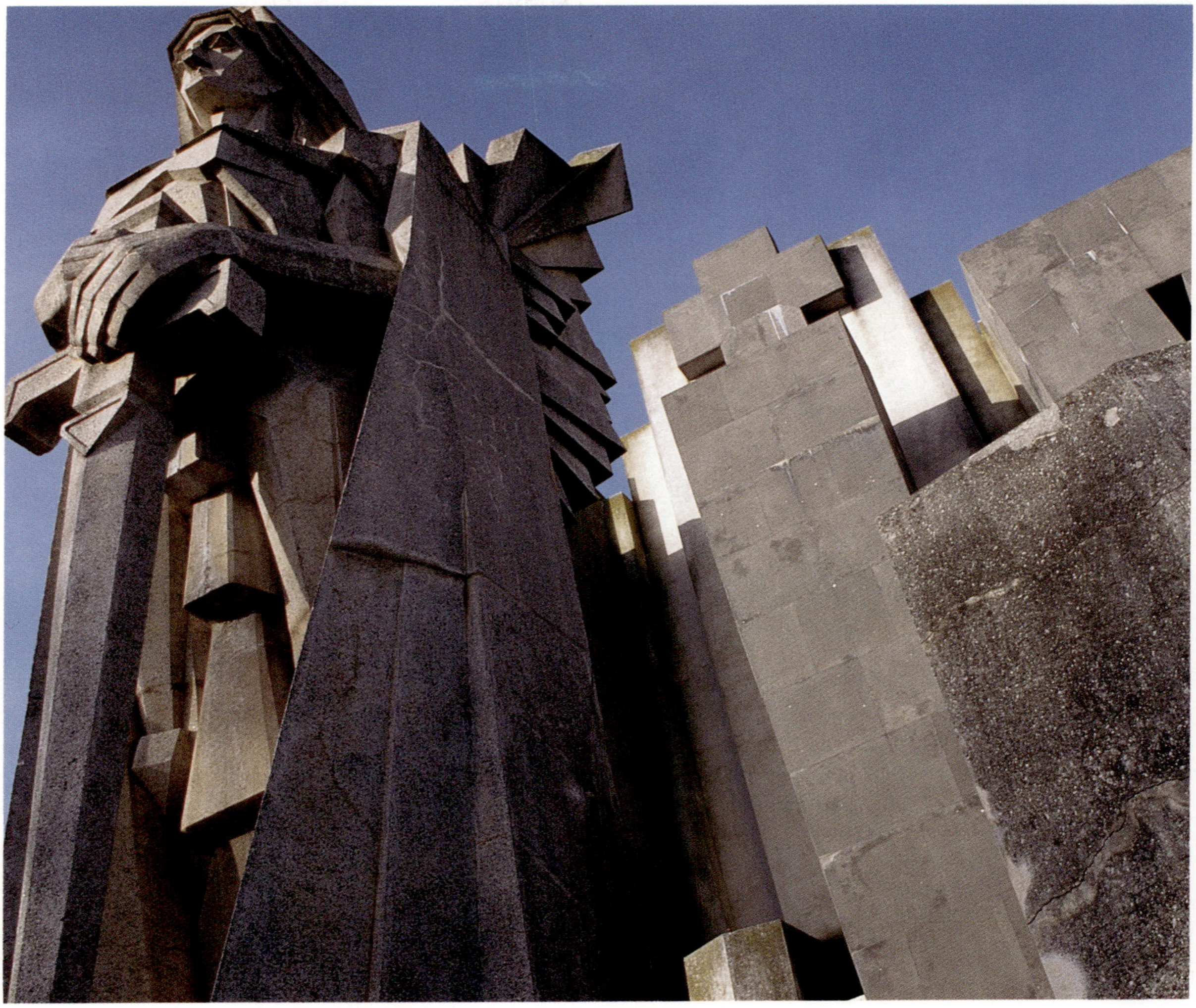

▲

Fig. 40. Azul cemetery, angel, sculpture in reinforced concrete.

◄

Fig. 41. Azul cemetery, angel, sculpture in reinforced concrete, detail.

Fig. 42. Credit for work on the cemetery of Azul. In the top line Governor Fresco is mentioned, in the middle line Salamone as "technical director and designer," in the bottom line the construction company.

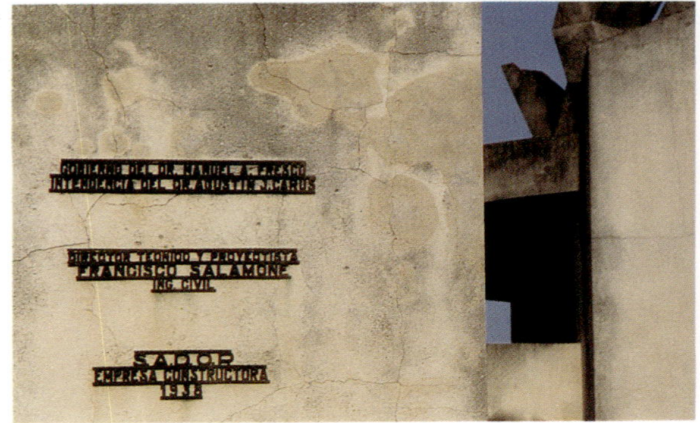

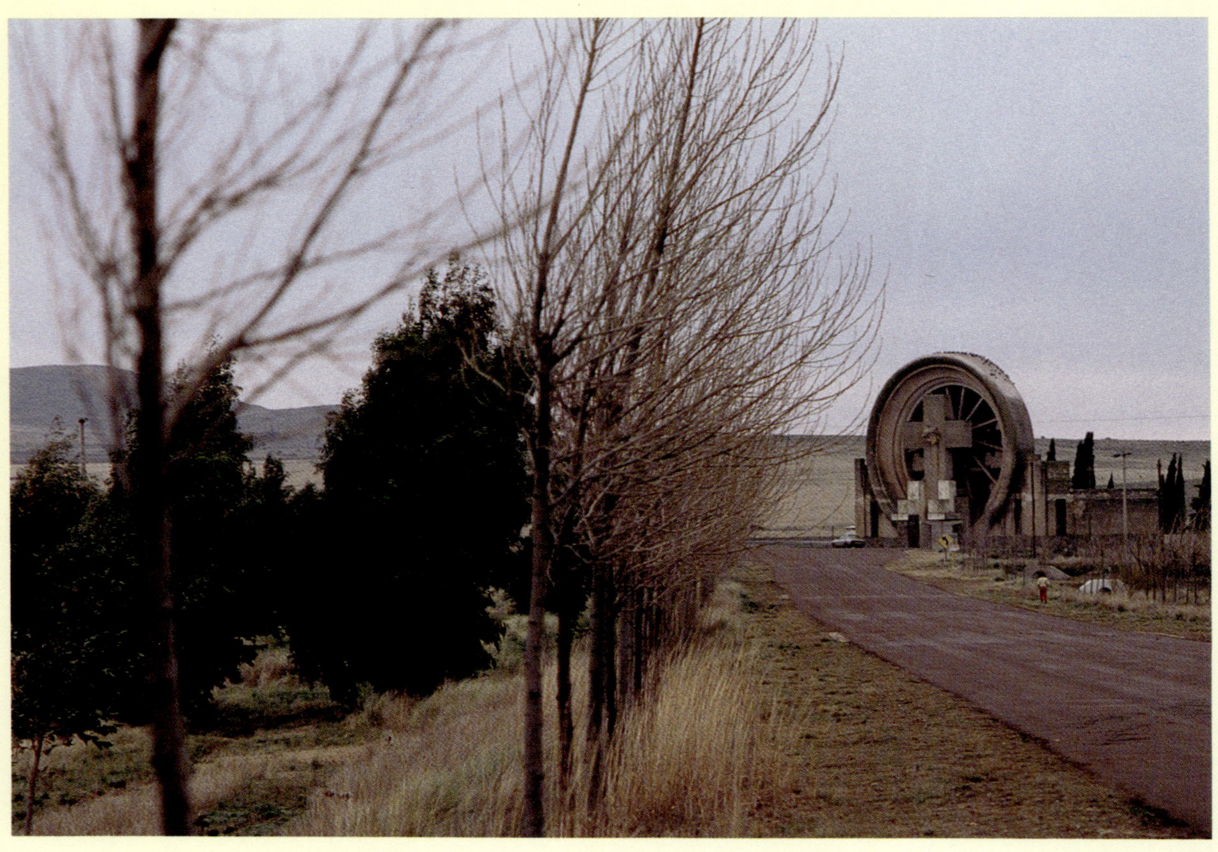

Fig. 43. Saldungaray cemetery, approach to the monumental portal.

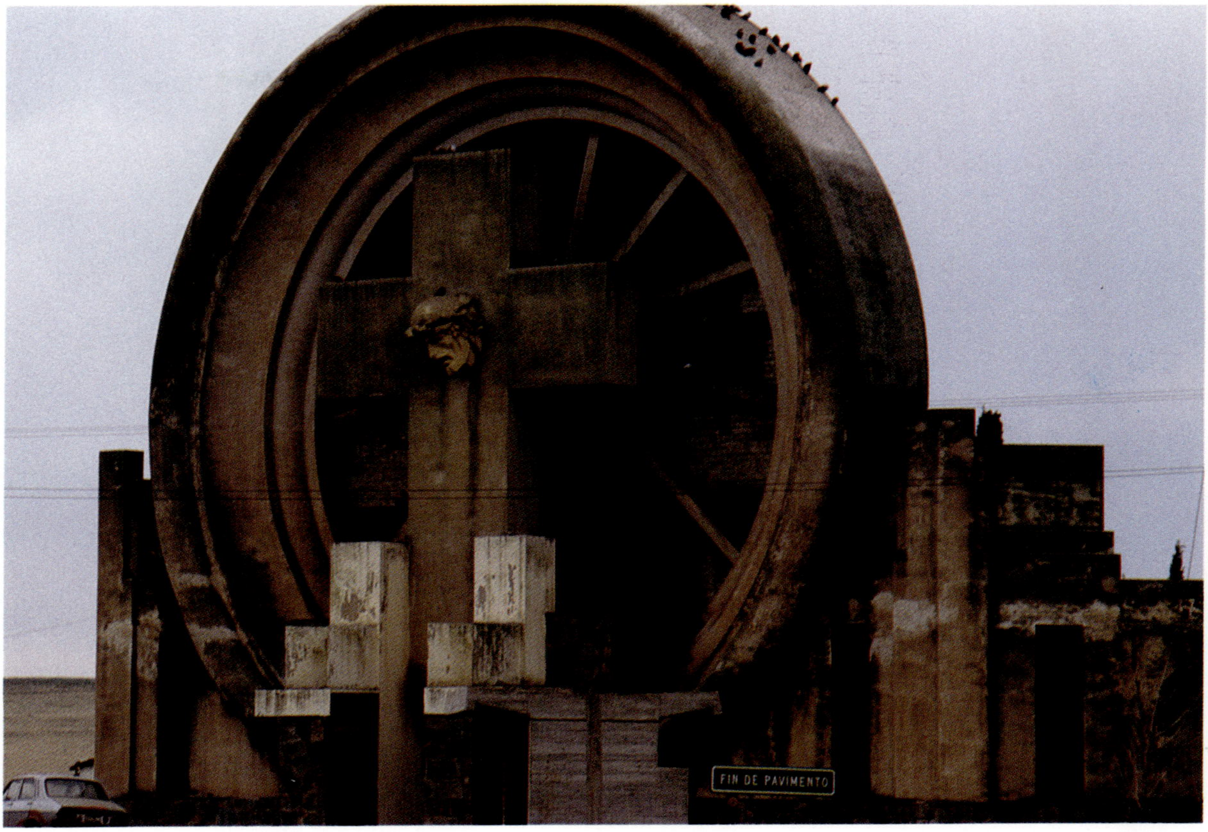

Fig. 44. Saldungaray cemetery, monumental portal.

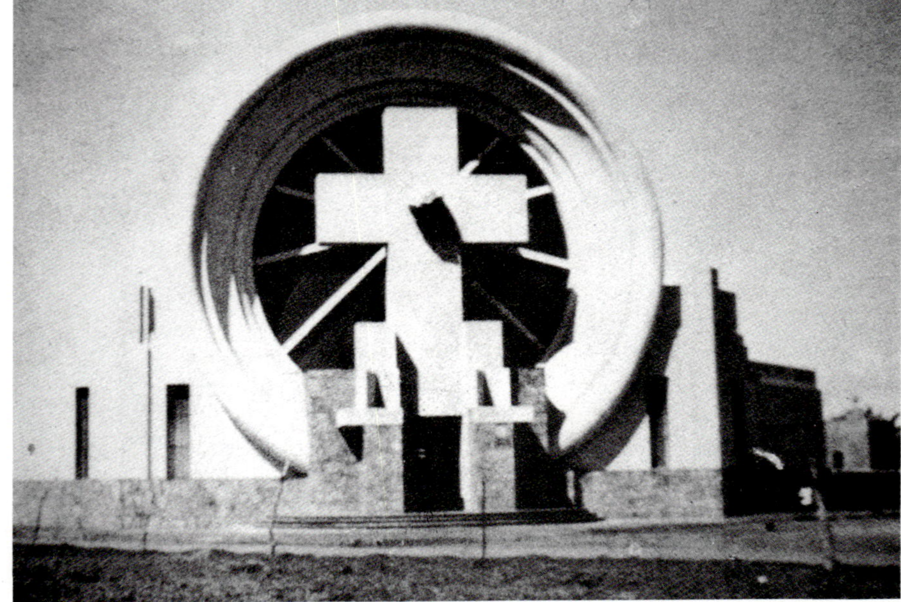

Fig. 45. Saldungaray cemetery, monumental portal. The disk is approximately 18 meters in diameter. Historic photograph.

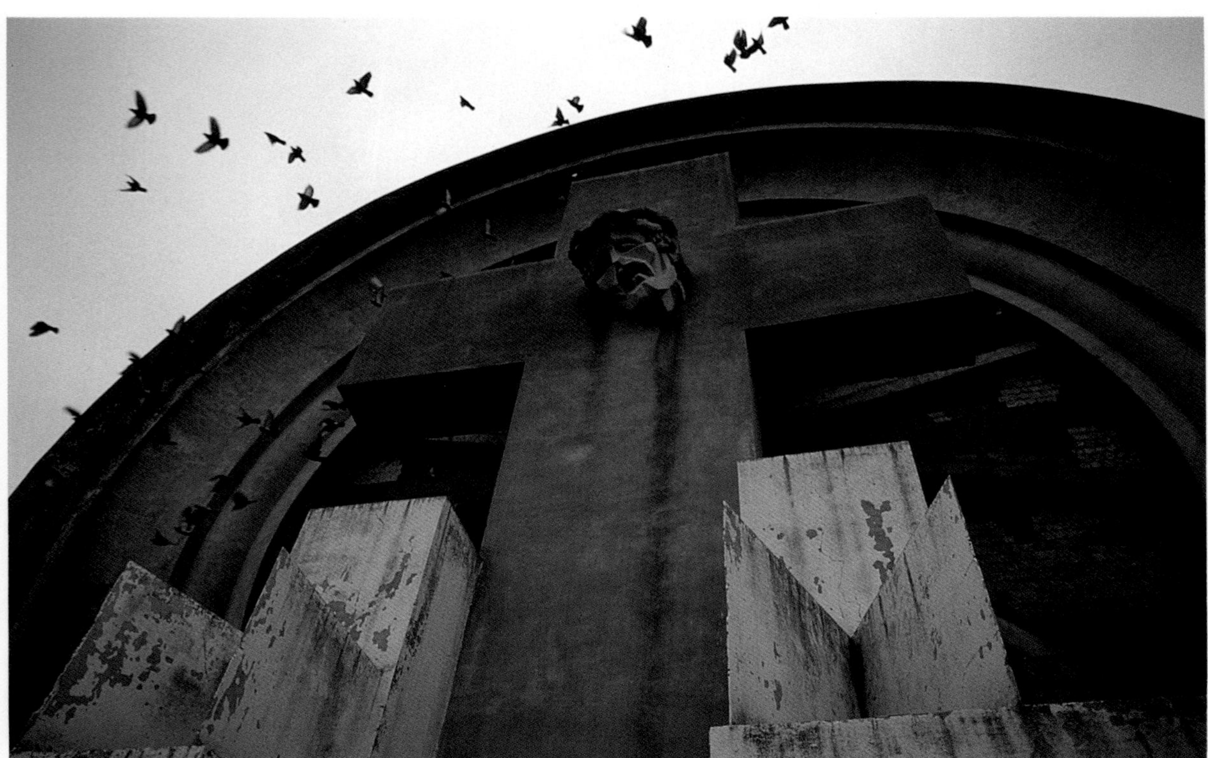

Fig. 46. Saldungaray cemetery, head of Christ molded in concrete, background of a cross with rays of masonry and stonelike plaster. The radial fields are covered with blue vitrified ceramic.

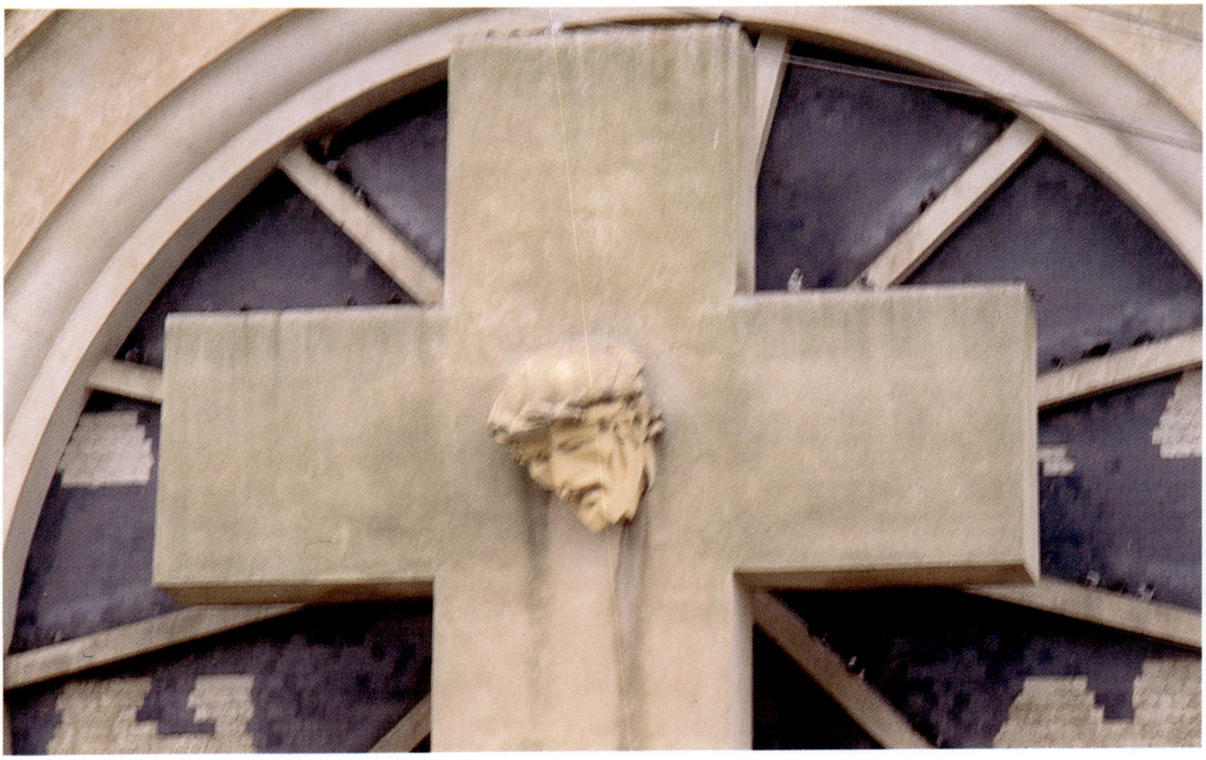

Fig. 47. Saldungaray cemetery, head of Christ molded in concrete, background of a cross with rays of masonry and stonelike plaster. The radial fields are covered with blue vitrified ceramic.

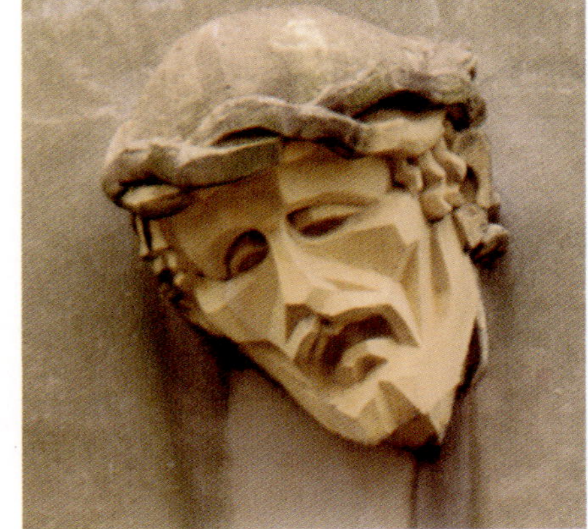

Fig. 48. Saldungaray cemetery, head of Christ, detail.

Fig. 49. Pirro Ligorio, gate of Hell, Park of Monsters, Bomarzo, ca. 1551, which is similar in character to the Saldungaray cemetery portal.

someone named Cacavelos built in 1922, with a double circular entrance decorated with garlands and geometric figures, halfway between Liberty and art deco (fig. 50). The relation between the images of the theater on Martín García and Saldungaray's entrance is obvious and one could have been the inspiration for the other. But we cannot discard as antecedent the monumental circular entrance to the house of the Grand Duke Ernst Ludwig in Darmstadt, designed by Josef Maria Olbrich in 1899. Salamone surely knew of this design as he was well informed about early twentieth-century German architecture. Four-and-a-half centuries separate and unite the mysteries of initiation and the circular entrances of the Dukes of Orsini and Darmstadt. Even farther away, from the pagan *bocca della veritá* in the Roman atrium of Santa Maria in Cosmedin, passing through the gate of Hell about which Dante chants "lasciate ogni speranza voi ch'entrate," come layered images of contact between daily reality and the indifference of eternity. With the plain, almost elemental realization of a spectacular project, Saldungaray continues to evoke this tremendous imagery, even in the twentieth century.

It has been more than fifty years since these works were built, but we still are

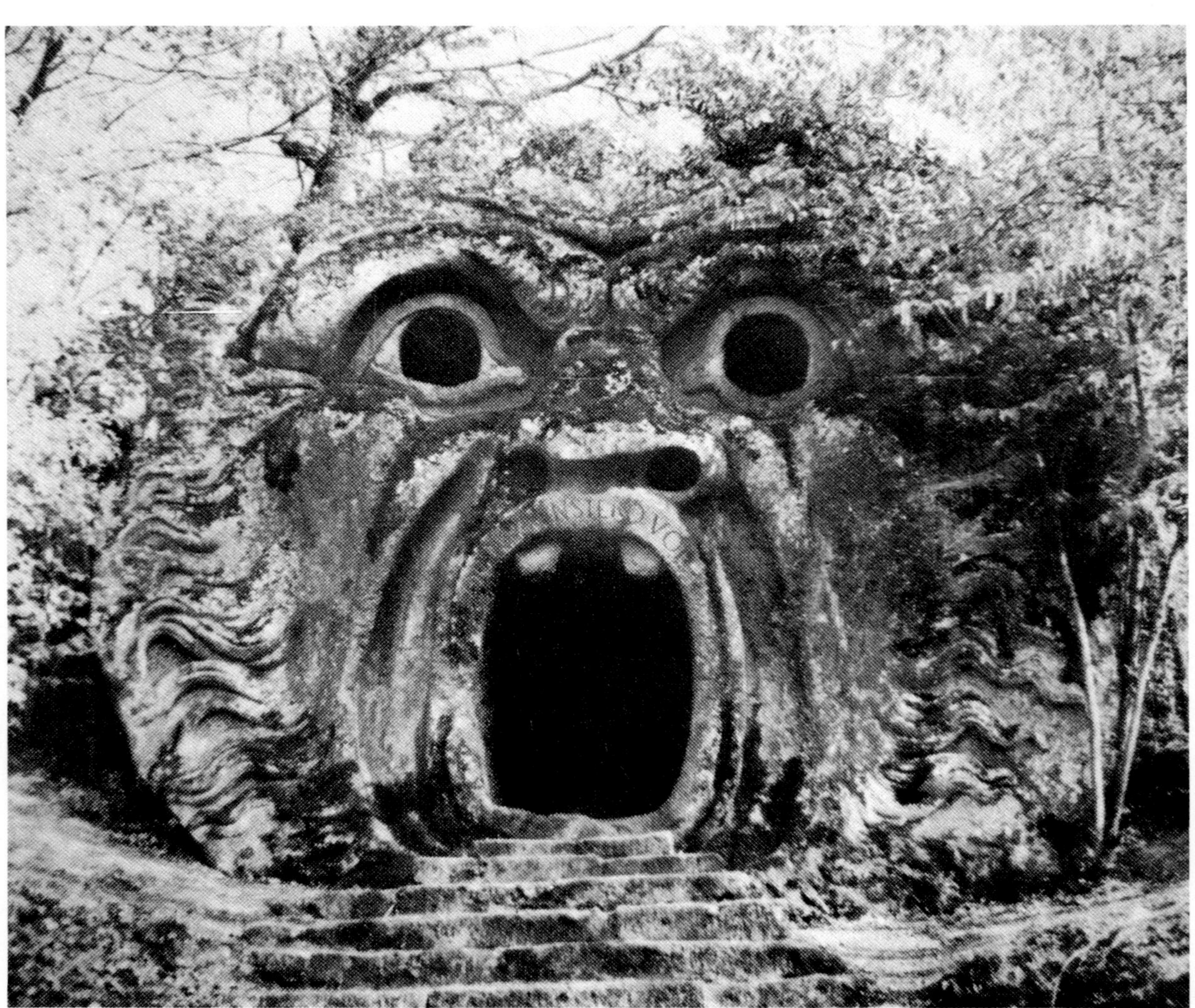

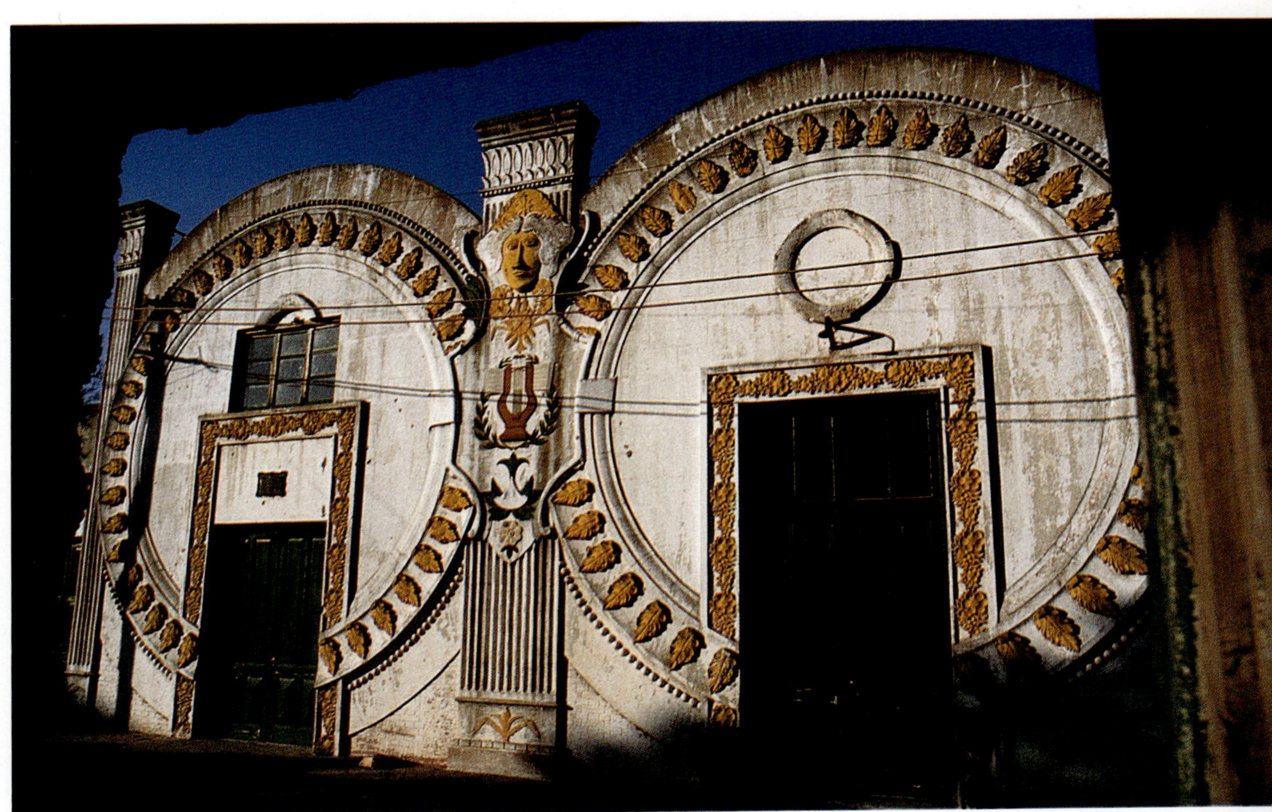

Fig. 50. Cacavelos, double portico of a theater on Martín García Island, constructed in 1922, which may have served as inspiration for the Saldungaray cemetery portal.

too close to certain authoritarian implications surrounding their creation to attempt a more dispassionate analysis based on specifically architectural, decorative, and communicative values.

In Europe and the United States, critical views of recent history have been approached from several different angles. As Charles Jencks reflects, "[W]e are becoming removed enough from the thirties to enjoy a Stripped Classicism without having to put up with the specter of Fascism. The attempt by those such as Aldo Rossi and Leon Krier to use Fascist and Stalinist forms in a new context has, precisely because of the many new uses, partially resemanticised the forms. We are slowly rehabilitating them, purging them of their negative associations through tentative distortions and tying them to new social institutions. This resemanticisation may be complete in another ten years, since the consumption of images today is much faster than in the past."[14] Twelve years have passed since these words were written, and the diagnosis has proved correct, beyond the coincidence or not of the historicist focus created by postmodernism. For us, in the southernmost part of South America, the time has come to rediscover the combined elements of surprise, size, evocation, and geometry in urban art that Salamone sowed in the pampas. They can validly be added to our future proposals for enhancing the urban scene. □

14. Charles Jencks, "Post-Modern Classicism," *Architectural Design*, no. 5/6 (1980): 6–7.

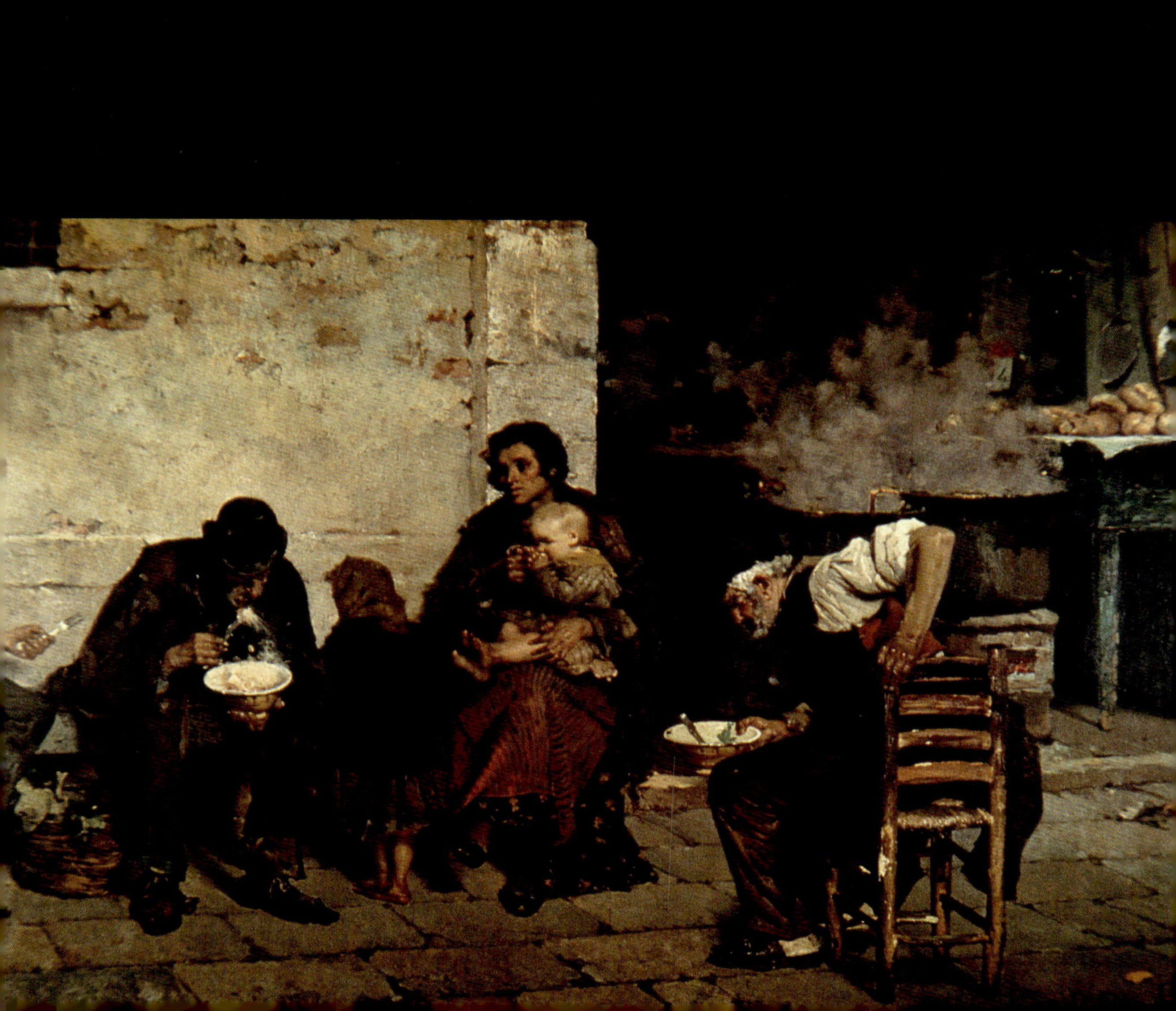

An Approach to Social Realism in Argentine Art: 1875–1945

By Marcelo Pacheco

Translated by Jon R. Snyder

Marcelo Pacheco is assistant director of the National Museum of Fine Arts in Buenos Aires. He graduated with honors from the National University of Buenos Aires and went on to earn a masters degree in art history. He has taught there and at other state and private institutions. A specialist in Argentine art, 1910–1940, he has contributed to publications at the National University of Buenos Aires and the National Museum of Fine Arts.

Most studies of Argentine art attempt to fit Argentine painting into the categories of European art. This process causes an almost literal extrapolation of those characteristics and fails to take into account Argentina's distance from Europe and the time needed for Argentine culture to assimilate European ideas. Thus, in the homologation or ratification of Argentine art, there is always a dichotomy: the divorce between written analysis of it, following pre-established theoretical models defined by the European experience, and the paintings themselves which respond to a creative dynamism in Argentine reality. Therefore, we must keep in mind that we are working with a "preconceived ratification," one which subordinates local artistic production to the principles of European art history.[1] Social realism is also a victim of this procedure, and it is important to note its extreme mobility in terms of time and stylistic definition.

Social realism appeared in the nineteenth century with the rise of modern industrialized societies in which social struggles began to emerge and the proletariat was first defined. In countries like Italy or France, some forms of realism or naturalism took a stance of criticism and commitment to social reality with the aim of denouncing and transforming it. Artists have incorporated into this image the themes of the defense of the worker and of marginal sectors of society. Then expressionism emerged, for example, in Germany, to be renewed in the language of the avant-garde. However, the tendency known as social realism, which is neither a school nor a style nor a closed historical category, is present—if not always visible—throughout the history of art, flowering in distinct moments and enveloped in various esthetic formal orders specific to certain groups or individual artists.

Therefore, we are not faced with the study of a local movement, stylistically and chronologically speaking, but rather with a vital attitude of commitment to the analysis of art's relation to reality and the world. The concept of homologation, and social realism as a constant tendency both open and variable, are two fundamental ideas to bear in mind in the following discussion of social realism in Argentina between 1875 and 1945.

Between 1862 and 1880, the successive rule of three constitutionally elected presidents—Mitre, Sarmiento, and Avellaneda—signaled in Argentina the onset of a new historical era marked by political stability and dizzying economic and

1. Marcelo Eduardo Pacheco, *Aproximación a la pintura argentina. Necesidad de una construcción teórica diferente* and Marcelo Eduardo Pacheco, *Malharro, Fader y Pettoruti según el criterio de homologación*. These papers were presented at the Primera Jornadas de Teoría e Historiografía del Arte, Buenos Aires, 1989.

social change. The so-called liberal republic began in 1880 with the first presidency of Julio Roca. This is frequently defined, as much in cultural as in political and economic terms, as the Generation of the '80s. It was the period of predominance of a recently formed social class, the paternalistic oligarchy, who retained power in every area of the nation's life for more than thirty-five years. This occurred within the framework of a republican presidential system whose elections were held without secret ballots. Throughout these decades, Argentina defined her economic and social as well as cultural profiles.

For the first time in history, the project of forming a country crystallized in a realistic way thanks to the overwhelming initiative of the ruling class, which was sure of its objectives, precise in its methods and strategies, and clear on its national as well as international models. A number of the endemic problems of Argentina in the nineteenth century were rapidly, although not always structurally, resolved. The modernization of the nation, synonymous with its europeanization, was undertaken in a decisive manner. During these years the system of public administration was organized; the first political parties emerged; Buenos Aires was declared a federal district; productive land was recuperated—15,000 square leagues, despite being occupied by indigenous peoples. This appropriation hastened the extermination of the native populace during the last military campaign in the desert in 1879. In the economic sphere, the export of beef products and later agricultural goods grew, and foreign investments guaranteed by the state arrived—especially British, North American, and German. The population rose notably because of immigration, largely Spanish and Italian. This changed the social, economic, demographic, and cultural profile in Argentina.[2] Furthermore, a keen opposition was defined between the ancient, colonial mentality and the new mentality of the river area; there was a sense of a profound difference between the large cities and the countryside as well as between the capital, now a cosmopolitan metropolis, and the rest of the country. There was the business of land speculation; successive loans were received by the state, and inflation generated; monetary stability was permanently altered by immense public expenditure bringing about constant economic crisis—for example, the financial crisis of 1890—within an apparently well-off and growing nation.

It was, in addition, the era of the discourse of nationalism, an ideological debate that subsequently appeared among intellectuals and artists. It was also the era of Comte's and Spencer's positivism and Zola's naturalism, of the evolutionary theories of Darwin, the influence of Taine, and the public debate between lay and Catholic factions.[3]

By the end of the century, socialism and anarchy appeared together within the newly born proletariat—especially in the food and textile industries. Workers began to use strikes as an active method in the fight against excessive workdays, low wages, unemployment, and electoral fraud. While wealthy classes believed in the "progress" that they saw taking place daily through the action of their government, the working classes (rural groups, immigrants, and children of immigrants in the cities), the middle class, small military groups, and a

2. In some places, such as the coastal areas of the country, in fifteen years the population increased up to 70 percent. In the census of 1895, the country had 3,995,000 inhabitants, 25 percent of them foreigners, and in 1914 the number had grown to 7,885,000, with 30 percent foreigners. The immigration process was unusual in that there was no colonizing policy; thus, immigrants moved into already populated sections, such as the coastal sections or Buenos Aires.

3. During the Generation of the '80s, Argentina sanctioned the laws of Civil Registration of Persons; the law of Civil Matrimony; and law 1420, which assured obligatory, free, and secular education.

dissident sector of traditional classes found themselves in opposition, generating a sense of restlessness that every day grew stronger.

Around 1910, the opposition between the interests of Conservatives in the government and the Radical party, between the upper class, the middle class who were growing more and more aware of their political power, and the working class became evident. The Roque Sáenz Peña law sanctioning secret and obligatory voting (based on military conscription lists) made possible the coming to power of the Radicals in 1916 with the election of Hipólito Yrigoyen as president of the nation.

Different social sectors, which until now had been marginal and powerless and which did not belong to the Generation of the '80s, came to occupy the centers of decision-making. The Creole population and the children of immigrants began a social process of economic ascension by way of professions such as medicine, law, and engineering; commerce; and the production of and access to public functions and positions. Immigration began again, the rural population declined,[4] and, proportionally, the concentration of people in the cities grew. There, where greater social mobility was possible because of the presence of the middle class, which tended to level out and integrate people independent of their origins, one found prospects for education and improved economic conditions. Since 1914, international prices of farm products had begun to decline, greatly affecting the local economy. Excessive public spending constantly caused budget deficits. The permanent rise of prices and the decline of real salaries raised the level of social tensions and increased the number of strikes as well as governmental repression, with its outbreaks of violence instigated by organizations of employers and managers. A high level of unemployment was, in large measure, related to the shrinkage suffered by those industries that had grown during the First World War. The structure by which Conservative groups held power remained intact in the provincial districts, in the parliament, and in the justice system, while the economic system continued its decline within the large landholding sectors and the cattle industry.

The First World War, during which time Argentina remained neutral, and the Russian Revolution of 1917 were the international events that most influenced the country. Protectionism, long sponsored by the upper classes, continued under the same paternalistic seal of the Radical government and the popular leaders. This was also the era of university reform (1918), the reaction against positivism, and the diffusion of neo-Kantianism, Bergson, and Croce.

In 1922, Marcelo T. de Alvear became president as a representative of radicalism; once in power, his politics was oriented toward a right-wing democracy closer to the interests of the traditional classes. In 1928, Yrigoyen was again elected president. However, internal pressure groups, including a politicized military and Conservatives who had been dislodged from power in 1916, returned to the political arena for a number of reasons, such as the influence of Italian Fascism inside Argentina, the pressure from international petroleum companies, and the sense of menace that the global crisis of 1929 had caused in local cattle dealers. These combined to trigger an institutional fracture, occurring with the Conservative military revolution of September 1930 and with electoral fraud in the election of General Augustín P. Justo, who assumed power in 1932.

What developed was a country closed to immigration, with an entrenched politics of internal and external loans, experiencing the readjustment of the

4. In 1914, the rural population made up 42 percent of the total; in 1930, it had been reduced to 32 percent.

economy in favor of large national producers and the interests of foreign investors. The tradition of private initiative, sustained until then by both the ruling Conservatives and Radicals, was altered by overt political interventionism through the creation of all types of government regulation. Industry grew and new social sectors sprang up around the cities, especially around Buenos Aires, altering the demographic configuration of the country and the outline of national union organizations.[5] In 1937, the General Confederation of Workers (CGT), originally founded in 1930, was consolidated. Opposition movements were persecuted by the government.

Electoral fraud was used again in 1938 to assure the continuity of this program via the election of Roberto Ortiz and Ramón Castillo. The Spanish Civil War and World War Two polarized opinions throughout Argentina. Ortiz decreed neutrality in the global conflict,[6] but broad sectors of the military sympathized with the Axis powers and distributed pro-Nazi newspapers throughout the country (subsidized by the German Embassy). In 1943, a military coup led by Pedro Ramírez, minister of war, led to the fall of the government. In February 1944, General Edelmiro Farrell replaced Ramírez. Next, a new protagonist began to appear on the national scene: Juan Domingo Perón, under secretary of war and secretary of labor and social services. Perón simultaneously looked to the military and the labor unions for support.

The basic components of the Argentine esthetic field were defined around 1870. These were the years in which a group of artists and intellectuals, especially writers, organized the local fine arts through the creation of the Sociedad Estímulo de Bellas Artes (Society for the encouragement of the fine arts) in 1877, with its exhibition halls, library, specialized journal, and Teacher's Academy. The Forum, with its courses in drawing and art history as well as its collective annual exhibitions and auctions, was inaugurated in 1892. The National Museum of Fine Arts was founded in 1895. The Witcomb Gallery was created in 1896, and the first important group of local collectors, in general not interested in Argentine art, appeared.

The same generation that formed and organized a political, economic, and social plan for the country also outlined and defined the essential nature of artistic institutions, the market, art collecting, teaching—all aspects of visual culture bearing on the subsequent development of Argentine painting. Also, the first theoretical model for the history of national art was established through the critical and historical work of Eduardo Schiaffino, who wrote columns in *El Diario* and *La Nación*. Working in the final decades of the past century were such painters as Eduardo Sívori, Angel della Valle, Ernesto de la Cárcova, Eduardo Schiaffino, Reinaldo Gíudici, and Graciano Mendilaharzu. Francisco Cafferata and Lucio Correa Morales were the first two native sculptors.

For this generation, travel to Europe in order to perfect technique was a fundamental step in professional development. And, in this respect, it is important to point out that despite the significance of France as a cultural model for the Argentina of 1880, in the case of the plastic arts, northern Italy exercised the greatest influence almost until the end of the century. Della Valle studied in Florence in Ciseri's studio between 1875 and 1883; Gíudici studied first in Rome with Maccari between 1877 and 1879 and later in Venice with Favretto

5. In 1947, 3,386,000 of the working class had moved from their place of birth, 50 percent to the suburbs of Buenos Aires (the origin of the overcrowded belt of Greater Buenos Aires), 28 percent to the coast, and 22 percent to other regions of the country.

6. Argentina did not declare war on Germany and Japan until March 1945.

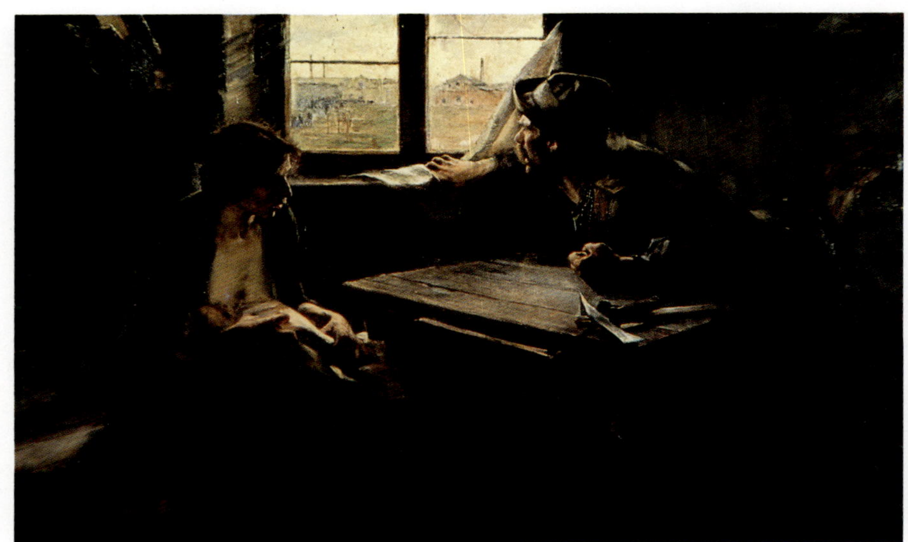

Fig. 2. Ernesto de la Cárcova, *Sin pan y sin trabajo* (Without bread and without work), oil on canvas, 126 x 175 cm, 1893. National Museum of Fine Arts, Buenos Aires.

from 1880 to 1886. De la Cárcova, before traveling to Paris in 1890, lived in Turin, studying with Grosso at the Albertine Academy. Correa Morales arrived on scholarship in Florence in 1874 to study at the Academy of Fine Arts with Lucchesi (who would also become Cafferata's teacher). Included in this group was Schiaffino, already the strongest defender of the French tradition before settling in Paris in 1885. In order to participate at the Colarossi Academy, he stayed for several months in Venice studying with Lancelotto. The youngest group, who journeyed to Europe at the end of the decade of the 1880s, would more frequently opt for Paris, a tendency almost exclusively adhered to by the generations that followed.[7]

Travel in Italy, and the influence of teachers from northern Italy, were keys to the theme of social realism for this generation. The artists lived their formative years in a country, namely Italy, that was convulsed by social struggles, and those struggles were reflected in the works of the naturalist painters. They took from reality that aspect of the social, either from within certain quasi-romantic tendencies that were not always distanced from anecdotal interpretation, or from within a critical posture that would go beyond the traditional "compositional frame."

As a result of this, three canvases, all produced in Europe, are most representative of this era in Argentine art: *La sopa de los pobres* (fig. 1) by Reinaldo Gíudici, made in Venice, 1884; *Sin pan y sin trabajo* (fig. 2) by Ernesto de la Cárcova, painted between Rome and Buenos Aires in 1893; and *El despertar de la criada* (fig. 3) by Eduardo Sívori, completed in Paris, 1887.

In the case of the first two works, their inclusion in the trend of social realism is clear. Gíudici describes the urgent situation of the working classes while avoiding anecdotal local color and concentrating on the effect of a painting with a strong naturalistic character. It depicts marginal figures gathered around a common pot in the midst of the street: children, elderly people, and a mother with her son are isolated by their own indigence and united by their shared misery. The painter knew how to create a composition in which each of its functions permits it to skillfully resolve the esthetic problems posed, while

7. We must point out, in addition, the importance Spain had for some artists, such as Jorge Bermúdez and Cesáreo B. de Quirós, in the first decade of the twentieth century.

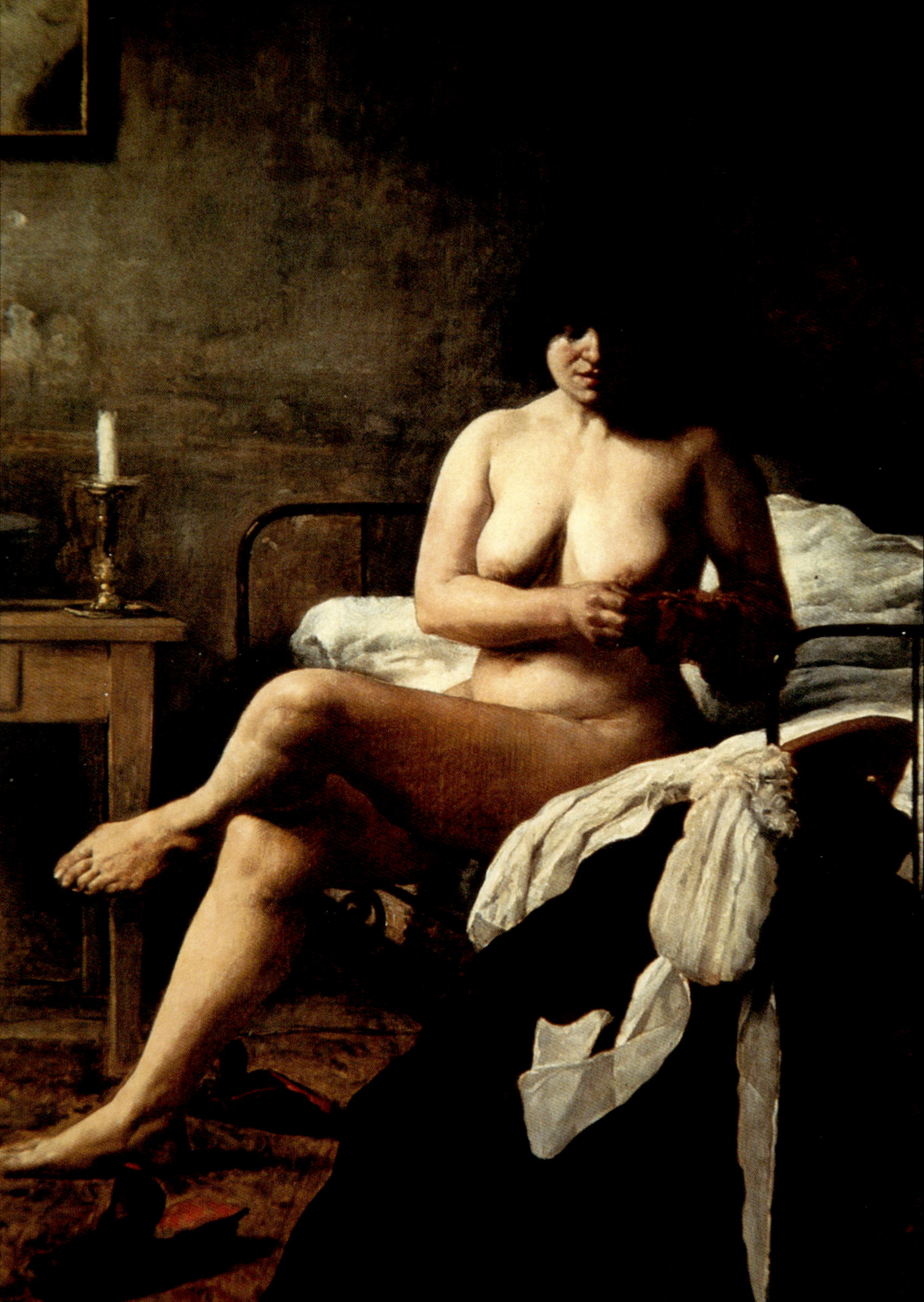

Fig. 3. Eduardo Sívori, *El despertar de la criada* (The maid's awakening), oil on canvas, 192 x 131 cm, 1887. National Museum of Fine Arts, Buenos Aires.

producing a scenario in which dramatic tension is neutralized, in part, by the predominantly regional tone and theatrical emphasis of the individual figures and their spatial resolution. The origin of the subject and the pictoral style, too, is clearly related to the work of his teacher from those years in Venice, namely Giacomo Favretto. In the case of *Sin pan y sin trabajo*, its strength of expression is ably displayed in the drawing, the brushstrokes, the light effects, and the choice of the principal elements of the picture: the helplessness of the worker pounding his fist on the empty table next to his useless work tools, the desolate mother who cannot feed her child, and the factory that one sees from the window with its chimneys extinguished while the army advances. In a synthesized account, free of descriptive details, de la Cárcova presents misery, hunger, unemployment, social injustice, and pain. In this case, the theatricality of gesture and space do not diminish the effect of the beating fist, but rather accentuate the esthetic and conceptual tension. The question is, what is the intention of the painter in his *Sin pan y sin trabajo*?[8] The same question is valid with respect to *La sopa de los pobres* of Gíudici. "Is it a question of scenes conceived with the intention of imitating reality for the viewer, to awaken his or her social conscience, or do painters see their subjects as representative of some aspect other than the multiple reality that surrounds them? Social realism or critical realism is the question."[9]

For example, Gíudici, upon his return to Buenos Aires, devoted himself primarily to teaching and to painting historical compositions, landscapes, portraits, and decorative works. In the case of de la Cárcova, figure paintings, landscapes, and portraits (fig. 5)[10] occupied the greater part of his production from 1893 on, parallel to his career as a public figure. There is no sign of social realism in his later works. We return to a key theme in this early social realism in Argentina: the lack of articulation of such works within the artists' production and the lack of a defined ideological stance.

El despertar de la criada tangentially approaches social realism when Sívori chooses the undressing of a maid as his subject. The atmosphere, the light of the room, and the objects arranged in the scene describe the way of life of a French servant at the end of the 1880s. Academic, romantic, and realistic elements coincide in the personal style of the Argentine artist. There exists here a message to decode. Reality is brutally synthesized. The social nature of the theme is expressed by the model chosen and also by the esthetic syntax. Here, without a doubt, Sívori paints a female nude, concentrating his energy and attention upon this task. And it is precisely this aspect (nudity) that provoked a scandal in Buenos Aires when the work was exhibited privately in 1887 in the Salóns of the Sociedad Estímulo de Bellas Artes. Criticism, at the time, was directed toward the unabashed and unusually realistic character of the nude.

"Now then, must we classify this picture as pornographic? We think that one could classify it thus without affecting in the least the intrinsic value of the work as a true reflection of reality."[11]

8. The work was exhibited to the public in the second Salón de El Ateneo in 1894, without his contemporaries seeing in it any reference to the situation of social tension apparent in Argentina in those years.

9. Marcelo Pacheco and Ana María Telesca, *Aproximación a la generación del ochento (antología documental)* Facultad de Filosofía y Letras, Universidad Nacional de Buenos Aires, serie Historia del Arte, vol. 6, no. 3 (Buenos Aires, 1988), 6–7.

10. The portrait of *Señora M. de la C. de Ferrari* (fig. 5) of 1894, exhibited together with *Sin pan y sin trabajo* in the second Salón de El Ateneo, is a typical portrait affirming social status, following the general lines established in the seventeenth century.

11. *Sud-América*, 6 September 1887, 1, col. 5.

However, the choice of the work's esthetic theme was negatively assessed because of the scant interest that it generated rather than because of its possible social reference.

"The awakening of the servant!

"To whom would it occur to paint such a silly thing, above all when the servant is as terribly ugly and dirty as the one whom the artist has chosen?"[12]

After those experiments with aggressively realist art, Sívori concentrated upon the painting of local customs, landscapes, portraiture, and certain mythic themes of almost symbolic origin.

In the case of contemporary sculpture, two artists, Lucio Correa Morales and Francisco Cafferata, devoted themselves particularly to sculpture and the creation of portraits, nudes, allegories, historical figures, and busts of leaders and heroes as well as portraits of specific ethnic types such as the Indian and the mulatto. In these, the language of the academy and the craft learned in the studios of Florence coalesced, as one observes in Cafferata's *Esclavo* completed in 1882, in which one finds certain realistic intentions and great expressivity without directly confronting the social theme (fig. 4).

In the approach of the Generation of the '80s to social realism, the central points to bear in mind are the intellectual projections of European positivism and scientism, the lack of definition of a program of social realism, and the appearance of an esthetic which could be realistic or naturalistic, depending on the particular case. This esthetic was, as we have seen, connected to the studies of those artists in Italy or France. Furthermore, we find an esthetic language that prefers themes of a social nature in a sporadic manner and with an attitude somewhere in-between the romantic, the theatrical, the documentary, and the anecdotal. This is especially true in works completed during the years of study in Europe. With respect to this last point, the following reflections of Sívori, published in 1894, are worth mentioning here:

> A painter goes to Europe, studies and works there for years, makes paintings in his own style, and thinks of composing them in his native land. When he returns home, he finds that there is no market.... Why should he produce paintings of local culture which no one will buy?... So, with this sad knowledge, he devotes himself to portraiture and makes portraits and more portraits, alternating this with giving painting lessons,...the only way of making a living.... That is why Argentine painters create works of spirit and courage in Europe but do not continue to do so here.[13]

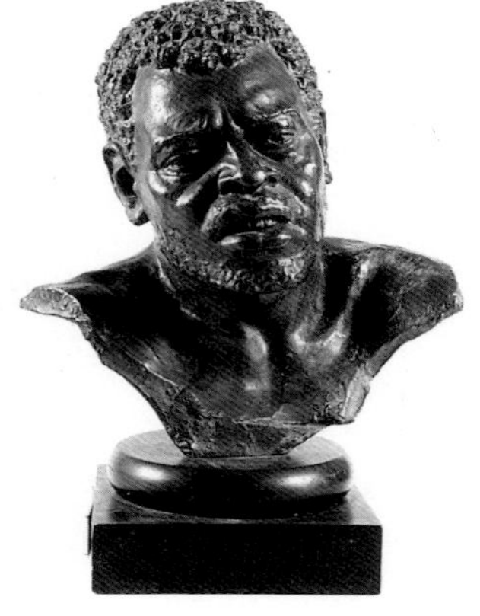

Fig. 4. Francisco Cafferata, *Esclavo* (Slave), bronze, h. 37", 1882. National Museum of Fine Arts, Buenos Aires.

The attitude marking the Generation of the '80s was prolonged in our century, although in a more modern pictorial style, in paintings such as *La hora del almuerzo* (fig. 6) by Pío Collivadino, painted in 1903.[14] A work such as this closed the first chapter of social realism in Argentina; but social realism still had not found its own language of confrontation or a functional ideological definition.

The early years of this century coincided with a call to impressionism in Argentina, issued first by Martín Malharro's one-man show in 1902 upon his return from Paris. These were also the years of a rupture with the positivism of

12. *El Censor*, 12 September 1887, 1, col. 2–3.

13. "II Salón de El Ateneo," *La Nación,* 5 November 1894.

14. Collivadino trained in Buenos Aires with the Italian master Francesco Romero at the Academy of the Society for the Encouragement of the Fine Arts and traveled to Rome in 1889 to attend the Academy of Fine Art.

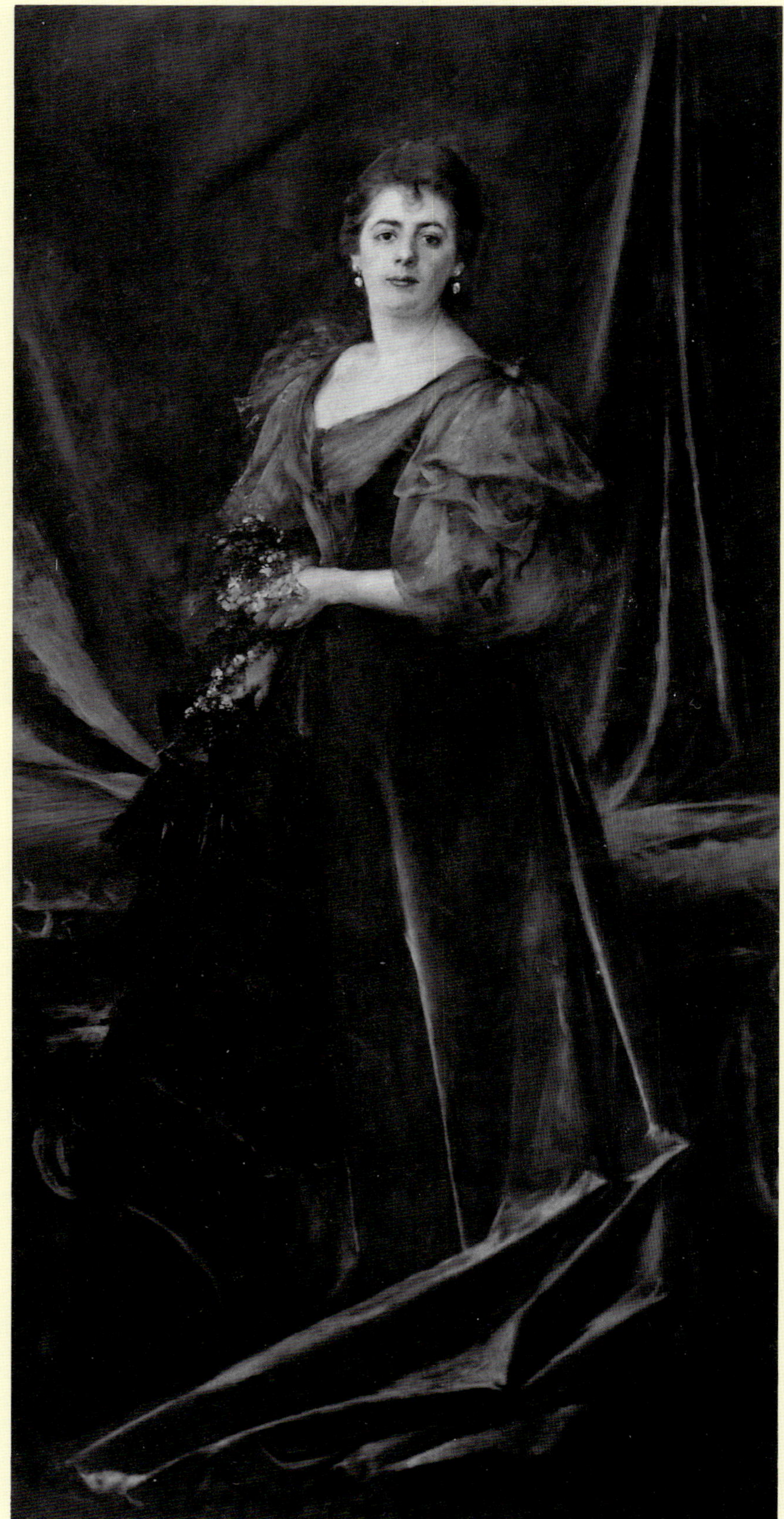

Fig. 5. Ernesto de la Cárcova, *Sra. M. de la C. de Ferrari*, oil on canvas, 251 x 126 cm, 1894. National Museum of Fine Arts, Buenos Aires.

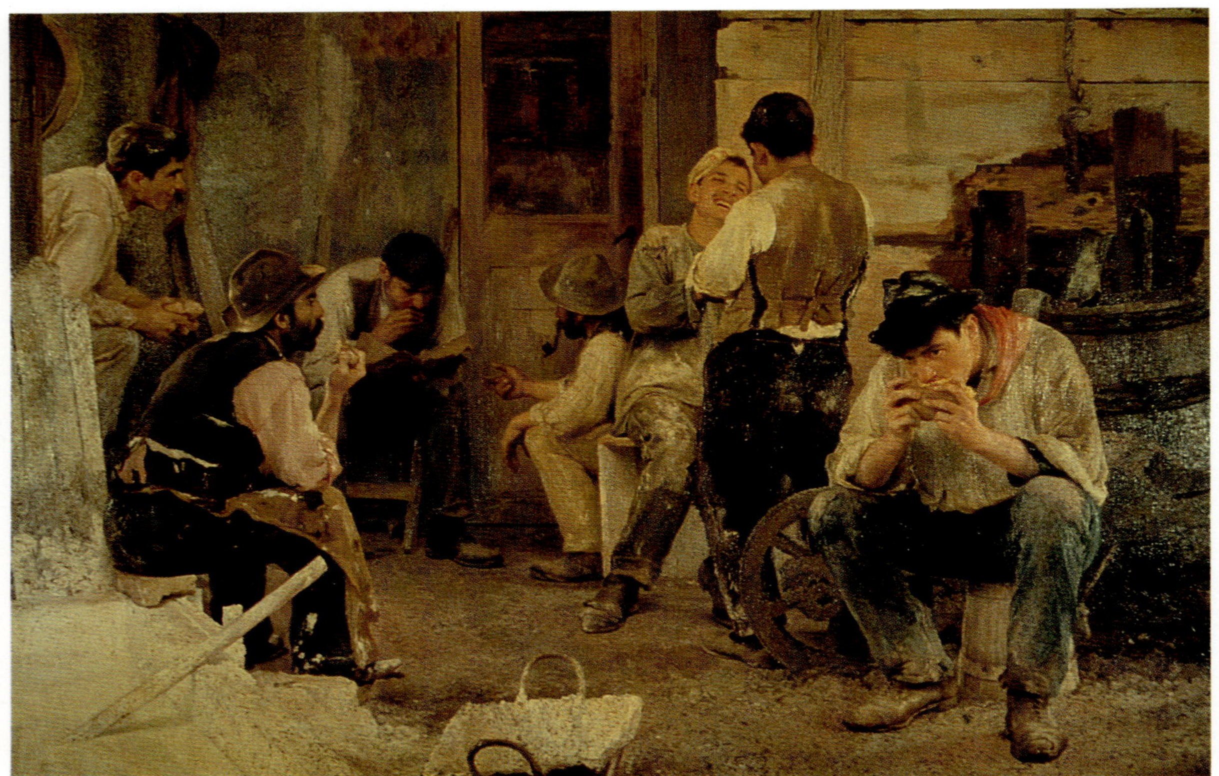

Fig. 6. Pío Collivadino, *La hora del almuerzo* (Lunch hour), oil on canvas, 160 x 252 cm, 1903. National Museum of Fine Arts, Buenos Aires.

the late nineteenth century and a revival of the discussion concerning the definition of a national art.[15]

While Malharro embodied the modern position at the time as much by his theoretical outspokenness as by his artistic work, the Nexus group,[16] active since 1907, offered local artists a different mode of incorporation of impressionism and a nationalist variant tinged with *criollismo*.

In this respect, Ana María Telesca and José Emilio Burucúa have discovered an important distinction between an impressionist influence, in terms of a style both dynamic and modern, and an impressionism reduced to its technical, scientific elements, at once closed and repetitive.[17] In this context, there appeared in Argentine art the concept of the avant-garde: thus, two simultaneous trends were created that both converged and differed. The first of these was the trend toward renewal, now identified with the impressionism of Malharro or the postimpressionism of his followers.[18] The second of these was the officialism of the Nexus group and its satellites, in which academic origins, close to naturalism, are combined with the techniques of impressionism. In those

15. "The fact of being an artist born on Argentine soil does not imply that his work is nationalistic; the fact of painting native scenes does not represent our art." Malharro, 1903, cited in José Emilio Burucúa and Ana María Telesca, *El impresionismo en la pintura argentina. Análisis y crítica*, (Buenos Aires: Fundación Caja Nacional de Ahorro y Seguro, 1989), 91.

16. This Nexus group, the second in Argentine art, was formed by Cesáreo B. de Quirós, Carlos Ripamonte, Alberto Rossi, Fernando Fader, and Pío Collivadino, among others.

17. Burucúa and Telesca, *El impresionismo*, 95–96.

18. These stylistic concepts, resulting from the presupposition of homologation, are extrapolated literally and need to be revised in order to acquire local validity since otherwise they appear to be sterile, artificial, and empty applications.

years, Malharro established a clear reaction against positivist objectivity, while searching for an alternative stylistic definition.

His point of departure was linked to a work of theoretical philosophy by the French philosopher Jean-Marie Guyau, published posthumously in 1889. Guyau considered art as a means of communication between humans, allowing individual consciousness potentially to communicate with all consciousness. "Do you know what love is? The artist makes you feel all the emotions of love. How? By showing us a being that loves. We watch, we listen, and, within what is possible, we ourselves will love. All the arts, at bottom, are but multiple ways to condense individual emotion by making it immediately transmittable to another, to open it up in a social way. The interest that we take in a work of art is the consequence of an association that is established between us, the artist, and the personages of the work; it is a new society."[19]

Thus, Guyau includes the esthetic within a new field, that of scientific sociology. The narrow relation established by the French philosopher, between esthetic emotion—always of a social nature—and the creation of a different world superimposed on the known world, changes art into a powerful means for the transformation of societies. "[H]istory teaches us the civilizing effects of the arts on societies, or at times the opposite, its effect on social disintegration."[20]

Such ideas predicted an ideological and esthetic path for the Argentine painter. Starting with his articles in *El Diario*, and in the journals *Ideas*, *Athinae*, and *Ideas y figuras*, Malharro explained his esthetic and political beliefs which seemed to be a result of the conjunction between anarchy and nationalism.[21] In *Ideas y figuras*, one of the anarchistic journals directed by Alberto Ghiraldo, the painter published a series of critical drawings (figs. 7 and 8) of the political and economic reality of the time. Here, his works seek to bring to light the hypocrisy of the clergy and army, for example, vis-á-vis the marginalization and exploitation of immigrants. Malharro described another side of the coin as well: the myth of an abundant America and the promised land is transformed to the collective frustration of immigrants who are subject to unemployment and misery. These drawings, published in 1911, are an interesting chapter in the history of social realism in Argentina.

The painter resorts to the construction of synthetic images through rapid and accurate sketches, looking for the essential in a forceful expressive deformation. Each illustration is accompanied by an inscription or a statement, thus establishing the unity of the signified image-word, as in the case of the drawing *Reflexión* (fig. 8): "Twenty years as washerwoman, ten as ironer, and in the most wealthy homes, the most aristocratic...and today I gather garbage for my little ones! Is this the America of which my grandfather spoke to me?"

Between the sociology of Guyau, the esthetic modernism of impressionism, anarchy, and nationalism, Malharro found an artistic solution that allowed him to denounce social reality. With political ideology, intellectual posturing, and the search for style, all these elements converged to form a single program for this artist. The way was cleared for the appearance of the group known as Cinco Artistas del Pueblo (The five artists of the people), who were the founders of social art in Argentina.

19. Juan María Guyau, *El arte desde el punto de vista sociológico* (Madrid: 1902), 64–65.

20. Ibid., 100.

21. Burucúa and Telesca, *El impresionismo*, 89–91.

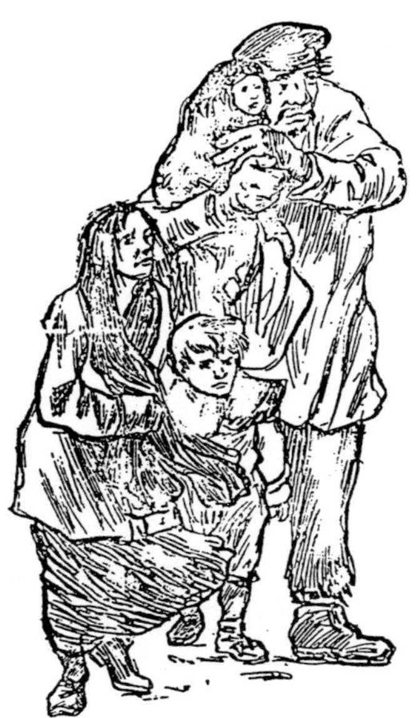

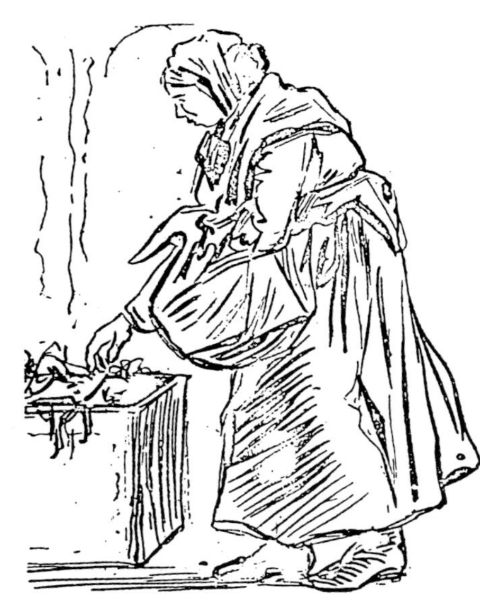

Fig. 7. Above left. Martín Malharro, *En el granero del mundo* (In the granary of the world), illustration for *Ideas y figuras*, vol. 3, no. 60 (26 October 1911). Private collection, Buenos Aires.

Fig. 8. Above right. Martín Malharro, *Reflexión* (Pondering), illustration for *Ideas y figuras*, vol. 3, no. 60 (26 October 1911). Private collection, Buenos Aires.

In 1911, the Salón Nacional Anual (Annual national salon) was created and became the space for an official consecration of artists. The tension already present in preceding decades between two artistic positions, one innovative and the other traditionalist, further increased, and there appeared two clear signs of the conflict underway: The Salón de Recusados (Challenger's salon) in 1914 and the Salón Independientes Sin Jurados y sin Premios (Salon for independent artists with neither prizes nor juries) in 1918.[22]

These offered an alternative space in which to exhibit artists' works that had been refused in the annual salons and in which to search for a different model in the face of the established practices of official juries and prizes. They were linked to a critical trend in local art: "[W]e come together in our endeavor to fill a void that exists in our nascent social arts."[23]

Already in those years, José Arato, Adolfo Bellocq, Guillermo Facio Hébequer, Abraham Vigo, and Agustín Riganelli shared nights of work, study, and discussion in a humble outbuilding of the Academy of the Society for the Encouragement of the Fine Arts. Also with them was Santiago Palazzo, who died prematurely in 1916 at age twenty-eight. These painters and graphic artists,[24] together with the sculptor Riganelli, formed the Baracas group, named for a neighborhood on the outskirts of Buenos Aires where they lived. They were also called the Boedo group and were linked to the leftist publication *Claridad*, whose writers were directly tied to them as much for their ideology as for their esthetic theories. Critics identified these young men as Artistas del Pueblo (Artists of the people), a pejorative denomination which they then proudly adopted as their own name.

> A profound psychological affinity unites us. We are what is called the *pueblo*, or people. [Around 1918,] we lived in the harbor area in solidarity with those workers dwelling there. We lived in the same dirty and inhospitable shacks and ate in the same foul places.... There, among the workers,

22. The Salón Independientes exhibition was the initial public presentation of the Salón Costa of the Sociedad Nacional de Artistas, Pintores y Escultores. Created in 1917, the Sociedad was the first artists' trade union.

23. Catalogue of the first Salón de Recusados, 1914.

24. Graphic art constituted the most important of their works and permitted its diffusion.

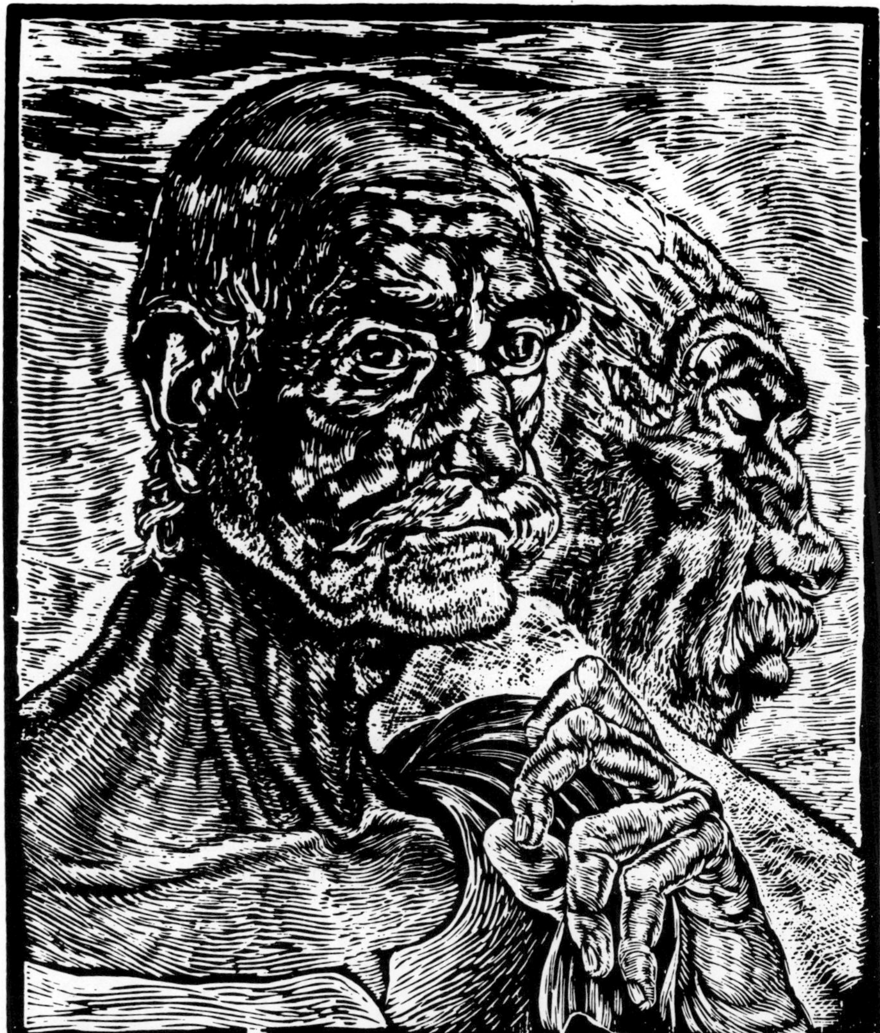

Fig. 9. Adolfo Bellocq, *Hurones* (Beggars), wood engraving, 1925. Private collection, Buenos Aires.

> I felt for the first time the shame of being no more than an "intellectual".... There we saw clearly the absurdity of the psychic masturbations occurring in art. In the face of this sad world of work and social misery, there is something superior to the "esthetic" and to "art"—that is the human being. Nothing separated us now from the right road.[25]

With the Artistas del Pueblo, a militant social realism was first defined and, for the first time in Argentina, reflection about the function of art in contemporary society acquired an active agenda of struggle and popular protest. Its painters and illustrators—especially wood-engravers, lithographers, and etchers—constituted the nucleus of an artistic group that, from a stylistic point of view, compelled social realism toward a deep-rooted, dramatic, and eloquent expressionism (fig. 9). Within the complex and rich panorama of the decade of the twenties, the Artistas del Pueblo established a clear alternative for Argentine art: an ideological vanguard proclaiming an art of ideas, centralized

25. Guillermo Facio Hébequer, 1935, cited in Miguel Angel Muñoz and Diana Weschler, *Los artistas del pueblo*, Galería Forma exposition catalogue (Buenos Aires: Sociedad Argentina de Artistas Plásticos, 1989).

Fig. 10. Ernesto de la Cárcova, *Naturaleza en silencio* (Nature in silence), oil on canvas, 73 x 92 cm. National Museum of Fine Arts, Buenos Aires.

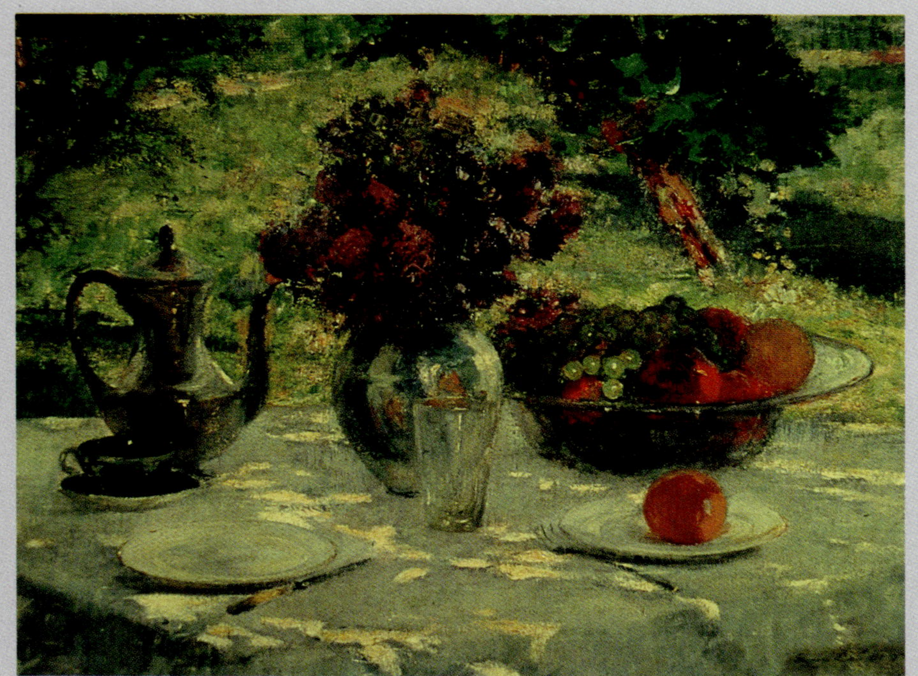

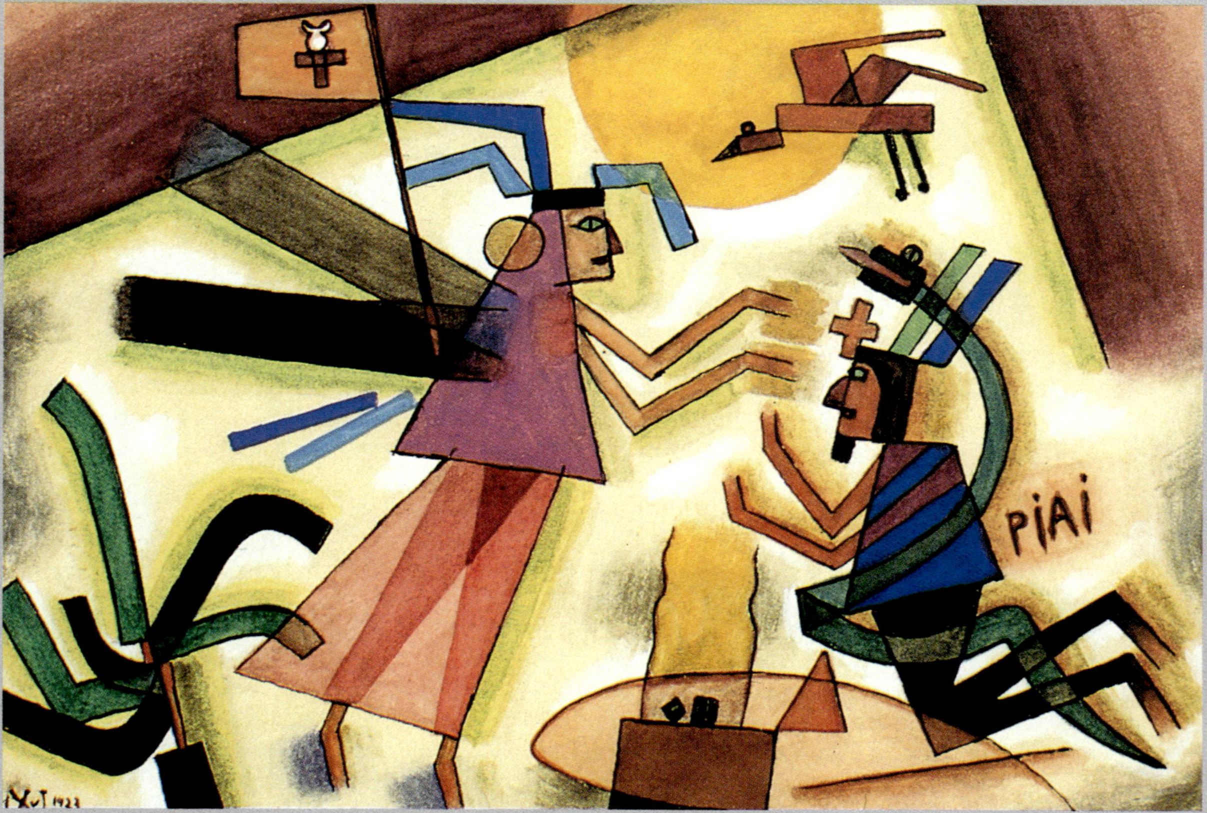

in content, capable of transforming society, and opposed to the esthetic avant-gardes, concerned instead with the esthetic renewal of art.[26]

However, in the context of the development of the visual arts in Argentina, we may also see that the expressionism of Facio Hébequer, Bellocq, Vigo, Arato, and Riganelli could be viewed as an esthetic avant-garde in relation to the official art of de Quirós and Collivadino or of the old master de la Cárcova, who had been active since 1926 (fig.10). What is most evident, however, is the modernist tendency of Pettoruti's neocubism and the fantastic paintings of Xul Solar (fig. 11).

In the intellectual and esthetic realms, the Boedo group was particularly concerned with reading such texts as *What is Art?* by Leo Tolstoi, *Art from the Sociological Point of View*, by Jean-Marie Guyau, and *Art and Social Life* by J. Plejanov.

Fig. 11. Xul Solar, *Piai* (Piai), 1923. National Museum of Fine Arts, Buenos Aires.

The increasingly violent social climate in Argentina during the period of Radical governments,[27] and the influence of the Russian Revolution of 1917 constituted the natural frame of reference for the action of the group. The following are basic characteristics that defined their agenda: exhibitions in theaters, clubs, libraries, and galleries; articles in the journal *La montaña*; the illustration of literary works for mass-market editions published by Editorial Claridad; the use of engraved illustration—a diverse craft as well as an inexpensive and artisanal product—as a fundamental medium of expression and diffusion; a social message and struggle for the transformation of a political and economic order based on marginality and injustice; an attack on the merely formal and intellectual avant-gardes, especially concerning nonrepresentational trends in art; a definition of the modern city as a place of exploitation, misery, and dehumanization; coexistence, although a polemical one, with other artistic and intellectual groups;[28] the choice of an expressionistic realism, in agreement with a critical and descriptive intent (neither anecdotal nor romantic) in the depiction of proletarian social groups (fig. 12); a dramatic representation of reality while seeking to establish models in which anonymous characters are transformed into prototypes (fig. 13); a restriction of the thematic spectrum to the human figure as sole protagonist and to areas of the suburbs, the harbor, or the city as a setting for the action and scenario of the drama; a belief in the future fraternity of humans and in the building of a better society; the union of esthetic form and thematic content in order to affirm a social message, always in accordance with the chosen graphic technique; and, finally, a belief in the art of ideas as an active transformer of society.

"There exists a definite orientation within the plastic arts that is inclined to paint the life of the poor as it is seen through the eyes and hearts of the proletariat."[29]

26. These are the artists of the Florida group, a name habitually used although vague and restrictive. The group was composed of independent painters and sculptors like Emilio Pettoruti, Xul Solar, Norah Borges, and Pablo Curatella Manes.

27. We may recall here the massacres in Patagonia and the general strike of 1919.

28. This was evidenced in the attendance of the Artistas del Pueblo at the Salón Anual de Bellas Artes where they had received remuneration since 1921, or in their exhibitions in the parlors of the Amigos del Arte, the same place where the works of the Florida group and the traditionalists were presented.

29. Ricardo Vázquez Paz, "El arte que preconizamos y estamos dispuestos a defender," *Claridad*, (10 August 1929).

Among the Argentine artists active in 1920, Eugenio Daneri is a good example of a certain elliptical movement in both style and theme of the period. In his works, we frequently find as subjects the suburb and the neighborhood known as La Boca (fig. 14), together with his series on the harbor. With a palette dominated by ochres, earth tones, browns, and a paint texture often forcefully three-dimensional, the painter captures with dramatic and silent pain the precariousness and misery of the outskirts of the large capital city. His paintings describe a marginal urban landscape revealing an alternative, skeptical point of view toward testimonial art and local color.

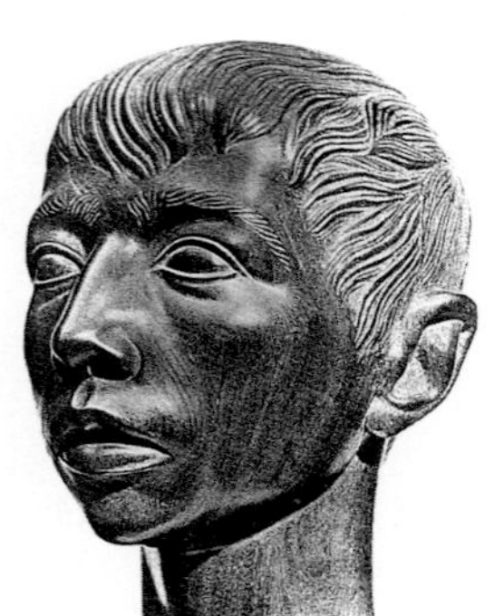

Fig. 12. Agustín Riganelli, *El niño de la calle* (Child of the street), wood, h. 39", 1913. National Museum of Fine Arts, Buenos Aires.

In regard to La Boca, no doubt the artist *par excellence* who is identified with the harbor and its workers is Benito Quinquela Martín. Abandoned by his parents at birth, Quinquela Martín worked from the age of nine as a coal worker and later as a laborer at the loading docks, where he participated in various important strikes to reduce the working day to eight hours. He began to study painting in 1907, and by 1914 had participated in the Salón de los Recusados; in 1917, along with Stagnaro and Facio Hébequer, he was one of the founders of the Sociedad Nacional de Artistas, Pintores, y Escultores (National society of artists, painters, and sculptors) and had a place in the Salón Independientes Sin Jurados y sin Premios the following year.

Thanks above all to Stagnaro's guidance, he rapidly familiarized himself with the works of Gorki, Balzac, Tolstoi, Proudhon, Bakunin, and Kropotkin. During those seminal years, he frequented Facio Hébequer's studio and met the individuals who subsequently founded the Boedo group. However, their positions subsequently grew apart. For Quinquela Martín, the themes of his work from 1916 on were almost exclusively concerned with La Boca, the dockworkers, and their labors (fig. 16). His style was characterized by its luminosity of color and thick paint textures, created by the alternating use of spatula and brush, which together formed an intense and visually dynamic image.

In the later career of this successful and popular artist, from 1930 on, his work became highly manneristic; his initial promise gave way to a reiterative formula of scant artistic interest. Collazo called this *quinquelismo*.[30] In his depiction of the dockworker, Quinquela Martín shows labor as a multifaceted activity, where there seems to be no lack of physical strength, no moral fatigue, no exploitation of the worker, and no rebellion. His vision is concerned more with the exaltation of the proletariat through labor rather than with documenting a marginal reality in social terms. Multitudes of workers, men loading and unloading, fishermen, boats, bridges, factories, chimneys, dockyards, sacks, sheets of metal, piles of wood; all the world of work is represented as an epic with neither beginning nor end. The painter resolves his relations with the social reality of La Boca in a world basically made of colors and textures, from which a single progatonist always emerges obsessively: the proletarian worker.

Within the field of American social realism, Alfredo Guttero, who returned to Argentina in 1927 after a long stay in Europe,[31] offered an alternative approach to this technique. His series of works on the harbor, the zone of the southern dock, and the island of Maciel show two variants. The first is an ensemble of small landscapes, often created on pasteboard, strongly constructive, and at times almost like Cézanne (fig. 15). They are composed in brilliant colors applied with visible brushstrokes and abundant paint. These harbor scenes

30. Alberto Collazo, *Quinquela* (Buenos Aires: Centro Editor de América Latina, 1980), 6.

31. From 1904 on, he lived in Paris and, after the war, traveled to Spain, Switzerland, and Austria. He spent the last two years of his life in Florence.

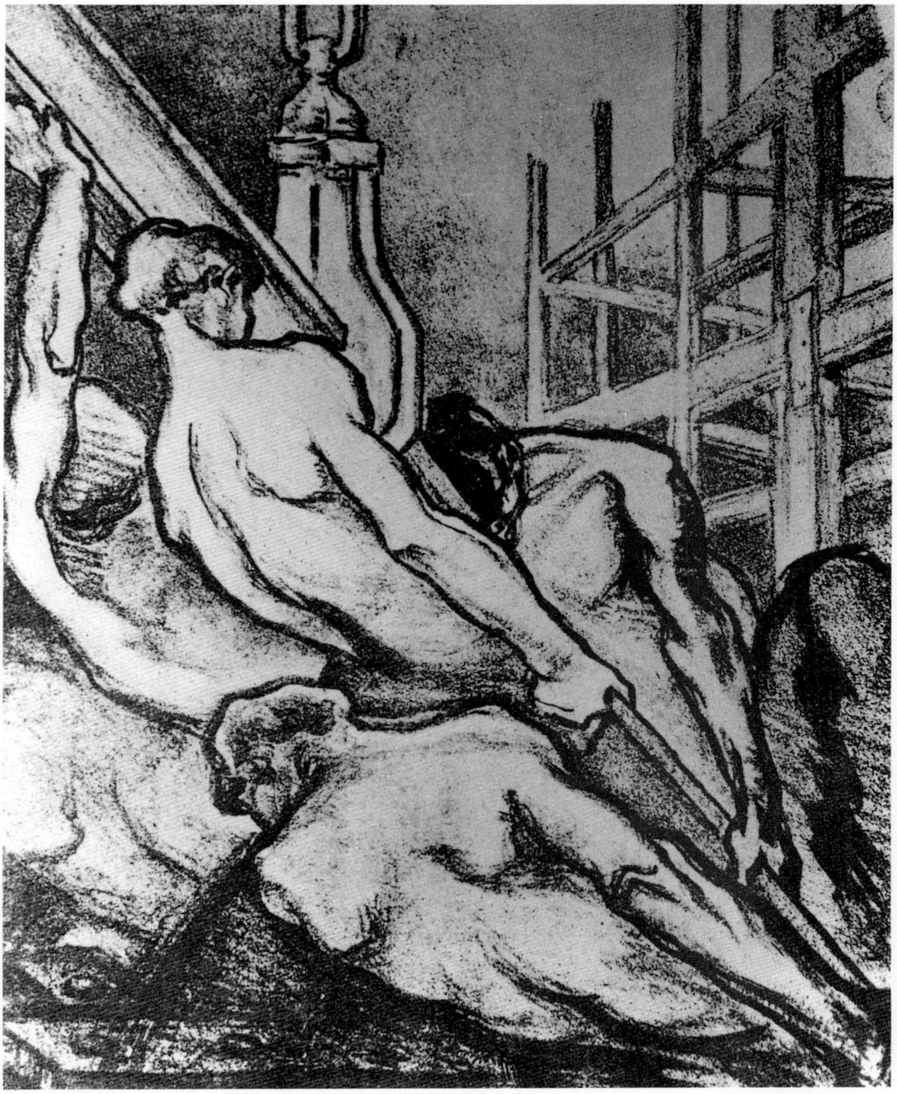

Fig. 13. Guillermo Facio Hébequer, *Tú historia compañero* (Your history, comrade), lithograph, 24 x 20 cm, 1933. Private collection, Buenos Aires.

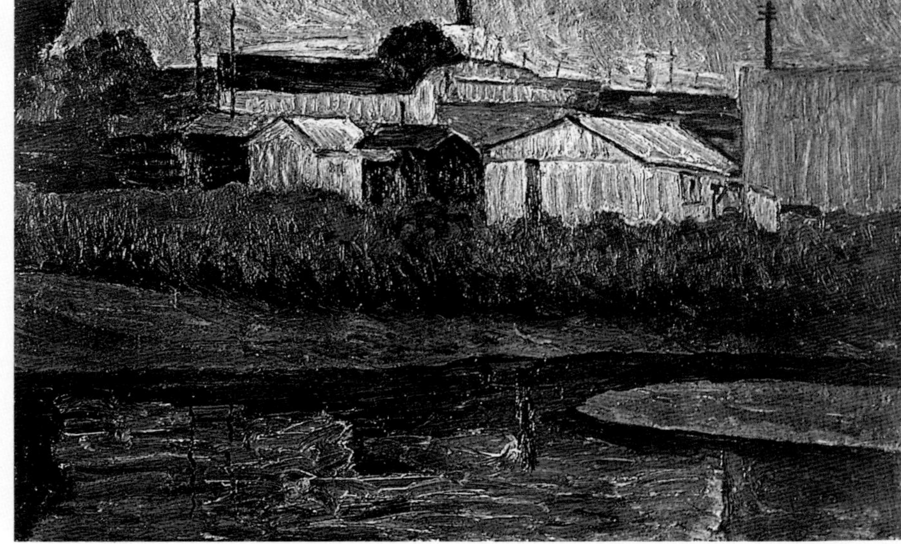

Fig. 14. Eugenio Daneri, *Viviendas obreras* (Workers' housing), oil on canvas, 42 x 66 cm, 1941. National Museum of Fine Arts, Buenos Aires.

Fig. 15. Alfredo Guttero, *Silos* (Silos), oil on pasteboard, 16 x 22 cm, 1928. National Museum of Fine Arts, Buenos Aires.

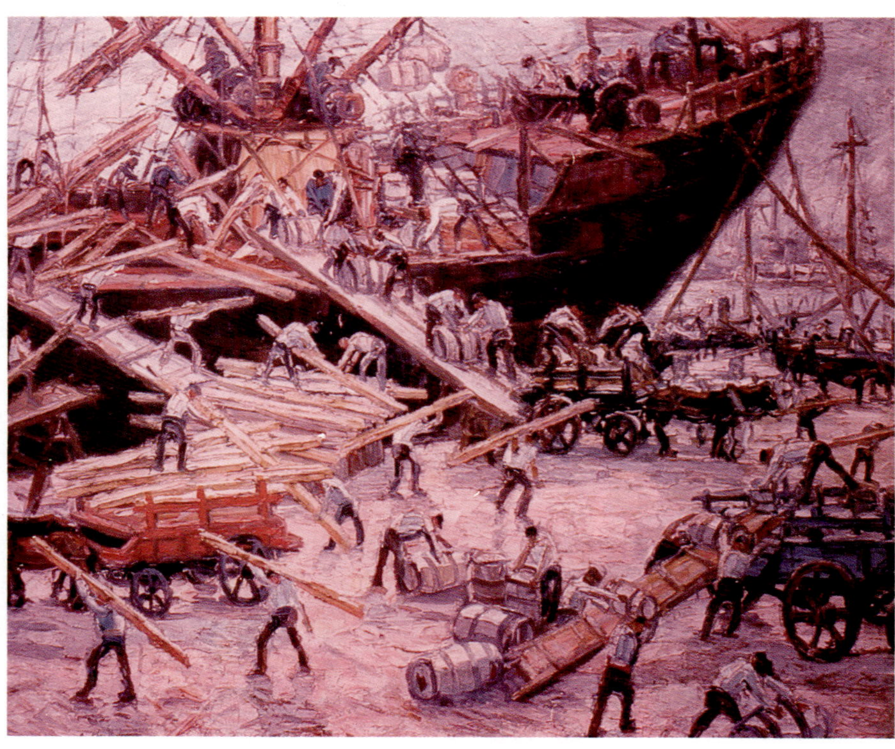

Fig. 16. Benito Quinquela Martín, *Descarga de madera* (Unloading wood), oil on canvas, 120 x 140 cm, 1926. Private collection, Buenos Aires.

date from 1928 and, in several of them, factories, silos, people, houses, and boats seem to acquire an air of unreality from the light and color that outline and congeal their masses and forms.

The other possibility offered by Guttero is the large canvas representing the crushing power of bodies devoted to work (fig. 17). The bodies are depicted with extensive decorative rhythm, and the compositions are crowded with strongly geometrical anatomies and clothing. These paintings contain a double image: of everyday life on the one hand, and a magical atmosphere that borders on the metaphysical on the other.

The years of study with Maurice Denis in Paris left a clear imprint on Guttero, especially in his tendency toward the monumental, even in his small pasteboard works. In the latter, easel painting is transformed and governed instead by principles closer to those of mural art. Construction, composition, and synthesis, in order to reflect a visible reality, are changed into pure esthetic forms. Social realism tinged with humanism serves as a basis for the eye of a painter seeking to reorder the world of the suburban harbor of Buenos Aires.

Ramón Gómez Cornet was one of the first to renew Argentine painting via his scandalous exhibition of 1921 in which he presented oil paintings derived from futurism and cubism. Subsequently, he developed an exceedingly personal style and a subtle equilibrium between the naturalism and modernism of contemporary images, focusing his work on the daily life of the inhabitants of the northern provinces of Argentina (fig. 18).

"A brief incursion towards the 'isms' tempted me when I was young.... But circumstances later carried me to the interior of the country, to my native province, Santiago del Estero...[where] I underwent a crisis of transcendence. I was taken by a new problem: humanity and our landscape."[32]

The result is images in which women and children in particular are shown completely stripped, conveying their poverty and their abandon, their profound and laconic sadness. Gómez Cornet presents an interesting variation in American social realism: here the message and the polemical and accusatory content is transformed into a magical but deeply documentary realism that is gently focused and sparing in its imagery. There is neither dramaticism nor expressive outpouring—all is contained, austere. The marginal characters of Gómez Cornet do not undertake any action, nor do they offer even a gesture; they pose as models for the artist and confront us with a limpid and transparent gaze. The spectator has no defense in front of the affective force that rises from the faces of abandoned and supplicant children. There is a union between apparent opposites—critical discourse and formal abstraction; the social theme and the immobility of the destiny of men of the soil; and realism of popular types and the category of the marvelous that resides within Latin American daily reality.

In the case of Lino Enea Spilimbergo, who completed his first individual work in 1921 in his native province of San Juan, and who traveled to Europe to study between 1925 and 1928 as did Gómez Cornet, one finds an eclectic esthetic language at work; it is a language in which contemporary lessons and historical inheritance—especially from Italian art—are united in the search for an identity. Among his images, defined by a rotund constructivism and by an at times metareal atmosphere,[33] we frequently find the disinherited as principle motif. An entire gallery of marginal figures, from the beggar (fig. 19) to the prostitute, from slumdwellers of Buenos Aires to rural workers of the northern provinces, inhabits the work of an artist aligned with the misery and the destiny of his fellow humans.

"Then I grasped the atmosphere of the world": thus Raquel Forner defined the beginning, in 1937, of her series on the Spanish Civil War. From then on, her works were filled with disturbing images in which the reality of destruction, death,

32. Rámon Gómez Cornet, "Unas palabras de Gómez Cornet," *Rámon Gómez Cornet* (Buenos Aires: Ediciones Galería Witcomb, 1965), 11.

33. During the twenties and thirties, various Argentine artists appeared in whom the transformation of daily reality into magical reality, with the suspension of time and space, is the common denominator, together with a constructive trend in their drawing and color. One of the reasonable explanations for this phenomenon is the strong influence that Italian art of the 1300s, the 1400s, and the early twentieth century had over them.

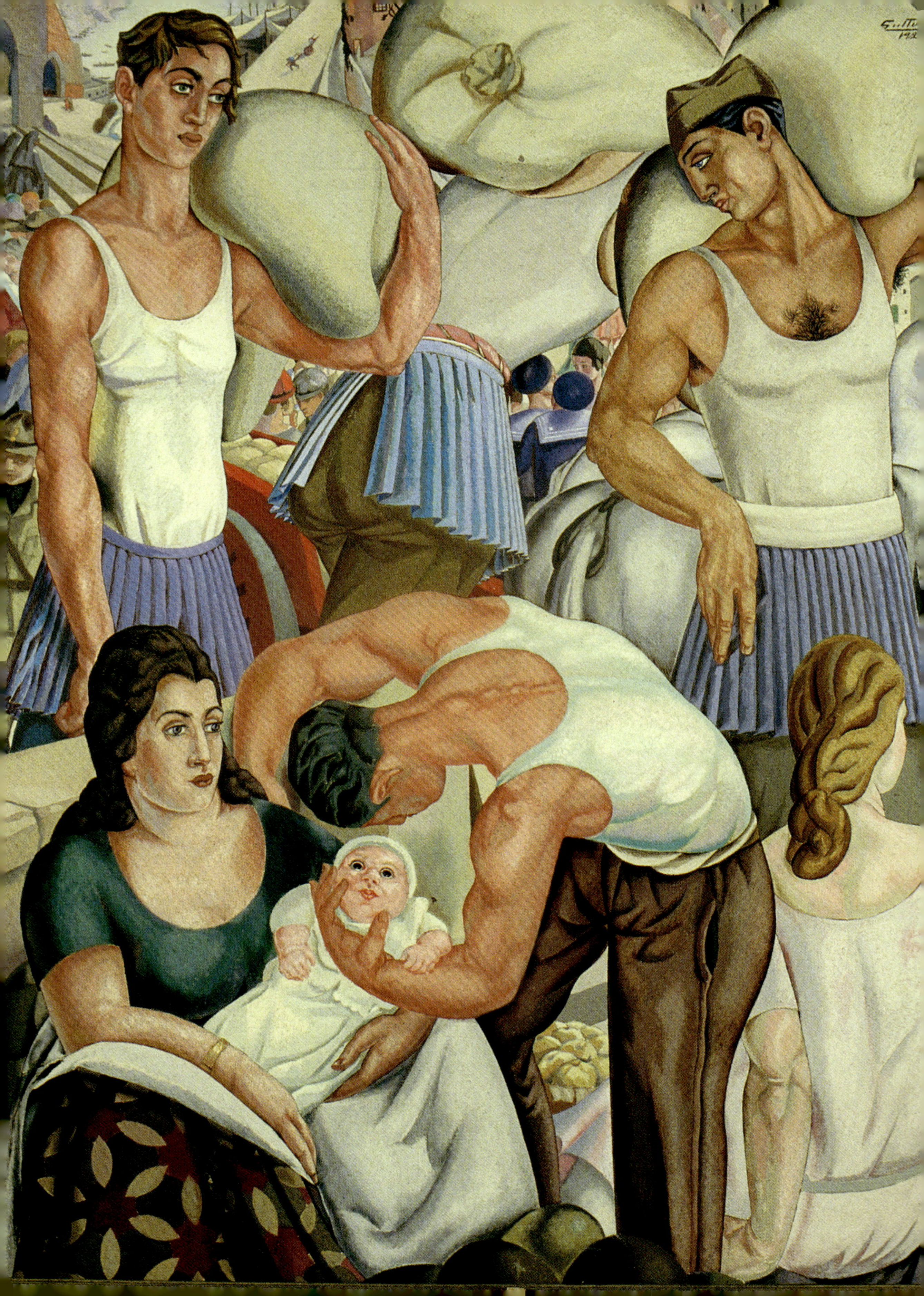

Fig. 17. Alfredo Guttero, *Cargadores ligures* (Ligurian stevedores), oil on canvas, 190 x 150 cm, 1926. Private collection, Buenos Aires.

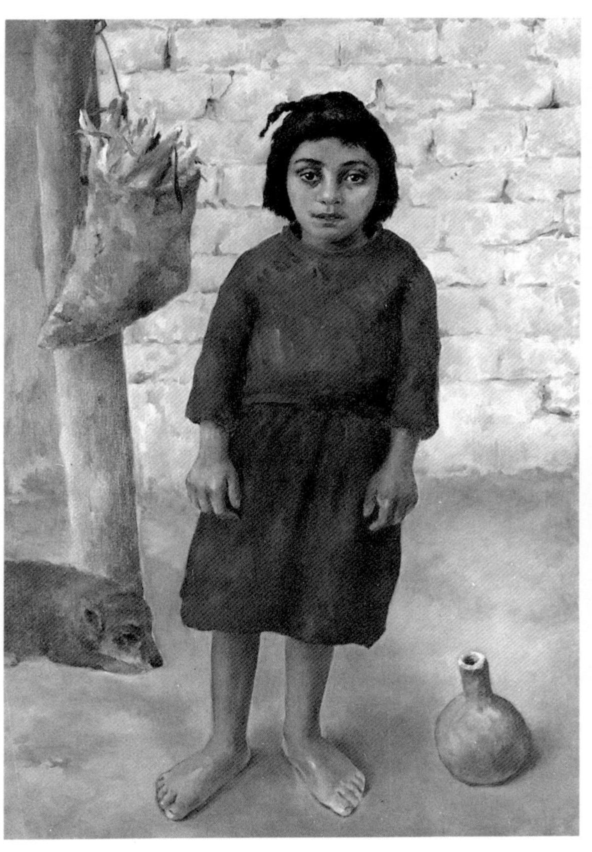

Fig. 18. Ramón Gómez Cornet, *La Urpila* (The dove), oil on canvas, 130 x 89 cm, 1946. National Museum of Fine Arts, Buenos Aires.

Fig. 19. Lino Enea Spilimbergo, *Momento feliz* (Happy moment), oil on canvas, 125 x 150 cm, 1926. Museum of the Boca, Buenos Aires.

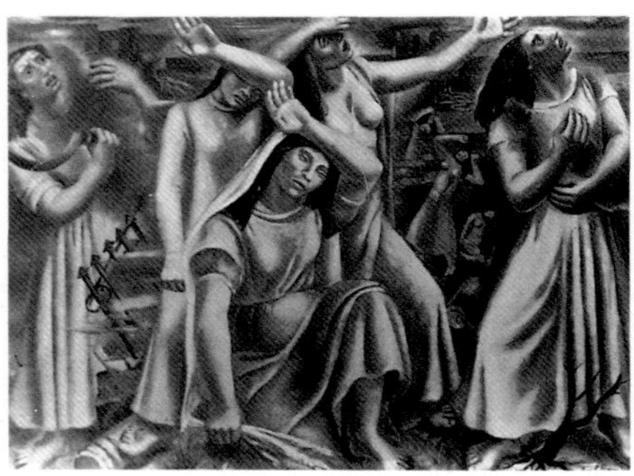

Fig. 20. Raquel Forner, *Mujeres del mundo* (Women of the world), oil on canvas, 170 x 238 cm, 1938. Forner-Bigatti Foundation, Buenos Aires.

hunger, and desolation is embodied in monumental and sculptural feminine figures whose cries express the agony and the conscience of the artist.

With Forner, social realism transcends the local documentary and reflects the pain and impotence of humanity faced with the tragedy of the world (fig. 20). With respect to *Mujeres del mundo*, she comments: "[T]he central figure is America bent over the earth with a bundle of stalks. America is at peace, but the clamor of the world reaches her. Behind her are China (to the left, with her face halfway covered by her forearm) and Spain (to the right) plainly in anguish. And, at the sides of the scene, I have positioned two figures of suffering: a mother who seems to rock her dead son (only suggested by a vague form) and a wife who, after having lost her companion, takes up the sickle so as not to lose the rhythm of work. In the background, beneath the terror of the receding planes, already finished with their mission of death, there is the panorama of a bombed-out village."[34]

During the first years of her career, Forner had taken as a theme the marginal social groups on the outskirts of Buenos Aires. However, after the Spanish Civil War, the artist needed to broaden her horizons and denounce the situation of the millions of disinherited humans punished by the war and the irrationality of power. Out of a vocabulary rooted in expressionism and through a dreamlike atmosphere, she constructed striking compositions with allegorical elements in which the painting of content asserts itself over stylistic functions and "isms." In *Retablo del dolor* (fig. 21), the external motivation of the work is World War Two. The image of a world darkened by destruction, desolation, and impotence when faced with the absurdity of slaughter, generates in the artist a strange mixture of reality and transformed reality.

Confronted by the war, her imagination responds by inventing fantastic limbs that are claws, or a humanity that suffers the martyrdom of the crown of thorns and the stigmata and lies mortally wounded. A realistic image could not express the consciousness of the abyss that Forner felt inside herself. The language of dreams was necessary in order to express the real.

In her canvases, this drama would go on developing until the 1955 series of the apocalypse. After that, hope arrived in the form of a space series, begun in 1958 with the apparition of an imaginary world of spacemen, labyrinths, lunar rocks, and creatures from outer space. Her work thus became open to the possible construction of a different world inhabited by terrestrial mutants.

34. *El Diario*, 1938, cited in Guillermo Whitelow, *Raquel Forner* (Buenos Aires: Ediciones de Arte Gaglianone, 1980), 23.

Fig. 21. Raquel Forner, ***Retablo del dolor*** **(Altarpiece of pain), oil on canvas, 152 x 137 cm, 1942. National Museum of Fine Arts, Buenos Aires.**

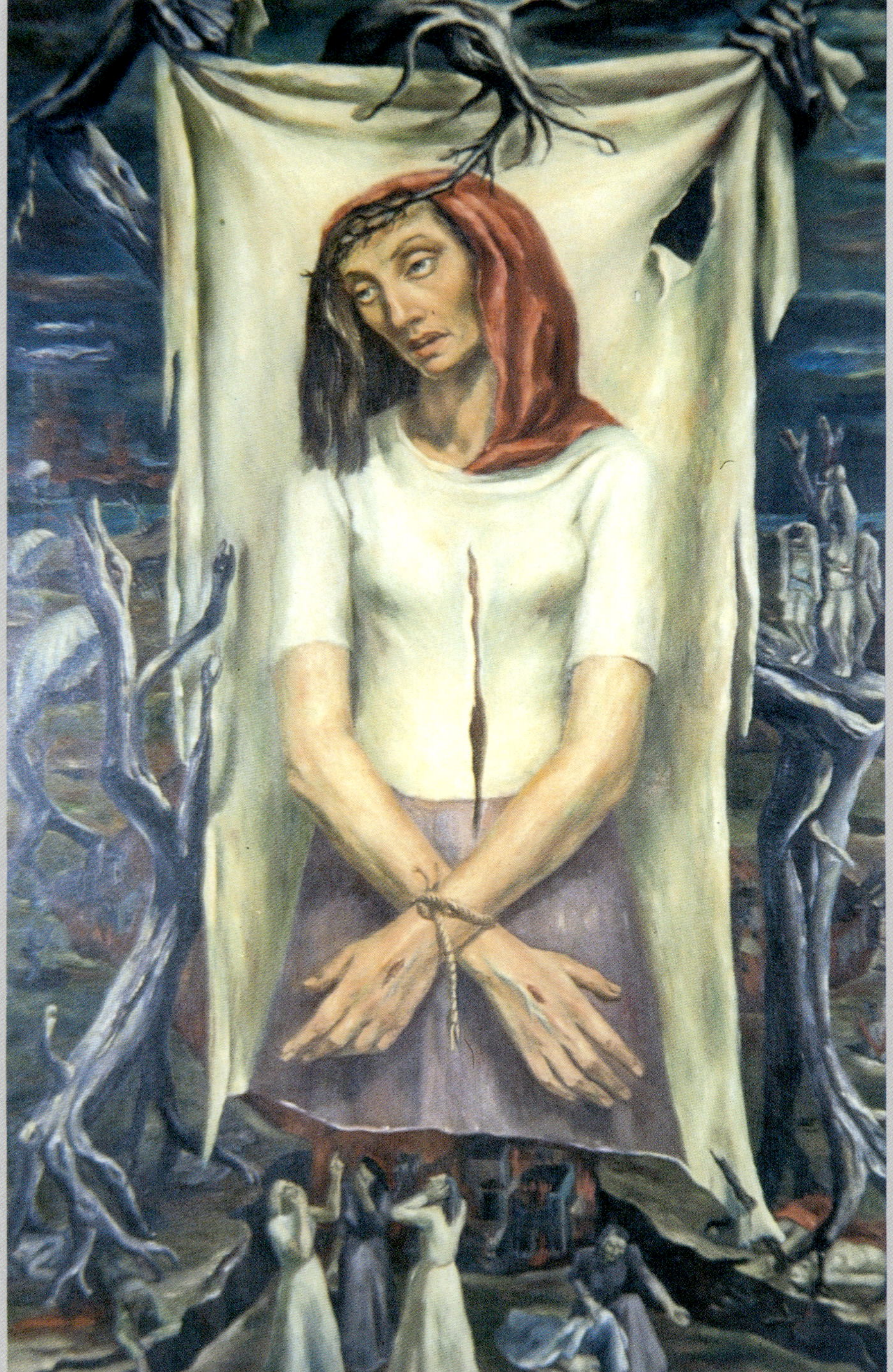

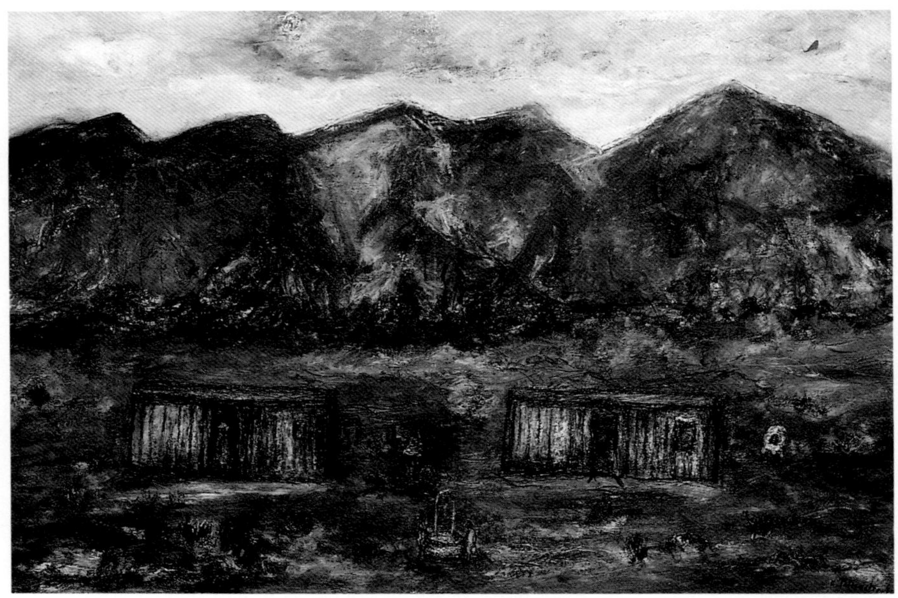

Fig. 22. Enrique Policastro, *Patquía* (Patquía), oil on canvas, 84 x 115 cm, 1960. Modern Art Museum, Buenos Aires.

Enrique Policastro, who for thirteen years worked in a factory, from the beginning of his career defined his thematic interest and esthetic images according to his genuine sense of solidarity with the dispossessed. A sober dramatic sense darkens his palette, enriches his texture, and gives expression to his tortuous drawing, whether in figures of workers of the twenties, in his suburban landscapes of the forties, or in his later northern compositions (fig. 22).

"He formed a quartet with Berni, Castagnino, and Urruchúa in exhibitions and publications. They were united in the same ideas and convictions, such as anti-fascism and anti-Francoism as well as sympathy for the Latin American revolutionary movements, just as they shared the same 'muralistic' formal tendency."[35]

Policastro belongs to a generation of artists, active since the twenties, who came from the middle or lower classes and made their living in areas not related to art, while at the same time devoting themselves to painting or sculpture (like Spilimbergo, who was employed as a mailman in his native province). Around this time, the number of artists coming from different provinces of the country increased, although the majority spent a large part of their career in the capital city.

"The goal that I pursue is a kind of intellectual nothingness. A painting is a shout proferred by the hand."[36] Taking this as his point of departure, Juan Carlos Castagnino's esthetic itinerary was evident, and evidently related to his friendship with and admiration for the works of Gómez Cornet and Spilimbergo. For him, there was no story he would rather capture on canvas than humanity and its surroundings. There, marginal figures acquire authentic presence while immersed in his everyday landscapes, in a rough and ready natural world (fig. 23). In Castagnino, social realism is an esthetic search contained within a basic thematics of solidarity.

Another painter related to the social realism of that time was Demetrio Urruchúa. Together with Castagnino, Antonio Berni, and Manuel Colmeiro,

35. Carmen Balzer, *Policastro* (Buenos Aires: Centro Editor de América Latina, 1980), 1.

36. Juan Carlos Castagnino, unpublished manuscript.

in 1944 he organized the Taller de Arte Mural (Studio of mural art). The debate over muralism was one of the key polemics in Argentina in the thirties and forties, especially in regard to David Alfaro Siqueiros's 1933 work in Buenos Aires, namely the mural for the villa of Natalio Botana. Because of the Mexican's visit, the controversy surrounding the topic of muralism remained alive.

In the work of Urruchúa, who made important decorative murals in Buenos Aires, Montevideo, and Resistencia, there consistently appeared a trend toward monumental figures and the simplification of scenery. He was searching for an effect that would strike the viewer in the way that great compositions conceived for giant wall surfaces are able to do. The content of his works shows a relation to the artist's intellectual formation; readings of Tagore, Strindberg, Ibsen, Tolstoi, and Nietzsche had piqued his interest in the social and had taught him a manner of relating self to the world.

With his choice of pictorial images, influenced in part by the strong personality of Eugenio Daneri, his teacher at the Academy of the Society for the Encouragement of the Fine Arts, Urruchúa opted for a palette of wide contrasts—dark in definition, but with violent outbreaks of yellows, violets, and greens. His firm designs defined his immense profiles; the oil paint was thickly distributed by forcefully administered strokes of the brush. In this manner, his art unified the esthetic weight and the "brutality" of avant-garde images with a polemical message. The result leaves the spectator with a sense of uneasiness.

Without a doubt, one of the Argentine artists bound up with social realism in Argentina is Antonio Berni. In fact, his artistic production occupies a privileged place. The quality of his work resides in the precise balance that he attained between narrative painting with strong social content and esthetic originality. For him, painting is basically thematic, and the theme is essentially the proposal of an idea. "[T]he course of my trajectory has been theme, and it is theme that has produced all formal and chromatic changes."[37]

Between 1925 and 1930, Berni was working in Europe: Madrid and Paris were his two places of residence, and in 1927 he traveled to Belgium, Holland, and Italy. From those years, he would retain the lessons taught him by Othon Friesz and Andre Lhote, as well as the direct influence of the historical avant-garde and its protagonists. He felt, too, the impact of Italian art, especially the muralism of the forties, and aligned himself with the ideology of the French Community party.

In the same period, other Argentine artists studied in Paris: Aquiles Badi, Héctor Basaldúa, Horacio Butler, Alfredo Bigatti, Lino Enea Spilimbergo (with whom Berni would form an intimate friendship), Raquel Forner, and Juan del Prete. All of these artists had studied first in Buenos Aires and then witnessed the brilliance of contemporary art while living in one of the most important cultural capitals of the day. Their travels to other European countries allowed them to experience "non-traditional" chapters in the history of art, different from those learned in the academic halls of Argentina. Primitive art, Etruscan art, art of the Near East, and pre-Columbian cultures appeared as alternative fields of study for all these young people. And, at the same time, the Italian masters of the thirteenth, fourteenth, and fifteenth centuries showed them a different esthetic point of view.

37. *Antonio Berni, obra pictórica 1922–1981*, catalogue (Buenos Aires: Museo Nacional de Bellas Artes, 1984), 20.

For many of them, the end result was an eclectic introduction to art in which elements of neocubism, neoexpressionism, and neofauvism intermingled in images of modern syntax. However, the avant-garde element appeared neutralized, thus establishing a resemblance with the works of the so-called School of Paris.

It was not so with del Prete, who was a follower of the abstract style at that time in both painting and sculpture. He introduced nonfiguration in Argentina with his exhibition of paintings in 1933 and sculpture in 1934, after his return from Europe.

Fig. 23. Juan Carlos Castagnino, *La mujer del páramo* (Wilderness woman), oil on canvas, 125 x 76 cm, 1944. National Museum of Fine Arts, Buenos Aires.

In the case of Berni, his choice was clear. His contacts with surrealism, along with the influence of the metaphysical work of Giorgio De Chirico, determined the nature of his first mature works. Upon returning to Buenos Aires in 1930, the artist continued working in oils and collages that adhered to the esthetic principles of André Breton. However, from 1933 on, his failure as a figurative artist was evident. He produced a series of large-scale paintings, monumental in conception, which functioned as a response, analysis, and denunciation of the social, political, and economic crisis that Argentina lived through in those years known as the decade of infamy.

For Berni, the point of departure for these 1934 works (figs. 24 and 25) was a number of photographs found in newspaper archives or taken by himself. He painted the theme of the worker, unemployment, strikes, and widespread hunger, not on canvas but on fine-grained burlap. The works are characterized by their gigantic size, monumental deformations of figures and space, severity and exasperation in the forms, disturbing atmosphere somewhere between documentary reality and a tense dream just before wakening, a cinematographical language of extreme contrasts, and the isolation and grimness of a compact mass of people.

In 1933, Berni collaborated with Siqueiros in Buenos Aires in the development of a mural for the Botana estate. This was the period of debate with Mexican artists about muralism and social painting, and about art and politics in general; and the year in which they, with Castagnino and Lazaro, signed the *Ejercicio Plástico* (Artistic exercise). When asked about the subject of Mexican muralism, Berni responded with his plans for *Manifestación* and *Desocupados* and, in 1936, published his manifesto of *Nuevo Realismo* (New realism) in the first issue of *Forma*, the journal of the Sociedad Argentina de Artistas Plásticos (Argentine society of plastic artists).

Berni's position is lucid in content and in what it proposes:

> Now a new language makes itself heard, expressing the necessity of a more substantial art. All the critical, philosophical, and esthetic digressions on pure art are substituted with realist reasonings concordant with the collective and social psychology of the time. In art, all that had been rejected by established prejudices and sectarian points of view returns to arise unstoppable, driven forth by its own unextinguishable vitality. The dramatic world, the social reality, conquers its rightful place in art, smashing the shell that covers it, contradicting all the artistic literature and all the criticism of this century dominated by the reigning impressionist or expressionist concepts. It was believed for the moment that subjects—the scenes on the canvases—had been forever eradicated from the domain of the plastic arts.... The true artist and the true art of the people open new doors propelled by changing objective conditions; on the other hand, leave those be who work according

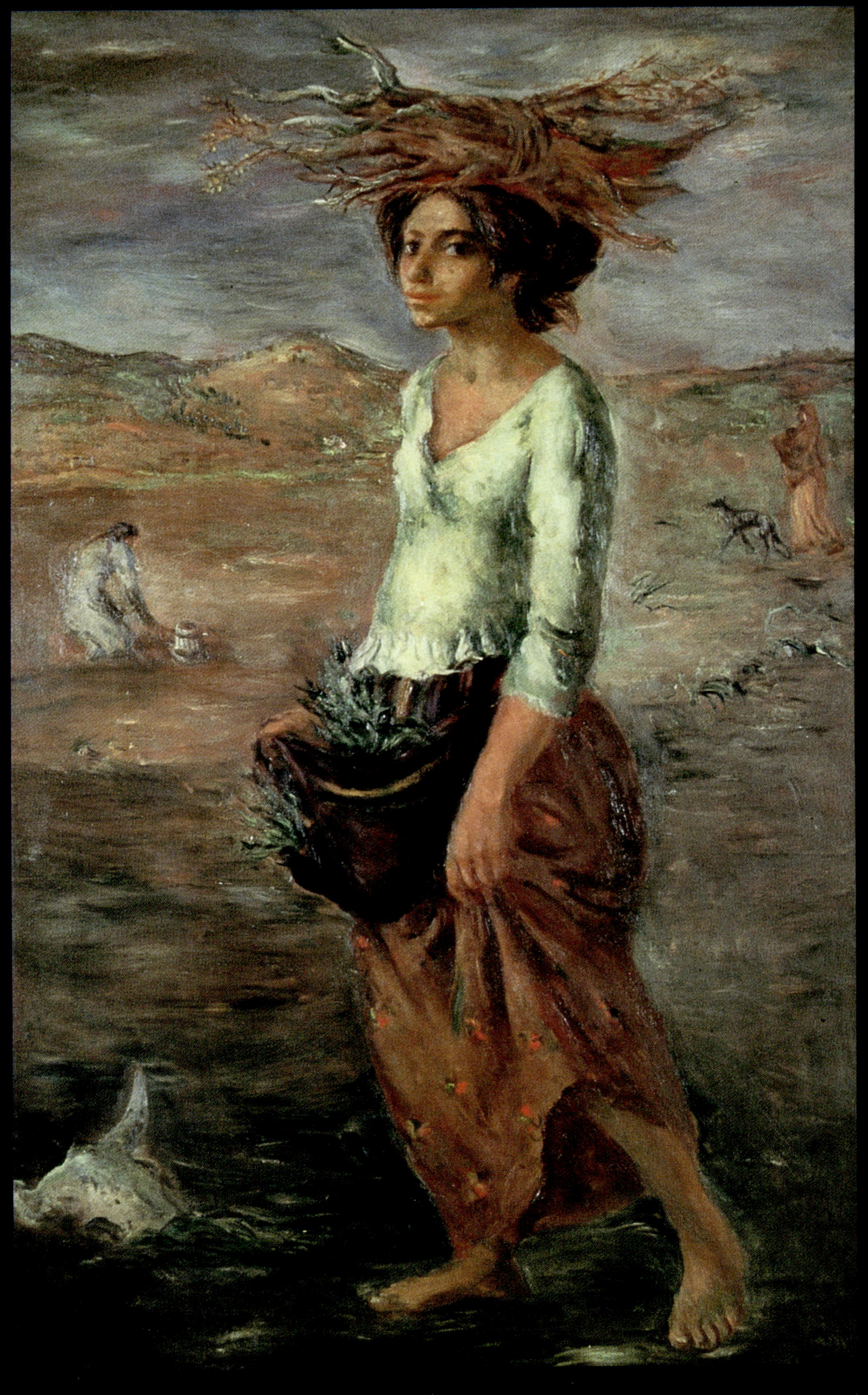

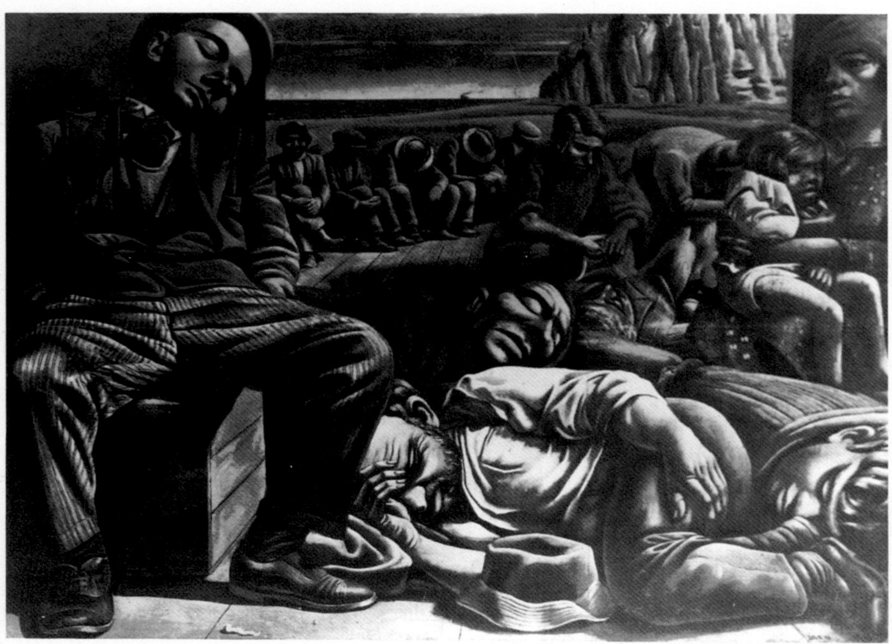

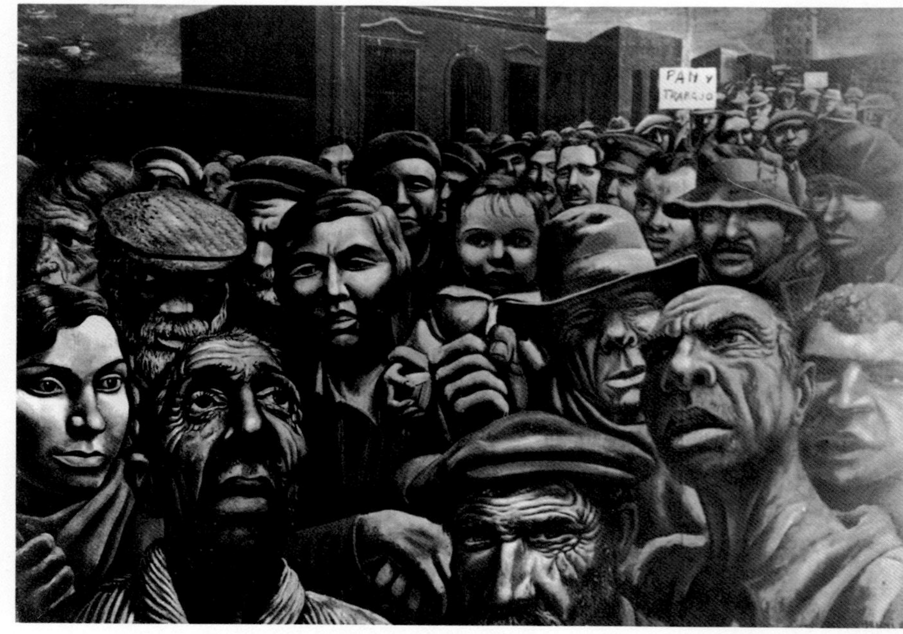

▲

Fig. 24. Antonio Berni, ***Desocupados o desocupación*** **(Unemployed), tempera on burlap, 218 x 300 cm, 1934. Berni Family Collection, Buenos Aires.**

Fig. 25. Antonio Berni, ***Manifestación*** **(Public demonstration), tempera on burlap, 180 x 250 cm, 1934. Berni Family Collection, Buenos Aires.**

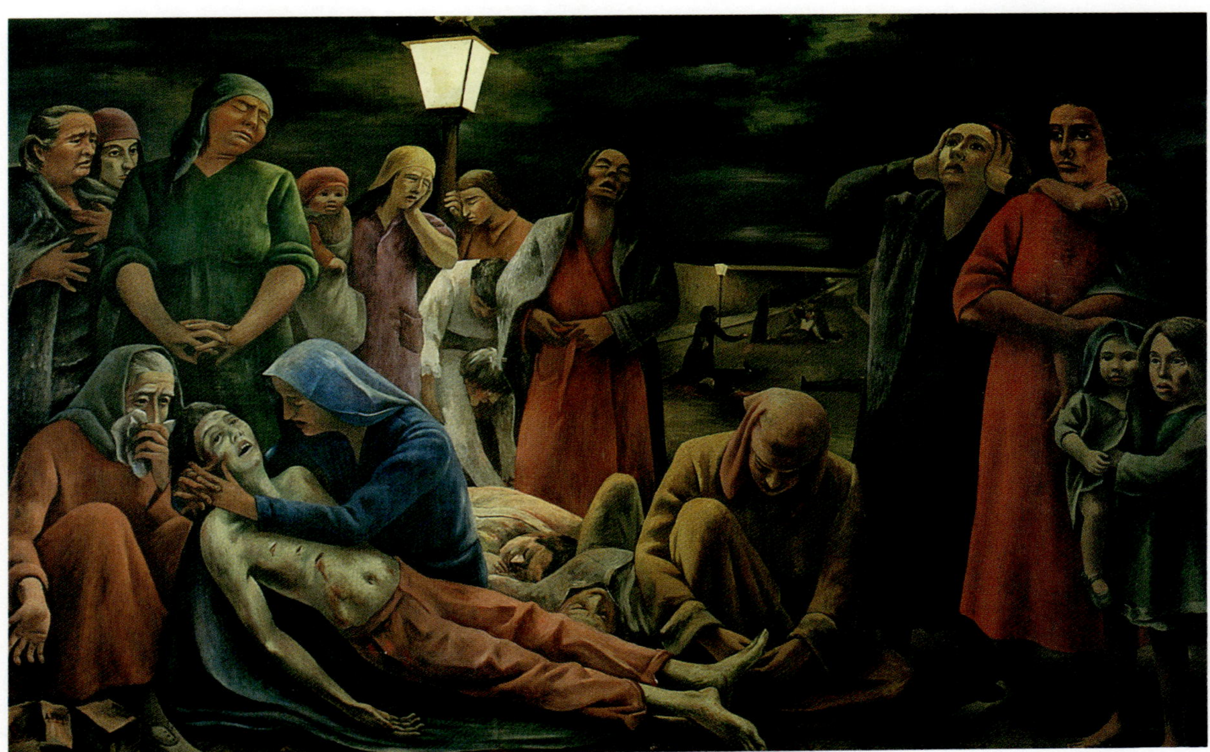

Fig. 26. Antonio Berni, *Medianoche en el mundo* (Midnight in the world), oil on canvas, 180 x 250 cm, 1936–1937. Private collection, Buenos Aires.

> to the established clichés, who continue working in outmoded forms that do not conform to any artistic or social reality. A new order, a new discipline, aided by a new criticism inspired by the concrete reality in which we live, must replace all that is defunct and that we today support.... In the new realism outlined in our medium, fabrication of action is most important; because it is not only the imitation of human beings and things that is portrayed but also the imitation of man's activities, his life, his ideas and misfortunes. The new realism is not simply a rhetoric or a declamation with neither basis nor objectivity; on the contrary, it is the subjective mirror of the great social, political, economic, and spiritual reality of our century.[38]

In 1937, Berni completed *Medianoche en el mundo* (fig. 26), in which his expressive force, already far removed from the geometric harshness and the tridimensional hypertrophy of his 1934 works, is concentrated on gesture and action. The human figures are now in motion; the close-up effect is eliminated and replaced by a space in which the figures are situated in the foreground of the scene, in the manner of fifteenth-century compositions, with accelerated flights of perspective toward the background. The white light, which before was uniformly extended over the canvas, now is changed into shadows and strong dark contrasts, creating stylistic tension in accordance with the thematic tension. Before, the images responded to the photographic point of departure; now the scene is more evidently theatrical.

However, the iconographic inversion of the traditional religious composition of the descent of Christ adds a complementary reading to the social content of the canvas. The dead Son of God is transformed into the victimized worker

38. Ibid., 8, 14.

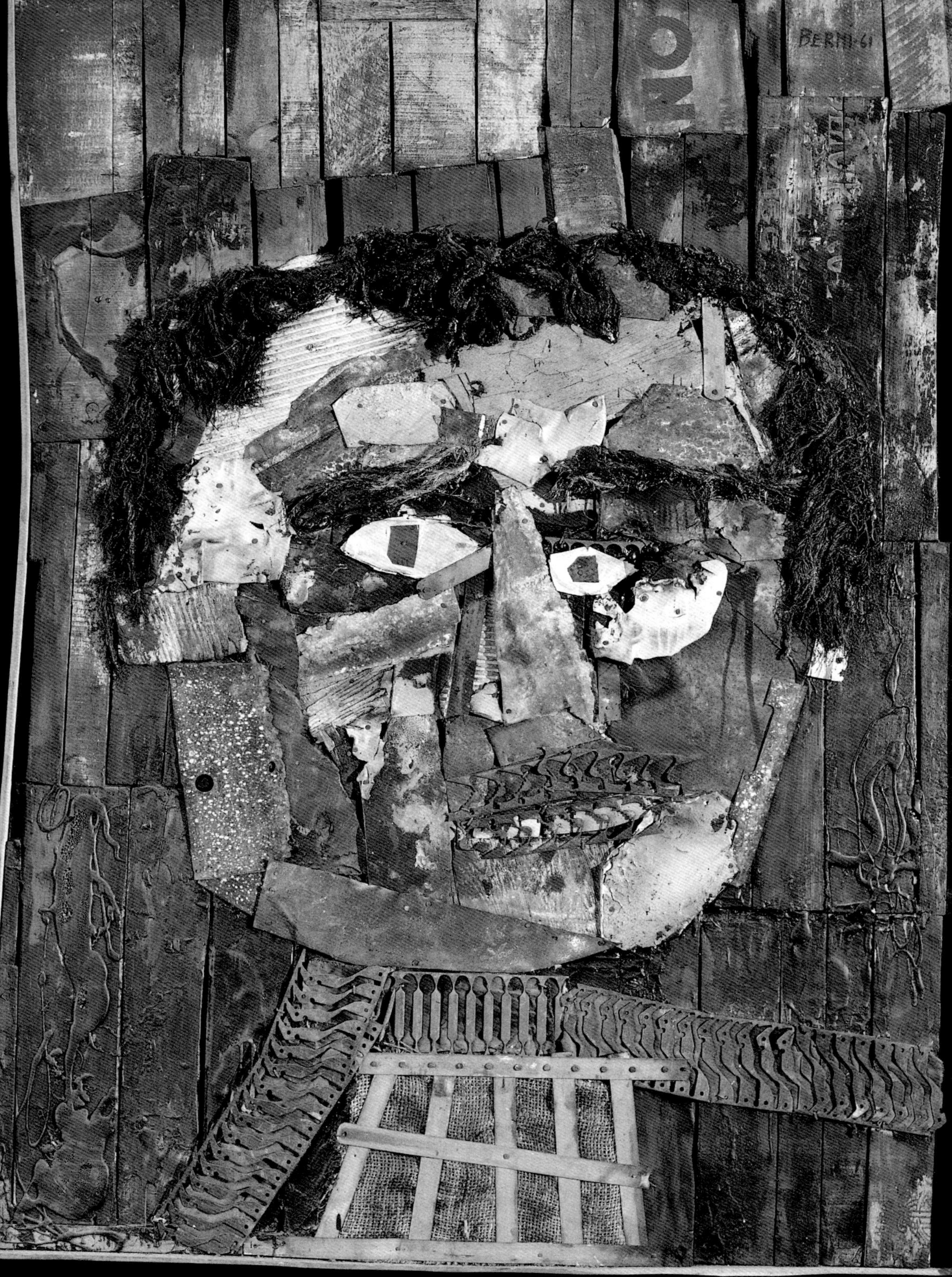
BERNI·61

and his disciples into the anonymous procession of village men and women who encircle the corpse and lament his sacrifice.

The definition of the new realism provoked polemical responses from other important painters of the time; they published in the same journal, *Forma*, their antagonistic points of view. Emilio Pettoruti, in a lecture delivered to the Sociedad Argentina de Artistas Plásticos, and later transcribed in the journal, defended avant-garde art and attacked Berni's ideas.

Fig. 27. Antonio Berni, portrait of Juanito Laguna, collage on wood, 145 x 165 cm, 1961. Guido Di Tella Collection, Buenos Aires.

"There are those who plead with us to accept that which they call the 'New Realism,' which is but an extension of photography, with all the defects of the camera, with its crudity and stiffness, its insensitivity, and its coloring. Are not the perceptions of artists infinitely superior to more faithful descriptions of reality?"[39]

The debate between these two painters signals two different conceptual and esthetic positions, and confronts two distinct ways of defining the function of art and its relation to reality. What is interesting is that two of the most important painters in Argentina arrive at esthetic solutions that are polarized in style and pictoralization, and unified in the quality of image and its expression.

In an article written in 1976, Berni maintained: "[E]very artist and all art is ultimately political, or we may say, using the terminology in vogue today, that all art 'also' admits a political reading. In my case, I recognize this; I think that the political reading of my work is fundamental, that one cannot leave it out, and that if one does leave it out, the work will not be understood in depth; and, moreover, I believe that a merely esthetic reading would be a betrayal."[40]

In Berni's work this definition of the link between art and politics is what led him permanently to the field of social realism. It is also what led him, at the end of the fifties, to the invention of that mythic character—mythic and terribly real at the same time—of Juanito Laguna (fig. 27), a synthesis of marginality and social injustice, an anti-hero who gave rise with his companion Ramona Montiel, a prostitute, to a series of collages and wood engravings in relief[41] which are key elements of American art in the twentieth century.

"The work is made by fully coexisting with the drama of humanity in its political, religious, and social totality; in the misfortune and in the shock of each day."[42] □

39. Emilio Pettoruti, *Forma* (1938): 4.

40. *Antonio Berni*, 21.

41. For a group of large-scale wood engravings, bearing in relief the theme of this series of Juanito Laguna and Ramona Montiel, Berni received the Grand Prize of Engraving in 1962 at the Venice Biennale.

42. *Antonio Berni*, 17.

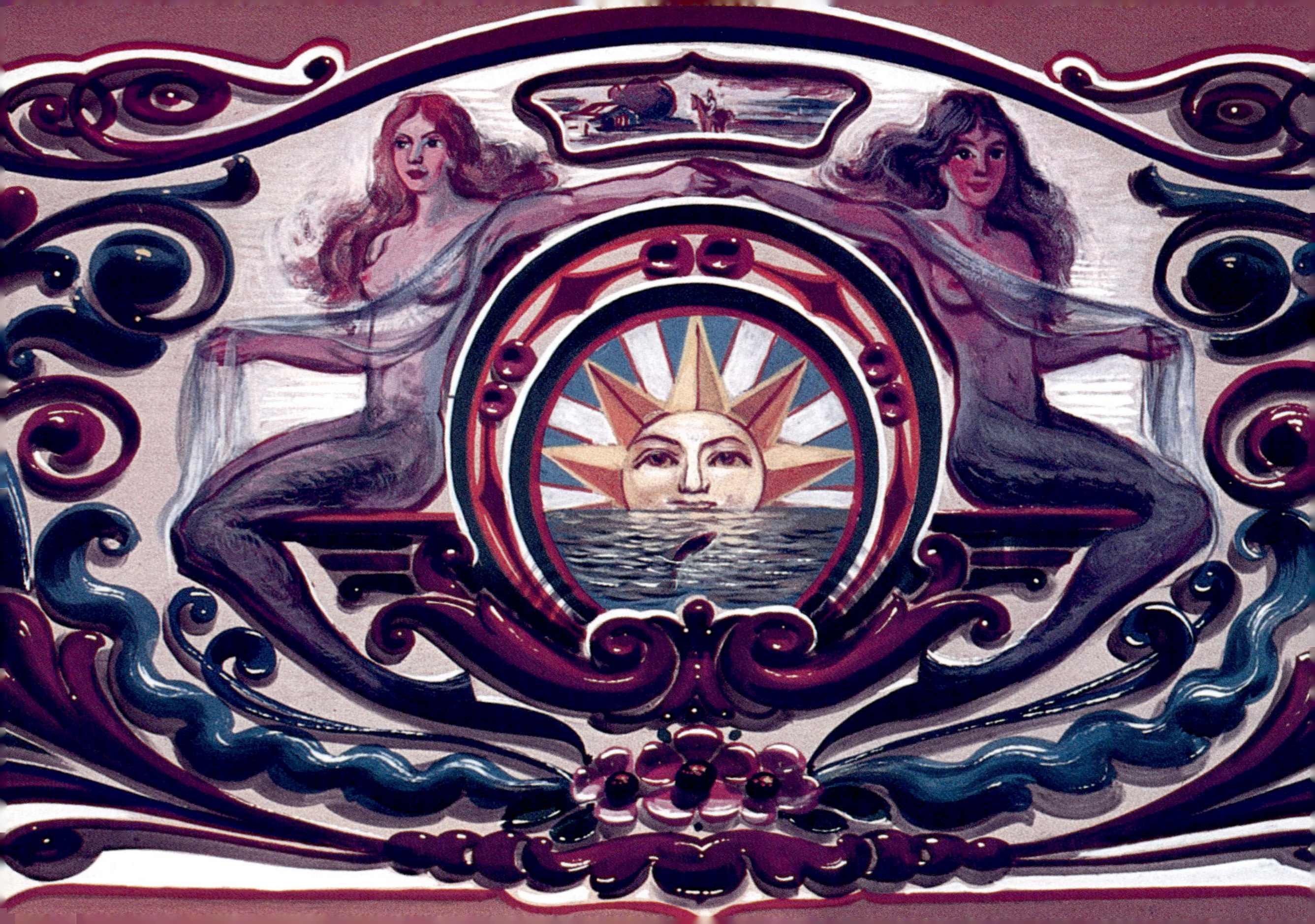

Rediscovering the Master *Fileteadores* of Buenos Aires

By María Estenssoro

María Estenssoro is an editor of the Argentine business magazine *Mercado*. She was with *Time* magazine for seven years, while writing for various other Buenos Aires publications. A graduate of Smith College, she has a masters degree in journalism from Columbia University.

Photographs by Nicolás Rubió.

Until the mid-1800s, Argentina was just one more country on the distant Latin American map. By the first decades of the twentieth century, thanks to an impressive economic, social, and cultural transformation, it ranked among the richest and most developed nations in the world. Those who set in motion such amazing progress were called the Generation of the '80s, a group of bright, Conservative statesmen, determined to build a replica of modern Europe in Argentina's vast and fertile territory.

Buenos Aires, the capital, became the symbol of this dream. British railways connected the city to the grain- and beef-producing pampas, far-off Patagonia, and the northern provinces. London-based shops and companies, like Harrods and Lloyds, set up subsidiaries in town. French architects and landscape designers, aided by hordes of European workers who settled in Buenos Aires, rapidly turned primitive colonial houses into an elegant city of *petit-hotels*, treelined boulevards, and lush parks. Soon Buenos Aires was dubbed "the Paris of South America." To this day, a popular joke defines the *porteño* (the native of Buenos Aires) as "an Italian who dresses in English clothes and speaks Spanish with a French accent."

And yet, as the city was clad in "civilized" European attire, two indigenous art forms developed in the poorer districts, where immigrants and *criollos* (people of Spanish-Indian descent) were brewing a totally new urban culture. These art forms were the tango, a popular song, music, and dance, and the *filete porteño*, the tradition of decorating horsecarts, trucks (fig.1), and, much later, city buses with colorful arabesques, Gothic inscriptions, and ingenious paintings (fig. 2). Over the years, the lament of the tango and the strident twirls of the *filete* became the musical and visual blueprints of the city, a unique expression of its heart and soul. However, in the beginning, both were despised and even banned by the official culture, which looked to Paris and London for models as it tried to forget its American roots.

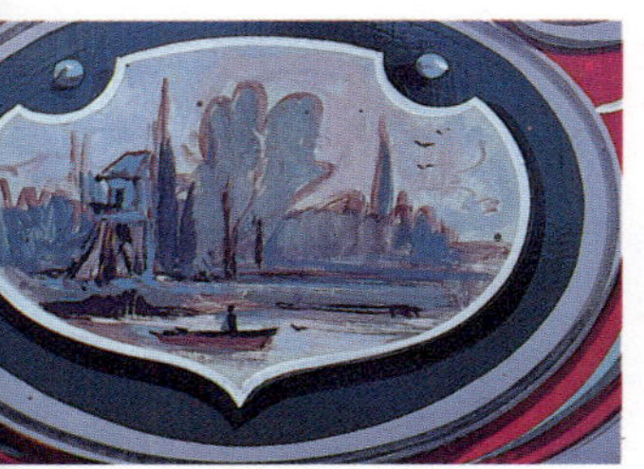

Fig. 2. León Untroib, truck panel, medallion with riverscape, detail, oil on wood, Buenos Aires.

The tango, born in the brothels and lowlife districts of Buenos Aires, was considered vulgar, erotic, and obscene by the ruling class and was prohibited on its dance floors. Not until the 1930s, when Carlos Gardel[1] took it to Paris, introduced it to the aristocracy there, and returned in black tie, was the tango admitted into the elegant ballrooms of the city.

1. Carlos Gardel, born in Toulouse, France in 1889, was raised in Uruguay and became a tango celebrity in Argentina early in this century. When he sang in Paris, he won immediate success and went on to make films in Hollywood. Then, at the peak of his career, he died at the age of forty-eight in a plane crash in Colombia. His sudden and premature death transformed him into a mythical figure for most Argentines and tango lovers.

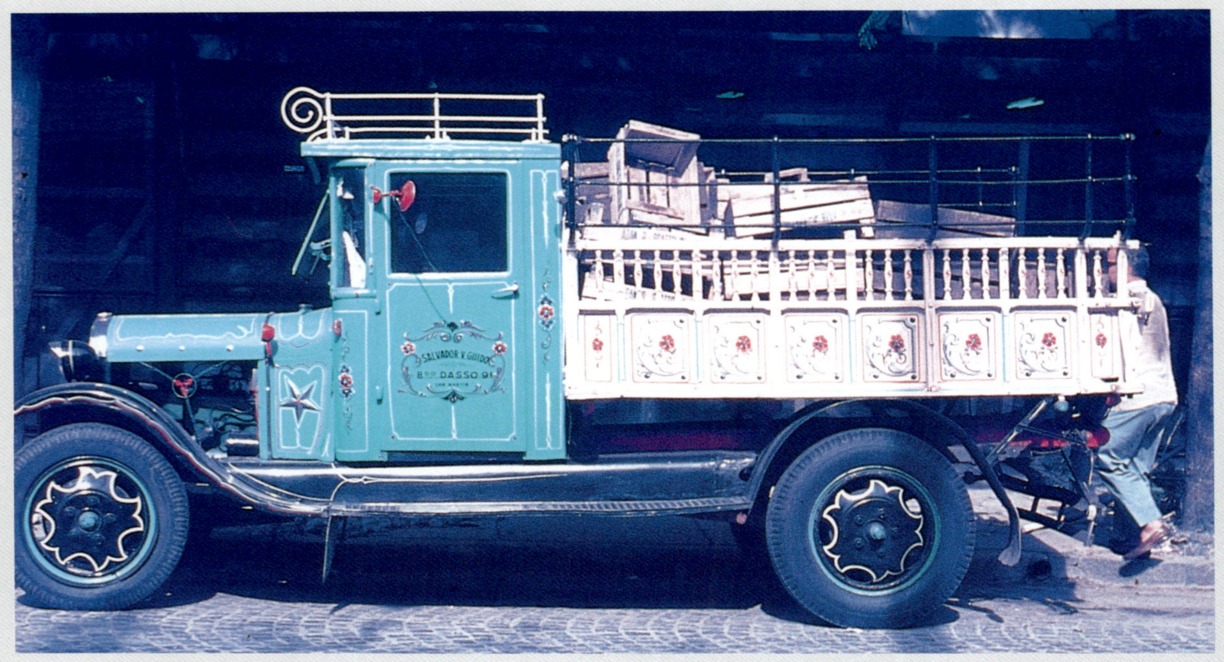

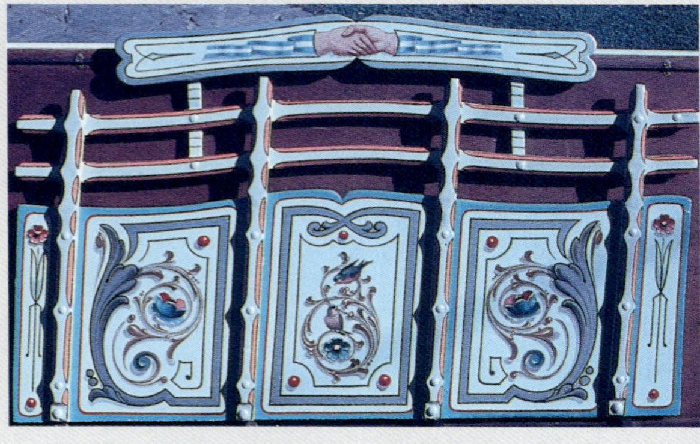

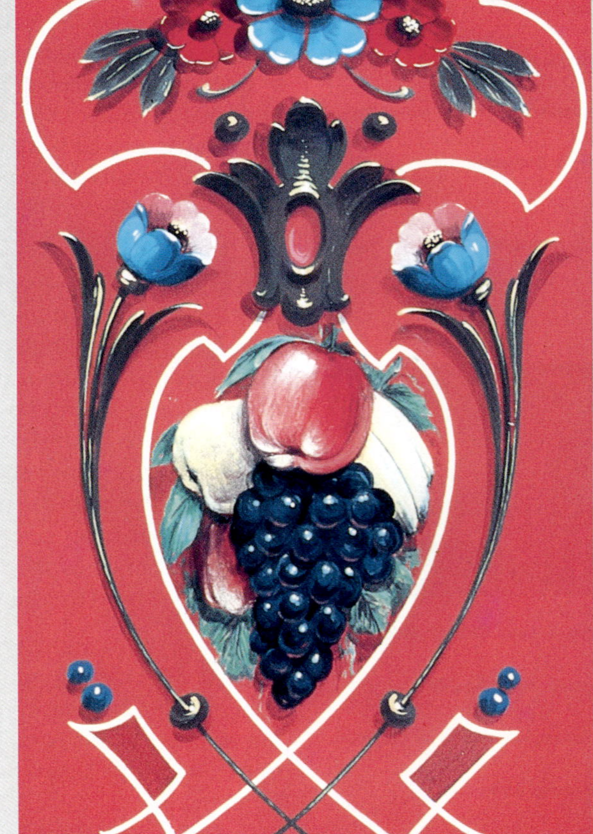

▲

Fig. 3. Carlos Carboni, horsecart side, oil on wood, Buenos Aires.

Fig. 4. Carlos Carboni, truck panel with fruit, detail, oil on wood. Museum of the City of Buenos Aires.

◄

Fig. 5. Typical grocer's cart, oil on wood, ca. 1930, Buenos Aires.

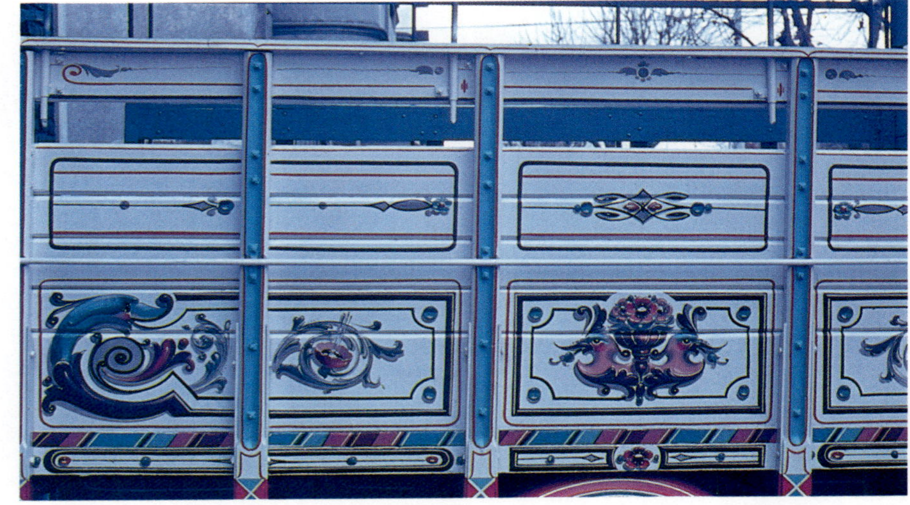

Fig. 6. León Untroib, truck panel with dolphin and dragons, oil on wood, Buenos Aires.

The *filete*, on the other hand, was simply ignored. Born in the food markets (fig. 5), it was perceived as a "thing of grocers and truck drivers."[2] Cultural officials, artists, and intellectuals did not even consider it a legitimate popular craft since, they assumed, it was only a bad copy of Sicilian cart paintings brought to Argentina by the Italians.

For almost eighty years, decorated horsecarts, trucks (fig. 4), and buses filled the streets of Buenos Aires with brightly colored mermaids, dolphin (fig. 6), birds, flowers, architectural ornaments, sophisticated arabesques (fig. 3), gaucho scenes, Gardel portraits (fig. 7), religious figures (fig. 10), flags, and pearled calligraphies. But no one ever wondered who painted the *filetes*, or where they came from. The flashy ambulatory paintings were so routine in the daily life of the city that most *porteños* ceased to see them. Then two artists, the Catalan painter Nicolás Rubió and his wife, the Argentine sculptor Esther Barugel, set out in 1967 to track down the anonymous authors, called *fileteadores* or *filete* painters.

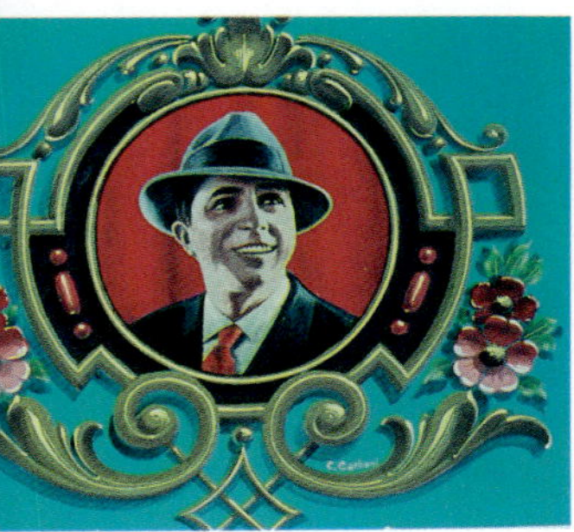

Fig. 7. Carlos Carboni, truck panel, Carlos Gardel portrait, oil on wood. Museum of the City of Buenos Aires.

The word *filete* comes from the Latin *filum* (thread) and the French *fil* or *filet*. It means—as does the English word fillet—a concave junction where two surfaces meet; a narrow flat architectural member; a flat molding separating others; or a design impressed in a book cover. In English, the verb fillet means "to adorn with or as if with a fillet."[3]

In his unpublished book, *Los maestros fileteadores de Buenos Aires* (The master *filete* painters of Buenos Aires), Nicolás Rubió recalls: "When I arrived in Argentina in 1948, I noticed that the carts and trucks of the city were vividly decorated. Every morning at dawn, at the train station in Floresta, I saw dozens of decorated milk carts loading milk from the dairy train (figs. 8 and 9). I assumed (certainly a logical assumption) that everybody knew about these paintings. I thought it undoubtedly was a well-researched topic. The horsecarts and trucks were everywhere. It was impossible not to see them. However, as years went by, and through my conversations with artists and others, I realized that

2. Nicolás Rubió and Esther Barugel, taped interview with author, 15 June 1991.

3. *Sopena enciclopedia ilustrada de la lengua Castellana*, 1961; and *The Random House Dictionary of the English Language*, unabridged, 2nd ed., 1987.

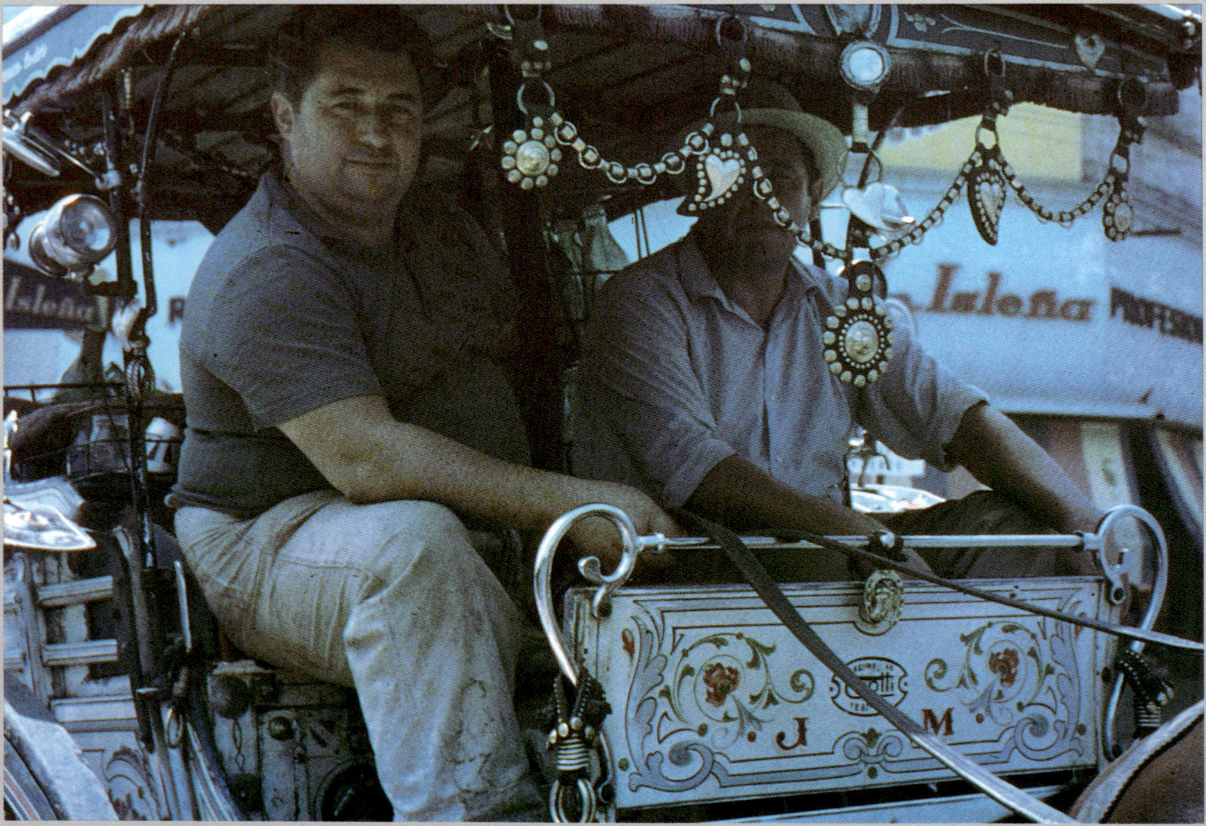

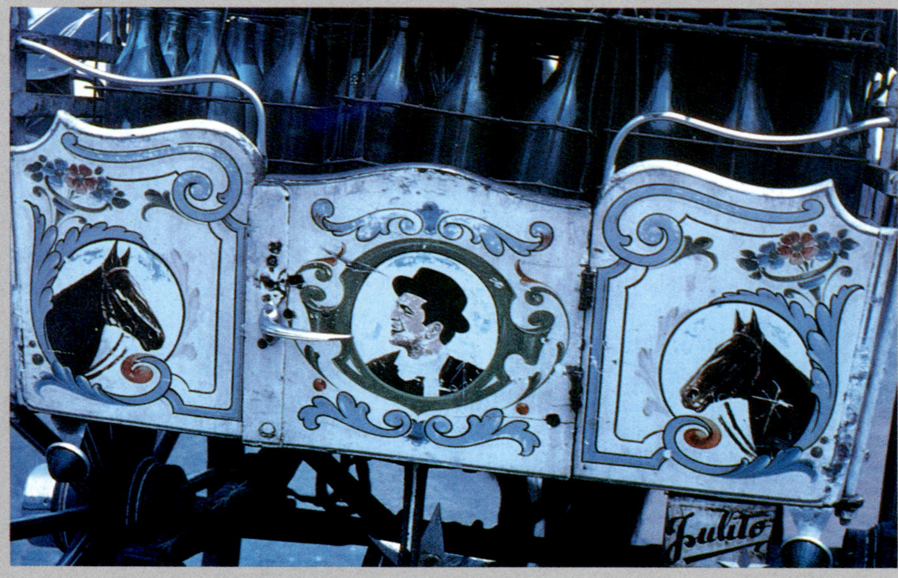

Figs. 8 and 9. Milkman's horsecart, oil on wood, Buenos Aires.

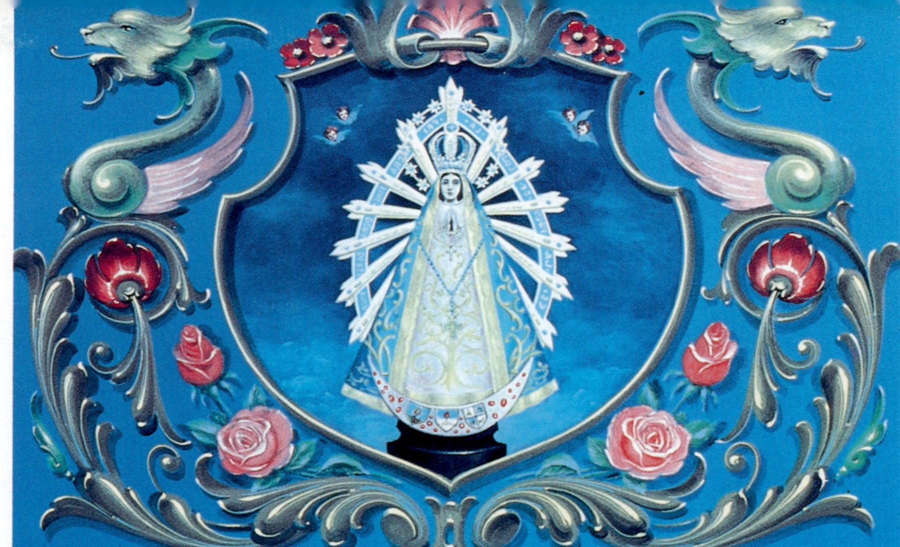

Fig. 10. Carlos Carboni, truck panel depicting the Virgin of Lujan, oil on wood. Museum of the City of Buenos Aires.

Fig. 11. Carlos Carboni, truck panel with mask, oil on wood. Museum of the City of Buenos Aires.

these decorations did not interest anyone. Such inexplicable indifference made the ornamentations all the more attractive to me" (fig. 11).

In late 1967, Rubió and Barugel decided to start a detailed research of the *filetes*. Their final goal was to curate an exhibition of the most important painters. "But when we talked with gallery owners, we could read in their incredulous stares that they thought we were absolutely crazy," Rubió says.[4]

They decided to try their luck at the Wildenstein Gallery,[5] where they had shown their own work. They felt instinctively that Lupo A. Stein, its director, would say no. Instead, Stein listened attentively and finally replied: "Okay, but keep it a secret."[6]

Their adventure had begun. For almost two years they photographed every horsecart and truck found in their long explorations of the city. (They were not interested in the buses since they could tell it was a simplified version of the craft.) "From the first slides, we realized that within one same style there existed no repetitions," writes Rubió. "The established formula was broken again and again by each artist's inventiveness. The photographs allowed us to compare types of flowers (figs. 12 and 13), different designs of doors and fronts....

4. Nicolás Rubió, *Los maestros fileteadores de Buenos Aires*, unpublished manuscript, 17.

5. The Wildenstein Gallery is a French gallery with branches in New York, Tokyo, and London. Their prestigeous Buenos Aires branch opened in the 1950s and closed in 1990.

6. Rubió, *Los maestros*, 17.

Fig. 12. León Untroib, truck panel with roses, detail, oil on wood, Buenos Aires.

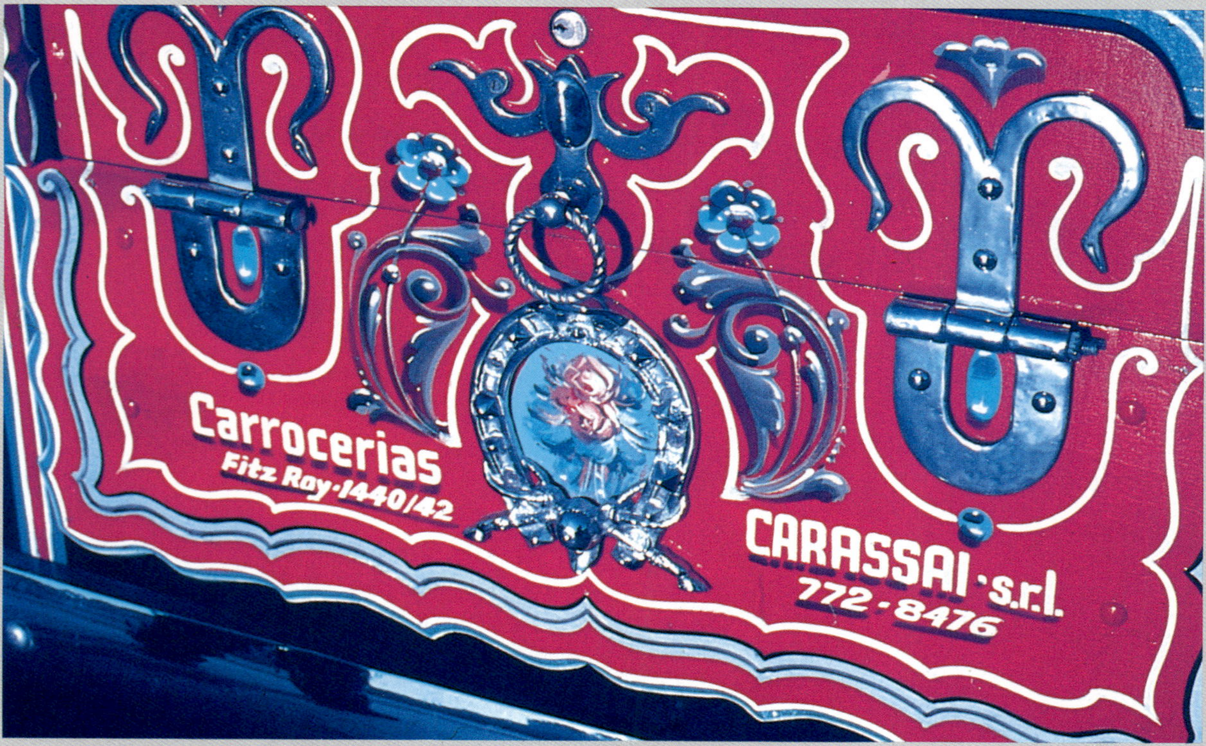

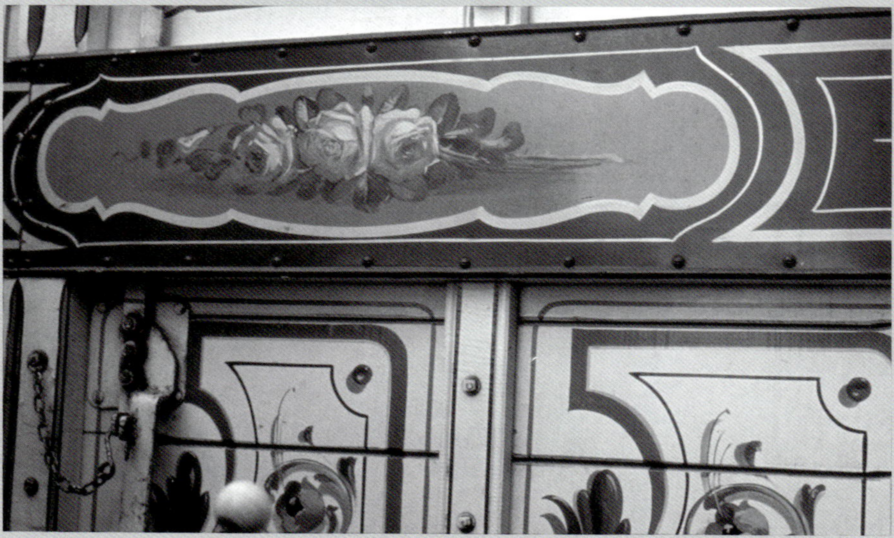

Fig. 13. León Untroib, wooden toolbox, Buenos Aires.

As we arranged the pictures, we were able to form our first hypothesis: this was a living art. The old stuff was thrown away or repainted. This explained why new images always appeared. The so-called experts kept telling us that it had no value, but we had stopped listening to them, so seduced were we by the *filetes*."[7]

With the help of Heriberto Arbolave, an art collector, they were able to discard the theory that the *filete* was a copy of Sicilian *carretto* paintings. At his house, Arbolave had a fragment of one of these carts, and it revealed scant similarities with the Argentine version. The sides of Sicilian carts were decorated with colored bas-reliefs, generally illustrating a legend or historical scene. It was a primitive, narrative art. The *filete*, on the other hand, was an essentially pictorial, graphic, and symmetrical art in which the careful use of lights, shadows, and contrasts of colors created an illusion of depth and volume. Its abstract ornaments could be traced back to the bell-shaped Corinthian capitals—with their acanthus leaves—and to the Pompeii decorations; but it had a definitively nineteenth- and twentieth-century flavor. The question remained: where had these Buenos Aires cart painters learned their craft?

In photo expeditions, when they asked the proud cart and truck owners who had painted their cars, Rubió and Barugel began hearing the same names over and over. "León painted it; Carboni did it; Arce, the Brunetti brothers...." Who were these people? Where did they live?

In January 1970, Barugel decided they should visit the cart and truck garages where the wooden structures of the vehicles were made and quite possibly painted. After several frustrating, failed attempts, at the Erdocia factory they finally met the *filete* painter León Untroib. "We expected to find a naive, humble, intuitive artist. Instead, we found a tall and venerable professor," says Rubió.[8] Untroib was a cultivated man, with a fine arts education. "When we told him about the exhibition and asked him to paint a panel for us, he did not say anything, but we could tell that he was more interested in being recognized as a canvas artist than as a *fileteador*," Rubió recalls. "Though he talked enthusiastically about his *filetes*, the intellectual prejudices dividing the Arts, with a capital *A*, from the mere crafts were so strong that we could sense Untroib did not want to appear in artistic circles as a truck painter."[9]

Despite his apprehensions, León Untroib gradually introduced them to the closely knit and undiscovered world of the car factories and the *fileteadores*. There they met the handful of men who had given life to this popular art since the late 1800s. The master painters were approaching their eighties and the younger disciples their fifties. Their names were Carlos Carboni, Alfredo and Enrique Brunetti (figs. 14 and 15), the Bernasconi brothers, Andrés Vogliotti (Figs. 16, 17, and 18), and Enrique Arce, among others. Like Untroib, most of them had studied drawing and painting at neighborhood academies and were passionate about their art.

Eventually, Alfredo and Enrique Brunetti revealed the true history of the *filete*. "The first *fileteadores* were my father, Vicente Brunetti, born in Agnone, Italy, in 1874, and his friend Cecilo Pascarella, also of Italian birth," says Enrique. Both men had come to Argentina with their parents at a very young age and, when they turned seven, began to work in a horsecart factory. There they did

7. Ibid., 12.
8. Ibid., 29–30.
9. Rubió and Barugel, interview, 15 June 1991.

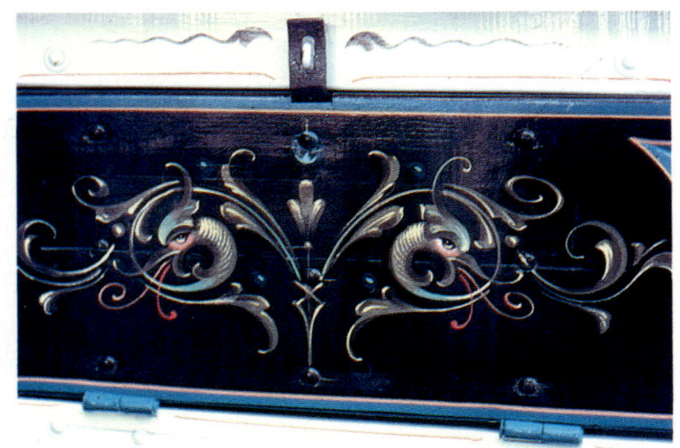

Fig. 14. Alfredo and Enrique Brunetti, wooden toolbox, Buenos Aires.

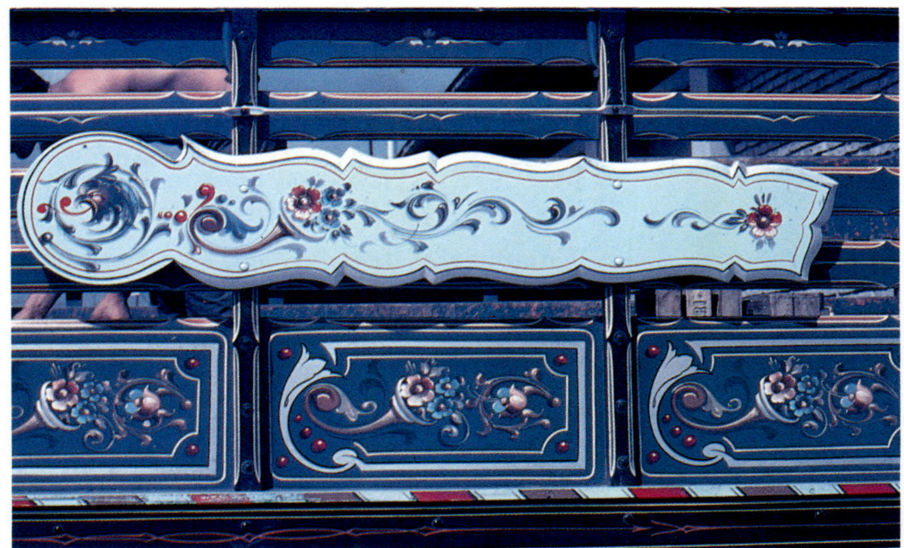

Fig. 15. Alfredo and Enrique Brunetti, truck panel, oil on wood, Buenos Aires.

errands, fetched tools, and prepared the mate (a local herbal beverage). After a few years, the garage owner asked if they wanted to paint the carts which, at the time, were done all in grey. Brunetti and Pascarella were delighted. "One day—probably in the early 1890s—my father decided to paint the concave edge of one of the cart's panels, known as the *chanfle*, in a different color," Enrique remembers. When his boss saw it, he liked it very much, and the owner loved it. "When the little cart arrived at the market place it caused a real sensation." From then on, every grocer, milkman, and bread deliverer wanted to have the prettiest cart in town (fig. 19).[10]

Pascarella was the skillful artisan who painted the letters incorporating the names of the cart owners and their firms. He carefully imitated the art of the French shop window and billboard calligraphists who worked in Buenos Aires at the time. Later, Rubió and Barugel were told that the elaborate Gothic letters characteristic of the *filete* were inspired by the Gothic calligraphy on peso bills. "For people in the food business, Gothic letters represented progress and wealth," explains Barugel.[11] They were also told that most *fileteadores* did not

10. Enrique Brunetti, interview with author, 21 June 1991.

11. Rubió and Barugel, interview, 15 June 1991.

Fig. 16. Andres Vogliotti, horsecart, detail, oil on wood, Buenos Aires.

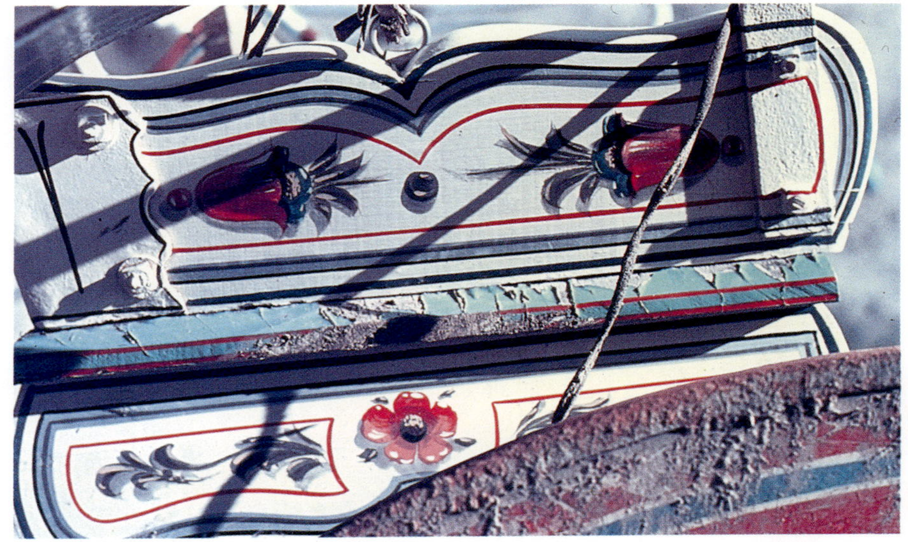

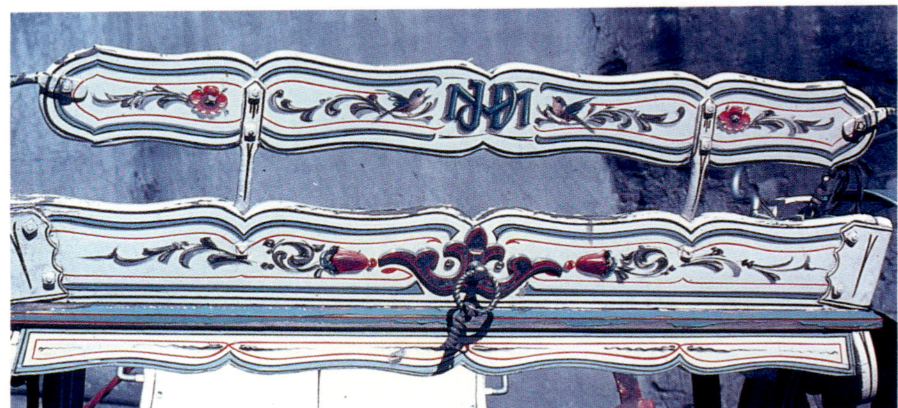

Fig. 17. Andres Vogliotti, horsecart, detail, Buenos Aires.

Fig. 18. Andres Vogliotti, horsecart, detail, oil on wood, Buenos Aires.

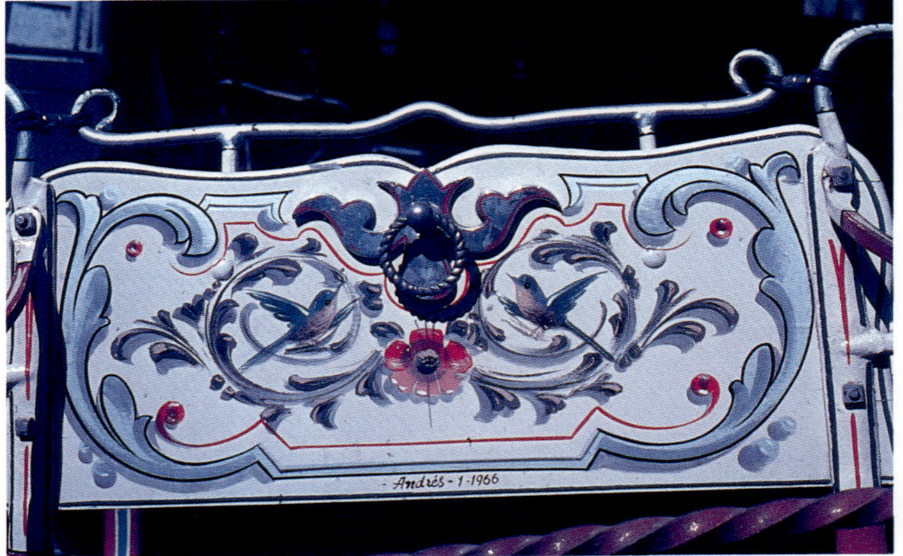

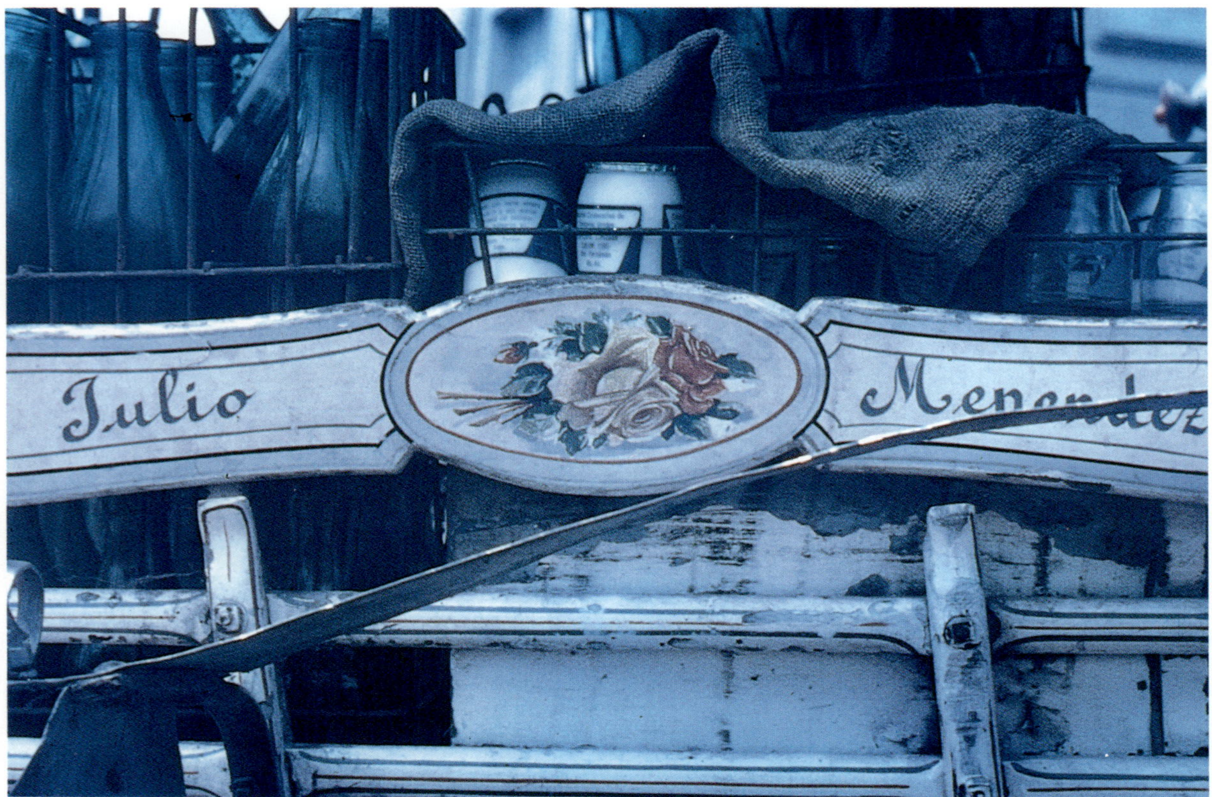

Fig. 19. Milkman's horsecart, detail, oil on wood, Buenos Aires.

like the witty phrases—such as, "Babe, kill me and come to my funeral"—that vehicle owners liked to paint on the front or back of their cars.

During long conversations in the truck factories (very few horsecart manufacturers were left), Rubió and Barugel also discovered that the man who "revolutionized" and fully developed the *filete* had been the late Miguel Venturo.[12] He was the son of Salvador Venturo, one of the first *fileteadores* at the turn of the century. Untroib (figs. 20 and 21), Carboni, and the Brunettis revered Miguel Venturo. They all said he was the master they emulated. In the early twentieth century, Venturo introduced a series of elements that became standard in the *filete*—dragons, diamonds, balls, birds, arabesques, medallions with gaucho scenes in them, and a rich assortment of architectural designs that he copied from the moldings and ironwork of the city's buildings.

Carlos Carboni, an outstanding *fileteador* who died in 1988 at the age of eighty-nine, once said of his master: "Venturo walked the streets. He got ideas by looking around. I think he took the dragons from the facade of the Cervantes Theatre. Have you ever looked at that theater? It's full of dragons and ornaments. What happens is that one passes by without looking."[13]

Carboni himself used to walk through the city searching for material for his *filetes*. His colleagues say that he salvaged objects from garbage cans.

12. Before Miguel Venturo, the *filete* was very simple—a few lines underscoring the edges of a cart, a flower or two next to the name of the company spelled in Gothic letters. Venturo began to fill every inch of the cart with sophisticated figures, drawings, and patterns. This information is from interviews with Nicholás Rubió, León Untroib, and Enrique Brunetti on 15, 20, and 21 June 1991, respectively.

13. Rubió, *Los maestros,* 84–85.

Fig. 20. León Untroib, truck panel with horses, oil on wood, Buenos Aires.

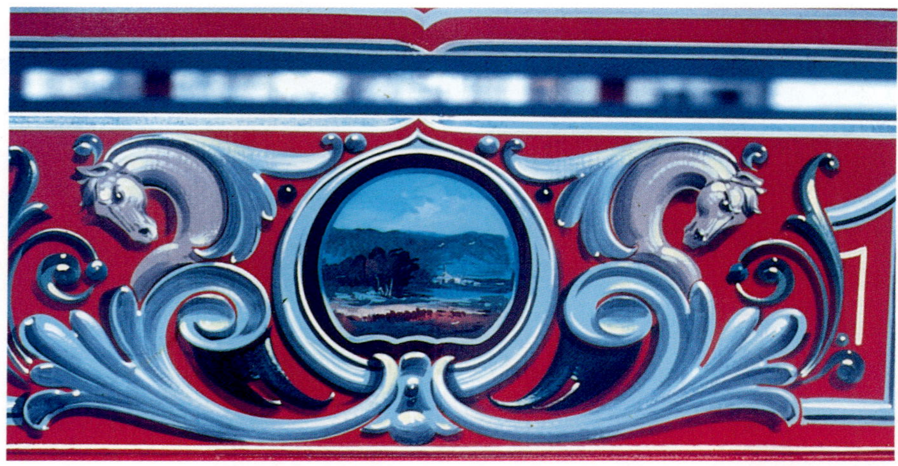

"The *filete* was created with chunks of the city," says Rubió, after more than twenty years of intense research in the field.[14]

In two generations, from approximately 1880 to 1940, a unique esthetic had developed. It resembled many different forms of popular painting found abroad, like the decorations of English Gypsy caravans, the Sicilian *carrettos*, or the painted buses and trucks found in Afghanistan, Haiti, and the Philippines. It even shared some common traits with the *peinture decorative* of the *pâtisserie* shop windows of nineteenth-century France. But the *filete* had its own particular formulas, images, and language.[15]

Technically, the *filete* is a complex art. León Untroib says that the *fileteador* "like the fresco painter must master several crafts at the same time." He must skillfully draw lines and elaborate arabesques with the longhaired fillet brushes (fig. 25). He must be a calligraphist and an artful draftsman and colorist as well.[16]

"Often, young men came up to me saying they wanted to learn the trade. But I would tell them that for the first two years all they would do is clean the paint cans and brushes," says Enrique Brunetti, now eighty years old. "It takes at least two months to learn how to draw the lines. One has to train the hand in the use of the fillet brushes," he explains. Besides, a good *fileteador* must spend several years in art school. "When we started out, my father told us: 'If you don't learn painting and drawing, you'll run into trouble.'"[17]

From beginning to end, the decoration of a vehicle involves at least seven stages. In the garage, a painter known as the *pintor de liso* paints the cart or truck in one color, the background color of the painting. Then the *fileteador* draws half of his design with chalk or charcoal directly on the panel. He folds tracing paper (called *spulvero*) in two and traces the drawing onto it (fig. 22). Then he pierces the drawing with a ravioli wheel (fig. 23), and, when he unfolds the paper, he has a completely symmetrical design. After erasing the first sketch from the panel, he spreads the *spulvero* against it and rubs the design

14. Nicolás Rubió and Esther Barugel, interview with author, 20 June 1991.

15. The FE, María Ofelia Escassany Foundation has an excellent video on the subject of the *filete*. Their address and telephone are Ombú 3061, 1425 Buenos Aires, Argentina, (541) 802-9188.

16. León Untroib, interview with author, 20 June 1991.

17. Brunetti, interview, 21 June 1991.

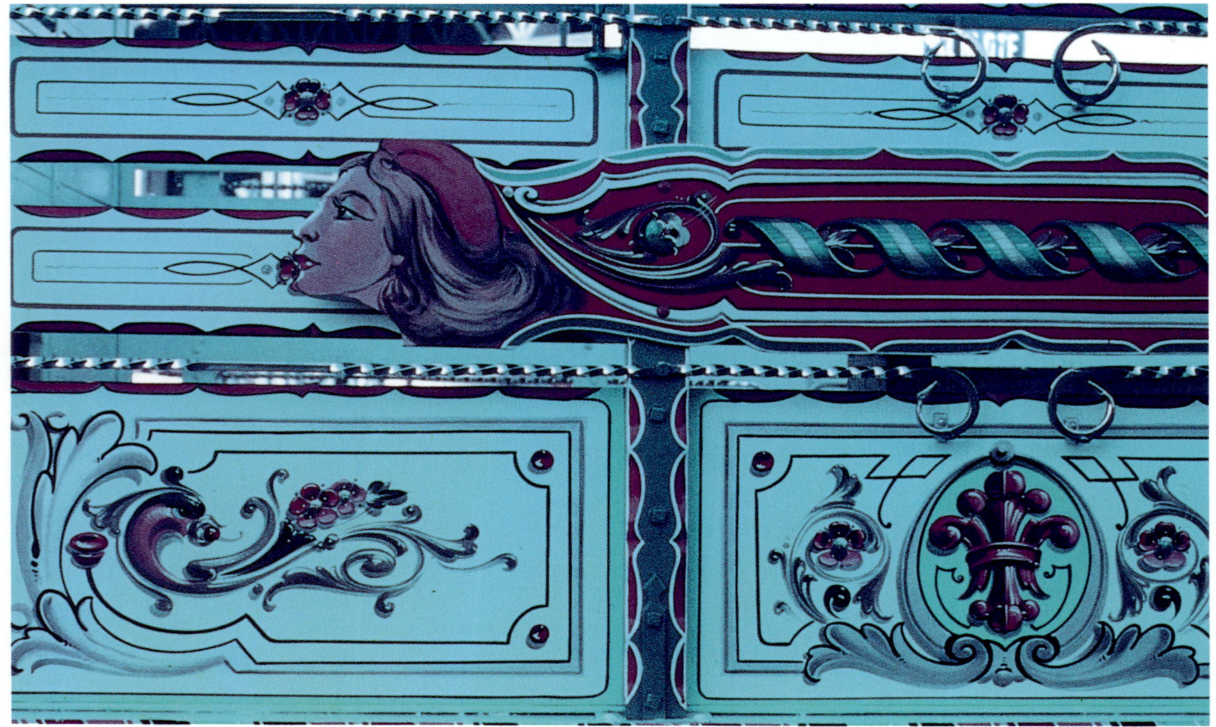

Fig. 21. León Untroib, truck panels, oil on wood, Buenos Aires.

with charcoal or chalk powder, tracing it onto the panel (fig. 24). He then paints the lines, ornaments, figures, and scenes with his longhaired fillet brushes (figs. 26 and 27). Finally, the *pintor de liso* paints the whole vehicle with a coat of glossy, protective, transparent enamel.[18]

On 14 September 1970, Nicolás Rubió and Esther Barugel inaugurated an exhibition called Los Maestros Fileteadores de Buenos Aires at the Wildenstein Gallery, right on fancy Florida Street. For the first time, the *filete* was leaving the markets and garages and making its entrée into the art scene. The show was a complete public and media success.[19]

Remembering that day, Rubió writes in his book: "As soon as the gallery opened its doors at ten that morning, journalists kept coming in one after the other, asking for information and pictures. The phone never stopped ringing. One reporter wanted to do an interview in a garage. Another asked to take the *fileteadores* to a radio show. A television station inquired what was the best hour to film.... By 6 P.M. the gallery was packed."

Perhaps the most significant effect of the show was the impact it had on the public. Rubió writes: "People kept saying, 'Thank you for giving us back our childhood, for making us see what we didn't see.' In an unconscious way, the *filete* lay dormant in the collective memory of the city."

Paradoxically, in the 1970s, as it rose to the status of a legitimate art form, the traditional *filete* began to die. The exhibition had been premonitory because, in that decade, the *fileteado* of trucks and buses began to disappear. Stifled by a

18. Rubió, *Los maestros*, 171–175.

19. *Fileteadores* who exhibited in the 1970 Wildenstein Gallery show donated that work to the Museum of the City of Buenos Aires, which has the most important collection of *fileteado* extant.

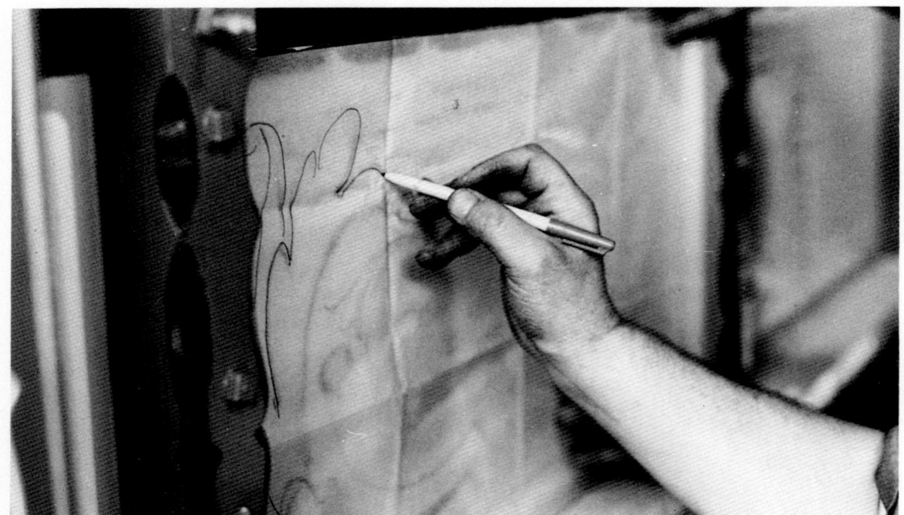

Fig. 22. León Untroib drawing on tracing paper.

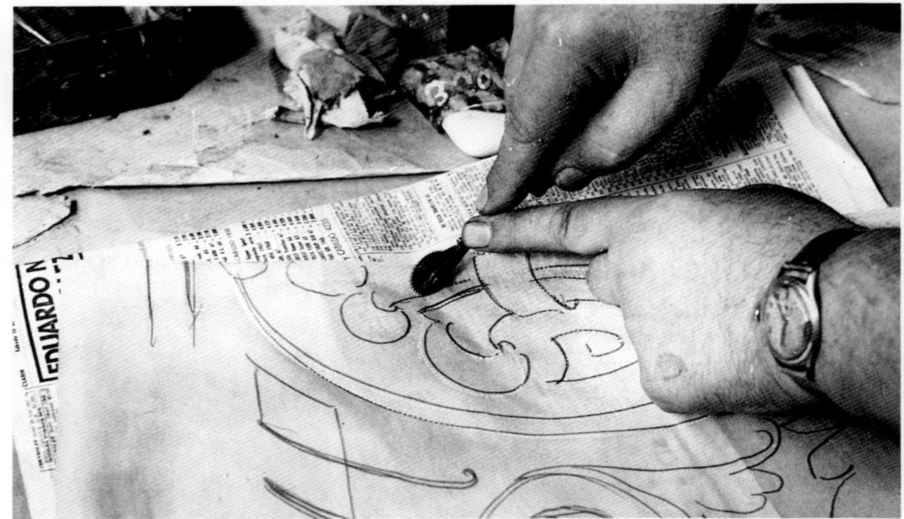

Fig. 23. León Untroib piercing a drawing with a ravioli wheel.

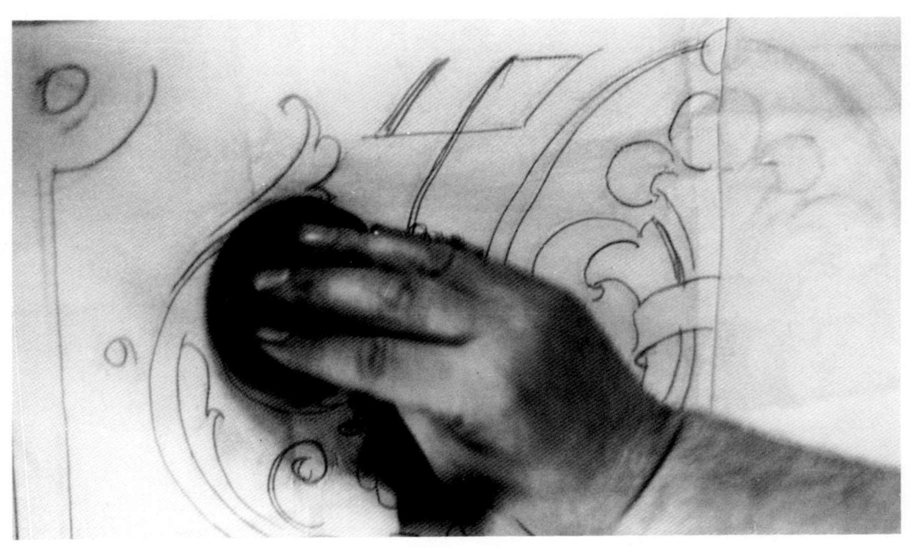

Fig. 24. León Untroib tracing a design onto a wooden truck panel by rubbing the pierced paper drawing with charcoal powder.

Fig. 25. León Untroib's fillet brushes.

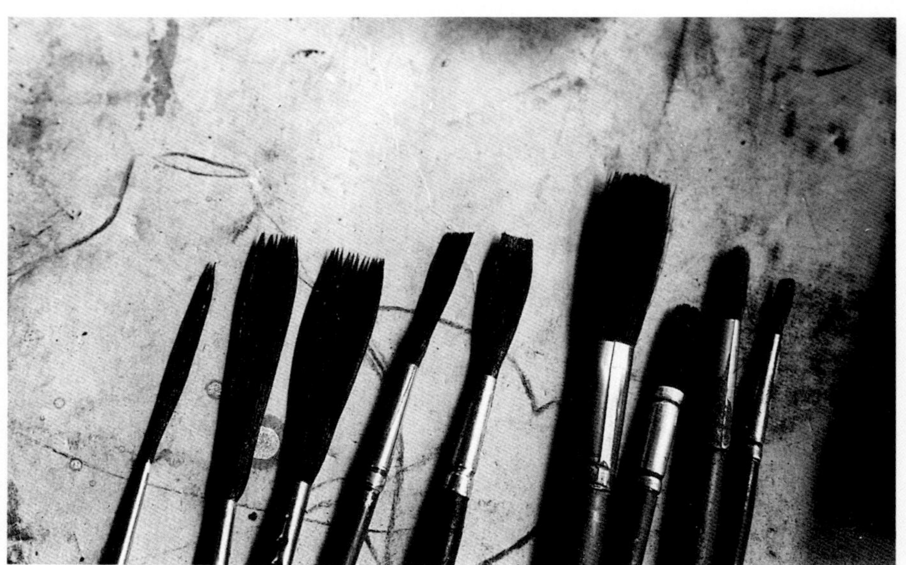

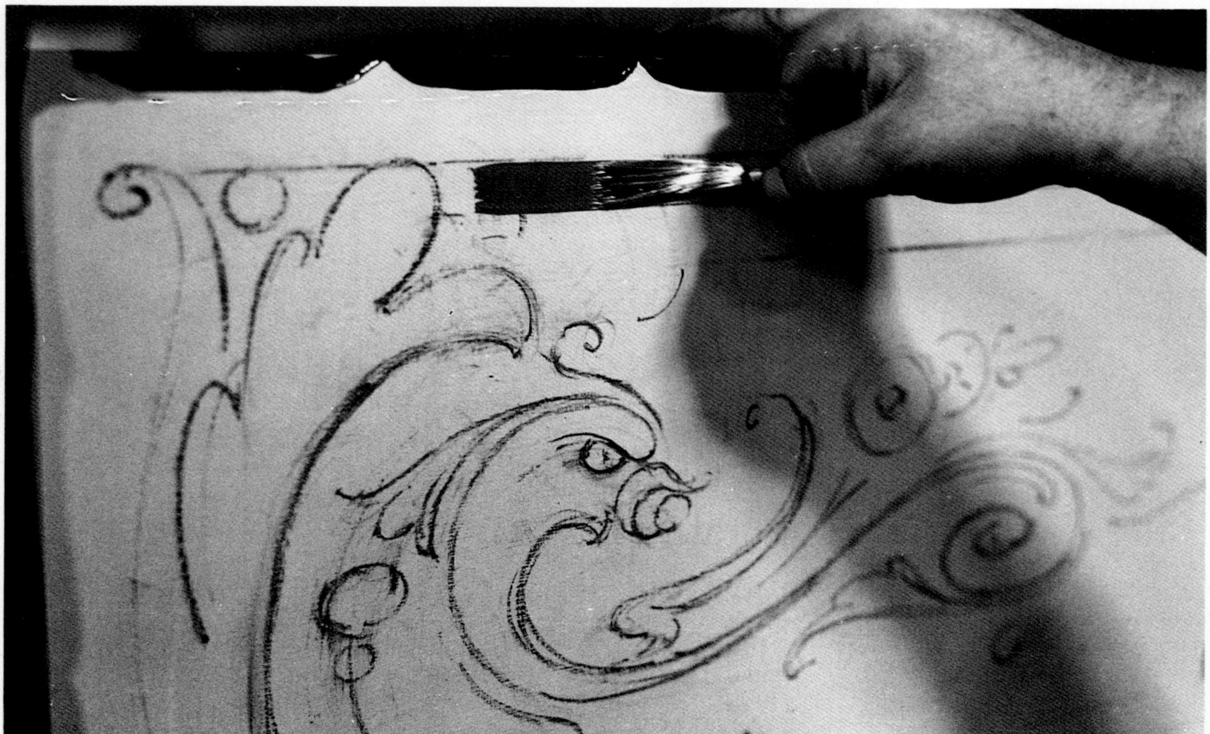

Fig. 26. León Untroib painting a *filete*.

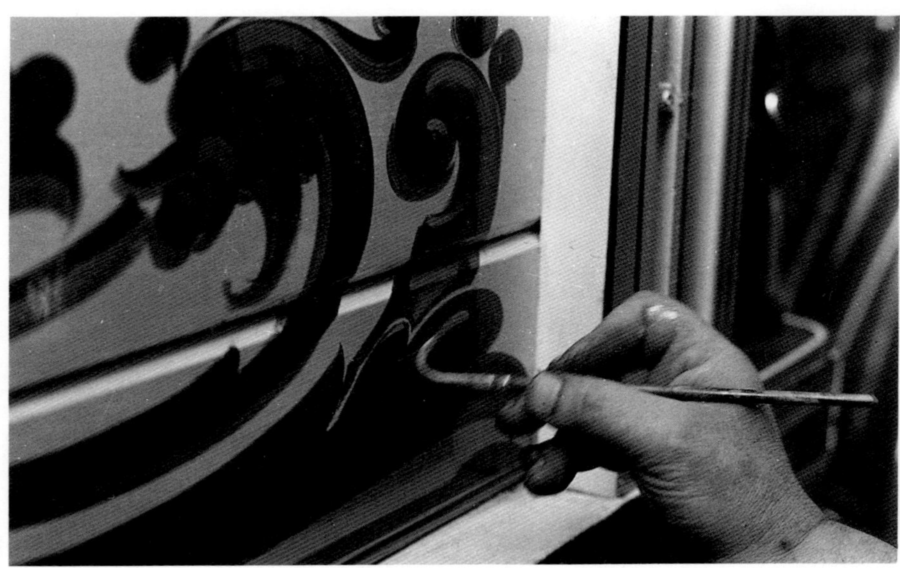

Fig. 27. León Untroib painting a *filete*.

growing economic crisis, grocers, truck owners, and food vendors were gradually forced to give up the relatively expensive decorations. Today, very few ornamented trucks remain.

The *fileteado* could easily have survived in the thousands of buses that crisscross the city. But, in 1975, the Department of Transportation issued a decree prohibiting all bus decorations. Roberto Caram, a member of the committee suggesting the measure, explains: "The *fileteado* had degenerated. The buses were full of flags, bleeding hearts, Gardel portraits. We had to put an end to all of that."[20]

Nicolás Rubió thinks that the real reasons behind the prohibition were more profound. "The official culture never appreciated the *filete*; there always was an animosity toward it," he says. "The fact is, to be 'cultivated' in Argentina, you have to have an English decal on your car."[21]

And yet, because the *filete* was such a vital art, it was able to survive in new media. Martiniano Arce, one of the best contemporary *fileteadores*, transformed it into a canvas art. He regularly exhibits his paintings in prestigious local galleries as well as abroad. A few years ago, in Holland, he decorated a whole bus in the *porteño* style. It was such a success that 150,000 people visited the show.

In recent years, the *filete* has reappeared throughout the city in restaurant and shop billboards, in shop windows and murals. Younger designers, like Luis Zorzs, are using it to illustrate the covers of tango magazines and records. Jorge Muscia, a thirty-three year old *fileteador*, used it in television set designs and video experiments. Optimistic about the future, Muscia says: "As long as the *filete* adapts to new places and new media, it will stay alive."[22]

More importantly, the *filete* will always live in the heart of every *porteño*. □

20. Roberto Caram, telephone conversation with author, 25 June 1991.

21. Nicolás Rubió, telephone conversation with author, 20 June 1991.

22. Jorge Muscia, interview with author, 20 June 1991.

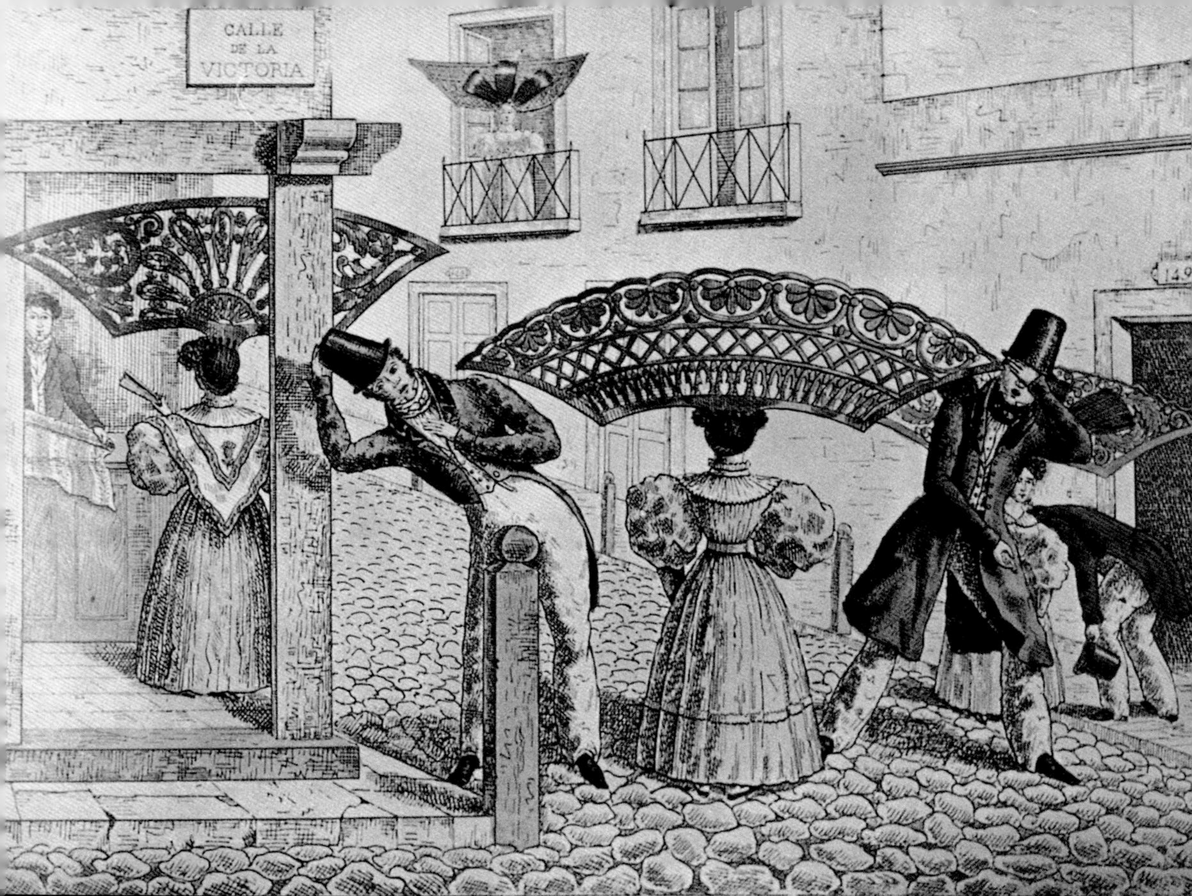

Fig. 1. César H. Bacle, *Extravagancias de 1834* (Extravagances of 1834), lithograph, no. 2 in a series, 8 x 24 cm. Ornamental combs worn on the streets of Buenos Aires. Isaac Fernández Blanco Museum, Buenos Aires.

Fig. 2. Carlos E. Pellegrini, *Juana Rodriguez de Carranza,* watercolor, 37.5 x 24.8 cm. National Museum of Fine Arts, Buenos Aires.

High Fashion: The Search for a Style

By Elena Moreira

Translated by Edward Shaw

Elena Moreira holds a degree from the School of Journalism of Buenos Aires and has been press coordinator for the minister of public works. In 1989, she joined the staff of *El Cronista Commercial* where she is fashion editor. She also edits their weekly supplement *Mujer*.

They were the Muses of poets like Apollinaire, Cendrars, and Darío, immortalized in portraits by Boldini, Sargent, Whistler, and Zuloaga, reincarnated in busts by Rodin or Trubetzkoy. The Argentine woman of this period, especially after 1914, was recognized by the entire world for her elegance. However, this distinction was not accompanied by an authentic local style. Rather, it reflected a special gift that Argentines have of assimilating people and patterns—call it mimesis if you will—which simultaneously stamped the country and its fashions with a special personality. The Argentine woman adapted fashions from other countries, taking what coincided with the idiosyncrasies of her own national character. Just as the mixture of many different nationalities formed an undeniably Argentine archetype, in the same way French, English, and Italian fashions eventually blended into a recognizable Argentine style.

Throughout the history of fashion, there were only two completely original Argentine contributions. One was the blood-red "Federal bow" which came in vogue in 1838 during the bloody reign of Juan Manuel de Rosas. Women wore it on the left side of their hairdos or on a lapel. Men wore it on lapels or hats. The other outburst revolutionizing the local look was provided by large ornamental combs called *peinetones* (figs. 1 and 2). They played a role of singular importance, so much so that they were depicted in virtually every mid-nineteenth-century engraving. Introduced around 1810 by a Spanish merchant, Manuel Mateo Masculino, their popularity continued until 1864. Some of them came to measure more than 120 centimeters. The materials preferred by *porteñas*—as ladies of this port city are called—were tortoise shell, bone, and ivory, carved or modeled artistically in relief.

After 1870, the last vestiges of colonial Buenos Aires vanished, and the society of the Río de la Plata grew more complex, modified by the phenomenon of immigration. To the enormous increase in population—6,500,000 foreigners between 1856 and 1930[1]—a tenfold explosion in foreign trade was added, provoking rapid growth in per capita income. *Porteñas* who followed to the letter the formal mandates of French styles, first filtered by Spanish taste, replaced their crinolines (those long starched skirts which in Spanish were *medriñaque*, and in the Río de la Plata became *miriñaque*) with the bustle and its hoops made with corset stays, generally independent of the dress itself. These dresses were also called *tapiceros*—Spanish for upholsterers—

1. Gino Germani, *Política y sociedad en una época de transición* (Buenos Aires: Editorial Paidos, 1974), 274–275.

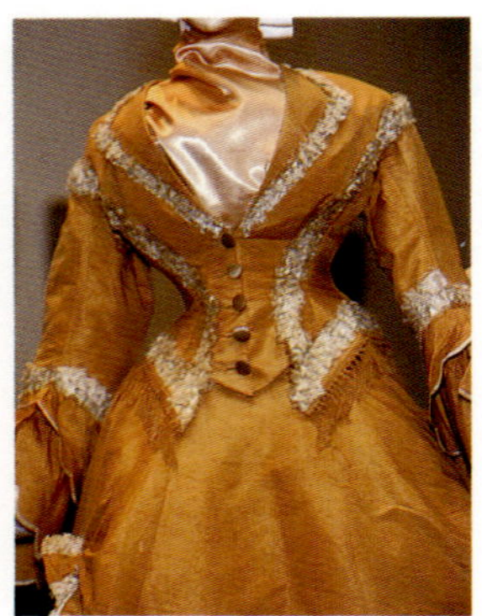

Fig. 3. Dress with a bustle, 1878. National Museum of the History of Costume, Buenos Aires.

since they were closed at the back with cords like those upholsterers used on venetian blinds.

In the collection at the National Museum of the History of Costume, one can find an 1878 dress with a bustle, composed of three pieces: jacket, skirt, and second open skirt on top, made of gold-colored silk and trimmed with silk fringe forming ruffles (fig. 3). The Polonaise, an elaborate dress popular in the eighteenth century, reappeared with its skirt that opens down the front and in the back sports a moderate train, trimmed around the edge with pleats, pleated ruffles, and bands of lace and passementerie (fig. 5). This style, so baroque and impractical, began to disappear around 1890 when contours became modified and skirts were narrower.

Upper-class families at the end of the century dressed formally at home. Ladies typically wore cotton or poplin dresses (fig. 4) decorated with lace, ribbons, and billowing sleeves called *globo* because of their balloon shape. Children's outfits stayed almost the same for the next several decades. A youngster's wardrobe was mostly made from piqué, buckram, and cambric, or lace with inserts of Valenciennes and satin ribbon. Little girls wore dresses of Irish lace, and little boys shirts and short pants of satin.

When Buenos Aires became the federal capital of Argentina in 1880, with a cosmopolitan population, a renovated architecture, cultured minorities, and an active port, it was the epicenter of changes sweeping the country.

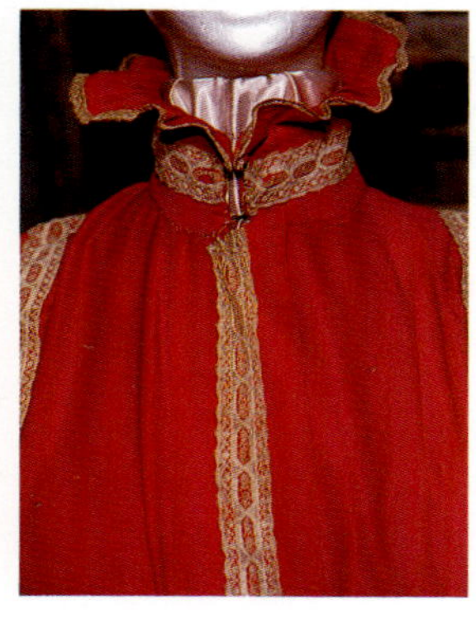

Fig. 4. Cotton and poplin morning dress, 1890. National Museum of the History of Costume, Buenos Aires.

> The first indicator of this new era erupted in the socio-political arena provoking a separation between the masses and the ruling class. The structure and traits of the masses had changed and, as a reaction, the ruling class essentially changed their attitude toward the masses. The liberal tradition acquired an increasingly conservative and aristocratic character. The masses took on a popular and democratic character....
>
> [T]he immigrant and the native-born began to intermarry in the lower class as well as in the middle class, which began to be formed by immigrants who were economically successful. The old republican aristocracy was transformed in this new framework into an oligarchy as they became the owners of the means of production.[2]
>
> A sense of privilege, of social superiority, began to appear in the men of the Generation of the '80s. Their...conviction that they had an unquestionable right, as a patrician class, to the wealth that the native and immigrant masses produced was strengthened. Wealth became the new goal.
>
> Austere habits [were swept away in] the fever for luxury and ostentation set loose by economic power. Further and further removed from the severe demands of republican virtue, they scorned the humble immigrant. At the same time, they succumbed without hesitation to the influence of the Europeans. From them, Argentines learned rules of the high life, along with a preference for French poetry and impeccable English tailoring with its solemn frock coat which ensured social credibility.[3]

These men followed the dictates of English style, an influence dating back to the times of independence. Guided by the dandyism of George Brummel

▸

Fig. 5. Polonaise dress. Illustration by Héctor Basaldúa for the program *Cabildo abierto de la moda* (Open fashion council), 1975.

2. José Luis Romero, ed., *Las ideas políticas en Argentina* (Buenos Aires: Fondo de Cultura Económica, 1987), 63–72.
3. Noe Jitrick, *El mundo del ochenta* (Buenos Aires: Centro del Editor de América Latina, 1982), 68–69.

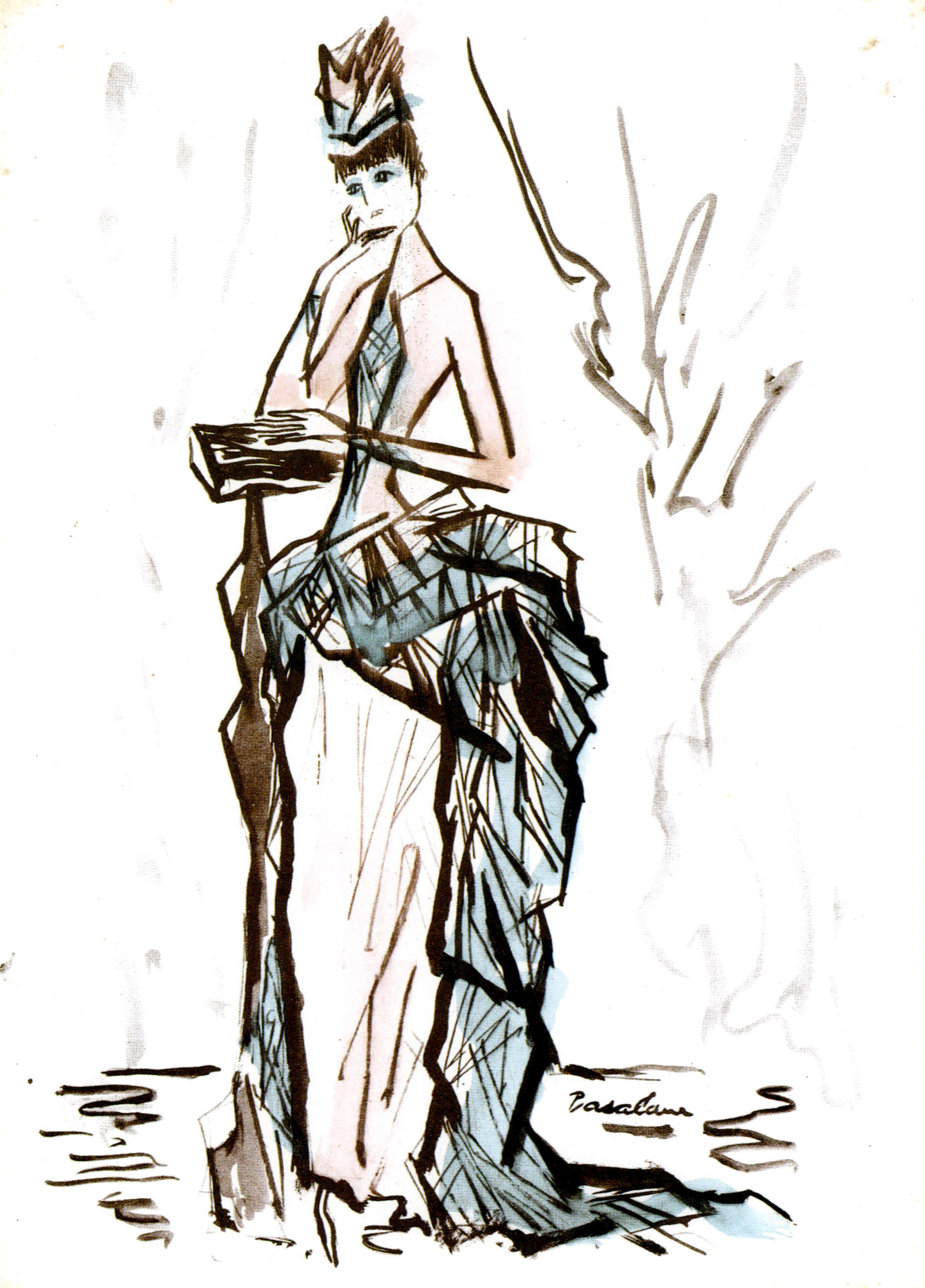

(1778–1840), England was the world leader in men's fashion. In Buenos Aires, dandies or fops set the style of men's suits that would endure throughout the nineteenth and into the early twentieth centuries. Their dark frock coats were worn with narrow-brimmed, tall top hats. The *cavour*, a sleeveless jacket with a single row of buttons and a short mantle, was worn over the jacket. Shirts with detachable fronts, collars, and cuffs were set off by wide neckties. "Attractive gentlemen, often slaves of appearance, wore their frock coats as the ideal outfit for social gatherings, and even government officials dressed this way to go to work."[4] The high degree of mobility of the society at that time, as much horizontal (migratory movements) as vertical (the ability to move easily between classes), reached a high point at this moment, and clothing was the principal way of manifesting it. According to what travelers reported, it was impossible to distinguish in the street between a millionaire and his employee. Among the former, dandies such as Lucio Mansilla, Jr. and Manuel Quintana preferred to wear a dark frock coat, top hat, gloves and the ever-present walking stick. At night they were in tails with a white silk or piqué vest and matching trousers. The necktie was white lace made of silk or linen. The shoes were patent leather with buttoned flannel or kid leather leggings. White gloves were obligatory. Some men preferred a dinner jacket made of black cashmere with a white vest and a piece of black lace used as a necktie.

This clear-cut citifying, and the progress that came with it, displaced that eternal symbol of the Argentine countryside: the gaucho, "who was confused when confronted by so many plows, so many *gringos* [the name given to recently arrived Italian immigrants], and so much barbed wire, none of which he had been taught to deal with. The gaucho let himself dissolve in drink, gambling, and the music of the last *pulperías*—countryside bars which became his almost permanent hangout. With the gaucho went his jacket, his *chiripá* [made from an embroidered woolen shawl with a corner drawn up between his legs] over his *calzoncillo cribado* [lace pantaloons], his pony-skin boots, *nazarena* [poncho], spurs, and *rastra* [a belt elaborately decorated with silver coins]. Urban fashions swept away any vestige of the modest expessivity achieved by the civilization of leather."[5]

In general, women of the countryside and of the city dressed in similar ways. It was only the quality of the cloth each used that set them apart from one another, together with the kerchief in the form of a triangle which rural women knotted around their necks. Masculine fashion, however, was totally different. At first native clothing was manufactured by a textile industry located in the interior of the country which supplied Buenos Aires. In every town, families had their own looms and, in some places, collective workshops spun wool, cotton, hemp, and even silk into thread. Catamarca, a northwestern province, was famed for its fine cloth, its table linen, robes for the clergy, and classical ponchos. In Corrientes, a northern province bordering on Brazil, weavers made fabrics for blankets and bedspreads.

After 1778, with the application of the Rules of Free Trade, local industry that had thrived in the interior suffered from the competition of products imported from abroad. Native textiles were replaced by those coming from England. Beautiful fabrics from London and Paris found in all the city's shops were living proof of the strength of the Industrial Revolution in Great Britain and the

4. García D'Agostino, Rebok, Asato, López, *Imagénes de Buenos Aires a través de los viajeros, 1870–1910* (Buenos Aires: Universidad de Buenos Aires, 1982), 100.

5. María del Carmen Tomeo, "La moda esa dulce tiranía," *Todo es Historia*, no. 30 (1972): 10.

importance that a new breed of businessmen—the importers—would soon have. In 1821, Alexander Caldlengh, an English observer, commented, "Right now there is no manufacturing in Buenos Aires.... [Local products] like rustic ponchos and blankets are brought from the provinces. It would not be strange to discover before too long that some article manufactured in England had come to replace the poncho, although up till now we have not been able to make anything that could be considered its equal."[6]

The dismantling of the provincial textile industry and the need to increase production of raw materials in order to supply the English industrial machine favored the city of Buenos Aires. Its customs authorities, who regulated the entry and exit of every product crossing the city's borders, even from within the country, were greatly enriched by this growing activity. The process was intensified by the arrival of products from France. The fashionable clothing market then was divided between England and France.

At the beginning of the nineteenth century, any development of local productivity was in direct conflict with European business interests who sought new markets. In general, the history of the textile industry has been the history of great struggles between foreign manufacturers and Argentine producers. The Argentine textile industry made cloth from imported thread. In 1872, the Primera Fábrica Argentina de Paños (First Argentine fabric factory) opened its doors, dedicated to weaving woolens. In 1879, a series of new factories were built in Buenos Aires, making shirts, hats, bags, and textiles in general. An industrially oriented consciousness began to spread, encouraged mainly by the growth of the local consumer market, owing to improved living standards in the city. By the end of the century, the textile industry began to flourish, and by 1908 there were eighty-six factories in Buenos Aires.[7]

The 1890s woman of Argentina's capital city decided to abandon the bustle and to turn her silhouette into the classical hourglass which, with important *gigot* sleeves and bell-shaped, trainless skirts, would reign as the predominant fashion until 1900. In the following decade, the romanticism of the S-shaped silhouette, achieved by squeezing the reluctant body into a tortuous corset, became a tempting alternative for those who chose to follow fashion's rigid codes. The corset combined with abundant skirts to accentuate a train which twisted in an amusing manner when the wearer moved.

Other highlights of the period were more contemporary, banishing the corset and imposing the imperial cut. These figure-hugging skirts made from cambric and buckram were tight at the hips and open in the shape of a bell, ending in a train which was used even in daytime. Voluminous petticoats disappeared, never to return. Just a single one survived, accompaning the flow of the skirt. Shoulders were explosions of pleats topping long, straight sleeves.

Blouses of linen cloth, though they had first appeared in 1880, were now used with bright collars and balloonlike sleeves, together with bell-shaped skirts and closed short boots. Embroidered dresses with high collars and Valenciennes decorations incorporated carefully elaborated tucks (fig. 6).

The excessive accumulation of wealth in certain sectors generated not only an avalanche of unscrupulous speculation but also the pleasures of showing off the luxury these riches could buy. The Buenos Aires market did not demand

6. Alexander Caldlengh, *Viajes por América del Sur, 1821* (Buenos Aires: Soler, 1943), 46.

7. "¿Recuerdan los porteños?" *El Hogar*, November 1947.

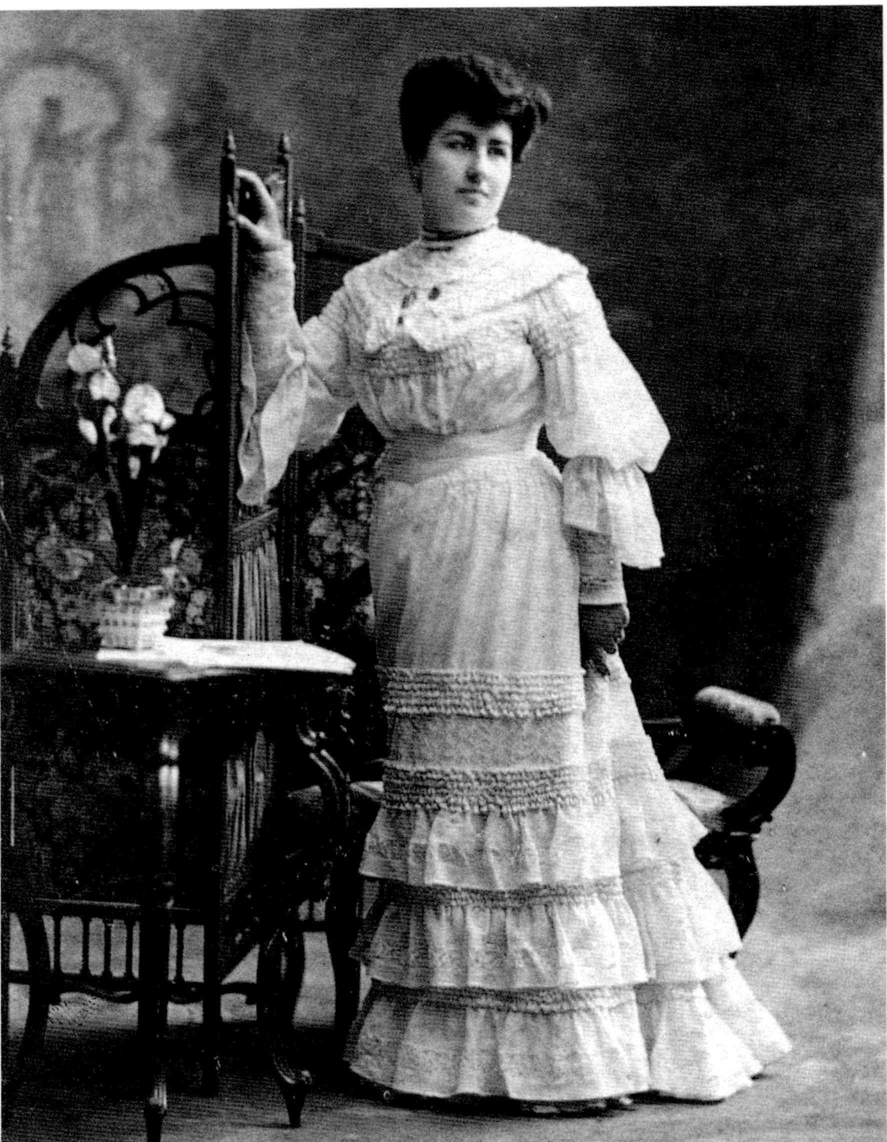

Fig. 6. Embroidered dress, 1905. Museum of the City of Buenos Aires.

good quality at this point, only outfits to produce an impact. Women copied the fashions of Paris and chose the most shocking.

Gone were the austere Spanish customs of an overgrown village. Now, ladies of the upper class no longer sewed their own garments. Tailors and dressmakers came to occupy a privileged position, as they were the ones to buy fabrics for their creations from department stores. In one model from 1905, we can see the silhouette molded into the form of an S by the corset. The dress is made of embroidered tulle with a colored slip of satin and a skirt with a train. The shirt front is adorned with lace needlework and the waistline with velvet (fig. 7).

The first fashion boutiques had appeared in Buenos Aires just before the stock market crash of 1890. La Porteña and Aux Armes de Paris were well known then. In 1878, the Brun brothers opened their shop, A la ciudad de Londres, on the

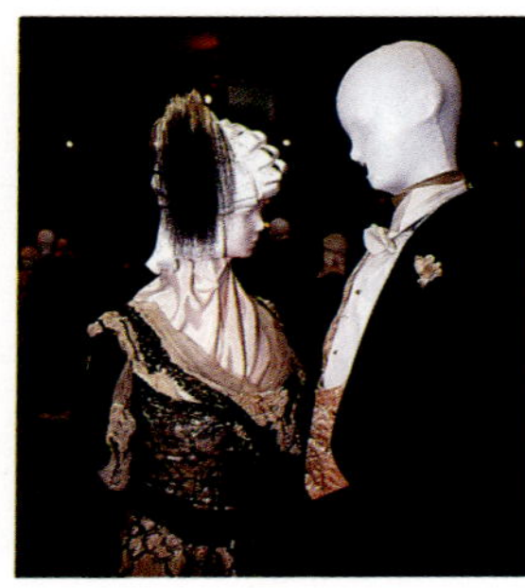

Fig. 7. Embroidered tulle dress, 1905. National Museum of the History of Costume, Buenos Aires.

corner of Peru and Victoria streets. Not everything was imported in this fine store. Ready-to-wear clothing was made mostly in large workshops which belonged to La Elegancia, the only shop publishing its own fashion magazine. In 1883, the renowned department store Gath & Chaves was founded. After the economic crisis, the store settled into its marvelous building on the corner of Florida and Cangallo. These establishments had buyers in Paris and workshops in Buenos Aires where they prepared garments based on designs bought abroad. In 1914, Harrods, the famous London department store, opened a branch on Florida Street.

After 1875, the upper class bought their clothing at the San Juan and their fabrics at the San Miguel on Suipacha and Bartolome Mitre streets. Little boys were dressed at El Niño Elegante, a shop belonging to Jeremy and René Saulquin. In 1889, A la ciudad de México opened. This new emporium specialized in a famous brand of corsets, the C.P. à la Sirène de Paris. Madame Carrau, another shop on Florida Street, declared publicly that the only dresses she made were based on "authentic French models." The system worked this way: famous dressmakers like Paquin, Doucet, Worth, Cheruit, Callot, and Doeuillet sent their products straight from Paris to the directress of Carrau, who, with her own supply of fabric, recreated them.

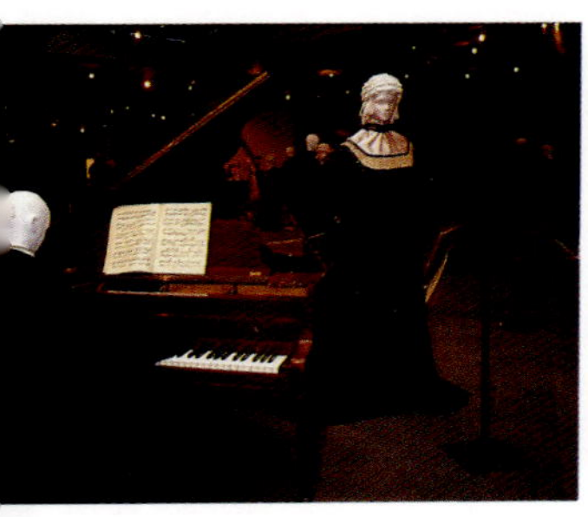

Fig. 8. Dress trimmed with guipure lace, 1910. National Museum of the History of Costume, Buenos Aires.

The centenary of the Revolución de Mayo was commemorated on 25 May 1910, and it was a great opportunity to show the world the degree of refinement Argentines had acquired. The impeccable organization of the ceremonies and festivities was enhanced by the presence of the Infanta Isabel de Borbón, sister of King Alfonso XIII of Spain. At the recently inaugurated Colón Theater, a full dress performance was held on the 25th, and a splendid dance at the theater two nights later was the principal topic in the newspapers for the follow-ing week. "The Theater's exterior was, like those enchanted palaces of Perrault, an outburst of radiance; its interior, a fascination of colors and lights. The gentlemen performed the service of acting as a backdrop for feminine grace emphasized by *toilettes* whose glories belonged to the nobility of Paris art and fashion—necklaces by the hundreds, splendid aigrettes, headbands, *rivières*, and all sorts of other jewelry worthy of an oriental fairy tale. The spectacle set one dreaming."[8]

For example, we can describe the dress that Mrs. Belén Tezanos Pinto de Olivier wore for the occasion: a broad décolleté neckline, trimmed with a band of guipure lace and entirely covered with tulle that was hand-embroidered with small beads and gold and silver thread. The skirt was shaped with transverse bands which grew larger in the shape of a corolla and ended in a velvet rim (fig. 8).

The ladies of this period wore dresses that tended toward trimness with soft, undulant contours. Most pleats had been done away with. In some cases, the skirt was whirled up in the back or given greater volume by the use of a train, fluffed out only at the hips. There was a great deal of fantasy employed in the styles: Greek tunics, kimonos, medieval gowns. Collars were adorned with boas, furs, or gauzes, while hats were either fitted and tilted or wide brimmed and adorned with feathers, flowers, and ribbons. Both skirts and hair were worn long.

8. Susana Saulquin, *La moda en la Argentina* (Buenos Aires: Editorial Emecé, 1990).

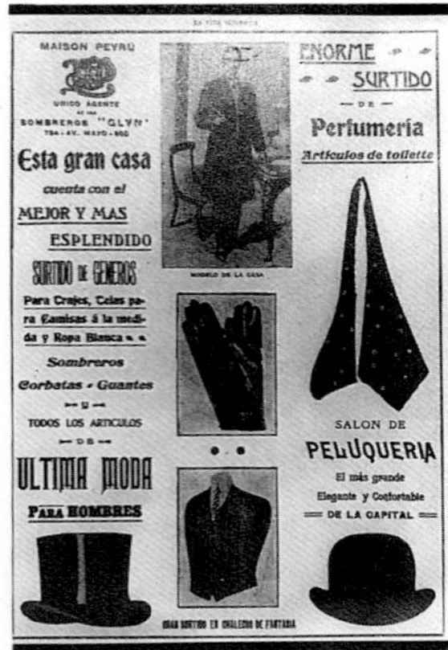

Fig. 9. Advertisement in *La Vida Moderna* (Modern life), Buenos Aires, 1907. Museum of the City of Buenos Aires.

Women began to enjoy a new spirit of freedom once released from the constrictions of the corset. Tunics appeared in 1911 and also the *trabada* style, which owed its name to a border that appeared at the height of the knees, holding in the flare of the skirt. But it was the tailor-made suit, worn during the day, accompanied by enormous, even exaggerated hats, that became the most characteristic outfit of the period.

A greater interest in leading a healthy life in the outdoors brought modifications to both masculine and feminine wardrobes. Ladies took bicycle rides or visited the country club dressed in blouses and skirts, light sweaters, and tailor-made suit jackets. It became more and more important for women to wear clothing that was not only elegant but practical. When it came to choosing shoes, they, too, had to meet standards of comfort and practicality. Men's jackets and *americanas,* or sports jackets, had become short and straight, without belts. The frock coat disappeared to make way for the dinner jacket or tuxedo—called a "smoking" in Buenos Aires: a black jacket for evening dress without the classical coattails. Trousers, up till now so tight, were made with stripes and cuffs. Slowly, the black top hat began to lose popularity (fig. 9), surviving only for use on ceremonial occasions, and a more flexible hat was adopted for every day use. (Argentines wore hats all the time, even at the cinema. This custom was not modified till 1940 when a law was passed prohibiting headwear in movie theaters.) The hats of Jipijapa became the rage, made from the delicate and flexible young leaves of *ambonaje*, a palm leaf which the English called Panama. (These hats, in reality, were made in Ecuador.) When Argentina approached the centenary of the founding of the republic, most men still wore moustaches and a stiff collar. In the first two decades of the twentieth century, the soft collar began to gain acceptance and totally shaven faces were the rule. The simplification of style was due not only to the importance given to sports and life in the fresh air but also to the accelerated rhythm of everyday activities in a city where the horse and carriage was rapidly being replaced by trams, cars, and railways.

This transformation, which occurred in only four decades—from 1870 to 1910—was based on the twin pillars of economic development and abundant immigration, fuel for a tremendous surge in the world of fashion. Argentina's rapid economic development created a multiclass system in which fashion exerted a strong influence on prestige. The real period of splendor for Argentine fashion started now, in this social framework. In the palatial homes of the Bosch Alvear, Saguier, Ortiz Basualdo, Anchorena, and Blaquier families, impressive parties were given for guests of honor such as Edward, the Duke of Windsor; the Maharajah of Kapurtala; Humberto of Savoy; and Louis Ferdinand of Hohenzollern. A spirit of modernness imported from Europe influenced fashion principally through the dresses worn at large parties by chic upper-class ladies, and later through accessories with surrealist symbols. Argentina's aristocracy continued to bring their wardrobes from Paris, but it was obvious that more shops were needed to cater to the realities of the market. High fashion, which had been born with Worth at the time of Napoleon III, now came to Buenos Aires. Before and after the First World War, social life accelerated to such a degree that, besides traveling to Paris, the ladies of Buenos Aires were visited by salesmen from French couturiers who arrived in the city with trunks full of gowns.

During the Belle Époque and up to the First World War, a select group of Argentines had gone to live in Europe. They divided their time between

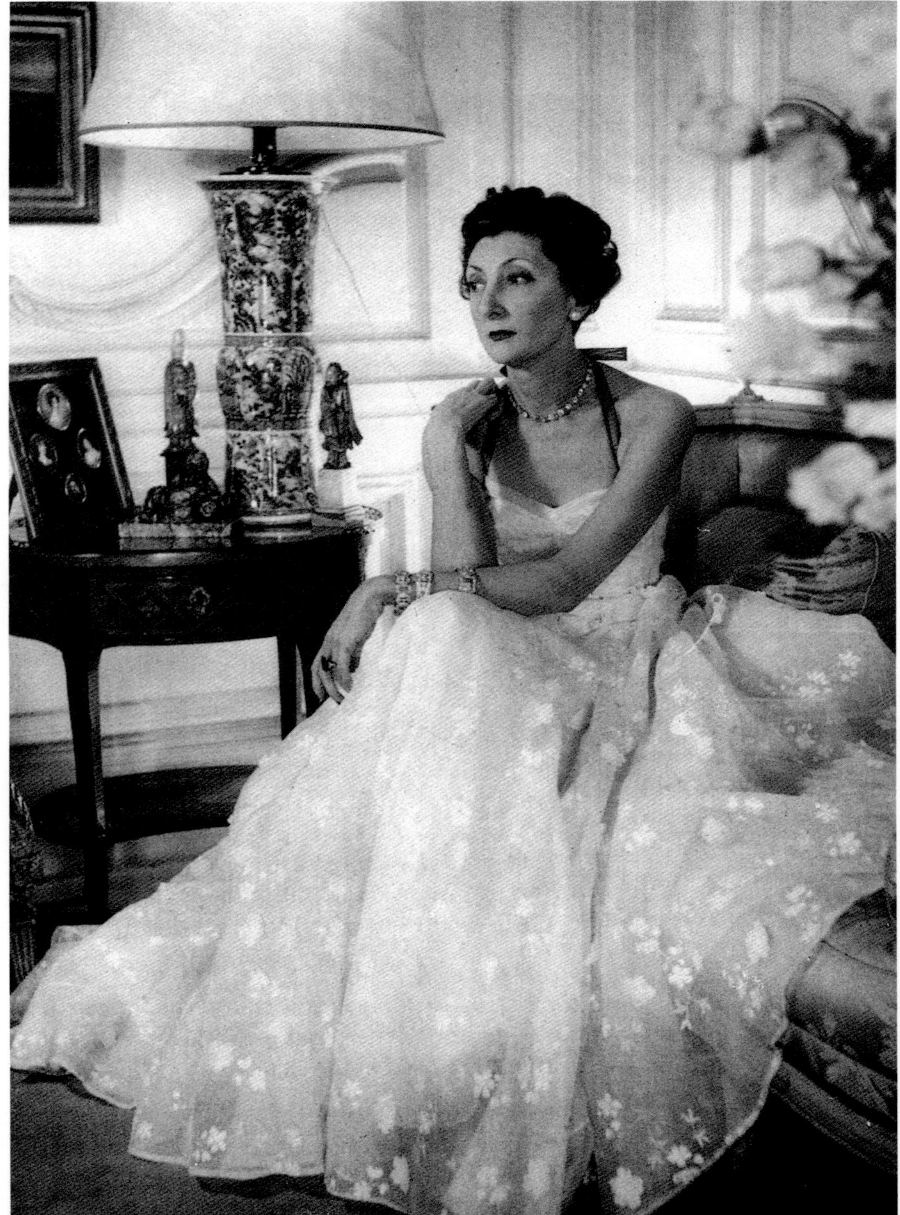

Fig. 10. Eugenia Huici de Errázuriz. Dress design by Maggy Rouff. ***París en America*****, (Buenos Aires) vol. 2, no. 7, (1948). Photograph by Dormen.**

homes in Paris, London, and Biarritz. Among this elite were Eugenia Huici de Errázuriz (fig. 10),[9] Amelia Riera de Pacheco, Mercedes Saint Felix, Rosita Alcorta, and the writer Victoria Ocampo. They were admired for the refinement of their dress as well as their intellectual and cultural development. Ladies in Argentina asked their distinguished friends living in Paris to send them the designs needed for the social round each season. This group exercised a definitive influence on fashion since they had been ordained to select and supervise what others ordered from dressmakers like Worth, Paquin,

9. Chilean-born, Sra. de Errázuriz strongly influenced European and Argentine fashion through her many friends on both continents.

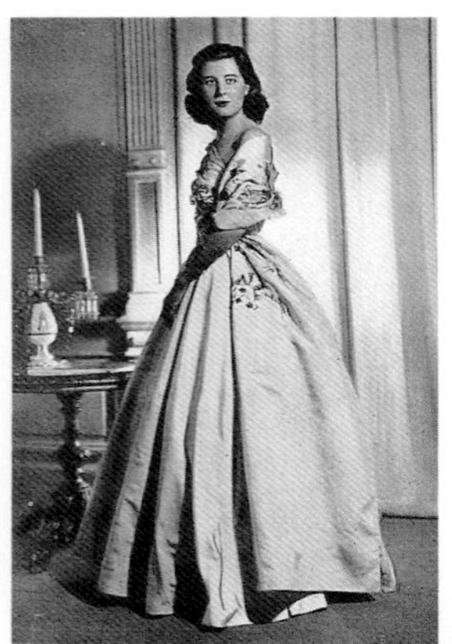

Fig. 11. María Teresa Giménez Melo de Frias Ayerza. Dress design by Saint Felix. *Galas*, (1948). Museum of the City of Buenos Aires.

Doucet, and Poiret. Tucked away in their princely lodgings in Paris, they became veritable arbiters of taste and style for Río de la Plata society. Although they never violated established criteria or imposed an original style of their own, they did have good judgment and chose with harmony and coherence, a gift found not only in upper-class *porteñas* but also in the middle class who bought their clothing from neighborhood dressmakers.

Beginning in 1914, important fashion houses opened in Buenos Aires. They bought patterns from the best designers in Paris and quickly distinguished themselves for the perfect cut and impeccable finish of their garments. Astesiano, Henriette, Campana, Jean et André, Palau, Saint Felix (fig. 11), Tomé, and Madame Suzanne were the best known *maisons*. They usually set up shop in *petit-hotels*, originally built as handsome single-family residences in the area of Retiro, and some grew to employ two hundred artisans at their peak. They had their own workshops where they kept mannequins made to the measurements of each of their clients. The owners traveled to Paris twice a year and bought original patterns, fabrics, and trims. Argentine-made cloth was rarely used.[10]

Enrique Astesiano recalls:

> I was born into the world of fashion and since childhood lived its magic. My parents, the founders of Astesiano, began with a hat shop in 1916. Back then, everyone wore a hat to work. In 1926, we decided to enlarge the business, bringing a collection of dresses from Europe that we planned to reproduce in our workshop. We put a high fashion shop on Florida Street in a four-story building. Years later we moved to the *petit-hotel* which had belonged to the Ocampo Alvear family. Amidst decorations of marble and bronze, within ornamented walls, we held our fashion shows. They were highlights of that epoch of splendor and luxury in Buenos Aires in the twenties and thirties. Then high fashion had its boom, but there wasn't any creativity in the country. We were all great at copying. There was so much copying going on that, in spite of the fact that it was a slow and difficult process, everyone was surprisingly speedy.[11]

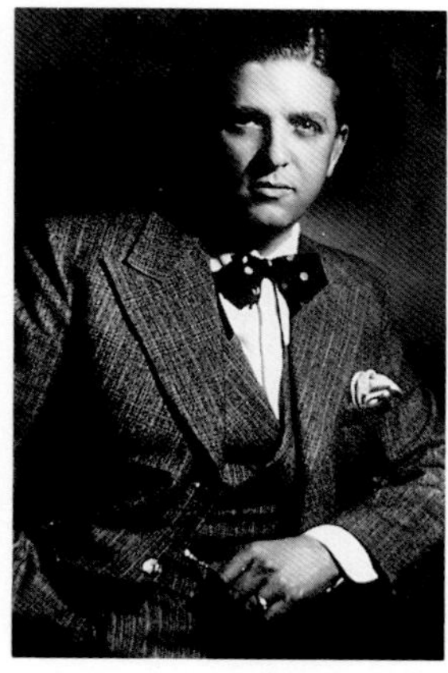

Fig. 12. Men's fashion, 1926. Museum of the City of Buenos Aires.

Son of the founders of this famous high fashion shop that opened in 1916, he lived through the great historical moments of Argentine fashion. The family firm finally closed in the sixties.

The First World War brought about another simplification in clothing design and style, changing the mentality of women who accepted a shortening of skirts, a final farewell to the corset, and shorter hair. This situation, shockingly new, took hold in Europe, but came to the Río de la Plata in an attenuated version. With the city's shops filled with imported fabrics and recently arrived French artisans, the cream of *porteña* society did not suffer the impact of the war. Before, during, and after the fighting, life was a constant party, with afternoons at the races, evenings in restaurants, and nights at the theater or dancing at balls.

Between 1914 and 1918, two trends shared the limelight: draped dresses, the upper part generally made of tulle, with pleated skirts; and tunics which were worn over straight sheathes, barely ruffled at the waist and embroidered with pearls or crystal beads. These tunics, worn morning and afternoon on top of suits, were tailored in flannel, serge, woolen velvet, or Scottish cheviot, and at night in velvet, tulle, gauze, or lace.

10. Ibid.

11. Enrique Astesiano, conversation with author, June 1991.

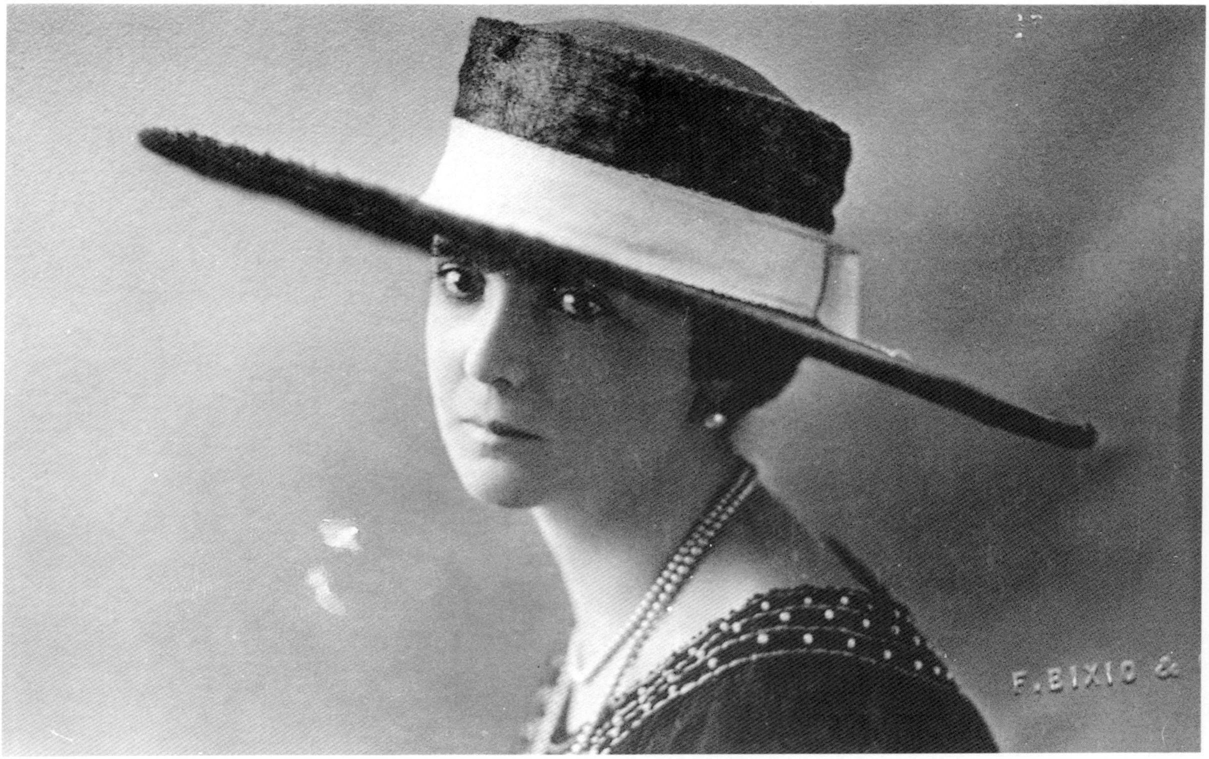

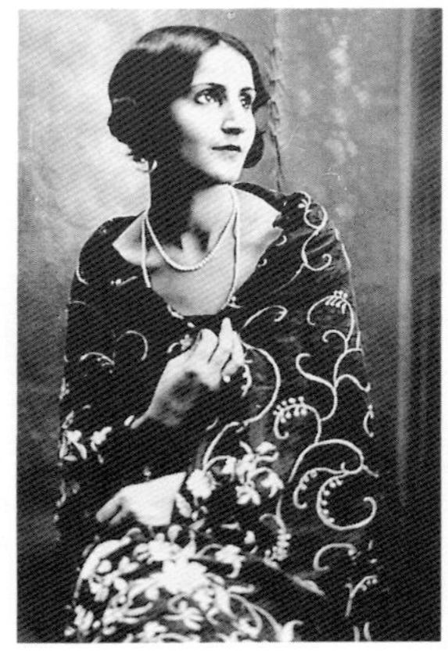

Fig. 13. Woman with an embroidered shawl, 1924. Museum of the City of Buenos Aires.

Fig. 14. Top. Woman wearing a hat, 1922. Museum of the City of Buenos Aires.

In 1916, the ideal wardrobe for sports consisted of a sheepskin jacket or a knit sport coat, which could be closed with three buttons and a belt. With this garment and a matching *boina* cap or beret, women completed their outfit with a long *portafolio* or wrap-around skirt of twill, which in summer was accompanied by a blouse and straw hat with ribbons.

The design of a man's wardrobe was also in the process of simplification. Double-breasted or not, suits had shorter jackets and no padding in the shoulders, lapels were wider and longer, and sleeves narrower than those before the war. Shirts usually had a rigid, white *palomita* collar; after 1914 detachable collars were discarded (fig. 12).

In exclusive clubs in Buenos Aires—like the Jockey and the Lawn Tennis—men took to the courts in long white trousers and jackets with wide blue or red stripes. Made of English flannel or white woolen jersey, these jackets were decorated with the colors of each club. They had *marinero* or sailors' collars trimmed with a double row of ribbon, white flannel sleeves, and mother of pearl buttons. Neckties and buttons were decorated with the insignia of the man's particular club.

Trends of the twenties reflected the enormous transformation women had been undergoing. A flattened figure, hairdos hugging the head, eyes highlighted in black halos, and cascading necklaces had become the synthesis of the look of the wild twenties (figs. 13 and 14). Luxurious shirtwaists were lengthened by daring fringes or dangling pearls from Mallorca. Women chose knee-length dresses which were straight and beltless, following the dictates of the style Molyneux presented in 1919. The line that began to be simplified when Paul Poiret liberated women from the corset had, by 1925, become a free-for-all for the most audacious. After that landmark year, when art deco allowed a more

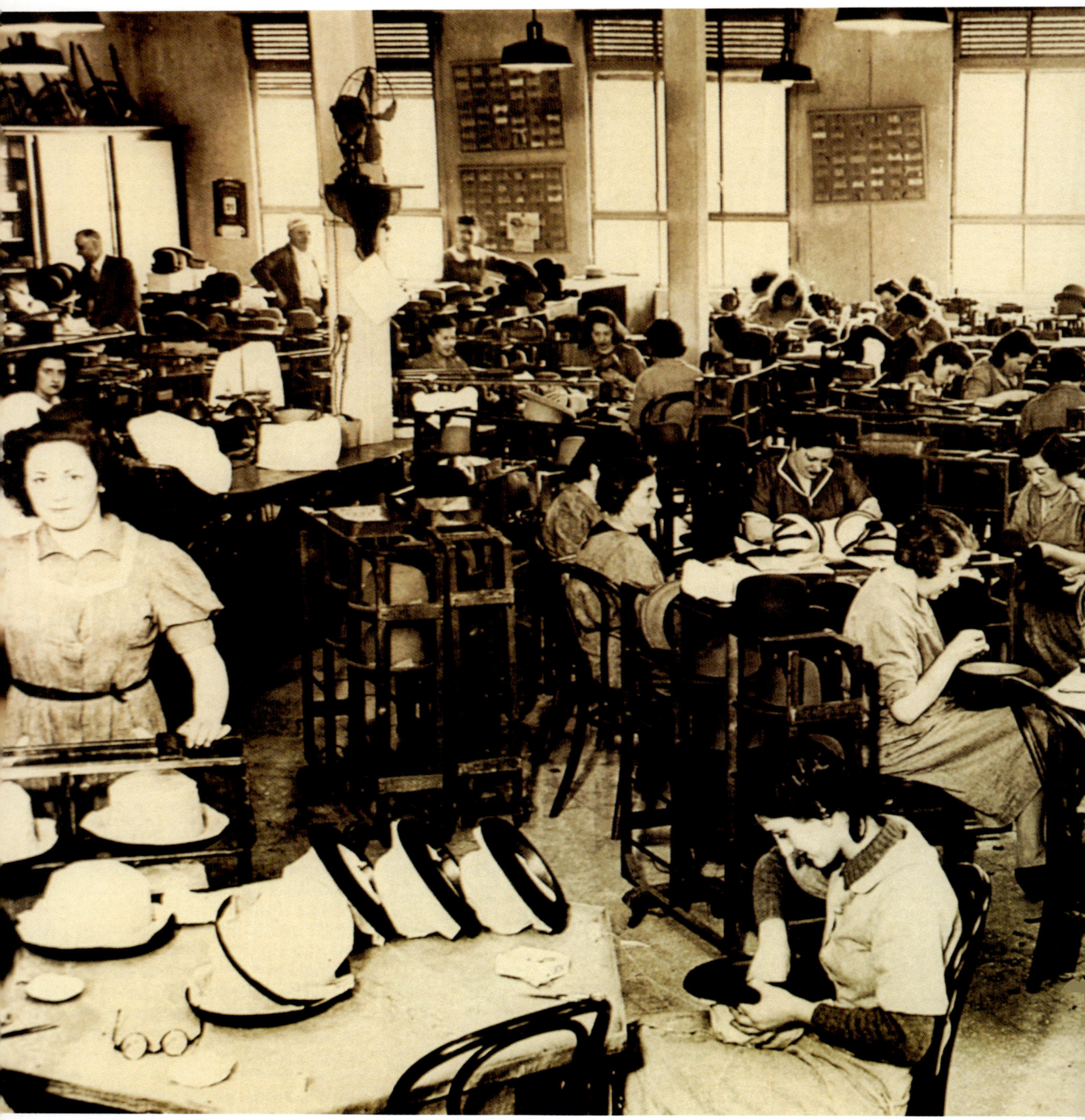

Fig. 15. Lagomarsino and Company hat factory, Buenos Aires, 1938. *Nuestro Siglo*, no. 13, September 1984. National Archives of Buenos Aires.

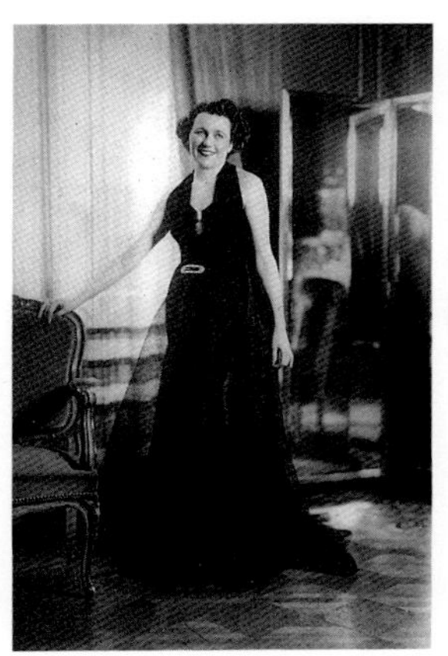

Fig. 16. Dress design by Astesiano, 1938. Photograph courtesy of Enrique Astesiano, Buenos Aires.

geometric, even cubistic modernism to emerge, the latest fashions in skirts—short and simple—replaced the more classic designs of the early twenties. The discovery of the tomb of Tutankhamen in 1923 gave a revitalized value to all that was Egyptian. These designs began to appear not only in architecture but also in fashions, especially in sweaters.

But the most important feature of the art-deco period was that it was conceived on the basis of a design totality. Nothing escaped the eye of the designer: everything entered into his potential realm. From clothing to tableware, all had to be submitted to the dictates of the new style. Geometrical motifs, taken from machines, automobiles, Egyptian tombs, ziggurats of Babylonia, and Incan and Aztecan monuments, all became the constants of art-deco design. Couturiers like Jacques Doucet and Paul Poiret took an active role in spreading the gospel of this new movement.[12]

The installation of high fashion shops in Buenos Aires, the reduction in time it took to travel to Europe, and the enthusiasm of the local press which dedicated a great deal of space to women, determined that styles would appear almost simultaneously in Buenos Aires. Argentines preferred the designs of Lucien Lelong, Doucet, or Maison Paquin in Paris—such as a black flannel suit with ermine collar and sleeves belonging to Elena Peña de Alzaga Unzue. Women of lesser social distinction wore knee-length, light-colored suits with belts of the same cloth, rounded necklines, short, tight sleeves trimmed with embroidery, and black shoes with a clasp on one side. Their short, straight hair was invariably covered by a cloche hat.

Underclothes were, primarily, long girdles without stays, made of elastic tricot, ending in four silk garters. The need to use a girdle in that period was accentuated because the majority of designs stressed an elongated silhouette. Fur trim and lightweight fabrics with beaded or paillette borders became popular, as did dresses whose lines hugged the body, a style soon the fashion for ladies of the upper and middle class countrywide.[13] Evening dresses were short, one-piece, and covered with sequins or pearls; they looked like untailored tunics, open at the neck and arms and ending at the knees. As for jewelry, a watch on a chain, bracelets made like fish scales, and pearls in chokers or strung in long strands with sapphires were the most popular items.

There was significant growth in the local textile industry in the decade of the thirties, especially in the manufacture of cotton goods. Industry production grew 26 percent in 1933 and reached 41 percent in 1937. For the most part, growth was concentrated in items that previously had been imported. By 1937, for the first time local products were at least as prevalent as imported goods (fig. 15). This was not a direct result of government policy but, rather, due to factors existing abroad. Another impending war was affecting Europe's industries, including textiles .[14]

After the rather asexual style of the twenties, the shapes of the thirties were fuller and more emphatic. Evening wear was long, narrow, and snug on the body, pepped up by interesting cuts, pleats on the bias, ruches, and bows (fig. 16). During the late thirties, what shaped the Argentine female's ideal of a woman were stars like Jean Harlow, Joan Crawford, and Greta Garbo, but they

12. "Más que un estilo el mundo art decó," *La Nación*, 8 September 1985, 12–13.

13. Gath & Chaves Catalogue, Buenos Aires, Spring 1922–1923.

14. Saulquin, *La moda*.

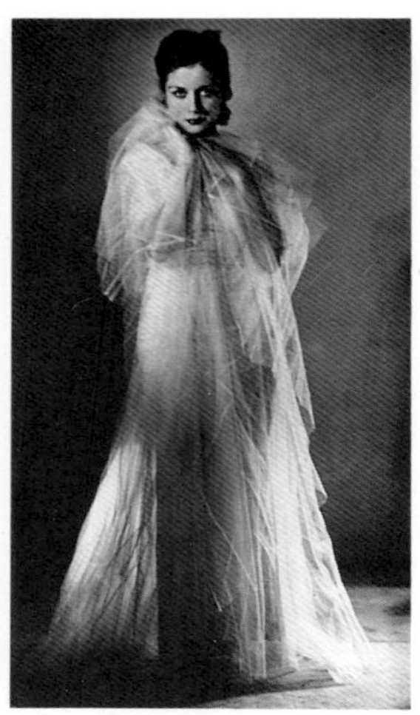

Fig. 17. Actress Mecha Ortiz, 1937. Museum of the City of Buenos Aires.

were considered models beyond imitation (fig. 17). Therefore, the local market looked to the style imposed by the upper class, as publicized in magazines such as *El Hogar* and *Atlántida*.

Now woolen jersey suits, narrow, medium length, and accompanied by coats trimmed in Astrakhan fur, were the predominant trendsetters. Toward the middle of the decade, skirts lengthened even more and plaid designs began to appear in dresses which were decorated with white crepe collars and belts, and Valenciennes or pleated collars of plain silk. One characteristic of the period was to line jackets with the same cloth as the accompanying blouse, another to edge jackets and overcoats with blue fox which descended vertically from collar to waist. Hats were discreet, worn tilted, like berets (fig. 18), alternating with large, broadbrimmed straw or velvet creations decorated with organdy flowers. No woman would be seen in the street without a hat; not even a maid or a schoolgirl, who combined her white pinafore with a blue beret.

The favorite precious stone of Argentine society was the diamond, especially one that would stand out in a tiara at a gala at the Colón Theater. Emeralds were set in rings, bracelets, and necklaces. *Plaquetas* were used on top of jackets or low-cut gowns.

The decade of the thirties in Buenos Aires seemed to mark the high point of the fame of local fashion designers, more numerous every day. The names prominent then were: Astesiano, Carrau (fig. 19), Palau, Naletoff, and Henriette.

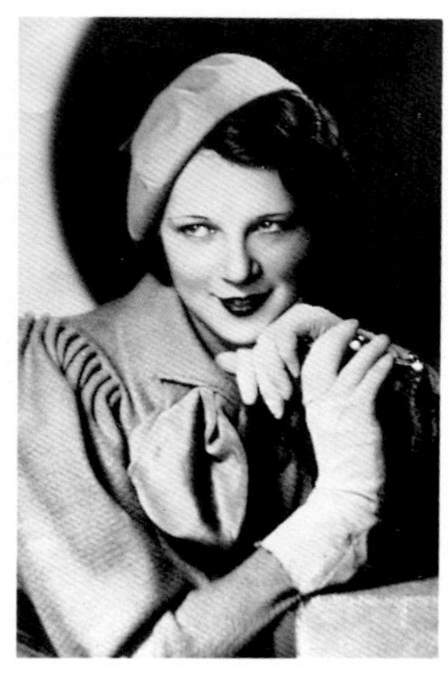

Fig. 18. Adela Stiro, 1934. Museum of the City of Buenos Aires.

The romantic style—draped, curled, and bejeweled—of the thirties ended with the Second World War. Influenced by the militarism of the period, fashion sought refuge in tailor-made suits of grey, black, and blue. Severe jackets with padded shoulders were accompanied by straight or box-pleated skirts which gradually shortened. These were dramatic years, years of a certain theatricality. Suits combined with eccentric hats, like the *canotier* with its extra-wide brim, feathers, and tulles. Neutral colors reigned supreme, especially black and grey. During those years, trousers made a tentative appearance: pleated, with cuffs, and very wide. The *porteñas* wore these pants with full shirts or very feminine blouses with pleats. The next furor was platform shoes, which appeared in the mid-forties, and pillbox hats. At the end of the forties, Christian Dior launched his famous New Look—immense ankle-length skirts, wasp waists, and accentuated shoulders (figs. 20, 21, and 22).

If, in the history of fashion in Argentina, most haute couture shops were clever copiers, at some point in this story an original creator had to make an appearance. This happened with the arrival of Paco Jamandreu in 1943. Jamandreu was an authentically creative individual, a designer for the stars, such as Zully Moreno and Tilda Thamar and, of course, for that figure who wore clothes like no other: Eva Perón. Jamandreu met Evita in 1944, and, until she was well launched in political circles, he designed her wardrobe.

On 15 March 1945, when the theater season commenced in Buenos Aires, Jamandreu dressed the stars of the five most important plays opening that night, including María Duval, Paulina Singerman, and Aida Luz. Traditional clientele of formal haute couture houses did not buy his designs, considering his style too theatrical and splashy.

Jamandreu made his name in fashion circles through his drawings of dress designs which, at the end of 1943, began to be published in *Mundo Argentino*, *Selecta*, and *El Hogar* magazines. In a newspaper interview he declared, "I work at everything with total irresponsibility, with irreverence. And perhaps

Fig. 19. Carlota Urquiza Anchorena. Dress design by Carrau. *Galas*, December 1948. Photograph by Gross.

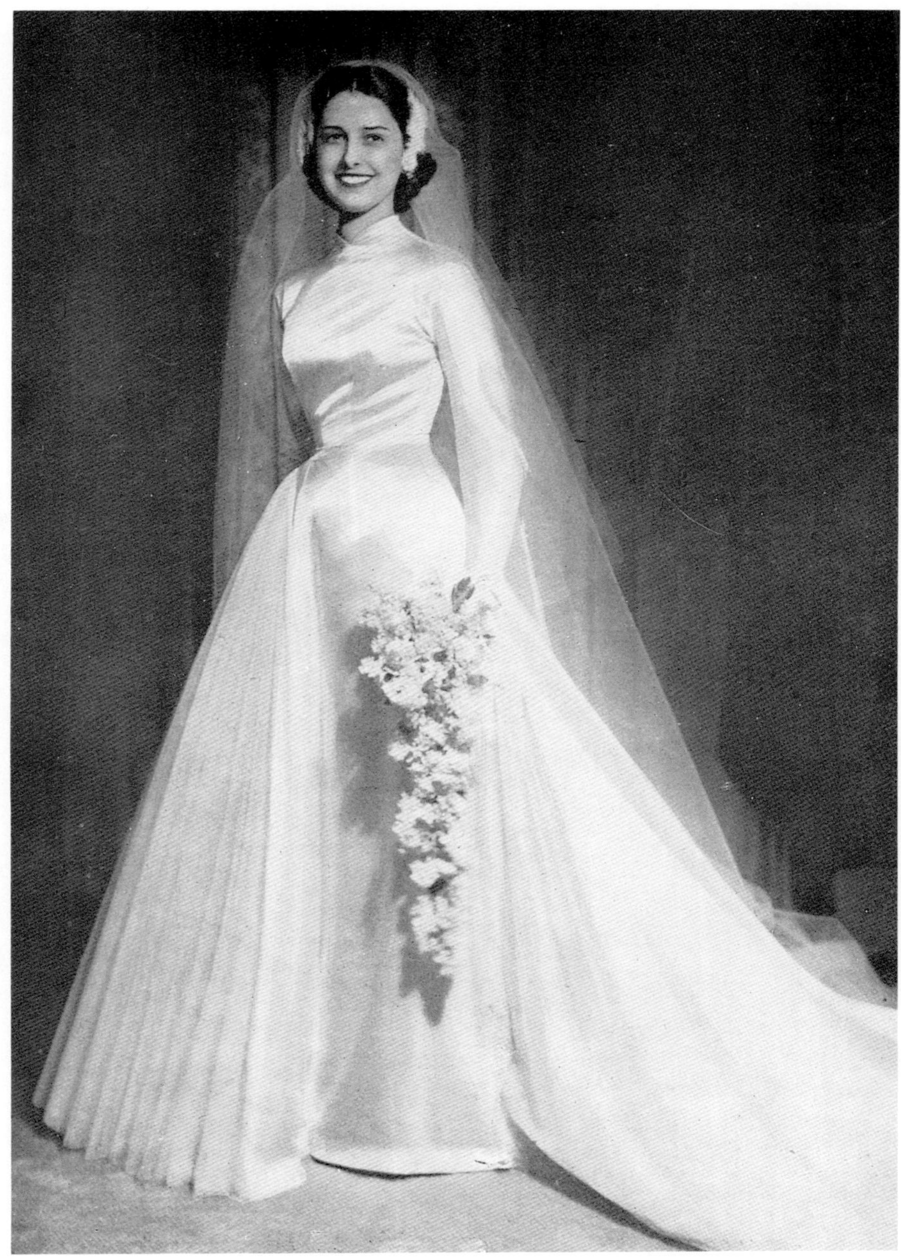

that is why there are some people in the world of fashion who hate me. I don't need to copy as so many of them do. I get all the ideas out of my own head, and I'm ready to reinvent myself every day."[15] The designer, who turned down a multi-million dollar contract to work in the United States and a similar offer from Dior in Paris, made his mark in the Argentine fashion world with his sophisticated and sumptuous evening wear, which was distinguished by the rich cloth he used—brocade, silk organdy, chiffon, and natural silk embroidered with gold thread.

15. Newspaper interview with Paco Jamandreu, *La Opinión*, 12 December 1975.

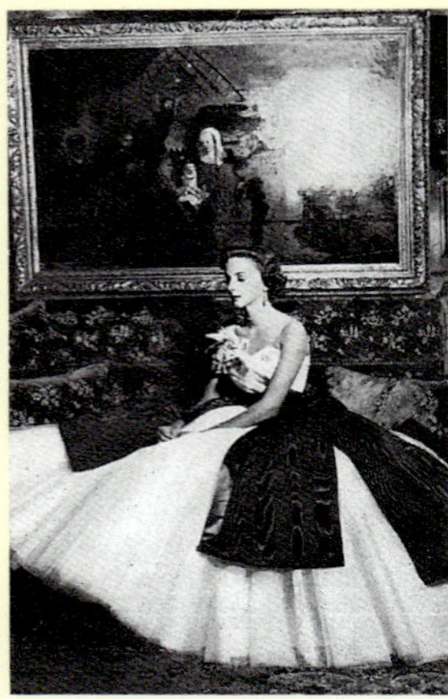

Fig. 20. Mónica De Ridder Perrier. Dress design by Paula Naletoff. *Galas*, January 1948. Photograph by Gross.

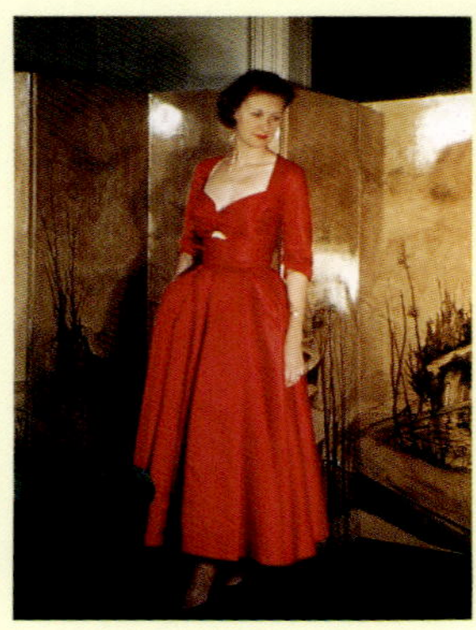

Fig. 21. Dress design by Astesiano, 1946. Photograph courtesy of Enrique Astesiano, Buenos Aires.

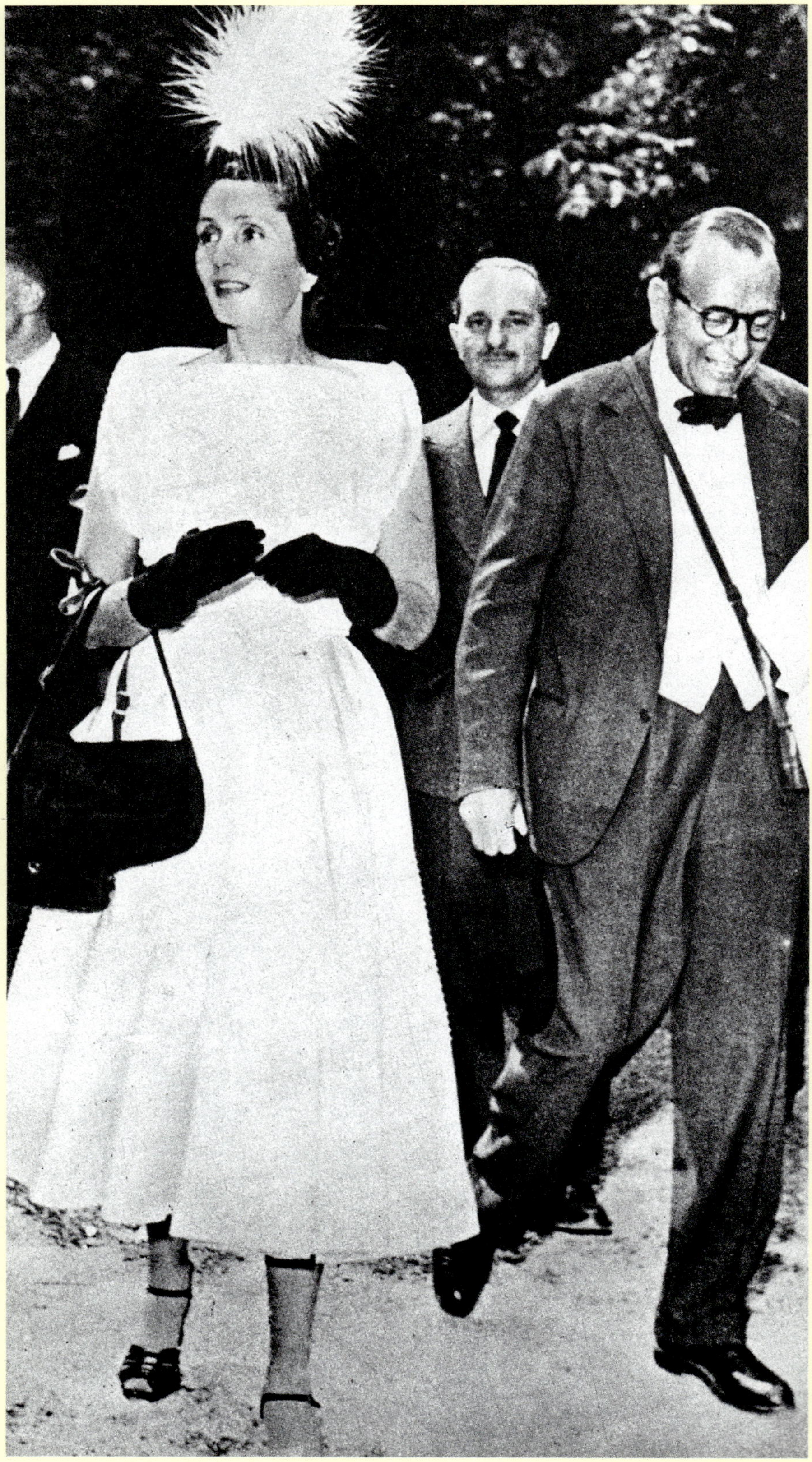

◂

Fig. 22. Dulce Liberal de Martínez de Hoz. Longchamps, 1949. National Archives of Buenos Aires.

▸

Fig. 23. Eva Duarte de Perón, 1949. *Nuestro Siglo*, no. 19, November 1984. National Archives of Buenos Aires.

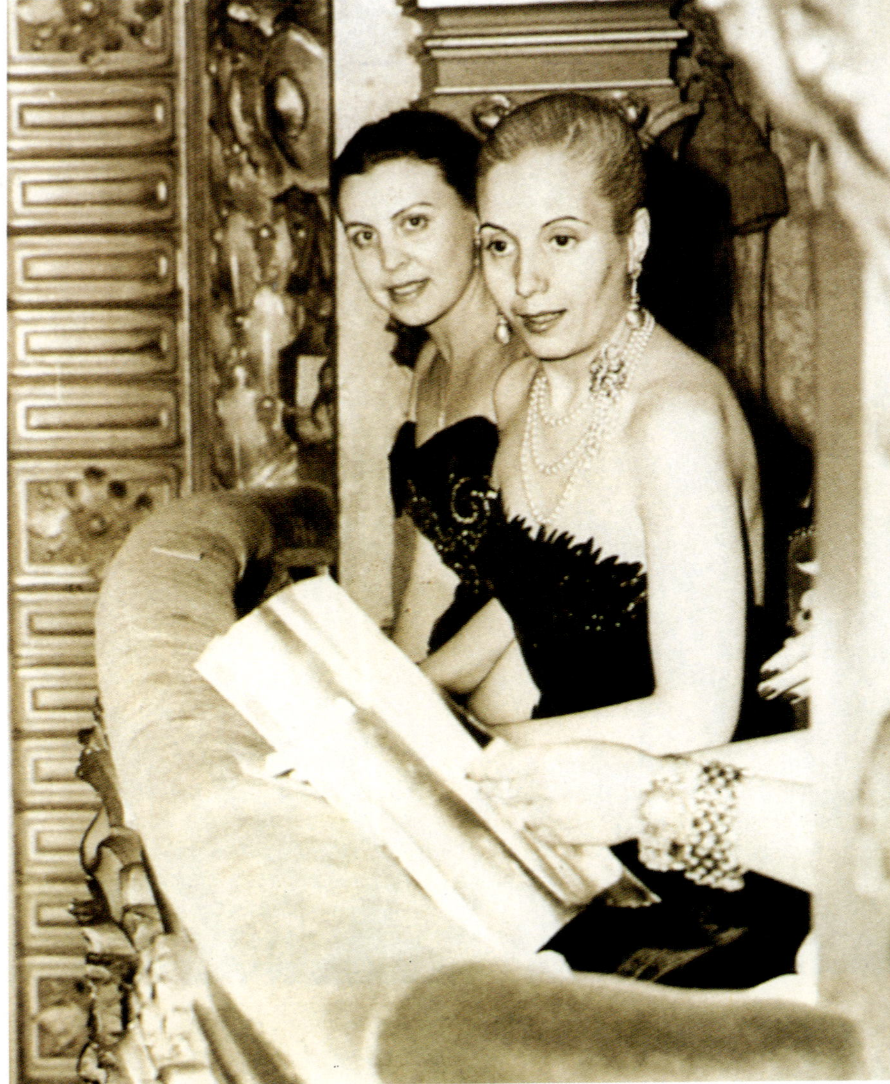

Evita was dressed exclusively by Jamandreu until 1946, when General Juan Domingo Perón was elected president. Then she chose the fashionable dress designers of the city like Paula Naletoff and Henriette to prepare her wardrobe. In 1947, Eva traveled to Europe in the company of her exclusive dressmaker, Luis D'Agostino. From then on, she preferred Dior's New Look or the creations of Jacques Fath (fig. 23).

Susana Saulquin, a sociologist dedicated to studying the role of fashion in society, stresses the fact that Evita used clothing as a tool for political expression and not as a means of personal self-revelation.[16] This meant that the Argentine fashion world and the country's textile and clothing industries lost their best opportunity to impose a truly Argentine style at home and abroad. □

16. Susana Saulquin, conversation with author, June 1991.

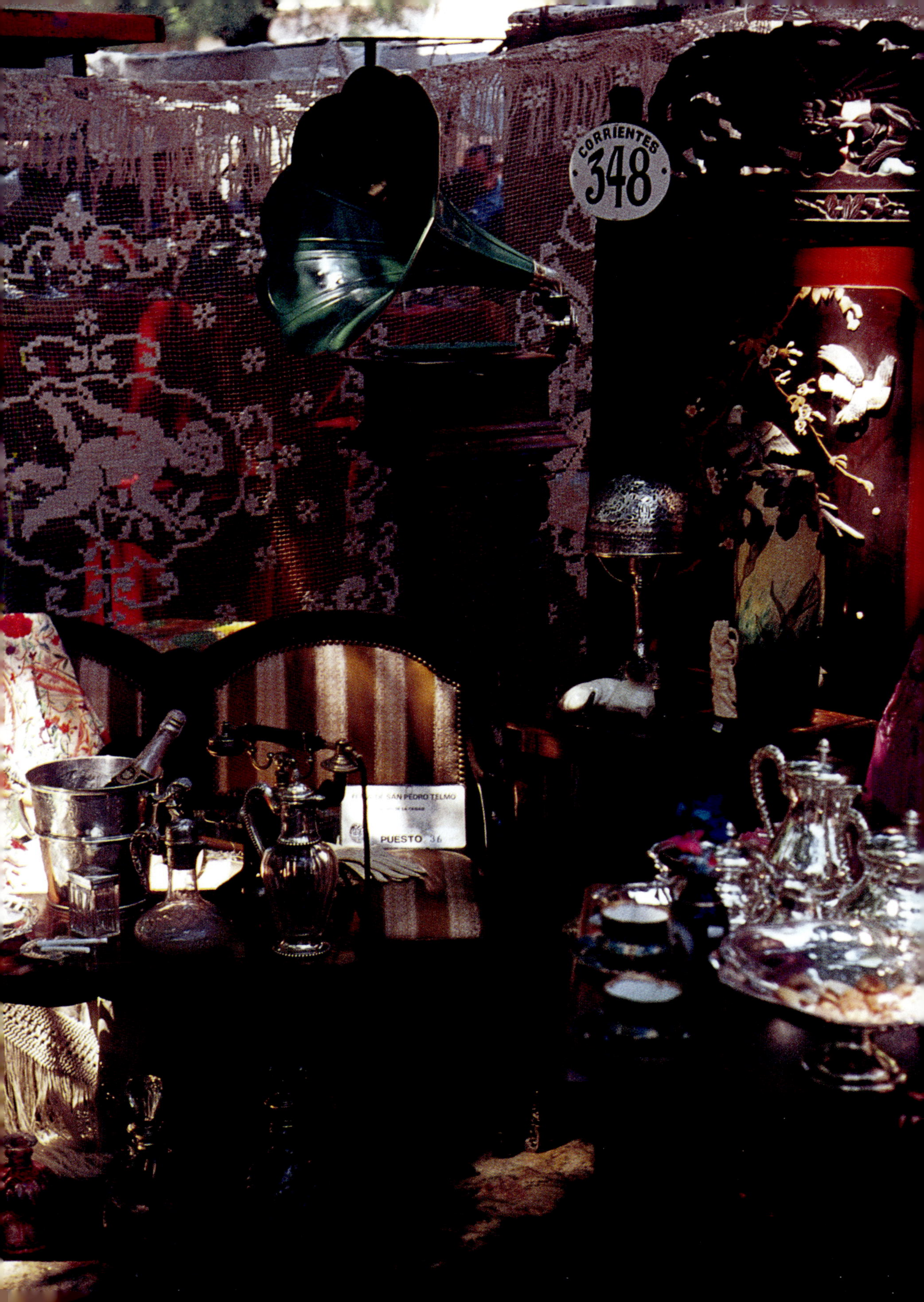
CORRIENTES
348
DE SAN PEDRO TELMO
PUESTO 36

An Interview with José María Peña

By Edward Shaw

Edward Shaw has written extensively on Argentine art. A director of the Nuevo Mundo Foundation and the Argentine Association for English Culture, he has served as juror for prizes sponsored by the Antorchas, Di Tella, and Fortabat Foundations and contributed introductions to numerous catalogues, the most recent for an Antonio Seguí retrospective. He is a graduate of Princeton University.

Photographs by José María Peña except where noted.

A steady stream of excited antiques dealers flowed down the steep stairs of the turn-of-the-century headquarters of the Museum of the City of Buenos Aires. Over a hundred hopeful candidates had gathered in the museum's modest main hall to witness a drawing which would award eight stands at the Sunday antiques fair in the heart of San Telmo (fig. 1), the city's designated historical quarter.

Periodically, death, exhaustion, or a quantum leap to a shop frees several of the 270 coveted stands, and in this city where corruption and cronyism are the order of the day, José María Peña (fig. 2), director of the Museum of the City, runs so tight a ship that no one gets a stand without winning it in these occasional low-key lotteries. Letters of recommendation go straight into the wastebasket, calls from Above—that bureaucratic demiparadise where most municipal fates are sealed—go ignored.

Early in his unorthodox career as a public servant, Peña set his own standards, and those wanting to do business with any of the offshoots of the museum do it straight. Most museum directors are not involved in managing flea markets, organizing block parties, decorating subway stations, and defending the city's vanishing historic patrimony against all comers—usually fleeting alliances of ambitious politicians and voracious builders. For twenty years, Peña, with his singular, unassuming style of counterattack, has defended his bailiwick better than any army could. He is revered by most of his neighbors, respected by an ever-mutating officialdom, and held in awe by all who come in tangible contact with his vocation.

In his mid-sixties, slim and agile, Peña has a profile that is a caricaturist's dream: abundant eyebrows standing permanently at attention, a nose that leaps forward, racing ahead of a receding brow, topped by a greying head of hair swept straight back in the manner of an earlier age. He dresses in a sweater, a striped blue shirt, a serious tie, dark trousers, and Indian-style beige moccasins, their matching laces trimming the border: hardly the attire expected of the dean of Argentine municipal museum directors; more like the uniform of a determined citizen who has withstood every form of government Argentines cleverly contrive to suit the nation's oft-altering circumstances.

◂ Fig. 1. Antiques stand at the San Telmo fair.

Culture courses through Peña's veins. Educated as an architect, he received his degree from the University of Buenos Aires in 1960, choosing investigation as his career. In Argentina about as many architectural investigators survive in the specialty as Americans walk on the moon. In a land where professorships

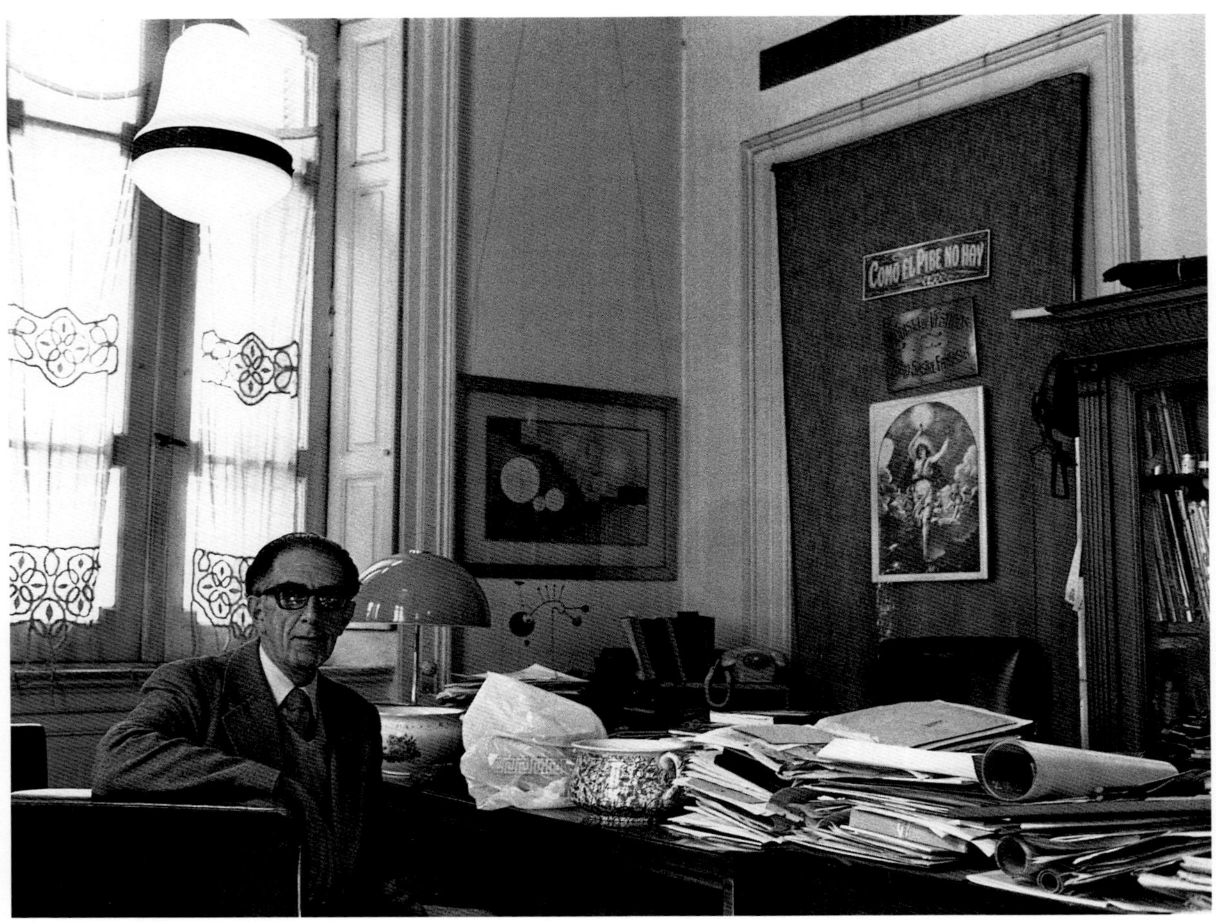

Fig. 2. José María Peña, director of the Museum of the City of Buenos Aires. Photograph by Aldo Sessa.

are generally part-time stipends for successful professionals, research is virtually unknown. To add to the difficulties, the National Library has been in the process of being built for forty years, and its collections struggle for survival in damp, rat-infested basements so sadly described so often by Jorge Luis Borges, once—in better times—the library's director.

Creating a career out of such chaos has made Peña an individual of great compassion and patience. The work of his early years as an investigator—a series of studies on architecture in Argentina in the nineteenth and twentieth centuries—was destroyed à la Savonarola when a change in political direction demanded an historic revision resulting in annihilation of previous scholarship.

Fortuitous chance led Peña out of academe and into the museum world. In retrospect, such a move was leaving the frying pan for a dip in the flame. Most museum directors—like ambassadors in many a politicized society—are temporary personnel, at the beck and call of their political patrons. Peña, early on, discovered how to avoid the pitfalls of playing politics. He would start his own museum and maintain a low profile; his fiefdom now operates in such impoverished conditions that no self-respecting pretender to power could covet his space.

After twenty-four years as director of the Museum of the City (technically not so, because it took City Hall fifteen years to grant him that title officially), Peña's office looks like the combination of a writer's cave and a junk dealer's storeroom. Donations to the museum are heterogeneous, to say the least, and the latest batch is always stacked up in a corner awaiting classification, a chore often entailing impossible decisions. Photos, texts, and old magazines stand like untidy recruits awaiting orders.

The only connection with twentieth-century technology is a 1970s typewriter. The nearest phone is across the exhibit space. All the tools of the trade of a state-of-the-art American museum director's office—a secretary, a fax, a computer, a copying machine, even a coffeemaker—are absent in Peña's anachronistic surroundings. Yet he manages to fulfill the responsibilities and obligations of a functioning museum administrator on a paltry annual budget of several hundred dollars, plus keep his prestigious image respected in a community where a week's absence from the firing line could mean a new decree annulling years of careful work to preserve the city's precarious architectural profile.

Peña is more artful than aggressive, more tenacious than tendentious. His quick mind cuts through all intellectualized prattle and bureaucratic gobbledygook. As his ambition is public, his goal is transparent. No one doubts the authenticity of his relentless crusade to save as much of the city's perplexing past as he can (figs. 3 and 4). Nothing escapes the vast scope of his curiosity, nothing is too minute or obscure to attract his attention and interest. The most humble token fits somewhere into his master plan for keeping life as conducted in Buenos Aires alive for future generations.

When it comes to preserving the flavor of what little remains of yesterday's city, Peña is crystal clear in his intention. "Buenos Aires has no really ancient sectors. Buildings built in the eighteenth century, for the most part, haven't survived (fig. 5). Homes from the early nineteenth century are few and far between. So, what we have is diversity of design, ranging from the remains of a Spanish colonial style through the modernism of the fifties, all standing side by side. This incongruous mix is what gives Buenos Aires its character. A commission I'm on [The Association of Neighbors and Friends of the Historical Center of the City of Buenos Aires] advocates that this relatively small nucleus—San Telmo and environs—be preserved as is (fig. 6).

"There are those who'd tear down everything not an architectural landmark in itself. Their main line of attack is that the *barrio* is filthy, rat-infested, and unhealthy. Offending buildings should be eliminated and pristine apartment houses built to replace them. We, on the other hand, believe cleanliness and order can be achieved without destroying what remnants of our past remain (fig. 7). At a public meeting on the topic, Rodolfo Livingston, an outspoken architect and the author of hilarious books, answered a crass real estate broker who called for immediate implementation of a cut-and-burn policy: 'When I'm dirty, I just take a shower; I've never contemplated suicide as the solution.' His graphic retort sent the audience into peals of laughter and saved the day for the conservationists."

Peña was born a part of that network linking affluent *porteños* in a closely woven, multipatterned community half a century ago. A certain position in society guaranteed access and precluded a need for introductions. Peña inherited his social contacts and earned his workaday credentials; now he is as familiar and as beloved—to most—as the landmarks he struggles to defend.

Thanks to his father's sister, María Rosa Peña, who held the honorary post of administrator of the city's Franciscan lay order, Peña found himself involved in restoring the San Roque Chapel at the Franciscan Convent. After many

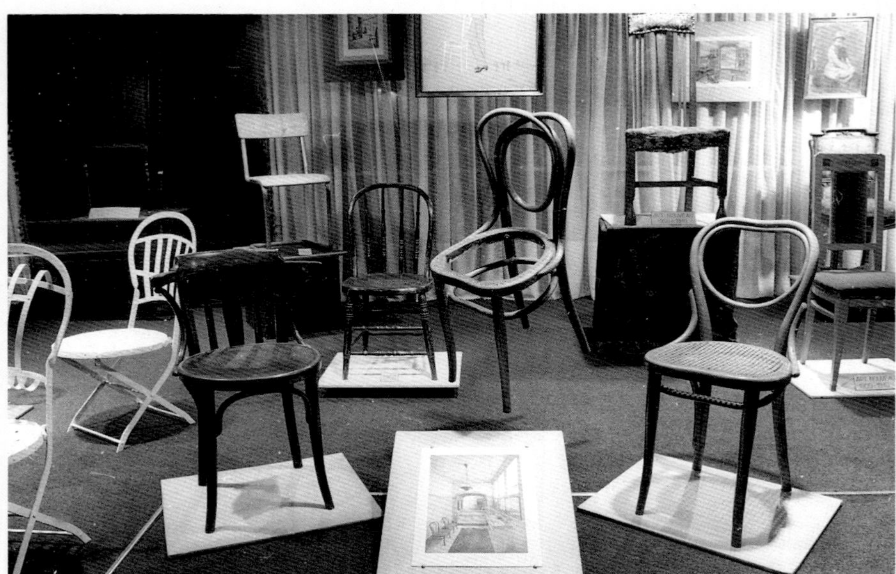

Fig. 3. An exhibition of chairs, prepared for the show windows of the Banco Popular Argentina by the Museum of the City of Buenos Aires, 1980.

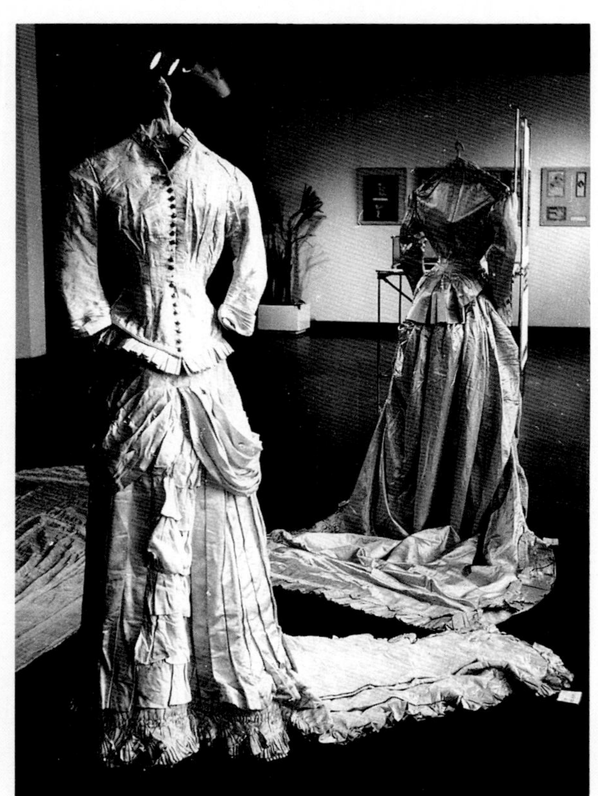

Fig. 4. An exhibition of clothing, original photographs, invitations, and other material related to weddings. Museum of the City of Buenos Aires, 1979.

nights of discussing the project with her nephew, Doña María Rosa decided in 1963 that it was time to urge the order's prior to undertake the much-needed restoration. Peña joined forces with the city's leading expert in colonial art, Héctor Schenone, and an equally knowledgeable brother-in-law, Juan Jaime Genoud. This erudite trio returned the chapel to its original glory and restored all the colonial woodcarvings that had decorated the convent.

When the restorers finished their job, Peña realized there were a significant number of statues with no assigned home. That was the instant of conception. *How wonderful it would be to make a museum*, he thought. The religious community maintained a modest library on an upper floor, beneath a magnificent vaulted ceiling. He convinced his aunt of the validity of the project; she in turn convinced the order to relocate the library downstairs.

Peña then appealed to his contacts to fill the handsome space with sufficient artwork to proclaim the place a museum in 1967: The Museum of San Roque. Other colleagues, friends, and enthused acquaintances lent what they could. Peña is possessed of a rare spirit of publicly oriented acquisitiveness. For him, a museum must be a creature in constant growth: stagnation is worse than death.

To maintain his desired growth rate, Peña devised a series of auctions. "A lady called me saying she had thirty religious statues to sell. I went to look at them. On the way, the idea of the auction occurred to me, and her collection was the core of the first one. What gave the whole idea credibility was that the museum offered a certificate of authenticity with each work."

He gathered additional material from his ever-growing contacts, catalogued and evaluated it, and brought in a professional auctioneer to conduct the sale. With his anticipated share of the proceeds, he, himself, bought pieces for

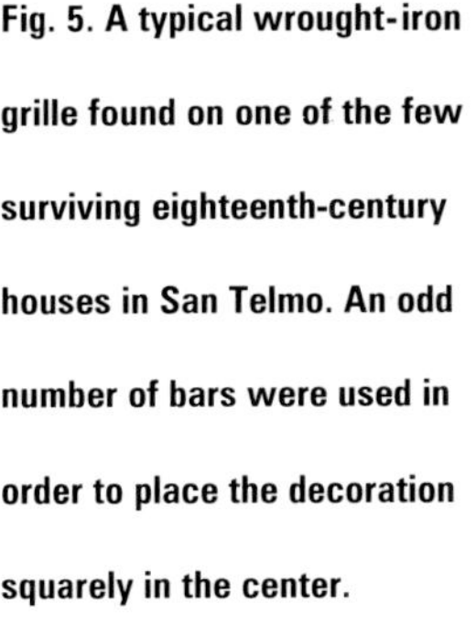

Fig. 5. A typical wrought-iron grille found on one of the few surviving eighteenth-century houses in San Telmo. An odd number of bars were used in order to place the decoration squarely in the center.

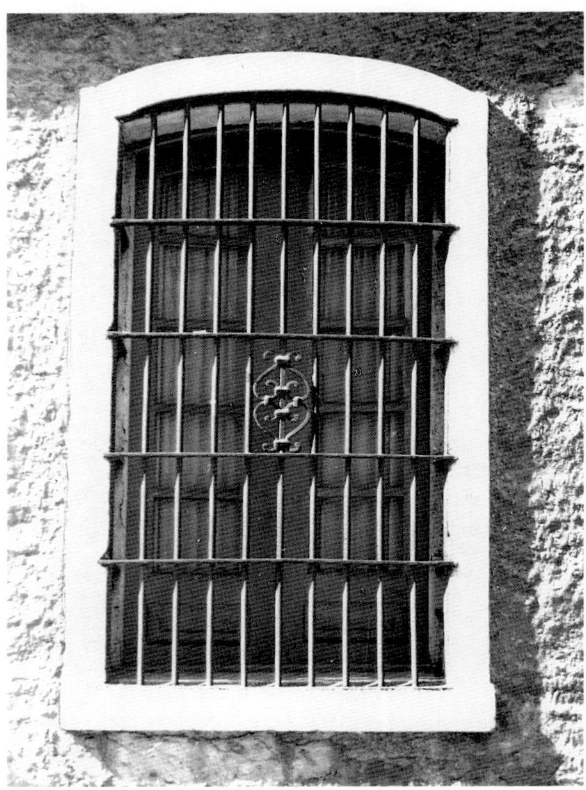

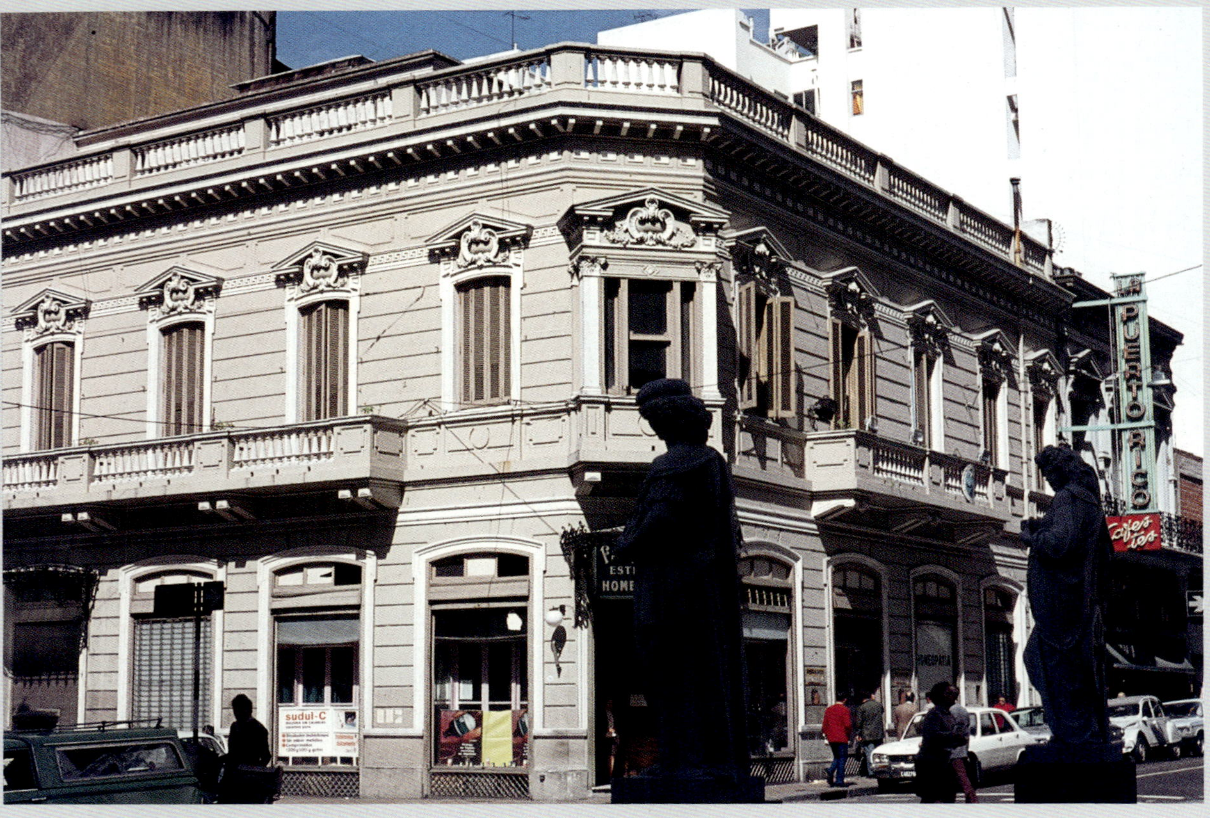

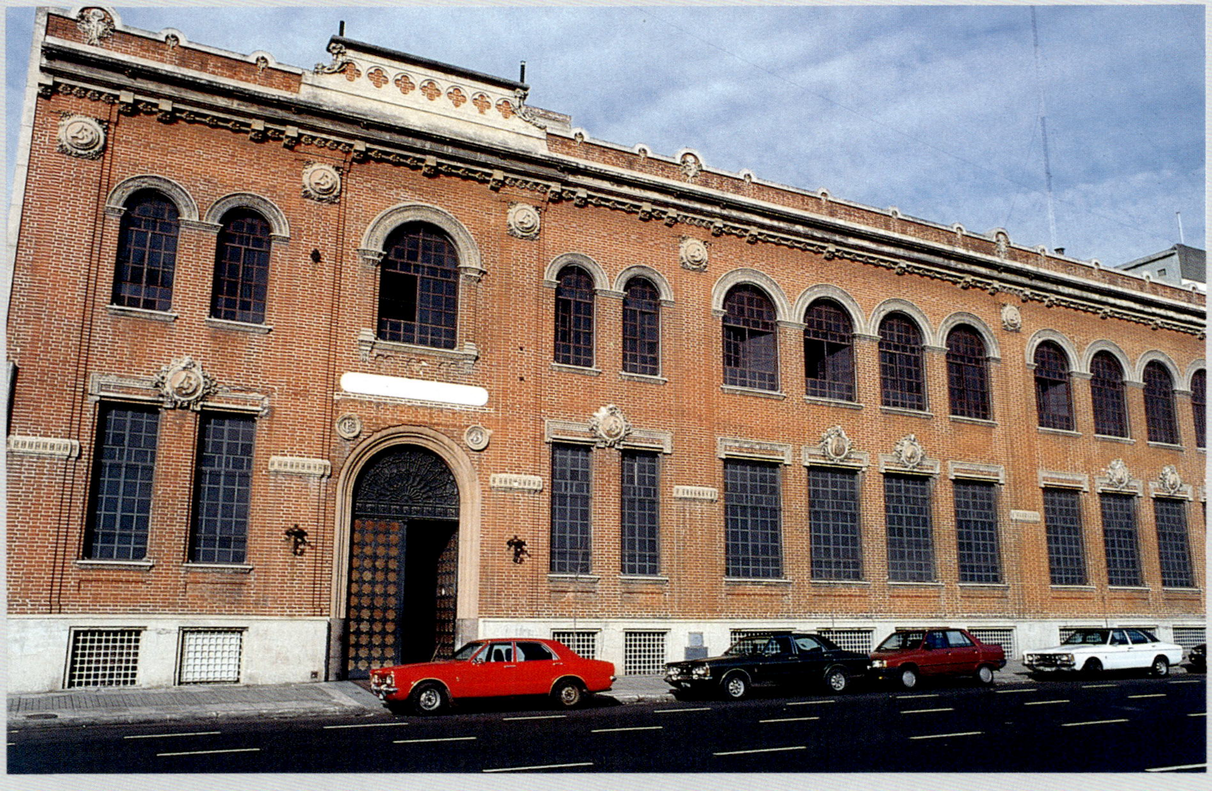

◂

Fig. 8. Exterior of the Museum of the City of Buenos Aires at 412 Alsina Street, San Telmo. The building dates from 1895. On the ground floor, there is still a pharmacy with its original painted ceilings and furnishings.

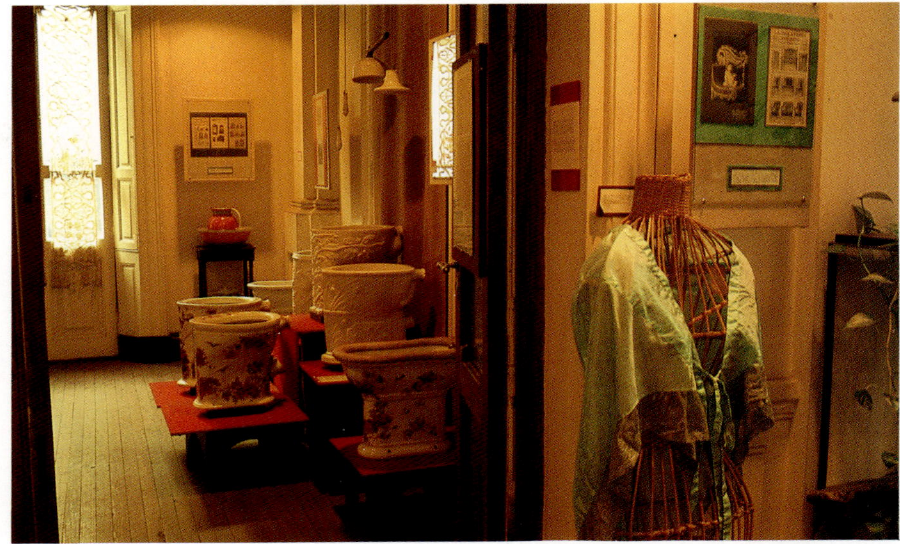

Fig. 9. Partial view of two exhibition rooms at the Museum of the City of Buenos Aires.

The original museum was housed in a cubicle in the General San Martín Cultural Center, where the Modern Art Museum (fig. 10) and the Sivori Museum (an entity dedicated to pre-modern Argentine art) each had a floor. Peña's project was confined to one room. He had become an expert on all that the city owned, sallying forth to save architectural fragments and stray statuary from the hammers of demolition crews and the hands of junk dealers. He was given a vacant lot to store his treasure, but his museum remained a tiny office in a modernistic structure built in the fifties. Peña kept his eye out for a likely site for his growing brainchild. At last, a wreck of an old house that stuck out like a sore thumb from the silhouette of the city's historical quarter became Peña's target for his future headquarters.

"Our part of the building was a shambles. On the ground floor, one of the city's oldest pharmacies still kept its nineteenth-century look. We moved in: for months we had no heat, electricity only in one corner, and a bathroom off a patio without a door. We arranged a series of verbal signals to guarantee a precarious privacy. Finally, a group of more modest workmen found us a door and installed it. Little by little, the building was transformed into our offices, a library, and three rooms for exhibitions (fig. 9). Now we have electricity and some heat. My office gets the morning sun, which has been a great help."

◂

Fig. 10. Modern Art Museum, now located at 350 San Juan Avenue, San Telmo. The building, ca. 1915, was a municipal tobacco warehouse belonging to a cigarette manufacturer.

If the building still lacks the basic amenities, it does have a certain character forged from overcoming adversity. Perhaps as a defense against chills and gloom, Peña developed the museum's outside activities with the same intensity he dedicated to conceiving and organizing exotic shows within its damp walls.

"The Museum of the City invites Municipal Radio's listeners to give a farewell send-off to the swallows gathered in Plaza de Mayo before they depart on their annual flight to San Juan de Capistrano, California." This upbeat message goes out once a year over the airwaves of a radio station just before thousands of swallows migrate north. Peña takes it upon himself to keep citizens aware of the more remarkable manifestations of both man and nature in the city.

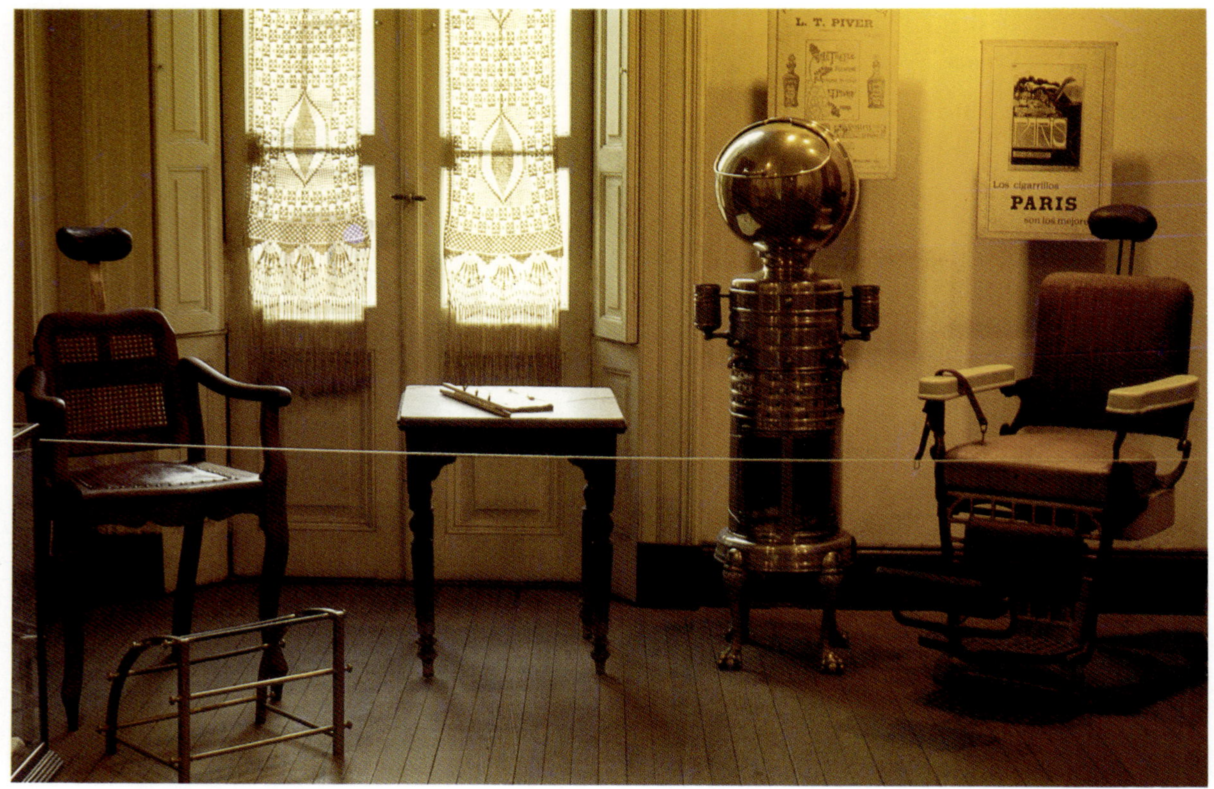

Fig. 11. The interior of an old barber shop displayed at the Museum of the City of Buenos Aires. The installation includes furnishings, magazines, and advertisements of the period.

July 22 is the Day of the Friend in Buenos Aires, and seven years ago Peña spent that evening at a dinner party celebrating the occasion. His tablemate was Margarita Porcel, director of community relations for the city's garbage removal monopoly known as MANLIBA (an acronym for "Keep Buenos Aires Clean"). He immediately accosted her with the description of a project he had been nurturing which needed MANLIBA's cooperation. Out of that serendipitous dinner came Clean-Up Week in San Telmo.

Although Porcel's bosses weren't quite sure what was going on, MANLIBA swept into San Telmo with all that United States technology had invented for carrying out municipal waste management. Highlights of the week were the election of the King and Queen of Cleanliness, the naming of the most spotless street in the neighborhood, and a contest for costumes whose theme related to tidiness. That first year, a lady dressed as a broom won the award and received "The Order of the Broom," an inscribed bronze medal. A boy was named King by virtue of his hygienic zeal. The garbagemen themselves voted a short alley the neatest thoroughfare. Peña had instituted another popular event.

Inside the museum, Peña gives his fertile sense of humor free rein. The museum probably owns the world's strangest permanent collection (fig. 11). A favorite in this retinue which never changes—perhaps because of the weight of these life-sized decorative statues—is a buxom lady in bronze, her breasts bared, who acts as an articulated signboard for each exhibit. Today she is partially covered in the trappings of a serving-girl, imitating the one on the wrapper of a popular brand of *yerba mate*, northern Argentina's favorite tealike infusion. For each show, her scanty wardrobe is adapted to the theme.

Peña prides himself on giving clever titles to his exhibits. Here Trod the *Porteños* was a show dedicated to mosaic tiles and turn-of-the century molds from which they were made. Years of Opening and Closing was a selection of those monumental carved and decorated wooden doors which are taller than the ceilings in most contemporary apartments. When the *Porteños* Gave Themselves Airs featured the breezy art of the fan. At the same time, Peña is practical. You can always recognize an envelope from his museum: it weighs half as much as that of any other art institution. His confidence in the quality and relevance of what he does allows him to send the city's cheapest invitations—a mimeographed form with the exhibit's title added by hand.

Donors to the Museum of the City are a mixed bag. A lady named Angélica Vázquez willed three trunks and two boxes to the institution. Months passed before Peña was able to get the court to grant an order to open these potential Pandora's boxes. When he finally received title to the bequest, he discovered that Vázquez had danced at the Colón in 1918, and the museum had been given all her costumes. A nun turned up one day in his office with a huge masonry statue: how she got it up the winding staircase was a mystery. She continued to be an active donor, appearing with valuable old dolls and, recently, an early Victrola. Another lady brought in a series of elaborate postcards with articulated figures attached to them. One had lost its head. Seven years later she came back with the missing head. "This kind of unexpected gesture makes the Museum special. We've never lost contact with the human dimension. People feel the museum is an extension of their home!" Peña proclaims, like a proud father (fig. 12).

"If the city is to have an auspicious future, citizens must regain the spirit of belonging to a small community, of participating in neighborhood activities (fig. 13). We need to form nonpolitical block committees responsible for keeping the streets clean, painting abandoned buildings, fixing signs. We need block parties, with everyone getting involved, even hanging treasures they want to share with their neighbors in their windows. On that day, there

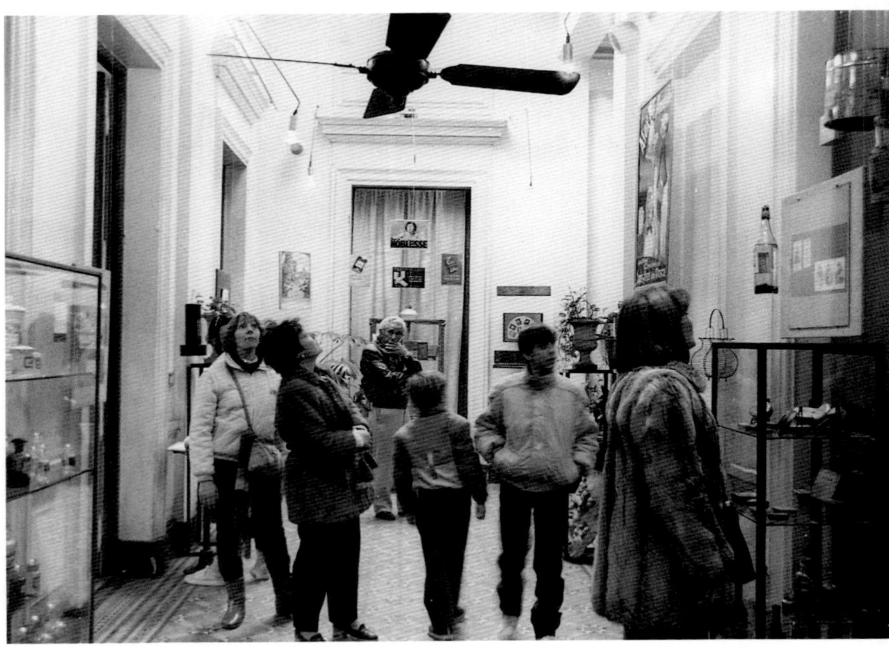

Fig. 12. An exhibition of containers and advertisements in which the packaging of a product is prominent. Museum of the City of Buenos Aires, 1989.

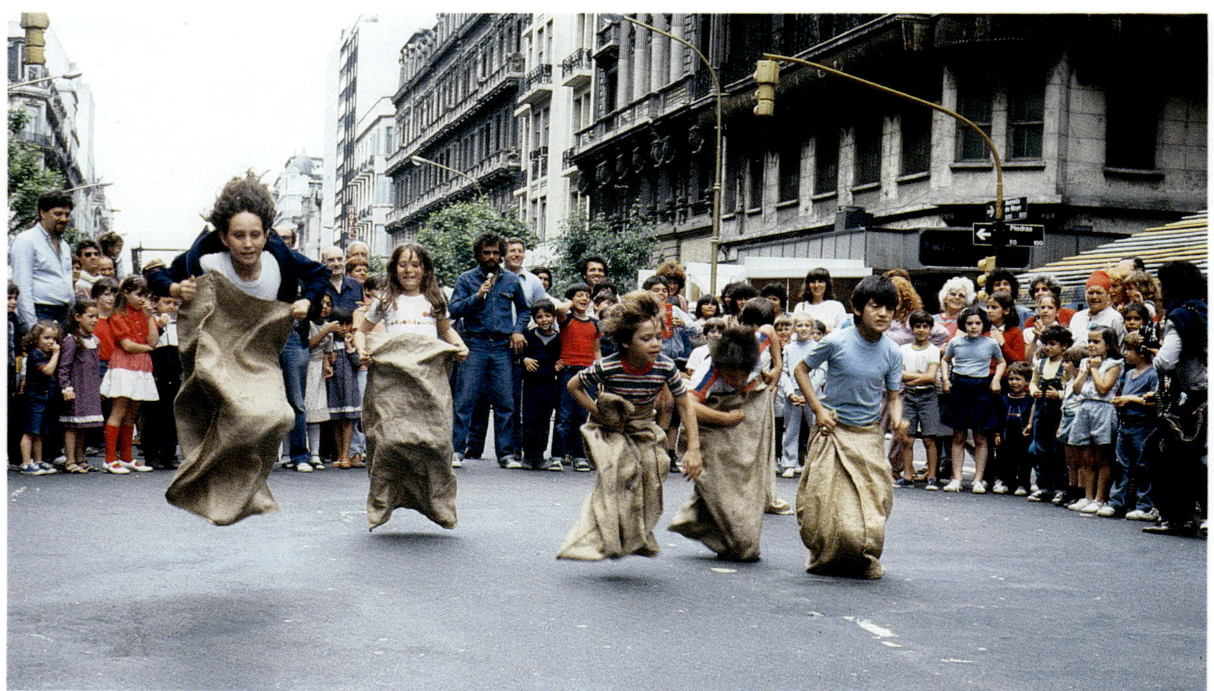

Fig. 13. Potato sack race. An event organized by the Museum of the City of Buenos Aires on the Avenida de Mayo, in the historic part of the city.

Fig. 14. Japanese parasols brighten a corner of the San Telmo antiques fair.

should be a band, wine and soft drinks, and artists and artisans with their creations—all spread out on the sidewalks for everyone to enjoy." Peña phrased these thoughts several years ago, and each year since he moves closer to his goal of communal integration.

Twenty years on the pavements have made Peña streetwise. He was in charge of the crafts fair in elegant Plaza Francia from 1971 to 1974. He envisioned the antiques fair in San Telmo in 1967. It took him three years to overcome bureaucratic indifference and adapt municipal regulations to his requirements. Having succeeded, Peña is personally responsible for converting a city's discarded bric-a-brac into instant antiques (fig. 14).

"Do you know what item has sold most consistently over the years? Milk cans! Those copperplated ten-gallon milk cans. Tourists keep on buying them even though they weigh a ton.

"There are only three or four left of the original cast of characters that manned the first stands back in 1970. My favorite is Roberto Tradatti, an engraver who is the classic bohemian. His father had a printing business and did reproductions of important artists. Roberto knows everyone and is a perfect gentleman, one of the few left of that endangered species.

"Many of the early standkeepers now have fancy antique shops in the neighborhood, like Macramé, La Ballesta, Gil and Rolo Polano (who recently had two Renaissance bronze horses that were extraordinary). How the market has changed over the years. And to think that none of them knew anything when they started. Not only have over one hundred antique shops opened since the museum initiated the project, but restaurants, cafés, and bars have flourished. Fortunately, most have tried to maintain a style that goes with the surroundings.

"When the fair began, there were just two good restaurants; people came in their cars from other parts of town and never ventured beyond the doors of

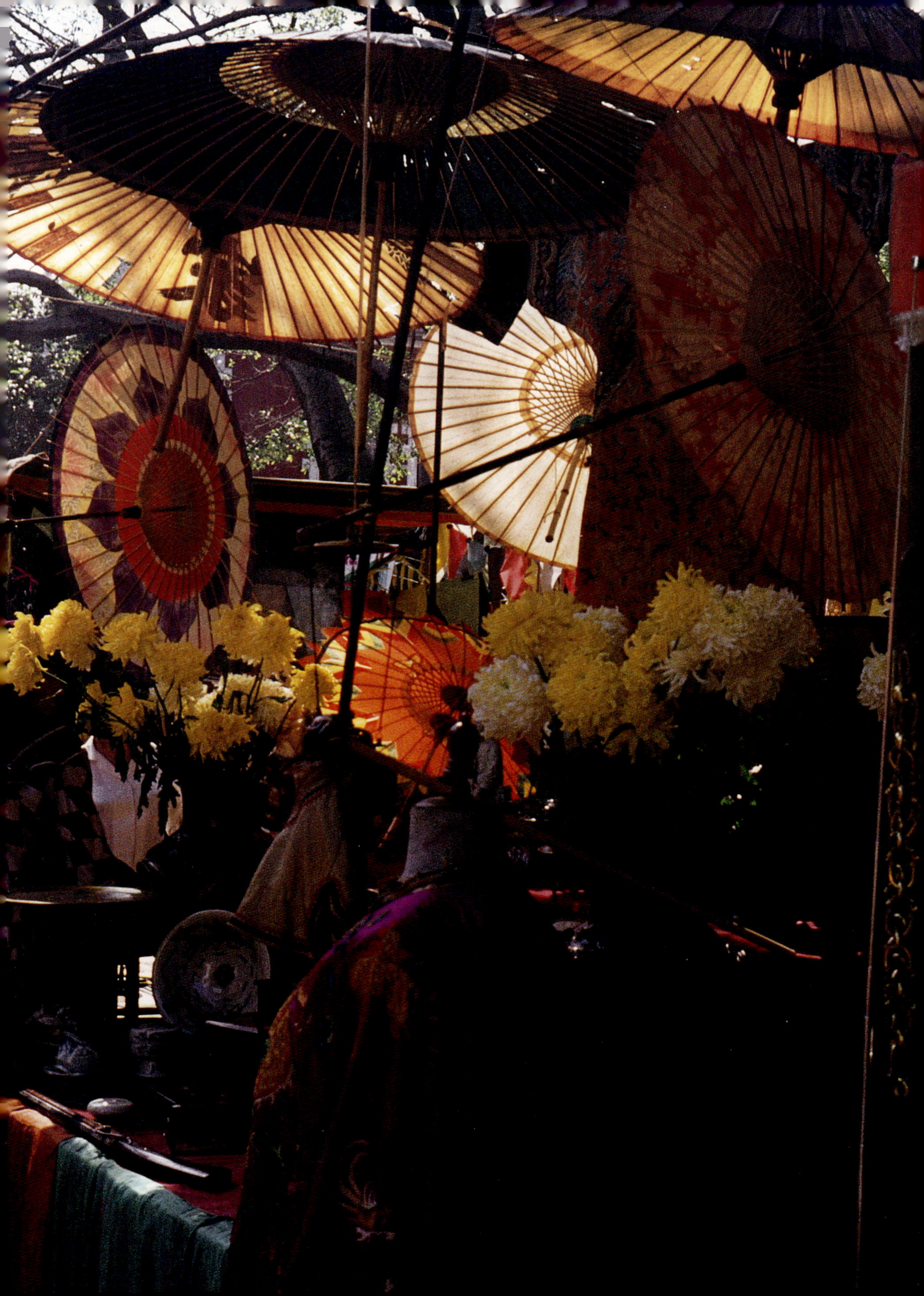

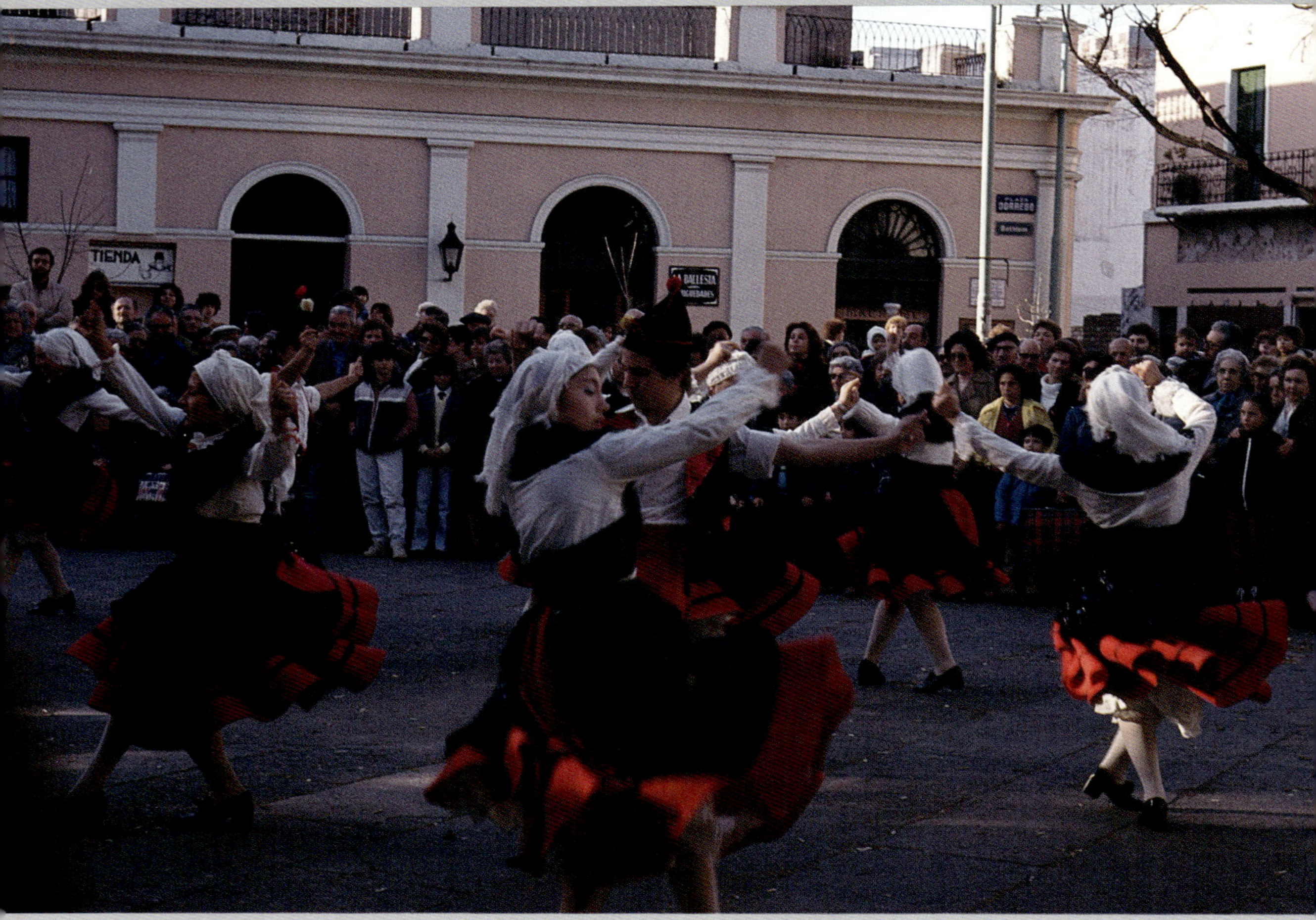

Fig. 15. ***Porteños*** **meet at Dorrego Plaza. This activity has taken place every other Saturday for three years. Here, a Spanish regional group is dancing.** **(See page 204.)**

the Repecho de San Telmo or the Viejo Almacén. Now there are dozens of choices, and strolling the streets is a socially acceptable pastime. San Telmo has developed a personality. In the mid-seventies, Osvaldo Giesso was one of the first architects to move to San Telmo. He rebuilt a house, organized a theater, and installed his studio. In 1979, Jorge Helft, an art collector and one of Buenos Aires's last benefactors, started the San Telmo Foundation. It's housed in a recycled building which has several showrooms and an auditorium. A decade later, the city's Modern Art Museum refurbished a warehouse and installed its headquarters in the *barrio*. Now a hundred artists, dozens of young couples, and even a few members of the local Establishment call San Telmo home.

"San Telmo was never sophisticated, and, without even trying, we've managed to maintain the neighborhood's traditional characteristics. Those who moved here didn't want to recreate the more elegant neighborhoods they came from; they wanted something absolutely different. While the impact of this immigration can't be seen from the streets, once you get inside the buildings it's surprising to see all the improvements.

"The fair itself is one of the country's most democratic institutions. From 1976 to 1983, it was virtually the only institution connected with government that was managed democratically. 'Practicing for the future.' That's how one of the members categorized the temporarily illegal activity called democracy that thrived at the fair. We had a precarious voting booth right in the Plaza where we've always held elections for the fair's governing commission.

"For fourteen years, the commission has voted an outstanding member of the community an honorary award called 'The Hand of Friendship.' The prize is often given to a prestigious personality whose dignity or integrity has been offhandedly questioned by the powers that be. This idea of giving a vote of recognition to an individual with a solid career caught in a moment of adversity due to some silly change in the political breeze seems important to me."

In 1977, Peña began to organize dances in the street. That was well before the return to democracy in 1983, when everyone took to the streets to celebrate their regained civil liberties. In Peña's part of town—San Telmo—the populace had been dancing all along. But Peña was a bit nervous that night in 1978 when the museum held its first masquerade. Nearly a thousand participants danced till dawn, while Peña himself surreptitiously guided the beat on his 78 rpm phonograph.

Permitting a masked crowd to dance in the streets produced no headaches, but his next dance did. For the festivities planned for the advent of autumn 1978, Peña requested a quantity of leaves from the city parks' administration. Sacks filled with foliage were duly delivered to the offices of the museum. When midnight came and the dancing was at its peak, Peña's plan was to let the autumn leaves fall romantically over the crowd gathered below the museum's balconies.

The bags were emptied. Peña watched in horror as damp leaves, dog droppings, and other sundries fell like so many mulch bombs onto the unsuspecting dancers. No one complained, and the bombardment became just one more anecdote in Peña's endless repertory of the ridiculous.

"Another of my favorite annual events occurs on the Saturday closest to the first day of Spring—The *Porteños* and Their Live Mascots. The audience chooses a jury from among themselves which votes four awards: the prettiest mascot, the most entertaining mascot, the most extravagant mascot, and the mascot that looks most like his or her owner. Usually over a hundred pets compete. One year a black ant named Summer won an award. A lady and her Siamese cat surprisingly won the look-alike prize, and, fortunately, a man who had threatened on the phone to bring his pet boa constrictor never appeared, much to the relief of the other contestants.

"The museum also instituted an award for 'The Living Testimony of Our Metropolitan Memory.' This prize goes to businesses or buildings which have preserved a patina of tradition. Often a bar or a shop wins it, or a special apartment house. The Bank of Boston's magnificent building won one year. Pharmacies, restaurants, and bars seem to be the most frequent winners. The owners of a bar in the Boca district never understood that they were being applauded for historical conservation. They hadn't modified the look of their bar because the idea didn't occur to them, and they never did grasp what the prize-giving ceremony was all about.

"The museum functions with a minimal staff. I have one assistant with an official title. Eduardo Vázquez is ranked as a 'department head.' We do have several colleagues who try to fulfill the roles of investigator, librarian, administrator of fairs, and photographer, plus someone who mounts our exhibits. What makes it all work is the wonderful disposition of the staff. Everyone does a bit of everything, from organizing children's games in the street to hauling exhibits to and from the plaza in the same day."

One of the museum's most recent achievements was coordinating the refurbishing of Dorrego Plaza (fig. 15), where the Sunday antiques fair is held. In 1989, the Association of Neighbors and Friends decided that repaving the plaza was a priority. The Antorchas Foundation, another institution which Jorge Helft directs, offered thirty thousand dollars if City Hall would chip in their share. When the government changed in mid-1989, the new municipal authorities declared a policy of total austerity, and the promise of a contribution was withdrawn. The Association managed to convince neighbors to put up part of the needed funding. Everyone was asked to give at least ten dollars; several generously gave more than five hundred. Many who could have given and who owed their success to the experience earned during years of Sundays at the Plaza didn't donate anything, which infuriated Peña. Finally, the last ten thousand dollars came from those who had stands and from several adjacent antique shops.

Peña pictures where his crusade is leading. "Rescuing the past can bring a greater awareness of what Argentina is. We have to start with the average citizen. I try to do all this in a good-natured way. A bit of humor makes the process flow more smoothly. First, the individual has to gain a consciousness of local realities before he can, in the abstract, fathom the concept of a national character. A resident of Buenos Aires, in order to integrate a truly national community, has to understand clearly his own reality and how it differs from that of the inhabitants of the mountainous northern province of Jujuy or Tierra del Fuego, down near Antarctica. There's no way to forge one common culture between these different regions. What's necessary is an awareness of the differences and a respect for them. The museum, and all my projects, aren't aimed at tourists. They're for Argentines to know themselves and each other better. First we have to revalue our collective memory, before we offer it to tourists" (fig. 16).

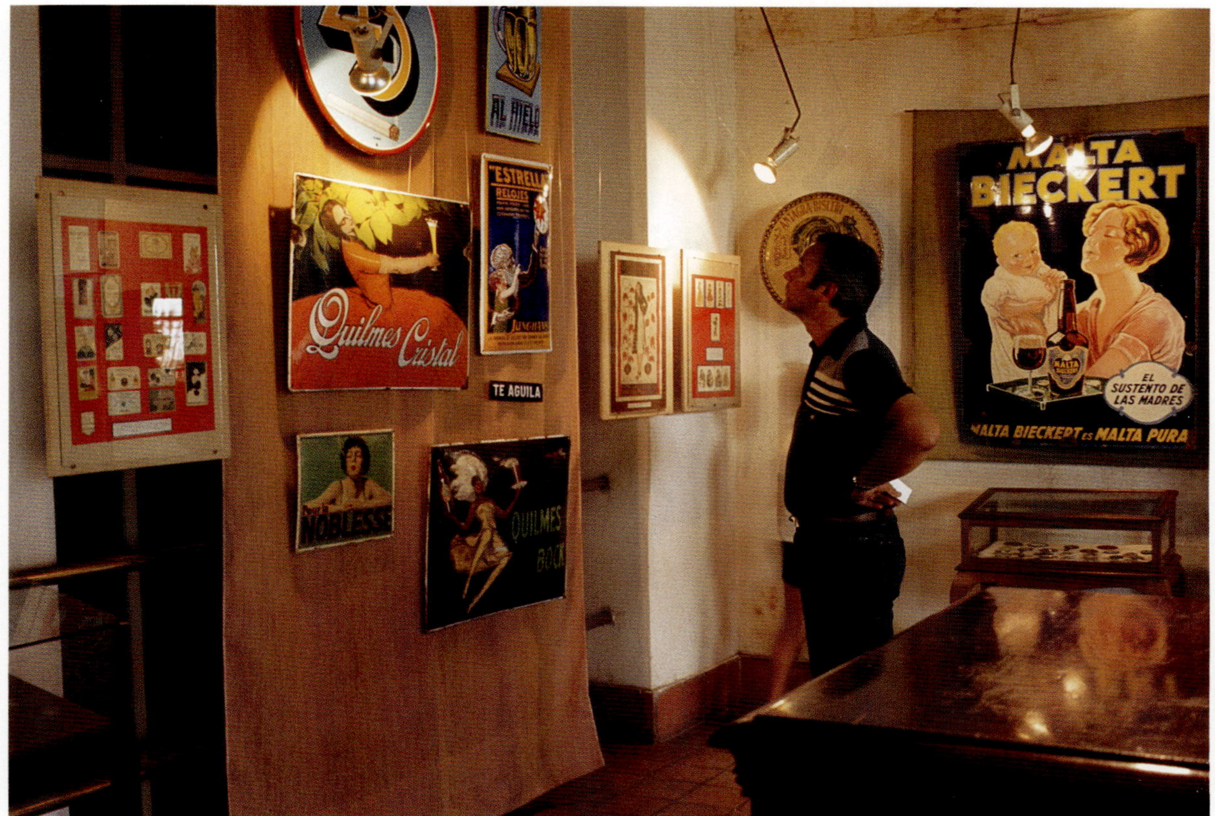

Fig. 16. An exhibition of antique advertising signs, enamel on metal. Museum of the City of Buenos Aires, 1983.

As for the much maligned *porteño*, Peña finds that "the irascible native of our city—as he's invariably catalogued by his fellow citizens—is in reality accessible, amiable, and even talks too much to strangers, inventing street directions if he's not sure what he's talking about. But he criticizes many minor details of urban life, and often fails to enjoy the city's special flavor." Peña loves to take foreign visitors to the bars on Avenida de Mayo, which seems like stumbling onto a corner of Barcelona fifty years ago; or strolling along Lavalle Street as thousands of moviegoers fill the pedestrian-only thoroughfares until well past midnight; or browsing in bookshops on Corrientes Avenue, vast spaces filled with tables offering the best and the worst ever printed; or, at last, to the *barrio* of Mataderos where the vast cattle market is held every morning, and people still use the sidewalks as their parlors and chat from window to window.

Peña's eaglelike expression brightens in delight as he recalls the details of his colorful past. He talks with conviction and enthusiasm, his eyes dancing behind the thick rims of his spectacles, sharing his experience and knowledge with a courteous generosity. His humor flickers constantly, interspersed with the outpouring of facts, reminiscences, dates, and figures. "The architecture of this city was designed, for the most part, between 1875 and 1945," he sums up. "Examples of each different moment coexist, and it is this ongoing testimony of a city in constant transition and growth that we must try to save." □

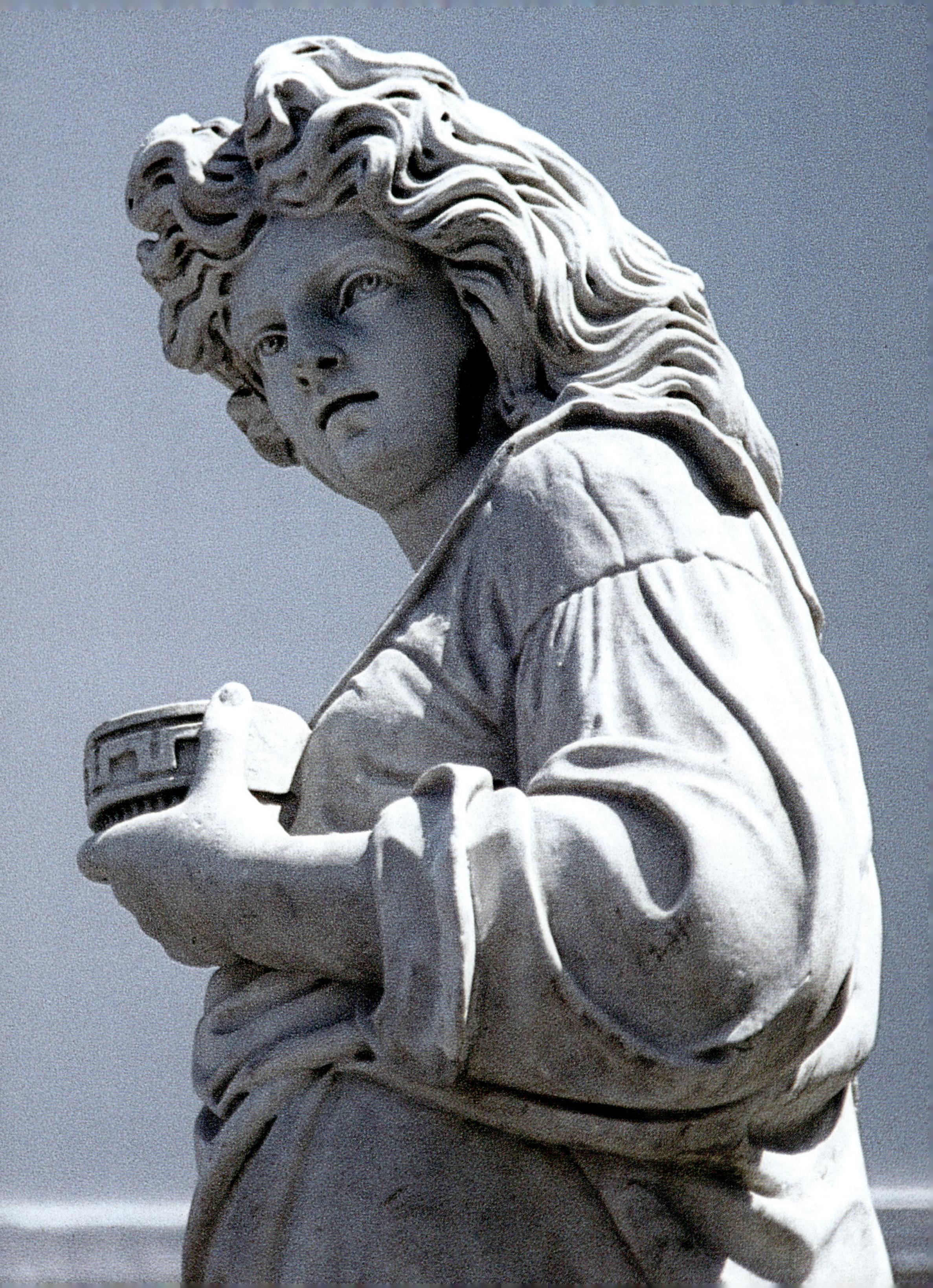

Public Sculpture

By José María Peña

Translated by Edward Shaw

José María Peña has been director of the Museum of the City of Buenos Aires for twenty-four years. A graduate of the University of Buenos Aires School of Architecture, specializing in the investigation of nineteenth- and twentieth-century Argentine architecture, he is active in historic preservation and urban planning.

Fig. 1. *Navegación* (Navigation), ca. 1870. One of four decorative sculptures in the Plazoleta San Francisco. Photograph by the author. **(See page 209.)**

The date chosen to open the period under consideration, 1875–1945, coincides almost exactly with the first appearance of sculpture within the perimeter of the city of Buenos Aires. For this study, we will concentrate on public plazas as a setting, although buildings and cemeteries are also sites for important statuary.

In accordance with traditional design, public squares began to appear in the early part of the 1820s. Before then, areas that later would be urbanized were just stretches of land without trees or any other element that could remotely inspire one to linger there.

In order to understand the evolution of Buenos Aires plazas and their design, we must situate ourselves in time, and ask why a country like the Argentine Republic, so far from Europe, adapted the essence of the layout of European plazas. First, the distance from the world of culture, which in those days the Continent alone was considered to be, was no obstacle to familiarity with its way of life. Second, since the 1820s, just after Argentina's separation from Spain, many foreigners trained in the liberal arts were invited to Argentina by local authorities, while others came on their own initiative. Once here, they made themselves at home. With them also came merchants and, after 1850, large waves of immigrants with their own particular customs and recollections.

Designs for plazas at first were unassuming, limited to pathways bordered by *paraísos* (a tree originating in the Orient known in English as the chinaberry), with a fountain in the middle, not excluding the possibility of a decorative sculpture. It is important to point out that soon after these humble beginnings, competitions began to be held for architects to create designs of greater importance. One of the most significant was by Julio Dormal (1846–1924), a Belgian architect and the man responsible for completing the building of the Colón Theater (two previous architects died during the eighteen years the project took to finish). Dormal focused on the vast Parque de Palermo in the center of Buenos Aires. Over the years, this has been and still is the principal outdoor site where numerous monuments and statues stand. It should be noted that the inspiration for the design of the park was the almost simultaneous creation of the Bois de Boulogne.

The first significant sculpture placed in a plaza was the work of French artist Joseph Daumas (1801–1887), who, with the help of contributions from the general public, created a monument in memory of the victories of Argentina's greatest hero, General José de San Martín. This work of San Martín on horseback, corresponding to then current styles, represents the General in an attitude of indicative authority with his right arm outstretched. It was inaugurated in 1862, initially on a low pedestal. At the celebration of the centenary of the Revolución de Mayo—one of the dates of Argentina's independence—the statue was shifted to a much more bombastic and hardly felicitous base designed by Gustavo Eberlein (1847–1926), a German artist.

It would be a long time before the city's public parks would see works by Argentine sculptors, with the exception of an equestrian statue to another hero of the Independence, Manuel Belgrano, creator of the nation's flag. This monument, inaugurated in 1873 and placed in what is now the Plaza de Mayo, is unusual in that it was done by two artists. The figure of Belgrano is by a Frenchman, Albert Carrier de Belleuse (1824–1887); the horse is by an Argentine, Manuel de Santa Coloma (1829–1886), son of an Argentine diplomat, who specialized in sculpting animals.

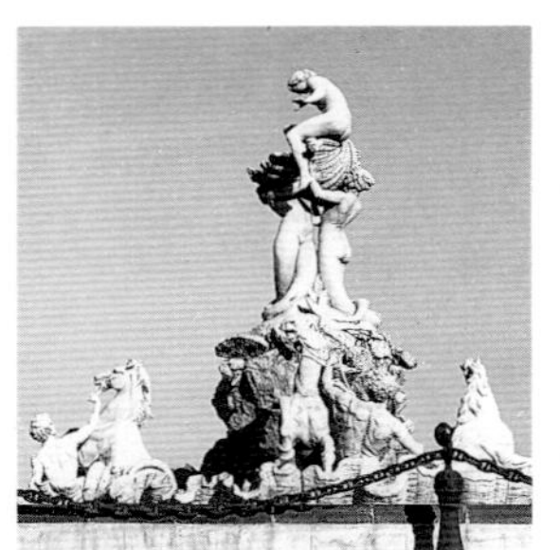

Fig. 2. Dolores Mora, *Fuente de las nereidas*, (Fountain of the sea nymphs), 1900. Photograph by Roberto Bunge.

These two monuments can be considered the first to gain popularity with the inhabitants of the city.

In 1880, Buenos Aires became the capital of the country, and change and movement were constants. Caught up in the giddy speed of growth, both recently arrived immigrants and established citizens began to mix. In 1887, statistics showed that the city had 204,734 Argentines and 228,641 foreigners. This differential is eloquent.

In Buenos Aires, it is impossible to avoid taking into account the relationship with the Old World when we consider the ornamentation of plazas, as in so many other things. This does not imply a lack of local artists (by 1889, there were thirty-seven workshops devoted to sculpture),[1] but rather that those who dedicated themselves to this art were, for the most part, trained in Italy and France. From this latter country came the two fountains which were placed in the Plaza de la Victoria. Built in 1868, this was the city's principal plaza. These first fountains were cast at the Du Val d'Osne Foundry, and they astonished the *porteños*—as the residents of portside Buenos Aires are known.

The Du Val d'Osne Foundry played a special role in that period for many cities of the world, and the fountains mentioned above were probably their most successful, judging from the importance given them in an article which appeared in the *Revue de l'Architecture et des Travaux Publiques* published in France in 1873. Fountains like these can be seen in French towns such as Troyes, in Spain in Valencia, and in Chile in Valparaiso. The fountains in Buenos Aires were built by uniting diverse figures and other decorative elements in cast-iron plates which serve as receptacles into which the water falls.

Back then, fountains in every form—those with figures, large vases, or whatever the foundry offered—produced an unexpected enthusiasm in the general public. Fountains became the rage, and the furor spread, spurring architects to use them to decorate innumerable gardens and plazas. Ordering them was easy; an illustrated catalogue offered all the models.

Here we should clarify that decorative sculpture, not to be confused with commemorative statuary, in the period from 1860 to 1900 in Buenos Aires was basically produced in series in cast iron, or carved in Carrara marble, usually in workshops in Italy. The figures found in the latter typically represented metaphorical symbols, for example, of the continents; classical reproductions;

1. F. Latzina, *Geografía de la República Argentina* (Buenos Aires: Felix Latjouane, 1888).

or perhaps allegories of industry: commerce, navigation, or geography. Four of these allegories in marble were placed on the Pirámide de Mayo (Pyramid of May) in 1876. This was not their first location; originally, with ten others, they crowned the main office of the Bank of the Province of Buenos Aires.

The four mentioned above, (replacing originals set on the Pirámide long before which deteriorated because they were made of stucco), were removed from the site in 1912. Today they can be found in the Plazoleta San Francisco, in the historical center of the city (fig. 1).

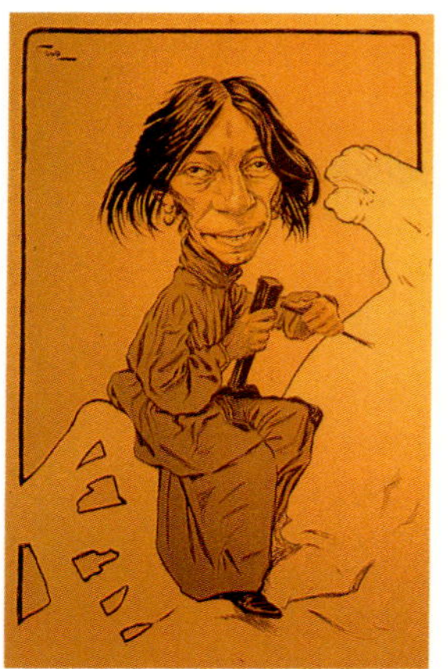

Fig. 3. Drawing of Dolores Mora by Cao, *Caras y Caretas*, 24 January 1903. Photograph courtesy of the author.

Another of the first statues to be inaugurated in the city was given by the Italian colony to honor Giuseppe Mazzini. The day before the event, *La Prensa* declared, "The circumstances through which a monument is erected to a man thousands of miles from his homeland, on shores he never knew...demonstrates the idea of human progress which tends to join men all over the earth in fraternal union." This fusion of nationalities and their cultures marked Argentine culture more and more, in spite of unleashing furious discussions about Mazzini's ideologies. His figure, on foot, next to a chair upon which one hand rests while in the other he holds written sheets of paper, strongly transmits the man's character. His image had such presence that Julián Martel wrote in his novel *La bolsa*, published serially in an important newspaper,[2] "the statue of Mazzini, white and erect, sharply outlined his marblelike profile on the reddish sky."

We should mention the sculptor, Italian artist Julio Monteverde (1837–1917), author of several works in the city, to be found predominantly at the Recoleta Cemetery. Monteverde was also the teacher of Argentina's first woman sculptor, Dolores Mora (1866–1936) (fig. 3). Her work, *Fuente de las nereidas*, was never called that because the public baptized it "The Fountain of Lola Mora" (fig 2).

Born in the Province of Tucuman in 1866, Mora was given a grant by the government of Argentina to study at Michetti's atelier in Rome. She soon decided that she wanted to continue her apprenticeship with Monteverde. Setting up her studio in Rome, she befriended many local figures, among them D'Annunzio. After winning a competition in St. Petersburg in 1899 (which she did not accept because the regulations demanded that she renounce her Argentine citizenship to accept that of Russia), she continued working in Rome until 1901, when the City of Buenos Aires commissioned her to do her well-known fountain.

The ensemble comprises two sections, the lower formed by a large shell from which three rearing horses emerge, held by young men who rise from water covering them to their waists. In the center, on a small rock hill, two mermaids with double tails hold a shell on which Venus is seated. Despite critical acclaim—"waists, hips, bellies, and thighs are treated brilliantly"[3]—it took only a short time for critics to complain about the audacity of the naked figures. Those who rejected the monument criticized its sensuality which transmitted more the softness of the feminine form than the traditional shapes of the classics.

Mora's selection of models for some of the male figures could be an important factor in judging the validity of the reactions. She chose the Marquis of San Giovanni, the son of the Uruguayan ambassador, and a handsome Italian fencer named Greco.

2. *La Nación,* 24 August 1891–4 October 1891.

3. J. Solsona, *La Ilustración Artística* (Barcelona) no. 1138 (October 1903).

In spite of the fountain's acknowledged virtues and the honor of being chosen to appear on the cover of a magazine printed in Paris,[4] just a few years after its installation two blocks from the Plaza de Mayo, the city's authorities deemed it necessary to look for a less conspicuous site for Mora's masterpiece. They chose the Costanera Sur, a promenade along the riverfront a little south of downtown Buenos Aires.

Another woman, Luisa Isella (1886–1942), was the author of a fountain placed in the Plaza Rodríguez Peña, a park known for its handsome trees. The first studies for this work were done in Monza, Italy, then continued in Chile, where she received a gold medal with a grant to study in Paris. There she received another prize in 1909.

Her sculpture, made from Carrara marble, represents the figure of a young nude bending down to drink water which springs from a rock (fig. 4). It was exhibited at the Exposición Internacional of 1910 in Buenos Aires and was purchased there by the city for the abovementioned plaza, where it still stands.

In reality, perhaps we should have started with the very first Argentine sculptors. They were Lucio Correa Morales (1852–1923) and Francisco Cafferata (1861–1890).

Correa Morales studied, as was often the case then, in Florence. Like all Argentines from what was called the Generation of the '80s, he had difficulty escaping the attraction of the Old World. His works of art and monumental statuary were executed in cities such as Rome, Barcelona, and Paris.

"His formation under the stylistic rules of regional realism, with a tendency toward the literary, a style in fashion in Italy at the time, was perfectly adequate for the Argentina he found on his return."[5]

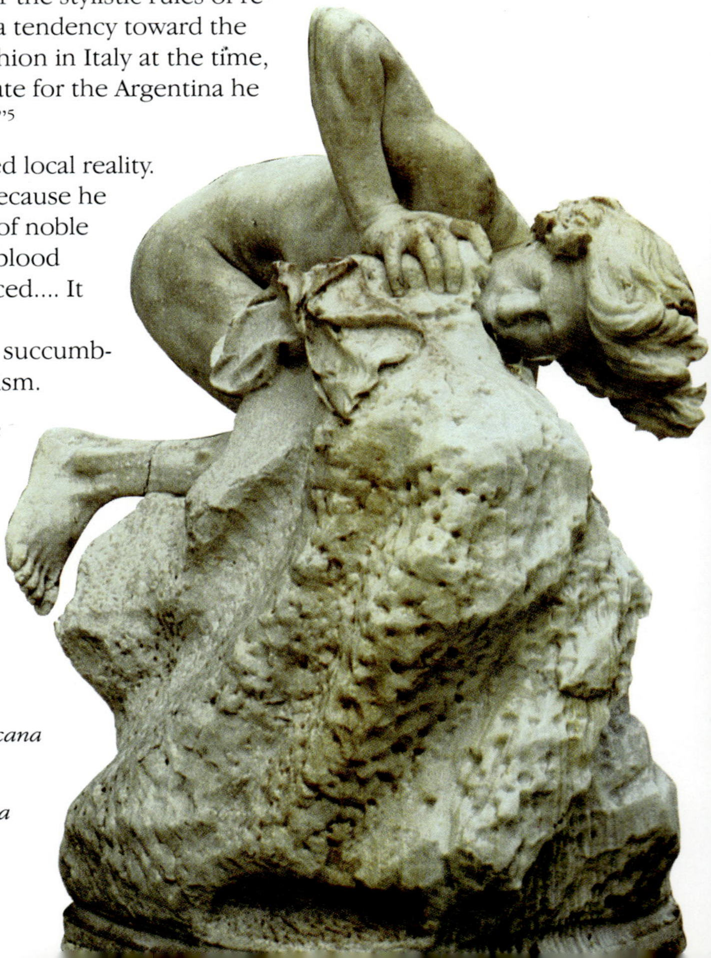

Fig. 4. Luisa Isella, *El bebedor* (The drinker), marble, 1910. Photograph by the author.

He rapidly assimilated local reality. "I love the gaucho because he represents the kind of noble being who shed his blood and was then displaced.... It is the last gesture of Argentine art before succumbing to cosmopolitanism.

"As for *Cautiva* [The captive] [1905], this is one of the works I most love. Do you know how it was born? One day I was with my children, and an old

4. *La Ilustración Sudamericana* (15 June 1903).

5. Jorge López Anaya, *Los comienzos de la escultura* (Buenos Aires, 1966).

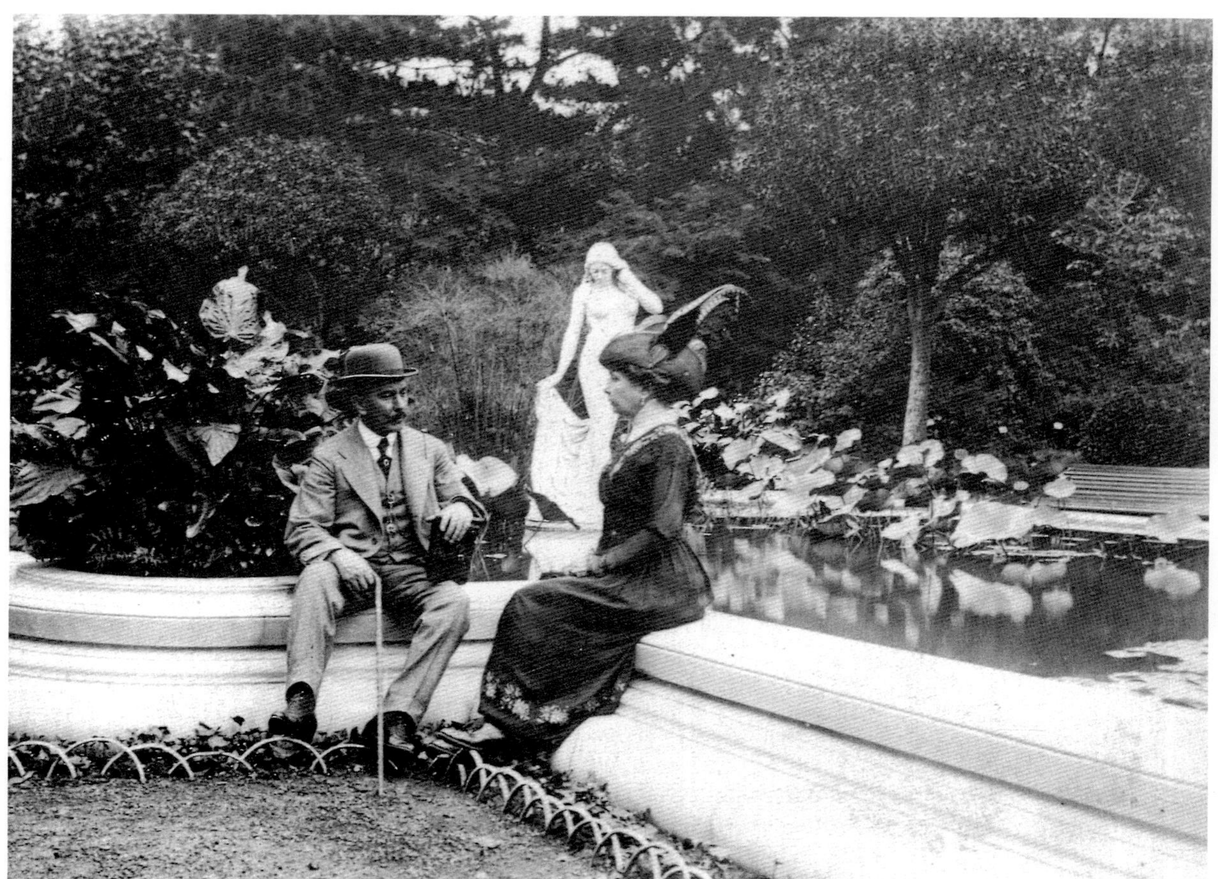

Fig. 5. Lucio Correa Morales, *La ondina del Plata* (The water nymph of the Río de la Plata), 1880. Photograph in the Botanical Garden, 1911. Courtesy of the Museum of the City of Buenos Aires.

Indian woman who stared at us for a long time with moist eyes let the following phrases fall from her lips, 'I also had child, pretty child. I don't know if alive. Or dead. Or where...'"[6]

In spite of this attraction to native themes, Correa Morales's sculpture continued its ties to Europe, with the exception of a few works, one of which was *La ondina del Plata*, done in 1880 (fig. 5). This statue has been placed in the midst of a pond with water lilies in our Botanical Garden.

His total immersion in realism was disturbing considering the modern tendencies of the times. Curiously, he who would be the master of Rogelio Yrurtia, Pedro Zonza Briano, and Pablo Curatela Manes once wrote in a notebook, "The Venus de Milo is/ changed and diminished:/ because of the unhealthy life/ to which modernism subjected her."[7]

Almost ten years younger, Francisco Cafferata had the same education as Correa Morales. He could not avoid the classical undercurrents which determined an artist's access to commissions for monuments venerating the heroes of the Independence. His death at twenty-nine prevented him from manifesting all that his early work promised. He was, however, the author of the first monument made by an Argentine, erected in homage to Admiral Guillermo Brown, inaugurated in the suburb of Adrogue in 1886.

6. Ibid.

7. *Correa Morales* (Buenos Aires: Academia Nacional de Bellas Artes, 1949).

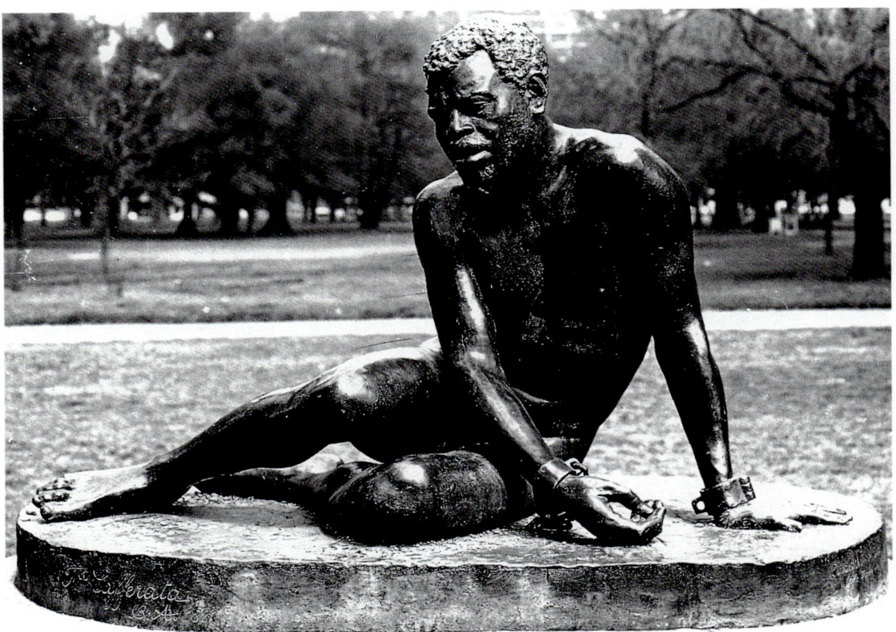

Fig. 6. Francisco Cafferata, *Esclavo* (Slave), bronze, 1882. Photograph by Roberto Bunge.

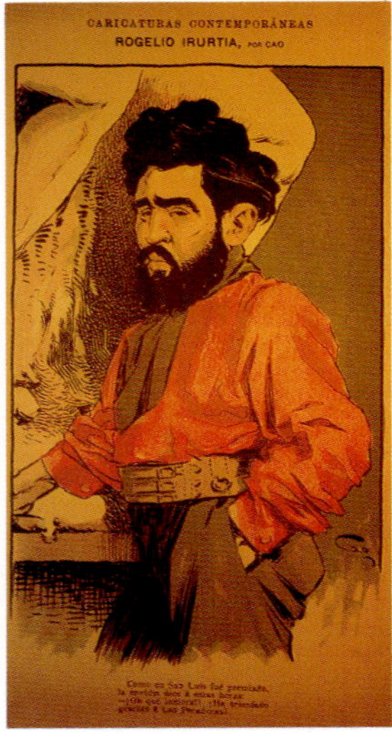

Fig. 7. Caricature of Rogelio Yrurtia by Cao, *Caras y Caretas*, 8 October 1904. Photograph courtesy of the author.

We cannot avoid mentioning his *Esclavo*, more inclined toward a naturistic style (fig. 6). The figure is of a naked black man seated on the ground in an attitude of resignation. This comes close to expressing a feeling of spontaneity, and the modeling of the body, beautiful from every angle, is especially so when observed from the back.

"We are talking about a great piece of sculpture. There is nothing at the Salón which could be considered its equal."[8] These were the words of Camille Mauclair, speaking of the presentation by Rogelio Yrurtia (1879–1950) at the Salón of the Société Nationale des Artistes Françaises in Paris in 1903. Yrurtia is perhaps Argentina's greatest sculptor (fig. 7). Fortunately, the city of Buenos Aires has his best works and a museum dedicated to the artist in what was once his home

As might be expected, Yrurtia began to work with Lucio Correa Morales when he was very young. Correa Morales learned a deep respect for Yrurtia's technique and discipline. Both the output and career of Yrurtia exemplify this artist's singular character. Proof of his will power came at the Universal Exposition held in St. Louis in 1904. He presented a sculptural group shown in Paris the year before and was awarded the Exposition's Grand Prize; but he did not accept it and, in addition, demolished the statue because it no longer satisfied his implacable standards.

Yrurtia was an artist who needed long periods of time to reach the definitive version of each of his creations. We will mention only three of the most important. *Canto al trabajo* (figs. 8 and 9), commissioned in 1907 by the city's mayor, Carlos T. de Alvear, underwent a series of successive alterations between 1907 and 1908. The sculpture began as one feminine and two masculine figures, grew to reach sixteen different figures in a variety of different studies, to end up, finally, at fourteen. This liberty of experimentation was possible thanks to the generosity and patience of Alvear.

8. Camille Mauclair, *París* (16 May 1903).

"*Canto al trabajo* is one of the few truly monumental sculptures that does not fall back on an epic theme.... Built on a low, rectangular base, the figures are distributed harmoniously. The size is twice that of real life, and the figures are assembled in descending heights on one side, the other side balanced by the large rock they are hauling. The bodies are in different poses, adapted to enhance the central scenography of the monument, which depicts the importance of work as a means of mastering the future."[9]

Fig. 8. Rogelio Yrurtia, *Canto al trabajo* (Hymn to work), bronze, 1908. Photograph by the author.

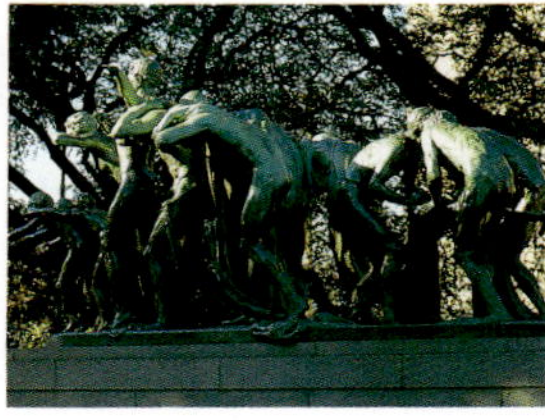

This sculptural grouping, balanced as it is, inspires a desire to study it carefully from every angle to enjoy the harmony of the bodies, which should be observed individually as they integrate into the group and, additionally, for the modeling and excellent patina. "[T]he figures are dynamic, anticlassical and germinative because of the tense structural curves and their unstable equilibrium."[10]

Yrurtia won a competition in 1907, and the outcome was another important monument which, for a variety of reasons, was not completed until 1926. It was made to commemorate Manuel Dorrego, a colonel who once governed Buenos Aires and who had been a legendary figure, dying tragically (fig. 10). The space the city designated for this statue was a small, untypical *plazoleta*. Here the monument is simultaneously a statue and a work of architecture. The axis of the composition is a grey granite pedestal, predominantly vertical in design in order to adapt itself to the small site. In the central part of the sculpture, Yrurtia has placed Dorrego seated on his horse led by a winged Victory. The figure is turning his head toward the left, holding the reins in his left hand, forcing the torso to twist in the same direction. At the sides, much lower and also mounted on blocks of granite, are two figures representing History and Fate. They are austere presences which are on foot. The former is serene and immutable; the latter represents a young man struggling in the coils of a snake (fig. 11). The patina is dark.

"All the creative talent of the sculptor is displayed in the principal group. The figures are joined in a dynamic composition organized by a strong diagonal tension. The movement generated at the foot of the horse finds its resolution in the ascending hand of Victory. This figure forms an arch which is a constant in the work of Yrurtia."[11]

Fig. 9. Rogelio Yrurtia, *Canto al trabajo* (Hymn to work), detail, bronze, 1908. Photograph by the author.

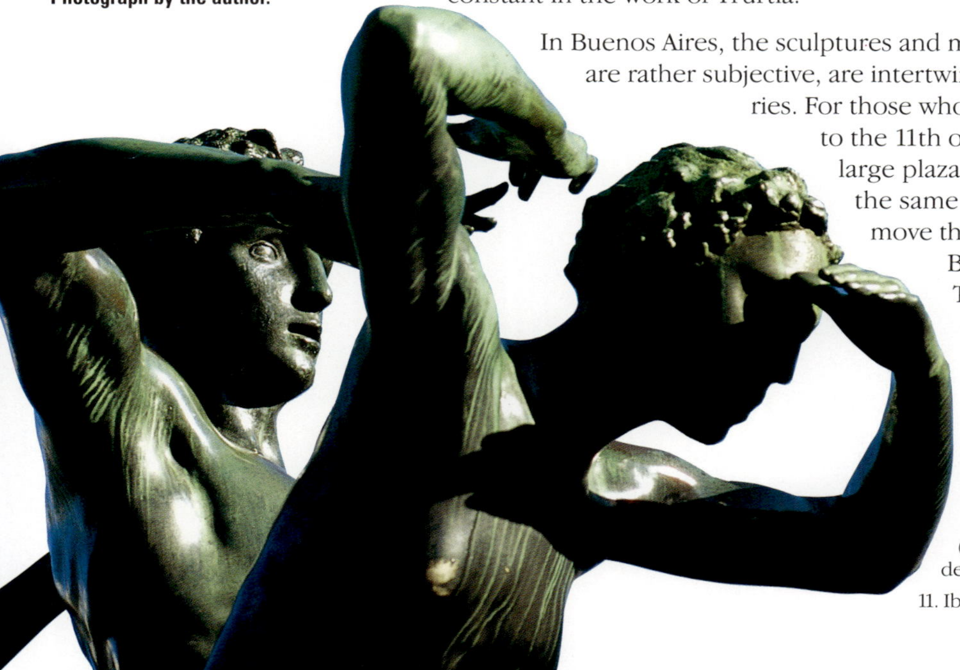

In Buenos Aires, the sculptures and monuments, since they are rather subjective, are intertwined with our vital memories. For those who travel by train every day to the 11th of September Station, the large plaza nearby would never be the same if someone were to remove the mausolem of President Bernardino Rivadavia. This monument is different from most we have discussed; here it is

9. Eduardo J. Santaella and José María Peña, *Escultura Buenos Aires* (Buenos Aires: Eduardo J. Santaella,1972).

10. Guiomar de Urgell, *Yrurtia* (Buenos Aires: Centro Editor de América Latina, 1981).

11. Ibid.

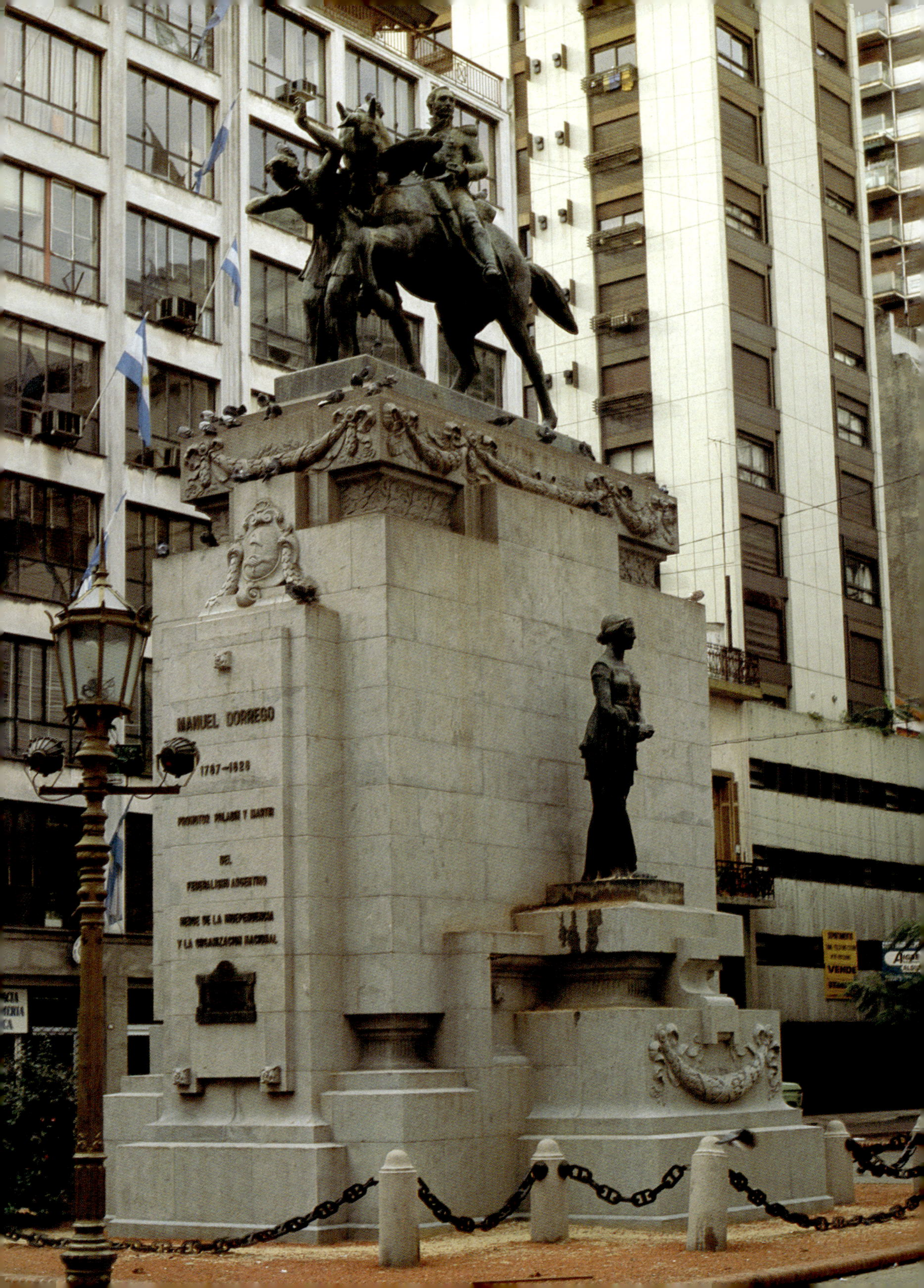
MANUEL DORREGO
DEL

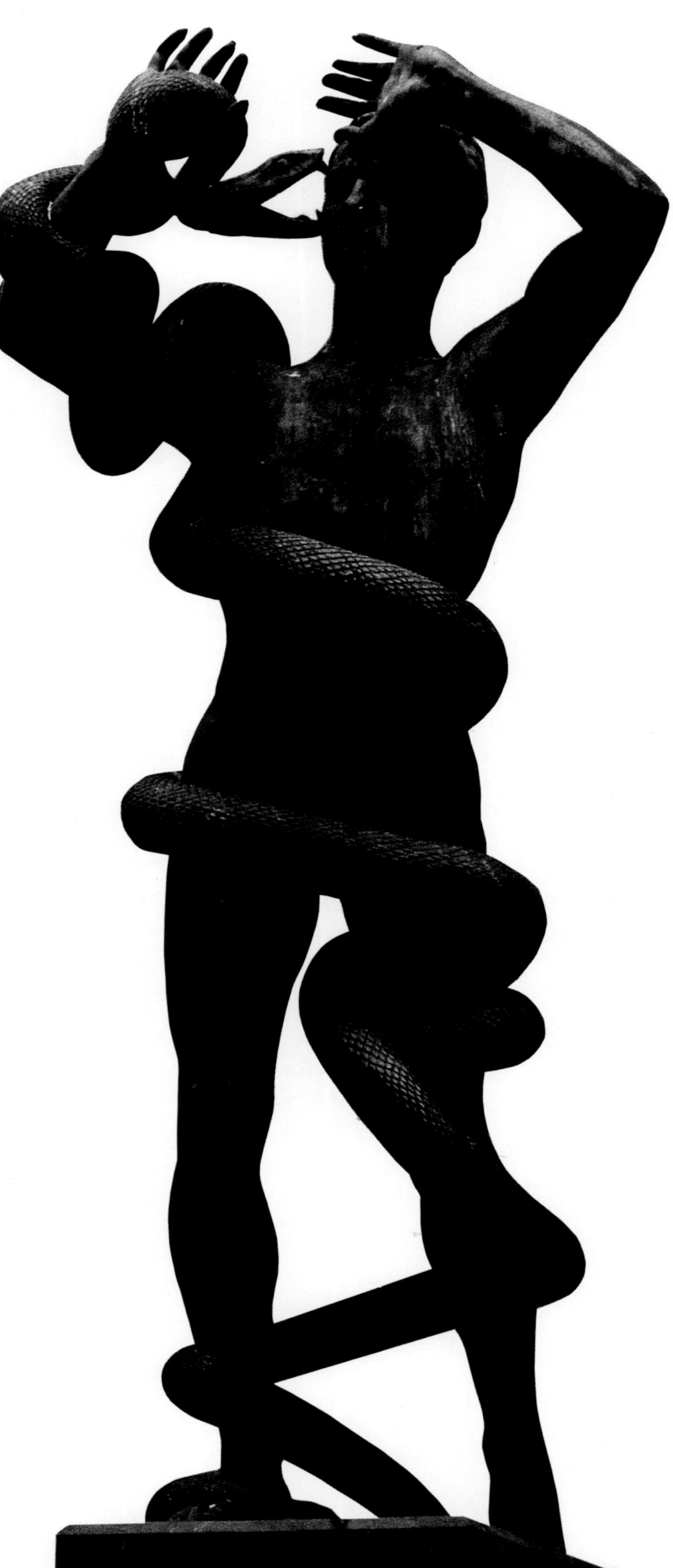

◂

Fig. 10. Rogelio Yrurtia, monument to Colonel Manuel Dorrego, 1926. Photograph by the author.

Fig. 11. Rogelio Yrurtia, monument to Colonel Manuel Dorrego, detail, 1926. Photograph by the author.

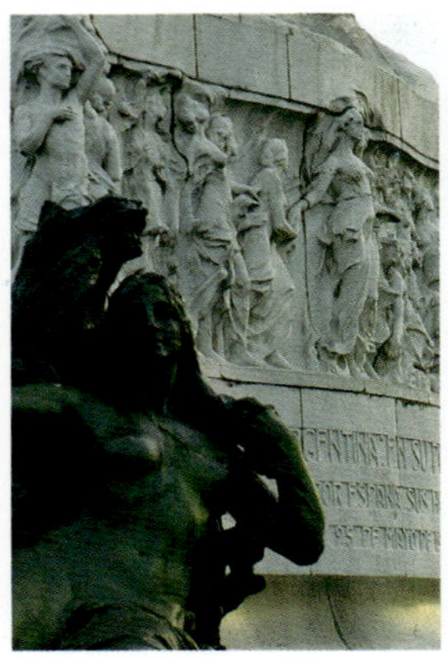

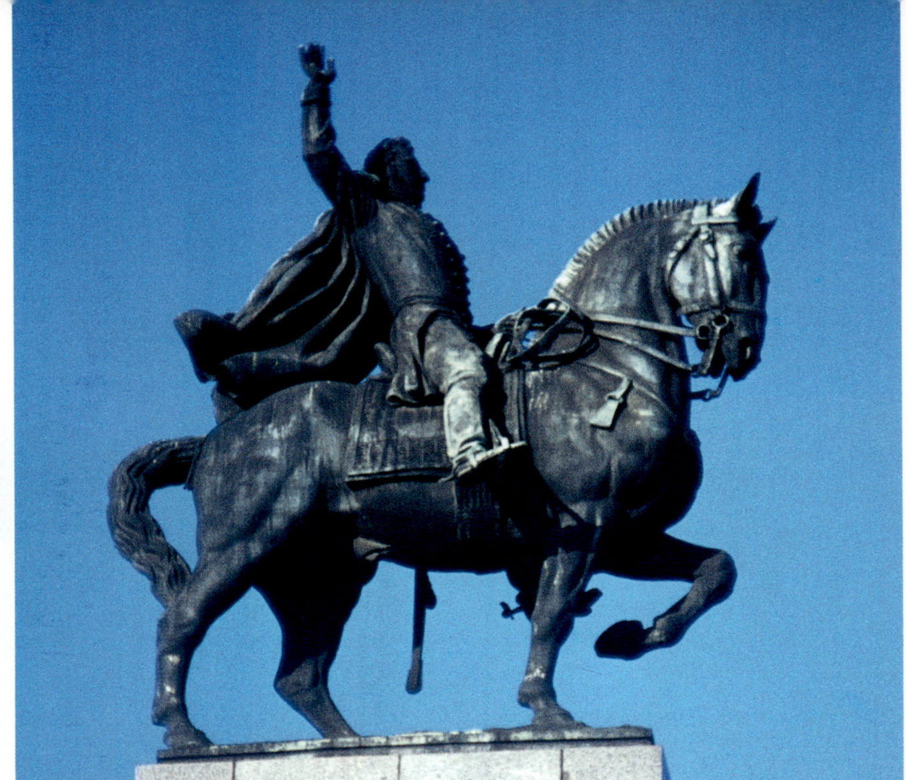

Fig. 12. Above left. Augustín Querol, *La Carta Magna y las cuatro regiones argentinas* (The Magna Carta and the four regions of Argentina), detail, 1910. Photograph by the author.

Fig. 13. Above right. Émile-Antoine Bourdelle, statue of General Carlos María de Alvear, 1926. Photograph by the author.

architectural volume that predominates. A solid grey granite base acts as the support for a prismatic body of rectangular proportions which appears to be an immense catafalque or platform. The effect is lightened by its seemingly being separated from the base, due to the shadow produced by deep grooves set into the perimeter. We could consider this an example of the intrusion of art-deco tendencies because of a superpositioning of geometric volumes.

Yrurtia avoided the personification of Rivadavia, representing him in two characteristic and imposing sculptural symbols: Moses and the Law, and Action. These allegories serve to transmit the personality of this public figure, one of our civic heros. Both figures are seated; the former, elderly, is wearing tailored clothes of refined subtlety which, instead of being a distraction, direct our attention to the strength of the body. In Action, Yrurtia has represented the ideal as the seated figure of a young man who typifies strength and self-assurance. Through the sculptor's treatment of the anatomy we are reminded of "the great Michaelangelesque torsos which manifestly aspire to interpret eternity."[12]

It is an injustice not to mention every worthy artist, but it is difficult to include them all in this short essay. Let me briefly mention two other foreign artists. The first, a Spaniard, Augustín Querol (1853–1909), is included because of the special place his work occupies in our city and its culture, in addition to the merits of the work itself. At the corner of Libertador and Sarmiento avenues stands *La Carta Magna y las cuatro regiones argentinas*, better known as "The Spanish Monument" since it was donated by this community in 1910 (fig. 12).

Querol imbued it with a spirit of Catalan modernism, making it a monument which is now an integral part of the city. Today, brides in wedding gowns line up to have their pictures taken there on the eve of the ceremony. Querol chose a vertical approach, setting the monument on a broad, low

12. Ibid.

which a quadrangular trunklike mass arises, crowned by a vigorous figure of the Republic with her robes streaming in the wind. The base is encircled by a wide frieze of figures carved in relief; fully carved figures symbolizing Work emerge at the base of the trunk, and, to achieve a union between all these figures and that of the Republic, all stand with their arms reaching high above their heads. "The figures in relief seem to blend into each other; the clothes tightly adhere to the bodies modeling them and, at the same time, dematerializing them, as if they were floating on the impulse of the wind."[13] Just after its inauguration, one critic attacked the monument saying that the figures seemed like smoke, a definition that today seems a precise justification of its merits.

At the other end of Libertador Avenue, where it crosses Alvear Avenue, we find a monument to General Carlos María de Alvear by the Frenchman Émile-Antoine Bourdelle (1861–1929), which was inaugurated in 1926 after a dozen years spent in previous studies, execution, and casting. Set on two platforms which are reached by steps, the statue rises as a tall prism of red granite into which four bronze allegories are set, one on each corner. They represent four qualities attributed to Alvear: Strength, Eloquence, Liberty, and Victory. Above these figures, Alvear is mounted on his steed, majestic and vigorous (fig. 13).

Fig. 14. Pedro Zonza Briano, bust of the sculptor Lucio Correa Morales, 1928. Photograph by the author.

There have been few sculptors like Bourdelle. On seeing the scale-model sent from Paris, the commissioners in charge questioned the fact that the general was not wearing a hat. The artist quickly and cleverly replied, "My general is a hero. He lost his hat in the heat of the battle." And with that, the discussion ended.

Returning to Argentine sculptors, we also should mention Pedro Zonza Briano (1886–1941) (fig. 14), who, although he did not have the personality of Bourdelle, in his own way introduced a break in the established dependence on classicism (fig. 15). As with his fellow sculptors, a stay in Paris gave him a chance to discover what was happening in Europe, even giving him a chance to exhibit. One of the works he did in Paris was sent to the Buenos Aires Salón Nacional in 1913, where it was rejected. *Creced y multiplicaos* (Grow and multiply), for its content and its execution, would not go unnoticed in the stiffly conservative society of Buenos Aires in those days. "Later, Zonza Briano was influenced by Medardo Rosso and, like him, softened the atmosphere in which his figures were done, letting them blend into a strange formal confusion. "[14] In 1925, his monument dedicated to Leandro Alem was inaugurated. Alem was an important politician of the Generation of the '80s, and the figures, especially the secondary ones, reflect the spirit of that era.

Fig. 15. Pedro Zonza Briano, *Flor de juventud*, (Flower of youth), bronze, 1929. Photograph by the author.

13. Santaella and Peña, *Escultura*.
14. Anaya, *Los comienzos*.

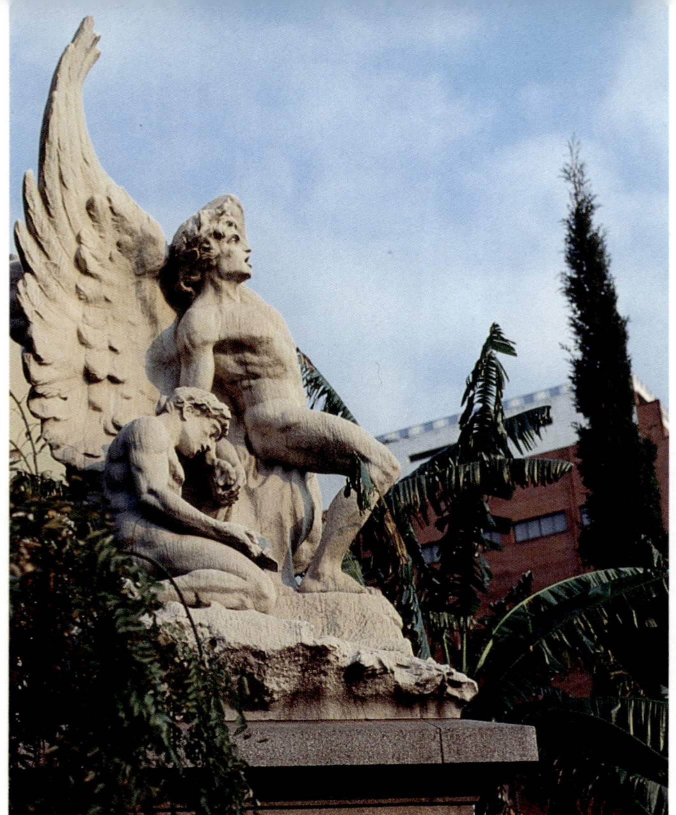

Fig. 16. Alberto Lagos, monument to Colonel Ramón Falcón, marble, detail, 1918. Photograph by the author.

Fig. 17. José Fioravanti, monument to President Nicolás Avellaneda, stone, 1935. Photograph by the author. (See page 221.)

Alberto Lagos (1885–1960) is proof that classicism and the new structural forms could live together when sensitivity and strength were an integral part of them. Like Zonza Briano, he also went to Paris, on a grant in 1909 and eventually twice more. Besides being influenced by Rodin, he shared the new sculptural language of Bourdelle and Maillol. This was the time of the School of Paris, which meant that the city was teeming with ideas and projects. Lagos, a passionate man from his youth, lived the euphoria of the period. "[He] listened to and respected the wildest points of view. But his own personality had been defined long before, his technical capacities established, and his style without doubts."[15]

His monument to Ramón Falcón, done in 1918, is one of his most distinguished creations. In it, Falcón himself vanishes before the presence of two symbolic allegories. One winged figure in marble, Fate, in a violent gesture gives his hand to Glory, seated with her head bent and her eyes closed (fig. 16). Colonel Falcón, ex-chief of police, has been assassinated by an anarchist's bomb.

El arquero de San Sebastian (The archer of San Sebastian) is another sculpture deserving comment. It is quite different from the main body of Lago's work, which is basically intimistic. Here, he chose a large-scale figure which lets us evaluate the tension achieved by the balanced anatomy. The positioning of the legs and the arms combined with the bow creates a continuous rhythm which gives the statue a special character and sensitivity.

Most recently represented in our plazas is Argentine sculptor José Fioravanti (1896–1977). Until 1925, Fioravanti modeled in clay, making a number of distinguished portraits. Then he decided to concentrate on carving, choosing stone as his material. The son of Italians, his early background was an important factor in the quality of the work that eventually was to grace the city's landscape

15. Clara Giménez, *Lagos* (Buenos Aires: Centro Editor de América Latina, 1981).

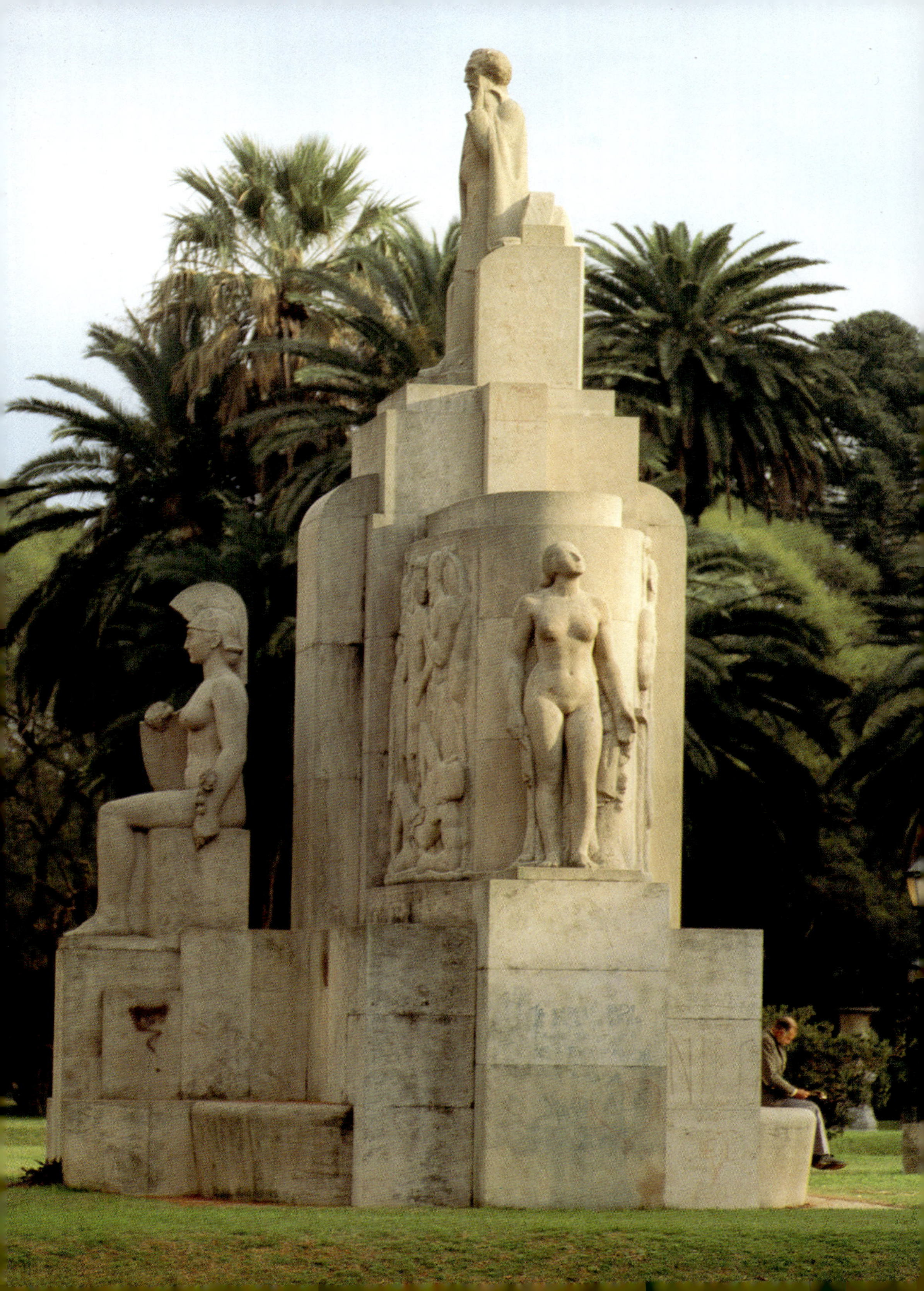

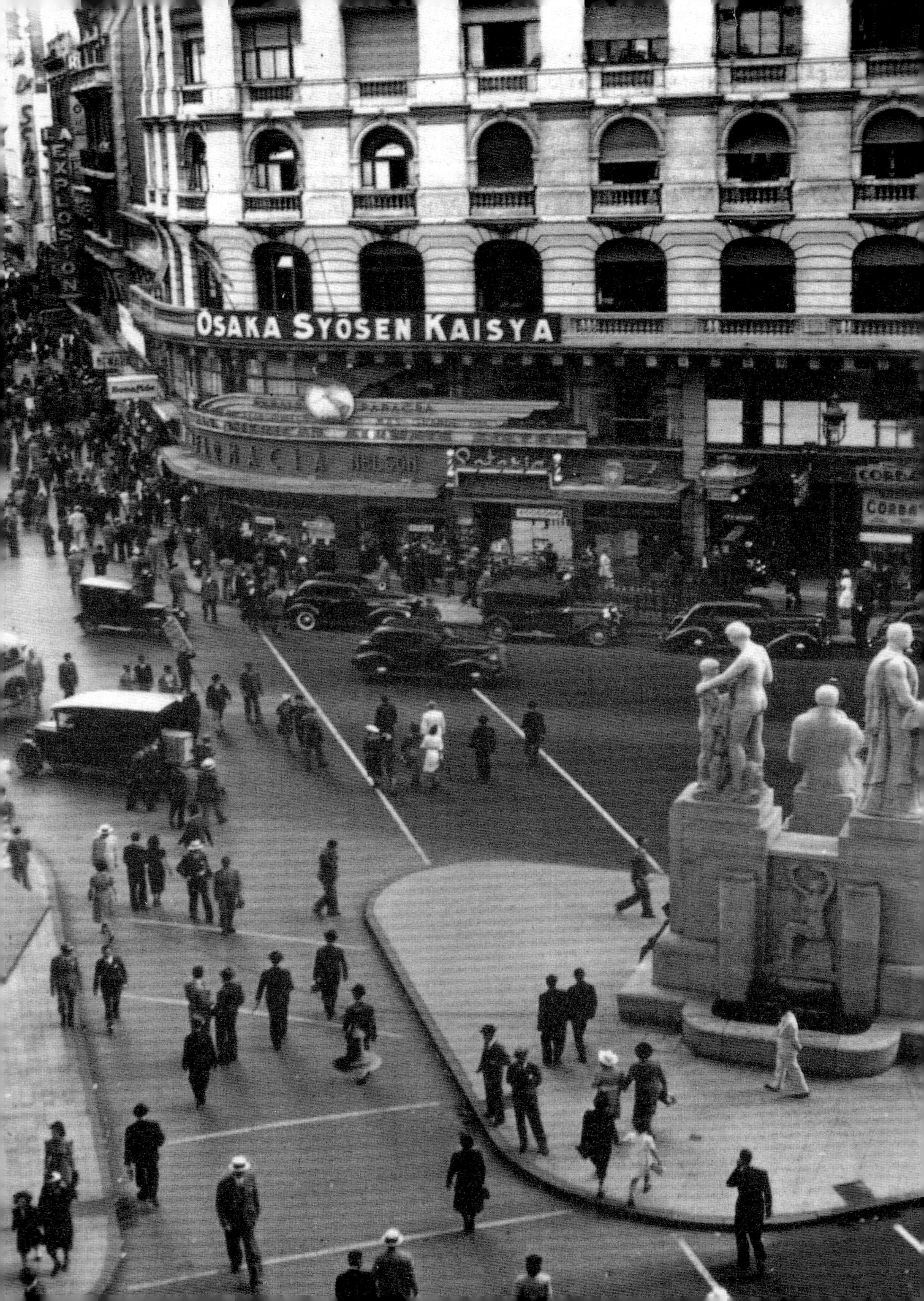
ŌSAKA SYŌSEN KAISYA
EXPLOSION

and to acquire a special identity through the specific sites chosen for it. As Guiomar de Urgell says, "The passage from one way of working to another originates in a decision generated deep inside the artist. He is able to feel by intuition what would be the monumental form,...the initial and primordial mass that emerges from the block of stone, the total integration of architecture, sculpture, and landscaping. He reaches a wise comprehension of the monumental work as a modifier of urban space and an integral part of its texture."[16]

Fig. 18. José Fioravanti, monument to President Roque Sáenz Peña, stone, 1936. Photograph courtesy of the author.

Only the tireless traveler avidly absorbs what he sees; Greece and Egypt, without any doubt, left their seal on Fioravanti, fortifying his resolution to endow his figures with a characteristic we might call compactness. It was a new conception of sculpture for the city. When he returned from Paris in 1927, President Marcelo T. de Alvear commissioned him to do two reliefs for Government House, which meant that, for the first time since the last century, contemporary art had been blessed with official recognition. Years later, in 1934, several of his reliefs and sculptures from the monuments to Presidents Roque Sáenz Peña and Nicolás Avellaneda were exhibited in the Jeu de Paume in Paris, "that place of honor reserved for the famous."[17]

The monument to Nicolás Avellaneda is placed in the center of a large plaza in the Parque de Palermo in front of Libertador Avenue (fig. 17). It is composed of a massive, geometric central body of rectangular appearance, split in the middle by another vertical form on which stands the figure of Avellaneda. On the rectangular form, we can see symbolic reliefs: the important figures are placed at the extremes, while the nude seated figure of the Republic appears in the middle, set forward and given the hierarchic importance of an Egyptian diety.

The monument was inaugurated in 1935. A year later, Fioravanti's monument to Roque Sáenz Peña, which was less volumetric but no less severe in the calculated rigidity of the figures, was installed in a very strategic and central spot: 100 Florida Street (fig. 18). Carved in sandy rose-colored marble in the Burgundy region of France, the monument was composed by placing Sáenz Peña in the foreground, seated on a schematic base. A pair of ubiquitous allegories were placed a bit behind, higher, and looking to the sides. At the back can be seen a fountain on which appears a bas-relief. This sector "constitutes the basis of a general idea that orders the rest of the architectonic parts of the monument and interprets the generosity contained in the phrase that this illustrious Argentine politician pronounced in Washington in 1890: America for humanity."[18] The monument, in memory of the leader who in 1911 gave all Argentine men over eighteen the right to vote, was paid for by funds raised through public donations.

The monuments to Presidents Avellaneda and Sáenz Peña mark a new sculptural-architectural focus in the city. The figures become more massive and are integrated into the whole sculptural ensemble as if they themselves—or the monument itself—could be envisioned as the original block before it was carved. No air filters between the figures; we could say that it collides against them. A feeling of roundness exists but is different from that expressed in the figures of the fountain by Lola Mora or in those of *Canto al trabajo*. It is not difficult to relate the monuments of this period to the rationalistic buildings of the moment; simple and serene but not at all ingenuous. It is another transformation in the treatment of symbolic presence. □

16. Guiomar de Urgell, *Fioravanti* (Buenos Aires: Centro Editor de América Latina, 1981).

17. "El desarrollo de la escultura," *La Prensa*, 18 October 1969.

18. *La Prensa*, 9 August 1936.

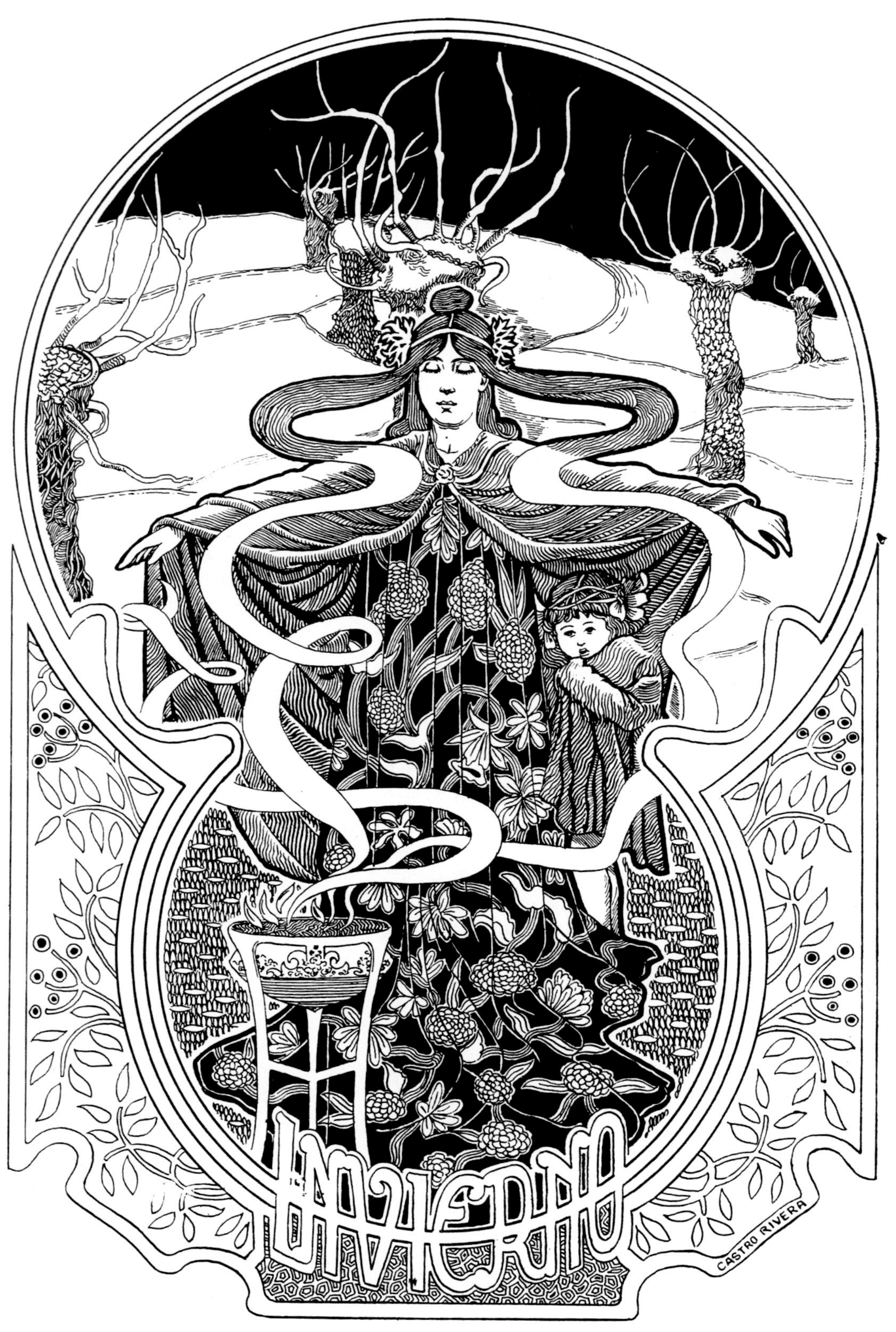
INVIERNO
CASTRO RIVERA

Art-Nouveau Stained Glass and Ironwork

By José María Peña

Translated by Jon R. Snyder

José María Peña has been director of the Museum of the City of Buenos Aires for twenty-four years. A graduate of the University of Buenos Aires School of Architecture, specializing in the investigation of nineteenth- and twentieth-century Argentine architecture, he is active in historic preservation and urban planning.

Photographs courtesy of the author.

"In an atmosphere illuminated by fiery light bursting amidst white drapery and glittering jewels, from the first flight of the splendid staircase where our gaze ascends as if magnetized, we are dazzled by the perfect grace of a white statue, serene as an apparition in a dream: the *Diana* by Falguiere. She illuminates the sumptuous gallery with the light of art, toward which all eyes converge, attracted by the ecstacy inspired by ideal form."[1]

This paragraph, which appeared the day following the dance inaugurating the Jockey Club, is the perfect introduction to an essay about a style not alien to the life of Buenos Aires despite its distance from what was happening across the sea in far-away Europe. In the case of France, the country most closely aligned culturally with Argentina, the tremendous alterations in Paris following the urban development carried out by Napoleon III also transformed Argentina in the image of this newness.

The country had established Buenos Aires as its definitive capital in 1880, and its rulers desired that it be known as the *Gran Aldea* (Big village). In order to achieve this, big changes were needed, changes that coincided with the arrival of a growing number of immigrants. There could be nothing better for a city of narrow streets and sidewalks than to open up boulevards in the style of those in Paris or Barcelona; thus, for the progressives, the idea of a wide avenue was a blessing.

After the expropriation of property needed for the project, and recovery from the bankruptcy of 1890, the Avenida de Mayo was inaugurated in 1894—the first sign of modernism in Buenos Aires. There was, finally, a thoroughfare with wide sidewalks upon which people could not only walk easily but also see and be seen, seated at tables arranged around the cafés. It would be one of the undisputed sites for buildings adhering to stylistic tenets that broke for the first time with established architectural canons.

But such dreams could not become reality in an ordinary or complacent city; the Avenida de Mayo, which grew rapidly, was joined to a new lighting system that "in 1895...in the Puerto del Riachuelo, already had activated 8,950 meters of wire."[2] Local and global reality was reflected in the 143 newspapers, magazines, and journals published in the city that year. One such publication, *Caras y Caretas* (Faces and masks), appeared for the first time in 1898 as the virtual introduction to *art nouveau* by way of its graphic art (figs. 1 and 2).

Fig. 1. Castro Rivera, *Winter*, illustration from *Caras y Caretas*, 1900.

1. *La Nación*, 1 October 1897.
2. Francis Korn, *Buenos Aires, 1895, una ciudad moderna* (Buenos Aires: Editorial del Instituto, 1981).

This weekly magazine carried news and information not only of Buenos Aires and the interior but of the latest events in the world, in fashion, and so on. Their advance in style was possible due to the capacity and quality of the journal's illustrators, a number of whom came from Barcelona. Each week people grew more familiar with the decorative borders, the drawings, and the caricatures of Cao, Mayol, Aurelio Giménez, and Castro Rivera which, without a doubt, at first disconcerted many readers.

It is not easy to date with precision the initial appearance of *art nouveau* in Buenos Aires, but certain isolated elements, such as ornamental tile, ironwork, and stained glass probably appeared in conventional buildings at the end of the last century. Adding to the natural makeup of the populace, basically Spanish and Creole, were others from many different countries. Thus, it is natural that artistic displays took diverse forms. To this cosmopolitan influence may be added decorations, toiletry articles, chinaware, musical scores, and numerous other objects that could be bought in emporiums such as Bazar La Luna, Bazar París, or the jewelry stores.

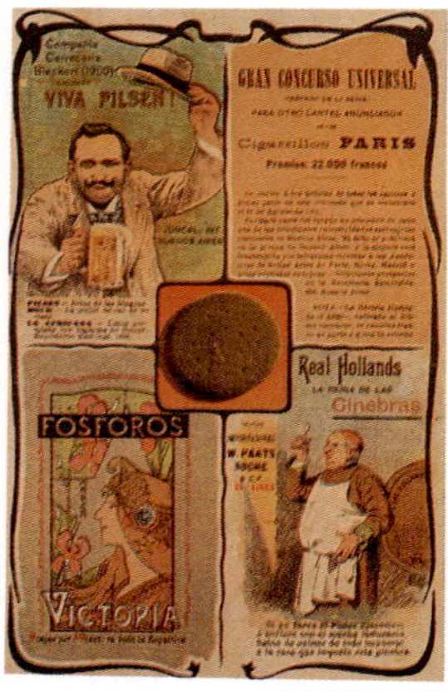

Fig. 2. *Caras y Caretas,* showing a border and advertising design that convey the *art-nouveau* image, 1900.

Contrary to what one might think, this everyday familiarity with objects where art design appeared did not necessarily mean that they were accepted. A personal experience may serve to clarify. In 1965, the Modern Art Museum commissioned us to organize the first exhibition on the theme of *art nouveau*. Visiting some ladies of a certain age, we asked if they had any *art-nouveau* objects that might be exhibited. One of them responded, "Absolutely not; our mother never permitted things of such doubtful taste to enter the house." She told us this while we drank tea in porcelain teacups that gleamed with a finish designed in that sinful mode.

In the same way, it is not rare to see in a traditional building details such as door knockers, floors, or windows that answer to the above style (figs. 3 and 4). The explanation for these details would probably be found in the decision of the architect, to whom a different trend was not acceptable; but he would say that the introduction of "modern" elements was merely a game that he played with convention.

This duality appeared in important public buildings such as the Colón Theater, where, in a design that could be called conservative, there appeared details in accordance with the new trend, as in the case of the mosaic floor in the entrance hall or certain designs for stained-glass windows. We can situate this period between the years 1895 and 1915 (for late examples).

In 1904, the municipality of Buenos Aires established a prize for the best facade which was won by a small hotel—today, unfortunately, no longer standing—designed by the architect Eduardo Lemonnier. Of interest, in addition to the treatment of the facade and the interior spaces, were the stained-glass windows (fig. 7), one of which the Museum of the City of Buenos Aires was able to save. Here the choice of colors (violet, lilac, and green) is clearly related to the chosen flower, the wisteria, a traditional species in the old courtyards of Buenos Aires.

In another now-demolished building, there was the opportunity to see a grand gallery enclosed by translucent glass panels alternating with Mucha designs. In this case, the painted glass was connected by leaded joints.

The architect Julián García Núñez especially favored the use of colored glass, but he did not use it in stained-glass windows alone. Many of his works are faced with panes containing glass mosaics. They were made by cutting out the

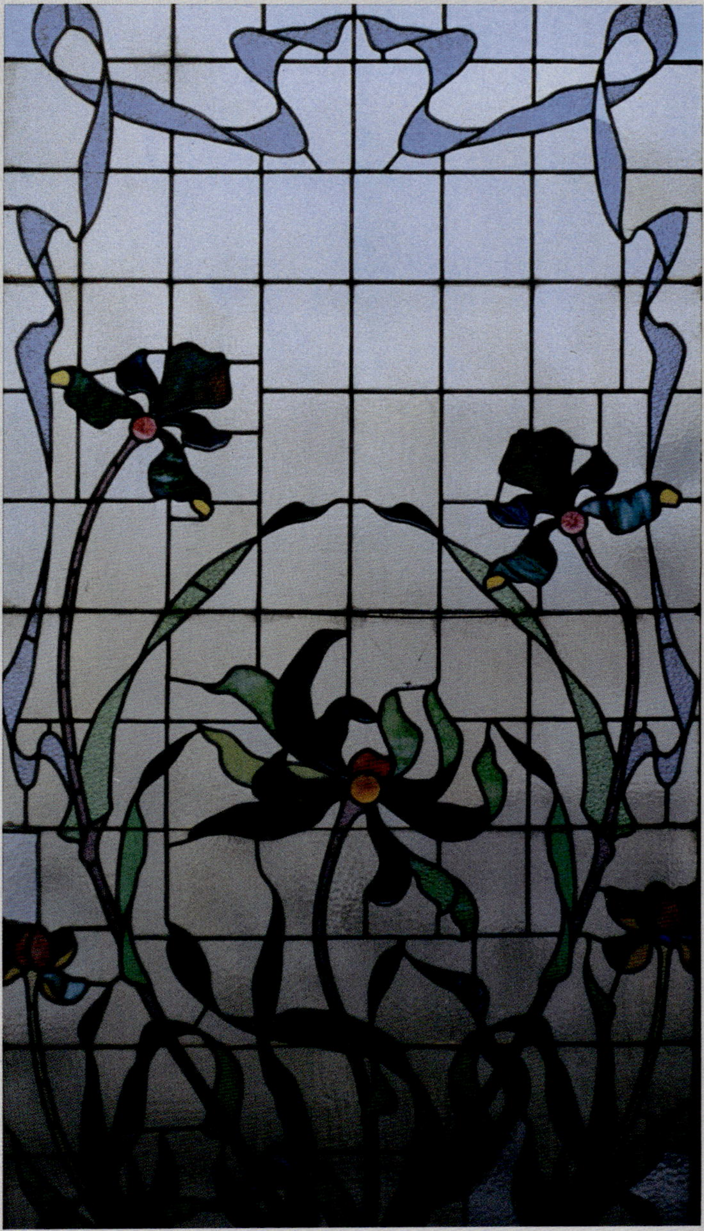

Fig. 3. ***Art-nouveau*** **stained glass, 2.18 x 1.06 m.**

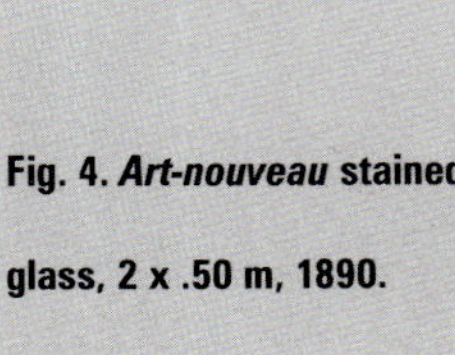

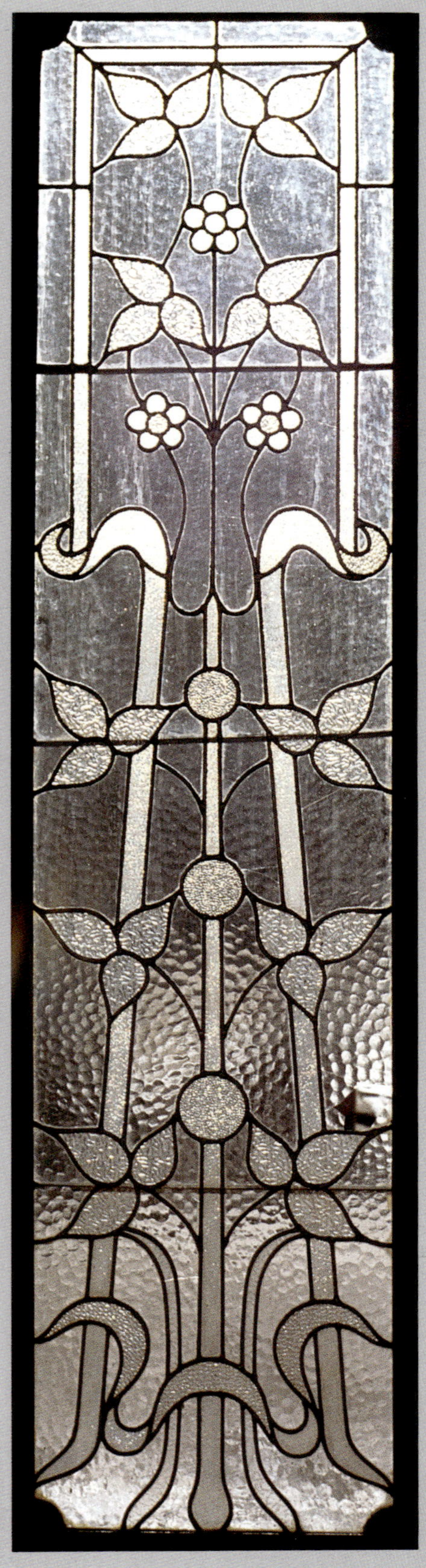

Fig. 4. ***Art-nouveau*** **stained glass, 2 x .50 m, 1890.**

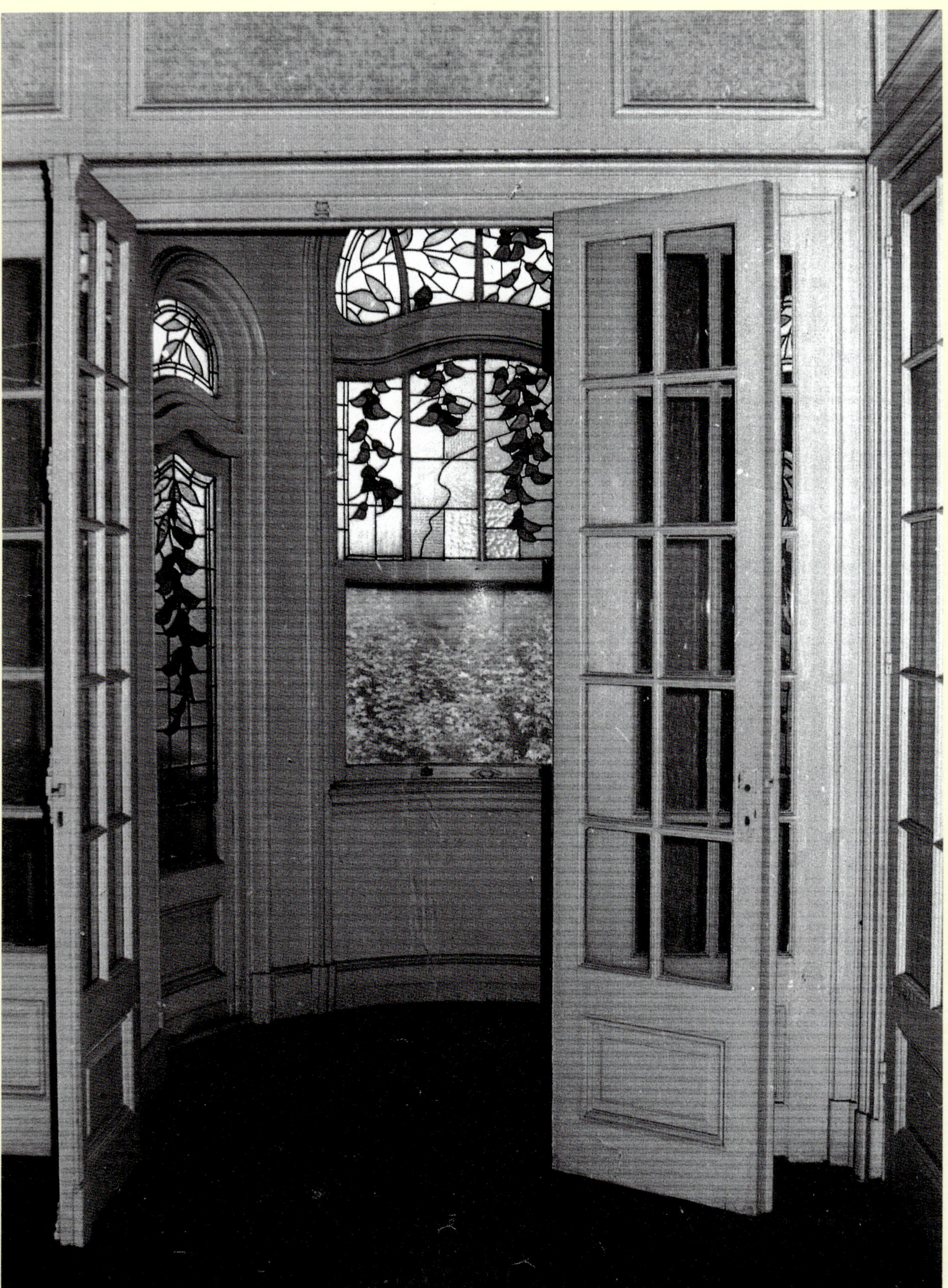

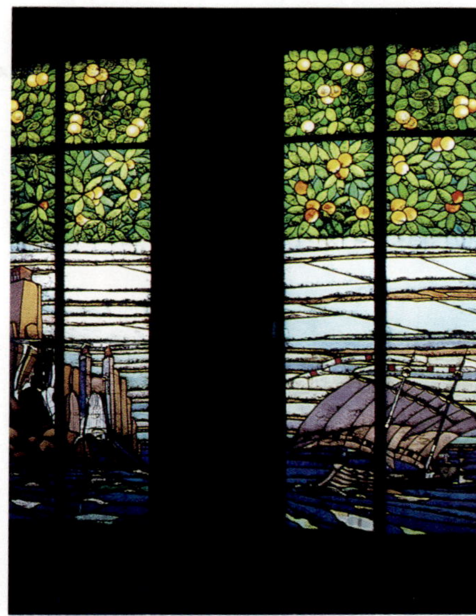

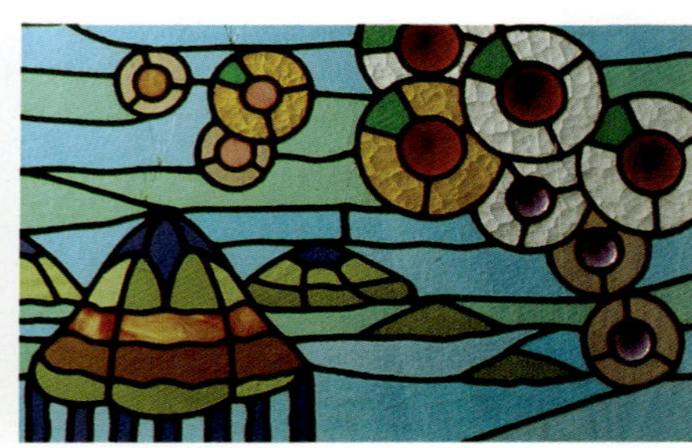

Fig. 5. Above. Julián García Núñez, stained glass in his residence, 1907. The motif of oranges is repeated in many rooms. Photograph by the author.

Fig. 6. Above right. Julián García Núñez, stained glass in his residence, .35 x .60 m.

◂

Fig. 7. Eduardo Lemonnier, stained glass in a building that won the Buenos Aires municipal prize in 1904. Demolished in 1970. Photograph by the author.

glass according to an original design and gluing it onto white cement.

His own house, regrettably demolished some years ago, gave evidence of the seduction that stained glass had for him. After passing through the front door, one encountered the *puerta cancel* (door screen) with its initial treatment of a motif that meant a great deal to him, namely the stylized figure of a rose. This was repeated on the floors, in the stucco work, and in other parts of the edifice.

In the drawing room, doors sported pennants in which numerous stylized oranges and leaves were woven together (fig. 5). In a principle area of that drawing room, García Núñez obtained one of his most attractive visual effects: the entire wall facing out onto a courtyard was enclosed in stained glass in which colors were combined with great intensity. In another section, he replaced the glass in a small window with an enigmatic stained-glass design (fig. 6).

García Núñez chose a different perspective for the stained glass illuminating the stairway and entrance hall of the Hospital Español (1906) located on Belgrano Street (fig. 9). Lamentably, the sector where these windows were found has been destroyed. Its design, contrasting those in his house, was decidedly abstract; it used junctions of lead as vertical lines, separating translucent, non-colored panes from others of a pale green; circles of amber-colored glass approximately twelve centimeters in diameter were inserted at intervals between them. This work in particular received international acclaim and was mentioned in a Spanish journal of the period.[3]

The only case in which García Núñez used landscape as a motif was in his own house. In the rest of his works, stylized figures were arranged within rectangular panes. The visual effect is remarkably attractive, and their arrangement on the top floor contributes to the notion of crowning the building.

3. *Arquitectura, Ingeniería y Construcción* (Madrid-Barcelona) (September 1910)

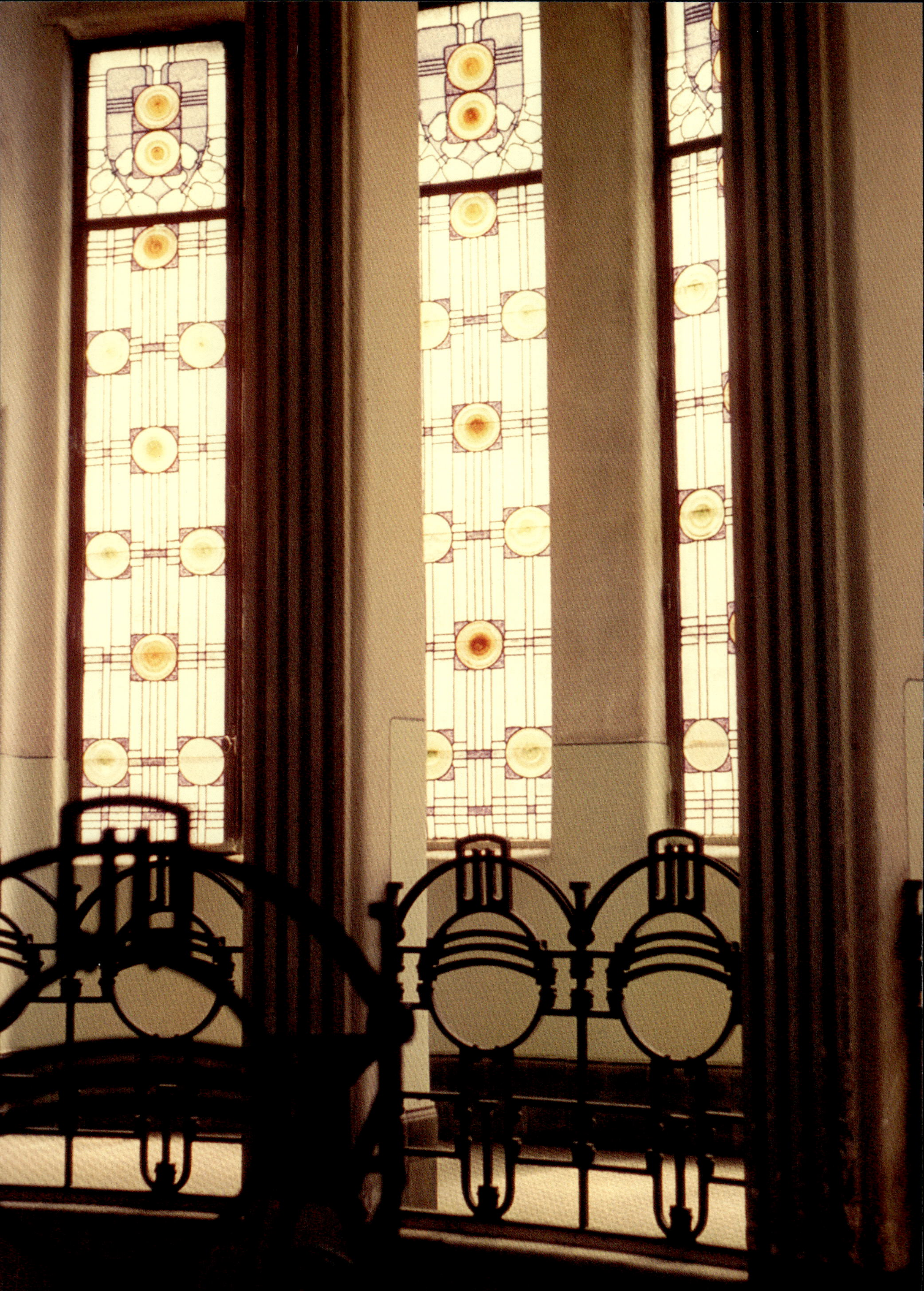

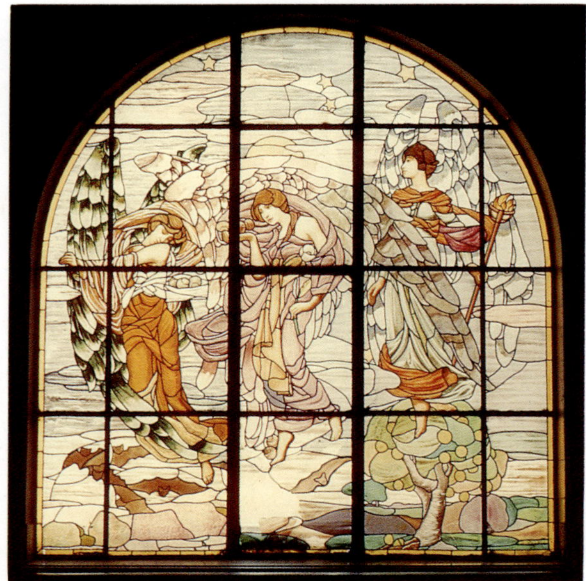

Fig. 8. Stained-glass window in a house at 1332 Moreno Street, ca. 1908. Photograph by the author.

The architect Virginio Colombo also used this decorative system in a building found at 3667 Rivadavia Avenue. His large panes in the vestibules represent mythological scenes. One refers to Orpheus, while the other symbolizes the dance of Salomé. Colombo was born in Milan and graduated from the Brera Academy. His career in Buenos Aires has left us some outstanding examples of *art nouveau*. His works testify to a genuine concern for the general coherence of the project, as can be seen in the precision of the details.

In another building constructed by Virginio Colombo at 2562 Hipólito Yrigoyen Street, in addition to the fine sculptures that appear on the facade and in the interior, he also used stained glass, among the most interesting found around the *puerta cancel* where the head of a woman with long hair appears in the painted glass.

In order to assess the ideas of those who chose this particular style, it is necessary to go back in time to understand the effect produced by these panes of colored glass that allowed light to pass into darkened areas, like the *palieres* in apartment buildings; such buildings were definitely a novelty.

◂

Fig. 9. Julián García Núñez, Hospital Español, stained glass and iron railing, 1906. Photograph by the author.

Two large stained-glass windows in the house at 1332 Moreno Street represent a special case in point, "where the hall that connects the rooms on the first floor, approached by way of the main staircase, is separated from the outside by two large stained-glass windows (fig. 8). These let the light in, shining through groups of angels, constructed in flat colors in the pre-Raphaelite style. [The windows] make up the center of attention of the space by perforating the wall and giving the interior a special appeal, complemented by a decoration with borders of flowers and frescos of people."[4] These two examples prove the excellence of the original design. Even the lead connecting the glass emphasizes the contours of the figures.

Born in the city of Turin, Francisco Gianotti completed his studies at the Royal Academy of Brussels. He began to work in Buenos Aires in 1908, during one of

4. José María Peña, *Los murales*, vol. 1, no. 7 of *Argentina en el arte* (Buenos Aires: Editora Viscontea, 1966).

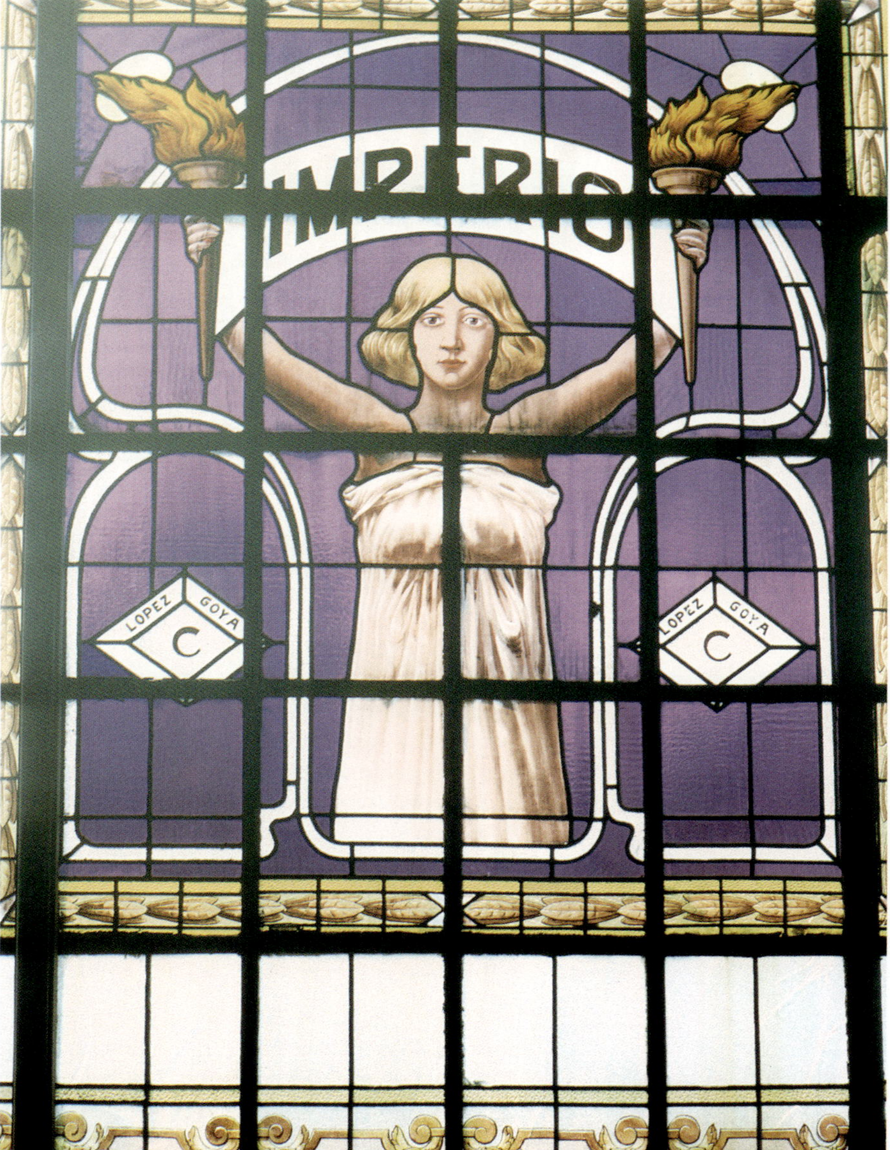

Fig. 10. ***Art-nouveau*** **stained-glass advertisement from a textile company building, approx. 2.20 x 1.20 m.**

the city's most vital periods, and built diverse buildings which, through time, have become important markers of the city's past. One of these, located on the corner of Rivadavia and Callao streets facing the National Congress, is known by the name of a sweetshop found on its ground floor: La Confitería del Molino. Here *art-nouveau* design occupies first place in its general plan and in many of its details. Noteworthy, in addition to the great perimetrical glass canopy constructed from the union of small contrasting colored panes of glass, are two stained-glass windows inserted in the walls that separate the bathrooms from the salon, in which the figures of women are found.

The vivid presence of stained glass was the principle reason it was used for the purpose of advertisement (fig. 10). Advertising design was one of the most perfect expressions of *art nouveau*; as mentioned before, an Argentine precursor of the style was the magazine *Caras y Caretas*.

Beginning in the eighteenth century, skillful ironwork was a hallmark of the artisans who worked in Buenos Aires. However, treatment of the material and designs completely changed over the course of the years. From grilles of thick iron in squared sections, common in the eighteenth century, the material began to grow lighter at the beginning of the nineteenth century, thus allowing more extensive decorative play in the ornamentation. In approximately 1850, iron was refined for work in the forge; small sheets resembling bands or strips were produced and used in making grilles for balconies, windows, and *puertas canceles*. This application was popularly compared to inlay work.

Grilles made of cast iron appeared simultaneously with those made of forged iron. It is worth emphasizing that, in this period, both systems were utilized indiscriminately. Cast-iron grilles were also undoubtedly used for industrial purposes, whether manufactured in Buenos Aires or imported from Europe. The most important foreign manufacturer was represented by the A. Motteau firm that had its agency and storehouses at 1272 Garay Street and its Du Val D'Osne foundry in Paris. This ancient factory had existed since 1810 and for many years provided the city with statues and decorative fountains, such as the two fountains placed in the Plaza de la Victoria in 1868.

The local counterpart of Du Val D'Osne was the Pedro Vasena Foundry. Vasena arrived in Argentina in 1865. For thirteen years he was a blacksmith, and later he worked for the Zamborini firm. His workshop grew rapidly after he founded it. "His establishment was given awards more than once: in 1898, the grand prize and diploma of honor from the Turin Exhibition; in 1906, the grand prize and diploma of honor from the Milan Exhibition. He was decorated by the government of Italy with the Cross of the Cavalieri del Lavoro (Knights of work)."[5] A large number of laborers worked for his firm, and its importance has been documented by a catalogue in which one can see different models including balconies, bandstands, gates, and storefronts (fig. 11).

5. Francis Korn, "La aventura del ascenso," in *Buenos Aires 4 Siglos* (Buenos Aires, 1983).

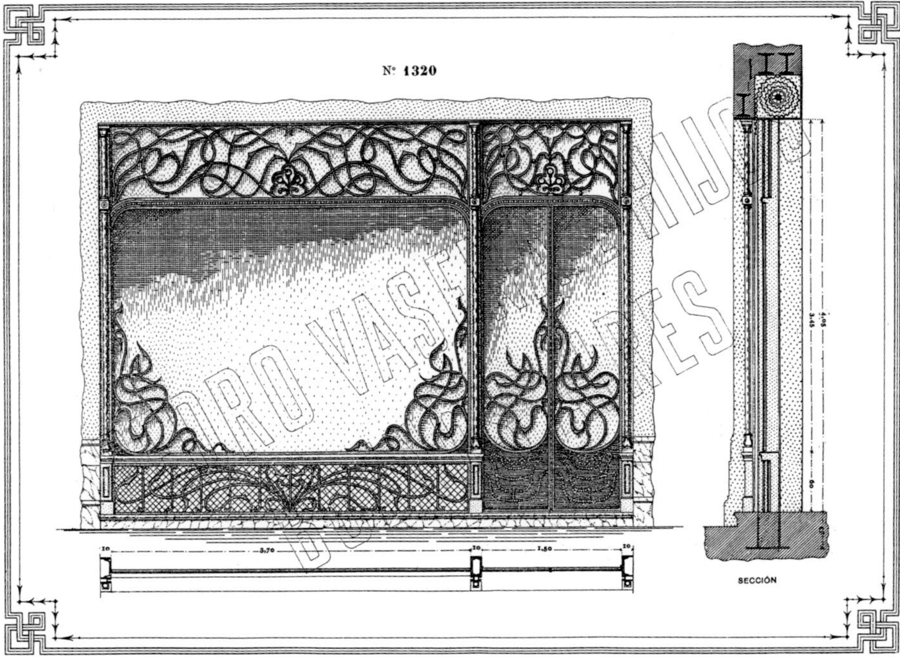

Fig. 11. Pedro Vasena and Sons, catalogue with example of *art-nouveau*-style iron show window, 1902.

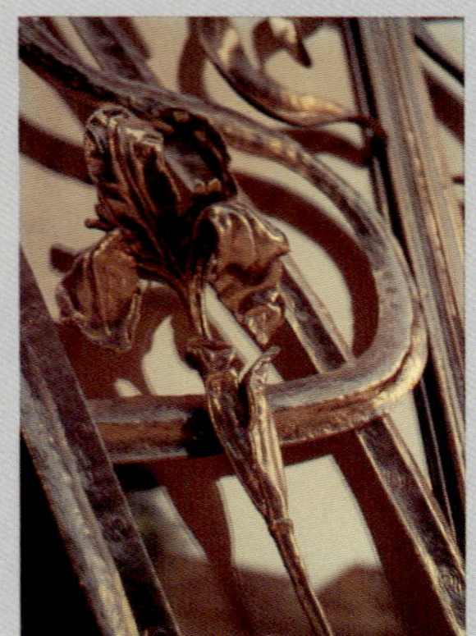

Fig. 12. E. Rodríguez Ortega, detail of an entry door at 2031 Rivadavia Street, ca. 1908.

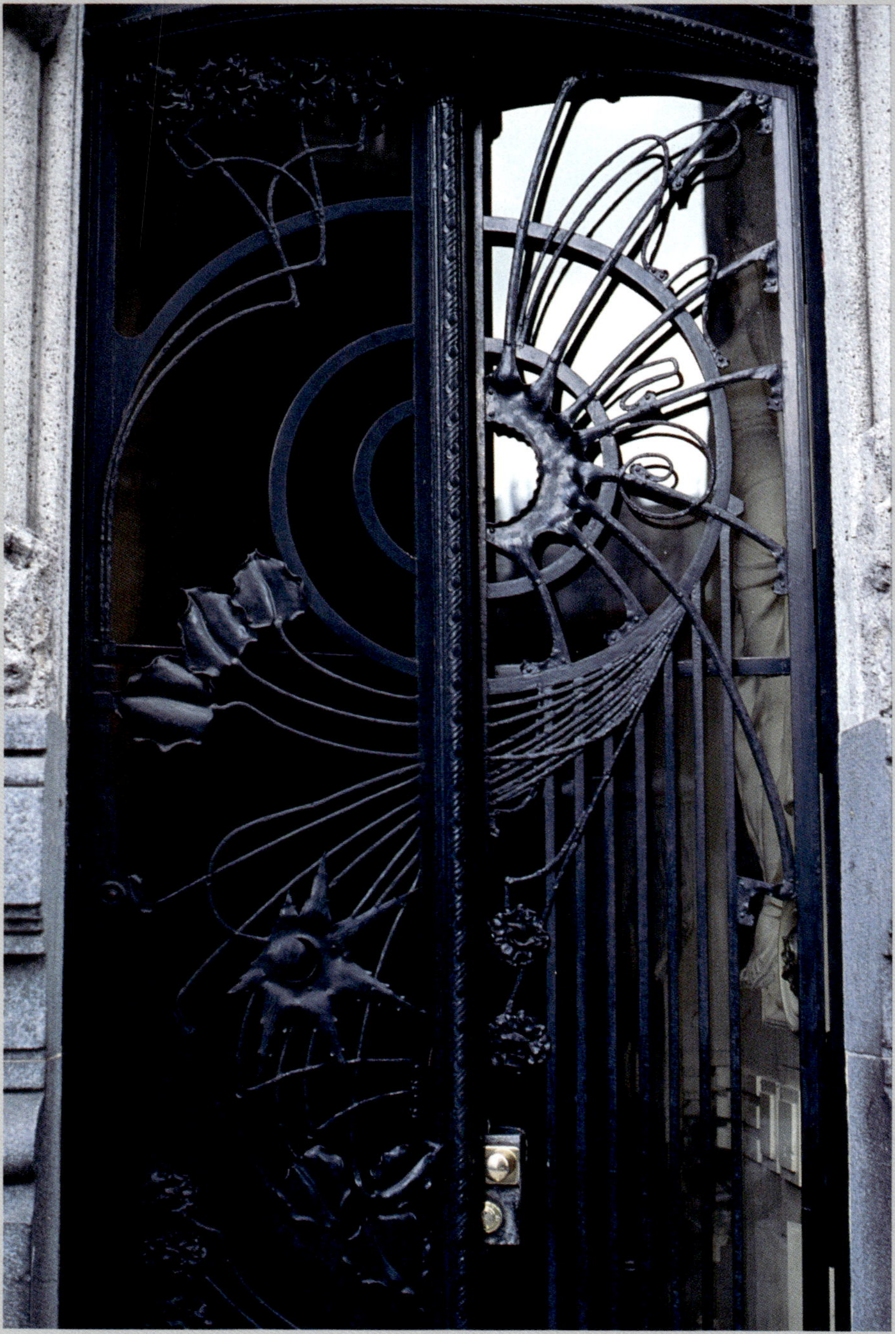

Fig. 13. Virginio Colombo, cast-iron entry door at 2562 Hipólito Yrigoyen Street, reminiscent of the works of Gaudí. Photograph by the author.

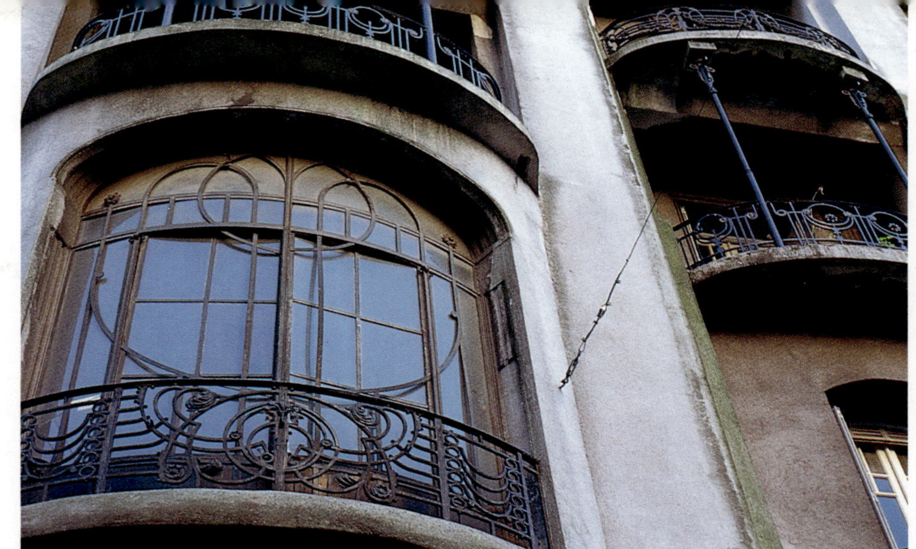

Fig. 14. Oscar Ranzenhofer, ironwork design at 761 Avenida de Mayo, ca. 1906. Photograph by the author. **(See page 234.)**

Evidently, certain architects designed doors and balconies themselves in order to compliment the rest of their buildings, and it is this particular style to which we refer when we speak of them as works in their own right. At 2031 Rivadavia Street, the architect E. Rodríguez Ortega built an apartment building circa 1908. It has a visually undulating facade; the balconies are constructed with fine strips of forged iron that ripple and interlace like stylized plant figures. In conjunction with this, it is essential to mention the front door, in which one sees large irises (fig. 12) that come forth from the main body of the door where delicately stylized leaves rise up and curl around as if growing on a balcony.

One of the most spectacular examples of *art-nouveau* ironwork is the front door of the building found at 2562 Hipólito Yrigoyen Street (fig. 13). This is the work of Virginio Colombo, who gave free rein to his imagination, requiring from the artisan a combination of iron with a forged lock. A fine strip of iron separates from the lower sector, curving slowly until it reaches the upper quarter where it dynamically forms a spiral from which emit, by centripetal force, delicate stems that end in flowers and leaves. The spiral finally bursts forth, creating a surprising image that imparts a strange marine presence.

While this work was being carried out, journals continued to publish articles referring to the new style. Some emphasized the particular nature of its lines, which many found unacceptable: "What is this *art nouveau*?

"According to some, it is the most refined blooming of esthetic sensibility; according to others, it is only a ridiculous style characterized by an extreme lack of taste, calling attention to itself by its vulgarity and the irregular extravagance of its lines. In spite of this, many notable artists openly admire it and are confident of its future."[6]

It is curious that this article appeared in the year 1908, when several *art-nouveau* buildings in the city had already been awarded prizes; the same journal had published a photograph of a Georges de Feure sofa, Gaillard chairs,[7] and Philippe Wolfers jewelry.[8]

6. *Caras y Caretas*, 22 February 1908.
7. *Caras y Caretas*, 12 January 1901.
8. *Caras y Caretas*, 30 January 1904.

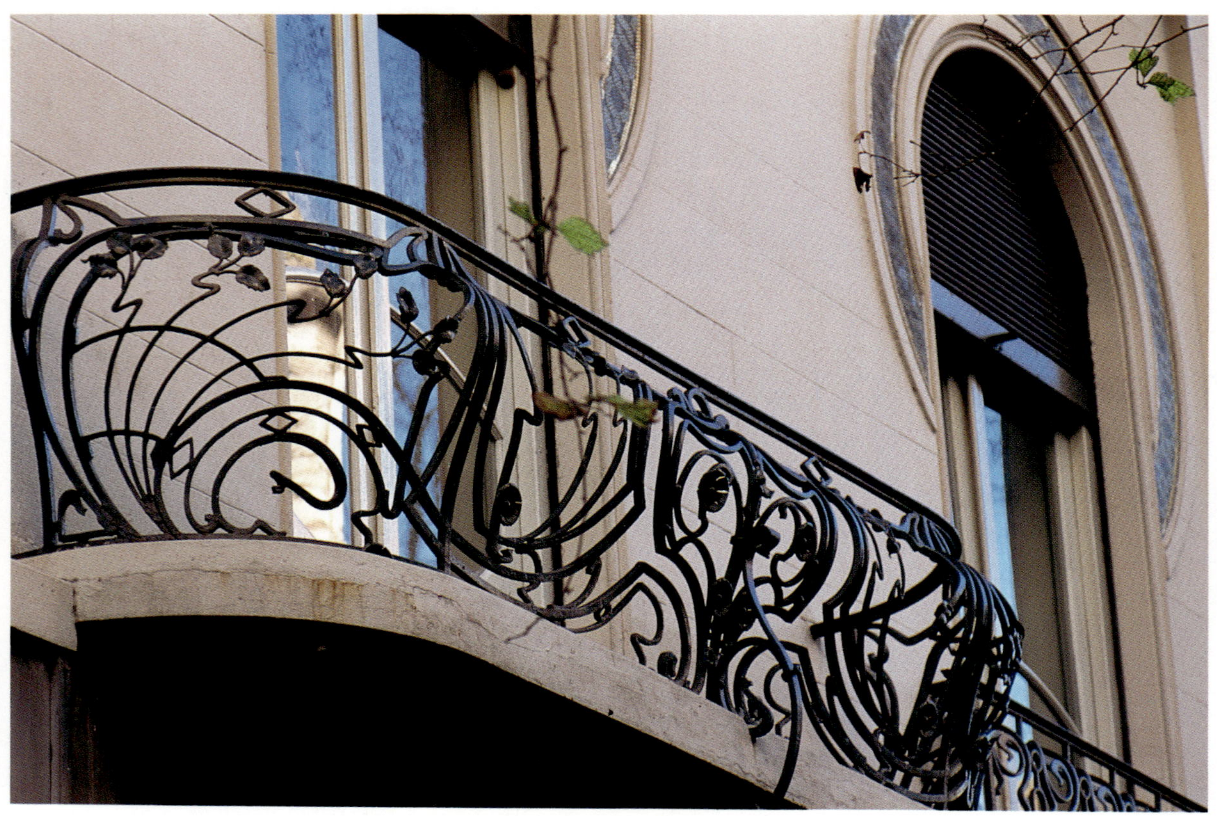

Figs. 15 and 16. Jules Dubois, iron balconies at 1297 Avenida de Mayo. One of the best *art-nouveau* facades in Buenos Aires. Photograph by the author.

The city grew uncontrollably and was open to all novelties, although many were not brave enough to accept them consciously.

On the Avenida de Mayo, there were notable examples of the *art-nouveau* style. The architect Oscar Ranzenhofer designed the building at number 761 (fig. 14); in it not only is iron used for the door and the balconies but the two are united by means of fine columns linking them together. Thus, the search for an integration of the facade is consummated. In this case, the ironwork follows a design inclined to geometric figures. Its placement on the corner contributes to the hierarchization of the facade, as is also found at 1297 Avenida de Mayo. The different ornamental treatment of the windows, which are crowned by colored mosaics, generates variety in the design of the ironwork. Balconies with right angles are seen next to those that curve, thus permitting the play with stylized plant figures (figs. 15 and 16).

A block farther, exactly on the corner of the Avenida de Mayo and Santiago del Estero, one finds another prime example of ironwork with glass that allows one to see the horizontal structure of iron. The work of architect Fausto di Baco is distinguished by the use of curious spirelike locks (if it is possible to call them that) bearing the unmistakable mark of *art-nouveau* design; less notable is the front door, where the iron and the lock are forged together.

In the year 1912, the new Club Español was opened. This building had a great impact at the time, despite the fact that its architect, Enrique Folkers, was Dutch; its lines were decidedly wedded with modernism. We will mention here only the balconies, the upper one made hierarchical to the first floor by the positioning of specially designed lamps of forged iron (figs. 18 and 19).

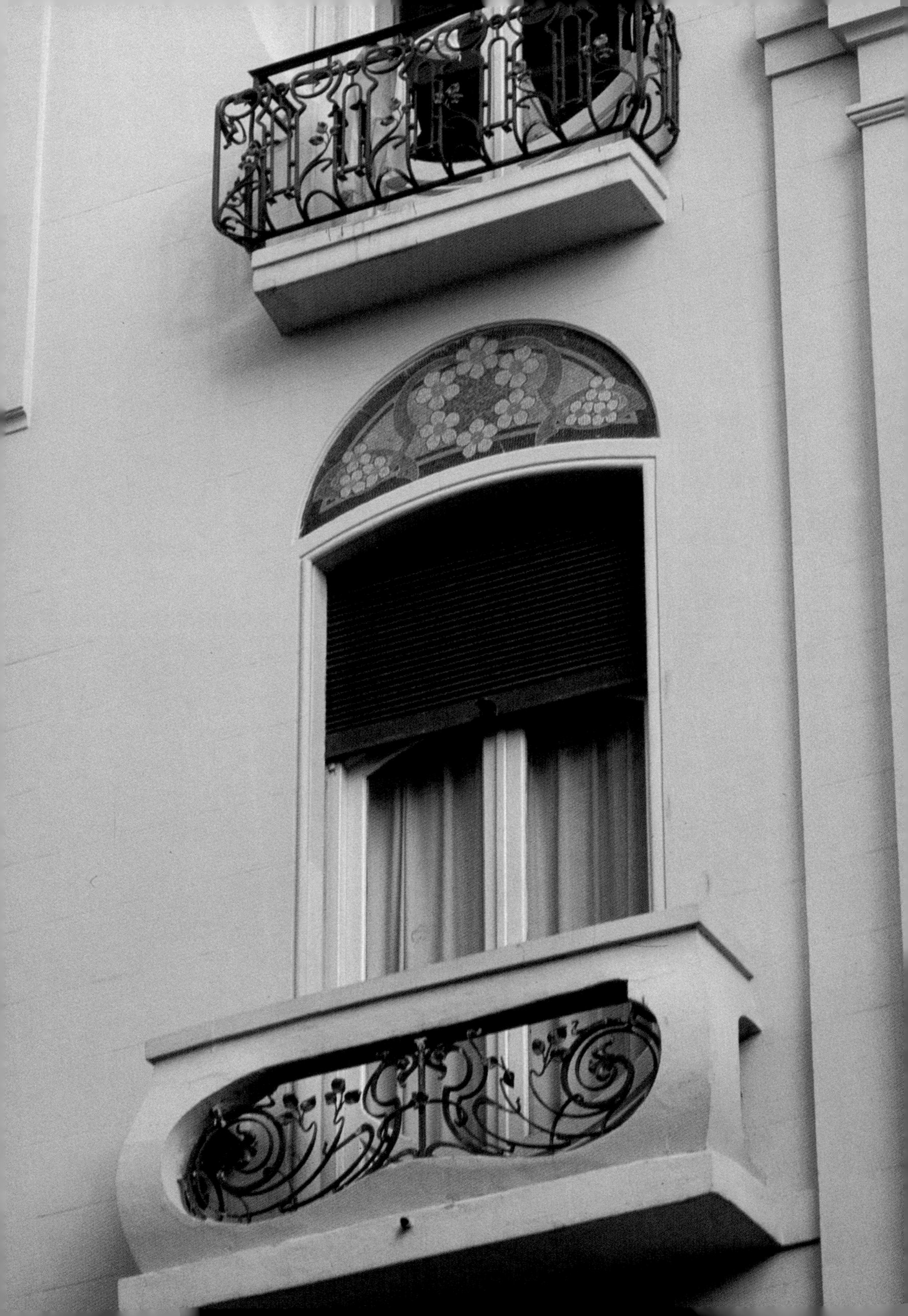

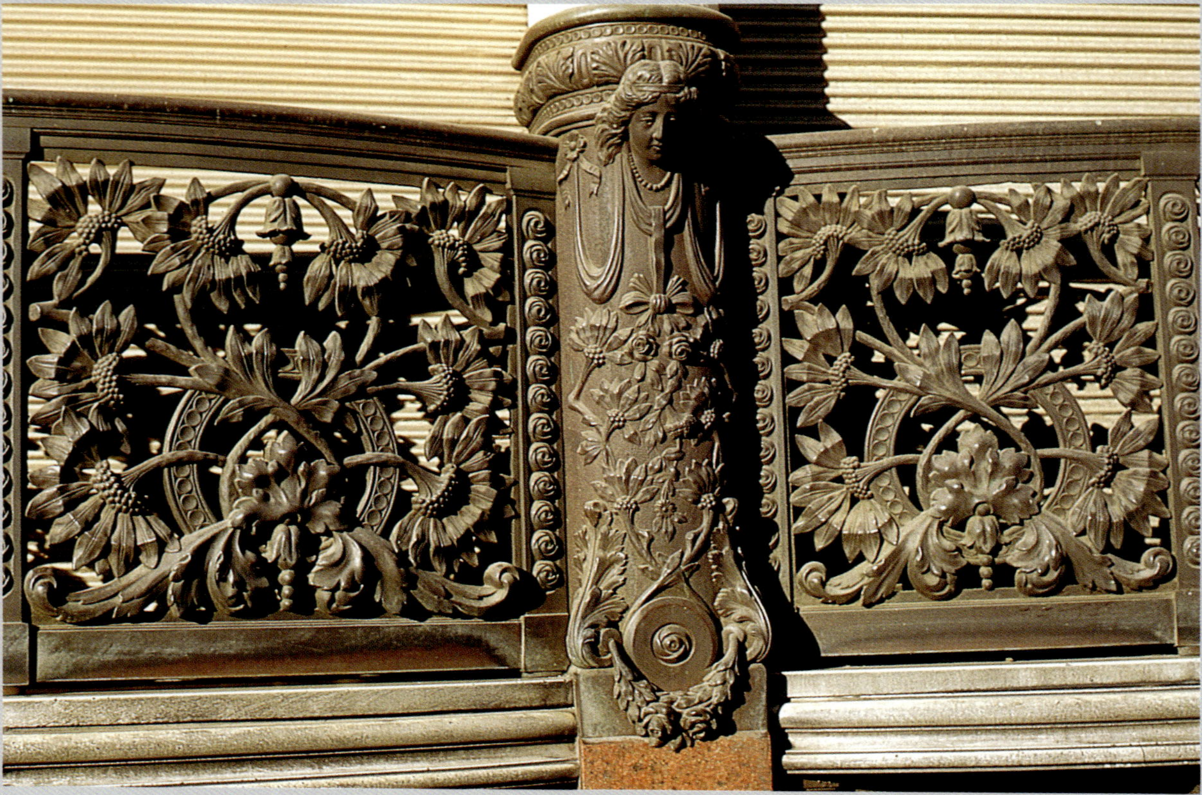

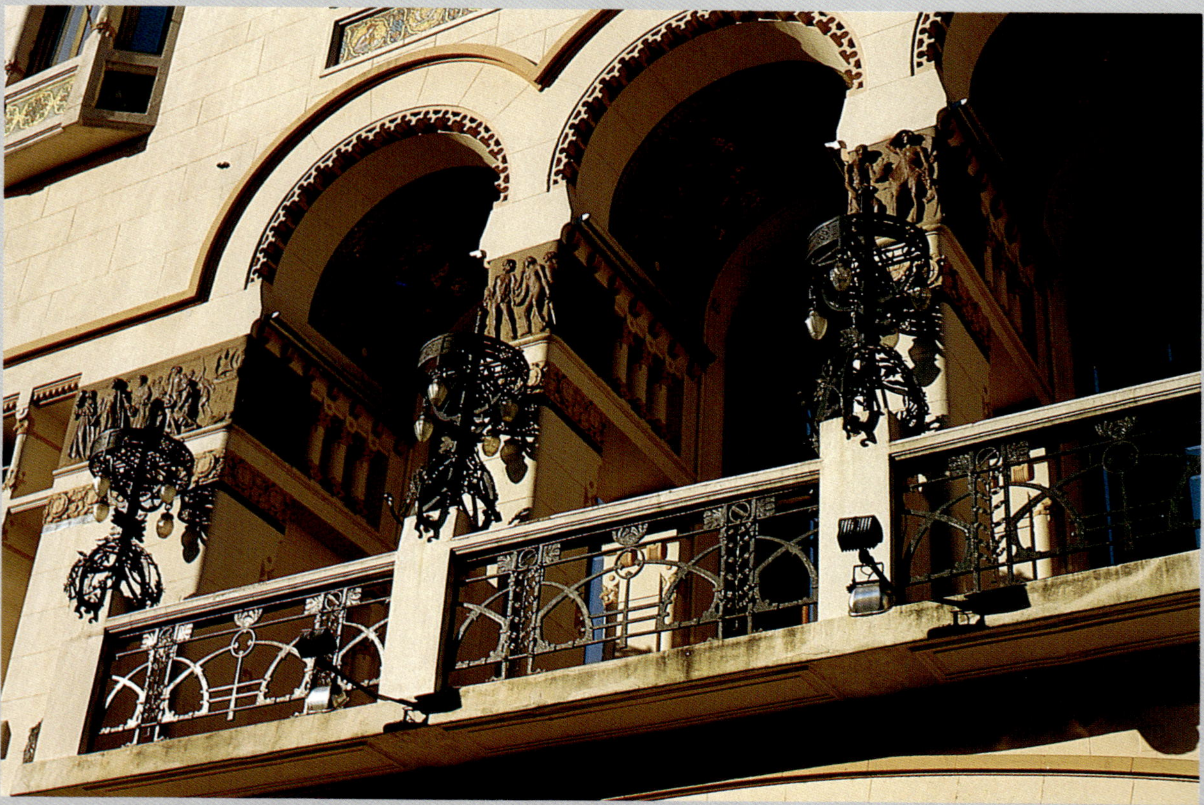

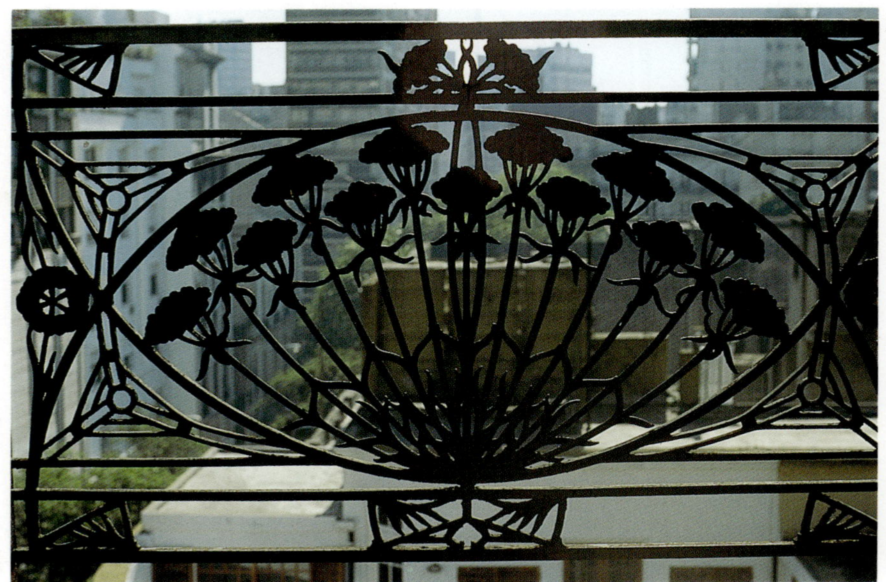

▸

Fig. 17. Pablo Pater, cast-iron balcony at 1175 Ríobamba Street, 1909. Photograph by the author.

Overlooking the ground floor was a balcony of continuous cast iron, especially designed for the building and taking the place of a strong base which was unique in a city "in which a minute examination finds itself inevitably rewarded by the discovery of a plethora of delicious details."[9]

Quite different is the plan for a three-story apartment building that the architect J. Trivelloni designed at 1330 Paraguay Street. The two upper levels are visually unified in the facade thanks to two large murals of ornamental tile at the sides of the central windows. The balconies are of iron and, in their turn, are united by fine columns. In its own way, as in the case of Club Español, this building is a unique example dating from 1911.

The traditional influence of French culture made the taste for the architecture of the École des Beaux-Arts natural in the first years of our century, but the permanent duality of conservatives versus innovators in the city resulted in several truly interesting works. Pablo Pater, a Frenchman, arrived in Buenos Aires while still very young to vie for a commission which he failed to win. However, a short time before returning to his country, he was commissioned to design an apartment building that was to be the first in a long series of such commissions.

As one of its means of expression, *art nouveau* took academic styles as points of origin in order to modify them later with total liberty. One of the best instances of this is the first work of Pater (1909), still standing at 1175 Ríobamba Street, which, if one looks casually, would seem to follow the accepted usages of the Parisian Beaux-Arts school. However, upon closer observation, one sees that there is neither element nor detail that has escaped transformation. Well-designed balconies of cast iron stand out from the whole. Each main panel consists of a rectangle whose measurements are formed by the crux of two semicircles. In the central space, and emerging from the lower midpoint, are thirteen stems ending in flowers opening in the shape of a fan. The rest of the ornamentation has been resolved with geometrical stylization (fig. 17).

◂

Figs. 18 and 19. Enrique Folkers, Club Español, details of the balconies, showing the influence of Catalan modernism, 1912.

9. José X. Martini and José María Peña, *La ornamentación en la arquitectura de la ciudad* (Buenos Aires: Instituto de Arte Americano, 1966).

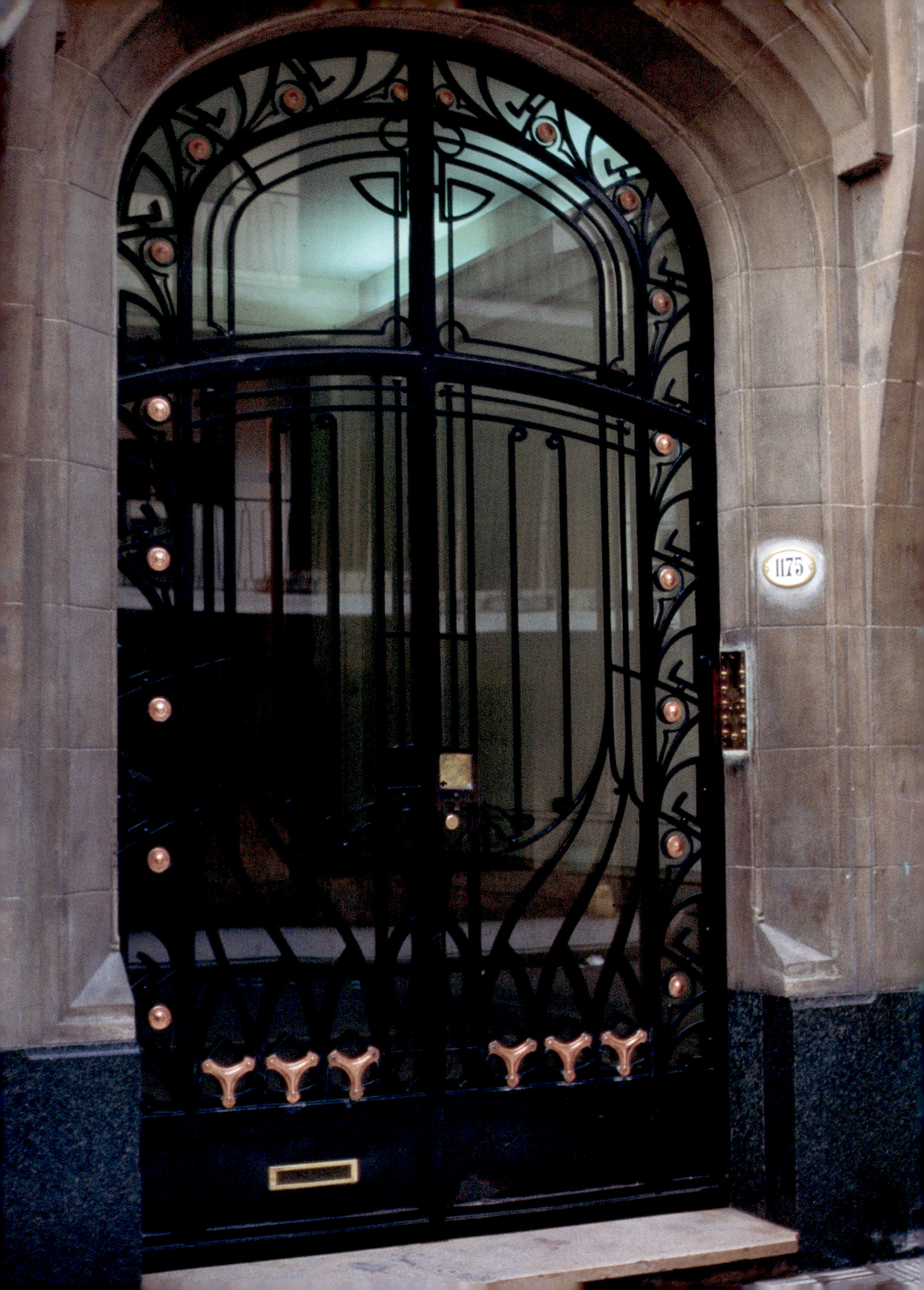
1175

▸

Fig. 20. Fausto di Baco, detail of the entry door at 390 Avenida de Mayo, 1909.

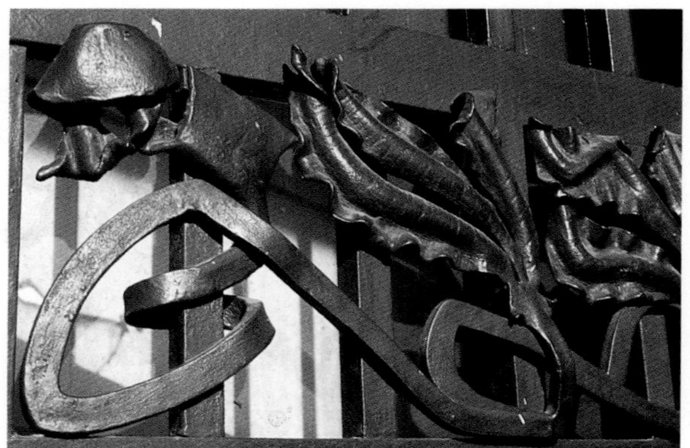

The front door is also significant for its geometrical design with copperwork (fig. 21). Originally, the structure carried stems and flowers of forged iron that, unfortunately, were removed years ago as a result of an erroneous desire to relieve it of "superfluous details." The difficult tasks of forging, embossing, and the subsequent soldering of components that make up such a door or balcony were completely overlooked by those who did such things out of ignorance.

> Among the diverse processes employed, the most important, the most precise, that which in the end allows the forger to execute his beautiful pieces, is heat soldering.... The iron can be soldered when the necessary temperature is reached. In his forge, the two pieces that will be joined must heat equally; he then turns them, spreading fine sand over the surface. This aids in the liquefaction of the iron. Once heated until they turn white, the pieces are put on the anvil and given several well-placed strokes of the hammer to join them finally in a manner that is indissoluble.[10]

No one would deny the decorative nature of the works generated by *art nouveau* (fig. 20), although, in the majority of cases in Buenos Aires, we are speaking only of exterior details. Its presence almost always was a response to the need for self-expression of a new economic class that sought to make a visual impact by way of the facade rather than the interior. People of recently acquired wealth lived in such buildings, and they were, in their way, as conservative as many others of the age. Designs were not born from inside to outside; first and foremost, they must not interfere with the daily routine of life. Functionality and the spatial structure of buildings continued to exist without impeding their claim that they also could be "modern." Cabria shares the view that "above all, *art nouveau* expresses itself on the surface; yet I think that in no way is it always a superficial style."[11]

◂

Fig. 21. Pablo Pater, entry doors at 1175 Ríobamba Street, 1909. Photograph by the author.

Along these lines, we have mentioned the balconies of the building constructed by the architect Pater, as well as those of the Club Español, as examples of unique cast-iron construction. Nevertheless this was not the norm; such balconies were generally made in series. In light of these last examples, we would like to make special mention of those works made from molds (figs. 22 and 23); this system facilitated a certain flexibility in the measurements that balconies could have. The system of molding for these railings naturally resulted in the proposed design remaining on the front of the balcony, while the rear was very simple and without ornamentation.

10. *Étude de la Plante; Son application aux industries d'art* (Paris: M. Verneuil, ca. 1900).
11. Robert Schmutzler, *Art Nouveau* (London: Thames and Hudson, 1964).

The continual state of change in Buenos Aires, long a part of city life, has resulted in the demolition of numerous buildings that today would offer valuable testimony to the times in which they were built and, therefore, to the vigor of artistic ironwork at the beginning of this century.

In classified ads in the journal *Arquitectura y decoración en Sud América* (Architecture and decoration in South America)[12] appeared the name of the French firm René Gueudet and Cie. They represented, in the Río de la Plata region, the Bricard Frères and the Schawartz and Meurer foundries, in addition to the previously mentioned A. Motteau firm. This would lead us to think that these firms were representative of the state of ironworking on the whole in this period.

In reality, the number of artistic ironworks existing in the city in 1913 was much greater. That year the commercial guide *Arlas*, (previously called the *Guía Gran Nacional*), boasted twenty-four pages dedicated to ironwork, including iron facades, balconies, doors, canopies, and related products (fig. 24).

One of the characteristics of the architecture of Buenos Aires, from midway through the last century until today, is a permanent superimposition of influences and styles. This is the result not only of the undeniable eclecticism of

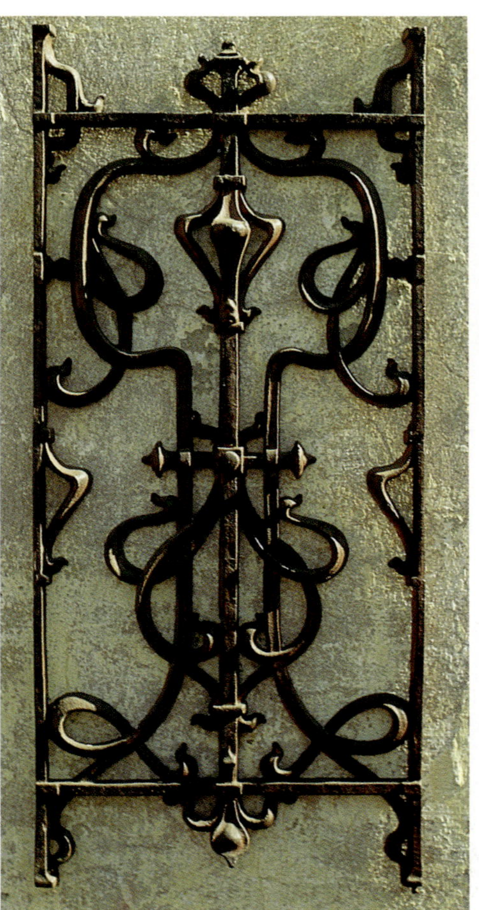

Fig. 22. Cast-iron module from which balconies are made. Photograph by the author.

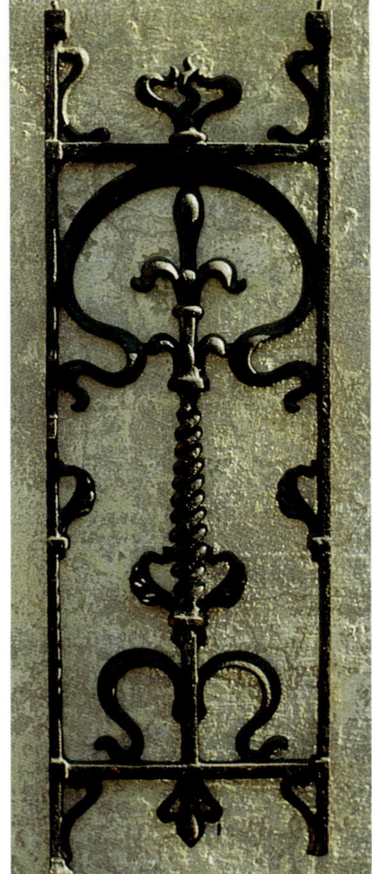

Fig. 23. Cast-iron module of a popular design, 1905–1910. Photograph by the author.

12. *Arquitectura y decoración en Sud América*, (ca. 1911).

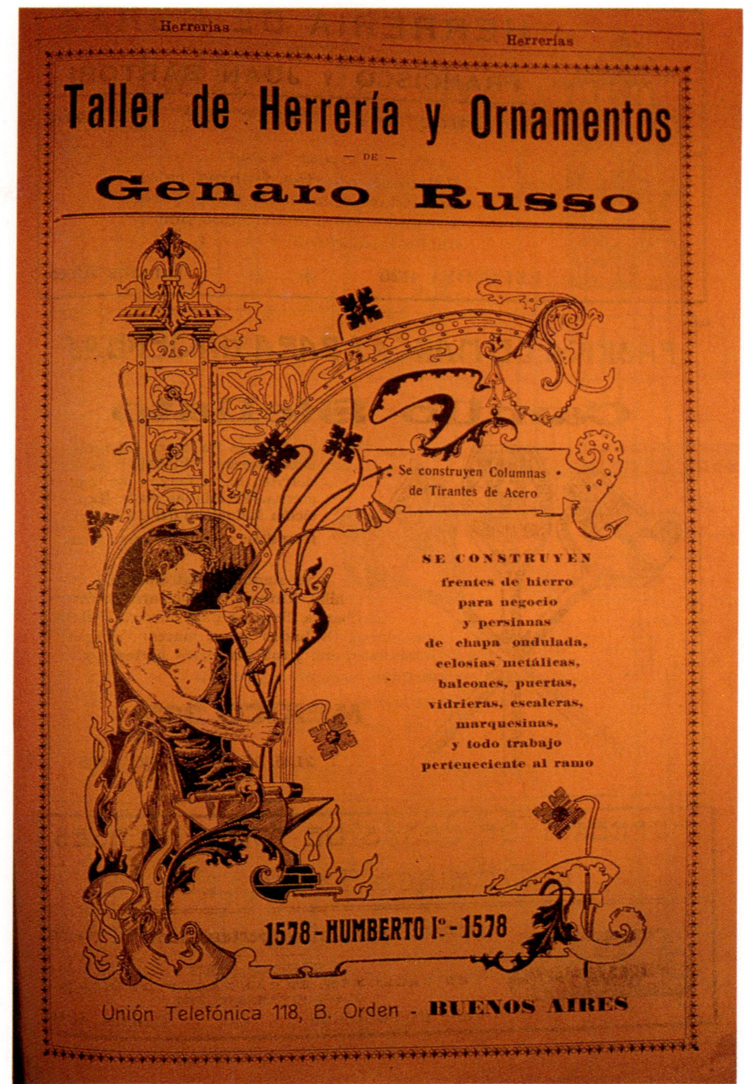

Fig. 24. *Arlas* business guide, advertisement for "Ironwork and Decorations Workshop Genaro Russo," Buenos Aires, 1913.

the first hundred years of the period but of the varied nationalities that settled in the country. This same observation could be applied to *art nouveau*, which was as much in accord with French fashion as with the Catalan versions of modernism, *stile floreale*, and *Jugendstil*. The architects who worked in Buenos Aires were not strangers to these influences. Julián García Núñez was a student of Lluís Domènech i Montaner in Barcelona; and we do not doubt the influence that *Jugendstil* could have exercised on Ranzenhofer.

These differences distinguish the balconies and the doors one from another. García Núñez did not use the inlaid locks that are found in the works of Colombo and in certain works of the architects Fasiolo and Storti. García Núñez stylized almost to the point of abstraction, while Rodríguez Ortega fashioned enormous lilies, carnally corporeal. But both played with iron, obtaining transparency, softness of form and—especially—the individualism that characterizes the artists of *art nouveau*. □

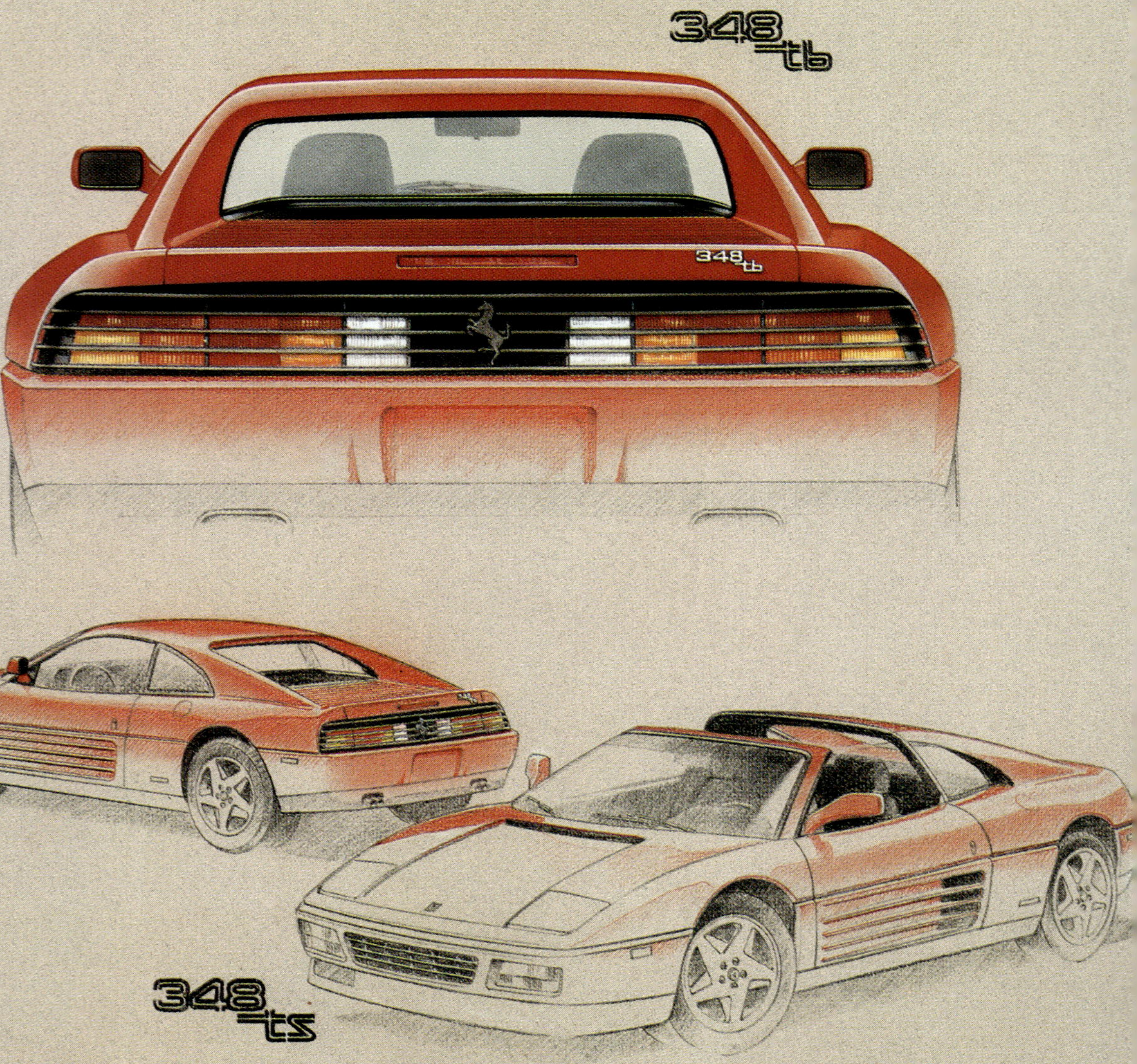

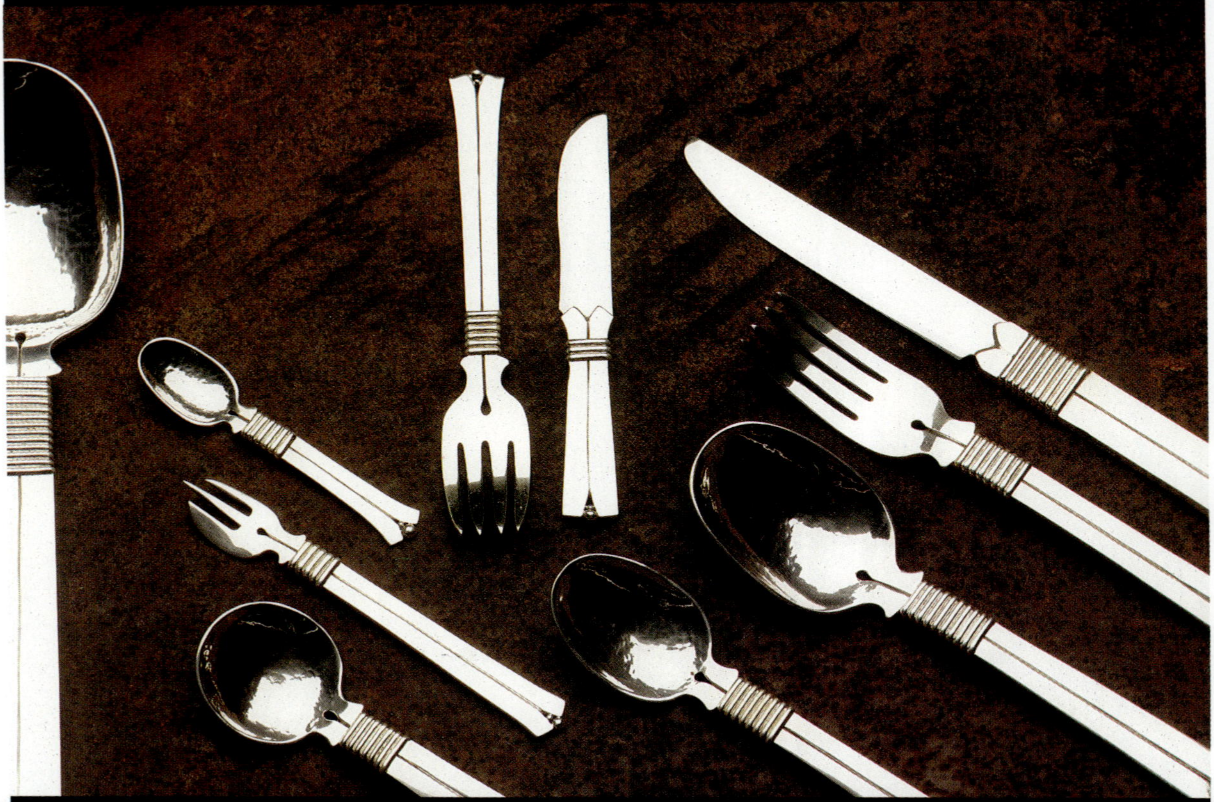

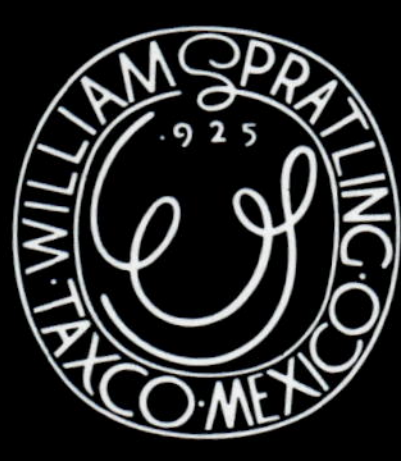

TS-24

Sucesores de
William Spratling, S.A.
Rancho Spratling
Carr. México-Acapulco, km. 177.5
Taxco el Viejo, Guerrero
Tel. (762) 200 26 y 245 07
México.

Milagros Inc.
7959 Broadway, suite 300
San Antonio, Texas 78209
Tel. (512) 821 5861

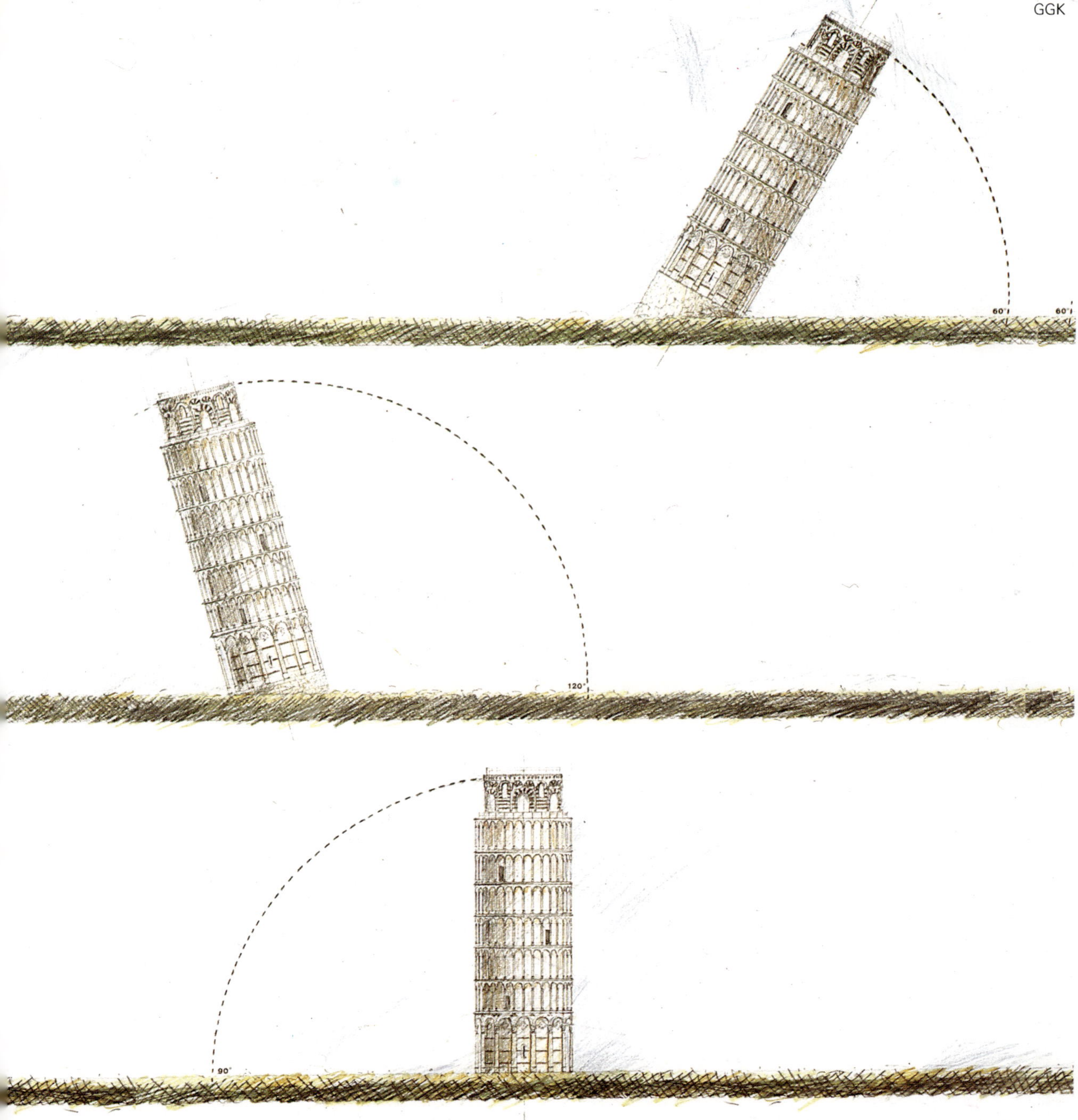

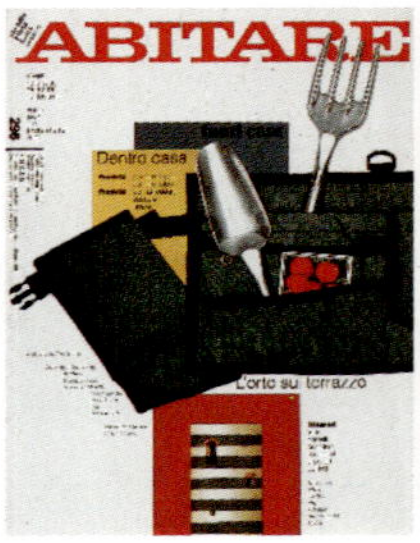

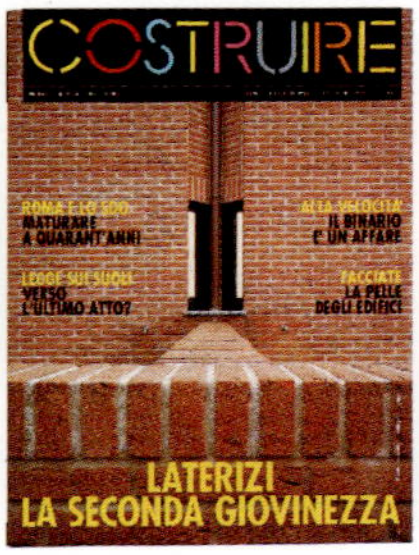

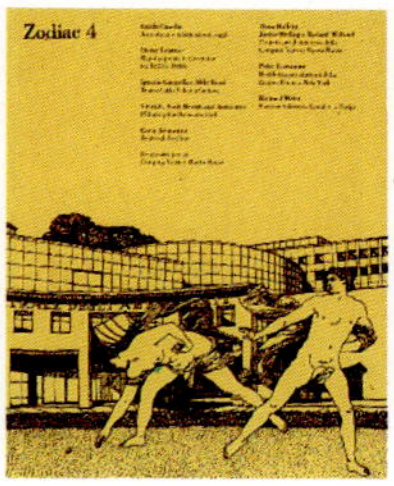

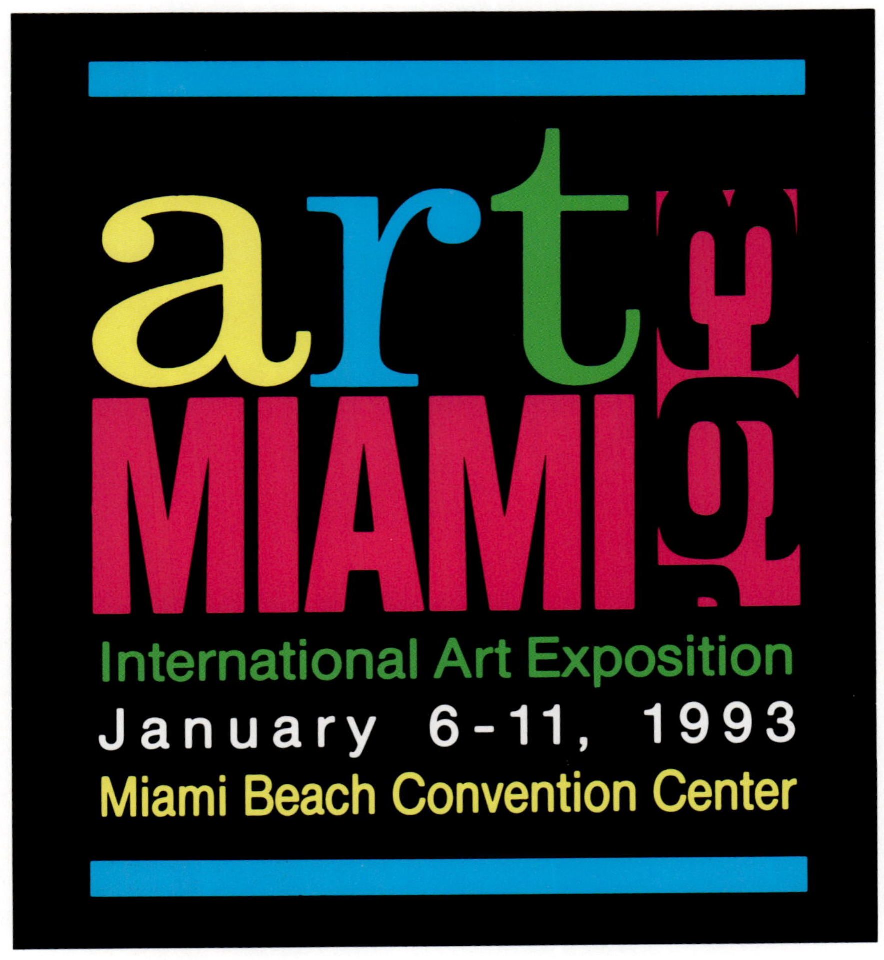

The International Exposition of
Contemporary, Latin American
and Emerging Art.

Fair Information: 310-820-0498 • Fax: 310-820-5426

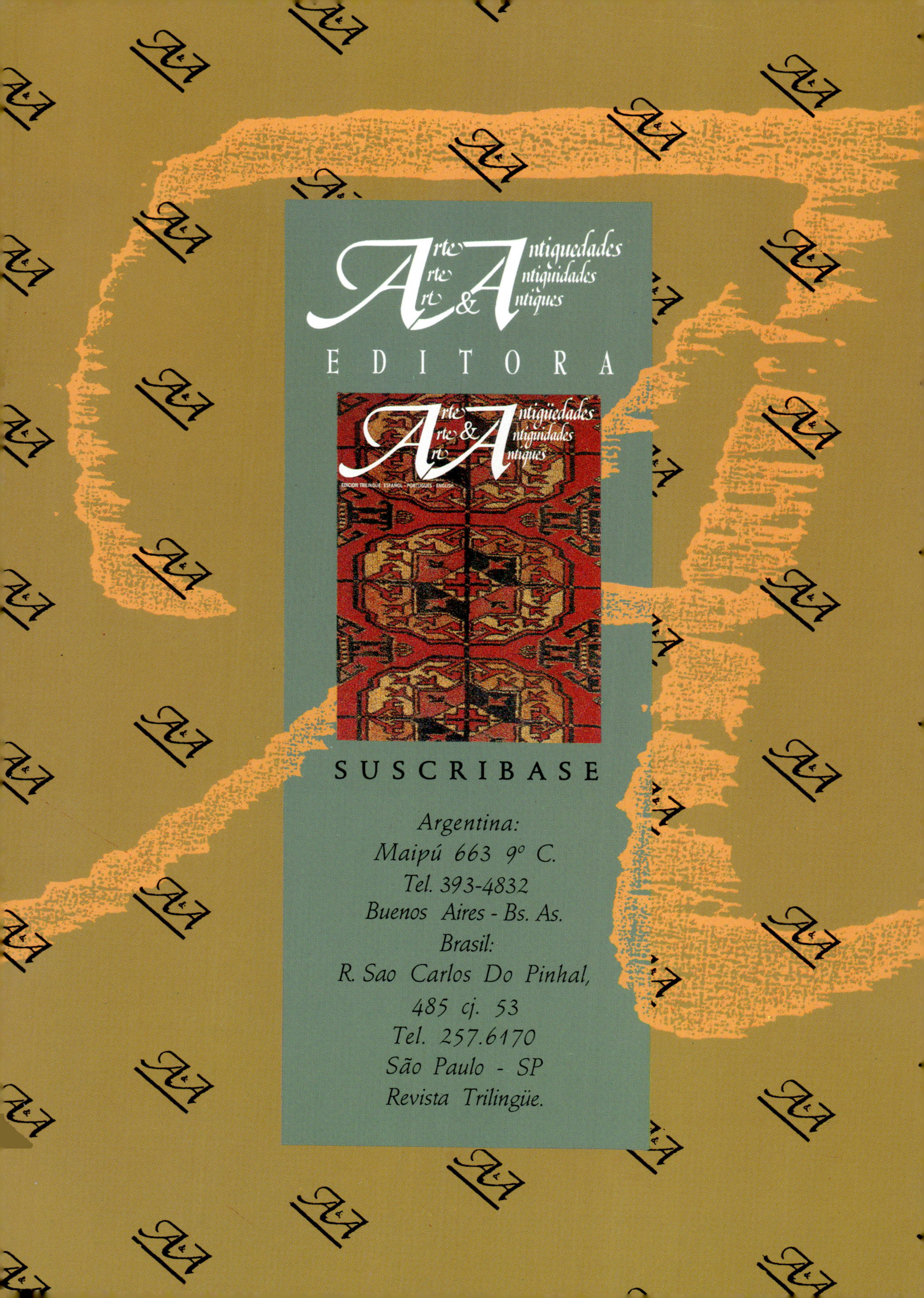

Arte Antiguedades
Arte Antigüidades
Art & Antiques
EDITORA
Arte Antigüedades
Arte & Antigüidades
Art Antiques
SUSCRIBASE
Argentina:
Maipú 663 9º C.
Tel. 393-4832
Buenos Aires - Bs. As.
Brasil:
R. Sao Carlos Do Pinhal,
485 cj. 53
Tel. 257.6170
São Paulo - SP
Revista Trilingüe.

revista

D&D

DISEÑO Y DECORACION
EN LA ARGENTINA

LA REVISTA
DE PRESTIGIO INTERNACIONAL

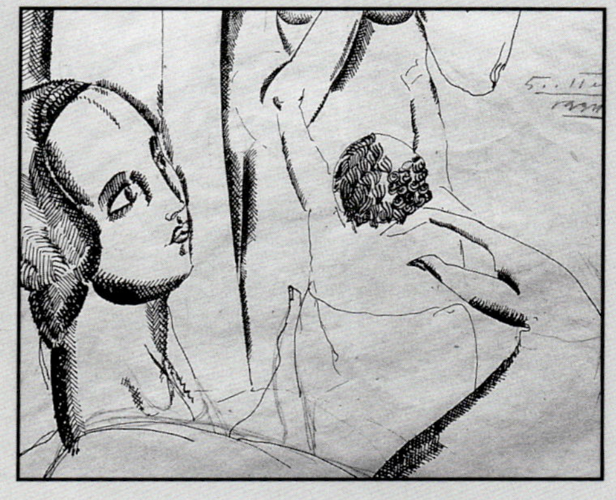

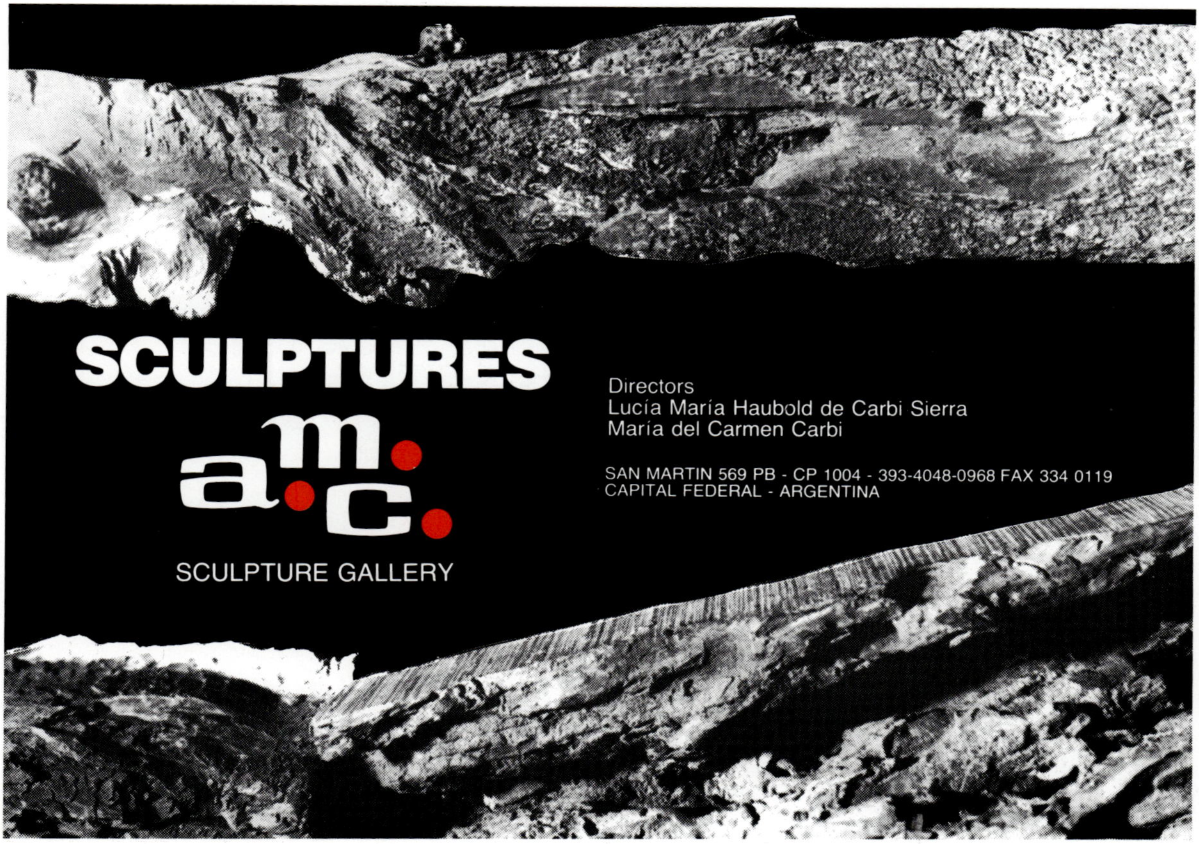

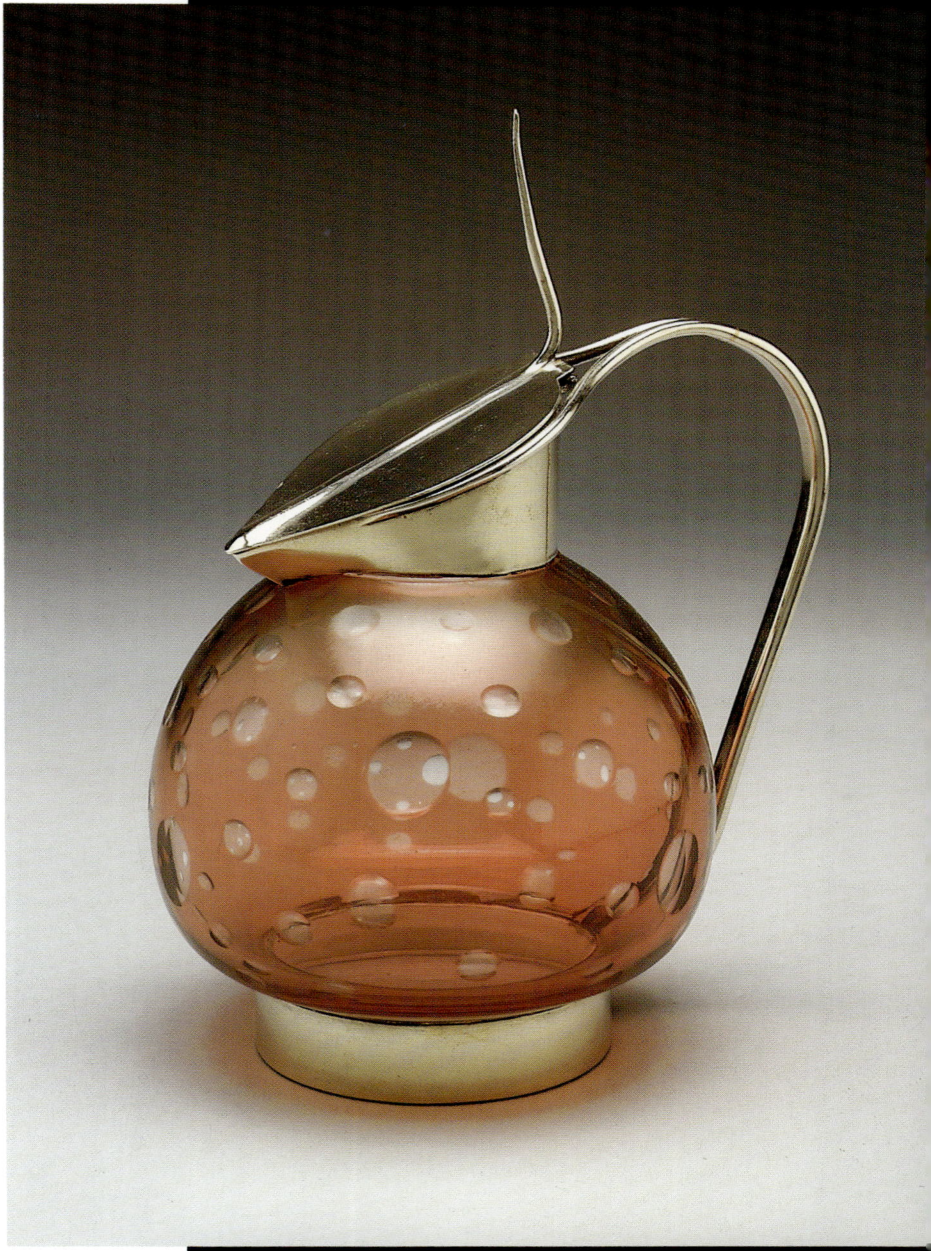

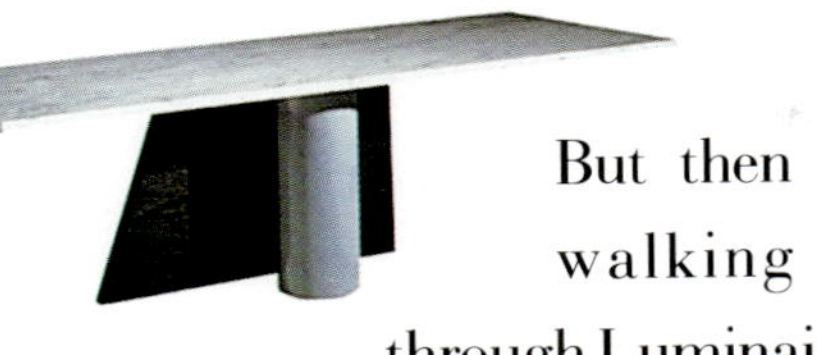

Not everything in the Museum of Modern Art has earned a place in our collection.

But then walking through Luminaire you might think you are in the Museum of Modern Art. At each of our locations you'll find contemporary design tended by intelligent, well-trained sales associates. As direct importers, we are able to offer the best possible price on a vast selection of elegant European design. And, an in-stock program makes this design available to you immediately, with local delivery and expert installation. So, if you just want to visit one of the great collections of contemporary furnishings, the Museum of Modern Art will do.

But if you want to buy from a great collection, come to Luminaire.

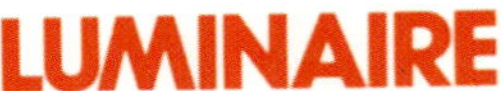

Miami 2331 Ponce de Leon, Coral Gables, FL 33134 T: 305.448.7367 F: 305.448.9447
Chicago 361 West Chestnut, Chicago, IL 60610 T: 312.664.9582 F: 312.664.5045

Swiss Theme Issue

19

The Journal of Decorative and Propaganda Arts

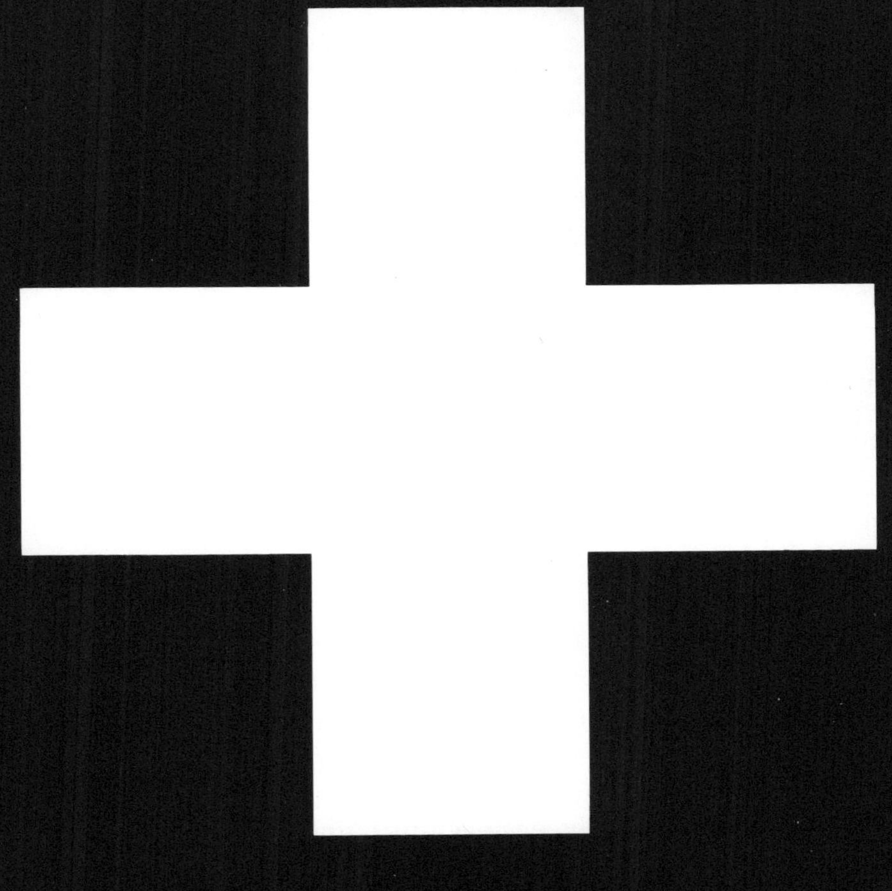

To be published in
Spring 199[illegible]

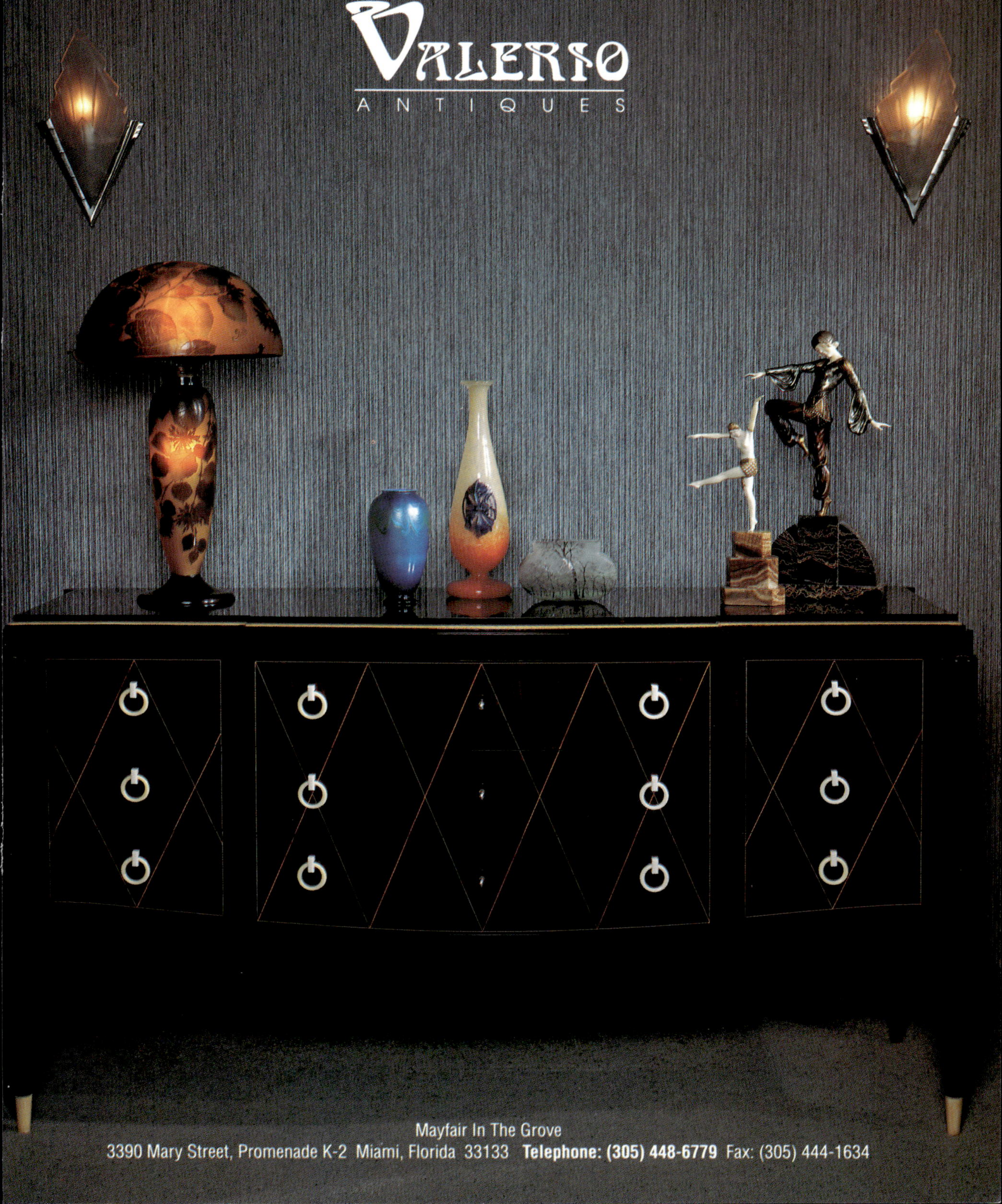

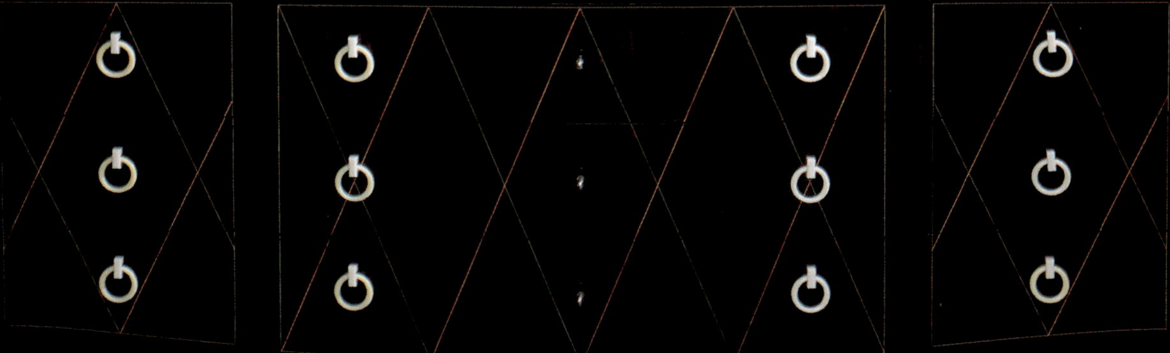

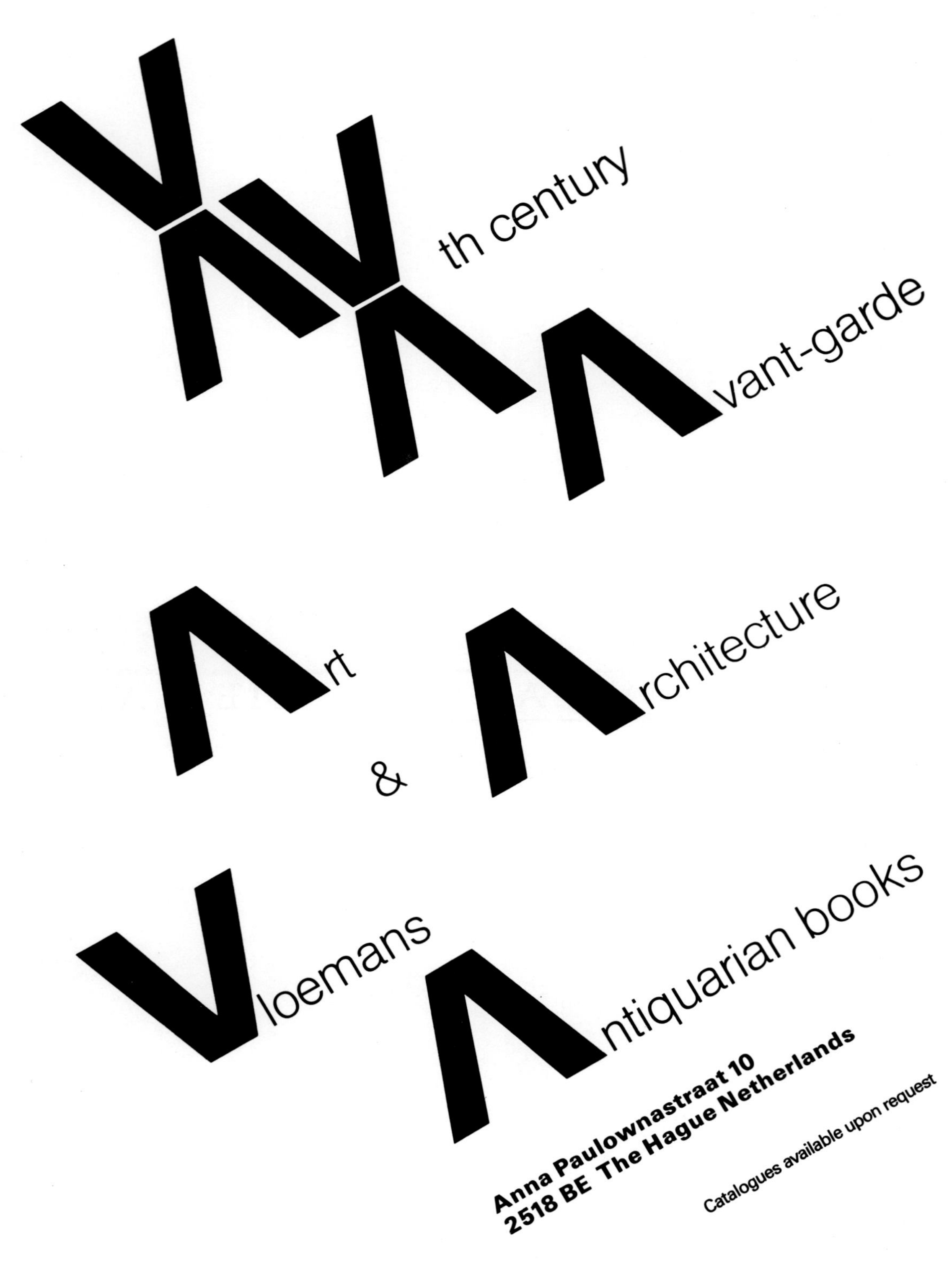

XX th century
Avant-garde
Art
&
Architecture
Vloemans
Antiquarian books
Anna Paulownastraat 10
2518 BE The Hague Netherlands
Catalogues available upon request

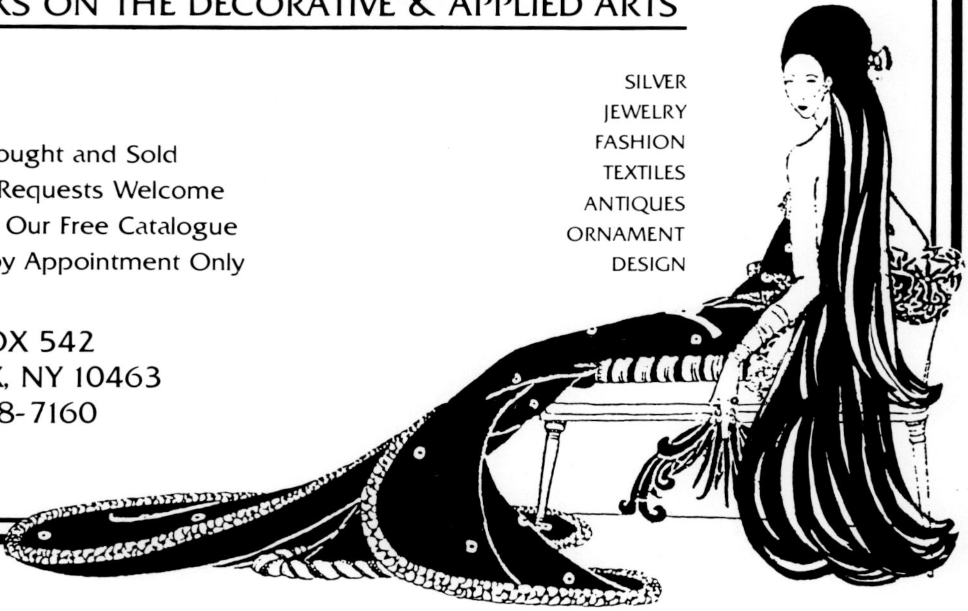

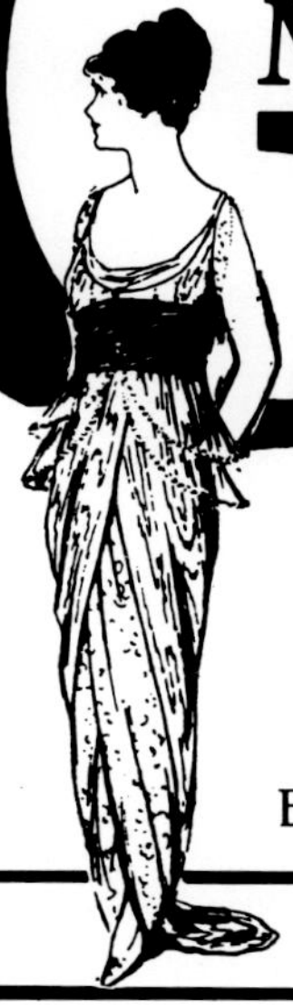